LOCAL GOVERNMENT IN JAPAN

KURT STEINER

LOCAL GOVERNMENT IN JAPAN

1965

STANFORD UNIVERSITY PRESS

STANFORD CALIFORNIA

To Kitty

Acknowledgments

In writing this study, I accumulated debts of gratitude to persons and organizations on both sides of the Pacific, and they are so numerous that I cannot hope to acknowledge them all. I benefited greatly from the comments of Professor Robert E. Ward of the University of Michigan. I am indebted also to some of my colleagues at Stanford University for their comments. Professor Nobutaka Ike read most of the manuscript in its present form; Professors Philip W. Buck and James T. Watkins IV read it in its original form as a doctoral dissertation; and Professor Thomas C. Smith gave me useful advice on the historical chapters.

Dr. Ukai Nobushige, President of the International Christian University in Tokyo, read major portions of the manuscript, put his immense knowledge of the subject freely at my disposal in many discussions, and was a constant source of encouragement. I am deeply grateful to him. Among the members of the faculty of Tokyo University with whom I discussed my work, I must give special thanks to Professor Tanaka Jiro—now a Justice of the Japanese Supreme Court—for his kind interest in my research and for the time he took, in spite of a schedule crowded by commitments of academic and public life, to illuminate specific subjects for me. My thanks go also to Mr. Takagi Shosaku, research associate of the Tokyo Institute of Municipal Research, for reading parts of the manuscript, for his valuable comments, and for his correspondence, which over the years kept me in touch with developments in the field.

Like many another American scholar, I owe a debt of gratitude to the Tokyo Institute for Municipal Research, to its former president, the late Mr. Maeda Tamon, its director-general, Mr. Tanabe Sadayoshi, and its managing director, Mr. Onogi Katsuhiko, for making available to me the assistance of its personnel in the gathering of material and the arranging of interviews, especially in the early stages of this study. Mr. Hirahata Terayasu helped me as interpreter and translator. Of the directors of the Institute at the time, I must thank especially Mr. Kojima Reikichi, now director of research of the Japan Association of City Mayors, for discussions that were invariably fruitful for me; and the late Mr. Ogura Kuraji, dean of the Faculty of Law and Economics of Tokyo Metropolitan University after leaving the Institute, who gave unstintingly of his time to make visits with me to cities, towns, and villages in the Kanto area.

It is impossible to mention all the national and local officials who willingly answered my questions in lengthy interviews. On the national level, I profited especially from the cooperation of officials of the present Autonomy Ministry. Mr. Suzuki Shunichi provided me with material and information at the earlier stages of the research, when he was Vice-Minister of the Autonomy Board. He was helpful to me again during my last visit to Japan in his new position as Vice-Governor of Tokyo Metropolis. During this last visit I was greatly aided by Mr. Omura Joji, Secretary-General to the Autonomy Minister, who was always able to find the proper person within the Ministry to answer an embarrassingly long list of questions with utmost efficiency. To Mr. Sato Tatsuo, formerly Chief of the Cabinet Legislation Bureau, and now President of the National Personnel Authority, I am indebted for many frank discussions and for a great deal of material.

My thanks go also to governors, mayors, members of prefectural and municipal assemblies, and prefectural and municipal officials in various areas of Japan. In Okayama I was permitted to use the facilities of the field center of the Center of Japanese Studies of the University of Michigan, which still existed when I began this study. I remember with particular pleasure my lengthy interview with Governor Ninagawa of Kyoto Prefecture in the summer of 1962. I am deeply indebted to Mr. Ishii Hajime—who had previously assisted me during his stay in the United States—for arranging a round-table conference with members of the Hyogo Prefectural Assembly and of the Kobe City Assembly, and interviews with Governor Sakamoto and his staff as well as with a number of members of the Diet in Tokyo.

Among my other research assistants, I must mention Mrs. Edna Crawford with particular praise and thanks. Mr. Kodaka Kenichi helped me both in the United States and in Japan. When the Pacific Ocean separated us, he continued to send me, with an unfailing grasp for what I needed at a given stage, information and material from Japan. I am indebted to him not only for his efficient service but also for his interest in the progress of the work, which sometimes seemed to him excruciatingly slow. Fate decreed that he should not live to see its completion.

At the outset I received a grant from the Ford Foundation Board on Overseas Training and Research. Funds from the Ford Foundation, administered by the Committee on East Asian Research at Stanford University, sustained the work thereafter. I am grateful to the Foundation and to the Committee for this assistance.

If this list of acknowledgments is insufficient because it does not mention all to whom I am indebted, it is also inadequate because it does not indicate my appreciation for the many courtesies and the hospitality that I encountered everywhere in Japan. In some cases, professional contacts established during the Occupation period were renewed in connection with the study and ripened into personal friendships, for which I am especially grateful.

I am well aware that many who were of great assistance to me may not agree with my conclusions. The acknowledgment of my debts should not obscure the fact that I alone am responsible for all errors and inadequacies.

J. G. Bell and Gene Tanke of Stanford University Press were unusually helpful—and unusually patient. And to Mrs. Isabel McKenzie and Mrs. Mary Johnson go my thanks for the efficiency and cheerfulness with which they typed and retyped the manuscript.

I have dedicated this book to my wife Kitty, for being at my side throughout the long period of its gestation, and during many a crisis before.

Contents

Local Government in Japan

Introduction

This volume is an attempt to present Western readers—especially students of Japan, of comparative local government, and of comparative politics in general—with a comprehensive introduction to Japanese local government. It is not a comparative study, but I hope that it may incidentally help generate concepts upon which future comparisons of local government structures and processes can be based. Perhaps, too, it will stimulate further studies of the relations between local and national politics, which have been largely neglected in favor of studies focused on the national level.

Local government has many facets. Because its institutions are based on law and designed to provide services to the public, a study of it must touch both public law and public administration. Local government is also politics. Relations between a central and a local government, for instance, are not only administrative but also political; and the answer to a question such as whether local autonomy is preferable to strict centralization—or, to give a more specific example, whether it is better to entrust control of a police force or an educational system to a central government or to local authority—will always depend to a large extent on political value judgments. Local government is also politics in the sense that the local unit is an arena of the political process, a place where elections are held, influences exerted, and decisions reached. Furthermore, cities, towns, and villages are not only political subdivisions of the country; they are also subsystems of the society, and the difference between the government and politics of a city and of a village can be understood only with reference to their different sociological bases. Hence any broad study of local government must look beyond political science to the sister discipline of sociology; and this is especially neces- sary where the social setting is relatively unfamiliar. Finally, to under- stand the law, administration, and politics of today, we must know something of their history. Thus a general view of local government should throw some light on its legal, administrative, political, sociologi- cal, and historical aspects.

Such a comprehensive approach can seldom succeed except at the expense of depth, and I am well aware that experts in such areas as intergovernmental financial relations, urban planning, and local poli- tics will find the treatment of their specialties far from exhaustive. Still, my primary purpose has been to present an introductory study, and I will be satisfied if this book raises some new questions and suggests some areas for further specialized research.

There are two general questions, however, for which I have tried to find answers. The first is in some ways the easier: How much local auton- omy actually exists in Japan today? Before the Occupation, Japan's local government system was highly centralized. The Occupation re- forms made local autonomy one of the principles of the new constitution; the basic law regarding the organization, powers, and activities of local entities is entitled the Local Autonomy Law, and the national agency in charge of national-local relations is now called the Autonomy Min- istry. The terms "democracy" and "local autonomy" have actually be- come "hurrah words"; only the political fringe fails to pay at least lip service to them. But we may still ask whether local entities really have sufficient freedom of action, and whether their inhabitants have suffi- cient control of that action, to warrant characterizing the system as one of local autonomy. If the actuality falls short of the constitutional ideal, it could be because the institutional arrangements themselves are defective; but it could also be because these arrangements, although sufficient in themselves, are not operating as they were intended to. An answer to our question thus requires an investigation into both law and actual practice.

The second question concerns the relationship between local auton- omy and democracy. This question is pertinent because the Occupa- tion's attempts to establish local autonomy were part of a larger effort to democratize Japan. According to the common view, which the Occu- pation accepted, the contribution of local autonomy to democratic gov- ernment is twofold. First, local autonomy serves a preventive function similar to that of federalism or of the separation of power among branches of the government; the creation of local power centers and vested local interests puts obstacles in the way of any who might want to control the state from top to bottom by authoritarian methods. Second, local autonomy has an important contribution to make to political socialization in a democracy and to the training of political and administrative leaders.

But an opposite view is also possible. At an early stage of modernization, local power elites may well be opposed to the modernizing efforts of the central government and to the broadening of citizen participation, and the resulting dispersal of power may delay rather than promote democracy; at a later stage, local autonomy may lose its significance for democracy because most of the governmental functions that come into being in industrialized countries are necessarily national rather than local in scope. As for the notion that local communities provide training in the ways of democracy, it may be well to compare the political socialization provided, say, by New England town meetings—which Tocqueville had in mind when he wrote that "town meetings are to liberty what primary schools are to science"—with that provided by a traditionalistic village community. In one case the political process is, so to speak, of one cloth; when the experience gathered in the local arena is applied to national affairs, democratic government is strengthened. In the other case, the political process is fragmented, and the attitudes and behavior patterns learned in the local community, when writ large on the national level, may not spell democracy. On the contrary, new and different attitudes and behavior patterns may have to be acquired to make a parliamentary democracy work. I have attempted to investigate this complex of problems only for Japan, but I hope that this investigation will contribute to a re-examination of the relationship between local autonomy and democracy in general.

Finally, a word about the methods I have employed in this study. In the beginning chapters a historical approach is used; the chapter on the constitution is in the main an essay in legal interpretation; in the chapters on local entities, on their organization and functions, and on financial and other relations between levels of government, the legal-institutional approach is emphasized; and in the chapters on neighborhood associations and on citizen participation I have taken a sociological approach. Deplorable as this eclecticism is in principle, it has in practice served my several purposes far better than a single approach would have.

I have stressed the legal aspect of local government to a greater extent than is customary today, for two reasons. One is that in non-Western countries which have adopted Western models for their governmental institutions the gap between law and actuality tends to be wide, and both law and actuality must be understood if one is to understand their interaction. The other is that the law may be seen as a record of the victories, defeats, and compromises of the various groups participating in the political process. In Japan, where the political process is commonly seen as a struggle, legislative victories and defeats assume a significance that goes beyond the immediate issue of changing a statute or the like. The passage of a controversial piece of legislation is seen as a landmark in the development of public policy, and public policy is in fact conceived as a succession of laws.

This Japanese approach may appear overly legalistic, but it has the great merit of suggesting how problems and issues are actually seen in Japan. Too often, meetings between foreign and Japanese specialists in the field of local government have a quality of unreality about them: the fact that their respective countries share a problem seems to establish a common ground for discussion, but the common ground soon proves to be located in a cultural no-man's-land. The discourse would be greatly advanced if the foreign experts could be expected to see things a little more through Japanese eyes, and I hope that my efforts to show the subject "from the inside out" will contribute something to that end.

PART ONE

A Historical Survey of Local Government

CHAPTER 1

Some Observations on Local Government in Feudal Japan

The local government institutions of modern Japan did not evolve naturally from their feudal antecedents. So great was the break with traditional institutions effected by the reforms of the Meiji era that a famous Japanese jurist once wrote that Japanese local entities have no history of their own.[1] But the question whether local units possessed autonomy before the Meiji period merits our attention, because such a precedent may influence attitudes toward local autonomy today.

Many writers assert that there was local self-government in Tokugawa Japan. It has been said that in the latter part of the era there was "complete local autonomy" in the fiefs.[2] It has also been claimed that below the fief level towns and villages were given "a generous measure of self-government" or allowed "a maximum of autonomy," so that rural communities, for instance, were "independent and democratic in the conduct and administration of their municipal affairs."[3]

Without questioning the existence of the arrangements that gave rise to these assertions, we may still ask whether these arrangements can fairly be described as amounting to "local autonomy." This is more than a problem of semantics. When we describe the institutions of other times or lands in the same terms we use to describe our own, we can easily impart to them alien qualities. It is quite possible that the same institutions that would have spelled "local autonomy" in a Western setting did not have that meaning in Tokugawa Japan. Lafcadio Hearn may have been right when he wrote:

Superficially the difference between Japanese social organization, and local government in the modern American or the English colonial meaning of the term, appears slight; and we may justly admire the perfect self-discipline of a Japanese community. But the real difference between the two is fundamental, prodigious, measurable only by thousands of years.[4]

The Shogunate and the Fiefs

A political map of the islands of Japan during the Tokugawa era shows a patchwork of fiefs, about 250 of them at the end of the period, with the Tokugawa domain lying in the approximate middle of the main island of Honshu. The Shogun's government, the *bakufu*, extended its direct rule beyond its own fief to all major cities and to some of the more important smaller islands. The rest of the fiefs were held either by *fudai daimyo*, lords who had fought on the side of the Tokugawa at the Battle of Sekigahara which established the Tokugawa supremacy in 1600 A.D., or by *tozama daimyo*, who had opposed the Tokugawa or remained neutral. The fiefs of the *fudai* were so allocated that they separated the *tozama* fiefs from each other and protected the main highways of the country.

Relations between the shogunate and the fiefs were not uniform throughout Japan nor static during the entire Tokugawa period. But before discussing the question of autonomy of the fiefs vis-à-vis the shogunate, we must glance briefly at Tokugawa legislation and administration outside the Tokugawa domain. Legislation followed the established class distinctions, which the Tokugawa were eager to maintain. Thus the Laws for the Military Houses (*buke hatto*) were considered of basic importance because they were addressed to the class that stood highest on the hierarchical ladder. The first of these laws was promulgated by Ieyasu, the first Tokugawa Shogun, in 1615. It later became the practice to summon the daimyo to Edo castle at the time of the succession of each Shogun to office. There they listened with bowed heads to the reading of the *buke hatto* of their new lord, which was always an adaptation of the original law.[5] One of the recurrent provisions of these laws dealt with the *sankin-kōtai* system, according to which the daimyo had to stay at Edo during specified periods and had to leave their families behind as hostages when they returned to their fiefs. Other provisions aimed at preventing political alliances. Thus the daimyo were prohibited from contracting marriages without shogunal permission and from approaching directly the Imperial Court. The *buke hatto* also decreed that structural innovations on castles were to be avoided and that even repairs had to be reported.

Not all provisions of the *buke hatto* were injunctions directed at the fief lords. There were also rules for the military class in general and for other classes as well, dealing in each case with aspects of the behavior proper for each class. On the other hand, the *buke hatto* were also less than complete codes governing relations between the Shogun and the fief lords. Not every specific order issued by the shogunate was based on them. If we look at some of these orders to individual fiefs we find, for instance, the practice of imposing a heavy burden of public works on the daimyo, frequently in order to reduce their financial war potential, but occasionally also in order to enhance Tokugawa power or to aid a *fudai daimyo* in an emergency at the expense of a *tozama daimyo*. A typical—and quite the best known—example of the type of work that drained the daimyos' wealth was the building of the temples at Nikko, in the precincts of which some of the Tokugawa were buried. The grandeur of these buildings is an impressive testimony to the amount of labor and material that the Tokugawa could exact from various feudatories. At one time the treasury of the lord of Satsuma, a *tozama,* was nearly crippled by a corvée for the benefit of the province of Mineo in *fudai* territory.[6]

The Laws for the Military Houses have sometimes been described as the constitution of Japan under the Tokugawa.[7] To the extent to which the description stresses the importance of the document, it is fitting; but the word "constitution" must not be given meanings that would not jibe with the general character of Japanese feudalism. As in early European feudalism, the relations between lords and vassals in Japan were not primarily based on rules delineating mutual rights and duties in a specific manner. They were based on personal loyalty, and in practice on the actual power that the lord possessed.[8] While Western feudalism, influenced in time by Roman law, increasingly defined and spelled out the mutual rights and duties of lords and vassals, Japanese feudalism was greatly influenced by Confucianism, which in its emphasis on morality tended to be antagonistic to the specificity required in the regulation of human relations by law. The Laws for the Military Houses, although containing complete norms for the behavior of vassals, did not replace the general moral concepts of the lord-vassal relationship. The Laws for the Military Houses, then, were not a constitution in the sense that Tokugawa orders which could not be traced back to their provisions were considered as somehow illegal or ultra vires. Such limitations on Tokugawa rule as existed were limitations in terms of power, not in terms of legal theory.

We know that *bakufu* officials—except for the censors (*metsuke*) and their traveling inspectors—were not stationed throughout Japan and did not interfere with fief administration. In regard to some of the *tozama* fiefs, Wigmore wrote:

Into a few of the fiefs of the powerful lords on the West and North no central administrative power entered. In fact, a Tokugawa man might not venture into the district of the great Shimadzu family, the lords of Satsuma, and its neighborhood without incurring more or less peril.[9]

The limitations of Tokugawa rule coincided with the ability of the Tokugawa to enforce their will and fluctuated, in place and time, with that ability. A strong *tozama* lord in a fief remote from Edo had more independence than a smaller lord within easy reach of the *bakufu*. Commands of the first three Shoguns had a different impact from those of Shoguns at the end of the era, when Tokugawa power was waning. While Tokugawa rule was thus limited, the limitations did not spring from or give rise to a recognition of baronial rights or immunities.

In short, it is difficult to find anything like a common denominator in relations between the shogunate and the feudatories. Arrangements and situations varied for more than two and a half centuries, and for a diversity of daimyo ranging from the proud Shimazu of Satsuma to the former personal retainer of the Tokugawa who had received a small fief for services rendered to Ieyasu. The task grows even more complex when we leave this plane and examine the governance of the *misera plebs*, the peasants and merchants both in shogunal territory and in the various fiefs.[10]

Governance of the Lower Classes

In the rural areas fiefs were divided into districts—named differently in different areas—administered by magistrates appointed by the fief government. Within these districts were the villages (*mura*). In the urban areas the arrangement was similar: cities and wards (*chō*) roughly corresponded to districts and villages, and villages and wards were generally subdivided into neighborhood groups of five or ten houses (*gonin gumi* or *jūnin gumi*).

The district magistrates—whose titles varied as widely as the names of the districts—were the points of contact between the fief administration and the people. Their functions were ill-defined, but it would probably be most accurate to call them "local administrators in charge of peasant (or townspeople) affairs."[11] They exercised legislative, executive, and judicial powers, which were of course not clearly distinguished, and they governed their districts under instructions of the vaguest sort.[12]

Even the term "govern" has to be considered in the particular setting of Japanese feudal society. The maintenance of morality, for instance, was a high governmental concern. Morality required that everyone behave as was proper for his status. If peasants wore *geta*, sported umbrellas, or spent extravagantly for *sake* at weddings, the moral order seemed to be threatened, and sumptuary laws were issued to regulate these minute details of the peasants' lives. On the other hand, "governing" did not include service activities. Feudal government was primarily government of the people by the lord's officials for the benefit of the lord. What the lord required above all was revenue and peace and order, which implied maintaining the basis of public order in morality. Beyond this, peasant life moved in its own circle, and its points of contact with government were few. In this sense it can be said that the scope of governmental functions was, in fact if not in theory, rather limited; or, to state it differently, that there was a low degree of governmental integration. This explains in part how one magistrate could control a district encompassing a few dozens of villages. The other part of the explanation lies in the indirect method of his control: the village was the smallest unit with which the government dealt. Taxes were laid on the village as a unit, and the village as a unit was responsible for the maintenance of peace and order. Normally it was up to the village officials to implement the magistrate's orders and instructions vis-à-vis the families in the village. The village officials—who were not members of the governing class, as were the magistrates and officials above them, but peasants— held a position of some sensitivity.[13] When the headman—whose task it was to deal with the "government" in the person of the magistrate— identified himself with the interests of the village in a crisis, as the villagers expected him to do, he risked incurring the wrath of the magistrate. When he leaned in the other direction, he lost the respect and support of the village and his usefulness to the fief government.[14]

The village and its officials, of course, did more than serve the purposes of the fief government. The village, as an association for cooperative living, owned and regulated the use of common lands, forests, and meadows, provided mutual aid and charity, arranged festivals, and engaged in a number of other social tasks. These activities were seldom considered governmental, but they were what made life in the village community meaningful to the peasants. Government was thought of as an external force, and the role of government was shrugged off with such sayings as *"tenka hatto, mikka hatto"*—"government laws are but three-day laws." Government demanded, exhorted, and punished; the course of wisdom was to stay away from contacts with it. It should not be assumed, however, that the villages were run internally on the basis of some agrarian type of egalitarian democracy. They were run on strict hierarchical lines, and only certain families participated in village affairs and filled village offices.

The Spirit of Local Government in the Tokugawa Era

We may now consider the validity of the statement that local autonomy existed during the Tokugawa era at both the fief and village levels. As for the fiefs, there was no specific grant of autonomy to the fief lords, either affirmatively or in the more negative form of immunities known to the West. In particular, the *buke hatto,* the "constitution of Japan," contained no such grant. It is not surprising that we find no assertions by the barons that actions by the *bakufu* constituted an infringement of the daimyo's right to govern the fief with a certain degree of independence. A delineation of individual jurisdictions would have been against the spirit of Japanese feudal relations, which were diffuse in nature. Whatever decentralization did exist arose not because the central government gave the right of self-government to lower units; it arose either because no interference in these units was necessary (as was the case where loyalty and benevolence really did govern relations between a fief lord and the Shogun) or because limits were set to shogunal interference by the actual power of those fiefs that were strong and distant from the seat of Tokugawa military strength. When the fief lords were left to administer their fiefs as they saw fit, it was because the Shogun literally could not or would not interfere, but not because he respected a right to independence which he had granted.

Similarly, there was no grant of self-government, explicit or implied, to towns and villages. A grant of rights usually springs from a recognition of power or social standing, and the peasant had little of either. The idea of allowing peasants to participate in government was certainly alien to the Tokugawa rulers, who began their ordinances relating to agriculture with such standard preambles as "since peasants are ignorant people," or "since peasants are people who lack sense and forethought." The same thinking applied to the merchants, who ranked even below the peasants in the social hierarchy. What might appear as self-government was really nothing but a sort of vacuum of government, a vacuum that grew larger the lower the position of the group and reached its greatest extent in the case of the outcasts, the *eta* or *hinin*.[15]

This governmental vacuum is not hard to explain. Little in the lives of the lower classes was of governmental concern; where there was a concern—as in collecting taxes and maintaining social order—the rural village and the urban ward were the smallest units with which the government normally dealt. This arrangement was congenial to a society with a strong collectivity-orientation and was also administratively convenient, but it lacked the political significance that characterizes the notion of autonomy.

The absence of the notion of a right to self-government reflected the absence of the notion of "rights" in general. For centuries in the West, "rights"—abstract norms which safeguard the interests of individuals and groups—have been used in the ordering of human affairs. The system of Roman law is an illustration of this fact. It is significant that parts of this system were borrowed by the Germanic conquerors of Rome, who played such an important role in the coming of feudalism, and that the revival of Roman law shaped the character of later feudalism. As a result, diffuse elements, inherent in a hierarchical structure in which those of lower status owe loyalty to those above, existed side by side with specific, contractual elements—a combination that may seem inconsistent in theory. The emphasis on the contractual element made it possible to obtain piecemeal concessions of right from those to whom loyalty was due. Changes in power relations could be articulated and systematized in a change of the system of rights. It was an aspect of this general process that the immunities and privileges, pressed for and obtained by manors and towns, became the basis on which the rights of local self-government developed.[16]

Japanese feudal culture did not incorporate a value system that placed emphasis on "rights." The ideal of harmony, not that of justice, stood in the foreground. To be harmonious one had to forgo insistence on one's interests, and peace in society was seen as the absence of strife between interests. The ideal of harmony was in accordance with the belief in the desirability of diffuseness in interpersonal relations, as indicated by the emphasis on such virtues as piety, loyalty, benevolence, and obedience; it was hostile to the development of any moral or political theory based on the notion of rights. It is highly significant that a word for that notion did not exist in the Japanese language until 1868, when Tsuda Mamichi, writing a treatise on Western public law, found it necessary to invent the word *"kenri."*[17]

The absence of the notion of rights explains to some extent certain differences in developments in the West and in Japan to which we alluded earlier. In the West, the cities with sufficient economic power to play the conflicting interests of the king and the feudal lords against each other emerged with charters granting them the right of self-government. But in a society without rights, it is not possible to advance to power by a claim of right or to translate power into rights. When the Tokugawa weakened and the power of the western fiefs increased, the fiefs did not demand concessions of expanded rights; they simply overthrew the Tokugawa. Similarly, the prosperous merchants in cities and towns did not play the conflicting interests of the Shoguns and the daimyo against each other and come forth with demands for rights of self-government. Such demands would have been more than politically subversive; considering the low position assigned to merchants and the moral postulate that everyone must "keep his proper place," they would have violated all concepts of morality. The politically frustrated merchant class found an escape by infiltrating the upper classes and by taking up cultural pursuits. In Tokugawa times the spirit of this merchant culture was conformist, not independent.[18]

Of course, the differences in historical development between the West and Japan were based on much more than differences in ideological structures. Western feudalism operated in an era of more or less continual strife and thus offered certain possibilities for the assertion of claims by underprivileged groups. Tokugawa feudalism, on the other hand, operated in an era of seclusion from the outside world and of peace within Japan. The isolation of Japan restricted the opportunities for Japanese merchants to accumulate wealth and power; their activities were limited to internal trade at the time when their Western counterparts were growing rich, powerful, and independent through trade with foreign lands.

It is thus significant that before seclusion and internal peace were established under Tokugawa rule, there were certain incipient tendencies toward the development of local self-government in Japan. The preceding period of internal strife—from the close of the fifteenth to the close of the sixteenth century—offers the example of the seaport of Sakai, near Osaka, which was described by Jesuit fathers who visited Japan in that period as "free and republican Sakai, the Venice of Japan." Sakai established an elective council that governed the area as an independent city-state, free from the exactions of neighboring feudal lords. While most cities were unprotected—lying outside the walls or moats that surrounded the residential castles of feudal lords—Sakai's citizens constructed walls and employed troops for their own security.[19] When the Tokugawa regime was established, Sakai, together with all the other important cities and ports, came under direct *bakufu* administration. The hostility of the Tokugawa to the merchant class, together with the loss of overseas trade caused by the seclusion policy, ended the tendency toward city self-government.

The stabilization of the country under Toyotomi Hideyoshi and the Tokugawa brought a similar reversal of tendencies toward local self-government in rural areas. In the fifteenth century these tendencies were unmistakable. In 1485 there was established in the province of Yamashiro an independent commune based on the principle that "the province of Yamashiro shall be ruled by its native people." Similar instances are reported for the provinces of Harima and Kii and for Kaga, Echizen, and Mikawa. This was an age when obscure antecedents were not insurmountable bars to political success, as was proved by the rise of Hideyoshi. The age ended when the same Hideyoshi, following the example of lesser lords, enforced a policy of suppressing peasant unrest by disarming the lower classes in his Great Sword Hunt of 1587.[20] In sum, neither the operative ideas in Japanese culture nor the circumstances of the time were propitious for the creation of a spirit of local self-government during the Tokugawa period.

We have noted that during Tokugawa times the lack of governmental integration created a "governmental vacuum" in which the lower classes shifted for themselves. During the succeeding Meiji era the vacuum began to be filled as government did project itself into the affairs of the village, sometimes even abolishing its legal existence and expropriating its property held in common. It is understandable that in retrospect the earlier period appeared as one of freedom. On the surface, the "vacuum of government" may have had a certain resemblance to local self-government. But the concept of a right to local self-government was lacking, and there was no theoretical underpinning for the notion of rights of "lower" against "higher." The prevailing attitude was one of subservience, not independence. The lack of such a spirit of independence may help explain the comparative ease with which centralization was achieved in the succeeding Meiji period.

CHAPTER 2

The Establishment of the Meiji
Local Government System

Tokugawa feudalism has often been characterized as "centralized feudalism." Although this description is useful in distinguishing Tokugawa feudalism both from earlier forms of Japanese feudalism and from European feudalism, it is also somewhat misleading. The relations of the *bakufu* to the daimyo were neither those of a centralized government to its agents nor those of a decentralized government to autonomous entities. The daimyo were "semi-independent sovereigns."[1] What Goethe said of Germany in 1830 may be paraphrased with equal truth for Tokugawa Japan: There was no town, there was no countryside of which one could say with certainty, "This is Japan." There were no Japanese subjects, only vassals loyal to their immediate lords, and the lower classes, whose outlook was equally limited and whose role in government was, in addition, a passive one. All ideas of an overriding national loyalty smacked strongly of subversion until the Meiji Restoration. There was no central legal, military, or fiscal authority in the modern sense.

But although the *bakufu* was not a central government, the "centralized" features of Tokugawa feudalism undoubtedly facilitated the establishment of a central government in the Meiji Restoration. Other factors were the existence of the imperial institution throughout the period of feudalism and the pressure from the West. In addition, the time was ripe because the decline of the power of the shogunate was accompanied by a weakening of the ties of loyalty that held the old order together. As far as the relations of the daimyo to the Shogun were concerned, there was at the end of the era only one case of unbroken allegiance, that of the daimyo of Aizu.[2] More important for our inquiry is the question of loyalty to the fief. There had been a time when it could be said of the feudal retainer that "his fatherland, his country, his world, extended only to the boundaries of his chief's domain."[3] But later, this narrow loyalty was subverted by the calls for a higher loyalty to the nation and to the emperor that came from such scholars of the National and Mito Schools as Motoori Norinaga and Fujita Tōko. Many of the leaders of the Restoration, such as Kido, Ito, Yamagata, Inouye, and Shinagawa, were disciples of men who had committed their lives to this higher loyalty, such as Sakuma Shōzan, Takano Nagahide, Yoshida Shōin, and Yokoi Shōnan.[4] It can be easily imagined that they embraced the new creed with fervor, for their self-interest coincided with it. The ambitions of the young samurai who managed the affairs of various daimyo—and many of the new leaders belonged to this category—were severely restricted by the existing division of the country into fiefs. The destruction of these barriers brought opportunities for new careers any-where in the empire. Thus at the time of the Restoration loyalty to the fief no longer stood in the way of centralization. Centralization was also consistent with the emperor system fostered by the Meiji leaders; the exalted position of the emperor as the true fountainhead of the nation's government made it difficult to advocate the exemption of certain affairs from the control of the central government.

The foundation of the modern Japanese state took place under conditions of grave external stress. The years before the Restoration had convinced the new Japanese leadership that local particularism meant weakness. The problem was to create a unified country strong enough to withstand onslaught from without. To "enrich the nation and strengthen its arms" became the primary aim, and little thought was given to ideas that might have weakened the country's defenses. This "siege psychology" prevailed for a long time, and when it was lessened, the revision of treaties with the Western powers became the chief concern. Only a unified nation, with uniform institutions that would impress the Western powers as modern and stable, could achieve this task. There had to be not only one army, one treasury, and one foreign office, but also one system of law and administration to which resident foreigners could be expected to subject themselves.

Thus everything pointed in the direction of centralized government. Only an ideological commitment to democratic ideas might have inclined the Meiji leaders to give the local citizenry freedom in the administration of local affairs, which in turn might have counteracted the centralizing tendencies. But there was initially no such commitment on the part of those who belonged to the mainstream of the Restoration. If anything, the vicissitudes of the time seemed to make it even more imperative than before that those fit to govern be able to perform their tasks without restriction.

It was only when the basic assumptions underlying oligarchic rule were being questioned by the Movement for Freedom and Popular Rights (Jiyū Minken Undo) that the role of local government became a political issue. At that time, the "siege psychology" was still strong. The term "local self-government" was used, but real self-government was in fact denied in various degrees to all levels of local government. The centralized system, established in what appeared to be a time of stress, continued long after the stress had lessened or disappeared.

Against this broad background we can trace some of the more significant developments leading to the establishment of the Meiji local government system.

The Abolition of Fiefs and Establishment of Prefectures

When the last Shogun, Tokugawa Keiki, submitted his letter of resignation in November 1867, he used such phrases as "the restoration of administrative authority to the Emperor" and "the unification of the whole people in support of the Throne."[5] He did not mean, however, that he was willing to abolish feudalism in general or even to relinquish his feudal rights over the shogunal domain. He expected rather that he would maintain a place of importance in the feudal hierarchy, even though his power would now have to be shared with other lords.[6] Other lords also believed at least that the feudal system would continue. But the Restoration swept the Tokugawa aside and eventually brought about the end of feudalism.

The first steps of the new government were faltering and uncertain. After a civil war had shown the impotence of the Tokugawa forces, the confiscated Tokugawa lands came under the control of the new government, which arranged them into nine urban prefectures (*fu*) and twenty rural prefectures (*ken*), each headed by an official, called the *chifuji* and the *chikenji* respectively. The rest of the country remained divided into 273 hereditary fiefs (*han*), which were virtually as independent as they had been in the declining years of the Shogun's government; their former lords simply governed under the new title *chihanji*.

In the *Seitaisho*, the constitution drawn up hastily in June 1868 to implement the emperor's Charter Oath, there are references to a central government of separated powers, to a deliberative body staffed by men from each urban or rural prefecture or fief, and to officials selected by public balloting for a limited term of office. But this evidence of Western influence on the constitution-makers was overshadowed in importance by the power and authority granted to the central government. According to Article 2, "all power and authority in the empire shall be vested in a council of state and thus the grievances of divided government shall be done away with." This theme was repeated in Article 9, which stated that "there shall be no private conferral of rank, no private coinage, no private employment of foreigners, and no conclusion of alliances with neighboring clans or with foreign countries, lest inferior authority be confounded with superior and the government be thrown into confusion."

To facilitate liaison between the central government and the fief governments and to represent the fiefs on the national level, the office of *kokunin* (later called *koginin*) was established in each fief. The *kokunin* were appointed by the various lords from among their retainers. A decree regarding the standardization of the fief administrations, dated December 1868, stressed that the *kokunin* and other fief officials, although appointed by the lord, were to be "subject to imperial authority." One may well wonder to what extent the authority thus claimed by the government was actually implemented. Simply proclaiming this authority was about as far as the new government could go at the time without risking the loss of important support from the anti-Tokugawa lords.

The path toward eventual unification of the country was broken primarily by samurai from the fiefs of Satsuma, Chōshū, Hizen, and Tosa, notably Kido, Okubo, Itagaki, and Hirosawa Sanetomi. They persuaded the daimyo of these four fiefs to surrender their fiefs to the Emperor as a patriotic gesture. This was done in March 1869 in a memorial in which the four daimyo recognized the supremacy of the central government. The memorial stated: "There must be one national polity and one sovereign authority." And again, "Now that we are about to establish an entirely new form of government, the national polity and the sovereign authority must not in the slightest degree be yielded to subordinates." By July 1869 the government was bold enough to demand the return of all fiefs to the Emperor. Following the cautious advice of Kido and Okubo—and against Ito's advocacy of immediately extending the prefecture system—the daimyo were reappointed governors of their fiefs and given an allowance of one-tenth of their former revenue. The power to tax was put under the complete control of the central government, but otherwise fief administration continued to be carried out by the lord's retainers without much reference to action by the central government, and the people continued to act and be treated as if their old feudal organization still existed.

After quietly and carefully laying the groundwork—which required patching up disagreements among the four western fiefs—and after assuring sufficient military strength by organizing a military force requisitioned from these same fiefs, the Gordian knot was cut in 1871. By imperial rescript, the fiefs were abolished altogether. In its wording the rescript showed the determination and strength of the men who wrote it. It stated bluntly that although *chihanji* had been appointed, there had been cases in which "the word only was pronounced, but the reality was not performed," and that the time had now come "when the fictions of the past must be abolished and realities substituted for them." The rescript declared that "in order to give protection and tranquillity at home and to maintain equality with foreign nations abroad" it was necessary that "the government of the country be centered in a single authority." It ended with these words: "With the object of diligently retrenching expenditures and of arriving at convenient working procedures, of getting rid of the unreality of names, and of abolishing the disease of government from multifarious centers, we now abolish the fiefs completely and convert them into prefectures."[7]

Institutionally, at least, Japan had become a unified nation. This was achieved at a price. The problem of compensating the daimyo and of assuring their acquiescence, first tackled in 1869, was solved more or less to mutual satisfaction. But the related problem of securing the livelihood of their retainers, who had yet to learn to be a productive element in the new and colder world that had dawned upon them, continued to vex the government for some years. Throughout this period the fear was latent that the prefectural governors might become a menace to the central government.[8] It would lead us too far afield to describe the solution to these problems. Suffice it to state that the new rulers, samurai themselves, showed a certain ruthlessness in dealing with their former peers,

and that they crushed the violent reactions which their measures engendered—the Saga Rebellion of 1874 and the Satsuma Rebellion of
1877—with the aid of the new national army. They emerged from these
struggles with a strengthened conviction that complete centralization
at the level of government that had replaced the fief was an essential
basis for creating a strong Japan.

In the emotional vacuum created by the breakdown of feudal loyalties
and the abolition of the fiefs, they could create and rearrange new administrative units as they saw fit. They established prefectures originally
on the principle that each one should have a yield of 100,000 *koku* of
rice; that smaller fiefs should be joined to neighboring larger ones; and
that each prefectural capital should be within a reasonable distance
from each part of the prefecture.[9] In 1871 there were 302 *ken* and 3 *fu*.[10]
Before the year was over, the *ken* had been regrouped so that there were
only 72 of them; by 1890 their number was 43, and the total number of
prefectural units—including the 3 *fu*—was 46. These numbers have remained almost the same ever since. The present prefectures are thus
artificial creations into which only time and a policy of self-government
could put the breath of civic life.

Conscription, Registration, and the System of Districts

The problem of their relations to the feudatories was a matter of immediate and grave concern to the Meiji leaders. There appeared at first
no necessity to introduce changes in the governance of peasants, arti-
sans, and merchants, to fill the "vacuum of government" surrounding
their lives, or to establish a new "system for the villages, towns, and city
wards in which they lived."[11] But once the commoner had been called
upon to participate in the defense of the country, the gap between him
and the government gradually closed. Compulsory conscription made it
necessary to keep some record of the population. For this reason, the
Council of State adopted a House Registration Decree in 1871. The
various *fu* and *ken* were divided into districts (*ku*) encompassing a
number of the natural villages of the feudal period, each under an official called a *kochō* and his deputies (*fuku kochō*). Originally, these
officials were given the task of completing the house register (*koseki*).
But what began as an ad hoc arrangement became soon a new system
of local administration, for the *kochō* and the *fuku kochō* took the place
of the traditional headman (*nanushi*), whose office was abolished to-

gether with the other traditional village offices in 1872. In 1874 the new officials were given semi-official status of varying rank.[12]

Three aspects of this development are worthy of note: first, the traditional offices of the natural villages, such as the office of *nanushi,* were first bypassed and then abolished; second, the new appointees, being government officials, assumed only the external functions of the traditional officers, not their functions as leaders in an arrangement for cooperative living (*seikatsu kyōdō tai*); and third, an area for purely administrative purposes, different from the natural village, came into existence. In other words, a wedge had been driven between the village as a cooperative living arrangement functioning in a governmental vacuum and the village as a unit that served the needs of the state.[13]

The new arrangements, on both the prefectural and district levels, were completely artificial, and thus illustrate a tendency in local government that persists even today. In the words of Royama Masamichi, the eminent Japanese political scientist, "the problem of local government was always treated as a problem of the local administration of the central government: what areas should exist, what authorities should be established for them, and what functions they should exercise."[14]

The National Scene

These arrangements of 1871 did not provide for any citizen participation. From this point of view, self-government had reached its nadir. In order to understand the first changes introduced into this system, it is necessary to glance at the national scene, where the struggles that shaped their character took place. In 1873 a Department of Home Affairs was established and Okubo Toshimichi assumed the post of Home Minister (*naimukyo*), which he held until his assassination in 1878.

In the controversy over constitutional government that began at about this time, Okubo was apparently influenced by German ideas of "Rechtsstaat." Government should not be arbitrary, but it need not be representative so long as it governed according to firm rules laid down in a constitution. The constitution would fix the powers of the emperor, which, while not unlimited, would be broad enough to allow a small group of able men around him to govern without interference. The people, whose rights would be limited, would nevertheless be protected against arbitrariness because the officials would carefully conform to regulations concerning the conduct of administration.[15] These ideas led

Okubo to concentrate his efforts on building a national bureaucracy. At a time when the memory of the poorly paid magistrate of Tokugawa times, who had to supplement his income by "squeezing" the villages under his control, was still fresh, it was not always easy to convince lower officials that the meaning of officialdom had changed. But inspections, reports, dismissals, and removals from one area to another drove home at last the lesson that they were no longer a law unto themselves but had become the creatures of a stern master. The officials of the Department of Home Affairs—later called the Naimusho—became an efficient bureaucracy, fulfilling their task with a jealous enthusiasm that prohibited the delegation of power to decide even the smallest details. From 1873 on, it put its indelible imprint on the development of local institutions in Japan. It has justly been said that the establishment of the Home Ministry helps to account for the peculiarly centralized nature of Japanese government and that local government in Japan cannot be understood without reference to this bureaucracy.[16]

The year 1873 was important in another respect. The Restoration ultimately put the power of government into the hands of small groups of ex-samurai who came from the four fiefs of Satsuma, Chōshū, Tosa, and Hizen, often referred to collectively as Sat-Chō-To-Hi. But the coalition that constituted this first "clan government" soon showed fissures and in 1873 it fell apart, mainly over the issue of a Korea policy. The two clans of Satsuma and Chōshū continued to hold the reins of power, while the ex-samurai from Hizen and Tosa resigned from the Council of State and went into opposition. Discontent was rampant in various quarters. The year 1873 saw peasants, hard put by the conversion of the land tax from a levy in kind to one in money, rioting in many parts of the country. These outbreaks could still be suppressed with the aid of samurai, but the unified support of the new regime by the samurai as a group was by no means assured. In early 1874, for instance, there were riots by samurai in Hizen and Saga. Disaffection grew year by year and reached a high point after the compulsory capitalization of samurai pensions in September 1876. In 1877 one wing of the malcontents, led by Saigo Takamori, who had fallen out with the government over the Korea policy and other issues, staged the ill-fated Satsuma Rebellion. During this restless time, when the new regime was also beset by the difficulties of treaty revision and by grave financial problems, a new political trend appeared as a result of the split in the original ruling coalition. The opposition of the ex-samurai from Hizen and Tosa took the form of an attempt to return to power by replacing the oligarchy of Satsuma and Chōshū (often called Sat-Chō) with a government constituted on a representative basis.

In 1874, Itagaki, Goto, Soejima, and Eto, who had resigned from the Council of State, presented to the throne a memorial urging the establishment of a representative assembly.[17] This was not the first time that the demand for some form of representation had been voiced. On the prefectural level, certain governors had already created assemblies without waiting for national sanction.[18] But the memorial was the first important effort by persons of power to urge representative government as an alternative to oligarchic rule on the national level. The Left Board of the Council of State—which was to represent public opinion on decrees proposed by the much more important Central Board—held out hope for a national elective assembly at a later time but promised local assemblies for the immediate future.[19]

In February 1875, Ito and Inouye took the initiative in persuading Itagaki and Kido—the latter having resigned from the government in opposition to the Formosan expedition of 1874—to meet with Okubo, the dominant figure in the government. The meeting, held at Osaka, was to arrange for Itagaki and Kido to return to the government and strengthen it. Part of the arrangement was a promise of governmental reorganization. The reorganization, which was carried out, included the establishment of a bicameral parliament consisting of an appointive Senate (Genrōin) as the upper house and an Assembly of Local Governors (Chihōkan Kaigi) as the lower house. Neither house became an effective legislative organ. The Chihōkan Kaigi, governed by regulations established as a concession to Itagaki and his followers as early as May 1874, was finally convened in June 1875. The opening ceremony, with Kido presiding, was held with considerable pomp at a temple in Asakusa in Tokyo, and the young Emperor gave a speech in which he characterized the gathering as a representative assembly. Such attempts to make the new institution appear more important than it was did not deceive the opposition. The press, a new force in public life, was openly hostile. After twenty-seven days of debate on items previously determined by the government, the assembly adjourned. One of the questions it had discussed concerned the establishment of local assemblies. The Chihōkan Kaigi was asked whether members of such assemblies should be local government officials or elective representatives. It favored the former alternative, but no action was taken by the government. The Assembly of Local Governors did not meet again until 1878, at which time it approved the Rules for Prefectural Assemblies discussed below. The new and detailed regulations for the Chihōkan Kaigi, issued prior to its meeting of 1878, provided for annual sessions thereafter, and after 1881 annual meetings became customary. But the character of the assembly changed. It was no longer considered an institution of representative government—a national parliament having been promised by this time—but rather a routine conference of local officials under the control of the Home Minister. As such it aroused little public interest, although it did play its part in the establishment of a comprehensive system of local government in 1887.[20]

The government reorganization of 1875, and more particularly the creation of the Assembly of Local Governors, failed to still the clamor for a national representative assembly. The opposition gained momentum and more definite form with the founding of such political organizations as the Self-Reliance Association (Risshisha) and the Patriotic Association (Aikokusha). It flourished on the discontent of the ex-samurai over the settlement of their claims, the resentment created by the attitudes of the national officials in the prefectures, who treated the populace like a conquered nation, and the appearance on the political scene of a new rural entrepreneur class of sake brewers and silk spinners. Itagaki, who had resigned from the government again in 1876, was at this point riding the crest of the Movement for Freedom and Popular Rights.

The oligarchs in power differed in their attitudes toward the demands for representative government, but none of them were disposed to give in to the opposition.[21] Repressive legislation was enacted against the press in 1873, and, on Okubo's instigation, more drastically in 1875. Some still denied the desirability of representative government for Japan, but others advocated a policy of gradual development in that direction. The main advocate of this policy was Kido, who had ordered Aoki Shuzo to draw up a draft constitution as early as 1872. After Kido died in 1877, his ideas continued to exert an important influence. One of these ideas was that the groundwork for the establishment of constitutional government should be laid on the local level. Aoki's draft had already provided for elected officials of the lowest local government units (*kumi*) and for management of *kumi* affairs by the residents. Officials at higher levels were to be appointed. But ad hoc conferences of the local inhabitants, convened with the permission of the government, were to allow for popular participation in some decisions also on these levels.[22] The establishment of local assemblies came to be desirable for other reasons, too. Kido himself felt that there was still enough truth in the idea that "*fu* and *ken* were like a type of independent country," as he wrote in his diary, to make it feasible to divert troublesome political agitation to the prefectural level and thus free the national government from its effects; he also believed that local government could provide an outlet for the energies of the restless samurai, and that local activities could be prevented from getting out of hand if the governors were given enough powers vis-à-vis the assemblies. Others who did not necessarily agree with the long-range purposes of the gradualists also felt that local assemblies might help placate the "public mind" and thus alleviate the pressure for a national representative assembly. Since those who demanded such an assembly also attacked the existing centralization—as shown, for instance, by the Risshisha memorial of 1877—the establishment of local assemblies appeared to be a reasonable compromise. Whether called into being as a step in the gradual development of representative government or as a concession required by the situation, the local assemblies were to be strictly circumscribed in their powers. There was thus some justification for McLaren's interpretation of the government policy:

If the two processes—the erection of a highly centralized local bureaucracy and the creation of local assemblies—be combined, as they must be in any attempt to understand the period between 1874 and 1885, we can see plainly the policy of the central government. The main purpose was to extend and consolidate its control over local affairs, and its second object was to enfranchise the people in as small a degree as possible—sufficiently to satisfy the popular demand for representation, while at the same time not endangering its own supremacy.[23]

This is the background of the second important period in the development of Meiji local government, the period that brought the first local assemblies into being. It is usually called the period of the "Three New Laws" (*Sanshimpō*).

The Period of the Three New Laws

As mentioned earlier, the government's drafts were submitted to the Assembly of Prefectural Governors in 1878 and approved by that body. The new laws were promulgated as Imperial Decrees Nos. 17, 18, and 19, on July 22, 1878. They were the Law for Reorganization of Counties, Wards, Towns, and Villages (*Gunkuchōson henseihō*); the Rules for Prefectural Assemblies (*Fukenkai kisoku*); and the Rules for Local Taxes (*Chihōzei kisoku*). A fourth law, promulgated as Imperial Decree No. 18 of April 8, 1880, completed the system. It was called the Law Regarding Ward, Town, and Village Assemblies (*Kuchōsonkaihō*).[24]

The first of these measures abolished the 907 large and 7,699 small districts existing at the time, apparently because Okubo—who had drafted the law but who was assassinated before it was promulgated—realized that such artificial creations were "not favorable to popular feeling."[25] The old districts were replaced by counties (*gun*), towns (*chō*), and villages (*son*). A new unit of local government, the ward (*ku*), was established within the three urban prefectures of Tokyo, Kyoto, and Osaka, and within five port cities. The heads of these units were called *gunchō, kochō,* and *kuchō* respectively. A *kochō* was the head of either a town or a village. The *gunchō* and *kuchō* were to be appointed by the government: the former because the *gun*, as a unit comprising a number of towns and villages, could be utilized as a link between the local and central government; the latter because urbanized areas were considered politically unsafe as potential breeding places of new ideas and demands. The heads of towns and villages, on the other hand, were to be elected, but this concession was severely modified by the requirement of prior approval by the governor. In May 1884 an even more restricted system was substituted by a Decree of the Council of State: the town or village assembly was permitted to nominate three candidates, of which the governor appointed one. Whenever the question of selection of chief executives had to be regulated during the following decades, similar considerations and solutions were certain to be brought up.

The Rules for Prefectural Assemblies of 1878 and the Law Regarding Ward, Town, and Village Assemblies of 1880 permitted elective assemblies on all but the county level. It is hardly necessary for our purpose to describe these laws in detail, but it should be pointed out that the active and passive franchise was restricted, that the vote was not secret, and that the agenda of the assemblies were limited mainly to matters of budget and taxes. Furthermore, the executive had the whip hand in his relations with the assembly; he alone could initiate action and his approval was required to put the assembly's action into effect; he could decide when the assembly had failed to act; and he could ask the Home Minister to dissolve the assembly when it became recalcitrant.[26]

Considering the complete autocratic centralization that had existed before, it is understandable that the promulgation of the Three New Laws was considered at the time as a victory for the opponents of the existing oligarchy. Actually, it was the sort of victory that Japanese liberals would win many times in succeeding decades: their opponents would grant a concession in form but not in substance, and what the government would give with one hand it would take back with the other. Thus, before actual elections for the local assemblies were held the powers of the governors were increased to enable them to deal with the local representative bodies.

Because the new system met few of the expectations and desires of the liberals, it also proved of little value to the rulers of the time as a tool for silencing the opposition. The clamor, far from subsiding, was strengthened as the Movement for Freedom and Popular Rights found in the prefectural assemblies a new weapon against the government. On the other hand, the Sat-Chō oligarchs used the governors in attempts to stem the growth of political opposition. Thus when Mishima Michitsune was appointed governor of Fukushima in 1882, he vowed publicly that the three things he would not tolerate in his jurisdiction were arson, burglary, and the Liberal Party, even though Fukushima was a Liberal Party stronghold. Mishima's ruthless and arbitrary regime led him into sharp clashes with the prefectural assembly, which voted down every one of his bills and refused to appropriate the expenditures he requested. But under the existing rules, Mishima could and did proceed to implement the programs in utter disregard of the assembly. The resulting disturbances in the prefecture were suppressed by the police, and the leaders of the Liberal Party, including the chairman of the prefectural assembly who had led it in its fight, were arrested, tried, and sentenced on the grounds of plotting to overthrow the government.[27] In December 1882, Iwakura advocated the suspension of the prefectural assemblies, but this step was not taken and the assemblies continued to press for an expansion of popular influence on government, occasionally establishing liaison among themselves until this practice was forbidden. In memorials submitted to the Home Minister, they urged, among other things, popular election of the *gunchō*. The System of the Three Laws, although often revised, essentially remained in force for ten years, from 1878 to 1888.

The Background of the Meiji Local Government Structure

Before we turn to the great codification of the rules for local government that replaced the Three New Laws in 1888, we must outline again, at least in general terms, the background for these proceedings. This time we must consider briefly both the national and international scenes.

On the international front, the problem of gaining a revision of the treaties with the Western powers achieved particular prominence in 1884 and the following years. Popular feeling ran high on the issue. Because the Western powers made the modernization of the legal and political institutions of the country a condition for treaty revision, this was a period of feverish legislative activity aimed at meeting this condition. It has been stated with justification that no legislation of the day can be understood apart from this aim.[28] Yamagata, the creator of the Meiji local government system, repeatedly referred to relations with foreign countries when urging the harmonization of Japanese institutions with Western ones.[29]

On the national scene, the Imperial Rescript of 1881 promised the promulgation of a constitution and the opening of a national representative assembly. In short order, the political associations became political parties: the Liberal Party (Jiyūtō) was formed in 1881 with Itagaki as its colorful leader; a year later the Progressive Party (Kaishintō) was organized by Okuma, who had fallen out with the rest of the oligarchs. It is true that the mere existence of two parties with substantially similar aims shows that personal relationships, then as now, were as important for Japanese parties as political principles. It is equally true that these parties were vehicles on which their leaders hoped to return to power, from which some had been largely excluded since the breakup of the Sat-Chō-To-Hi coalition. But when all this is said, it remains true that these parties aimed at replacing a government without any popular mandate with a government that had received such a mandate through the elective process; that they used the ideas and terminology of liberalism (especially John Stuart Mill's variety) with apparent conviction; and that they thus differed sharply from their opponents, whose "modernism" was devoid of enthusiasm for the ideologies of the West. It is interesting to speculate what a victory of liberal ideas at this formative stage of Japanese politics would have meant for the future of the country.

For the observer of the Japan of later decades it is also important to note that this was the time when the schism between the bureaucracy and the political parties originated. The bureaucracy, still hailing chiefly from Satsuma and Chōshū, was as intent on retaining its power without regard to the parties as the parties were bent on dislodging the bureaucracy by political means. The bureaucracy was not motivated solely by a thirst for power. They viewed the prospect of success by the political parties with serious patriotic concern. As long as the reins of government were in the firm grasp of reliable men, as they were, they felt optimistic about the future of the new empire they had built; but what would happen once they were replaced by those who were chosen by the uneducated populace, which had never borne the responsibility of governing?

It is not surprising, therefore, that the period between the Imperial Rescript of 1881 and the opening of the Diet in 1890 saw repressive measures on a large scale. Various disturbances in Ibaragi, Saitama, Fukushima, and other places led to the disbanding of the political parties in 1884. But the political ardor, once aroused, did not subside, and in 1887 the Peace Preservation Law marked a high point of suppression. To keep political movements "under control" became one of the tasks of the Home Minister. Yamagata held that post during most of this time.

A glance at some of the draft constitutions proposed by officials, political societies, parties, and individuals shows various degrees of interest in the question of local government. The platform of the Constitutional Imperial Party (Rikken Teiseitō), founded as a bureaucratic counterweight to the popular parties, the Jiyūtō and the Kaishintō, said nothing on the subject. The drafts of the Finance Ministry and of the Senate (Genrōin) left provisions regarding local government in general and regarding the functions of local assemblies in particular to determination by law. But Okuma's Kaishintō adopted a platform containing the following plank: "We endeavor to establish a basis for local self-government, restricting the sphere of interference by the central government." As early as June 1877, the Self-Reliance Association (Risshisha), a forerunner of the Jiyūtō, had pointed out the "evil of centralization" in a memorial and accused the government of "endeavoring to decrease what little power is possessed by local authorities and to concentrate it wholly in its own hands." In its draft constitution, written between May and September 1881, it placed more stress on citizen participation in the designation of governors and other local officials and in the determination of matters of local interest, including finances. The most extreme form of decentralization—a federal union of states—was proposed in a private draft by two liberals, Nakajima Nobuyuki and Furuzawa Shigeru, in 1885. The nature of this document is suggested by Section 13: "The United States of Japan shall not interfere with any state of Japan concerning intrastate affairs nor with the municipalities in any state concerning their organization." It should also be noted that the press sometimes expressed hopes for the establishment of local self-government.[30]

When we turn to the deliberations and investigations of those in power, we find considerations and opinions of a different sort expressed by Ito and Yamagata. By this time, Okubo, Kido, and Saigo, the members of the original triumvirate of the Meiji Restoration, had all passed away. Ito Hirobumi, who hailed from Chōshū, had been close first to Kido and later to Okubo, with whose views he increasingly identified himself. After Okubo's assassination in 1878, Ito succeeded him as Home Minister, and he took an important part in the early discussions of the future constitution. Early in 1882 he was sent to Europe to study various systems of government in operation. The last item on the list of subjects that he was to investigate was "local administrative systems." He returned in 1883 and became Minister of the Imperial Household Department and Chief of the Bureau for the Study of Institutions, a bureau which had been established within the department. In 1885, when the Cabinet replaced the Council of State, he became Prime Minister. He resigned from that post in 1888 to become President of the Privy Council in order to see the ratification of his constitution draft through this new organ of government.

Yamagata Aritomo was also a Chōshū samurai. Together with Saigo he was sent to Europe in 1870 to study Western military organizations and he became War Minister in 1872, when the Department of Military Affairs was divided into separate war and navy departments. He was instrumental in preparing the Universal Military Conscription Ordinance in 1873. His first contribution to the Meiji reforms was thus in the military field. However, in the first decades of the modernization effort in Japan, all available talent could be used in a wide range of endeavors, and no clear lines of demarcation were drawn between the civilian and military functions of government. Thus, during the Saga Rebellion of 1874 and again duing the Satsuma Revolt of 1877, Home Minister Okubo was invested with full military powers for the restoration of peace and order, including the command of troops. On the other hand, military men engaged widely in purely civilian tasks. Yamagata became Home Minister in 1883 and held this post for six years.[31] In due time he and his followers became the core of a military bureaucracy which competed with the civilian bureaucracy under Ito for decision-making power in all national affairs. Although an open break between the two leaders did not occur until 1898, their rivalry had long been in the making and it explains in part the opposing positions they took on the question of the establishment of a new local government structure.

When Ito had journeyed to Europe in quest of models for a Japanese constitution, he had been most impressed by the Prussian system. In Berlin he attended lectures by Rudolph Gneist and by his disciple, Albert Mosse. Yamagata, who was equally fascinated by Prussia, brought Mosse to Japan as an advisor in 1886. He explained this by saying that since Western nations had made institutional modernization in Japan a condition for treaty revision, it was necessary to have the local government system fixed by law, and that the Prussian model was "the soundest way."[32]

It is thus not surprising that there was no sharp disagreement between Ito and Yamagata on questions of substance. Men trying to create a new state naturally focus their attention on the interests of the nation, even when they are dealing with the status of local entities or of individual citizens. This is implicit, furthermore, in the form in which the problem presents itself to them. A local government system that has grown up from below may emphasize the idea that the citizens of a community should be given an opportunity to realize their own interests within that community and that the state should exercise self-restraint for this purpose. A local government system imposed from above will put the interests of the state first, and will stress the duties, not the rights, of citizenship.

Ito did not approve of the notion that the state should exercise the self-restraint which a policy of local autonomy implies. On August 27, 1882, in a letter to Yamada Akiyoshi, Yamagata's predecessor as Home Minister, he stated in part:

> In order to organize local government, we must be able to interfere with the regulation of prefectures, counties, and wards. The organization of autonomous bodies must not be in accordance with opinions and hopes recently expressed in the press. The central power must not be divided and mixed up with local government. Local government must have its bounds, and the central power shall absolutely not be restrained by it. Local government shall be limited by the Imperial Edict which permits its existence. This shall be true for the administration of regions, prefectures, and counties. These matters need no further explanation. . . .[33]

Yamagata, steeped in concepts of a basically inequalitarian, hierarchically ordered society in which all relationships are expressed in terms of duties toward a collective body, saw a close connection between the two tasks that he had made his life work: the building of a national army based on conscription and the creation of a local government system. The common basis was the fulfillment of the individual's obligation to the state: just as it was the duty of the lower orders to bear arms, so it was also their duty to carry out such tasks of government as were assigned to them. It was, in fact, the essence of local government that it provided for a discharge of the latter obligation.[34] Like Ito, Yamagata looked at local government from the standpoint of the interests of the state.

While thus sharing a common outlook on the character of the local government system, Ito and Yamagata disagreed on the question of when to establish it. Yamagata held that the local government system should be set up before promulgation of the constitution, and Ito wanted to see the constitution passed first. The argument was frequently carried on in academic terms—for example, whether it was not more proper that the general (the constitution) precede the specific (the local government system)—but such language obscured the real issue.[35]

The reasons for Yamagata's stand were in fact highly realistic.[36] At the time, the opening of the first Diet was imminent. There was no way to avoid popular participation in public affairs altogether, but those who governed had to ensure that the people had learned the lessons necessary for such participation. In Yamagata's mind the need for such preliminary education loomed large, and local government appeared to him a suitable vehicle for it. In his treatise entitled "History of the

Establishment of the Conscription and Self-government Systems" he paraphrased the Prussian statesman, vom Stein, with approval:

Local self-government raises the public and cooperative spirit, unites the ideas and hopes of the people and the policy and aims of the bureaucracy, and fosters patriotism and a sense of independence and honor in the people of the entire country.[37]

Yamagata felt that the people had to be imbued with this spirit before a constitution and parliament could be granted. In his explanation of the new municipal codes he stressed the training that popular participation in local public affairs would provide and stated: "Thus the people's ability will be nurtured to the point where they may gradually be entrusted with national affairs." Addressing a conference of local officials in February 1890, two days after the promulgation of the constitution, he sounded the same note:

If sound self-governing bodies are established, the spirit of self-rule developed, and the people in the cities, towns, and villages given experience in public administration, so that they might gradually acquire the ability to assume the nation's duties, then the fundamental basis of constitutional government will have been laid and the foundation of the nation will have been strengthened.[38]

Another reason for Yamagata's stand reflected his deep distrust of parliamentary institutions. He detested political parties and their divisive influence in government. Realizing that it would not be possible to stem indefinitely the tide of rising political consciousness, he was determined to guard certain areas of public life against the effects of party politics. The military establishment was one of these areas, and this explains partly his efforts to keep the armed services independent of the civil administration. Similarly, he wanted to keep local government isolated from the flood of party politics. More specifically, he hoped that it would be possible to have the local administration controlled by nonpartisan bureaucrats, even after party cabinets had replaced the oligarchic "transcendental" cabinets on the national scene. In the above-mentioned address in 1890, Yamagata stressed this point:

A sound administrative system for the cities, towns and villages—one which will steer a middle course and produce good results—will not be affected by the political upheavals of the central government.

There is an indication of this line of thinking in the reference to "uniting the ideas and hopes of the people with the policy and aims of the bureaucracy" in the quotation from Yamagata's treatise cited above. The passage that follows is more explicit:

Not only does local self-government aid the realization of constitutional government by raising the public spirit of the people and by giving the experience of participation in the administration, but it has also the considerable advantage that the influence of changes in the central administration does not extend to local administration; that is to say, under a constitutional government it occurs not infrequently that in connection with the tendencies of the members of the Imperial Diet, a change in the Cabinet is urged. Therefore, as the time for the establishment of the Constitution draws close, the establishment of local self-government as a preparatory step for it cannot be neglected for even one day.

The need for haste stemmed from the imminence of the establishment of the first Diet. A local government system of the type desired by Yamagata could not be expected to result from the deliberations of that body. Parliamentarians would not only fail to isolate local government from party politics; they would also stress—as Mosse suggested to Yamagata—the rights rather than the duties of local self-government. This could be anticipated because of the connection of the parliamentarians with the upper classes in their localities; the upper classes, as bearers of the greatest financial burdens of local government, would certainly want more independence than Yamagata and Mosse thought proper from the viewpoint of the state.

There were other reasons of a somewhat subsidiary nature in Yamagata's mind. The creation of a modern state would bring a tremendous increase in governmental work. Some of this work could be transferred to the localities so long as these were sufficiently controlled. At the same time, a certain amount of dissatisfaction with the central government could be deflected to the local bodies. Thus, he stated, "the cargo of the government could be lightened and a safe voyage and good speed could be achieved." And just as the citizens could be trained in public affairs by serving in local government, so could the officeholders. At a time when much of the discussion about the national government was couched in ideological terms—which were rather obnoxious to the practical men in government—Yamagata hoped that local officeholders would learn to keep their eyes on practical questions.

Ito—who, it should be noted, later became the first of the oligarchs to make peace with the parties—was less rigid in his attitude even then. He was more confident than Yamagata that the new parliament which he devised would not disrupt strong leadership. Ito considered himself a moderate and he probably wanted to steer a middle course between Yamagata's intransigence and the more radical demands of the opposition. Yamagata's idea that local government ought to be carved out of the body politic as an area of bureaucratic control may have been suspect to Ito, because as Home Minister, Yamagata would exercise that control, and at a time when he was becoming Ito's own main rival for power. Whatever Ito's motives, a desire to anchor local self-government in the constitution was not among them. He insisted that the local government system should be based on the spirit of the constitution and that therefore its establishment should follow, not precede, the promulgation of the new charter. Since the constitution is silent on local government, the course of the argument remains somewhat obscure.[39]

At any rate, Yamagata went ahead with his plan. His predecessor in the post of Home Minister, Yamada Akiyoshi, had ordered an official of that ministry, Murata Tamotsu, to draw up a draft for a local government system. Yamagata discarded this draft—which was characterized by the use of many indigenous Japanese elements—and in 1884 created an Investigation Committee for a Law of Towns and Villages (Chōsonhō Chōsa Iinkai). Its draft on the organization of municipal government, completed in 1885, was considered inadequate.[40] Later developments bear the mark of the participation of Mosse, who in July 1886 recommended the establishment of a special organ to lay down definite principles first. This was the Local System Compilation Committee (Chihō Seido Hensei Iin), over which Yamagata himself presided. The General Principles for the Reform of the Local Government System (*Chihō Seido Hensan Kōryō*) drawn up by Mosse were approved by the committee with some amendments strengthening central control, and later by the Cabinet. In March 1887 they were submitted to the Assembly of Local Governors. In spite of strenuous criticism there, Yamagata proceeded along the lines of the general principles, and Mosse drafted a System of Autonomous Entities (*Jichi burakusei*) dealing with cities, towns, and villages. The committee divided Mosse's draft into two parts, one for cities (*Shisei*), the other for towns and villages (*Chōsonsei*). The draft was submitted to the Cabinet in September, and to the Senate in November 1887.

The opinions expressed in the Senate give such an insight into the thinking of the time that we may note a few of them. Tsuda Shindo felt, like Ito, that the establishment of the constitution should precede the creation of a local government system. He argued that in Japan every-thing had to fit the "national polity" (*kokutai*) and that, since the Em-peror ruled the entire country, everything had to spread from the center. He opposed local self-government as a potential exception to this com-plete rule of the Emperor. Miyamoto Shoichi also saw dire consequences if the government should establish a right to self-government by law. Others, like Kato Hiroyuki and Ozaki Ryozo, simply stood for postpone-ment of the enactment of the draft, either until a system for the larger divisions, prefectures, and counties had been established or until the people could submit petitions indicating whether they wanted self-government or not.

The question whether mayors of cities, towns, and villages should be paid or honorary officials was discussed at length, for, along with the question of how they should be selected, it had great bearing on the problem of bureaucratic control. The selection of city mayors became the subject of a heated disagreement between the Cabinet and the Senate. The final solution was a system under which control increased with the importance of the entity: mayors of towns and villages were to be elected, but those of cities were to be appointed from among three candidates whose names had been submitted by the City Assembly. The three biggest cities—Tokyo, Osaka, and Kyoto—were to have no mayor at all, but were to be administered by the prefectural governor, an appointed official.

The Senate approved the Town and Village Code (*Chōsonsei*) in January 1888 and the City Code (*Shisei*) in the following month. Cabi-net approval followed in March and promulgation on April 17, 1888. Enforcement was to be gradual, starting in April 1889. It turned out to be gradual indeed, for it was far from complete at the time of the first major revision in 1899.

The Code for Urban and Rural Prefectures (*Fukensei*) and the County Code (*Gunsei*), also based on the general principles drawn up by Mosse in 1887, passed the same procedures as the other codes. They were promulgated on May 17, 1890, just two months ahead of the election of the first Diet and five months ahead of its first convocation.[41]

These codes constituted the main pillars of Japan's local government structure, which was to endure, with occasional alterations—including a large-scale revision in 1911—until 1947.

CHAPTER 3

A Survey of Local Government in Prewar Japan

The Meiji local government system was stricken from Japan's statute books in 1947. The purpose of our study would not be substantially furthered by going into its provisions in great detail. But because the past explains much of the present—and in this particular case, perhaps of the future—some remarks about its characteristic features are necessary.* No system is in force for over half a century without creating certain attitudes, among officials and the population at large, which outlast the validity of the law. If there was a long tradition of looking up to the national level and down to the local level, if the national official habitually considered the local entity as a ward and himself as the guardian, and if the local official customarily expressed his desires as humble petitions rather than as legitimate demands, then no legal fiat could immediately make national and local officials equal in their everyday dealings. Even where the law imposes limits on the powers of national officials, the attitudes of the past will often prove stronger than

---

* Japanese lawmakers are prone to look into the armory of the past for devices with which to execute new policies. This is so partly because the policy-makers of Japan have in general been conservative; but, in addition, legal technicians, especially in a country in which the law is codified, delight in using tried and proven terminology, lest they disturb the legal system. On the other hand, when such devices are used, they are immediately recognized, and opposition feeds on earlier, bad experiences with them. To cite an example: in the amendment of the Local Autonomy Law in 1956 the Prime Minister was granted powers to take supervisory measures of limited extent in case a local entity acted in a manner "injurious to the public interest." The mere employment of this phrase, which was also used in the prewar local government codes, seemed to stamp the amendment as an expression of the "reverse course" in post-Occupation Japan, which is anathema to the progressive opposition.

the law, and the fine line between legal and unwarranted interference, as drawn by the lawmaker, will be disregarded.

We have seen that the magistrates of the feudal era and their successors in early Meiji days needed only their official appointment and the loosest type of instructions in order to govern. Since then there has of course been a gradual progress toward more specific arrangements in law.[1] But as shown by Ito's letter (quoted in the preceding chapter), law was considered primarily as a framework within which the central government organized the exercise of its power, not as a restraint on that power. The adoption of a system of administrative rather than of statutory or judicial control was in line with that concept.[2]

Yamagata called the system that he created a "local *self*-government" system, and to those who measured it by the standards of the unbridled bureaucratic authoritarianism of earlier Meiji days it may have appeared as such. By comparison with other countries, Japan was highly centralized, but the term "local self-government" has nevertheless been applied ever since to any system of local administration, even when centralization reached its ne plus ultra in 1943.* As this suggests, there is widespread confusion over the meaning of the term. In the Japanese word for it, *chihō jichi*, the syllable denoting "self" (*ji*) is habitually used, but it has lost its significance. The lack of a clear concept has greatly hampered the endeavors to make local self-government a reality in the full sense of the term.

The Meiji local government system underwent repeated changes prior to the war, and a word needs to be said about the direction of these changes. In general, local autonomy showed some progress when democracy advanced, especially in the twenties. Further demands for local independence were voiced by scholars, and between 1926 and 1932 these found their way into the platforms of such leftist parties as the Social Democratic Party (Shakai Minshūtō), the Japan Mass Party (Nihon Taishūtō), the Labor-Farmer Mass Party (Rōnō Taishūtō), the National Mass Party (Zenkoku Taishūtō), and the Social Mass Party (Shakai Taishūtō). Although some of these platforms were rather general in nature—advocating, for instance, the "democratization of local government" and the "establishment of autonomous local government," —others demanded specific changes, including the popular election of

---

* At that time, the Home Minister referred to the wartime centralization measure as "elevating the true essence of local self-government." See Chapter 4, p. 61.

prefectural governors, mayors, and all other local public servants, the extension of the authority of the assemblies, and the curtailment of the powers of the governors and mayors to execute their policies over the heads of unwilling assemblies. These demands were not fulfilled in pre-Occupation Japan. The revision of 1929 stood, as has been aptly stated, on the watershed.[3] As Japan came under the sway of militarism the tendency was reversed. The connection between the notions of democracy and local autonomy, when stressed by the Occupation, thus found some basis in the history of prewar Japan. The Occupation abolished the Meiji local government system so as to further democratization. Similarly, those who wish to defend democracy in Japan today find it necessary to oppose the attempts of conservative Japanese governments to return Japan to a semblance of the prewar system. In thus continuing a role which they had played earlier in this regard, they are also willy-nilly siding with the now-defunct Occupation.

The Hierarchy of Government

Because national power cannot be exercised directly on the thousands of localities in a unitary state, an intermediate organ is a prime requisite of centralization. In pre-Occupation Japan the prefecture was that organ.[4] The prefectures were subordinate to the central government, and they in turn exercised control over the municipalities. The hierarchy of government under the Meiji system may thus be diagrammed as follows:

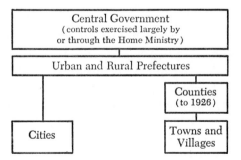

We speak of the relationship of the central government, the prefectures, and the cities, towns, and villages as a "hierarchy," because the upper level controlled the lower. But it is well to remember that such control presupposed a monolithic view of governmental functions. All levels of government could be considered parts of the same structure, because all were engaged primarily in carrying out functions assigned by the top level, the central government. All local units were, in effect, "distribution centers of the central authority."[5] This was always most conspicuous in the case of the prefecture, but the lower units differed from it only in degree.

Within the central government, the controls exercised by the Home Minister were based on the local government codes and were thus open to the view of the most cursory observer. But there were also other laws and regulations that intensified and broadened the scope of central government control, directly over the prefectures and indirectly over all local government. Thus the laws regarding the central government organization gave not only to the Home Minister but also to each minister within his jurisdiction the power to issue directions and instructions to the prefectural governors, who in turn had the same power vis-à-vis the mayors.[6] Furthermore, a great number of special laws, each dealing with a specific function of the various ministries, contained similar authorizations. As the range of governmental functions expanded, these laws multiplied. Thus, contrary to the impression gained by studying only legislation dealing specifically with local government, the thread of central control did not lead exclusively to the Home Ministry. Nevertheless, the Home Ministry remained the dominant organ in central-local relations because some of the controls of the other ministries were customarily exercised through it.

The difference between urban and rural prefectures was marked until 1899. Characteristically, the most developed cities—Tokyo, Osaka, and Kyoto—had the most restricted measure of self-government. They were not allowed to elect mayors of their own, but had as their chief executives the nationally appointed governors of the prefectures in which they were located. Opposition to this arrangement began as early as 1891 during the sessions of the second Diet. It did not come to fruition, however, until 1898, when the big cities were first allowed to have their own mayors. Throughout this century the same movement has pressed for a more complete exemption of the big cities, now swelled to the number of six, from the control of the prefectures, but the efforts have thus far met with no success.[7]

Two prefectures had peculiar features under the Meiji system. In Tokyo a Metropolitan Police Board had been created in 1874; jurisdiction over police functions was transferred from the Justice Ministry to the Home Ministry, and the Board's Superintendent-General came to be directed and supervised by the Home Minister. This direct chain of command, which bypassed the governor of Tokyo Prefecture, was retained under the new local government system. In other prefectures the Home Minister exercised his general jurisdiction over police affairs through the governor. The arrangement in Tokyo was thus identical with that in Paris, with its Prefect of the Seine and Prefect of Police.

Arrangements that differed from those for other areas were also made for Hokkaido, Japan's frontier for colonization and development. For one, the island was not subject to the municipal codes of 1888; instead, its towns and villages were divided into two classes and governed by special regulations enacted in 1897. For another, until 1890 the administration of Hokkaido was entrusted to a board under the Prime Minister, and the area was thus exempted from the control of the Home Ministry. When Hokkaido was placed under the Home Ministry, the area became similar in its administration to a rural prefecture. But it continued to be governed by special laws that gave its executive more authority than was possessed by governors elsewhere.[*]

The prefectural governors were not only national administrators but also the political agents of the central government in power. In an earlier period, when the Sat-Chō oligarchs were still trying to prevent the participation of parties in government, the governors had been exhorted to stand aloof from the parties and had been used to stem their growth within the prefecture by any means available. Later, when political parties became an inescapable reality, their task was to "deliver elections" to the government party. Their control over the police provided them with an effective means to this end. In Toyko, the Metropolitan Police Board could similarly be relied upon.

The City Code of 1888 applied to localities which the Home Minister had designated as cities. In 1889, 36 localities were so designated. Subsequently, additional localities were made cities on the basis of a population of first 25,000 and later 30,000 inhabitants. Urbanization was one of the prominent sociological developments in this period, so that the

---

[*] During most of this period these special laws were the Hokkaido Assembly Law and the Hokkaido Local Expense Law, Laws No. 2 and 3 of 1901. The main differences between Hokkaido and other prefectures were removed in 1922. Since 1946 Hokkaido has been governed by the same laws that apply to other prefectures.

number of cities increased rapidly, until there were about 200 at the end of World War II.[8] Until 1926, when the *gun* was abolished, one of the major differences between cities on the one hand and towns and villages on the other was that the cities were separated from the *gun*. A prefecture was thus composed of city areas and *gun* areas, the latter encompassing the towns and villages. This is still reflected in Japanese statistics, which continue to refer to these areas as *shibu* (city or urban part) and *gumbu* (county or rural part).

There was, and is, no difference in the legal status of towns and villages. Both are primarily rural units, although towns frequently have a more or less extended area of shops in which not only the townspeople but also the farmers from surrounding villages do their trading. Almost all of the towns and villages existing at the end of the period had come into being as the result of repeated large-scale amalgamations, carried out by the central government in order to create units capable of handling the functions assigned to them. As an association for cooperative living, the village of old served its purpose. As a unit of government— e.g., for purposes of conscription, census, education, and the repair of highways—it was too small. Since the old village had significance to its inhabitants mainly in the former capacity, and since the villagers, tightly knit together by a variety of bonds, had a feeling of "exclusiveness" toward neighboring settlements, such amalgamations were often executed against the will of the residents. The first wave of amalgamation between 1874 and 1886 reduced the number of towns and villages by 7,346, somewhat less than 10 per cent. Actually, the decrease would have been greater if the government had not sometimes permitted, especially from 1879 to 1883, the separation of towns and villages amalgamated earlier under duress. It is thus noteworthy that the Town and Village Code of 1888 expressly permitted amalgamations of towns and villages "regardless of the objections of interested parties when a town or village does not possess the capacity of fulfilling the obligations made incumbent upon it by laws, or when it is necessary for the public interest." In 1888 a Home Ministry Ordinance fixed standards of amalgamation for the guidance of the local officials, and by the end of the succeeding year 55,494 towns and villages had been absorbed, leaving a total of 15,820.[9]

However, the old village did not disappear altogether. It remained the center of loyalty and identification for its inhabitants, retained its social importance as a unit of cooperative living, and stayed as independent within the new administrative units as was feasible. Without any legal recognition until 1940, it lived on, usually under the name of an *ōaza* or *buraku*.* Thus a Japanese town or village became a governmental unit covering a comparatively large area and usually encompassing a number of scattered settlements, the old villages.

Besides a governor and a mayor, the other organs of government in prefectures and cities were councils and assemblies. The prefectural assembly was at first indirectly elected. In the counties, joint sessions of the county assemblies and county councils met for this purpose under the chairmanship of the *gunchō* (county head), and in the cities there were corresponding joint sessions of the city assembly and city council under the chairmanship of the mayor. This system of staffing prefectural assemblies was replaced in 1899 by direct elections. The prefectural governor, in whose selection the electorate had no voice, was always a true executive. The prefectural council, indirectly elected by the assembly, served as a secondary deliberative organ. In the cities, on the other hand, the city council was originally a collegiate executive body. The mayor was a member of the council, convoking it, presiding over it, and representing it. In many ways the city councils at that time were thus similar to the councils of British local bodies. But when the City Code was revised in 1911 the city councils were given the same subordinate role as their prefectural counterparts and the executive power was lodged in the mayor. As mentioned earlier, the mayor of a city was appointed from among three candidates nominated by the city assembly. Of course, the appointment could be denied to all three candidates, in which case the Home Minister called on the city assembly to nominate more candidates. This system continued until 1926, when city assemblies were permitted to elect a mayor in the same way as town and village assemblies. The mayor was a salaried official serving for a fixed term— first six and later four years. He played a dual role, for in addition to his duties as an official of the city, he carried out the administrative work of the prefecture and of the central government in his locality.

The members of the city council were elected indirectly by the assembly. Their positions were honorary, but as in the case of many honorary

---

* In some cases old villages retained their communally owned forests or meadows. In these cases they had the legal status of "property wards" (*zaisanku*). See Chapter 9, pp. 201–3.

positions, there was a legal duty to serve, and it was enforceable by sanctions—usually a suspension of citizenship imposed by the city assembly. Only citizens (*kōmin*)—as distinguished from residents (*jūmin*)—had the franchise and the right and duty to serve in honorary positions. Citizens were those who had resided in the city for two years or more, had contributed to the city's revenue, and had paid national taxes of, originally, more than two yen. The city assembly was directly elected by them on the basis of a three-class system patterned on the Prussian model: the holders of the franchise were divided into three classes on the basis of their taxpaying ability, and each class, regardless of its numerical size, elected one-third of the assembly. The vote was thus heavily weighted in favor of the larger taxpayers. The number of assemblymen, which ranged between a minimum of thirty and a maximum of sixty, depended on the population of the city.

In the towns and villages the mayors or headmen were elected by the assembly. Until 1926 the choice had to be ratified by the governor, who had to consult the prefectural assembly but was not bound by its opinion. An appeal against a disapproval by the governor was allowed to the Home Minister. Towns and villages had no council. The mayor was their chief executive. As the city mayor, he also administered prefectural and national affairs in his locality. Normally the position of the mayor of a town or village was honorary. The village assembly, again varying in numerical size according to population, was directly elected by a restricted electorate, which was divided into two classes according to taxpaying ability.

Although the class election system is basically a conservative device, its institution, in rural Japan at least, was also a measure of social change. The law sanctioned a shift of the basis of political leadership from family status regardless of wealth to wealth regardless of family status. Egalitarian considerations did not become victorious until 1926, when the class election system was abandoned after the establishment of universal male suffrage.

Until 1926 there existed between a prefecture and the towns and villages within it another level of government, the *gun*, or county. The *gun* had historical antecedents, but in its modern form it was modeled after the Kreis in Prussia. It exercised control functions over towns and villages but not over cities. Its head, the *gunchō*, was appointed by the central government, as had been the case during the period of the Three New Laws. The *gun* was thus "an imperfect autonomous entity." In addition to the *gunchō*, there was a county council (*gunsanjikai*) elected indirectly by the county assembly (*gunkai*). The county assembly itself was elected in part by the town and village assemblies and in part by the big landholders within the county until 1899, when a system of direct elections was established. But even after 1899 it remained subject to far-reaching controls exercised by the *gunchō*, who in turn was answerable to the governor and the Home Minister. Dissatisfaction with the role of the *gun* in the scheme of local government led to efforts in two directions: some proposed that the autonomy of the *gun* be increased by permitting election of its head; others advocated the abolition of the *gun*. Both ideas were anathema to Yamagata, who saw in the *gunchō* a useful tool for bureaucratic control below the prefectural level. In 1921 a law was passed that did away with the *gun* as a level of local government but retained the *gunchō* and his office (*gunyakusho*) as agencies of central administration; the law became effective in 1923, after Yamagata had died. Finally, in June 1926, the *gun* offices were also abolished. The *gun* was still used as the name of a geographical area, as an election district, and for other purposes outside the area of local administration. In 1942 it became the jurisdictional area for the local offices of prefectural governments. It still exists as such, in fact if not in law.[10]

Functions and Controls

The basic local government laws stated that prefectures, cities, towns, and villages should deal with "their public affairs" and with such affairs as they were made responsible for by laws or ordinances or by custom and practice. All this was qualified by two phrases: "subject to limitations by laws and ordinances" and "under the supervision of the government."[11] The phrase "their public affairs" might seem to suggest a considerable number of local functions, but this was not the case. Charles Beard, writing in 1923, observed that "the city government of Tokyo has very limited municipal powers,"[12] and the same thing could have been said of Japanese cities, towns, and villages in general. According to the terminology of Japanese public law, the "public affairs" of a municipality—usually called "proper functions"—are limited to activities that are designed to enhance the welfare of the inhabitants but which do not require the exercise of governmental authority over them. Such activities as budget-making, collecting local taxes, fees, and rents, and building roads, canals, and bridges are examples of "proper functions."[13]

Outside this category, local entities had authority over their citizens only as agents for the central government. There could be no local police, no local control of nuisances, no enforced zoning, not even a local dogcatcher, unless a national law or ordinance assigned the respective functions to the specific type of local entity in question. Police and education were kept strictly within national channels. Police functions included such matters as fire prevention, flood control, building inspection, sanitation, trade licensing, and the administration of factory and labor laws. All police officers and all schoolteachers were national officials, answerable only to national agencies. The scope of "proper functions" was thus exceedingly narrow. In addition, it did not denote an area of more or less independent local activity: both "proper" and "assigned" functions were subject to interference from above.

The duty of participating in the administrative affairs of higher levels of government—national or prefectural—was assigned either to local entities as such or to their chief executives. In either case it was always understood that the assignee acted in the interests of the assignor. The assignments continually created new links between the local entities and the various central ministries concerned with the assigned functions.

If the participation was assigned to the chief executive, his actions became completely independent of the assembly and of the local entity over which he presided. But even if the participation was assigned to the local entity itself, there was no choice: assigned functions were generally "obligatory functions," and the assembly acted simply as a rubber stamp of the assignor.

The delineation of functions was further blurred by laws that made certain "proper functions" also "obligatory functions." In this case, the local entity had no choice of acting or not acting, and when it acted, as it was obliged to do, it did so under supervision and control from above. There were national laws regarding water supply, drainage, and other proper functions which occupied these fields. As a matter of fact, there were few decisions that a locality could make on its own initiative. Most of the activities of local organs were predetermined from above. Viewed from the point of functions, there was deconcentration of the national administration, but no local self-government.[14]

Controls resulted, first of all, from legal provisions that granted the higher authorities powers to interfere in the administration of the lower levels of government. They ensured that, by and large, not the will of the lower entity but that of the supervising authority prevailed in the making of important decisions. The supervising authority for the prefecture was the Home Minister; cities, towns, and villages were supervised by the prefectural governor in the first instance and by the Home Minister in the second instance.[15]

In the literature of Japanese public law it was customary to classify the principal types of controls as inspection, preventive control, and corrective control, and we shall follow this classification.[16] Inspection was a general and preliminary control. The supervisory authorities could demand reports and documents, examine receipts and expenditures, and actually inspect the supervised localities as such.[17]

Preventive control included the granting of permits and approvals, on the one hand, and the reservation of the right of decision by the supervising authority, on the other. An example of the latter type of control was the selection of the city mayors until 1926. As we noted, the city assembly could nominate three candidates, but the appointment—i.e., the real decision—was reserved to the Home Minister.[18] The right to give permits included the right to modify the local action proposed. The number of acts requiring a permit or approval was decreased by various amendments until in 1926 only two remained in the basic codes: the raising of loans and the passing of all bylaws.[19] Yet in spite of the decline in the number of legal provisions regarding permit and approval, no important action could be taken without the consent of the prefectural or national authorities.[20] For where a sweeping inspection power and extensive powers of corrective control (which we shall presently describe) are accompanied by a firm grip on the purse strings and by a traditionally accepted higher status, the temptation to solicit approval from higher authorities, even when the law no longer makes this necessary in a particular case, can be overwhelming. In a different social and legal context, the remaining provisions regarding permits might have required only sporadic contact between a prefectural government and a village. In Japan, however, there was probably a more or less continuous liaison between them.[21]

Correction was exercised in various ways. The supervisory organ could issue orders (*meirei shobun*) or annul actions of the supervised entity on the grounds that they were ultra vires, or in contravention of laws and ordinances.[22] In addition, there was the "power of decision or execution by delegation." This power was usually exercised at the request of the chief executive of the supervised entity. For example, if the assembly failed to act or if the local chief executive considered an act of the assembly "injurious to the public interest," he could apply to the supervising authority for directions. The directive then took the place of the lacking or faulty assembly action. This was called a "discretionary disposition" (*senketsu shobun*).

A special case of this substitution was the so-called "enforced budget." If an assembly decision relating to the budget was deemed "impracticable," and particularly if the assembly failed to vote funds necessary to meet emergency expenses or to carry out "obligatory functions" (in most cases, assigned functions), the directive of the supervising authority could supply the lacking authorization for the expense by the assembly. Since the result was that the original draft measure could be executed, this device became known as "execution of the original draft" (*genan shikkō*). In 1929 about fifty per cent of the prefectural budgets were enforced in this manner.[23]

In what was called "execution by delegation," an act incumbent on the local entity could be carried out by the supervising organ or a person acting on its behalf. Two examples may illustrate this device. When a city mayor failed to include in the budget estimate one of the obligatory expenses mentioned above, the governor could add the item to the budget estimate. Similarly, when a mayor or other executive city official was unable to act, the Home Minister could dispatch a national government official to act in his stead.[24]

The dissolution of prefectural, city, town, and village assemblies was another control device. Normally, the power to dissolve the legislature is granted to the executive, and it is thus an element in the internal relations of the two branches of government. But under the Meiji local government codes, this power was not given to governors or mayors, but reserved to the Home Ministry as the supreme supervisory organ.[25] Finally, the governor could impose disciplinary punishment on mayors and other officials of cities, towns, and villages.[26]

These, then, were the principal provisions for the control of local government under the Meiji system. Their aim was clearly and openly to permit interference by the higher levels of government in the administration of the lower levels. But there were other arrangements that served the same purpose in a less conspicuous manner. One of these was that representatives of the electorate in the assembly were made subordinate to the executive. The relationship of the local executive to the assembly is usually seen as a problem of internal organization within the local entity, but under the Meiji system it had a direct bearing on relations between the lower and higher levels of government. The executive could be guided more easily than the assembly, and so by rendering citizen participation less effective the possibility of bureaucratic interference was increased. In other words, the scheme protected the executive from controls from below in order to facilitate his control from above.

Thus, the subjects on which the prefectural assembly could act were limited, while the governor exercised a "general control"; the town or village mayor was also chairman of the town or village assembly; and the executive on all levels called the assembly into session and, until 1929, had the exclusive initiative in the submission of bylaws. The executive could also annul the assembly's decisions—the device of "decision by delegation" by the supervisory authority being a last resort—when he considered an action of the assembly ultra vires, illegal, injurious to the public interest, or financially impracticable; and in certain cases he could put into effect proposals that had been submitted to the assembly or council but not acted upon. Finally, the threat of dissolution by the Home Minister could be used against a recalcitrant assembly. Dissolution put on the assembly members the burden of running for re-election; the executive, on the other hand, could not be removed by the assembly once installed in power.[27]

The regulations concerning local finances further ensured the impotence of local governments. They were not devised primarily to provide revenues for local activities, but rather to enable local entities to fulfill their assigned national duties, to make certain that national revenue could be poured into the important tasks of the time, such as developing armaments and building railroads, harbors, and mines. In financial matters as in general, the relationship between national and local government, as envisioned by the creators of the local finance system, was that between guardian and ward, but it would be equally appropriate to compare it to that between master and servant. The right of compulsory defrayal, which the central government had in case of obligatory functions, whether assigned or proper, is an example of this relationship.[28] Once the compulsory expenses were paid, few local entities had any money left for tasks they might have wanted to perform on their own initiative.

According to the law, the first source of local revenue was to be income from properties, use charges, fines, and so forth; only in case of shortage was income to be derived from taxation or the raising of loans. But there was always a shortage, and so taxation became a general source of income. The types of taxes that a local entity could impose were determined by national law, originally in the codes themselves and later in the Local Tax Law.[29] These consisted primarily of surtaxes to national taxes and—in the case of cities, towns, and villages—also of surtaxes to prefectural taxes. The Home Minister and Finance Minister controlled tax rates and collection as well as borrowing. Local initiative was thus effectively stifled. Since the revenues from these sources did not fully cover the expenses for tasks imposed by the national government, local entities had to be given subsidies, which increased in number and amount as the years passed. This made the localities dependent on the national treasury and subjected them still further to central government control.

Finally, the legal and financial submission of the local entities to the will of the central government was reinforced by the difference in prestige enjoyed by national and local officials. This difference found expression on all occasions. To cite examples, the mayor of the city of Tokyo occupied a very modest role at any official function at which the governor of Tokyo Prefecture was present. The passage of a governor through a town or village was a state affair, anticipated by the mayor with trepidation and preceded by frantic preparations. The clean-swept streets, the flags, the children lined up in their school uniforms, the mayor in morning coat and white gloves, and the deeply bowed heads—all gave acknowledgment to the exalted status of His Excellency, who represented the State and the Emperor, and to the lowliness of his subjects and their chosen officials.

Local government was thus entangled in a mesh of restrictive legislation, financial disability, and social inferiority. Some amendments to the codes—especially those made in 1926—loosened one or the other strand of legal control. But this alone could not bring about a substantial change. Although officially described as "local self-government," the system remained one of almost complete centralization, regimentation, and submission.

CHAPTER 4

Wartime Local Government

The Meiji leaders had hoped to restrict popular political participation so that the ruling oligarchy could do what seemed necessary and best for the country. In time, however, this concept of governing became unworkable. On the one hand, the rising political consciousness of larger and larger population groups had to be dealt with in some manner. On the other hand, governmental integration increased during the Meiji and Taisho eras in the sense that government reached into more and more aspects of the daily lives of the people.

As Japan prepared for war and faced the problems of large-scale planning in the organization of industrial and agricultural production, the allocation of manpower and material, and the rationing of food and consumer goods, the government had to mobilize the masses and channel all their energies into the war effort. This meant integration on a new scale and of a new and modern type. The use of such indigenous institutions as the *tonarigumi* was somewhat deceptive. The new *tonarigumi-chō* had his counterpart less in the village elder of Tokugawa times, from whom he took his title, than in the Blockwart of Nazi Germany. The *burakukai*, which was charged with promoting martial spirit and assisting in such governmental tasks as food rationing, was a far cry from the natural social unit of cooperative living which had kept contact with the government at a cautious minimum.

The establishment of neighborhood associations in 1940 was the capstone of several earlier measures to tighten government control over the economic and social life of the nation. Economic and social organizations had been increasingly regulated from the top even before the war in China,[1] but now, with a bigger war approaching, they were integrated into the governmental structure. In due time, local public entities assumed a new role: they became, in the language of Japanese observers, "collective entities." The strands that connected the individual with a variety of associations—the local entity as an inhabitant, the agricultural association as a producer, the *buraku* as a participant in the "cooperative life"—were all gathered together and linked with the big strand that connected him with the government as a subject of the Emperor. This "gathering" was one of the two chief trends in government during the period.

The other trend was toward application of the executive leadership principle on all levels. The revisions of the local government laws of the twenties had tended to increase the power of the assemblies, but now the trend was sharply reversed. In addition, the executive was given the authority to direct the various associations, which had been integrated into the local entity.[2] He was thus much more of a "leader" than his predecessor. This trend reached its climax in the creation of the position of superintendent-general, who headed the newly created regions until the end of the war.

A "reformation of the local government system" was demanded by Japan's military leaders as early as 1936, when a "Plan for the Renovation of the National Government" was submitted by the War and Navy Ministers to Prime Minister Hirota. The announced purpose was to free the government from "individualistic institutions and liberalistic policies" and to establish a totalitarian country "in accordance with the needs of national defense and the spirit of Japan." In 1937 the first Konoye Cabinet established a Local Institutions Research Institute. Later, the National Spiritual Mobilization Movement proposed plans to "bridge the gap between the people and the government." A number of drafts resulted from all these projects, but none was submitted to the Diet, because it was feared that there was not enough political backing for them.[3] It was not until 1940 that any measures affecting local government were actually put into effect.

The System of Neighborhood Associations

The political parties, which had supplied most of the prime ministers of the twenties, gradually lost their feeble hold on the government of the country to the exponents of militarism and totalitarianism. In the summer of 1940 they meekly submitted to the demands for a "new po-

litical structure" and disbanded. The new look in Japanese politics was
the Imperial Rule Assistance Association, a pet project of Prince Konoye,
who formed his second cabinet at the time. This association was to be
organized at the lowest level on the basis of the *buraku* and the *chō*
(town precincts).

In September 1940, a month before the inauguration of the Imperial
Rule Assistance Association, Home Ministry Ordinance No. 17 called
for the establishment of a net of neighborhood associations.[4] These associations had both a political and an administrative raison d'être, and
it is thus not surprising that there was some rivalry over leadership of
them between the Imperial Rule Assistance Association and the Home
Ministry. The Association saw them primarily as cells for political integration, whereas the Ministry considered them primarily as small-scale
local agencies for such administrative purposes as rationing, civil air
defense, and fire fighting. The declared political aim was to provide
channels for transmitting government policies down to the people and
popular feeling up to the government, which was to unify the nation
spiritually. The emphasis was definitely on the channel that led from the
top to the bottom, rather than on the one leading the other way. Government control was to be strengthened and extended to cover all phases of
the life of the people, including their "spiritual life." The neighborhood
associations were to cultivate conservative sentiments and to stem the
inroads of new forces wherever they existed.*

The government's scheme was to graft the new associations onto
existing groupings.† We have noted that the natural villages of feudal
times often survived the amalgamations of the Meiji era and retained
their social importance for their inhabitants. Sometimes the shrine of a
protecting deity (*uji*) formed the nucleus of a small grouping. In some
rural areas *goningumi* or *jūningumi*, encompassing from three to thirteen houses and serving a number of cooperative functions, also existed.
Of later vintage were the Young Men's Associations, Young Women's
Associations, and Women's Associations, which were frequently organized at the lowest level in areas smaller than the smallest legal local

---

* Functionally, this was probably their strongest similarity with their Tokugawa
counterparts.

† In the following discussion, the term "neighborhood associations" will be used
for the entire system and the term "block associations" for the *burakukai* and *chōnaikai* level; Japanese names will be used for specific components of the system.

government unit, the village. There were also various types of economic groups, usually called *kumiai,* such as the Agricultural Cooperative Association (Nōgyō Kyōdō Kumiai), which were normally organized on the village level and carried out purchasing, storing, marketing, and credit functions for the villages. These agricultural cooperative associations had shown signs of spontaneous development in the twenties and were assiduously fostered by the government in the thirties, until one of them existed in nearly every agricultural village. In addition there were Associations of Agricultural Households (*nōkai*) at various levels, starting with the village. They concerned themselves, at least on the local level, primarily with improving agricultural production. There were also similar groups in the fields of sericulture and fishing. In the course of the thirties all these organizations lost whatever spontaneous character they had originally possessed. They became part of an organizational hierarchy, governed by laws and ordinances and used for the execution of the government's economic policies.[5] In the cities, street groupings (*chō*) frequently existed within the administrative wards established by Article 82 of the City Code.

The areas of these groups formed a highly irregular patchwork, and their names varied considerably. As stated earlier, the area of the old natural village was sometimes called *ōaza* and sometimes *buraku.* Often an *ōaza* was in turn divided into *buraku.* In some cases *goningumi* or *jūningumi* existed as part of a larger unit, such as the *buraku,* but sometimes they were the only unit below the village. Sometimes the areas of the economic and social groups, which had come under government regulation, coincided with those of one or the other natural community, but this was not always the case.

Most important, the natural communities did not exist everywhere. Especially in the cities, *chō* and *tonarigumi* covered only part of the urban areas, being most prevalent in the districts of small shopkeepers. In the past, there had been occasional attempts to keep them alive or even to revive them, especially at such times of stress as after the Russo-Japanese War, after the first World War, and during the depression of 1930–32. Sometimes they had sprung up more or less spontaneously after a calamity, as after the great earthquake in Tokyo and Yokohama in 1923.[6] But this had always been a temporary phenomenon. Whereas the *buraku*—in the wider meaning of the larger natural unit below the village level—could look back on a more or less continuous and widespread existence, small units of a size comparable to the *goningumi* could be found only in about a third of the towns and villages.[7] Sweeping generalizations regarding the traditional and indigenous character of the entire neighborhood association system and the social needs that it fulfilled are thus somewhat misleading.

We shall return to the natural groupings and their social and political significance in later chapters. Here it is sufficient to record that such existence as they had at the time was utilized in 1940 to create new echelons of local government below the city, town, and village level.* These echelons were the *tonarigumi,* the rural *burakukai,* and the urban *chōnaikai.*

In general, about ten households formed a *tonarigumi* and ten to twenty *tonarigumi* a block association (*burakukai* or *chōnaikai*). In cities, or in the wards of the larger cities, federations of *tonarigumi* were sometimes set up. Where such groupings did not exist, they were artificially created without any semblance of support by social or economic need or any traditional community spirit. Nevertheless, the job was speedily accomplished; in April 1941, only seven months after the initial ordinance, the Home Ministry announced that the system was in complete operation throughout Japan. A total of 199,700 block associations and 1,120,000 *tonarigumi* had been created.[8]

The *tonarigumi* disseminated official instructions, usually by means of a *kairanban,* or "circulating bulletin board," reported on compliance with them, distributed rations, collected taxes and contributions, and performed a number of similar services.[9] The block associations served as channels for the distribution of orders and such essential papers as ration books, and directed agricultural and welfare work. Heads of block associations met at regular intervals to receive instructions from municipal, prefectural, and national officials.

Control from above was rigid. The leaders of the block associations were appointed by the mayor, although "nomination or other suitable ways of recommendation" by the associations were permitted. Regular monthly meetings, called *jōkai,* had to be attended by all members on the day and hour prescribed by instructions.[10] These meetings served as much for indoctrination as for the conduct of any business of immediate

---

* Strictly speaking, this status was given to them by a law passed on February 27, 1942; but in actuality they had functioned in this capacity since their inception.

practicality, and the participation of the membership consisted almost exclusively of being present.

The leadership of these groups often fell to the most conservative and nationalistic elements within them, who gladly used their position to suppress all criticism of the existing regime and to berate any lukewarm attitude toward it. In many instances, the local "boss" or his henchmen achieved official recognition in this way, and submission to them thus became unavoidable, because they could easily deny food, fuel, and other necessities to a recalcitrant individual or family. Often the block association heads became petty tyrants and the position they held was resented, especially where it had no roots in tradition or in acknowledged local needs. In the urban centers, in particular, where artificial face-to-face group patterns had to be superimposed on the natural anonymity of city life, the *tonarigumi* often created more friction than neighborliness and there was a good deal of hostility against the system.

Revision of the Basic Local Government Codes

Within the conventional levels of local government, the tendencies toward integration and the establishment of the executive leadership principle found expression in the revision of the basic laws in 1943.[11] According to the government statement at the time of the submission of the revision to the Diet, cities, towns, and villages were now to become primary organs of national administration, assuring success to the central government's emergency programs for prosecuting the war and securing the people's livelihood. Mayors were given authority to direct the economic and social units, such as the youth organizations and the *nōgyōkai,* which had been created by legally merging the various agricultural associations and cooperative societies into one nationally controlled, compulsory, and strictly hierarchical organization. Mayors were given enlarged control over the neighborhood associations and were authorized to delegate matters under their jurisdiction to the chiefs of these associations; on the other hand, the scope of matters that they were required to submit to the assembly was curtailed and, in general, the powers of the assembly were reduced.

At the same time, central government control over the local executives was strengthened. Mayors and other municipal officials could now be dismissed by the Home Minister and the governor if they were considered unfit for their office. The number of acts requiring a permit or authorization by the supervising authorities increased.

Under a new law called the Code for Tokyo Metropolis, the Prefecture of Tokyo absorbed Tokyo City.[12] Tokyo Metropolis comprised the thirty-five wards of Tokyo City and the various cities, towns, and villages previously under the supervision of the Tokyo prefectural government. The governor of Tokyo Metropolis was nominated by the Home Minister and then formally appointed by the Emperor. The chiefs of the Tokyo wards also became government-appointed officials. The new metropolitan assembly had only one hundred members, approximately one-third of the combined membership of the erstwhile Tokyo prefectural assembly and Tokyo municipal assembly. In general, the nation's biggest city was given less self-government than other units, in this sense reverting to the status it had when the Meiji system was first established.

While thus bringing centralization to a new high, the government talked of "calling from local self-government all potentialities to have national policies penetrate throughout Japan and to obtain the security of the people's livelihood," and officials were exhorted to "make local self-government respond to the needs of the state and thus elevate its true essence."[13] There was some opposition to these measures in the Diet, and Representative Nakatani Takeyo, calling a spade a spade, insisted that the new laws amounted to a complete suppression of local self-government.[14] But under the circumstances of the time, such opposition could be only a brave but futile gesture.

Regional Administration

With the exception of the brief interlude of the twenties, the measures of the Japanese policy-makers in the field of local government usually had two mainsprings: one was the need to organize the tasks of government, the other the desire to keep popular participation under control. In the establishment of the neighborhood associations, both political considerations and considerations of public administration played an important role. The revision of the Basic Code in 1943 was avowedly designed to simplify local administration and make it more efficient. But it was clearly also an element in the authoritarian trend of the time. In creating a new top organization in 1943, considerations of public administration were probably in the foreground. It was felt that such problems as the expansion of war production and the distribution of foodstuffs and other commodities could be solved more expeditiously within areas larger than the existing prefectures. At the same time, the establishment of regions served to reduce incipient tendencies toward local

self-government on the prefectural level, which the government decried
as "sectionalism." Referring to the demands for popular election of governors which had been frequently voiced in the past, a commentator,
writing in 1943 in praise of the new regional system, stated:

> The popular opinion is that an elected prefectural governor or an elected
> mayor of a big city would naturally endeavour to serve the interests of his sup-
> porters and thus display sectionalism. On the other hand, if a prefectural gov-
> ernor or a mayor is appointed by the Government, he will not have any sec-
> tional interest to serve, and so he would stand a better chance to prove himself
> a non-attached administrator. Inter-prefectural sectionalism emanates from
> provincial autonomy. If the latter is dispensed with, the former will automati-
> cally disappear. It is gratifying to note that the tightening of State control over
> all branches of national activity has considerably straitlaced the scope of pro-
> vincial autonomy.[15]

The regional system was established by a series of Imperial Ordinances and thus without consultation of the Diet. The country was
divided into nine regions (*chihō*): Hokkaido, Tohoku, Kanto, Tokai,
Hokuriku, Kinki, Chugoku, Shikoku, and Kyushu. With the exception
of Hokkaido, each region comprised a number of prefectures. In each
region a regional administrative council (*chihō gyōsei kyōgikai*) was
set up. This council was headed by a president, who was always the
governor of the most important prefecture. He was appointed to the
post by the Prime Minister and was under his immediate control. The
other members of the council were the other governors of the region, the
chiefs of police, and the chiefs of regional bureaus of various central
government ministries, such as the bureaus of home affairs, financial
affairs, taxation, forestry, mine inspection, munitions, fuel, communications, railways, and of the offices of the monopoly corporation. While it
was claimed that the system thus provided the machinery for collabora-
tion between central and prefectural authorities, in actuality the councils were agents of the central government. The president, frequently a
former minister, was given wide powers by the Wartime Administrative
Special Measures Law. He could not only request the various ministers
to issue necessary instructions to the chiefs of their bureaus within the
region, but also require the other governors within it to comply with his
orders. The executive officers of the councils, the regional councilors,
were appointed by the Home Minister and responsible to him. A secretariat was provided for the councils.[16]

In June 1945 the possibility of an invasion raised the specter of a country so divided by actual fighting that communications with Tokyo could not be maintained. To prepare for this emergency the nine regional administrative councils were replaced by eight regional superintendencies-general (*chihō sōkanfu*), each coinciding with a military and air defense district.[17] The superintendent-general had his counterpart in the military district commander. The new units were given "the complexion of a centralized government with the object of administering local affairs with authoritarian thoroughness."[18]

The wartime developments demonstrated that totalitarianism necessarily leads to complete centralization. The ease with which the revisions were achieved also showed clearly how weak local self-government had been in the past. Commenting on these revisions, a Japanese political scientist observed that just as men expose their defects in time of crisis, so do national institutions. The mere outward trappings of autonomy, which Japanese local entities had worn since the Meiji period, fell under the impact of total war, exposing nakedly the true character of the system.[19] When the Occupation of Japan began, it encountered Japan's local government in its most thoroughly centralized form.

CHAPTER 5

Occupation Reforms in Local Government, I

The Occupation reforms in the field of local government cannot be really understood or fairly appraised unless they are considered within the framework of the Occupation's overall aims. These aims were strongly colored by the character of the war and of the enemy against whom it was fought. For the United States, the power that almost single-handedly carried out the Occupation, that war—as the one before it—was to a large extent a war "to make the world safe for democracy." It is thus not surprising that "democratization" was the primary aim of the internal reforms in Japan. This was particularly true during the first phase of the Occupation, when most of the local government reforms were put into effect.

"Democratization" is a political aim. The civilians and officers who staffed the sections of the headquarters of the Supreme Commander for the Allied Powers* in the years after the surrender have justly been compared to a band of devoted revolutionaries.[1] Like all revolutionaries, they tended to subordinate other concerns to the imposition of their beliefs and ideals on the country and to the eradication of practices that stood in the way.

This raises the question whether their aims were realistic. After all, their power was that of a foreign occupying force, and the ideals that motivated them were drawn from a cultural heritage developed in the West. Could democracy and local autonomy, in the sense of a right of local entities to govern local affairs, be expected to find roots in Japan?

---

* Hereafter the Supreme Commander for the Allied Powers will be referred to as SCAP, the abbreviation by which the persons occupying that position—i.e., successively Generals MacArthur and Ridgway—and their staff organization became known.

We may admit at the outset that no alien system, imposed by a foreign power and bearing no functional relationship to the realities of the indigenous society, is likely to endure. But how alien were the Occupation aims to Japan? To what extent were the reforms related to trends in Japanese society? The answers hinge on one's view of contemporary Japanese society and, more generally, on one's view of the nature of culture. At the risk of oversimplification, we must consider various possible views and indicate our own.

The Occupation tended to negate the importance of cultural differences. In the statements emanating from headquarters, we find frequently the assumption that all men desire freedom and that they will use free institutions, once established, to increase their freedom. Occasionally, public relations releases even equated the establishment of such an institution with successful democratization. It is not necessary to argue at length here that this was an overly optimistic and untenable view. As this study will show, most reforms were opposed by those who feared that they would undermine traditional ways, and once the reforms were "on the books," traditional attitudes had a braking, modifying, and sometimes nullifying effect.

On the other hand, the importance of cultural differences is sometimes overrated by critical observers of the Occupation. A distorted view may result, in particular, from an excessive stress on the traditional elements in culture. These are often considered the prime reality of a society. A fixed Eastern pattern of culture is constructed out of elements of the great tradition and then compared with an equally fixed Western pattern. Thousands of years of cultural heritage on either side seem to confirm the notion that "never the twain shall meet." In gauging the compatibility of Western ideas and Eastern ideas, this essentially static view of culture leads to the assumption that what was incompatible yesterday is also incompatible today and probably will be so forever. Those who hold this view naturally conclude that the Occupation was parochial and highly unrealistic when it endeavored to transplant Western notions like democracy into a Far Eastern setting. It is difficult, however, to reconcile this view with the social and cultural change that is taking place in Japan today. The effects of the growth of commerce, industrialization, and urbanization on the culture of this recently agrarian society are obvious enough, but a static view of culture is simply unable to account for them.

According to a different, more dynamic view of culture, culture is not permanently fixed, and cannot be extrapolated for all time from a few great classics of the past. It changes in time, with the later accretions being related to the changing circumstances of the society. Tradition thus retains significance as the base point for adaptation, but its influence is counterbalanced by the influence of social change. Such a view of culture avoids the distortion inherent in a neglect of either cultural tradition or of social change. It also does away with the dichotomy of fixed Eastern and Western culture patterns. When we view the Asian scene from this vantage point, we no longer see simply the encroachment of one culture on another. We recognize that after the original impact of foreign contacts, cultural change develops its own dynamics. The direction of the change is dictated not by alien impositions or by native imitation, but by the functional prerequisites of the society at any given time. Whatever has no relation to this direction is alien; whatever fits in with it is not.

It follows from this view that the Occupation reforms were not necessarily unrealistic whenever they ran counter to Japanese tradition. One also has to ask whether they found, or are still finding, support in some trends of social change in Japanese society. Only when this question must be answered in the negative can a specific reform be considered culturally inept.

We cannot attempt here to answer all the complex questions raised by this view, but it is pertinent to note that few of the reforms "introduced" by the Occupation were completely unfamiliar to the Japanese. The aims of most SCAP reforms had been supported in the past by various groups within Japan, which had simply lacked sufficient power to realize them. In the field of local government, for example, there had been endeavors to increase local autonomy by providing for the election of governors, for the strengthening of the assemblies, and for the curtailment of the controls of the central bureaucracy. The Occupation supplied the necessary power to translate these aims into reality. The reforms have thus had their Japanese supporters and defenders, and the more thoughtful SCAP policy-makers recognized the opportunity of working with them and through them. They saw the need for assuring the survival of their reforms by strengthening those forces in the body politic that supported them. They realized that once the power of the Occupation was withdrawn, the interplay of political forces might lead to a measured return of the pendulum, involving certain modifications of their work; but they felt certain that the results of their labor would not be tossed aside wholesale as a foreign imposition. Their expectation was apparently justified. Up to this time, twelve years after the end of the Occupation, only piecemeal attempts at a return to the status quo ante have been attempted, and these have often met with heavy opposition.

SCAP assumed from the beginning that the democratization of Japan would be furthered by placing emphasis on local self-government. Since the advances in democracy in Japan during the twenties had been accompanied by advances in local autonomy, and since the authoritarian trend of the thirties and forties had led to increasing centralization, SCAP's assumption was a reasonable one. The circumstances, however, were not auspicious for the introduction of local self-government. Revolutions in general are not friendly to local self-government; revolutionaries realize that a strong central government can facilitate their work throughout the country, whereas all kinds of intermediary associations could hinder their work and tend to keep pre-revolutionary—and thus potentially anti-revolutionary—sentiments alive. (The French Revolution is a clear illustration of this.) During the Occupation some of the most zealous Japanese supporters of reform were lukewarm to local autonomy for similar reasons. Quite possibly, an indigenous revolution might have pushed aside the memory of past experiences with centralization and concentrated on making sweeping changes in the constellation of power at the center, rather than on curtailing the strength of the central government, regardless of its character. Still, taking a long-range view, there was much to recommend a policy of decentralization. For one thing, insofar as local self-government created vested interests in preserving itself, it constituted an insurance against an easy reversal to totalitarian patterns; for another, if social change— and the concomitant political change—was to be permitted to follow its natural course, it sooner or later had to express itself on the local level, and local autonomy set the stage for an uncoerced development in this direction. Finally, the Occupation was as sure of the educative merits of local self-government as Tocqueville, Stein, Gneist, and Yamagata had been, whatever the differences in the content of the desired education.

It has been claimed that the Occupation remodeled Japanese local government in the image and likeness of American institutions.[2] Certainly, there were some Occupation officials who could not or would not understand any system that differed from what they had known in the United States, or in their home states. But this element of provincialism did not result in an "Americanization" of the Japanese local government structure; that structure, in its main elements, still bears a much closer resemblance to its own antecedents than to any American counterpart, and it may be well to recall that even these antecedents were anything but indigenous.

If SCAP's local government reforms were less than a complete success, it was not because the idea of local self-government was utterly alien to the Japanese or because the structure established by the reformers followed an American model too closely. The reasons lie elsewhere. For one thing, the piecemeal opposition of conservative Japanese governments, closely allied with the prewar bureaucracy, sapped the effectiveness of the reform from the start.[3] For another, the reformers failed to tackle early enough and vigorously enough such vital problems as the reallocation of governmental functions and the establishment of an independent and viable local finance system. As a result, local self-government remained incomplete. Even a fully established system of local autonomy would have had to overcome social inertia and traditional attitudes in order to work effectively, and the partial reforms accomplished by the Occupation could hardly serve as the basis for such a development.

A different and more germane sort of question remains to be answered: could progress toward a greater degree of local freedom be expected to occur in Japan in the mid-twentieth century? Would it find a basis in the requirements of contemporary Japan? Did the exigencies of the modern state, which elsewhere had created a "crisis of local autonomy," permit it? Was it too late to try to establish a system that ran counter to the new collectivism of the national welfare state? No simple answers can be given to these questions; it seems to me that they have to be answered not in absolute but in relative terms. The new collectivism may not support the degree of local freedom known in the past in older democratic countries, but does it demand the degree of centralization that characterized pre-Occupation Japan? If we admit that local functions have shrunk and national functions have expanded in industrializing societies, need we abandon the idea of local self-gov-

ernment functions altogether? Ultimately, the balance between centralization and local autonomy is influenced, within the range of feasibility,
by value judgments. The idea of local self-government has political
advantages for a democratic society, and the Occupation professed to
put a high premium on these advantages. Some Japanese have seemed
to agree, as shown by their opposition to later efforts to revert to a
semblance of the centralization of the past. Others, however, have
found the advantages too unimportant and the price for them too high.
If the Occupation had succeeded in establishing the prerequisites for
a system of local autonomy, even within the narrower limits dictated by
the needs of a modern state, the outcome would have depended on the
strength of these competing forces. As it was, the battle never reached
such a tentative balance.

Basic Occupation Policy

Neither the Potsdam Declaration of July 26, 1945, nor the Presidential
Policy Statement on Japan of September 6, 1945, required expressly that
the democratization of Japan include the establishment of local autonomy.[4] But when the Government Section of SCAP was established, on
October 2, 1945, one of its functions was to make recommendations for
the decentralization of the Japanese government and the encouragement of local responsibility.[5] A policy of changing national-local relations in Japan had thus been decided upon in Tokyo before the Occupation was one month old. A month later, on November 3, 1945, it was
apparently sanctioned in Washington. The Joint Chiefs of Staff's Basic
Initial Post-Surrender Directive for the Occupation and Control of
Japan, forwarded to SCAP on November 8, 1945, stated: "Local responsibility for the local enforcement of national policy will be encouraged."[6]

This was a somewhat cryptic sentence. It considered local entities only
in their relation to the execution of national policy—a viewpoint that had
been the bane of local self-government ever since the Meiji Restoration.
The enforcement of national laws by local public bodies, which it envisioned, was hardly a new departure. It apparently aimed at loosening
national controls, even where localities enforced national policy, but
the word "responsibility" puts some doubt even on this interpretation.
Thus while the statement lacked precision, its tenor did not seem to
prohibit a policy aiming at the establishment of local autonomy.

Such a policy was in fact adopted by SCAP. Its ideological basis may be seen in General MacArthur's statement on the occasion of the Diet's approval of the local government reform of September 1946. Here are some excerpts:

Democracy cannot be imposed upon a nation. . . . It must swell up from the people's will to be free, from their desire and determination to govern their own local affairs without domination by individual strong-men, by minority pressure groups or by an entrenched bureaucracy. . . . It is essential, therefore, that the people in every prefecture, city and village be given complete opportunity to express their will, and by assuming full responsibility to learn procedures of democratic government. Such direct participation in local government will profoundly influence the shaping of national policies, will provide a checkrein against arbitrary governmental controls and a safeguard to individual freedom. . . . It is axiomatic that such experience in government will develop the dynamic and enlightened leadership and initiative essential to the vigorous and progressive building of a democratic nation.[7]

Similarly, the Government Section Report states:

It is on the local level that the individual citizen gains his experience in participating in public affairs. It is on the local level that he most directly comes in contact with his government. . . . Representative government reaches its fullest expression when the citizens of a local community, through officials elected by and responsible to them, determine the policies and manage the affairs of that community. . . . The local arena thus becomes a training ground for leadership in national affairs.[8]

These are, of course, variations on Tocqueville's theme that town meetings are to liberty what primary schools are to science. They show that to the Occupation the establishment of local autonomy was a means to the end of democratization.

The enthusiasm for decentralization and local self-government was not shared throughout SCAP, however. The exigencies of war and its aftermath create a particularly unhealthy climate for the dispersion of governmental power. In the early years of the Occupation the economic situation of Japan was critical and economic controls were essential, and it is not surprising that the SCAP sections in charge of this field of governmental activity were opposed to a weakening of these controls by limitations on the powers of the central government. But even later, when the economic crisis had passed, staff sections engaged in certain practical and ostensibly non-political programs—public health, public safety, social security, development of natural resources, and so on—

were often in favor of centralized controls for their particular projects.[9]

Nevertheless, the Occupation was publicly committed to the establishment of local autonomy, and we may now review the steps it took, or failed to take, in that direction.

Some Negative Steps

As a new local government structure was erected, some parts of the old order were destroyed. The abolition of the regional superintendencies-general and the system of neighborhood associations did away with innovations of the immediate prewar and wartime periods. But the abolition of the Home Ministry struck at an institution with a history of seventy-five years, an institution which had occupied a position of great importance, second perhaps only to that of the Army and Navy, ever since Japan's emergence as a modern state.

In all three cases, the abolition was not ordered immediately but was the result of a series of developments. In regard to regional administration, the Japanese government requested on September 28, 1945, SCAP's permission to replace the superintendencies-general, created in anticipation of an invasion emergency, with regional administrative affairs bureaus. There was some feeling in SCAP in favor of immediate dissolution rather than replacement, but the opinion that the bureaus might prove useful in the application of necessary controls prevailed, and the permission was given.[10] The new bureaus, established in the areas of the superintendencies-general by Imperial Ordinance No. 622 of November 26, 1945, were in their functions and structure similar to the former regional administrative councils. They continued to exist until April 30, 1947, a few days before the enforcement of the Local Autonomy Law.

The abolition of the neighborhood associations raised a more delicate problem. When the war ended, the activities of these associations, including those of rationing and thought control, were at their height. Some of these activities ceased with the end of the war, but the continuation of controls on production and consumption held the system together. The Home Ministry, furthermore, considered the neighborhood associations an essential part of local government.

The first steps regarding these groups did not involve any change in their position. Not even the amendment of the basic local government laws in September 1946 affected their legal status. As before, the local executive could delegate administrative business to them.[11] At the time, the Japanese government replied to a question in the Diet by stressing that neighborhood associations would remain the lowest branch of local administration and would play an important role in the execution of assigned national functions.[12] Control by the local executive was retained and public subsidization continued.*

But, in keeping with the demands of the hour, the government thought it necessary to create the appearance of a "democratization" of the neighborhood association system. The Vice Home Minister therefore instructed perfectural governors to encourage election or other methods of selection of officers of neighborhood associations that would reflect the will of the constituency.[13] This step, which did not bring about a significant change in local leadership, failed to satisfy SCAP.† The Japanese government was faced with the alternatives of either abolishing the neighborhood associations or else providing by law for the public election of their chiefs. At the time an extension of the original purge directive to local levels was under consideration. If the purge was to be extended to the level of the neighborhood association chiefs, their public election would have required the examination of the eligibility of some 220,000 persons. The Japanese government had various misgivings about the extension of the purge to the local level in general, but it particularly wanted to exclude the neighborhood association chiefs from it. It finally submitted a plan for the extension on October 21, 1946. The memorandum from the Chief of Government Section, General Whitney, to the Japanese government, reviewing the government's plan, insisted on the free election of heads of block associations, but demanded screening only for "all holders of important executive policy-making positions in the local government, including chiefs of departments, bureaus, and sections in municipal and town governments." The demand for election was based of course on the governmental character of the neighborhood associations. In an effort to deny this basis, Prime

---

* Between August 1945 and May 1946, a single *chōkai* (an alternative name for *chōnaikai*) in Tokyo received 512 instructions, mainly from the metropolitan and national governments. The subsidy for all *chōkai* in Tokyo in 1946 amounted to more than six million yen. These figures are based on unpublished reports of the Tokyo Metropolitan Office.

† Until November 1, 1946, only 208 out of 1807 Tokyo *chōkai* leaders had been replaced. This figure includes replacement of leaders who died, changed their residence, or for other reasons had become unavailable.

Minister Yoshida described the neighborhood associations in his letter
to General MacArthur of October 31, 1946 (which dealt with the extension of the purge) as "entirely voluntary associations." But this picture
was hardly in accord with reality; membership remained compulsory as
long as a person's residence had to be certified by neighborhood associations for rationing purposes, and as long as the actual distribution of
rations was carried out by them. Yoshida's plea against the requirement
of election of neighborhood association chiefs failed. The purge was
extended to the local level by a series of imperial ordinances of January
4, 1947. In regard to block associations, Imperial Ordinance No. 4 provided for the election of heads by universal adult suffrage. Reluctantly,
the government thus reached its decision to divest the neighborhood
associations of their public character in order to obviate the necessity
for the election of their chiefs, which would otherwise have been part
of the local elections scheduled for April 1947. Government control
over the system was abolished on January 22, 1947. On that day Home
Ministry Instruction No. 4 rescinded Home Ministry Instruction No. 17
of 1940, which had instituted the system. Administrative tasks, such as
the issuance of residence certificates, were to be transferred to cities,
towns, villages, or wards by April 1, 1947. At the end of March 1947 the
Ministry of Agriculture and Forestry decided to issue staple food rations
directly to the individual consumer, rather than to the *tonarigumi* as
before. Neighbors could, however, pool their ration cards to receive
their rations jointly if they wished.[14] But while ostensibly stripping the
neighborhood associations of their governmental functions, the government made it clear that it favored the continuation of the associations
on a voluntary basis. The Chief of the General Affairs Section of the
Home Ministry's Local Affairs Bureau stated that only the character of
the neighborhood associations as terminal administrative agencies had
been abolished, and that this did not imply that the organizations had
been a bad thing. He stressed that there existed no obstacle to their
continuation as voluntary associations.[15] A few days later Home Minister Omura released a statement in which he explained the abolition
of the wartime system. He referred to the original evolution of the
neighborhood associations through a natural and voluntary process.
Then he mentioned that because of their ties with the Imperial Rule
Assistance Association during the war they "were considered as a
perpetuation of a system born of war whose aspects recall wartime

regimentation and chauvinism." The alteration of the structure had been administratively unwise up to now in view of the exigencies of rationing, but now the "continuation of the present structure is considered not only contrary to the principle of local autonomy but may also permit unscrupulous individuals to exercise improper influence over the forthcoming elections." The considerations to which Omura referred were, indeed, uppermost in the minds of the Occupation reformers. But Minister Omura was quick to add that the abolition of the *chōnaikai* and *burakukai* "opened the road for reformation of free voluntary organizations of the citizens for the satisfaction of their needs."

Another point in the statement deserves attention. After explaining the transfer of functions from the neighborhood associations to city, town, village, or ward offices, the Home Minister stated: "In order to effect this . . . subordinate members of a staff of city, town, or ward officers may be assigned to suitable districts." Since the "suitable districts" turned out to be those of the former *buraku* and *chō*, the ground was laid for their continuation as administrative units, represented by a resident or liaison officer having the status of an official of the local entity.[16]

It is thus not surprising that the changes effected by the Home Ministry Instructions did not go very deep. Repeated violations were reported in the press. A great many neighborhood associations thought it desirable to change their names—for instance, to "cooperative living guilds" (*seikatsu kyōdō kumiai*)—but otherwise they carried on as usual under the same leadership.

As the failure of the attempt to change the neighborhood associations into voluntary, democratic, and independent organizations became apparent, SCAP's attitude stiffened and its policy shifted toward compulsory abolition. A Cabinet order "with teeth" was promulgated on May 3, 1947. All heads or assistant heads of *buraku* associations who had held office continuously from September 1, 1945, until September 1, 1946, were barred for four years from any municipal office that had similar functions. Officials were forbidden to issue orders to the chiefs of either the original association or its successor and these chiefs were forbidden to issue orders to the membership. The prohibited acts and the refusal to issue rations to a consumer who was not a member of such an association were made punishable. All block associations, similar groups, and "liaison offices" formed after January 22, 1947, to take up the slack created by Home Ministry Instruction No. 4 were to be disbanded by May 31, 1947. The governors were given the task of liquidating those that did not disband voluntarily by the prescribed date.[17] Thus the neighborhood associations were not simply to be deprived of their public character, but actually abolished. The wisdom of this step has been questioned on various grounds. To some, it seemed that if the associations had been stripped of their objectionable wartime features and placed under new leadership, they could have become a nucleus for real local self-government. Others were convinced that the "democratization" of the system was a hopeless task.[18]

At any rate, as Chapter 10 will show, the step was not successful. In rural areas, where the *buraku* was more firmly entrenched in the needs and customs of the community, it retained not only its social but also its political significance, and, to some extent, its connection with the village office. In the cities, the abolition of the *tonarigumi* and *chōnaikai* was welcomed by many, especially among the intelligentsia. But here and there various organizations, voluntary only insofar as government regulation was replaced by social pressure or pressure by "bosses," took over some of their tasks, often with the aid of municipal subsidies of doubtful legality. The overt step of reestablishing a neighborhood association system on a legal basis, while frequently discussed, has not been taken. Here, as elsewhere, successive conservative governments have been too uncertain of the extent of public support and too sure of the existence of opposition to risk a political battle.

The abolition of the Home Ministry was also the result of a lengthy development. To the decentralization-minded officials of SCAP's Government Section, the Japanese government existing at the time of the surrender was a monster that reached with thousands of tentacles into the home and private life of every individual Japanese. If the abolition of the neighborhood associations aimed at shortening the tentacles, the abolition of the Home Ministry was meant to strike at the very heart. It was more than a measure of administrative reorganization; its significance was primarily political.

Although the blow did not fall until more than two years after the beginning of the Occupation, the handwriting had been on the wall for a long time. As early as October 4, 1945, SCAPIN No. 93 (known as the "Bill of Rights Directive") had deprived the Home Ministry of its former peace preservation and censorship functions and had led to a reorganization of the Ministry which included the abolition of its Police Bureau.[19]

The Home Ministry officials had long been regarded—not only by foreign observers—as the very incarnation of Japanese bureaucracy, possessed of their own importance as pillars of the emperor's rule, disdainful of the masses of subjects who had to be governed, well aware of their strategic political position, tightly knit as a result of professional inbreeding and strict discipline, and generally opposed to changes in the existing social and political order. The relationship of Government Section with the Home Ministry was not a happy one. The Government Section Report is eloquent in its denunciation of the endeavors of Home Ministry officials "to sabotage as far as they could or dared." It states: "Attempts by outright action, or more subtly by evasion and delay, to undermine the transfer of power from the national government to local entities . . . marked the efforts of the Home Ministry to retain its former domination over the lives and liberties of the people."[20] The question arose whether the reforms could be carried out with any promise of success under these circumstances. Characteristically, an attempt was made to solve the problem—which was only a ramification of a much larger one presented by the policy of working through Japanese agencies and their officialdom—by an institutional change.

It was not until the end of April 1947, a few days before the new constitution and the Local Autonomy Law were to go into effect, that the future existence of the Home Ministry was brought openly into question. On April 30, 1947, General Whitney, Chief of Government Section, sent a "Memorandum regarding the Decentralization of the Ministry of Home Affairs" to the Japanese government, in which he referred to the Ministry as the "focal point for centralized controls within the governmental structure of Japan" and requested that plans for its reorganization be submitted not later than June 1, 1947.[21] The wording of the memorandum made it clear that little of the old Home Ministry would remain after the reorganization was effected. On June 27, 1947, the Government Section Report states, the Japanese Cabinet "recommended" its abolition.[22] Even then, some haggling continued over which agencies were to take up the functions of the Home Ministry. Under the original bills of the Cabinet, a newly created Local Autonomy Commission would have inherited, among other tasks, those of managing elections and coordinating prefectural administration, and a Public Safety Board would have supervised the police. These bills had to be withdrawn after they had already reached the committee stage in the House of Representatives, and when the Cabinet resubmitted its program, it included such far-reaching changes as the new Police Law and the National Election Management Commission Law.[23] The Law Concerning the Abolition of the Ministry of Home Affairs and of the Imperial Ordinance Governing Its Organization and Other Ordinances and a second law providing for adjustment in other laws—such as a transfer of functions from the defunct Home Ministry to the various other "competent ministers"—were finally passed on November 28, 1947, by the House of Representatives and on December 8, 1947, by the House of Councilors.[24]

All that remained of the Home Ministry was a temporary caretaker agency called the Office of Domestic Affairs, which was scheduled to function for only ninety days. For part of this time it assumed jurisdiction over the police system until the National Public Safety Commission was formed in accordance with the new Police Law.

On December 27, 1947, a brief ceremony brought to an end the seventy-five-year history of the Home Ministry. The incumbent Home Minister, Kimura Kozaemon, became Chief of the Construction Board, which had taken over the functions of the Home Ministry's Public Works Bureau together with those of the War Damage Rehabilitation Board; the Chief of the Home Ministry's Local Affairs Bureau, Hayashi Keizo, became Director of the Office of Domestic Affairs. Other high-ranking officials were given various positions in the national and prefectural governments.[25]

Since then there has been a measured and partial return to the past in accordance with the desires of the conservative governments that have been in power since the end of the Occupation. The Local Autonomy Agency was followed by the Autonomy Board and then the Autonomy Ministry. These developments will be discussed in Chapter 13 under the heading "Successors to the Home Ministry"; it may suffice to state here that while the importance of the central government organ dealing with local administration has increased over the years, the Autonomy Ministry still does not have the legal powers once possessed by the Home Ministry.

The Local Government Reform of 1946, the New Constitution, and the Local Autonomy Law

The 90th Imperial Diet adopted the first revision of the local government laws under the Occupation in September 1946, a little more than a month before it adopted the new constitution. Just as it was somewhat strange that the original codes preceded the enactment of the Meiji constitution, so it seems strange that their amendment in 1946 could not have waited this brief period until the enactment of the new constitution, particularly since the constitution was to contain provisions regarding local self-government.

This curious parallel to the Meiji experience was made explicit for a brief moment in the deliberations of the Diet, when Homma Shinichi, representing the Progressive Party, questioned Prime Minister Yoshida on the purpose and reason of putting the revision before the Diet "with such haste." With characteristic curtness, the Prime Minister referred in his answer simply to the "inevitable situation of affairs at home and abroad," a phrase often used to indicate that a measure was the result of pressure by SCAP. Home Minister Omura added that there existed already a legally unauthorized tendency to elect mayors which should be put "on its proper track." He cited the necessity of changing the law before the anticipated local elections and expressed his conviction that no essential change in the proposed law would be necessary after the enactment of the constitution.[26]

The bills for revision of the Prefectural Code, the City Code, the Town and Village Code, and the Code for the Tokyo Metropolis, which were submitted to the Diet on July 5, 1946, were the result of conferences since March between SCAP officials and representatives of the Home Ministry. They introduced some features that were new to Japan, such as direct demands by local voters for the enactment of bylaws or the recall of officeholders, the management of local elections by local committees, and the appointment of inspection commissioners. In general, however, they constituted the type of amendment that had been advocated in the twenties. Thus the power of the assemblies was increased, their position vis-à-vis the executive was substantially strengthened, the franchise was extended, and all local executive positions became elective.

In this last regard, demands for the election of the prefectural governors had been voiced repeatedly in the past, and in 1946 the platform of almost all political parties contained a plank concerning the matter.[27] As the process of drafting the new constitution progressed, the fulfillment of these demands became a foregone conclusion, as we shall note later in this chapter.

The question whether the prefectural governor should be appointed or elected is, of course, closely connected with the issue of centralization versus decentralization. But a decision in favor of election does not necessarily determine the issue. To a certain degree, election places the governor in the service of a new master, his constituency. But so long as he remains a national official, he is also subject to central government orders in the entire range of his activities. He has thus two masters instead of one, and the problem arises as to whose mastery will be stronger. His status as national or local official is thus of great import, and the question of the future status of the governors thus aroused a great deal of controversy. The government made it clear from the outset that it wanted the prefecture to remain an "incomplete autonomous entity" and that it would insist that the governor, in spite of his election, remain a national official (*kanri*).[28] In the deliberations of the Diet this stand was repeatedly attacked. One representative, Yao Kuzaburo, went so far as to say that the proposed bill was "not a revision of, but rather a gross transgression on, local autonomy . . . a bill to keep the status quo under the cover of a 'reform.' " "What is the difference," he asked, "between a publicly elected governor put under restraints as a government official by the government service regulations and a former governor, appointed and pressed upon the people by the government, equally under bondage by the same government service regulations?"[29]

Home Minister Omura never tired of repeating the reasons for the adamant stand of the government, referring to the need for harmonizing national and local demands, to the fact that the delegated national business of the prefecture outweighed in quality and quantity the local business, and to the necessity of securing to the various ministerial authorities the power of supervision and control.[30] The government won a temporary victory, and as a result the supplementary provision of the amended Prefectural Code contained the brief sentence: "The governor of an urban or rural prefecture shall be a governmental officer for the present."

The grant to the local electorate of the power to recall local executives also filled Japanese bureaucrats with apprehension. The Home Minister originally suggested that successful recall petitions should be submitted to him for decision, but in the end the decision was put into the hands of the constituency. Parenthetically it may be noted that only the Communist Party declared itself opposed to local self-government in principle. Its spokesman, Tokuda Kyuichi, argued in the tradition of the

French Revolution that in a real democracy there could be no intermediary autonomous unit between the people and the representatives of their will in the Diet.[31]

The House of Representatives passed the four bills with some forty amendments on August 31, 1946, and passage by the House of Peers followed three days later. The reform legislation became effective on September 27, 1946.[32]

Although it retained the basic framework of the old codes and preserved strong elements of bureaucratic government, the revision was a big step in the direction of local self-government. When the measure was passed by the upper house General MacArthur issued a statement full of exultation and optimism, which said in part:

The Diet's approval of local government reform legislation strikes the bonds which have prevented the full emergence of the nation's democratic forces and prepares the way for eventual full realization of the most lofty ideals of a democratic society.[33]

The House of Representatives was more sober in its appraisal. It attached a seven-point resolution to the passage of the bills, calling, among other things, for the creation of a Local Institution Inquiry Council to advise the government on further reforms, and for the submission of measures making the governors prefectural officials, decentralizing the police, establishing independent sources of local revenue, and decreasing central controls.

We noted earlier that Home Minister Omura predicted at the time of the discussion of the revision of the local government codes that the enactment of the constitution would not require any essential changes in the laws. Although the amended codes were formally abrogated in May 1947 by the Local Autonomy Law, his prediction proved correct in a sense. The constitution did not lead to a replacement of the original continental European model for local government by an Anglo-Saxon or American model. This was an important and somewhat surprising development, because the Occupation had originally aimed at establishing a system of "home rule." To understand how this aim was thwarted or abandoned, we must look into the local self-government provisions of the constitution.

The genesis of the Japanese constitution is fairly well known in its general outline.[34] Neither the basic points for constitutional reform required by SCAP (and presented by political advisor George Atcheson to Prince Konoye in September 1945), nor the ill-fated Matsumoto draft, nor the notes of General MacArthur of February 3, 1946, which served as a minimum standard for later drafts, contained any reference to local government.* But when it was decided that the Matsumoto draft was unacceptable, the SCAP Government Section was divided into various committees for the purpose of writing, in closely guarded secrecy, its own draft for the various parts of the constitution; one of these committees was a Committee on Local Government. This committee's first report, providing for "a form of local sovereignty with residuary powers reserved to local public entities," ran into opposition even within Government Section, where some felt that "Japan was too small to permit a form of state sovereignty" and that "the Diet and the courts could be trusted to protect local communities."[35]

The opposition, backed by the Deputy Chief of the Section, Colonel Kades, won, and the committee draft was extensively revised. But while a system resembling "states' rights" was thus discarded, the idea of giving to the local entities "home rule," including the right to adopt their own charters, was retained. Article 87 of the original Government Section draft—which ultimately became the basis for the present Article 94 of the Constitution—guaranteed to "the inhabitants of metropolitan areas, cities, and towns" the right "to manage their property, affairs, and government and to frame their own charters within such laws as the Diet may enact." Quite logically, it contained no article which provided that the organization of local entities should be fixed by national law, as does the present Article 92.

A reference to a national law fixing the organization of local entities appeared for the first time in a draft prepared by Sato Tatsuo of the Cabinet Legislation Bureau after consultation with Minister of State Matsumoto and Vice-Chief of the Bureau Irie on February 28, 1946. The draft was slightly revised on the following day, but the provision regarding the organization of local entities by national law, contained

---

* Prince Konoye's draft also did not refer to local government. However, a draft submitted by Professor Sasaki Sōichi to the Lord Keeper of the Privy Seal on November 23, 1945, contained three articles on the subject, providing for a measure of self-government within the limits prescribed by law and under the supervision of the national government. These drafts have not been published, but are contained in the materials collected by the Constitution Research Committee (No. 26 of July 1956 and No. 53 of March 1961).

in the draft of February 28, remained basically unchanged. It was substantially this revised draft that was presented to Government Section on March 4, 1946, as the first official Japanese government draft after the rejection of the Matsumoto draft. Since it provided for a determination of the organization of local entities by national law, the draft quite logically contained no reference to freely chosen local charters. Article 87 of the Government Section draft (renumbered as Article 103) was changed so that it now gave inhabitants of local entities simply "the right of self-government" and permitted them to "enact bylaws and regulations within law." There was thus no inconsistency: national law was to determine the organization of local entities, and, acting through this organization, local entities were to regulate the affairs placed under their jurisdiction.

But the second draft of the Japanese government, dated March 6, 1947, contained an apparent inconsistency: on the one hand, it provided in its Article 88 that "regulations concerning the organization and operation of local public entities shall be fixed by law in accordance with the principle of local autonomy," which implied uniformity; on the other hand, its Article 90 gave local entities the right "to frame their own charters," which implied a diversity in the forms of local government organization and a choice among them by the citizens. It is strange that this inconsistency was not noticed or not explored by the American draftsmen and that they did not object to it. Apparently they were so favorably impressed by the reference to the "principle of local autonomy" that they failed to grasp the potential implications that the article as a whole held for their aim of permitting "home rule." The Japanese draftsmen, on the other hand, seemed to have realized the existence of an inconsistency, but preferred to make no issue of it.

The subsequent drafts, the last of which was submitted to SCAP on April 15, 1946, contained no change in the provisions regarding the organization of local entities. That is to say, they still contained, side by side, references to national laws fixing the organization of local entities, and to the right of local entities to "frame their own charters within such laws as the Diet may enact." SCAP's Government Section still believed that this wording allowed for home rule. This is shown by a memorandum dated April 30, 1946, which stated that one of the major objectives of the local government reform was to provide

opportunity for the people of a city or town to select the kind of governmental organization they preferred by elimination of the rigid structure established by law and dominated by the central government. A variety of forms of local government and an opportunity for the people to choose among them would help develop the public's political consciousness.

But when the new constitution emerged from the Diet it did not provide for such an opportunity. The inconsistency in the March 6 draft and its successors was resolved: Article 88 of the draft of March 6, now Article 92, remained as it was. It stated that "regulations concerning organization operations of local public entities shall be fixed by law in accordance with the principle of local autonomy." However, in Article 90 of the draft (now renumbered Article 94) the word "charter" was changed to "regulation," thus returning to the wording of Article 103 of the first Japanese government draft of March 4, 1946. Together the two articles assured the continuation of uniform local government organization. Yet one would look in vain for any Diet debate or for the adoption of a motion to amend the draft submitted by the government on this point.

The key to this mystery can be found only by comparing the English drafts with the Japanese drafts. When the Government Section draft— commonly referred to by the Japanese as the "MacArthur draft"—was translated into Japanese by the Foreign Ministry translators, the word "charter" was rendered as *kenshō*, a word implying a fundamental rule of the nature of a constitution. As noted, in the first Japanese government draft, presented to Government Section on March 4, the word "charter" had been replaced by "bylaws and regulations," and consequently in the Japanese version the word *kenshō* had been replaced by *jōrei oyobi kisoku*. The change was intentional and its significance was clear to the Japanese drafters. Mr. Sato later stated in his article "Memoranda on Chapter 8 of the Constitution": "As for the word *charter* in the GHQ draft, it was thought it presumably anticipated home rule charters, but this was revised to *jōrei oyobi kisoku*."[36] A discrepancy between the English and Japanese versions appears for the first time in the draft of March 6, which was the result of conferences between Japanese and SCAP officials. The English version refers again to "charters," but the Japanese version retains instead the word *jōrei*, meaning "bylaws." The discrepancy had not been removed by April 17, when the final draft constitution was made public, nor when the draft constitution, after approval by the Privy Council, was put before the 90th Extraordinary Session of the Diet on June 20. Thus the English version could still provide a basis for the above-mentioned Government Section Memorandum of April 30, 1946, which stated that the reform aimed at allowing people to choose among a variety of forms of local government. On the other hand, the Japanese version discussed in the Diet provided that national laws would determine the organization of local entities and that local entities, thus uniformly constituted, had the right to enact bylaws. Consistent in itself as it was, the Japanese draft did not raise the question of a choice of home rule charters. All that was needed to remove the inconsistency in the English version was to retranslate *jōrei* into "regulations" or "bylaws." This was done by the translators of the Central Liaison Office of the Japanese Government on August 26, 1946, while the House of Representatives was still debating the draft. Of course, this "correction" of the English draft had no effect on the Diet's deliberations.

The implications of this legislative legerdemain were apparently not recognized by the American participants in the drafting until much later. Mr. Sato states that the Japanese felt from the beginning that the constitution should not grant the right to establish charters; yet no one in SCAP objected to the change from *kenshō* to *jōrei* in the Japanese version and the subsequent change in the English version by which "charter" was replaced by "regulations."[37] As a matter of fact, as late as February 1947 the Local Government Division of Government Section envisioned the enactment of laws providing that "within the pattern of democratic government, local communities will select the form of government which they desire."[38] But neither the constitution nor the Local Autonomy Law that was enacted barely two months later established the basis for such a selection.*

---

* The grant of a free choice of organizational forms would have been a drastic deviation from the pattern of the past. It should be noted, however, that the freedom of choice would have been limited at any rate by Article 93 of the constitution, which required the popular election of chief executives. In this regard SCAP was bound by a policy statement of the Far Eastern Commission of July 2, 1946, which directed that the new constitution should provide for "the popular election of heads of institutions of local government such as prefectures, cities, towns, and villages." Thus the adoption of a pure commission system or of a city-manager plan would apparently have been impossible. Since popularly elected local assemblies were also required by the constitution, the choice of charters would have been restricted to some forms of the mayor-and-council plan. The Japanese were apparently aware of the discrepancy between the constitution's requirement of a "presidential system" in local government, based on separate elections of executives and legislatures, and the grant of a choice of charters.

In the light of later developments the genesis of Article 93 also deserves some comment. Article 86 of the Government Section draft provided for direct popular election of

governors of prefectures, mayors of cities and towns, and of the chief executives of all other local entities having the power to levy local taxes, as well as of the members of prefectural and local legislative assemblies and of such other prefectural and local officials as the Diet may determine.[39]

The Japanese drafters felt that the enumeration of the types of local entities might prove "legislatively inconvenient" and that it might be better to refer to local entities collectively. Thus in the draft prepared on February 28 the reference was to the popular election of "the chief executive officers and the members of assemblies of local public entities." This was repeated in Article 101 of the first Japanese government draft of March 4 and in Article 89 of the second draft of March 6 (with the addition, based on the MacArthur draft, of the words "and such other local officials as may be determined by law"). Home Minister Omura felt that the draft went too far in providing for direct election of prefectural governors. There was some sentiment in the Cabinet in favor of an indirect election of governors and possibly of other local executives. (One plan envisioned the election by prefectural and municipal assemblies of electors who would then in turn elect the governor.) But discussion on this point with Colonel Kades, Deputy Chief of Government Section, did not bring about a change, and such a change would at any rate have been made impossible by the policy statement of the Far Eastern Commission of July 2, 1946, requiring the popular election of local chief executives.[40] Thus all subsequent drafts retained this wording: "The chief executive officers of all local public entities, the members of the legislative assemblies, and such other local officials as may be determined by law shall be elected by direct popular vote within their several communities." This is the wording of the present Article 93 of the constitution. (The adjective "legislative" was dropped in the final English translation.) It is significant that there are no references to prefectures or any other specific types of local bodies. An enumeration would have anchored the existing types of local entities in the constitution; failure to enumerate them opened the door to the interpretation that the constitution leaves the definition of the term "local public entities" to law. If so, it can be argued, a simple legislative act may change the scope of that term. Without change in the constitution, the prefecture could thus be abolished or, a fortiori, made again an "imperfect autonomous entity" under an appointed chief executive.*

The draft constitution was submitted to the House of Representatives on June 20, 1946. Prime Minister Yoshida's explanation of the draft in general and in regard to the local autonomy provisions in particular is a marvel of brevity. He stated simply: "In view of the importance of local self-government, new provisions have been made."[41] This brevity was matched by the dearth of interpellations on these new provisions throughout the proceedings. Many pages of the record deal with the question whether the new supreme law changes the "national polity" of Japan, especially by providing in Article 1 that the emperor derives his position "from the will of the people, with whom resides sovereign power." There was also much discussion about the changes in the family system, foreshadowed by Article 24, and about the renunciation of war in Article 9. But the local autonomy provisions evoked little interest. Except for the passing announcement by one or another interpellator that he might have some question to bring up in committee session, they were never mentioned in plenary session.

The House of Representatives adopted the constitution on August 24, 1946. The House of Peers approved it with minor amendments on September 6. The amended version was approved by the House of Representatives on October 7 and by the Privy Council on October 29. November 3, the birthday of Emperor Meiji, was fixed as promulgation date. The new constitution became effective six months later, May 3, 1947.†

In the meantime, work had also progressed on the drafting of the Local Autonomy Law. It will be recalled that the resolution which the House of Representatives attached to its passage of the amendment of the existing local government codes in September 1946 called for the creation of a Local Institutions Inquiry Council to advise the government on further reforms. The Council was duly created by a Cabinet ordinance. It consisted of Diet members, specialists in various fields, such as police, education, finance, agriculture, industry, welfare, and

---

* For later use made of this argument, see Chapters 7 and 8.

† For reasons of legal continuity, the constitution of 1947 was given the appearance of a revision of the Meiji constitution. Nevertheless, it seems appropriate to refer to it as a "new constitution," as has been done here.

labor, together with a few scholars in public law. Somewhat incongru-
ously, the Commission proper included only one representative of local
entities as such—and a governor, at that—but six representatives of Japanese womanhood.* Representatives of the six big cities and prominent
national officials were appointed as special or temporary members. Officials of various ministries served as secretaries. The Council started its
work on October 24, 1946, and submitted its recommendations in late
February 1947.[42] Simultaneously conferences of Government Section
continued with five groups in Tokyo: ministerial officials, especially of
the Local Affairs Bureau of the Home Ministry and of the Finance Ministry; party representatives; women members of the Diet; men and
women from educational institutions and learned societies; and the appropriate Diet committees. Government Section also had to coordinate
its local government policy with other sections of SCAP. Finally, field
investigations by military government teams, supplemented by field
trips by members of Government Section, were to test the opinions gathered in Tokyo against the comments of people in local areas. The result
of these labors, the Local Autonomy Law, was promulgated as Law
No. 67 on April 17, 1947, and became effective, together with the new
constitution, on May 3, 1947. Basically, the Local Autonomy Law was
a consolidation of previously existing local government laws, with occasional innovations, into one comprehensive code. Reviewing the enactment of the Local Autonomy Law, Government Section found that

it provides the basis for a democratic system of self-governing local public entities, fully empowered to manage all affairs of a purely local nature and to discharge their local responsibilities in matters of national concern. The people
are given an opportunity to participate in local political and governmental
affairs; local answers can be developed to local problems; local officials and
representative bodies are given opportunities to participate in the shaping of
national policies.[43]

Although the Local Autonomy Law has since undergone close to fifty
amendments, it still forms the cornerstone of the present local govern-

---

* The women representatives may have been appointed in accordance with the
precepts current among Japanese bureaucrats at the time: "Let's put some women
in; that will please SCAP." On the other hand, the entire composition of the Council
may have reflected the groups that Government Section actually consulted in draw-
ing up a policy for the Local Autonomy Law. As will be noted, the women members
of the Diet were one of these groups.

ment structure.* Its provisions, the origins of the various amendments, and, where necessary, their legislative history will be dealt with in Part Two of this study. There we will also show to what extent the hopes put into the law by its drafters were fulfilled in reality. But since neither the provisions nor the effects of the law can be fully understood in isolation, the following chapter reviews briefly other Occupation measures affecting local government.

---

* Japanese commentators usually call the amendments of September 1946 the "first reform," and the Local Autonomy Law the "second reform." Before the year 1947 was over, there occurred what is commonly referred to as the "third reform," a rather substantial amendment of the Local Autonomy Law occasioned in part by the dissolution of the Home Ministry. This amendment was Law No. 169 of 1947. A description of the main features of the Local Autonomy Law up to the middle of 1948 is to be found in *Government Section Report,* Vol. I, pp. 273ff.

CHAPTER 6

Occupation Reforms in Local Government, II

In February 1947 the Local Government Division of Government Section planned a review and, if necessary, a revision of all existing laws, imperial ordinances, and other regulations affecting local government.[1] Such a review, if carried out, would undoubtedly have brought into sharp focus the problem of allocation of functions. A broad frontal attack on this problem was of decisive importance if the concept of local autonomy was to be made meaningful to the citizen. He had to be enabled to distinguish between the acts of his local community and the acts of the central government; he had to learn to allocate his praise and blame for an existing situation accordingly; and he had to become aware of the more immediate control he was now supposed to exercise over the local leadership and over local affairs. The local officials also had to be enabled to distinguish between the areas of national and local affairs, to consider the central government as their master only in the former area while deciding local affairs freely within the mandate of the local citizenry. As it was, all this was impossible because the local entities had long been primarily the extended arm of the central government, and both officials and citizens had been accustomed to consider them as such. The notion of a clearly separated area of independent local action was practically nonexistent.

The broad frontal attack on the problem of function, although envisioned in 1947, was not attempted until 1950. In the meantime, the new Local Autonomy Law operated within the environment created by the laws and regulations of a time of centralization. New laws continually assigned additional national functions to the local entities and required additional local expenditures. While lip service was paid to the "principle of local autonomy" now anchored in the constitution, a functional area of local responsibility was not established. Piecemeal attacks on the problem of separation of functions were undertaken on only two fronts, the areas of police and education.

Decentralization of Police and Education

An overall reallocation of functions would have involved the difficult task of devising some standard for distinguishing between national and local affairs. In the decentralization of police and education, the primary consideration was not that these are, by their nature, local functions. The centralized education system had been used for indoctrination in a narrow nationalism and the centralized police system had been used for the control of "dangerous thoughts." The decentralization of police and education was thus thought of primarily as a step in eliminating specific evils of the past and in preventing their recurrence, and only incidentally as a step in a general program of reallocating functions.

Certain police functions and organs were abolished at the very outset of the Occupation.[2] As was frequently the case, the Japanese government then sought to forestall more drastic action by SCAP by taking some action of its own. In early 1946 plans for improvement of the quality of the police and for its "democratization" by a system of civilian advisers were discussed. The new slogan for the police was "Respect human rights, keep alert, always be kind and popular."[3]

In SCAP, the responsibility for public safety was with G-2, a section whose interest in democratic reform and decentralization was tempered by grave concern over the threat of communism. There was thus a certain pulling and hauling between G-2 and Government Section, which had responsibility for the reform of local government. While the zeal of the various sections for the implementation of their own programs was, in general, a characteristic feature of the early Occupation, in this particular case the rivalry between two section chiefs, Generals Willoughby and Whitney, also played a role. The first step was undertaken by G-2, or more specifically by the Public Safety Division of the Civil Intelligence Section of GHQ. It called on two police experts, Lewis J. Valentine of the city police of New York and Oscar G. Olander of the state police forces of Michigan. From their reports originated the division between "autonomous police" and "national rural police," which characterized the Japanese police system during the next years.

The Japanese Cabinet submitted a draft plan, based to some extent on the Valentine and Olander reports, to SCAP on February 28, 1947. While loudly condemning the obviously dying past by the use of such phrases as "improper functions" and "excessive centralization," the plan was essentially a plea against "hasty reorganization of the fundamental system." It would have left control of the police force unchanged until "local government officials have demonstrated efficiency in self-government," at which time the police forces were to be reorganized "in cities with populations capable of supporting them" and controlled and operated by these local self-governing bodies. The government's preoccupation with "stabilizing the condition of the nation" and with the use of the police force as "the only stabilizing influence available to the Japanese government" is apparent throughout the plan, which also envisioned an increase in overall police strength from about 94,000 to 125,000.

The plan did not find favor with Government Section. In a lengthy memorandum for the record, dated July 17, 1947, Government Section set forth its objections and called for "decentralization of the police force without delay and not at the expiration of any period of probation."[4]

The early part of 1947 was a period of momentous developments. After a general strike had been averted at the last minute by SCAP intervention, elections were called for and they brought the downfall of the Yoshida Cabinet and the formation of a coalition Cabinet under a social-democratic Prime Minister, Katayama Tetsu.

As soon as the Katayama government was formed, the discussions on police reorganization were resumed. On September 3, 1947, Prime Minister Katayama presented a new plan to General MacArthur. In his letter he referred to the draft plan of his predecessor of February 28, 1947, but stressed that the government had striven for "the formulation of a reform plan of its own from an independent standpoint." He also discussed two proposals that had emerged in the appropriate Cabinet committee, one termed a "progressive plan" and the other a "conservative plan." According to the progressive plan, all uniformed police would have been transferred to the six big cities and the prefectures; only certain technical functions would have been left to the central government, and the Prime Minister would have been granted limited control over the local police only in case of emergency. The conservative plan would have established a metropolitan police in cities of over 200,000 population and would have placed it under the national police, which would have been far more numerous and important. The plan approved by the Cabinet and submitted to SCAP was a compromise. It envisioned a national police of 30,000 and a municipal police of 95,000, the latter to be established first in cities of more than 200,000 population, but to be gradually extended to all cities of more than 50,000 population. In thus limiting the autonomous police to the larger municipalities the plan conformed with the Valentine and Olander reports and took cognizance of a problem that was to vex the new police system later: the financial inability of small entities to maintain their own forces.

In SCAP, joint conferences were held between G-2 and Government Section, and as a result General MacArthur replied to Katayama in a letter which, in effect, not only disapproved of the Cabinet plan of gradual decentralization but also went beyond the proposals of the progressive plan. The letter presented a blueprint for a new police law, which was to be enacted by the current session of the Diet and to be completely enforced within a period of ninety days thereafter. With the framework of the new legislation thus established, Government Section and G-2 cooperated closely in the drafting of the law, which was promptly passed on December 17, 1947.[5]

The salient features of the Police Law were: (1) the division of police functions between the National Rural Police and the police of the autonomous entities; (2) the division of controls into operational and administrative controls in the case of the national police; and (3) the institution of Public Safety Commissions on all levels.

The national police was to be in charge of the police communications system, of criminal identification, and of police training. Otherwise its operations were limited to rural areas and to towns and villages with less than 5,000 inhabitants. The autonomous police was to operate in cities, towns, and villages with more than 5,000 inhabitants.[6]

The control of matters relating to organization, budget, and personnel management of the police (administrative control) and control over the activities relating to maintenance of public order, prevention and suppression of crime, and traffic and judicial police affairs (operational control) were separated in the case of the National Rural Police. Administrative control was to be exercised at the national and regional level—the country being divided into six police regions—by the National Public

Safety Commission and the directors of the police regions; operational control was to be exercised at the prefectural level by the prefectural public safety commissions. In the case of the autonomous police, both controls were lodged in the local entities, more specifically in the local public safety commissions.[7]

The establishment of public safety commissions was intended to limit the control of the executive over the police, which had been so strong in the past. For this reason, the commissions were assured a certain independence of status. When the Prime Minister wanted to appoint a member of the National Public Safety Commission, he needed the consent of both houses of the Diet. The same was true for dismissals, which had to be for cause. Not more than two of the five members of the commission could belong to the same political party. The chairman of the commission was to be co-opted by its members. Similar provisions were made for the public safety commissions of prefectures, cities, towns, and villages, all of which consisted of three members.[8]

As indicated earlier, there was a basic difference between the prefectural commissions and those of cities, towns, and villages: the former were within the framework of the national police, the latter outside it. For the autonomous police the chain of command ended, generally speaking, within the boundaries of the respective localities. Within those areas, local control was complete. Article 154 of the law stated explicitly: "There shall be neither administrative nor operational control by the National Rural Police over the police of cities, towns, and villages." Since a simple lack of authorization frequently failed to prevent national officials from interfering in local affairs, a provision of this type, making such interference clearly illegal, was perhaps not a superfluous precaution.

The decentralization of police raised great problems in dealing with large-scale internal unrest. Japan had been stripped of its army and had renounced the right to maintain land, sea, and air forces or other war potential.[9] In cases of widespread internal unrest amounting to a state of emergency, the national government had no way to "call out the militia" for its suppression. Until the creation of the National Police Reserve Corps in 1950 it had to rely on the regular police. For this reason, the National Public Safety Commission was authorized to prepare and execute plans for integrating the police to cope with a state of national emergency, which was to be proclaimed, on the commission's recommendation, by the Prime Minister. The proclamation had to be ratified by the Diet within twenty days to remain valid. In such an emergency, the Prime Minister would assume control over the entire police system down to the autonomous police of towns and villages.[10]

With some changes—including one in 1951 that led to the virtual abolition of the autonomous police on the town and village level—this police system of 1947 remained in force for seven years. The dramatic developments surrounding its replacement by a new, more centralized police system in 1954 are described in Chapter 11.

In the field of educational reform, as in the field of police reform, some preliminary steps were taken shortly after the beginning of the Occupation. These involved a ban on the spreading of militaristic and ultra-nationalistic thought, a purge of educators, a revision of texts, and the suspension of the teaching of certain courses, especially the course in morals (*shushin*).[11] The decentralization of the Japanese school system was recommended by the United States Education Mission, which stayed in Japan during March 1946. The Mission suggested that prefectural and local administrative agencies, to be elected by popular vote, should be put in charge of educational functions, while the Ministry of Education, which had been in principal control of local schools, should in the future provide them only with professional and technical counsel. A Japanese Educational Reform Council, created in August 1946, approved these recommendations in general. The recommendations went far beyond the vague and timid steps, such as the establishment of local advisory councils,[12] that had been under consideration by the Ministry of Education since the end of the war.

In March 1947 the Far Eastern Commission stated in a directive to SCAP that "responsibility for the local administration of educational establishments should in due time be decentralized." But this decentralization was to be tempered by two considerations: first, that the Japanese government should retain enough control over the educational system to ensure the achievement of the objectives of the Occupation; and, second, that the Japanese government should be responsible for the maintenance of an adequate level of education throughout Japan and should thus assume a major burden of the required finances.[13] These statements created a certain element of ambiguity in the position of the staff section concerned—the Civil Information and Education Section—

with respect to questions of local autonomy, and this became more apparent as time went on.*

As frequently happened, the Far Eastern Commission's directive—which had actually been developed in close cooperation with SCAP officials in Tokyo—came somewhat late. By the time it was issued, the Diet was already considering the first legislative measures to implement the recommendations of the United States Education Mission and the Japanese Educational Reform Council. One of these measures was the Fundamental Law of Education, adopted on March 31, 1947. The sweeping and unenforceable generalities of this "educational charter for a new Japan" offer a curious parallel to the Imperial Rescript on Education of 1890. Its spirit was, of course, prodigiously different. Where the Rescript aimed at the indoctrination of youth with Confucian principles and at the creation of "good and faithful subjects of the Emperor," the new charter proclaimed the "full development of personality" and "the rearing of people . . . imbued with an independent spirit" as the aims of education.[14] Another reform measure was the School Education Law, passed by the Diet on March 27, 1947. It changed the Japanese school system to what is commonly called the 6-3-3-4 system and made three years of middle-school education compulsory in addition to the six years of elementary schooling. It also foreshadowed the decentralization of education.[15]

The climax in the process of decentralizing education came with passage of the Board of Education Law, adopted on July 15, 1948. Its purpose was to free education from direct control by the Ministry of Education, to place responsibility for education on the local citizenry, and

---

* The position of the Civil Information and Education Section sometimes brought it into conflict with Government Section. An example occurred in 1950. As a result of the Shoup Mission, a block grant system had been established to minimize the "strings" so easily attached to specific financial subsidies by the central government. Shortly thereafter the Japanese government proposed to exempt educational grants from the block grant system. The proposal was strongly supported by CIE on the basis that a specific grant, accompanied by central controls, would ensure the allocation of sufficient funds by local entities for educational purposes, and thus the maintenance of acceptable standards. Government Section, on the other hand, saw the proposal as an attempt to create a breach in a barely established policy which it considered essential for building up local independence. In the absence of evidence to the contrary, Government Section was willing to assume that Japanese local entities were interested in the education of their children. The problems of national grants in general are discussed later in this chapter and in Chapter 12.

to make educational administration within the locality independent of the general local administration. For this purpose, boards of education were put in charge of all schools except private schools and higher educational institutions.[16] Their control was to include, among other things, the curriculum, the selection of textbooks, and the hiring and firing of personnel. The members of the boards of education—seven in the case of prefectural boards, five in the case of municipal boards—were to be elected locally for terms of four years. The election was to be direct, except that one member of each board was to be elected indirectly by the assembly of the prefecture or municipality. The board members were made subject to the recall provisions of the Local Autonomy Law. The boards were given the power, not attributed to other commissions created by the Occupation (such as the public safety commissions), to participate in the compilation of the budget, a function otherwise reserved to the chief executive.[17] The Ministry of Education was to cease its direct supervision of education and become an advisory body, giving technical guidance.

The boards of education were first established in the 46 prefectures and the five big cities.* Elections in these localities took place on October 5, 1948. The voting rate was 56 per cent, a low turnout for Japanese elections on the local level, indicating a lack of interest on the part of the voters and of the forces that usually "get out the vote." The new boards began functioning on November 1, 1948.

The law originally required establishment of boards of education in the remaining cities and in towns and villages by November 1, 1950. But the Japanese government was doubtful about the extension of the system to these smaller local bodies, and with SCAP's approval it postponed the establishment of municipal boards from 1950 to 1952. During this period, various advisory councils of the government expressed themselves against the establishment of municipal boards, and there was much discussion, both inside and outside the government, about a further postponement. The government and the majority Liberal Party were both divided on the question. The Ministry of Education obtained Cabinet approval for submission of a bill to the 13th Diet, then in session, which would have postponed the election for one year. The

---

* The "five big cities" were Osaka, Kyoto, Nagoya, Kobe, and Yokohama. Tokyo stands on the same level as a prefecture.

measure passed the House of Councilors, but in the House of Representatives opposition arose within the ranks of the Liberal Party. The argument was raised that the municipal boards, which would presumably be dominated by conservatives, would create a desirable counterbalance to the influence of the leftist Japan Teachers' Union on the prefectural boards. The Japan Teachers' Union, probably for similar reasons, protested the immediate establishment vigorously, even to the point of staging a hunger strike. The National Association of Governors, the National Association of Mayors, and the national top organization of the existing boards of education also favored the postponement bill. Before the differences of opinion within the Liberal Party were resolved and before a floor vote on the bill was taken, the Diet was suddenly dissolved for political reasons. The postponement bill was thus not passed, and the elections to the municipal boards of education were held according to schedule on October 1, 1952. On that date 9,950 new boards came into being and the system went into full operation.[18] It continued to exist in its original form until 1956, when the Board of Education Law was drastically amended, as will be related in Chapter 11.

The revisions of the Police Law in 1954 and of the Board of Education Law in 1956 are landmarks in the political history of post-Occupation Japan, not only because they partially nullified the Occupation reforms but also because they met violent opposition. At any rate, in the two fields of police and education—to which may be added the field of fire defense—the Occupation had accomplished the aim of decentralization.[19] But what about the broad frontal attack on the general confusion of administrative responsibilities, the criss-cross of assigned functions and the encroachment on supposedly proper local functions by national laws?

In April 1950, three years after the enactment of the Local Autonomy Law, it was still justifiable for the Osaka Municipal office to state:

Apart from the epoch-making decentralization of police, fire, and education services by the Police Law, Law of Fire Defense Organization, and the Board of Education Law, the old state of affairs still remains and almost all the other administrative functions are treated as national functions. For example, public works administration, which embraces rivers, roads, harbors, urban building, and city planning; public health, which includes prevention of epidemics and other diseases and disposal of refuse; and other services, such as examination of domestic animals, are all closely related to the local community and yet are subject to strict control and supervision by the central government with the

Road Law, River Law, Canal Law, Public-Owned Waters Reclamation Law, Port Regulations Law, City Planning Law, Infectious Disease Prevention Law, Refuse Disposal Law, Waterworks Regulations, Disaster Relief Law, Lunatics Protection Law, Child Welfare Law, Weights and Measures Law, Law Concerning Prevention of Infectious Diseases of Domestic Animals, and many other laws.[20]

The report from which this quotation is taken was published at a time when public attention had finally come to be focused on the entire problem of redistribution of functions. (This was largely a result of the Tax Mission of Dr. Carl Shoup, about which more will be said later.) But by 1950 it was too late for a comprehensive reorganization. A task of such proportions required a sustained effort of the sort that the Japanese government was obviously not willing to make. The Occupation, obviously approaching its end and with its democratizing fervor largely spent, was no longer able to undertake it. As will be shown, the problem has yet to be solved if vigorous local self-government is to exist in Japan.

The Purge of Local Officials and the Land Reform

Although the preceding sections of this chapter have dealt with the chief institutional changes in the field of local government, the story of the Occupation reforms would be incomplete without mentioning two other measures that had important effects on local leadership. The first of these was the extension of the purge to public service personnel below the prefectural level; the other was the land reform program.

The original purge directive of January 4, 1946 (SCAPIN 550) applied only to "government service," which was defined as including "all positions in the central Japanese and prefectural governments and all of their agencies and local branches, bureaus, and offices." The SCAPIN was accompanied by a memorandum which stated that it would be necessary to extend the purge to the local government level at a later time.

This need was felt most strongly when the reform legislation of September 1946 was under way and when the first local elections were in the offing. On January 4, 1947, the purge was extended to "assembly members and personnel of the local public organizations" by Imperial Ordinances Nos. 1 to 4 and by Home Ministry Ordinance No. 1 of 1947. Of these, Imperial Ordinance No. 1 contained the basic rules; No. 2

dealt with procedures; No. 3 prohibited mayors and their deputies who held office prior to the surrender from succeeding themselves in office; and No. 4 dealt with the heads of block associations. The screening system was reorganized, and prefectural and municipal committees, the latter in cities with a population of more than 50,000 inhabitants, were established.

Under Imperial Ordinance No. 3, some 1,160 former local chief executives were prevented from running for election. Of the 299,429 persons who were screened for elective local positions, 1,841 were disqualified from holding office. Of 351,971 persons screened for appointive local positions, 2,204 remained purged.

These are rather small percentages. Besides, those who held or aspired to local office—and were thus touched by this purge—were not always the real powers in the community. On the other hand, the purge of local government officials was only one part of a vast operation. Thus of 16,854 leading local officers of the Imperial Rule Assistance Association all but 201 were disqualified. While this number may have included many who held their office only for reasons of prestige, it is also likely to have included a large portion of the real local leadership.[21] A survey conducted in thirteen villages, for example, showed that 28 of the 39 persons who had been most influential before the surrender had become "purgees."[22]

The purge, however, prevented individuals only from holding office; their power as community leaders, and even the entire leadership structure, was not necessarily affected by it. Furthermore, the purge could do little to prepare a new group of people to function as leaders.

As far as the countryside was concerned, a step in the direction of training new leaders was made with the execution of SCAP's land reform program. In pre-Occupation Japan the power elite of the rural areas was the landlord class. Its leadership extended beyond the realm of local government proper into cooperative agricultural societies and other organizations, and it also formed the backbone of the conservative political parties on the national level. The number of landlords in pre-Occupation Japan has been estimated at roughly 1,700,000, of whom about 1,000,000 were non-farming. In 1941, 46 per cent of Japan's cultivated land was worked by tenants and only 30 per cent of the peasants owned all the land they tilled. The war and the immediate postwar period brought about a decrease in tenancy, but it was not a decrease of major proportions. While the relations between landlord and tenant were customarily idealized in the diffuse terms of harmony and cooperation—the landlord was to be a paternalistic master, the tenant an obedient servant—tenancy was beginning to be felt as a problem as early as the 1890's. In the twentieth century, tenancy disputes, accompanied by the growth of tenant unions, rose to a high pitch in 1935; but nationalism, fostered by "spiritual mobilization," temporarily restored the old virtues of resignation and submission, at least on the surface. Some steps in the direction of agricultural reform were undertaken in the 1930's, culminating (if that is the proper word for so conservative a measure) in the Agricultural Land Adjustment Law of 1938.[23]

Shortly after the beginning of the Occupation, the Japanese government began to consider a land reform program, probably in anticipation of a SCAP demand for one. But the conservative Shidehara government did not want to enact any measure that might threaten the economic basis of the traditional rural leadership. Its reluctance to make land reform a vehicle of social and political change was shown in some of the features of its plan. This plan provided for compulsory transfer of all land owned by absentee landlords and of all tenanted land of other landlords in excess of five *chō,* but the transfer was to be effected by land commissions of eighteen members, only five of whom were to be tenants. Moreover, the plan encouraged direct negotiations between tenants and landlords, a procedure that held little promise of equity in hierarchically minded rural Japan. According to the estimates of the planners, the reform would have resulted in the sale of about 39 per cent of the total tenanted land over a five-year period.[24]

The enactment of this plan, in the form of an amendment to the Agricultural Land Adjustment Law of 1938, took place on December 29, 1945. It proved to be a dead letter, however, because it was considered unsatisfactory by SCAP. On December 9, 1945, three days after submission of the Japanese bill to the Diet, the Occupation issued SCAPIN 411, which directed the Japanese government "to take measures to insure that those who till the soil of Japan shall have more equal opportunity to enjoy the fruits of their labor" and ordered it to submit on or before March 15, 1946, a program of rural land reform. The wider purpose was "to remove economic obstacles to the revival and strengthening of democratic tendencies."[25]

The program submitted by the Japanese government on March 15,

1946, was similar in its main features to the law already passed in December 1945. In a continuing series of conferences, members of SCAP's Natural Resources Section raised in detail their objections to this plan. In the meantime, the issue was raised before the Allied Council for Japan, and in June 1946 the Council reached agreement, with some reservations by the Soviet delegate, on a number of points, including disapproval of the program presented by the Japanese government. After the elections of April 1946 the Shidehara Cabinet was replaced by the first Yoshida Cabinet, in which Wada Hiroo, a sincere advocate of land reform, was Minister of Agriculture. There ensued a period of Allied-Japanese cooperation. The resulting program was submitted by Wada to the Cabinet on July 26, 1946, and was endorsed by it. On August 14 General MacArthur announced his approval of the plan. The implementing legislation, in the form of the Owner-Farmer Establishment Special Measures Law and the revised Agricultural Land Adjustment Law, was passed by the Diet and promulgated on October 21, 1946.[26]

Under these laws, lands subject to transfer were to be purchased by the government at a fixed low price and resold to eligible buyers—in practice, to the tenants actually cultivating the land—through local land commissions. Direct negotiations between tenant and landlord were rendered unnecessary. The land commissions at the lowest level were created in towns and villages and consisted there of five tenants, two owner-cultivators, and three landlords. The various groups elected their representatives separately. At the prefectural level, the ratio between the groups was identical, although the commissions were twice the size of the town and village commissions. (In addition, prefectural commissions had five neutral members, town and village commissions could co-opt by unanimous vote up to three neutral members.) At the national level a Central Land Committee was appointed as a policy-making body. It consisted of eight tenants, eight landlords, two representatives of farmers' unions, and five university professors.

The plans for the purchasing of tenant land were drawn up by the town and village land commissions and approved by their prefectural land commission. In most cases, paying for the land was not too difficult for the new owner-operators. As is usually the case at the end of a lost war, the shortage of food in the cities allowed the farmers to make substantial earnings despite economic controls. Economic conditions in the countryside thus showed a sudden improvement, while city dwellers led an "onion existence," peeling off layer after layer of heirloom kimonos and shedding tears in the process. In addition, the inflation of the early postwar years made it easy for the tenant farmers to buy the land at the legal purchase price, which was fixed on the basis of the rental value of 1938.[27] Within two years tenant lands shrank from 46 to 12 per cent of all cultivated land, the owner class rose from 36 to 70 per cent of all farmers, and landless tenants dropped to 4 per cent of the total farm population.[28]

In addition to its economic purposes, the land reform had political aims; the preamble to the Owner-Farmer Establishment Special Measures Law states these as "the promotion of democratic tendencies in the rural communities." Not the smallest effect of the reform was a broadening of the strata of village leadership. Since one-half of the members of the town and village land commissions had to be tenants, many tenants were given a chance to participate for the first time in public affairs of immediate interest to them. The experience gained by this participation tended to break down the attitude that such affairs were best handled by those higher up in the hierarchical order. With the disappearance of the economic dependence of the tenant on the landlord, his subordination in terms of status crumbled away.[29] Although the landlord often remains an important figure in the town or village, on the whole his group does not exercise its prewar dominance nor enjoy the exalted social status it once possessed.[30]

The land reform has deprived left-wing parties of their most important issue in the countryside, and the leadership of the owner-farmers is by and large conservatively inclined. Thus the Japanese village remains a stronghold of conservative politics. This explains in part why the post-Occupation attacks on the land reform program, instituted by landlord groups, failed to obtain sufficient political support in party councils and why the Agricultural Land Law of 1952, enacted after the end of the Occupation, preserved the new land system essentially intact.[31]

Reforms Following the Shoup Mission

The reforms described thus far were substantially completed by the middle of 1948. Around this time there occurred a change in the priority of Occupation objectives. Partly as a result of the international situation, the gravamen shifted from democratization to economic stabilization, which was deemed necessary to make Japan a strong ally of the West in the struggle with the Soviet Union. In its methods the Occupation turned, in General MacArthur's words, "from the stern rigidity of a military operation to the friendly guidance of a protective force." Its initiative and supervision were relaxed. One aspect of this policy was the abolition of the prefectural Civil Affairs Teams.[32]

In the field of local government reforms, too, there ensued a comparative lull. A few minor amendments were made to the Local Autonomy Law; as the national government organization was consolidated by the various laws regarding the establishment of the national ministries, national agencies on the local level were somewhat reduced; and the Local Autonomy Agency was established as an external organ of the Prime Minister's Office for the purpose of liaison between the state and the local entities and as a paternalistic protector of local interests. But these measures were essentially adjustments, and sometimes even retrenchments, rather than new reforms.

However, in the latter part of 1949 and during 1950, local autonomy again came into the public limelight. Its promotion was again undertaken by the Occupation, and a promising start toward considering its problems from a practical viewpoint was made. The impetus came not from a renewed ideological fervor of the Occupation; characteristically for the second phase of the Occupation, the renewed drive toward local autonomy was a byproduct of efforts toward financial stabilization. These efforts were highlighted by the recommendations for a deflationary program put forward by the Dodge Mission in the spring of 1949. To hold or abolish the "Dodge line," to follow or not to follow the "Nine-Point Economic Program," became the primary political issue of the day.* One effect of the trend toward austerity was a drastic lowering of the rate of the local distribution tax, i.e., the percentage of the national income and corporation taxes distributed to local entities in the 1949 budget. Suddenly deprived of a major part of their normal revenue, the local entities were in dire financial straits.

At this time SCAP requested the formation of a Tax Mission, which

---

* Joseph Dodge, a Detroit banker, was invited to Japan to develop plans for coping with the postwar inflation. These plans, embodied in a "Nine-Point Economic Program," led to a temporary economic retrenchment, and, in spite of its generally beneficial effects, to certain hardships, since many employees lost their jobs. The efforts of the Dodge Mission were subsequently offset by the inflationary impact of the Korean War.

was to submit a report and recommendations on Japanese taxation. The mission, known by the name of its director, Dr. Carl Shoup of Columbia University, presented its report in September 1949.[33]

The five great weaknesses in the field of local finance, as the Shoup Mission saw them, were: (1) the lack of a clear separation of functions; (2) the lack of a clear tax structure and the excessive control of local tax sources by the central government; (3) the insufficiency of financial resources of local bodies; (4) the arbitrariness and unpredictability of national subsidies and grants, the lack of equalization between richer and poorer areas, and the strain placed on local resources by the requirement that national payments be matched locally; and (5) the excessively severe limitations on the borrowing power of local authorities.[34]

In regard to the first weakness, the Mission pointed out that the existing allocation of functions failed to fix political responsibility for providing particular governmental services on any specific level of government. The citizen could not see a clear connection between the various taxes he paid and the services rendered by the recipient of each of those taxes. To overcome this shortcoming, Shoup recommended the establishment of a commission to undertake the long-neglected task of reallocating functions across the board and in detail. Principles to guide such a commission were set forth in the report.

The second weakness stemmed from the fact that in spite of a major reform of the local tax system in 1940, the major local taxes were surtaxes, as they had been ever since the establishment of the Meiji local government system. Thus the prefectures would levy a tax, such as the prefectural land tax, at a certain rate prescribed by law and the municipalities would add a percentage to it (usually a hundred per cent). The mission believed that each local level should have its own kind of tax and should have the power to raise or lower tax rates in response to the needs of the local electorate. If this were the case, the citizen would know which set of government officials to hold responsible for the rates of the various taxes. In addition, if the functions of each set of officials were clear to him, he would be enabled to judge their performance. In accord with these principles, the mission made detailed recommendations for revamping the tax structure. These will be discussed in Chapter 12.

The insufficiency of local financial resources had been the bane of local independence even under the new Local Autonomy Law. It had led not only to an excessive dependence on national subsidies; to gain revenue, local entities had also resorted to the use of lotteries and other forms of gambling, and to the collection of quasi-voluntary contributions. The mission's recommendations aimed at raising the revenue from local taxes—particularly municipal taxes—by an additional forty billion yen. Other measures proposed to relieve the revenue shortage were connected with the changes in the system of grants and subsidies.

The mission found that in 1949–50 about 350 subsidies were in effect; they were provided for by a host of different laws, controlled by fourteen different ministries, and totaled about eighty billion yen. These subsidies were of three kinds: (1) One hundred per cent subsidies for services considered national in character, of which there were about 130. (2) Partial subsidies, which numbered about 210. Some of these were granted under the theory that certain services were partly of national and partly of local concern; others aimed at providing an inducement for local entities to undertake new services or to improve the quality of existing services. The percentage of the national share was arbitrarily fixed—usually at fifty per cent—without any reference to the degree of national interest, and the richest and the poorest area received exactly the same percentage. (3) Payments for public works, including specified rehabilitation activities following natural disasters, in which latter case the rate was two-thirds of the total cost.

The mission recommended that except in cases of clear necessity, the practice of having national services performed by local government, which was the basis for the hundred per cent subsidies, be discontinued. This was to be one of the guidelines for the redistribution of functions by the proposed commission. As a result of its work, ultimately all functions would be carried out *and paid for* either by the national or the local level. Hundred-per-cent subsidies would thus no longer be necessary and they would, in general, be abolished. A few of them would remain in force for the exceptional cases in which the execution of national services by local governments was unavoidable; but in these cases the national government would also pay a fair share of the local overhead, so that the work would involve no financial sacrifice by the local entity.

The proposed commission was also to reallocate those functions for which most partial subsidies were given. Recognizing the difficulty of weighing the preponderance of national or local interests, the mission recommended that functions be assigned completely to the level of government best equipped to undertake them. Only "promotional subsidies"—partial subsidies granted for the purpose of encouraging new local functions—were to continue, together with consultation and technical assistance. They were to be "a tool of leadership and not an instrument of domination."[35] Other subsidies were to be absorbed in a block grant, as described below, and disaster rehabilitation was to be completely paid from a national government fund.

Besides granting subsidies, the national government had been supplying the balance of the required local revenue in the form of the so-called Local Distribution Tax. This system had originated in 1940, but it had undergone a number of revisions by 1948, when the Local Distribution Tax Law of 1948 was established.[36] It was this law that was in effect at the time of the Shoup Mission. The Local Distribution Tax—misnamed because it was not a tax but a national grant to local entities—was comprised of a portion of the National Income and Corporation Taxes and a portion of the Amusement and Admission Taxes. The size of these portions varied. According to the law of 1948, 33.14 per cent of the Income and Corporation Taxes was to be transferred to the local entities. But, as noted earlier, the central government decreased this percentage for the fiscal year 1949 to 16.29 per cent, thus upsetting all local budgets at the time and creating bitter frustration among local officials.[37] Shoup aimed at eliminating this element of unpredictability.

There was another major flaw in the system. Half of the Distribution Tax was given to the prefectures and half to the municipalities even though this distribution did not necessarily reflect the relative needs of these two classes of local government. Within each class the tax was distributed according to a rough yardstick of financial need and capacity: the revenue from certain local taxes (land, house, and business taxes) was considered a criterion of financial capacity and distribution was made in inverse proportion to it; the size of the population was considered a criterion of need and distribution was made in direct proportion to it. Shoup considered this formula arbitrary and faulty, and he thus felt that the system failed to reduce the inequalities between local entities. To obviate the unpredictable fluctuations in the amount of support and to achieve a more effective equalization between wealthy and poor localities, the Shoup Mission recommended the replacement of the Local Distribution Tax by a Local Finance Equalization Grant. This grant was also to remove the shortcomings of the existing system of specific subsidies. The Shoup Mission viewed this system with a jaundiced eye because specific subsidies lent themselves to administrative controls of various types, and could also be used for purposes of political control. To meet the costs of specific services, local entities had to send their officials, hat in hand, to Tokyo to petition for a subsidy. Those who were politically close to the government party could use influence with persons in the government or in the Diet to get a subsidy where others would have failed. Needless to say, they made sure that this point was understood by their constituents at election time. Specific subsidies could thus be used to keep supporters of the government party in power on the local level. The Shoup Report recommended the absorption of most of the specific subsidies in the Local Finance Equalization Grant.

The Local Finance Equalization Grant will be discussed in greater detail in Chapter 12. Here it may suffice to state that according to the Shoup plan the grant to each local entity was to be determined objectively on the basis of a formula that gave recognition to inequalities of financial capacity and need. The amount of the grant was to be the difference between the amount needed for standard services, calculated on the basis of a system of unit costs, and the amount yielded by 70 per cent of the available taxes at the standard rates. The local entity would have to spend the grant with reasonable efficiency and to raise the amount of revenue that could be obtained by levying standard taxes at standard rates. But beyond this it could freely determine what kind of local services it wanted to provide, the extent to which it would provide them, and, on the other side of the ledger, what kind of local taxes it would levy and at what rates.[38]

Finally, the Shoup Report dealt in its chapter on intergovernmental fiscal relations with the problem of local loans. It recognized that a limit on the total scope of local borrowing would be unavoidable for reasons of national financial policy. The mission's recommendations therefore aimed at a change in the form of the limit, from a limit on the debt principal to a limit in terms of debt interest—for example, to ten or fifteen per cent of the average operating budget.

The report of the Shoup Mission was transmitted to the Japanese government on September 15, 1949. On the next day, Prime Minister Yoshida acknowledged the receipt of it, calling it a "monumental work, which is bound to mark a new era in Japan's fiscal policy." A few days earlier, in a statement on the surrender anniversary of September 2, 1949, General MacArthur had referred to a remedy for the pressing problems of local government finance, which he said was being evolved as a safeguard against the re-emergence of autocracy as the prevailing philosophy of government in Japan. With such blessing from the head of the Occupation, it is little wonder that the year 1950 was greeted with high hopes by those SCAP officials who were devoted to the establishment of local autonomy.

The primary laws, which were enacted as a result of the Shoup report, were the Local Tax Law, the Local Finance Equalization Grant Law, and the Local Finance Commission Establishment Law.[39] The first of these, the Local Tax Law, was submitted to the Diet in December 1949 and created tremendous agitation. The public was in no mood to countenance anything resembling an increase in taxes in any field after the austerity measures associated with the Dodge program. The opposition was strong against the new "value-added" tax and the new municipal property tax, which subjected machinery, tools, etc., to taxation and thus affected business, large and small. The political parties were not prepared to resist these pressures, and it may well be that the government was not eager to push the bill too hard for the sake of a reform about which it was not enthusiastic. An almost unprecedented situation arose: the regular budget was delayed. It passed the House of Representatives on March 11, but was held up in the House of Councilors until April 3, 1950, three days after the beginning of the new fiscal year. The Local Tax Bill was finally passed by the lower house on April 20, but only after the opposition walked out.* Even then the upper house did not go along. The Japanese suggested the idea of breaking the deadlock with a "Potsdam Declaration Ordinance," probably hoping that this would direct the criticism toward the Occupation.

Instead, SCAP issued a statement on May 3, 1950, that the Diet had acted within its prerogatives. It became necessary to call a special Diet session to cope with the problem. After 19 days of deliberation, a slightly modified bill was passed on July 31, 1950, the last day of the session. But this merely transferred the fight from the Diet to the street: the Communists, happy over the issue, instigated anti-tax riots, and it took a long time for public sentiment to subside.

* A last-minute attempt by the government to amend the bill met with rejection by SCAP.

During this time, the Shoup Mission returned to make another survey of the situation. It made recommendations for some amendments of the new law. It also found its system already endangered by certain measures contemplated by the government, such as a return to the old system under which disaster rehabilitation was to be borne in part by the local entities. There was a note of gloom in the mission's prediction that 1951–52 would be a critical year for local finance. It felt certain that inadequate finances could kill local autonomy, but it believed that there were still ways to solve the problem and anticipated that the reallocation of functions by the newly established Local Administration Investigation Commission would be of great importance in that respect.[40]

The Local Finance Equalization Grant Law was drafted, on the basis of the Shoup Report, in many lengthy conferences between Japanese and Occupation officials, the former largely from the Local Autonomy Agency, the latter mainly from Government Section and the Public Finance Division of the Economic and Scientific Section.* Throughout the discussions, the Japanese participants expressed deep concern over the effects the scheme would have on national controls. Nevertheless, Article III of the final draft, which became law, stated: "In delivering the grant, the national government shall respect the principle of local autonomy and shall not attach any conditions nor shall it specify how any portion of the grant is to be used."

A very important feature of the Shoup Report was the recommendation for a Local Finance Commission. This commission, which according to Shoup was to be "one of the most important organs of government," was to play a vital role in the calculation and distribution of the equalization grant and in the adjustment of financial relations between the national and local levels in general. The Shoup Report stated that this commission "must be so constituted as to represent local interests adequately, something that the existing committees of somewhat similar status seem not to have done."[41]

In the drafting of the law that established the new commission, a heated controversy arose over the issue of its independence. The Economic and Scientific Section of SCAP sided with the Japanese govern-

---

* I participated in most of the conferences on the Local Finance Equalization Grant Law and the Local Finance Commission Establishment Law as representative of SCAP's Legal Section.

ment in proposing that the commission should be under the chairmanship of a Minister of State, and in arguing that this would give local interests a voice at the highest executive level. Government Section and other staff sections were equally adamant in opposing this and in pressing for a considerable independence of the commission from the Cabinet. Essentially they saw the Local Finance Commission as an arbiter between the local entities, which might occasionally request more than the national economy could tolerate, and the Cabinet, which might not be willing to pay sufficient attention to local needs. Government Section proposed that in case of a divergence of views between the Cabinet and the commission—for instance, regarding the total of the grant to be included in the national budget—the Diet should make the ultimate decision. This was feasible only if the commission was separate from the Cabinet.

The question was finally settled in favor of the view of Government Section by one of General MacArthur's infrequent letters to Prime Minister Yoshida. The new commission was then hamstrung by the Japanese government, which refused to assign to it sufficient personnel to carry out its task. When Dr. Shoup returned to Japan, he issued a press statement on September 21, 1950, in which he noted: "There is probably no more important step toward local autonomy to take at this moment than the addition of a large number of capable personnel to the staff of the Local Finance Commission." The step was not taken.

The effort to reallocate functions in accordance with the Shoup recommendations came to a close before Japan regained independence, and we shall dwell on it here as a melancholy epilogue to the Occupation's endeavors to establish local autonomy.

The Local Administration Investigation Committee, which was to perform the vital task, was established by law in December 1949.[42] Its chairman was Dr. Kambe Masao, a former mayor of Kyoto and professor of Kyoto University. Under SCAP auspices, three of the five members of the committee undertook a journey to the United States to inspect local administration there. Then the group settled down to do a prodigious amount of careful and painstaking work.

It submitted its first and principal report to the Cabinet and to both houses of the Diet in December 1950. This report was based on the three principles for the redistribution of administrative affairs, as set forth in the Shoup Report, namely:

1. So far as possible or practicable, the functions of the three levels of government should be clearly demarcated, and each specific function should be assigned exclusively to one level of government. The level of government would be then fully responsible for performing the function and for financing it from general funds.

2. Each function would be allocated to that level of government which is equipped by virtue of its size, its power, and financial resources to perform it efficiently.

3. In the interests of local autonomy each function would be given to the lowest appropriate level of government. Municipalities would have first priority in the sense that no function would be given to the prefecture or national government which could be performed adequately by municipalities. The prefecture would be given second priority, and the national government would assume only those functions which cannot be administered effectively under local direction.[43]

The committee put its finger on almost every problem that had thwarted the development of local autonomy, and its report can be read with profit for an understanding of both the former and the present systems. It envisioned a more cooperative and less hierarchical relationship between the state and the local entities. "The state," it said, "should give no guardian-like attention to or have no solicitude about the performance of such [local] affairs." In local matters that might also have nationwide bearing, the state should be responsible for information, assistance, the adjustment of inequalities, and the maintenance of minimum standards. None of these should involve "authoritarian supervision."[44]

National affairs were defined in accordance with specified criteria. The commission recommended that their delegation should be kept to a minimum and that the state should bear full costs in such cases. There was nothing equivocal in the parts of the report dealing with the participation of the state in the affairs of local bodies. A few quotations show the spirit:

In regard to those affairs which are related exclusively to a particular local public body or its people and which have little effect upon other local public bodies or the nation as a whole, the state should have no part. Provisions should be made to preclude even the non-authoritarian participation of the state, to say nothing of the enactment of laws establishing standards or making the performance of certain affairs obligatory. . . .

The ill effects that may arise when the local public bodies neglect the execution of affairs or when the manner of execution is not appropriate should be criticized or corrected by the people of the local public bodies concerned through election or the system of various direct demands, or by arousing public opinion. The maintenance of the integrity of law should be made secure finally through the judicial system, and the state should be patient enough to refrain from hasty intervention and wait for the occurrence of the voluntary criticism of the people. . . .

The so-called authoritarian supervision by the state in the form of permission, approval, authorization, direction, cancellation, alteration, subrogation, etc., which are the manners of state participation with the local public bodies, should be abolished as a matter of principle.[45]

The committee advocated that the delegation of national affairs to the executives of local entities, or "agency delegation," be avoided, and spelled out exceptions to this rule. The entrusting of national affairs to local entities as such, or "entity delegation," should not be compulsory but should be made on the basis of agreement. In principle, state responsibilities should be performed by agencies of the state.

Prefectures were not considered to have a higher status than cities, towns, and villages in the hierarchy of local government, but it was envisioned that they would provide liaison between the state and the municipalities and adjust extraordinary inequities among the municipalities. The report also made recommendations for increasing the efficiency of local administration, for rationalizing the scale of local public bodies, and for promoting cooperative relations among them.

These general observations were followed by particular recommendations regarding the various functions. The principal laws concerned were specified and the lines along which they should be amended were laid down. This was, indeed, the sort of overall review of laws affecting local government that had been planned, but not carried out, in 1947. As the foregoing outline will have shown, the report constituted a clean break with the prevalent bureaucratic thinking about national-local relations. It was a constructive and careful blueprint for a system of genuine local self-government. The reaction of the various associations of local public bodies was uniformly in sympathy with the report.* Nevertheless, two undercurrents were noticeable in the words of praise: one was the

---

* These six organizations are the National Association of Prefectural Governors, the National Association of Prefectural Assemblies, the National Association of City Mayors, the National Association of City Assemblies, the National Association of Town and Village Mayors, and the National Association of Town and Village Assemblies.

doubt whether the government would show the necessary "enthusiasm" in implementing the recommendations; the other was a certain apprehension about the yet unexperienced situation in which local units would find themselves when the mass of delegations—and with it the mass of subsidies, insufficient as they were—would dwindle. Everyone agreed that the existing situation put local government in a squeeze and that certain steps were necessary, but there was little spirit of optimistic experimentation among the local leaders themselves.

When Prime Minister Yoshida submitted his appointments for the Local Administration Investigation Committee to the Diet, as the law required, he stated that the government intended to fully respect and implement their recommendations. But in fact, the Kambe Report was shelved in all but a few minor recommendations. Some SCAP sections were as unwilling to insist on implementation as were their Japanese counterparts. The real problem, however, was the general trend of the times. Decentralization, along with democratization, had lost its importance as an Occupation aim. The work of the Kambe Committee should have been carried out in 1947, when the Local Autonomy Law was drafted. By 1950 it was too late.

The Kambe Report was the flowering of the last rose in the Indian summer of local autonomy reform, which had begun with the Shoup Mission. With the imminent conclusion of the Peace Treaty and the departure of the Occupation forces, the climate was no longer propitious for new reforms. The Indian summer was over.*

---

* The Local Tax Law and the Local Finance Equalization Grant Law have frequently been revised since 1950. The latter law changed its title to Local Distribution Tax Law in 1954. The new nomenclature—harking back to the pre-Shoup era—is indicative of a change in the character of the block grant. We shall deal with the fate of these laws and of the Local Finance Commission in Chapter 12.

PART TWO

An Analysis of Contemporary Local Government

CHAPTER 7

The Constitution and Local Autonomy

In the first part of this study, we traced the development of local government in modern Japan through the period of the Occupation. In the second part we shall describe and analyze the present system and its actual operation. Our interest will continue to focus on the degree of local self-government existing in law and in reality.

We begin with a discussion of Chapter VIII of the new Constitution, which makes local autonomy one of the basic principles of government in Japan. Our aim is to find an answer to the question: Does the Constitution safeguard local autonomy? We are interested not only in the meaning of the provisions of Chapter VIII *in abstracto,* but also in their concrete practical significance. Are the safeguards provided in the Constitution effective? Are they being invoked in the courts? Does their existence put a brake on centralizing tendencies at the national level? Or are the constitutional provisions really a dead letter?

In Japan, constitutional guarantees may be invoked through the system of judicial review familiar to Americans. In the United States the doctrine of judicial review was established in 1803 by Chief Justice Marshall in his famous decision in Marbury v. Madison (1 Cranch 137). In Japan, the Constitution itself provides for judicial review *expressis verbis.* Article 81 states: "The Supreme Court is the court of last resort with power to determine the constitutionality of any law, order, regulation or official act.*

* In spite of the wording of Article 81, the power of judicial review is given not only to the Supreme Court but to the lower courts as well. Thus the Court Organization Law (Law No. 59 of 1947) provides, in Article 10, that appeals on cases in

Because in the United States a large body of constitutional decisions has grown up, we are used to looking to these decisions for the meaning of constitutional provisions: they mean what the Supreme Court declares them to mean. The Constitution of Japan is, of course, much younger than its American counterpart, and there have naturally been fewer constitutional decisions by the highest tribunal. In particular, the Japanese Supreme Court has been called on only very rarely to interpret the meaning of a provision of Chapter VIII and to apply this interpretation to a national statute.

What then is the meaning of the provisions of Chapter VIII of the Constitution? It would of course be possible to attempt an independent interpretation, but this would be of little use for our purposes. The important thing is to find out how these provisions are understood in Japan. For this reason, we shall focus our attention on the interpretations of Japanese legal scholars and on the actions of the national government that indicate its interpretation.

Article 92 and the "Principle of Local Autonomy"

Japanese jurists have concentrated to a great extent on finding a philosophical basis for the relationship of local entities to the state as laid down in the Constitution.[1] Throughout the Constitution—especially in the preamble and in the bill of rights—there are traces of the theory of natural law, and some commentators assume that the provisions regarding local self-government are also colored by it. According to this theory, local bodies antedate the state; they have their own purposes; and the rights necessary for the achievement of these purposes are inherent in them. These rights—the *pouvoir municipal*—are not created but only recognized by the Constitution and laws of the state.

In most countries where this theory developed, it had some support in historical and sociological facts. In Japan this is not the case; practically all existing local entities are artificial creations of the state, which

---

which the lower court has determined the constitutionality of a law, ordinance, regulation, or disposition are heard by the Grand Bench of the Supreme Court. According to Article 7 of the same law, the Supreme Court has only appellate jurisdiction. See Hōgaku Kyōkai, *Chūkai Nipponkoku kempō* (Tokyo, 1953), Vol. III, Part 2, pp. 1216, 1231. (This detailed commentary by the Juridical Society of Tokyo University will be cited hereafter as Juridical Society, *Commentary*.)

even preceded them in order of time.* Moreover, as has been shown in the first chapter, the local units of the era before the emergence of the Japanese state were not conscious of having "rights." The application of the natural law theory to local government in Japan thus does not seem well-founded.

But even if one rejects the natural law theory and holds that there can be no rights in the state above or outside of its sovereignty—so that ultimately the existence and rights of local entities depend on the will of the state—constitutional guarantees are possible. By anchoring the existence and rights of the local entities in the Constitution, the state may restrain its legislative and executive organs from interfering with them, not because of any higher order but as a matter of a chosen fundamental policy. In this case, the extent of local rights depends on the will of the state as expressed in the Constitution. Considerations of this type have some relevance to each of the four articles that make up Chapter VIII of the Constitution. They have been applied to the definition of that elusive concept the "principle of local autonomy," mentioned in Article 92; to the determination of the scope of the term "local public entities," as used in Articles 93 and 94, and of the rights and functions of these entities, as stated in the latter article; and to the problem of special legislation, dealt with in Article 95.

Of these four articles, Article 92 has probably been most widely discussed. It will be recalled that this article underwent a number of changes in the drafting process and that in its final version it reads: "Regulations concerning organization and operation of local public entities shall be fixed by law in accordance with the principle of local autonomy." The general meaning of this article is clear. The words "shall be fixed by law" have a dual significance. First, they call for uniform regulation of the organization and operations of local entities by the state, and thus exclude the free choice of diverse local charters; second, they prohibit the regulation of these matters by ordinances, instructions, etc., as was customary before and during the war.† The

---

* The only traditional local unit, the *buraku*, is not recognized by law and partakes of none of the guarantees of the Constitution.

† As was noted in an earlier chapter, neither the system of neighborhood associations nor the system of regions was established by law. In limiting the regulation of the organization and operations of local entities to law, Article 92 echoes the general rule of Article 41, that the Diet shall be "the sole law-making organ of the State."

words "in accordance with the principle of local autonomy" constitute a limitation on the legislature; it is generally acknowledged that a law violating this principle would be unconstitutional.

The difficulty lies in determining the meaning of the "principle of local autonomy." The Constitution contains no definition, and the commentators differ widely in their interpretation, as a few samples will show. In general, the principle of local autonomy is seen as a combination of two elements: the right of local entities to administer their own affairs freely in accordance with their own will, and the right of the local citizens to determine that will. The former element is called "corporate autonomy," the latter "civic autonomy." The Juridical Society's comprehensive *Annotated Constitution of Japan* states this view as follows:

What is called "the principle of local autonomy" means, in a word, that the existence of local public entities, independent of the state as far as the local administration is concerned, is recognized, and that these entities, in principle, carry on local administration free of supervision by the state, independently and autonomously, either directly or indirectly in accordance with the will of the inhabitants and in response to local conditions.[2]

According to this commentary, adherence to the principle of local autonomy requires, in the area of corporate autonomy, a separation of functions, a policy of strengthening local finance, and a relaxation of central controls. In the area of civic autonomy it requires that local organs, constituted by the inhabitants or their representatives, determine the activities of local entities, and that local administration be controlled by the inhabitants and not by the central government.[3]

The worldwide trend toward expansion of national functions has led other commentators to stress the need for greater flexibility than the foregoing view would allow. According to them, the principle of local autonomy requires some decentralization; but the Constitution wisely leaves to law the determination of the degree of decentralization. The degree may change in accordance with national policies.[4]

An extreme minority view has been put forward repeatedly by Professor Yanase Ryokan. To him the principle of local autonomy means that "local administrative affairs," i.e., affairs affecting only one locality, should be freely disposed of by that locality. But whether affairs of this type actually exist has to be answered differently at different times. The "principle of local autonomy" is not independent and fixed, but stands in a functional relationship to the existence of "local administrative affairs," expanding and contracting with them. Professor Yanase can imagine a time when local administrative affairs in this sense "have decreased to zero" and at such a time, he contends, the "principle of local autonomy" will also be reduced to zero. Thus Article 92 becomes almost meaningless as a guarantee of local self-government, as Professor Yanase realizes. According to him, the real significance of that article is that it *permits* a system of local autonomy, i.e., the handling of governmental matters by organs other than the central government. If it were not for Article 92, he states, all executive power would have to be vested in the Cabinet in accordance with Article 65 of the Constitution.[5]

Perhaps the most significant aspect of all these interpretations is the fact that they are all on a conceptual plane. Little has been written about the compatibility of specific laws with the "principle of local autonomy." The question could easily have been raised in relation to existing laws passed before 1947, when the "principle of local autonomy" was not recognized in the Constitution and did not guide governments and legislators. It could also have been raised in relation to more recent legislation. Even in the case of laws that state in their preamble or first paragraph that their aim is the "realization of the principle of local autonomy," the question whether their substance fulfils that promise could have been investigated. Specific laws have rarely been subjected to scrutiny from this viewpoint. More important, there are hardly any court decisions which draw the line between laws that are in accordance with that principle and those that violate it.* The yard-

---

* Only two decisions of the Supreme Court mention the "principle of local autonomy." In one case (Decision of the Grand Bench of July 20, 1959, *13 Supreme Court Reports (Civil Cases)*, 1104) the question was a rather narrow one: Did the fact that the provision of Article 243–2 of the Local Autonomy Law (according to which the inhabitants may demand a special inspection regarding unlawful expenditures or misuse of public property) was not established until 1948 constitute failure to comply with Article 92 of the Constitution, which according to the plaintiffs was to be construed as an order to the Diet to fix by law "regulations concerning . . . the operation of local public entities . . . in accordance with the principle of local autonomy"? If so, was Article 243–2 to be applied retroactively to a case that had occurred prior to its enactment? The Supreme Court denied both questions, pointing out that the Constitution did not spell out the meaning of the "principle of local autonomy" and that it was therefore up to the legislature to determine whether the right, embedded in Article 243–2, was a necessary part of this principle or not.

The other case was more important: In March 1962 the Supreme Court had to rule on the question whether the transfer of the police from the municipalities to the prefectures by the New Police Law of 1954 was a violation of the "principle

stick provided by the Constitution has been widely discussed, but it has rarely been applied.

Article 93 and the Scope of "Local Public Entities"

As noted in the preceding chapter, some articles of the original Government Section draft of the Constitution mentioned the various types of local entities. But the Constitution as adopted refers only generally to "local public entities" and gives no definition of the term. We have touched on the inferences that may be drawn from this lack of enumeration or definition. So far, discussions on this question have mainly centered around Article 93, which reads:

The local public entities shall establish assemblies as their deliberative organs, in accordance with law.

The chief executive officers of all local public entities, the members of their assemblies, and such other local officials as may be determined by law shall be elected by direct popular vote within their several communities.

The core of the issue is: What are the "local public entities," in the sense of this and other articles of the Constitution?

One view is that, in spite of the lack of enumeration or definition, the Constitution guarantees to all recognized local entities, first, their continued existence, and second, the rights that flow from its provisions.[6] The theory of *pouvoir municipal* would sustain this view: if the state did not create the local entities, but only recognizes their existence, which is actually grounded in a higher order, then it cannot abolish them or take away any of their rights, which are inherent in them. But even if one does not accept this theory, there is force in the argument that the local entities to which Chapter VIII of the Constitution applies are those existing at the time of its adoption. It is highly significant that the Local Autonomy Law came into effect on the same day as the Constitution. To determine what the Constitution means by "local public entities"—so the argument ran in its original form—

---

of local autonomy." The Supreme Court again showed reticence to interfere with the interpretation of that principle by the Diet, pointing to the separation of powers in the Constitution. But it also stated that the new police law did in fact not violate the "principle of local autonomy." The majority of the Supreme Court seems to hold the view regarding the relation of the Supreme Court to the national legislature that in the United States has been associated with Justice Frankfurter.

we need look only at the local Autonomy Law, which, as is generally conceded, was enacted to bring the regulations regarding local government into conformity with the new Constitution.

This argument would have more force if the Local Autonomy Law dealt only with prefectures, cities, towns, and villages. But as it stands, the Local Autonomy Law also provides in its Volume III for certain "special local public bodies"—such as "associations of local public bodies" and "property wards"—to which the provisions of Article 93 of the Constitution regarding public election of chief executives and assemblies are not applied. Not all local public bodies mentioned in the Local Autonomy Law are therefore "local public entities" in the sense of the Constitution. Even accepting the general tenor of the argument, the question remains which local entities are the subject of the constitutional guarantee.

This problem came into sharp focus in 1952, when the Local Autonomy Law was amended in such a way as to abolish the direct election of the chiefs of the special wards in Tokyo, which belong to the category of "special local public bodies." A resident of Setagaya Ward brought the question to the courts, asking for a declaration that the revised law, insofar as it replaces direct election of the ward chief by indirect election by the ward assembly and requires the consent of the governor of Tokyo, was invalid as a violation of Article 93. This implied, of course, that special wards were local public entities in the sense of Article 93. The case ultimately reached the Supreme Court as the first case invoking a provision of Chapter VIII of the Constitution. The Supreme Court did not answer the question of constitutionality. In its decision of February 17, 1956, it found that there was no actual controversy concerning a concrete legal right of the plaintiff, and that in the absence of such a controversy it had no authority to review the constitutionality of the law.[7]

In a more recent case, however, the question of constitutionality has been answered. The case arose in August 1957, in connection with the selection of the chief of Tokyo's Shibuya Ward, which according to the amendment of the Local Autonomy Law of 1952 was made by indirect election by the ward assembly. Three candidates for the post were indicted for giving bribes and four assemblymen for accepting bribes in connection with that election. The Tokyo District Court acquitted all seven in a decision of February 26, 1962. It stated that the Tokyo wards are "local public entities" in the sense of the Constitution, that the provisions of Article 93 apply to them, and that the present system of electing ward chiefs is therefore unconstitutional. It found that there was no case against the accused because the ward assembly had no power under the Constitution to elect the ward chief. On appeal the Supreme Court reversed the decision of the Tokyo District Court. In its decision of March 27, 1963, it pointed out that the special wards were not in any sense the centers of the daily lives of their inhabitants; in regard to their economy and to transportation and other services they were rather parts of another local entity, Tokyo Metropolis. Since they were not independent local entities, the constitutional provision of Article 93 did not apply to them. The amendment of the Local Autonomy Law in 1952 was therefore constitutional.

As for the leading commentators, some claimed at the time of the amendment that the abolition of the direct election was not a violation of Article 93 of the Constitution. Anticipating to some extent the reasoning of the Supreme Court in 1963, they found that special wards are not local public entities in the sense of the Constitution, namely entities exercising governmental powers and administrative rights of a general nature over the inhabitants of a certain area. In this regard, it was felt by some that special wards are more like property wards than like cities. The Constitution affords protection not to them, but to the Metropolis, of which they are subdivisions.[8] In general, the exponents of this interpretation nevertheless contended that, with the qualification noted, the local public entities in the sense of the Constitution are the existing local entities.

Others held from the outset that the amendment was unconstitutional, because special wards were local public entities in the sense of the Constitution. In connection with the criminal case mentioned above, they pointed out that the local government system is characterized by a division between the basic local entities, namely cities, towns, and villages, and the intermediary local entities, the prefectures. If the Tokyo wards are not recognized as basic local entities, their inhabitants do not live in any basic local entity at all. They are discriminated against in comparison with the inhabitants of Tokyo Metropolis who live outside the wards. Not only do the latter elect the mayors of their basic local entities directly, but they also determine indirectly the selection of the ward chiefs—in spite of the fact that they live outside the wards—because they participate in the election of the governor, who has to give his consent to the selection of the ward chiefs. Another argument, advanced by Professor Ukai Nobushige, goes back to the legislative history of the Constitution. Article 86 of the Government Section draft, which became Article 93 of the Constitution, provided for direct popular election of the chief executives of prefectures and "of all other local entities having the power to levy taxes." In the negotiations with Government Section the Japanese side stated that it would be sufficient to write "local public entities" because all enumerated entities would then be included. Since at that time the special wards had the "power to levy taxes," the argument runs, they were clearly encompassed by the provisions of Article 93.[9]

The government's stand has been essentially to deny the contention that the local public entities in the sense of the Constitution are those that existed at the time of its enactment. The argument runs briefly as follows: The Constitution does not define the term "local public entities." It therefore leaves the determination of the scope of this term to law. This seemed desirable to provide for a greater degree of flexibility than an enumeration would have permitted. Without offending the Constitution, the law can abolish existing types of local entities and substitute new ones for them. It follows, a fortiori, that it can also do a lesser thing: it can attribute to some types of local entities a smaller degree of autonomy than to others. As to the specific case of the amendment of the Local Autonomy Law in 1952, the Diet could have abolished the special wards altogether; therefore, it could, a fortiori, also provide for their continued existence under a chief executive who is not directly elected.[10]

The same argument can be used to support the constitutionality of a reestablishment of the prewar system of appointment of prefectural governors, and it was in fact so used when the government began to plan such a step after 1952. It can also be applied to matters outside the scope of Article 93. To cite an example: There has been some dissatisfaction with the existing division of the country into 46 prefectures and much discussion of a regional arrangement called the Dō-Shū system.[11]

Under this arrangement, the regions would be superimposed on the existing prefectures or would replace them. According to the government's view, this could be done without amending the Constitution by a mere revision of the Local Autonomy Law, since the law is free to determine what the country's "local public entities" shall be.

Another opinion follows the government's argument to a certain point, but reaches a different conclusion. Like the government, the exponents of this view see the lack of a definition of "local public entities" in the Constitution as grounds for inferring that the scope of the term must be fixed by law. But from this they reason that the constitutional guarantees therefore apply to all local entities created by law. The Constitution, in requiring that the law must be based on the "principle of local autonomy," aims at safeguarding a decentralized, autonomous, democratic system; it negates a centralized, bureaucratic system. It may be constitutional to abolish the prefectures, but it is unconstitutional to make the prefecture or its successor less than an autonomous entity—as by providing for the appointment rather than the election of the chief executives.[12]

Article 93 states that in addition to chief executives and assembly members, "such other local officials as may be determined by law" are to be directly elected. Up to 1956 this provision applied to the members of boards of education; in that same year the Law Concerning the Organization and Management of Local Educational Administration replaced the former Board of Education Law, and not even the boards were directly elected. (They are now appointed by the chief executive with the approval of the Assembly.) The question was raised at the time whether the Constitution does not require that there be, in addition to the chief executives and the assemblymen, some "other local officials" who are directly elected. But this point has not been contested in the courts, and the reference in Article 93 to the election of "such other local officials as may be determined by law" remains without concrete meaning.

Article 94 and the Scope of Local Functions

Article 92 establishes the general rule that "regulations concerning the organization and operation of local public entities shall be fixed by law in accordance with the principle of local autonomy." If Article 93 elaborates on that rule in regard to the organization of local public entities, Article 94 would seem to do the same concerning their operation.

The scope of local operation could have been defined in the Constitution in one of two ways: in general and abstract terms or in specific and concrete terms, i.e., by an enumeration of local functions. Both methods have been tried in various constitutions.[13] The drafters of the 1947 constitution chose the abstract method, either because they felt that the enumerative method was too drastic a departure from the past, or because they wanted to provide more flexibility than the enumerative method allowed at a time when national functions were expanding everywhere at the expense of local functions.

Article 94 reads: "Local public entities shall have the right to manage their property, affairs, and administration and to enact their own regulations within law." The first part of Article 94 deals with the administrative rights of local public entities, the second with their legislative rights.*

According to the first part, local public entities have the right to manage their property, their affairs, and their administration. What does each of these words encompass? Little need be said about the right of local public entities to manage their property. There is no new departure in this; local entities were in the past considered primarily as economic units, and there was no doubt that the management of their property belonged to their "public" or "proper" affairs. It was equally clear that it did not involve any coercive authority. But what is the difference between the management of their "affairs" and the management of their "administration"? One interpretation could be that the former term refers to "proper local affairs," the latter to affairs delegated by the national government. However, this interpretation was firmly rejected by the government spokesman, Home Minister Omura, when Article 94 was discussed in the special Diet committee on the revision of the Constitution. "The management of affairs," he stated, "includes both proper affairs and delegated affairs. The management of administration involves coercive power."[14] Unclear as this explanation was, about one point there was little doubt: Article 94 extended the coercive authority of local entities over their inhabitants; it insured to

---

* In the Japanese version, the qualifying phrase "within law" appears to apply only to the second part.

them, in American terminology, "police powers" of their own, which they did not have before. There was some question whether a local entity should be permitted to provide in its bylaws for penalties as sanctions of this police power.[15] This question was answered in the affirmative, and the Local Autonomy Law in Article 14 now contains this permission and sets the limits of the penalties that may be prescribed by local entities.*

* The exercise of local police power attracted widespread attention in case of bylaws regarding mass meetings, demonstrations, and parades, usually referred to as "public peace ordinances" (*Kōan jōrei*). The first of these was adopted in July 1948 by Fukui City, which had just been partially devastated by fire. This was followed by an ordinance for Osaka City, where various unruly demonstrations had occurred. These ordinances were adopted on the basis of instructions from the local Occupation authorities. They limited, of course, the freedom of assembly and of expression, guaranteed by Article 21 of the Constitution, and the question was debated whether the limitations they imposed were constitutional. With the memory of abuses of their authority by the police fresh in many minds, any system of limitations that gave the police, or even the newly established Public Safety Commissions, the right to refuse permits or attach conditions freely seemed to be fraught with danger for the civil rights of the Japanese people.

Within the Occupation there was some concern over these dangers in Government Section and Legal Section of GHQ, but G-2 and the local commanders were more concerned over the fact that in the absence of any provision for martial law, the political situation might become uncontrollable unless mass meetings, demonstrations, and parades were regulated by local bylaws. The upshot was that the draft of a "model ordinance" was presented to various local authorities. This had the expected results. In April 1949, for instance, eight cities in Osaka Prefecture adopted public peace ordinances based on a model ordinance handed down by the governor, who in turn was guided by the forcefully expressed desires of GHQ. Other local entities were similarly "guided," often by visiting teams from Tokyo which included representatives of the Public Safety Division of G-2 and the Metropolitan Police Board—a type of activity that surely was not in accord with the emphasis on local self-government, which was Occupation policy at the time. At the time of the Peace Treaty, 130 public peace ordinances were in force in Japan. The adoption of these ordinances was sometimes accompanied by disorders within the assembly halls and riots outside, notably in Tokyo, where one of the demonstrators fell from the ledge of a window of the Metropolitan Government Building and died.

The question of the constitutionality of some of the ordinances was brought to the courts. The Grand Bench of the Supreme Court dealt with that question in regard to an ordinance of Niigata Prefecture on November 24, 1959, and in regard to the ordinances for Tokyo, Hiroshima City, and Shizuoka Prefecture in its decision of July 20, 1960. In both, it declared that the ordinances were not an unconstitutional limitation on the freedom of assembly, speech, and expression. Referring in particular to Article 12 of the Constitution, according to which "the people shall refrain from any abuse of those freedoms and rights and shall always be responsible for utilizing them for the public welfare," the Court stated in its decision of July 20,

Another question of more fundamental significance did not receive sufficient attention. According to Article 98 of the Constitution, "no law, ordinance, imperial rescript, or other act of government, or part thereof, contrary to the provisions hereof, shall have legal force or validity." In the case of the basic codes—especially the Civil Code, the Criminal Code, and the two Codes of Civil and Criminal Procedure—the problem of bringing earlier statutes into line with the new fundamental law was met by enacting some makeshift devices between the promulgation of the Constitution on November 3, 1946, and its enforcement on May 3, 1947. These "laws for temporary adjustment" were to be valid until a permanent revision of the basic codes could be worked out.[16] In the field of local government, the old codes were abrogated and the new Local Autonomy Law came into force simultaneously with the Constitution. As far as the framework of local government organization was concerned, there was thus no need for the enactment of a temporary adjustment.

The situation was different in the area of functions. Many laws on the statute books that dealt with specific functions had been enacted during an era of rigid centralization. Did they conform with Article 94 of the new Constitution? Were they all "in accordance with the principle of local autonomy," as provided by Article 92? The "principle of local autonomy" would seem to require—even if we assume that flexibility is the aim of the Constitution—that a function be attributed to the state only where there is a reasonable need for doing so, considering the

---

1960, that the proper delineation between freedom and public welfare was to be established in individual cases by the courts. In the cases in question the majority of the judges (there were two dissenters) found that the bylaws were proper means for the protection of the public welfare. (English translations of these decisions are in John M. Maki, *Court and Constitution in Japan*, Seattle, 1964, pp. 70ff.) In September 1960 the Supreme Court decided along the same lines in a case involving the ordinance of Kyoto City.

At the time of the Supreme Court decisions the number of public peace ordinances had decreased to 67, primarily because many municipal ordinances had been abolished after the transfer of the police function from the municipalities to the prefectures. It is interesting to note that 22 of the 23 prefectures that have such ordinances are located in the eastern part of Japan, while 38 of the 41 cities that have public peace ordinances are located in the western part of Japan. For a discussion of the Supreme Court decisions and of the problem of public peace ordinances in general see, for example, the special issue of *Jurist*, no. 208 (Aug. 15, 1960) and *Municipal Yearbook 1961*, p. 60. As will be noted in Chapter 16, attempts to abolish some of the public peace ordinances by means of a direct demand were unsuccessful.

prevailing objective circumstances at a given time. The existence of this need would thus have to be examined in the case of each individual law dealing with such functions. As noted earlier, the Occupation planned at one time to carry out this task, but in the end it failed to do so. The revision of the police and education systems could have been the first step in implementing the requirement of Article 94 by Diet action, and a large-scale revision of laws, as envisioned by the Kambe Committee, could have continued the process. But the connection between the decentralization measures and the demands of the Constitution was never consciously established, and the Kambe recommendations were never realized. With much justification, the Juridical Society's *Annotated Constitution of Japan* states, after referring to the failure to reallocate functions: "When this problem has been solved, the rights determined by this article [94] will, for the first time, become a reality."[17]

In the absence of a large-scale reallocation of functions by legislation, the decisions of the courts, rendered in the exercise of the power of judicial review, could have established the line dividing those functions that are in accord with the "principle of local autonomy" from those that violate it. The line would have been "pricked out by the gradual approach and contact of decisions on opposing sides."[18] By this process, Article 94 could have been gradually filled with concrete meaning. But although the local entities, especially the large cities, have bemoaned the situation regarding functions, they have not taken it to the courts, and Article 94 still fails to guarantee a scope of independent local activity.*

Article 95 and Special Legislation

Of the four articles comprising Chapter VIII of the Constitution, only Article 95 shows unmistakable traces of American origin.[19] It reads: "A special law applicable only to one local public entity cannot be enacted by the Diet without the consent of the majority of the voters of the local public entity concerned, obtained in accordance with laws." It is generally acknowledged by the commentators that the words "applicable only to one local public entity" do not mean that special laws applicable to more than one entity do not have to be submitted to a

---

* The situation created by this failure is described in Chapter 11.

local vote. Diet practice conforms to this interpretation. Thus the procedure required in Article 95 was followed in the case of the "Law for Conversion of Former Naval Ports," which applies to four cities.[20]

While some State Constitutions in the United States prohibit special legislation, Article 95 of the Japanese Constitution permits it. It requires only that the approval of the electorate of the local entity affected be obtained. This shows the raison d'être of Article 95: to prevent passage of special legislation by the Diet that discriminates against a local entity, particularly by imposing an unequal burden on its inhabitants. In practice, most of the special laws on which a referendum in accordance with Article 95 was held seemed, at least prima facie, to bestow financial benefits on the localities involved.[21] In such a case, the outcome of the referendum is a foregone conclusion, and the expense for the referendum seems wasted as far as the public is concerned. Of course, the local representative who proposed the law and achieved its passage benefits from the publicity that his actions receive through the referendum. He is normally a member of the conservative majority in the Diet, and if the locality is also dominated by conservatives—which is likely to be the case—the passage of the special legislation creates no problems.

It is different when the special legislation affects a local entity whose government is in the hands of the opposition party. In this case the special legislation may well be politically motivated and have discriminatory effects. Article 95 was meant to play a role in preventing discrimination in such cases. In this connection the Hokkaido Development Law, passed by the Diet in 1950, is of particular interest.[22] Hokkaido then had a Socialist governor who commanded considerable popular support. If he chose to oppose the law in a referendum, the consent of the majority of the voters of Hokkaido was by no means a certainty. The question whether such a referendum was necessary was thus of great importance. The government contended that only a law that regulated the authority, rights, or organizational system of a local entity was a special law in the sense of Article 95. The Hokkaido Development Law, so the argument ran, did not answer that description. It did not deprive Hokkaido of any authority, but merely centralized already existing national powers for planning and supervision of Hokkaido's development in one agency, the newly established Hokkaido Development Agency.[23] On the basis of this reasoning the Hokkaido

Development Law was not put before the voters of Hokkaido. The question of the constitutionality of this procedure was not brought before the courts.

A year later the situation became exacerbated. Hokkaido's Socialist governor had been re-elected in April 1951 against a Liberal opponent. In May 1951 the government prepared an amendment to the Hokkaido Development Law which gave the national government, in addition to its previous powers, jurisdiction over the execution of the Hokkaido development program. The central government was authorized to set up a Local Development Bureau of the Hokkaido Development Agency and various construction offices, all of them located in Hokkaido, but directed from Tokyo. In practical terms, this meant the transfer of some 3,000 employees from prefectural to national jurisdiction. The Socialists felt that the bill was designed by the Liberals to get revenge for a defeat and to create an important patronage job for a member of the Liberal party.[24] They contended that the amendment was without doubt a special law, even if Article 95 was restrictively interpreted, because it deprived Hokkaido of certain powers possessed by other prefectures under such laws as the Road Law, the River Law, and the Port and Harbor Law. However, the government and its majority in the Diet denied this, using the reasons given in 1950. The law was passed without any provisions for a referendum in Hokkaido.[25] It would have made a good test case for the meaning of Article 95, but the Hokkaido prefectural government did not grasp this opportunity and the issue was not brought to court.

The Capital Construction Law, which provided that city planning within the Tokyo area could be executed, when necessary, by the Minister of Construction or the Minister of Transportation with the consent of Tokyo Metropolis and the local public entities concerned, was submitted to the vote of Tokyo Metropolis. On the other hand, when this law was replaced in 1956 by the Capital Region Development Law, the new law did not provide for a referendum. Various arguments were used to prove that the law of 1956 was not a special law.[26] But none of them—the earlier abolition of the Planning Law for Special Cities to which the Capital Region Development Law would have been an exception, the lack of authoritative interference, the applicability to an area extending beyond the borders of a single local entity—was really convincing. They demonstrated only the government's desire to apply Article 95 selectively and to interpret it restrictively.

Questions of interpretation of Article 95 were also raised in connection with the provisions of the Local Autonomy Law regarding special cities. As will be noted in greater detail later, the Local Autonomy Law provided until 1956 that such cities be designated by law. Would such a law, if enacted, be a special law, and if so would the "local public entity concerned" be the designated city or the prefecture in which it was located and from whose jurisdiction the designated city was to be exempted? For the five cities that aspired to the status of special city, the second question was vital: if the designation law was to be passed on by the voters of the entire prefecture, the chances of obtaining a majority of affirmative votes were greatly diminished. Nevertheless, when the Diet amended the Local Autonomy Law in December 1947, it added a provision to that effect.[27] Because no designating law was passed by the Diet, no city was in a position to test the constitutionality of the new provision. When the provisions regarding special cities were deleted altogether in the revision of the Local Autonomy Law of 1956, the issue died without having been solved.

Plans for Revising Chapter VIII of the Constitution

Since the end of the Occupation in 1952 a number of conservative plans for revision of the so-called "MacArthur Constitution" have been made public.* The proposed changes in the constitutional provisions regarding the position of the Emperor, the maintenance of war potential, the limitation on civil rights, and the decree powers of the Cabinet have attracted much attention.[28] But the plans also deal with the provisions on local government and are thus of interest to us.

The first of these plans was published by the Liberal Party on November 5, 1954. In the same year the Progressive Party issued the report of its Constitution Investigating Committee. In August 1955, Hirose Hisatada, a member of the House of Councilors belonging to the conservative group known as the Green Breeze Society, published a third

---

* The term "MacArthur Constitution" is more frequently used by those who want to revise the Constitution than by those who want to keep it unchanged. The latter prefer to call the Constitution the "Peace Constitution" with particular reference to Article 9, its "no-war clause."

draft. This was followed in May 1956 by the draft of a private group known as the Constitution Study Committee.[29]

The Liberal Party draft and the Hirose draft tackled the problem regarding the scope of the term "local public entities," which we discussed in connection with Article 93. The Liberal Party draft proposed to clarify the point by having it stated in the Constitution that not only the organization and operation of local entities but also the types of local entities shall be fixed by law in accordance with the "principle of local autonomy." The intention of the drafters was probably to exclude the prefectures (or the new regions that would replace the prefectures according to the Dō-Shū system) from the constitutional provisions regarding local entities. Hirose showed this intention more clearly, for he proposed that serious consideration be given to the possibility of limiting the scope of local public entities in the sense of the Constitution to such "basic entities" as cities, towns, and villages.

The Liberal Party proposed further that the present standardized system of direct elections of local chief executives be changed so that chief executives would be selected (the change in terms is significant) in accordance with the provisions of law. The Progressive Party favored abolishing the direct election of chief executives, which had allowed a degree of executive independence from the legislature, and establishing indirect election by the Assembly, which would tie the local chief executive to his assembly in the same manner in which the Cabinet is tied to the Diet. Hirose was less specific, but he also advocated a loosening of the system under which the chief executive was directly elected. Finally, the Constitution Study Committee (which favored retaining Article 92 in its present form) would have kept the direct election system for the chief executives of towns, villages, and of most cities. But, in accordance with a law to be passed by the Diet, the chief executives of other local public entities—including certain cities designated by law —could be appointed by the Cabinet from a list recommended by a selection committee established at the national level. Both the Liberal and Progressive Party drafts would also have eliminated from Article 93 the requirement of direct election for "other local officials as may be determined by law." As stated earlier, this requirement has been without concrete meaning since 1956, when the Law Concerning the Organization and Management of Local Educational Administration replaced the Board of Education Law and eliminated the direct election of members of these boards. Since there are at present no laws that provide for the direct election of local officials not mentioned in the Constitution, amendment of the Constitution would appear technically unnecessary. The proposals were probably based, however, on two other considerations. One was a desire to indicate a general reversal of policy by making it clear that the circle of elective offices was not to be widened in the future. The other was a consideration of internal consistency. Should the Constitution require not even the direct election of the local chief executives (as would be the case according to the Liberal and Progressive Party drafts), there would be no reason to provide for the direct election of lesser local officials. The direct election of assembly members was retained in all proposals, but the Constitutional Study Committee would have made the Constitution limit the number of assemblymen in any one assembly to between 10 and 80. Within this range a law would determine the appropriate number for the various types and sizes of local public entities, as the Local Autonomy Law does now.

As for intergovernmental, administrative, and financial relations, the Hirose draft suggested simply and somewhat vaguely a clarification of the position of the state "within the scope that decides the adjustment between the government of the nation and local self-government." The Constitution Study Committee was somewhat clearer. Article 113 of its draft echoed the Meiji local government codes by providing that the activities of local public entities shall be under the control of the state. It thus denied any notion of local independence, although Article 101 of the same draft still paid lip service to the "principle of local autonomy." Under the control of the state the local public entities would manage their property, affairs, and administration. They would also be able to enact bylaws "within law and in accordance with standards decided by law." The reference to legal standards was an addition to the present Article 94.

Finally, the drafts of the two conservative parties also dealt with special legislation in the sense of the present Article 95. The Progressive Party referred to the alien origin of that provision and declared that there is no need for it in Japan. The Liberal Party would have emasculated the declaration as a constitutional guarantee by limiting the requirement of a referendum in the affected locality to cases provided by law.

The plans to revise the Constitution in general are often characterized as a manifestation of the "reverse course" in post-Occupation Japan. The revisionist proposals regarding local government discussed above are clearly part of this trend. They do not strike out in any new direction, and the net effect of their realization would be a return to the past. This would, of course, thwart such expectations for the development of local self-government as the present situation still permits.

There is no indication, however, that any of these revisionist programs is likely to be realized in the near future. The only official step taken up to now was the establishment in 1956 of a council "to carry out a complete examination of the present Constitution of Japan from a new national viewpoint." Boycotted by the Socialists and unable to obtain the services of a number of eminent constitutional lawyers and other scholars, the Constitution Research Council devoted itself first to a painstaking investigation of the circumstances under which the Constitution was created. It published an interim report in 1961, in which it found that the basic law could not be characterized as one that was "forced on Japan."

As of this writing, the Council has not yet disclosed whether it will recommend a constitutional revision. Even if the majority of the Council ultimately expresses itself in favor of a revision in principle, there is likely to be some disagreement—even within that majority—about the specific articles to be revised. It is by no means certain that a revision of the articles dealing with local self-government will be recommended by a majority.

The real though unavowed purpose of the establishment of the Constitution Research Council in 1956 may well have been to lay the groundwork for a revision of the Constitution. The Council may have been expected to respond to this purpose with greater alacrity than it has displayed up to now. But the government's posture has also changed. Prime Minister Ikeda has adopted a "low posture" that differs significantly from the clear revisionist attitude of his predecessor, Mr. Kishi. He has been very cautious in his statements regarding constitutional revision and has avoided giving the impression that he is strongly committed to such a policy. A wait-and-see attitude is also in accordance with the present chances for gaining the votes required to allow constitutional revision. Amendment of the Constitution requires a concurring two-thirds vote in both houses of the Diet and ratification by a majority of the voters in a special referendum. Since 1956 the opponents of revision have had more than one-third of the votes in each house, and it is also doubtful whether the conservatives would be able to obtain a majority in a referendum.

Summary

We may now attempt to answer the question: How far does the Constitution actually go toward safeguarding local autonomy? One way to do this would be to look for court cases in which the Constitution was invoked by the litigants and applied by the courts. We would then find a dearth of such cases. Only in a very few cases has the Supreme Court been called upon to interpret any of the pertinent constitutional provisions, and in none of these has the Court held that a statute is unconstitutional because it violates a provision of Chapter VIII.

It is, of course, possible to attribute the scarcity of court cases to the comparative newness of the basic law. But it is doubtful whether this time element is a sufficient explanation. The Japanese courts, including the Supreme Court, have been called upon repeatedly to deal with various other constitutional issues. Occasions for litigation that would test the meaning of the provisions of Chapter VIII have repeatedly arisen. For instance, all the elements of a test case were present in the issue of the Hokkaido Development Law and its subsequent amendment. The governor of Hokkaido was well aware of this possibility, but no suit was brought. The chiefs of the Tokyo special wards threatened to contest the abolition of the direct election for their position in 1952, but they failed to do so.* Certainly some of the laws dealing with individual functions that were enacted during a period of strict centralization must raise questions of constitutionality under a constitution devoted to the "principle of local autonomy." Yet no action involving this question has ever been brought to court.

When we ask why local government officials have not attempted to give to the guarantees of Chapter VIII the practical significance that comes from using them in court proceedings, our earlier consideration of the notion of "right" and the status of law in Japanese society becomes pertinent. We have shown that the mutually related concepts of

---

* As noted, the issue was later brought before the courts as a by-product of a criminal case.

hierarchy and harmony are antagonistic to an elevation of the status of law. It is only in societies in which these notions are waning, and in which the mutual power positions of the parties involved are such that a victory in the courts would not be a pyrrhic victory in life, that the weak may find protection in the law and in the courts. Applying these considerations to the relations between the central and the local governments, we find, first of all, that hierarchical notions are still strong in Japan. Besides this, local entities realize that they cannot carry on without the financial support of the central government. Fears of disapproval of legal action against the central government and of the possibility of financial reprisals deter local entities from submitting their grievances to the judiciary. It matters little whether these fears are fully justified. A local official who knows that he risks alienating the respect of his constituents—either because they subscribe to "harmony" more strongly than he does or because they are unnecessarily cowed—is not likely to carry the fight for local self-government to the courts.*

The "rule of law" is intimately connected with the status of the judiciary in society. Both reach a high mark when controversies between levels of government are submitted to the courts. Litigation of this type is common in the United States, England, Germany, and other countries, but it is rare in Japan. The Japanese failure to use legal procedures stems in part from a feeling that an executive has a higher standing than a judge, which leads to a reluctance to call upon the judiciary for assistance. The slight regard for the importance of the judicial process seems to disincline local leadership to look to the courts for protection against the central government.[30]

It would be unrealistic, however, to gauge the effect of the constitutional provisions only by the frequency with which they are invoked in court cases. The government cannot ride roughshod over them just because it is safe in the assumption that its actions will not be tested in the courts. It must anticipate the possibly undesirable political consequences of these actions, and this anticipation has a restraining effect.

There is no doubt that some conservative governments in Japan have strongly desired a return to a greater degree of centralization. As later

---

* It is symptomatic of the existing relationship between the levels of government that legal questions arising at the prefectural level are most frequently solved by submitting the question to the Autonomy Ministry and by accepting its interpretation as binding.

chapters will show, in some cases this desire has been translated into legislative action. But in nearly every case, the price for such legislation has been disorders in the Diet, a decline in the prestige of parliamentary government, a wave of public agitation, increased distrust and hostility by the opposition, and the alienation of some population groups. Constitutional provisions, whatever their more overt functions, serve as symbols in the political struggle—much like regimental banners on the battlefields of yesterday. Their successful defense nurtures the morale of one side; their capture is a token of impending victory to the other. So far, the opposition has been able to set limits to the "reverse course," and the Constitution has given them moral support. The revisionists have shown that they recognize this by their proposals for constitutional amendment. In this context the Constitution is obviously not ineffective.

CHAPTER 8

The Prefecture and Its Future

Prior to 1947 three separate codes regulated the prefectures, the cities, and the towns and villages. The prefectures were different from the other local entities in two ways: as the highest level in the local government structure, they exercised control over the lower levels; and they were "incomplete autonomous entities," for their governors were appointed by the central government and had the status of national officials. The prefectures thus occupied an intermediary position between the central government and the municipalities.

In 1947, when the Local Autonomy Law replaced the three Meiji codes, the difference between prefectures and municipalities was done away with. The local entities were divided into two groups: ordinary local public bodies and special local public bodies. Prefectures, cities, towns, and villages constitute the first group. In principle, prefectures are thus governed by the same rules as municipalities.* However, there are exceptions to this principle. Prefectural bylaws, for example, take precedence over those of cities, towns, and villages; prefectures may establish conditions, in addition to those enumerated in the Local Au-

---

* The Local Autonomy Law—hereafter abbreviated LAL in footnotes—is divided into three volumes, the first containing general provisions, the second dealing with ordinary local public bodies, and the third with special local public bodies. Special local public bodies are special wards, associations of local public entities, and property wards. Before the amendment of the LAL by Law No. 147 of 1956 there existed also provisions for special cities; but in the absence of the required legal designation of any city as a special city, these provisions had always been dormant. An English translation of the Local Autonomy Law was published by the Local Autonomy Section of the Prime Minister's Office in the form of a loose-leaf handbook in 1948 and brought up to 1950. The most substantial revisions of the LAL are those of 1952 and 1956.

tonomy Law, that must be met by a local unit desiring to become a city; and they participate in the process of dissolution, division, and alteration of the boundaries of municipalities. Furthermore, the governor of a prefecture may delegate functions to the mayors and may supervise them whenever they are acting as organs of the national government.[1] The amendment of the Local Autonomy Law in 1952 added in a number of ways to the exceptions from the principle of equal treatment for all ordinary local public bodies, but the principle itself still stood.

In December 1952 the Local System Investigation Council was established by law. In its first report, published in 1953, the Council recommended the reestablishment of two levels of local authorities—the prefectural level and the city, town, and village level—and it stressed the "intermediary position between cities, towns, and villages, and the state," occupied by the prefectures.* It is in accordance with this report that the Local Autonomy Law, as revised in 1956, differentiates between the cities, towns, and villages as "basic local public entities" and the prefectures as "large-scale local public entities, encompassing cities, towns, and villages." The prefectures are now charged with maintaining liaison between the state and the municipalities, with assisting in the rationalization of organization and management of the municipalities, and with similar tasks. The prefecture thus holds again, in law as in fact, an intermediary position in the local government structure.

Of course, this position is by no means identical with the position the prefecture held under the Meiji codes, when it was truly the pivot of centralization in Japan.† But because of this historical background, any law changing the position of the prefecture is immediately seen in the terms of the issue of centralization versus decentralization. Thus, it will

---

* The Local System Investigation Council (Chihō Seido Chōsa Kai) was established by Law No. 310 of 1952. Partly because of the divergent interests of the local entities that are represented, the national government has the stronger voice on the Council. The preliminary report, submitted in October 1953, constitutes a series of compromises, which accounts for its remarkable vagueness on important issues. The report did, however, advocate that important functions, such as police and education, be largely concentrated in the prefectures. The Council's life was extended every two years, which explains the references in Japanese sources to the first, second, third Local System Investigation Council, etc. The Council delivered a number of reports.

† On the position of the prefecture within the scheme of Japanese local government, see my report, "The Japanese Prefecture: A Pivot of Centralization," delivered at the 1956 meeting of the American Political Science Association (mimeo.). A summary appeared in *Toshi mondai*, Vol. 48, No. 4 (April 1957), pp. 107–16.

be recalled, the status of the prefecture was the point at which the exponents of centralization fought a rearguard action during the local government reform of 1946. On the other hand, the Shoup Mission, aiming to put decentralization on firmer foundations, stressed the allotment of functions and finances to the municipal rather than the prefectural level of government. To write about the plans for the future of the prefecture only in terms of greater or lesser efficiency or rationality would give only part of the picture. Neither the advocacy of these plans nor the opposition to them would become fully understandable without reference to the issue of centralization.

To be sure, not every change in the position of the prefecture is a step in the direction of centralization. Not even a closer relation between the prefecture and the central government is necessarily detrimental to the sound development of local autonomy. If, together with the establishment of such a closer relationship, the local functions of the prefectures were to be abolished or transferred to the municipalities; if national assignments, on the other hand, would be concentrated primarily in the prefectures; and if, simultaneously, the prefectural controls over the municipalities were to be curtailed—then the confusion of functions within local government might be rationalized, to the benefit of local autonomy. The prefecture would assume more clearly the character of an agency for the local execution of national administration with appropriately close ties with the central government, while the municipalities could devote more of their time, money, and effort to local affairs, largely unfettered by such ties.

Many mayors and other city officials, especially in the larger cities, advocate a change of the status of the prefecture along these very lines. According to them, the prefecture today serves largely national purposes, its legal status as a local public entity notwithstanding. But among the national purposes, they feel, too much stress is put on the control of the municipalities and not enough on the direct execution of national affairs. At least as far as the larger cities are concerned, this control is an unnecessary and costly infringement on local autonomy. The change would lessen the importance of the prefecture in the overall scheme of local government.* Plans of this type have also been proposed at times by the Socialist Party.[2]

---

* Many officials of the large cities, who chafe under prefectural controls that they consider superfluous, would like to see the prefectures abolished altogether. If assistance, liaison, or supervision is necessary with regard to towns and villages—so

Proponents of reform in the local government system in the national bureaucracy, on the other hand, aim not only at strengthening the ties of the prefecture with the central government but also at increasing the prefecture's importance in the scheme of local government. The amendment of the Local Autonomy Law in 1956 and the transfer of the police functions to the prefectures in 1954 were steps in that direction.

The most far-reaching plan for forging closer links between the prefecture and the central government would have returned the prefecture essentially to its pre-Occupation status by putting the executive function into the hands of a nationally appointed governor. The plan had the determined support of former Prime Ministers Yoshida and Kishi.* Those who advocated that governors should be appointed rather than elected stressed considerations of economy and efficiency. They stated that elections are a luxury which the prefectures, in their straitened circumstances, can ill afford; that elected governors have to cater to the interests of their constituencies and thus tend to make promises of nonessential public works; that these promises are followed by much unnecessary competition by the prefectures for national grants; and that political campaigning and fence-mending require so much time that the governors are apt to neglect their national duties.†

---

their argument goes—these could be provided by a national organ, preferably on a regional basis. These schemes raise, of course, the constitutional questions discussed in Chapter 7 in connection with Article 93 of the Constitution. If the argument that all existing types of local entities are protected by the Constitution is valid, is it possible to abolish the prefectures or to change their character?

* Yoshida proposed it first at a Cabinet meeting in December 1953. (See *Shakai Times*, Dec. 16, 1953.) As noted in Chapter 7, it was then argued that the return to the appointment system was possible under the present Constitution; at the same time changes for a revision of the Constitution were deliberated.

† Sometimes the argument showed more clearly the aim of centralization. It was pointed out that national duties constitute most of the work of the prefectures. These duties, it was said, would be executed more smoothly if the governor would be an appointed national official with only one master. The dissatisfaction with the status quo stemmed from the fact that the elected governors serve as a buffer between the central government and their constituents. For instance, when rice quotas are assigned, the governor may negotiate with the central government in the interest of the farmers within his constituency in order to achieve a modification of its demands. From the viewpoint of the central government this appears as a "lack of smoothness" in the execution of one of its programs. On the arguments against the election of governors see, e.g., *Yomiuri shimbun*, January 12, 1954, p. 1, and January 13, 1954 (editorial). The arguments imply that what is necessary, good, or fair should not be determined by the interplay of competing forces, but by a dictum from above; they reveal a general bias against democratic government.

Economy and efficiency, however, were not the only motivations of the advocates of a return to the system of appointed governors. Political considerations also played a role. Thus Prime Minister Yoshida stated in a press conference that "the administration takes the stand that the relations between the central and local governments are likely to be hampered by the present system, under which Socialists could serve as prefectural governors while the Liberal Party is in power."[3] Besides, a prefectural governorship has always been one of the choicest patronage plums.

The opposition did not believe that the elimination of the "evils" of the popular election of governors was the real purpose of the conservatives. They felt that the proposal had to be seen as part of a larger scheme. Having accomplished the concentration of the police in the hands of the prefectures, which was another part of the same scheme, the central government was now planning to dominate the prefectures through appointed governors, in order to reestablish its control of the police and, ultimately, to become an authoritarian regime.[*]

Public opinion on the plan was largely unfavorable, with over 76 per cent of those polled in Tokyo Metropolis favoring the retention of direct elections.[4] To progressives the plan was a typical example of the "reverse course," commonly referred to in Japanese as *gyaku-kōsu*. But even the conservative press and parts of the Liberal Party were opposed. When Minister Tsukada, then in charge of the Autonomy Board, discussed the plan at the conference of governors in 1954, he encountered some opposition from governors belonging to the Liberal Party. The bill to amend the Local Autonomy Law in accordance with the plan, drafted early in 1954, was not submitted to the Diet because it was felt that "public opinion did not yet support the change."[5] There were predictions that the government would make a determined effort to realize the plan prior to the local elections of 1955 or 1959, but the government did not act. Prime Minister Ikeda's "low posture policy" put an end, at least temporarily, to such speculation.

At the same time that the plans for reestablishing the appointment of governors were being discussed, a second type of proposal was brought forward. This aimed at the establishment of regions, either as superstructures over the prefectures or as replacements for them. We shall

---

[*] At times the parties of the Left even saw a link with the plans for rearmament and for revival of the conscription system on a prefectural basis.

deal with the problem of regionalism after a brief discussion of the existing prefectural units.

The Present Prefectures

Japan is divided into 46 units: one *to,* or metropolis (Tokyo); one *dō,* or district (Hokkaido); two *fu,* or urban prefectures (Kyoto and Osaka); and 42 *ken,* or rural prefectures. All 46 are thus called To-Dō-Fu-Ken, a string of nouns that appears constantly in all laws affecting local government. In spite of the difference in denomination, all these units have basically the same legal status, and in this study we shall refer to them simply as "prefectures."

The prefectures differ greatly in size, population, population density, degree of urbanization, and financial capability. Table 1 presents the prefectures in the order commonly used in Japanese sources, starting at the northeastern extremity of the arc of islands and continuing in a southwesterly direction. The degree of urbanization is indicated by the percentage of the population living in areas designated as cities (*shibu*), and by the percentage of the population engaged in secondary and tertiary occupations (i.e., not in agriculture, fishing, or forestry).*

A few words may be said about the units which do not share the general denomination as *ken,* namely, the district of Hokkaido, the two urban prefectures of Osaka and Kyoto, and the metropolis of Tokyo.

Hokkaido, Japan's northernmost island, is still very much Japan's frontier. Not only the arrangement of villages but also the construction of dwellings differs from those in the older areas. Some traditional social practices, such as village ostracism, are virtually unknown. In the postwar years, the population has frequently voted farther to the Left than the rest of Japan. We noted that Hokkaido elected a Socialist governor in 1947 and reelected him in 1951. In 1955 he ran as an independent on a progressive platform and again found favor with the voters. In that year there were 36 Socialists in the prefectural assembly as compared with 34 members from the two main conservative parties. Not until 1959 were the conservative Liberal Democrats able to unseat him and to capture more seats in the assembly than the Socialists.

---

* The percentage of the population living in cities is not a completely reliable indicator of urbanization. As a result of recent mass amalgamations—about which more will be said in the next chapter—there are many "new cities" that are essentially rural in character.

TABLE 1
The Prefectures of Japan

Prefecture	Area in sq. km	Population			Tax receipts (in 1,000 yen)	Industry[a]		
		Total	Per sq. km	Per cent in shibu		Primary	Secondary	Tertiary
Hokkaido	78,664.48	4,773,087	61	42.9	40,407,342	42.4	22.1	35.5
Aomori	9,611.52	1,382,523	144	42.3	3,360,844	62.9	9.8	27.2
Iwate	15,309.50	1,427,097	93	43.6	3,363,791	63.3	11.8	24.9
Miyagi	7,285.70	1,727,065	237	37.2	4,678,197	55.1	12.7	32.3
Akita	11,611.48	1,348,871	116	38.7	4,010,378	60.5	14.2	25.3
Yamagata	9,325.15	1,353,649	145	45.9	4,247,468	58.4	15.6	25.9
Fukushima	13,781.82	2,095,237	152	37.4	5,772,688	58.4	16.2	25.4
Ibaraki	6,078.30	2,064,037	340	35.2	5,003,318	63.2	13.2	23.6
Tochigi	6,449.13	1,547,580	240	47.6	4,735,299	53.1	18.2	28.6
Gumma	6,331.86	1,613,549	255	47.9	4,939,824	51.1	21.8	27.1
Saitama	3,802.42	2,262,623	595	50.1	7,358,304	45.5	24.2	30.3
Chiba	5,024.92	2,205,060	439	49.7	6,371,015	55.7	14.1	30.2
Tokyo	2,020.88	8,037,084	3,977	93.7	62,486,142	3.8	38.2	58.0
Kanagawa	2,362.37	2,919,497	1,236	87.1	18,533,377	15.5	31.6	52.9
Niigata	12,544.52	2,473,492	197	46.6	9,324,933	56.0	17.5	26.5
Toyama	4,248.75	1,021,121	240	55.3	4,668,787	46.1	23.4	30.5
Ishikawa	4,190.62	966,187	231	48.8	3,686,284	45.3	24.1	30.6
Fukui	4,264.70	754,055	177	52.0	2,768,268	46.5	25.4	28.1
Yamanashi	4,455.62	807,044	181	44.5	2,098,365	52.5	20.3	27.3
Nagano	13,628.16	2,021,292	148	36.0	6,820,202	56.8	16.2	27.0
Gifu	10,477.67	1,583,605	151	47.2	5,797,756	43.2	27.1	29.7

Shizuoka	7,768.75	2,650,435	341	54.6	11,594,922	39.3	27.9	32.8
Aichi	5,057.55	3,769,209	745	68.6	20,833,273	26.9	36.8	36.3
Mie	5,765.85	1,485,582	258	55.7	5,505,998	48.5	22.7	28.8
Shiga	4,016.00	853,734	213	36.1	3,515,320	51.9	21.5	26.5
Kyoto	4,633.61	1,935,161	418	78.7	10,120,009	22.5	30.4	47.1
Osaka	1,809.93	4,618,308	2,522	87.4	34,288,678	7.8	42.3	49.9
Hyogo	8,312.96	3,620,947	436	66.6	18,869,302	28.1	31.4	40.4
Nara	3,692.11	776,861	210	30.5	2,488,289	41.3	23.8	35.0
Wakayama	4,712.99	1,006,819	214	42.0	3,708,461	39.8	26.5	33.7
Tottori	3,488.50	614,259	176	40.3	1,720,229	56.8	12.9	30.3
Shimane	6,625.04	929,066	140	43.0	2,735,666	58.3	15.0	26.7
Okayama	7,061.93	1,689,800	239	50.6	5,706,218	51.0	21.6	27.4
Hiroshima	8,431.22	2,149,044	255	46.7	8,128,766	39.9	23.1	37.0
Yamaguchi	6,074.88	1,609,839	265	62.2	7,680,048	43.9	21.4	34.7
Tokushima	4,142.85	878,109	212	28.5	2,267,382	54.0	17.7	28.4
Kagawa	1,859.36	943,823	508	36.0	2,898,594	49.2	17.4	33.4
Ehime	5,651.18	1,540,628	273	48.0	4,411,146	50.4	20.3	29.3
Kochi	7,114.24	882,683	124	39.4	2,287,348	58.8	12.9	28.3
Fukuoka	4,899.47	3,859,764	788	60.3	17,708,414	27.5	31.6	40.9
Saga	2,403.50	973,749	405	46.5	2,979,639	49.1	18.6	32.4
Nagasaki	4,086.38	1,747,596	428	48.8	5,089,317	48.3	17.2	34.5
Kumamoto	7,527.43	1,895,663	252	39.5	5,246,333	56.1	14.2	29.7
Oita	6,176.41	1,277,199	207	47.8	3,858,707	56.2	13.9	29.9
Miyazaki	7,733.59	1,139,384	147	45.7	3,446,794	59.8	14.1	26.1
Kagoshima	9,190.91	2,044,112	222	36.5	3,969,520	68.7	8.5	22.9
All Japan	369,765.89	89,275,529	241	56.3	381,490,955	41.1	23.8	35.1

a Base: employed persons of 14 years of age or older.

sources: Population Census of 1955; for tax receipts, Japan Statistical Yearbook 1957, p. 416.

Hokkaido covers some 21 per cent of Japan's territory, but in 1955 its population amounted to less than 5 per cent of Japan's total population. The island's population density (about 61 per square kilometer) was about one-fourth of the average population density for the country (241 per square kilometer). The development of Hokkaido is thus a continuing concern of Japanese governments. We mentioned the Hokkaido Development Agency, established in 1950, as an adjunct to the Prime Minister's Office to develop and execute plans for a fuller use of the natural resources of the island. In October 1951 the first five-year program was established. It aimed at developing electric power resources, expanding roads and port facilities, and increasing food production. The actual results were not very satisfactory; only a little over half of the planned targets were reached. A second five-year plan was established in 1958, paralleling the nation's new long-range economic program. It placed emphasis on the development of major industries, including exploitation of untapped resources. A new eight-year plan is to get under way in 1963. The largest city on the island is Sapporo, the prefectural capital, a modern urban center with a population of roughly 600,000 people. There were nineteen other cities on the island in 1955.

Kyoto-fu comprised in 1955 the city of Kyoto, Japan's ancient capital, six other cities, 34 towns, and 22 villages; Osaka-fu consisted of the city of Osaka and 20 other cities, 32 towns, and 51 villages. More than half of the population live in the cities of Kyoto and Osaka, and most of the prefectural taxes are collected there. It is thus not surprising that the question of the proper relationship between these cities and the prefectural administration has long been an issue. Officials and citizens' groups in the city of Osaka, in particular, have long considered prefectural control of certain functions as an anomaly of the "tail that wags the dog" variety. They have thus always stood in the forefront of the "Special City Movement," about which more will be said in the next chapter.*

More recently other problems have engaged the attention of the

---

* Sometimes aims which go beyond those of the Special City Movement—exemption of the big cities from prefectural control—are proposed. For example, in 1959 the Osaka Chamber of Commerce and Industry called for a merger of Osaka's prefectural and municipal governments into a single administrative unit. It pointed out the undesirable economic effect of the division of the area into small units and underlined the wastefulness of maintaining unnecessarily a prefectural and a city government. It estimated the waste at between 5,000 million and 7,000 million yen per year. (*Japan Times,* May 17, 1959, p. 3.)

people in the area. As most newly developing industries poured into the Tokyo-Yokohama complex, the relative economic position of the cities of western Japan began to deteriorate. It became clear that counter-measures had to be devised on some regional basis. There are a number of regional plans that have not been handed down from Tokyo but developed locally. We shall discuss some of these later in this chapter. But we may note here that their very existence seems to confirm the reputation of the people of the area for an independent, imaginative, and enterprising spirit.

Tokyo-to differs from Kyoto-fu and Osaka-fu. A city of Tokyo—paralleling the cities of Kyoto and Osaka in their relations to the prefectures in which they are located—existed until 1943. In that year the present metropolitan system was created and municipal administration was absorbed by the prefecture.[6] There is no governmental unit, embracing only the urban core of the metropolis and intervening between it and the metropolitan government. Rather, the urban core is divided into 23 units, the special wards. These have less self-government than the ordinary public entities on the municipal level, that is, cities, towns, and villages. In addition to the 23 wards, Tokyo Metropolis encompassed, as of April 1955, eight cities, 22 towns, and 20 villages, as well as a number of islands such as Oshima, Hachijojima, and Miyakejima. About 86 per cent of the metropolitan population, which reached the ten-million mark in 1962, live in the 23 wards.

The relationship between the wards and the metropolitan government creates certain problems of a political and administrative nature. But these are overshadowed at present by the fact that the metropolitan community is growing at a terrific pace and is expanding far beyond the administrative boundaries of Tokyo-to. We shall discuss these problems later in this chapter and in Chapter 9.

The existing prefectures are at present not legally subdivided into *gun* or counties. As noted in earlier chapters, the *gun* was abolished as an area of local authority in 1921 and as an agency of central administration in 1926; but in 1942 it was revived as a jurisdictional area of prefectural branch offices. Today the *gun* is first of all a geographical area. A town or village is usually referred to by its own name, then by the *gun* and the prefecture in which it is located (e.g., Okisato-mura, Sakata-gun, Shiga-ken). The *gun* also serves as election district.[7] Welfare agencies, public organizations of various types (such as agricultural cooperatives), labor unions, business corporations, and other groups use it as an administrative district. The Local Autonomy Law does not indicate what a *gun* is or what purposes it serves; it deals only with the question of how a *gun* may be created or abolished, and how its name or its area may be changed.* The *gun* nevertheless has a certain governmental importance. According to Articles 155 and 175 of the Local Autonomy Law, the governor may, through a bylaw, establish local affairs offices, staffed by local secretarial officials who act under his direction. Although the law does not require it, in practice the area of jurisdiction of the local affairs offices almost always coincides with a *gun* area. There are prefectural welfare offices, tax offices, infectious diseases prevention offices, and so forth, all on the *gun* level. Cities, which are outside the *gun* boundaries, usually deal with the prefectural government directly, but towns and villages have contact primarily with the local affairs office for the *gun* in which they are located. It is the local affairs office, for instance, that receives town and village applications for national subsidies, investigates them, guides them through the higher authorities, and distributes the subsidies received. A similar process is followed when towns and villages wish to obtain permission to raise loans. The mayors of the towns and villages within the *gun* meet regularly at the local affairs office and under the chairmanship of its chief. Thus the *gun* continues to serve the function it had served in 1942, and it remains, in actuality and in the consciousness of officials and citizens, a level of administration between the prefecture and the towns and villages.

The recent amalgamations of cities, towns, and villages have again raised questions about the continued existence of the *gun*. To give an extreme example: when all the towns and villages of an existing *gun* are amalgamated into one city, the *gun* becomes clearly superfluous. What if only one town remains, or two towns or villages? Is it necessary to maintain the prefectural local affairs offices on the *gun* level in such cases? The example is not too farfetched. In 1957 only three per cent of the *gun* embraced more than five towns and villages. The fourth Local System Investigation Council concerned itself with this problem, but in

---

* LAL, Article 259. The steps required are a resolution of the prefectural assembly, a subsequent determination by the governor, and, since the amendment of 1952, the issuance of an official notification by the Prime Minister. From the wording of Article 259 it is clear that the *gun* area shall, as before, not include the areas of cities.

spite of some sentiment in favor of abolishing or reorganizing the *gun* (e.g., by increasing their size and by including smaller cities within the *gun* areas), the decision was to retain the *gun* in its present form while continuing the study of the problem through a committee of the Council.[8]

Regionalism

The existing division of the country—which in its entirety is approximately as large as the state of California—into more than forty prefectures dates back to a time when modern means of communication and transportation were lacking in Japan. It is said that the sizes of the prefectures were determined with the idea in mind that it should be possible for a man on horseback, setting out from any part of the prefecture, to reach the prefectural capital within one day.[9] Clearly, this standard has little relevance today. The present prefectures also do not coincide with any areas that share common economic problems or needs. To cite examples: The northern part of the island of Honshu forms a natural unit in terms of climatic and crop conditions, but it is divided into seven prefectures. The industrial and commercial complex that has developed in the Kinki-Kansai area is similarly carved up into prefectural units. A new, more rational division of the country into a smaller number of regions or prefectures seems to be called for. Such a rearrangement could also contribute to economy and administrative efficiency.

The idea of regionalism is not new in Japan. The Tanaka Cabinet (1927–29) planned the establishment of regional boards on the basis of six regions.* The problems of the northern part of Honshu, where the depression had led to a flight of the impoverished rural population into

---

* The plan grew out of the election platform of the Seiyūkai, of which General Tanaka was President. It would have made the prefectures autonomous entities under an elected governor, carrying out local functions; national functions would have been concentrated in the regional boards, whose chiefs would have been appointed by the central government. Hokkaido would have remained a unit, separate from the six regions. It must be remembered that at the time the prefectures were "incomplete autonomous entities." The change in their character would have been a step toward local autonomy.

For the text of the Tanaka plan, drafted by the Administrative System Deliberation Council, see *Jichi ronshū*, Vol. II (November 1954), p. 173. This issue, entitled *Dō-shū seiron* (On the Dō-Shū System), is devoted in its entirety to the problem of regionalism.

the cities, which could not absorb the influx because they lacked sufficient industrial establishments, prompted the Okada and Hirota Cabinets (1934–37) to establish an Office for the Development of the Tōhoku Region, attached to the Cabinet. In 1940 Regional Liaison Councils were established for eight regions. We have already referred to the Regional Administrative Councils and the Regional Superintendencies General, established during the war, and to the Regional Administrative Affairs Bureaus of the early Occupation period. When the local self-government provisions of the Constitution were before the committee of the House of Representatives, the desirability of a regional arrangement was brought into the discussion, and when the lower house passed the Local Autonomy Law it attached a resolution which, among other things, called for a readjustment of the areas of the prefectures.[10] Although this step has not been taken yet, administrative divisions of the country which encompass a number of prefectures are being used by various agencies as jurisdictional areas of their local branches, such as Local Finance Offices, Regional Preventive Medicine and Narcotics Control Offices, etc. The Police Law organizes the national rural police on the basis of regions; similarly, the country is divided into regions for the purposes of the Electric Power Enterprise Law. In the organization of some of the national associations of local executives and legislatures a regional level exists between the prefectural and the national levels. Unofficial liaison organs between the prefectural governments in various regions have also sprung up.*

The Local Administration Investigation Committee, established on the basis of the Shoup recommendations, found it desirable to enlarge the scale of the prefectures in accordance with economic, social, and cultural realities. It proposed that this be done by amalgamating some of the prefectures, which would not change the structure of local government as such. It opposed the establishment of regions, whether these were to be superimposed on the present prefectures or were to replace

---

* Voluntary cooperation between prefectures could overcome some of the disadvantages of the present small size of the prefectures. But such cooperation is not well developed. To cite an example: A number of prefectures could join their efforts to establish a great, modern cancer center for a certain region of the country. The governor of Hyogo promoted such a plan for an area encompassing Hyogo, Osaka, and Wakayama prefectures. It came to naught—partly because the idea of contributing money to a center located in another prefecture was politically unattractive— and each prefecture has decided to set up its own center on a more modest scale.

them; it felt that the former plan would only complicate the existing administrative system and increase administrative expenses, and that the latter plan would weaken rather than strengthen local autonomy.[11]

Prime Minister Yoshida, on the other hand, declared himself publicly in favor of a regional system in April 1952 and repeatedly afterwards.[12] He did not make it clear which of the two alternatives considered by the Local Administration Investigation Committee that he favored. He also did not indicate what the relationship of the regions to the national government and to the municipalities would be, and, in particular, whether the heads of the regions would be appointed or elected. The intentions of the government became clear, however, on July 24, 1954, when the head of the Autonomy Board, Mr. Tsukada, commented on the matter before the Local Administration Committee of the House of Representatives. At that time the Local System Investigation Council was deliberating the issue. Without wanting to prejudge these deliberations, Minister Tsukada said, he personally believed that for a country as small as Japan a regional system would be desirable. This system should be realized in a number of steps. He linked the mass amalgamation movement of towns and villages, then in progress, with the feasibility of creating larger administrative units at a higher level, and cited Hokkaido as an example of what a future region might be like. Then he added: "Since such regions would be incomplete autonomous entities, it would be proper not to hold elections for the chief executives, as is the case at present. It is important, however, to establish assemblies. I think that the old prefectural system may be applied to the regional system."[13] Of course, this statement did not come unexpectedly. From the beginning, most observers had felt that the government's proposal for the establishment of a regional system was inextricably linked with its desire for a return to a greater degree of centralization.

The issue of centralization versus local autonomy also loomed large over the activities of the Local System Investigation Council. The Council had dealt with the status of the prefecture in its first report of October 1953, as noted earlier in the chapter. It had then concentrated its attention largely on the urgent problems of local finance. Its long-awaited report regarding rationalization of prefectural areas was submitted on October 18, 1957.

In this report two different solutions were proposed. The "Regional Plan" represented the view of the Council majority, the "Prefectural

Plan" that of the minority.* The two plans are different both in substance and in spirit.[14] Majority and minority are agreed that the present
prefectural system is outdated and that the unequal administrative and
financial capabilities of the present prefectures constitute a problem.
Both realize that larger units would avoid these shortcomings, would
contribute to efficiency and economy of administration, and would be
able to carry out large-scale development and other functions for which
the prefectures are too small. But while the minority believes in the desirability of an adjustment of the prefectural system, the majority advocates its replacement by a system that differs on essential points.

The majority proposal starts out with a declaration of fundamental
policy, which first recites the reasons for the reform. Governmental functions have expanded and there is a need for their unified and standardized execution. This calls for cooperation between the state and local
entities. Financial considerations demand a rational, efficient, and economical administration of governmental functions. Some of these functions require the establishment of local administration for large areas.
To forestall the criticism that the proposed system would weaken local
autonomy, the point is made that the cities, towns, and villages are after
all the "basic local entities," and that a reconsideration of the local government system is necessary if their local autonomy is to be strengthened.† The majority report then states that a discrepancy exists between
the functions and the legal position of the prefectures: prefectural functions are largely national in character, but the postwar prefecture is a
fully autonomous entity under a governor who is an elected local official.
According to the report it was because of this discrepancy that the national government felt it necessary to establish more and more branch
agencies of its own. While the prefecture in its present legal position is
inadequate for the fulfillment of its national functions, its local functions
and the functions of the municipalities are frequently overlapping. Thus

---

* At the plenary session which adopted the report, 33 of the 53 members of the
Council were present, and 17 of them expressed themselves in favor of the "Regional
Plan." Twelve of the members present expressed themselves in favor of the "Prefectural Plan," and the minority report was submitted to the Prime Minister for his
reference. The remaining four members who were present opposed both plans.

† In this connection, reference is made to the administrative and financial capabilities of the big cities, and to the results of the town and village amalgamations of the
preceding years, which led to the establishment of larger municipal areas while the
comparatively small prefectural areas remained unchanged.

the report considers the present system faulty as regards the size and the character of the present prefectures.

Then the main points of the majority recommendation are revealed: the prefectures are to be abolished and "blocks" are to be established between the state and the cities, towns, and villages. These blocks are characterized as new "intermediate entities" and as "consolidated national branch agencies." One and the same person is to head the block in both its aspects.

The second part of the report spells out these recommendations in greater detail. The new unit is tentatively called a district (*chihō*). As for the number of districts, the report suggests seven, eight, or nine. Maps and tables showing these alternatives are appended.* In principle, the districts are to be established without dividing up existing prefectural areas. Natural, social, economic, and cultural conditions are to be primary considerations. In all the alternatives proposed, the districts would still differ markedly from each other in terms of population, area, income, and taxation potential.

As noted, the district is to be both a local public entity and a national agency. As a local public entity it would have a district assembly of 40 to 120 members (depending on the size of the population) elected directly for four-year terms. As a local public entity, the district would also have a chief executive; but the incumbent of this position would at the same time head the district in its aspect as a national agency, tentatively called Chihō-fu (District Board or Superintendency). He would be a national official, appointed for a three-year term by the Prime Min-

---

* In each case, Hokkaido would form one district, the six northeastern prefectures of Honshu another, and all of Kyushu a third. Shikoku—the smallest of Japan's main islands, now divided into four prefectures—would be a district if the country is divided into at least eight districts. Otherwise it would form a district together with the present prefectures of Okayama, Hiroshima, Yamaguchi, Shimane, and Tottori, all located on the main island of Honshu. The division of the center of Honshu differs markedly in the seven- or eight-district plans, on the one hand, and in the nine-district plan, on the other hand. For example, in the former case a district encompassing Kanagawa, Tokyo, Chiba, Ibaraki, Yamanashi, Saitama, Tochigi, Gumma, Nagano, and Niigata would spread from the Pacific to the Sea of Japan. In the latter case, the eight first-named prefectures would be one district, but Nagano and Niigata would be combined with Fukui, Ishikawa, and Toyama to form another district. The Council's recommendations are tentative on this point. The Council suggests that further consideration be given to the question to which district all or part of Niigata, Nagano, Gifu, Fukui, and Mie prefectures should be joined.

ister with the approval of the district assembly. In order to assure the apolitical character of the office, officials of parties or other political organizations would be disqualified from holding it. The chief executive could be dismissed by the Prime Minister for violation of his official duties. The assembly could not dismiss him or force him to resign, but it could make a demand for his dismissal to the Prime Minister, who would accede to the demand only when he recognized the existence of proper reasons for it.*

As for the remainder of the executive branch of the district, some of the district officials would be national public officials, others local public officials. The administrative commissions established during the Occupation—as in the fields of public safety, education, election management, and personnel administration—are to have no counterparts in the new district, but commissions limited in function to the decision or review of individual cases may be created. Finally, the plan envisions the establishment of district branch offices within the areas of the present prefectures or within other appropriate areas.

The majority proposal then turns to the functions of the district in both its aspects. Its functions as a local public entity would consist, on the one hand, of such national functions as can be transferred to it, and, on the other hand, of such functions of the present prefecture as cannot be transferred to cities, towns, and villages. Within the scope of these functions the district would have the right to establish bylaws. It would also have the right to levy taxes and float loans. In its aspect as a national agency (that is, as a *chihō-fu*) the district would consolidate those national functions now exercised by the various national branch agencies that cannot be transferred to the district as a local public entity. The various national branch offices would be abolished. In the planned redistribution of functions, cities, towns, and villages would thus have priority in the sense that they would obtain all the national and prefectural functions that can be transferred to them.†

So much for the majority recommendation. As noted earlier, the minority has no quarrel with the argument of the majority for enlarging

---

*No demand could be made within one year from the appointment of the chief executive or within one year from the last demand for dismissal.

† An appendix to the report gives examples for the proposed redistribution. Special regulations for the big cities and for Tokyo Metropolis are envisaged.

the areas of the present prefectures. But leaving this consideration aside, it finds that on the whole the defects in present-day local government should not be attributed so much to the existing system as to the manner in which the system has been operated by the central government. This being the case, it suggests that institutional reforms be kept to a minimum. In particular, it opposes the abolition of the prefectures and their replacement by districts that differ from them in their essential character. Instead, it proposes the consolidation of three or four prefectures into one. Maps appended to the report show as three possible alternatives the division of the country into 15, 16, or 17 prefectures. The minority shows itself eager to retain the fruits of the postwar democratization of local government, including the position of the prefecture as a "perfect autonomous entity," the popular election of governors (with a new proviso, however, that governors should not be allowed to succeed themselves), the status of prefectural officials (including the governor) as local and not national civil servants, and the existence of local administrative commissions such as boards of education and election-management, public-safety, and public-service commissions.

The minority advocates a clear separation of the functions of the various levels, and, in particular, avoidance of the present overlapping of municipal and prefectural functions. National functions would be curtailed, and the cities, towns, and villages or their organs would perform those functions that directly affect the daily lives of the people. The prefectures would exercise as independent local functions many of the functions that are presently classified as assigned functions. On the other hand, where a prefectural function remains an assigned national function, the method of national supervision would be simplified and, in effect, strengthened. National branch offices would be abolished wherever possible. The redistribution of functions would be accompanied by a large-scale redistribution of financial resources.

First reaction to the majority report was overwhelmingly unfavorable. The Socialist Party was, of course, against the proposed plan, and even some segments of the Liberal Democratic Party were lukewarm or cool to it because of vested political interests in the existence of the prefectures. The National Association of Prefectural Governors did not favor the proposals of the majority. These proposals involved also the very serious constitutional question to which we referred in Chapter 7, namely, whether the present local entities, including the prefectures, are not protected in their essential character by Articles 92 and 93 of the Constitution. Under these circumstances the government did not push for an immediate implementation of the plan, and the present prefectural system, condemned by both the majority and minority reports, continues in force.

The problems created by that system have come into sharp focus again in recent years for two closely related reasons. On the one hand there was the continuing growth of the great urban and industrial centers around the Tokyo-Yokohama complex and the Osaka-Kobe complex. This growth did not respect administrative boundaries, and if chaos was to be avoided and some orderly development assured, planning had to be conducted for areas encompassing a number of prefectures. On the other hand, comprehensive national plans for economic development received a new impetus from Prime Minister Ikeda's scheme to double incomes within ten years. These plans, too, transcended by their very nature the boundaries of individual prefectures. The emphasis thus has changed from attempts at restructuring the general scheme of local administration to attempts at creating ad hoc devices for the planning and the execution of certain functions closely related to the development of certain regions in regard to their land and water resources, transportation and industrial facilities, housing and community facilities, and so forth.*

A case in point is the planning for redevelopment of the national capital region around Tokyo. The population of Tokyo is increasing at a rate of from 200,000 to 300,000 persons annually; this is equivalent to adding the population of a city the size of Honolulu or Coventry to the

* Occasionally a certain uneasiness with such a pragmatic, function-oriented approach becomes apparent. Thus it is sometimes proposed that a new ministry or a national agency under a state minister be put in charge of the redevelopment of the national capital region. According to some proposals this ministry would replace the present metropolitan government altogether. The Local System Investigation Council proposes that the national government assume responsibility for the national capital and refers in this regard to the examples of the District of Columbia and Brasília. See, e.g., *Japan Times*, May 10, 1962, for a proposal by the assistant director of the Administrative Management Agency, Mr. Okazaki, according to which the metropolitan functions would be split between a new ministry and the special wards, which would again elect their ward chiefs. A resolution of the Tokyo Metropolitan Assembly in June 1962 called the idea "a reckless and unconstitutional trampling on local autonomy." (*See Tokyo Municipal News*, Vol. 12, No. 4, August 1962.)

population of Tokyo each year. At least 70 per cent of this increase is social increase, i.e., the influx of people who are lured to Tokyo by its higher living standard.* Governmental agencies, industries, businesses, and educational institutions are concentrated there.† For this reason about 450,000 commuters come into Tokyo from nearby prefectures every day.‡ Since the physical capacity of Tokyo in terms of land and water supply is severely limited, the problems created by these facts are staggering. Housing, sewage, traffic—whatever service we consider, we find a crisis situation.

The first attempts to deal with this problem were limited in their application to the administrative boundaries of Tokyo Metropolis. On the basis of the Capital Construction Law of 1951 an emergency five-year plan was started in 1952. But its implementation was too slow and it was replaced in 1956 by a new three-year plan. In the same year a new law, the Capital Regional Development Law, was enacted. Abandoning the former approach, this law aimed at the comprehensive planning for a region within a radius of 100 kilometers from the center of Tokyo. The region thus encompasses the whole of Tokyo Metropolis, all of Kanagawa, Saitama, and Chiba prefectures, and parts of Tochigi, Gumma, Ibaraki, and Yamanashi prefectures. Plans for the development of this region—which is a planning area, not an administrative unit—are worked out on the national level. A Capital Region Development Commission, headed by a minister, was established as an external organ of the Prime Minister's Office. A deliberation council of 43 members, including the

* According to statistics of 1958 the average per capita income in Tokyo was about twice the national average and about three times that of such low income prefectures as Kagoshima in southern Kyushu. The average Tokyo resident spends about 53% more per year than the average Japanese and saves nearly three times as much. As long as such inequalities exist, the influx will continue. In interprefectural migration, seven prefectures—Tokyo, Kanagawa, Aichi, Kyoto, Osaka, Hyogo, and Fukuoka—are on the receiving end. See the series "The City in Crisis" by Hani Gyo in *Japan Times,* March 10–23, 1962.

† In 1959 there were in Tokyo 52,000 factories; 47% of the entire foreign trade of Japan was centered in Tokyo. Tokyo has 13 out of 72 national universities, 68 out of 135 private universities, and 71 out of 272 junior colleges; 280,000 of Japan's 600,000 university students attend universities there. See the pamphlet *Metropolitan Administration in Tokyo,* prepared by the Metropolitan Government for the 1961 EROPA seminar.

‡ At the same time some 150,000 go out of Tokyo to places as far as seventy kilometers away. See Masamichi Royama, "Tokyo and Osaka," in W. A. Robson, *Great Cities of the World* (2d edition, 1957).

governors and assembly chairmen of the eight prefectures concerned, serves as an advisory organ. The Commission is empowered to prepare redevelopment programs, designate industrial development areas and facilitate their development, impose restrictions on construction or extension of industrial plants within existing urban areas, and coordinate the execution of the redevelopment program.

In 1958 the Commission adopted a Master Plan which is to be fully implemented by 1975. The plan anticipates that the region will by then have a population of 26.6 million people, and according to current trends it could be expected that 14.3 million of them will be living in the presently existing urban areas. To check the excessive concentration of industry and population in these areas, the plan imposes restrictions on the construction and extension of large-scale industrial plants and of school buildings for certain higher schools within built-up areas.*

In this way the population of the existing urban areas is to be limited to a maximum population of 11.6 million. The difference of 2.7 million is to be absorbed into the new industrial development areas or satellite cities. The designation of these industrial development areas and the selection of the specific industries to be located there depend on a number of factors, such as availability of the appropriate resources, including industrial water. But in every case certain public facilities, such as housing and transport, must be provided. A number of ten-year work programs for the period from 1957 to 1967 have been adopted. One of these aims at the construction of a network of major trunk highways connecting the industrial development areas with existing urban areas and with other industrial development areas. The government has designated ten areas as "satellite cities." Six additional areas are under consideration. Some of these, such as the Maebashi-Takasaki area in Gumma prefecture, the Utsunomiya area in Tochigi prefecture, and the Mito area in Ibaraki prefecture are a considerable distance from the existing urban area. Others, such as the Omiya-Urawa area in Saitama prefecture, are very close to it. The designated areas receive subsidies from the government to develop the necessary facilities.

The execution of this aspect of the plan is certain to bring about far-reaching sociological changes in the affected areas. Some of these areas

* The Law of Industrial and Other Restrictions in the Built-Up Area of the National Capital Region (No. 17 of 1959) requires the permission of the governor of the metropolis for such construction and extensions within the 23 wards and the adjoining cities of Mitaka and Musashino.

are still predominantly rural, both in appearance and in the attitudes of their inhabitants. Now they are to become major industrial centers, and the land that only yesterday was almost exclusively farmland is to be studded by factories and huge apartment complexes (usually referred to as *danchi*) inhabited by newcomers who do not share the communal spirit of the farming population. It would be reasonable to expect some resistance to this change. It appears, however, that the resistance is not as strong as one might anticipate. Far from resisting designation as "satellite cities," many mayors—whose opinion has to be heard prior to designation—are actively seeking it. In this they have the support of many of their citizens who stand to benefit economically. Shopkeepers may see benefits in the influx of people who will become customers, and farmers, especially those whose land is needed for the development, may welcome the rise in the price of land which is the immediate consequence of designation. If these incentives are added to the traditional tendency to acquiesce in the acts of the government, the acceptance of the scheme becomes understandable.

As for the existing urban areas, the Master Plan aims at functional decentralization of central business districts, maximal use of house lots, and extension of public services. Work programs thus aim, among other things, at the replacement of low-storied buildings by high-storied buildings in the central districts, at the relocation of some offices of the national government,* at the development of land for residential uses and the construction of houses for 338,000 families, at the extension of the sewage system and the water supply system, at the construction of expressways and roads, and at the improvement of the existing public transportation facilities.†

* In August 1962 the Commission considered the establishment of a private company to build a city in which government offices with a combined staff of 35,000 employees would be relocated. The city would also house universities and private research institutes with a student body and staff of 120,000. Altogether, the new city would have a population of 300,000. The company would have a capital of 2,000 million yen; the government and private interests would each invest half of this amount. It would be subject to checks by the Board of Audit. See *Asahi Evening News*, August 15, 1962, and *Japan Times*, August 16, 1962.

† No visitor to Tokyo can miss the evidence of activities in these directions. From time to time the existing subway lines are being extended to more and more outlying districts. The streets are being torn up as subway lines are being constructed below. If the congestion of vehicular traffic is one of the visitor's first impressions, he will soon find evidence of efforts to ease that congestion by construction of expressways radiating from the center of the city. A powerful impetus was given to these activities by the decision to hold the 1964 Olympic Games in Tokyo.

Finally, the Master Plan calls for the development of suburbs between the existing urban areas and the industrial development areas. The suburban area is to provide a greenbelt and agricultural land to secure a supply of vegetables and other produce to the urban population. The greenbelt is to make up for the noticeable shortage of parks and open spaces in the urban areas.[15]

The development of the national capital region should not be considered apart from other development programs. The development of new industrial areas in other parts of Japan would, in fact, be an effective means of lessening the influx of migrants into Tokyo. Existing planning is based on the Comprehensive Land Development Law of 1950 or on special laws.[16] Planning based on the Comprehensive Land Development Law had a number of false starts, and produced little more than interim reports that were not implemented because there was no agreement among the various ministries concerned.* But when the government adopted its income-doubling program in December 1960, nationwide planning achieved a new prominence. One aim of this planning was to eliminate the crass differences between more advanced and less advanced regions, i.e., to stem the excessive concentration of population and industry in the former and to promote the development of the latter. The tentative plan adopted by the Cabinet divides the country into eleven regions. Each of these regions would have some large-scale industrial centers, which would constitute the core of the development areas. Around these would be grouped zones of medium- and small-sized industries, all interconnected by a road system with the center, with each other, and with their rural hinterland.† The new industrial centers will probably have populations of 500,000 to one million.

---

* The first report, entitled "The Concept of a Nationwide Comprehensive Development," was published in 1954. The "Interim Report on the Nationwide Comprehensive Development Program," published in 1958, recommended a ten-year program. It divided the country into eight blocs: Hokkaido, Tohoku, Kanto, Chubu, Kinki, Chugoku, Shikoku, and Kyushu.

† As a step toward implementation of this plan, the Law for the Promotion of the Construction of New Industrial Cities was passed in May 1962 (Law No. 117 of 1962). The Local System Investigation Council wanted to put the designation of the sites for the new industrial centers into the hands of the prefectural governors. The law, as passed, provides for screening of applications of prefectural governors by the Ministry of International Trade and Industry, the Construction Ministry, and the Transportation Ministry and other agencies, and for designation by the Prime Minister.

We are already familiar with some of the plans based on special laws. The National Capital Region Redevelopment Program, just discussed, belongs in this category, as does the Hokkaido Development Program. A difference between the two lies in the fact that the former cuts across the boundaries of existing prefectural units whereas the latter is confined to the area of one of them. A third program is the Tohoku Development Program. The Tohoku region has long been trailing other regions in economic growth. Its agriculture suffers from unfavorable weather and crop conditions; an Office for the Development of the Tohoku Region was established as early as 1935, following a drastic crop failure. In 1957 the Tohoku Development Promotion Law, the Tohoku Development Company Law, and the Hokkaido and Tohoku Development Corporation Law were enacted. They aim at a greater utilization of the region's resources—among which are natural gas, coal, limestone, and water power —in order to create an industrial base. Similar laws were enacted in 1959 and 1960 for the promotion of the development of the Kyushu, Shikoku, Chugoku, and Hokuriku regions. Other programs deal with the development of the outlying islands and the reconstruction of the Amami Islands, which were returned by the United States in 1953.

One program that has already achieved significant results is the development of the water resources of the Kiso River basin for the benefit of the prefectures of Aichi and Gifu. The Aichi Irrigation Public Corporation was established by law in 1955, with capital furnished by the International Bank for Reconstruction and Development, the Japanese central government, the two prefectures involved, and the Kansai Electric Power Company. The corporation was supervised by the central government, and its principal officials were appointed by the Minister of Agriculture and Forestry. The work projects were primarily executed by the corporation itself, but some were delegated to the two prefectures and to the Kansai Electric Power Company. As a result, 2,500 hectares of new paddy fields were opened up for cultivation, the irrigation system was extended and improved, the supply of drinking water and industrial water was greatly increased, and the generation of electric power was boosted to a new high.

This sketchy outline of development plans has taken account only of central government plans that include some aspect of regionalism. There are, however, some regional development plans in which the initiative did not come from Tokyo. A number of economic and civic organizations concerned about the competitive economic position of parts of the Kinki area found themselves increasingly drawn toward development planning on a regional basis. In the government, at least the prefectural executives began to share their interest. There now exist an Osaka Economic Progress Deliberation Council, a Kansai Economic Friends Association, a Kinki Economic Cooperation Organization, a Council for the Osaka Conurbated Area, and a Hanshin Metropolitan Region Council.

The Kinki Development Promotion Council, established in 1960, consists of the governors of the prefectures of the region; the mayors of Osaka, Kyoto, and Kobe; the chairmen of the prefectural and municipal assemblies; representatives of government agencies and public corporations operating in the area; and representatives of industrial, financial, and commercial organizations and various civic leaders and experts. The development plans for the Hanshin Metropolitan Region, Japan's second largest industrial area and the economic center of western Japan, are of particular interest. Since 1958 a research team of Japanese experts established by the Hanshin Metropolitan Region Council and the Council for the Osaka Conurbated Area has been working together with a team of experts appointed by the United Nations Bureau of Technical Assistance Operations.* Their planning and action program of June 1962 contains specific recommendations concerning such general problems of economic development and transportation as the development of capital-intensive industries, the reorganization and redistribution of labor-intensive industries, and the wholesaling, retailing, banking, and head office functions; it also makes recommendations for housing and land acquisition, the utilization of land and water resources, and regional administration and financial policies. Space does not permit us to discuss these here, but it is clear from this and other programs that regionalism, far from being a dead issue, has received a new impetus from the emphasis on economic development which has replaced the former emphasis on finding more economical or efficient administrative arrangements.

---

* Mr. Oya Sōichi in his article in *Chūō kōron* suggests that the local planners borrowed the prestige of the U.N. to facilitate implementation of their plans in the face of expected opposition from the national bureaucracy, which might have looked askance at such independent planning activities.

Summary

The prefecture holds an intermediary position in the local government structure. The resulting ambivalence is particularly apparent in the influences to which the executive branch of the prefectural government is subjected. On the one hand there is the influence of the national government, which stems from a number of sources. Before the Occupation reforms, the governor was the agent of the Home Minister. After the reforms were instituted, many of the elected governors had served as governors under the old system or had been officials of the Home Ministry, and a complete change in their attitudes toward the central government could hardly be expected under these circumstances. Since 1956 the prefecture is charged again with liaison between the state and the municipalities; but because the prefecture serves primarily as a channel downward, its liaison function tends to draw it close to the central government. The governor is also subject to the influence of the national government because most of the work of the prefecture is done on the government's behalf and with funds from the national treasury.

On the other hand, as long as the governor is elected he will be subject to the influence of local political forces. The extent of this influence may vary according to place and time. In an urban prefecture such as Kyoto or Hyogo, the governor may feel quite strongly about his role as the representative of the interests of his politically sophisticated constituency. His power and political future may well depend on the skill with which he seems to perform this role. In other prefectures local influence may be slight. A traditionally inclined constituency, accustomed to ratifying decisions made "above," may make few demands on its executive, and the representational role of the governor may thus be of lesser importance in the minds of the inhabitants and of the officeholder. As for the time dimension, it may be anticipated that the farther political development proceeds, the more closely the less developed areas will resemble the presently more developed areas in political sophistication. The actual role played by each governor is a function of the relative strength of the pressure from the central government on the one hand and the pressure from the constituency on the other. The attempts of conservative governments to abolish the election of governors have to be seen in this light.

The governor's role as representative of prefectural interests is, of course, also influenced by other factors. His relation to the officers of the prefectural government is one of these. Before the war, the governor and the prefectural officials were national officials, but now, at least in principle, they are officials of the prefecture. The deviations from this principle are significant in this context: the stronger the ties of officials of the prefectural government with the central government, the more difficult it is for the governor to perform his representational role. We shall return to this point in a subsequent chapter. The relations of the governor to the prefectural assembly are significant inasmuch as the assembly may articulate various prefectural interests. As we shall show in the concluding chapters of this study, individual assemblymen may be elected because they represent certain interests or they may be elected for other reasons. The degree to which the assembly as a whole performs its function of representing various interests differs in various prefectures, depending on the character of the constituency. An assembly reinforces the representational role of the governor to the extent to which it itself represents various prefectural interests. Where it fails to do so, the governor may see himself more in the role of an executor of the policies of the central government.

As for the attempts to establish a regional system, we noted that these became at first enmeshed in the controversial issue of centralization and decentralization. On the surface, these attempts were a quest for units of local government that are more rational, more viable, and more efficient than the present prefectures. But they were soon recognized as a part of the struggle about the future direction of the country in which those who espoused a "reverse course" were opposed by those who feared a revival of the authoritarianism of the past. They were not spearheaded by some private or semiprivate civic organization concerned with the improvement of administration and thus above suspicion of ulterior motives; nor were they initiated by prefectural governments that could not perform certain functions in isolation from other prefectures in their region. The movement came from the central government. Because the government was conservative and because the object of the reform was the prefecture, which in the past had been the pivot of centralization, an entire chain of associations came into play. The question was raised immediately whether the proposals for regionalism, emanating as they did from this source, were not in fact attempts to return by an alternate route to the system of appointment of governors. This question overshadowed all discussion of the relative merits of the prefectural and the regional system.* A stalemate was reached and the issue of regionalism lay dormant for some years. But in the meantime the atmosphere had changed to some extent. Regionalism became tied to development plans, and in this form it has not encountered the same type of opposition. The issue of central control is present, but it is not forced into the open. Ad hoc solutions to practical problems stand in the foreground, and regional development plans are beginning to emanate from sources other than the central government.

There are, of course, pitfalls in this direction as well. Regional development planning is a complex jigsaw puzzle with little of the neatness of the earlier proposals for regionalism. Older and newer programs overlap or follow different directions and aims.† A subtle shift in national-local relations is involved in the frequent establishment, by national law, of new public development corporations with regional jurisdiction but subject to national controls. The effect of the activities of these corporations on prefectural functions is yet to be explored.‡

One may well argue, in the abstract, the relative merits of the more systematic approach of yesterday and the more pragmatic approach of today. Certainly, the proliferation of ad hoc authorities elsewhere has sometimes led to exasperation and to a longing for a simpler, more lucid, less overlapping structure. There may well be diminishing returns in the continuation of pragmatic solutions. But in Japan the tendency toward pragmatic solutions is still a novelty. In the past, rigid structural thinking was strong, particularly in the central bureaucracy. In the postwar period, the powerful position of that bureaucracy became a contro-

---

* These considerations need stressing because the non-Japanese specialist in public administration, in discussing a problem with which he is somewhat familiar at home—such as the rationalization of local government units—is prone to overlook crucial differences in context.

† In this regard it should be noted that early planning on the basis of the Comprehensive Development Law emphasized the development of food and water resources and of measures for the prevention of disasters. Scant attention was given to industrial development. Most of the areas under this program were designated by the Prime Minister, after consultation with the Council for Comprehensive Land Development, in 1951.

‡ Examples not mentioned heretofore are the Hanshin Superhighway Construction Corporation (1962) and the Water Resources Development Corporation (1961). This development has a counterpart in the establishment of local public corporations and joint-stock companies for development purposes by prefectures and major cities. We shall return to this point in later chapters.

versial political issue, and plans emanating from it were suspect. The more clearly these plans involved changes in the governmental structure, which seemed like a return to the past, the harder they were fought. The new emphasis is more on functions than on structure, more on problem-solving than on politics. This shift may be a reflection of the shift from Prime Minister Kishi's "reverse course" to Prime Minister Ikeda's "low posture." But it may well be more than that. Both shifts may be a reflection of a major sociological change. The tremendous growth of Japan's economy in recent years, the country's continued prosperity, and the increasing extent to which consumer demands are being satisfied may usher in a decline in the influence of ideology on the various aspects of the governmental process. The changes in the approach to regionalism may well illustrate a general trend away from dogmatism toward pragmatism.* In a country torn asunder by ideological conflicts and haunted by dreams (or nightmares) of the past, such a new start must be welcomed, even if the price for it must be a certain loss in the neatness of the administrative structure.

* This would also involve a subtle change in the self-image of the bureaucracy and, ultimately, in how the bureaucracy is viewed by others.

CHAPTER 9

Municipalities and Special Local Public Bodies

The municipalities of Japan are cities (*shi*), towns (*machi* or *chō*), or villages (*mura* or *son*). Before the postwar reforms towns and villages were regulated by the same code. There remains no legal difference between them today, although towns are normally somewhat larger and more urban in character than villages. The designation of city, on the other hand, is given to municipalities that fulfill certain legal requirements in terms of their degree of urbanization. A city exercises certain social welfare functions that are performed for towns and villages by the prefecture.

We noted that the area of each prefecture is customarily divided into its urban part (*shibu*) and its rural part (*gumbu*). The former consists of the areas of the cities within the prefecture, the latter of the areas of the towns and villages which together make up the various counties (*gun*) of the prefecture. In other words, every part of the prefectural area belongs either to a city or to a town or village. There are no "unincorporated" areas. Increasing urbanization thus cannot be reflected in the incorporation of a new area, but only in the change of status from town or village to city.

But we should not assume too quickly that such a change in status always reflects increasing urbanization. That assumption, after all, would be based on a whole series of notions: that industrialization leads people engaged in secondary or tertiary occupations to concentrate increasingly in places with industrial establishments; that these places thus become, in fact, urban settlements; that in due time this social development is recognized by giving the legal status of cities to these urban settlements; and that the change brings the legal status into conformity with socio-economic reality.*

But are these notions applicable in Japan? Was the great increase in the number of cities in recent years a natural reflection of a socio-economic development? Did the government, in creating new cities, simply adjust the legal or administrative situation to existing reality, or did it instead create the new cities for administrative purposes or for other reasons having nothing to do with socio-economic considerations? The latter course would be another example of the role that government customarily played in the past, when it freely determined "what areas should exist, what authorities should be established for them, and what functions they should exercise."[1] If the new cities were created artificially, and if they therefore do not coincide with existing socio-economic units, what effect will this have on local autonomy? For example, can one expect that the inhabitants of such an artificial unit will share the civic spirit on which "civic autonomy" is based?

Similar questions can be asked about the amalgamations of towns and villages that did not result in the creation of new cities. To what extent were these mergers directed from above? To what extent did they create a new gap between legal and socio-economic units? These are some of the questions that we must consider in this chapter.

Cities

The trend to urbanization is unmistakable in Japan. The casual foreign visitor never fails to be impressed by the tall and modern office buildings, the large department stores, the myriads of neon lights, the traffic-congested thoroughfares, the subways, and the other paraphernalia of urbanization and westernization in such cities as Tokyo or Osaka. With regard to population mobility, a survey shows that only 20 per cent of the inhabitants of the 23 wards of Tokyo, 43 per cent of the inhabitants of Osaka, 47 per cent of those of Nagoya, and 55 per cent of those of Kyoto were born within these cities.[2] We have noted earlier the rapid increase in the population of Tokyo Metropolis, and,

---

* If we accepted these notions we would also be tempted to see the amalgamation of surrounding towns and villages with an existing city as a correction of the lag between socio-economic reality and the legal or administrative situation. We would then assume that the amalgamated towns and villages, having lost their rural character because of the proximity of the city, had become in fact a part of an urban socio-economic unit before their amalgamation made them also a part of the same unit of local government.

in particular, the rapid "social increase"—the influx of population from the outside. Between 1950 and 1955 the population of five out of Japan's six largest cities grew by 20 per cent or more, while the national population increase amounted to only 7.3 per cent. The difference is accounted for by an actual decline in the population in some rural prefectures (notably Nagano, Yamanashi, Yamagata, Shiga, Tokushima, Ehime, and Tochigi) and by a population increase well below the national average in others (such as Aomori and Kagoshima). In 1955 Japan had five cities with more than one million inhabitants; by 1957 a sixth city, Kobe, was added to their number.[3]

In 1920 about 18 per cent of the total Japanese population lived in local entities designated as cities (*shibu*). In 1940 the percentage had increased to 41.1 per cent. Under the impact of wartime dislocations, as thousands of families left the cities for rural areas in quest of food and safety from bombings, this figure fell to 28.7 per cent in 1945. Then a steady upward climb started. By 1950 the figure had risen to 37.5 per cent. In 1955 those living in cities outnumbered those living in towns and villages. The population figures for this year were 50,298,342 and 38,977,187, and the percentages of the total population were 66.3 and 43.7 respectively.[4]

The increase in the number of cities during the same period was spectacular as shown by the accompanying graph. From 39 in 1889 the number of cities rose to 81 in 1920, to 166 in 1940, and to 248 in 1950. During the following decade the rise became steeper: from 248 in 1950 to 383 in 1954, to 491 in 1955, to 496 in 1956, to 505 in 1958, and to 556 in 1960.[5] Thus the number of cities, which had doubled in the 20 years between 1920 and 1940, doubled again in the 6 years between 1950 and

TABLE 2

Number of Cities in 1920, 1940, and 1960

Population	1920	1940	1960
1,000,000 or over	2	4	6
500,000–999,999	2	2	3
100,000–499,999	12	39	104
50,000–99,999	24	53	156
Under 50,000	41	68	287
Total	81	166	556

source: Pamphlet by the Autonomy Ministry entitled *Local Government in Japan*, prepared for the 1961 EROPA Seminar, Tokyo, p. 5.

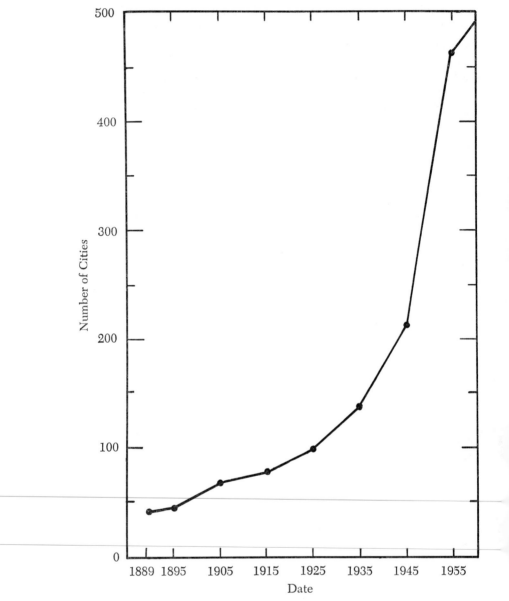

Increase in Number of Cities in Japan, 1889–1955
Source: *Municipal Yearbook 1956*, frontispiece.

1956. Table 2 shows the breakdown of the cities existing in 1920, 1940, and 1960 into categories according to population. The number of cities with a population under 50,000 increased more sharply between 1940 and 1960 than in the preceding two decades.

Of course, as the number of cities increased, these cities occupied an increasing percentage of the total area of Japan. Again we note that this increase was gradual at first: from 0.4 per cent in 1921 to 0.8 per cent in 1930, to 2.3 per cent in 1940, to 4.3 per cent in 1947, and to 5.4 per cent in 1950.* But between 1950 and 1960 the total city area jumped to 18.0 per cent. This increase in the total city area stands in contrast to the changes in population density in the cities. In 1921 it was 7,326 per square kilometer, in 1930 it had dropped to 5,220, in 1940 to 3,109, in 1947 to 1,627, and in 1950 to 1,574. In 1955 it was 747. Thus while the total city area nearly tripled between 1950 and 1955, the population density in cities decreased by nearly 50 per cent.[6]

These figures show that the creation of new cities between 1950 and 1955 was not based on growing population concentrations. An investigation of the occupational breakdown of the population of the cities demonstrates that it was not the result of increasing industrialization either. Of course, even highly industrialized cities may contain within their city limits a rural area inhabited by people engaged in agriculture or other non-commercial and non-industrial pursuits. The percentage of inhabitants so engaged is typically small: 1.5 per cent in Osaka, 5 in Nagoya, 5.8 in Kyoto, 7.3 in Kobe, and 12.1 in Yokohama.[7] But when the rural population is more substantial, the assumption that city status is a reflection of industrialization becomes more questionable.

As noted earlier, Japanese statistics usually divide occupations into three groups: primary, secondary, and tertiary. Primary occupations are agriculture, forestry, and fishing; secondary occupations are mining and industry; and tertiary occupations are business, transportation, communication, services, and the professions. In every Japanese city with a population of more than 300,000, the percentage of inhabitants engaged in primary occupations is less than 20 per cent. But when we look at the cities with populations of less than 50,000, we find a strikingly different picture: in about one-fourth of them the percentage of those

---

* In 1947 the Local Autonomy Law established new qualifications for local entities which were granted city status. These are explained below.

TABLE 3

Occupational Changes in City Populations

Area	Total Population	Primary Occupations		Secondary Occupations		Tertiary Occupations	
		Number	Per cent	Number	Per cent	Number	Per cent
City areas (*shibu*) as of Oct. 1, 1950	11,697,084	1,616,414	13.8	4,121,554	35.2	5,959,080	51.0
Areas amalgamated with *shibu*, Oct. 1, 1950, to Oct. 1, 1955	1,735,401	1,125,030	64.8	294,150	17.0	316,221	18.2
Cities newly created, Oct. 1, 1950, to Oct. 1, 1955	4,093,056	2,185,453	53.4	854,134	20.9	1,053,469	25.7
City areas (*shibu*) as of Oct. 1, 1955	17,525,505	4,926,897	28.1	5,269,838	30.1	7,328,770	41.8

SOURCE: *Municipal Yearbook*, 1956, p. 36.

in rural occupations exceeds 60 per cent, and in some cases is as high as 80 per cent.

Taking the city populations as a whole, we find an interesting development in the years between 1950 and 1955. In 1950 some 13.8 per cent of the total city population was engaged in primary occupations; by 1955 this percentage had risen to 28.1. Table 3 gives the explanation for this phenomenon. It shows that in the areas merged with existing cities, 64.8 per cent of the population followed rural pursuits. In the cities newly created as a result of amalgamations, the percentage was 53.4.

It is the mass amalgamations that explain the increase in the total city area and the decrease in the population density of the cities, which we noted above. Large areas lacking the dense concentration of a population engaged in urban pursuits, which we usually associate with cities, have nevertheless been designated cities. As a result there are tremendous differences among the cities of Japan. Some of them are huge urban centers with a high population density and a high degree of industrialization, as reflected in the occupations of the inhabitants. Others are, by the same criteria, cities in name only.

It should be noted that the Local Autonomy Law did not favor the development of these quasi-cities. According to Article 8, as originally enacted in 1947, a local entity had to have the following qualifications to become a city: (1) a population of at least 30,000; (2) a central urban area comprising at least 60 per cent of the total number of houses; (3) a population of which at least 60 per cent was engaged in commerce, industry, or other urban pursuits, or belonged to the households of persons so engaged; (4) urban establishments and other conditions necessary for a city as provided in prefectural by-laws.

Applications of towns or villages desiring to become cities were to be submitted to the prefectural governor, who was to determine, upon the basis of a resolution of the prefectural assembly and after consultation with the Prime Minister, whether these requirements were fulfilled. The actual change in status was effected by publication of an official notification by the Prime Minister.* Thus the initiative for a change to

---

* Within the Prime Minister's Office there was always an agency that handled the affairs of local governments. For the changes in the name and character of that agency, see the section on "Successors to the Home Ministry" in Chapter 13. In 1960 it became a separate ministry called the Autonomy Ministry. At the time many of the functions formerly exercised, at least in a formal sense, by the Prime Minister were transferred to the Autonomy Minister.

city status rested in the hands of the local entities, and a degree of urbanization was the main criterion for the designation.

The amendment of Article 8 that became effective on May 1, 1954, increased the minimum population for cities from 30,000 to 50,000, but left the system otherwise unchanged. Between April 1, 1953, and April 1, 1954, 97 additional cities were created.[8] It would be possible to assume that these were entities that met the lower population requirement and thus tried to get in "under the wire." In this case, the spurt would have been followed by a slackening in the increase of the number of cities. But, as the graph on page 172 so clearly demonstrates, the number of cities continued to rise steeply during the next two years. The fact of the matter is that not one of the 97 cities created in 1953–54 had been a town or village that had grown in population and urbanization until it met the requirements for a city; all of them were the result of amalgamations. These amalgamations did not occur spontaneously, but were the result of a planned drive conducted by the central government. We shall have more to say about this drive later, but we may note here that, in pursuit of its aim, the government made rather light of the legal criterion of urbanization. According to an editorial in the newspaper *Mainichi* (March 28, 1954), one of the new cities created between 1953 and 1954 consisted mainly of paddy fields and farms. This may have been an extreme case, but more often than not the new cities are artificial creations without any basis in social and economic reality.

The existence of this type of city side by side with dynamically expanding, real urban centers has a number of consequences for local self-government. We shall discuss here only two of them, one in the area of "civic autonomy" and the other in the area of "corporate autonomy."

It is part of the idea of local autonomy that the inhabitants of a local entity are granted the right to manage its affairs because they supposedly feel that the local community is "theirs" in some sense. Therefore the inhabitants must, first of all, recognize the community as a unit that is meaningful to their lives. This recognition may spring from the closeness of a face-to-face group, in which case the feeling that the inhabitants belong together and that the local community is "theirs" is likely to be endowed with emotional intensity. It may also spring from a perceived identity of certain needs shared by the inhabitants, and from common efforts to meet them. While the emotional intensity may not be quite as high in the latter case, civic spirit is nevertheless possible in such an associational setting so long as the local unit provides a focus for it. However, when a number of urban, semi-urban, and rural settlements are lumped together under outside pressure, none of these bases for a civic spirit exists. The government was able to combine the natural villages of the Tokugawa era and to create the new administrative village of the Meiji era; it can now combine these units with other villages and towns and make cities out of them. But it cannot create a civic spirit in these cities at the same time.

The artificial creation en masse of new cities also has important consequences for "corporate autonomy," or the freedom and capability of local entities to administer their own affairs. The centers of business and industry that really constitute urban Japan have little more than name in common with the new agglomerations of rural and semi-urban settlements. Certainly they are different in their administrative and financial capabilities. But since they all have the same legal status they are supposedly all to be treated alike, and the question arises: which type of city provides the standard? Are all cities being treated as equally competent or equally incompetent? Without going into this question in detail, two things are clear: if a medium standard is adopted, the new cities are not a spur to corporate autonomy but a drag on it. Their existence adds plausibility to the argument that cities need to be controlled or supervised because of their financial weakness, their lack of general administrative capability, and the poor educational background of their personnel. If no medium standard is adopted, all cities must be treated as being either as competent as the largest and most urbanized ones or as incompetent as the smallest and most rural ones. In either case, violence will be done to existing realities.

The way to avoid this dilemma would seem to lie in recognizing in the law the differences that exist in actuality. This would mean the creation of classes of cities. Thus it has been suggested that the five big cities should be one class, cities with more than 150,000 inhabitants the second, and the rest the third.[9] A reluctant step in this direction was finally taken in 1956 when Special Regulations Concerning Big Cities were inserted into the Local Autonomy Law. This step constituted a compromise with the aims of the Big City Movement, which we mentioned in earlier chapters. This was originally a movement of six big cities, but since Tokyo was given a special status in 1943—not in accor-

TABLE 4

Population of the Five Big Cities

City	1953	1955	1960
Osaka	1,956,176	2,547,316	3,011,553
Nagoya	1,030,635	1,336,780	1,591,914
Yokohama	951,189	1,143,687	1,375,100
Kyoto	1,105,734	1,204,084	1,284,746
Kobe	813,642	979,305	1,113,901

SOURCE: *Municipal Yearbook, 1961,* pp. 6ff.

dance with the aims of the movement, it should be added—the number of cities aspiring to special status decreased to five. These are the cities of Osaka, Kyoto, Nagoya, Yokohama, and Kobe.* Table 4 shows their populations as of 1953, 1955, and 1960 and their rapid growth during this period. Between Kobe and Fukuoka—the next largest city, with a population of 647,115—there was a gap of more than 400,000 inhabitants. The five big cities thus formed a distinct group among Japanese cities in terms of population.[10]

As was noted in Chapter 3, special provisions applied in Tokyo, Osaka, and Kyoto from 1888 to 1898. The aim of this differentiation was not to give to these cities a greater degree of self-government but rather to put them under stricter control. They were not permitted to elect their chief executives, for example, and the prefectural governor acted also as mayor. After 1898 the big cities were treated on an equal footing with all others.

Subsequent efforts for the creation of a special city system, first only for Tokyo, but since 1907 for Osaka as well, failed mainly because of the opposition in the House of Peers. As the big cities increased in population and wealth during and after World War I, the movement for their liberation from prefectural control—a sort of county-borough movement—gathered momentum. The wealthy cities of Japan finally began to assume the role that their European counterparts had played in the coming of local autonomy some centuries earlier. After 1917 several member bills applying the special city system not only to Tokyo and Osaka but also to Kyoto, Yokohama, Nagoya, and Kobe were pre-

* Since 1960 a new city with a population of more than a million inhabitants has been created in northern Kyushu by the amalgamation of existing cities, as discussed below.

sented to the Diet. All were frustrated by the House of Peers. Finally, in 1922 a Law for Special Treatment of Administrative Control of the Big Cities was enacted, and the supervisory powers of the Home Minister and of the governors were substantially reduced.[11]

But the tide turned again after the Manchurian Incident, which foreshadowed the end of the liberal tendencies that had existed during the twenties. A bill for establishing a Tokyo Metropolitan System, with appointment of the head of the Metropolis to be made by the central government, was proposed by the government in 1937. The six big cities combined in opposition and the bill was not passed. But the government had its way in 1943, when, as part of the general tightening of controls "to win the war," Tokyo City was absorbed into Tokyo Prefecture and the newly established Tokyo Metropolis was put under the control of a nationally appointed governor.[12]

After the war, success seemed to be within grasp of the big cities. The Local Autonomy Law, in its Articles 264 to 280, provided that cities having a population of 500,000 or more were to be designated as special cities. When so designated, they were to be outside the jurisdiction of the prefecture and were to exercise prefectural as well as city functions. The aim of the big cities now was to make these provisions of the Local Autonomy Law operative by another law that would designate them as special cities. Their case was impressive.[13] In regard to functions and controls, they could point out that they were being treated as incompetent even though their administrative machinery and personnel were equal or superior to those of the supervising prefectures in size and quality, and that there was a good deal of needless overlapping between the work of the cities and the prefectures. In regard to finances, the cities felt aggrieved because they had to carry not only the tax loads for their own complex administrations but also a load of prefectural taxes, which then were spent largely on other parts of the prefecture.

The last argument explains in part the resistance of the prefectures concerned: they stood to lose important financial resources by the designation of special cities.* There were of course also the normal difficulties of adjustment of areas. The city, in fact, is not a self-contained unit.

---

* Connoisseurs of Japanese desserts will appreciate the comment of the governor of Aichi that without the big cities the prefectures would become *"ankō hikimarete kawa bakari no manjū"* (a bun with its bean-jam stuffing removed so that only the outer crust remains).

The reservoir of employees working in the city, for instance, extends even beyond the prefectural limits. So does the necessary transportation system. If cities were to be made special cities, cooperation between them and the surrounding prefecture would be essential. But fears were voiced that such cooperation might not be forthcoming once the system was in force: the prefectures would not accept a cooperative relationship because they had hitherto enjoyed a superior position. The cities, on the other hand, would be inclined to demonstrate their newly won independence. In addition, the central bureaucracy was not overly eager to activate the provisions for special cities. Their predilection for uniformity, their conservative preference for the status quo, and, especially, their concern for strengthening rather than weakening the prefectures outweighed their consideration for the demands of social change.

When the House of Representatives passed the Local Autonomy Law, it adopted a resolution calling on the government to submit a bill designating the five big cities as special cities. But no such bill was forthcoming. Instead, a further roadblock was thrown into the path of the Big City Movement. We have noted that according to Article 95 of the Constitution, a law "applicable only to one local public entity" is to be submitted for approval of the voters of the "local public entity concerned." A law designating a city as a special city obviously fell into that category. But was the "local public entity concerned" in this case the city, or was it the prefecture out of which the special city was to be carved as an independent entity? This question was answered by the amendment of the Local Autonomy Law in December 1947 which provided that designating laws were to be submitted to the electors of the prefectures concerned. This was a major defeat for the movement because in most cases the cities had little hope of outvoting the rest of the prefecture. The cities thus worked for the deletion of the amendment. At the same time the opponents of the movement tried to eliminate the provisions for special cities from the Local Autonomy Law altogether. Member bills reflecting these contradictory aims were introduced in the Diet, but all failed to pass.

It is possible that time would have worked in favor of the Big City Movement even if the referendum was to be taken in the prefecture as a whole. In time, the growth of the urban population could have reversed the relative voting strength of the urban and rural components of the prefectures. The same result might have come about through the progressive merger of neighboring towns and villages with the big cities; but the control of the mergers was exercised by the prefectural governors, and those mergers that took effect worked greatly to the disadvantage of the prospective special cities. In the meantime various suggestions for a compromise solution were made. The Kambe Commission advocated in 1950 the transfer of some prefectural functions to the big cities without making them altogether independent of the prefectures. The first Local System Investigation Council, while holding in abeyance a decision on the general issue, recommended that the big cities be given a special status in regard to certain functions.*

The amendment of the Local Autonomy Law in 1956 enacted a compromise of this type. The legal situation created by the amendment is as follows: Chapter 1 of Volume 3 of the Local Autonomy Law, dealing with special cities, was deleted. Instead, Special Regulations Concerning Big Cities were inserted into Volume 2 of the Local Autonomy Law. The change makes it clear that the big cities are not to be "special local public bodies," as the special cities would have been, but "ordinary local public bodies" not different from other cities except where special regulations apply. These special regulations are to be found in two Articles, one dealing with functions, the other with the establishment of wards. According to Article 252–19, cities of a population of more than 500,000 inhabitants may be designated by Cabinet order as empowered to exercise certain functions of the prefectures or their organs.[14] The list of these functions contains sixteen items, which include welfare functions (such as care for children, the physically disabled, and the indigent); health functions (such as prevention of infectious diseases and food sanitation); the functions of city planning and land readjustment; the regulation of hotels, places of entertainment, bathhouses, and outdoor advertising; and the administration of building standards. In regard to these matters, the cities are exempted from the control of the prefecture and subjected instead to the control of the appropriate central government ministry. The list itself, however, is

---

* Thus the Council recommended that the big cities should retain their autonomous police, while otherwise police administration should be concentrated in the prefectures. The government's bill for revision of the Police Law did not contain this exception. A compromise was finally reached according to which the police of the big cities continued until July 1955.

not automatically operative. The Cabinet order designating the big cities may qualify the list by reserving certain matters within the enumerated functions to the prefecture. Cabinet Order 254 of 1956 designated Osaka, Nagoya, Kyoto, Yokohama, and Kobe—the five big cities—in accordance with these provisions. Article 252–20 provides for the establishment of wards, ward chiefs, and ward officers by city bylaw. The ward chiefs are to be appointed city officials and not elected officeholders, as was provided for in the now abrogated Article 271 concerning ward chiefs of the special cities.

The stalemate that lasted from 1947 to 1956 was broken by the enactment of these provisions. Considering that during this period the big cities had been given no special treatment at all, any step may have appeared as a step forward. But considering the differences between the special regulations enacted in 1956 and the provisions for special cities, which were abrogated, it is questionable whether this development can be termed an unqualified victory for the Big City Movement.

Let us now return briefly to the consideration of the rapid increase in the number of cities. We have shown that this increase was caused primarily by the government's drive for amalgamations of towns and villages, which led to the creation of the so-called "new cities." The motivations behind that drive were primarily administrative. The amalgamations, which boosted the number of cities, reduced the number of towns and villages and the total number of local entities. Thus the number of cities increased from 81 in 1920 to 166 in 1940 and to 556 in 1960; the number of towns and villages fell during the same period from 12,107 to 10,966 and finally to 2,955. As a result, the total number of local entities changed from 12,188 in 1920 to 11,232 in 1940 and to 3,511 in 1960.[15] This was considered desirable for reasons of administrative convenience, efficiency, and economy. More recently other plans for the creation of new cities have come to the fore and found expression in legislation. The motivation behind these has been economic rather than administrative, raising a parallel to the plans for regional solutions discussed in the previous chapter.

The impetus came again from the economic development plans related to the Ikeda Cabinet's National Income Doubling Program of 1960. These plans envision a progressively higher rate of urbanization. The migration away from the farms will continue at increased speed as a more appropriate ratio of manpower to available land will be established by reducing the present number of agricultural producers to about one-third. Unless urbanization, industrialization, and urban migration are guided by some plan, the metropolitan centers will soon be unable to absorb the influx. The development of the National Capital Region constitutes a plan of this type. Equally important are other plans, briefly mentioned in Chapter 8, to decentralize industrial locations and thus siphon off some of the influx into other areas. These involve the development of industrial cities in various regions. As a step in this direction the Diet passed in May 1962 the Law for the Promotion of the Establishment of New Industrial Cities.[16] The procedure for designation of the areas of new industrial cities raised some problems. The Autonomy Ministry wanted to put the initiative into the hands of the prefectural governors, but some other ministries preferred that the designation be initiated on the national level. A compromise aimed at satisfying both demands was worked out: the governors may apply for the designation, in which case the application is submitted to all ministries and agencies concerned; but some of the ministers—the Chief of the Economic Planning Board, the Ministers of Agriculture and Forestry, of Commerce and Industry, of Transportation, of Labor, and of Construction, as well as the Autonomy Minister—may also request a designation, in which case the agreement of the governor concerned has to be obtained. In either case the designation is made by the Prime Minister after consultation with the newly established Local Industrial Development Council. The law deals with the policy, basic plans, and financial resources for the establishment of new industrial cities. In the designated area a Council for the Establishment of the New Industrial City under the chairmanship of the governor is created. It includes the chiefs and officials of national branch agencies in the area, the mayors of affected cities, towns, and villages, the managers of port and harbor establishments, and the ubiquitous "men of learning and experience" appointed by the governor. A prefectural bylaw determines details of the Council's organization and operation. Ultimately, the affected municipalities are, of course, to be merged into the new industrial city. Since this will frequently mean that existing cities will be amalgamated with each other, a second law was passed establishing special regulations for such amalgamations.[17] Areas likely to be designated include the southern part of Okayama Prefecture around the city of Kurashiki, where, according to some plans, 7 cities and 26 towns and villages will make up a new industrial city, which, at least in terms of area, will be among the largest in Japan. In northern Kyushu the industrial complex encompassing the cities of Moji, Kokura, Yawata, Tobata, and Wakamatsu has already become the city of Kitakyushu, a center of Japan's steel industry and the seventh largest city in Japan with a population of more than one million inhabitants. Other industrial core cities are likely to be established in Oita, Aichi, Shizuoka, Miyagi, and Toyama. Because these industrial cities will absorb existing local entities, the total number of local entities will further decrease, but this time the decrease will also involve a reduction in the number of cities.

Although the motive behind these plans is different from that underlying the creation of new cities in earlier years, the initiative came in both cases from the central government. It is thus interesting and important to note that some planning is also going on on lower levels. It has become clear that economic development planning is not possible within the confines of the existing political subdivisions. Cooperation on various levels and between various levels has become necessary. The functional type of regionalism, aiming at cooperation beyond the prefectural level, is only one example of this fact. The problems of providing services for an "exploding metropolis" show that cooperation among the municipalities of an "intra-prefectural region" is also necessary.* The arrangements for such cooperation in the Local Autonomy Law—such as partial affairs associations—are too cumbersome and ineffective. Amalgamation, on the other hand, may be too drastic a step and may require a degree of coercion from above that is undesirable from the viewpoint of local autonomy.

Two middle-of-the-road programs are being worked out in Hyogo Prefecture for the Hanshin and Harima Regions.† In each of these an inter-municipal conference of regional administration, consisting of the

---

* In some cases—such as the case of the National Capital Region—intraprefectural arrangements are, of course, insufficient.

† The Harima Region constitutes the southwestern part of Hyogo Prefecture, along the coast of the Inland Sea. It was designated as an industrial zone by the national government in 1957. Its center is the city of Himeji (328,689 inhabitants in 1960 as compared to 300,204 in 1955). It comprises 6 other cities, 5 towns, and 1 village. The Hanshin Region lies between Osaka and Kobe. Its largest city is Amagasaki (405,955 inhabitants in 1960 as compared to 335,475 in 1955). It comprises 5 other cities and 1 town. The term Hanshin Region is often used in a wider sense to include Osaka, Kobe, and their surroundings.

mayors and the assembly chairmen of the cities, towns, and villages in the area and of some co-opted experts was established in 1961. This was a voluntary organization, financed by the participating local units. Its primary aim was to plan the joint establishment and utilization of water supply and drainage facilities, of hospitals, schools, parks, residential dwellings, of a coordinated road system, and of ports and airports. For the Hanshin Region a more ambitious program, aiming at the establishment of a "federated city," is being considered. The seven local entities in the area (six cities and one town) would cooperate to provide certain area-wide services while retaining separate control over strictly local services. The federated city would be authorized not only to plan but also to execute public works related to the rationalization of industrial location, housing, and school facilities; to consolidate the road network and arrange for traffic control on the roads; to consolidate water supply, sewage, and waste disposal facilities; to provide recreation centers and green belts; and to arrange for prevention of air pollution and disasters. It would have an assembly that would combine legislative and executive functions through a commission system. The mayor would be directly elected, but an appointed assistant mayor would actually perform the functions of a city manager. The expenditures would be financed by federated city taxes (comprising certain taxes now levied by the prefecture or the municipalities), by grants from the central government under the Local Distribution Tax Law, by contributions of member entities in proportion to the benefits they derive, by local bonds, and by subsidies.

The establishment of the federated city as a local entity would require national legislation, either in the form of a special law in accordance with Article 95 of the Constitution or in the form of a general law (probably an amendment of Volume 2 of the Local Autonomy Law), and such a general law would presumably allow other municipalities to federate according to the same model. Whether the program will be realized in either form is not certain, but it deserves attention for two reasons. First, it constitutes an effort to overcome the gap between the existing adminstrative divisions and the functional requisites of the present time, and it was initiated on the prefectural, rather than the national level. Second, it shows a degree of imagination and a preference for a function-oriented, pragmatic, and eclectic solution that contrasts favorably with the relatively inflexible, dogmatic, structure-oriented character of many solutions initiated at the national level.*

Towns and Villages and Their Amalgamation

In Chapter 3 we referred to the mass amalgamation during the Meiji period, which reduced the number of towns and villages to 15,820 in 1889, the year of the enforcement of the Town and Village Code. After that year the number decreased gradually while the number of cities rose. At first, this was a natural reflection of the increasing urbanization of the country. But in 1940–41 the process was speeded up by the government, which launched a minor amalgamation drive on the occasion of the 2600th anniversary of the mythical foundation of the Empire. In 1940, 58 towns and villages were absorbed into 21 existing cities, 52 towns and villages were merged to create 24 new cities, and 96 towns and villages were rearranged into 37 larger units without changing

---

* The program could forestall the amalgamation of the seven local units of the area into two large cities, which is also under discussion. Such a merger is bound to run into difficulties. The character of the various units differs widely: Amagasaki is industrial, Ashiya is residential, and Takarazuka is best known as the home of the Takarazuka Girls' Opera and as a tourist attraction. The program described above is often associated with the name of the chief of the Local Affairs Section of the Hyogo prefectural government, Mr. Honjo Yukito. It weaves together elements of the Metropolitan Toronto Plan and the Winnipeg Plan and of the commission system and the city manager system of city government. For example, 10 of the 17 members of the assembly would be directly elected, each one from an election district comprising approximately 10 per cent of the population of the federated city (Winnipeg Plan). The other 7 members—the "special members"—would be the mayors of the member units (Toronto Plan). The votes of the latter members would be weighted in accordance with the population of their unit. (Thus the mayor of Amagasaki would have 4 votes, 1 for each 100,000 inhabitants. The mayors together would control a total of 11 votes.) Under the mayor and assistant mayor (city manager) of the federated city there would be a Finance Bureau, a City Planning Bureau, a Construction Bureau, an Education Bureau, and a Waterworks Bureau. Opposition to the program comes from city assemblymen. The solution of the waste disposal problem of the region may well be the establishment of a plant within the limits of the city of Amagasaki. City assemblymen have already voiced opposition to the "conversion of the city into a dump for the benefit of others."

The description of the plan is based primarily on conversations with former Governor Sakamoto, Mr. Honjo, and other officials of Hyogo Prefecture and on material supplied by them. The article by Oya Sōichi in the August 1962 issue of *Chūō Kōron* also refers to it. The plan for the Hanshin Federated Regional City should not be confused with the broader Planning and Action Program for the Development of the Hanshin Metropolitan Region of the joint Japan–United Nations Team, which was mentioned in Chapter 8.

their denomination. In 1941, 111 additional towns and villages were re-arranged in the same way to form 43 units. The aim of the drive was twofold: on the one hand, it was to lead to increased administrative efficiency and to savings in terms of personnel and finances; on the other hand, it was to promote the mobilization of the industrial resources of the country by expanding the industrial centers.

As of October 1, 1950, there were 10,166 towns and villages in Japan. More than 60 per cent of the towns and villages had a population of less than 5,000 inhabitants; 85 per cent had a population of less than 8,000.[18] As functions increased after the war, much concern was felt on the question of whether small units of this type could adequately perform their tasks with their scant resources of money and personnel. Moreover, in a country as poor as postwar Japan, the maintenance of a separate administrative machinery for a small number of people seemed a wasteful luxury. Could not a good deal of money be saved by having one mayor, one assembly, and one village office instead of four or five of them? The Shoup Report suggested that the consolidation of munic-ipalities—or of prefectures—should be encouraged wherever it seemed likely to promote increased efficiency of operation. The Kambe Com-mission followed up with a recommendation that towns and villages should have a population of at least 7,000 to 8,000 in order to handle their own affairs rationally. But the Commission realized that large-scale amalgamations, while solving some problems, would also create new ones. It therefore suggested that the creation of rural villages of extensive area, except where the settlements are close together, should be avoided, because otherwise the village office would be too far away from most of the people; it urged that joint administration of affairs by associations of towns and villages should be given consideration, and that the advantages and disadvantages of merger of rural villages into cities and towns should be carefully evaluated. In particular, it recom-mended that the possibility of cultivating a community spirit should be given some weight, saying that this spirit "is the essential requirement for the formation of an autonomous entity."[19]

The government soon started a vigorous promotion of amalgamations. Under its prodding, some prefectures set up Amalgamation Accelera-tion Committees, and a number of amalgamations were effected in 1950. In January 1951 the Local Autonomy Agency instructed all the prefectural governors, then assembled in Tokyo, to follow this example.

But amalgamations did not proceed fast enough to suit the government. When the Local Autonomy Law was amended in 1952 it required that local entities plan necessary adjustments among themselves. Ostensibly to assist the towns and villages in their planning, the prefectural governors were given authority to devise plans for mergers and to recommend these plans to the local entities concerned.[20] Persuasion was to be replaced by guidance from above. The initiative was now in the hands of the prefecture. By 1953 the number of towns and villages had dropped to about 9,600. Still, the governor had to obtain the opinion of the local entities concerned when he drew up his plan, and the implementation of the plan required an application of these entities on the basis of a resolution of their assemblies. But what if the assembly should oppose the merger? How could local apathy or resistance be overcome? How could the entire process be speeded up?

These questions suggest the reasons for the enactment of the Law for the Promotion of the Amalgamation of Towns and Villages in September of 1953. The law stated in Article 1 that the realization of the "principle of local autonomy" in regard to towns and villages was one of its aims, and many commentators agreed that the law was a step in this direction. Yet the initiative came from the central government, not from the autonomous entities; the more efficient administration of national functions was a primary consideration in the minds of the drafters, and the government was intent on removing all local resistance to the plan.[21]

This suggests certain parallels between the mass amalgamations of the later Meiji era and the more recent ones. But there is also a striking difference. In the planning of the earlier amalgamations, the will of the inhabitants was hardly considered. This cannot be said of the more recent mass amalgamations, which were accompanied by a great deal of publicity. Between May and October 1954 two weeks were declared "Amalgamation Weeks." Exhibitions were held and movies were shown. Strenuous efforts were made to give the mergers a coloring of spontaneity to match the evocation of the "principle of local autonomy" made in Article 1 of the law. This was no easy task, for the small Japanese local entity is often a hotbed of parochialism, and its citizens frequently look on neighboring communities with suspicion if not with outright animosity. To overcome this attitude, the law engaged first of all in moralistic exhortations. It stated that amalgamation plans should be decided in such a manner that the people will live in harmony and will have a positive and cooperative attitude toward the construction of the new city, town, or village. It called for the "sincere cooperation" of the public organizations in the area (such as the agricultural cooperatives). When the Headquarters for the Promotion of Amalgamation of Towns and Villages adopted a "Policy for the Construction of New Cities, Towns, and Villages" in 1956, it stated that the inhabitants of the new units should give up "the feeling of the old towns and villages," sweep away conflicting local loyalties, and develop a new community consciousness. The Law for the Promotion of Construction of New Cities, Towns, and Villages, which resulted from this policy and replaced the Amalgamation Law in 1956, admonished citizens to be mutually harmonious and to be conscious of being citizens of one local entity.[22] In thus exhorting the citizenry, and in extolling such traditional virtues as harmony, sincerity, and cooperation, the government assumed a traditional stance to overcome an essentially traditionalistic resistance.

However, appeals to local interest were not neglected to make amalgamation more attractive. The promise of special subsidies and preferential treatment in regard to national assistance was used as an incentive. In order to soften the opposition of incumbent assemblymen, some of whom stood to lose office after the merger, the law assured them of continuation in office for a limited period. To make merger more palatable, communities antagonistic to it were offered the possibility of retaining a certain separateness; in cases of clear inequality between property holdings, communities with the larger holdings were permitted to retain separate control over parts of their property through the establishment of property wards.* One may wonder whether this was entirely consistent with the exhortations to develop a new community consciousness, but logical consistency does not seem to have been an overriding consideration. Later, when the possibility of establishing separate property wards began to be seized upon too avidly, the towns or villages to be merged were enjoined in an amendment to the Amalgamation Law in 1954 not to do so in violation of the spirit of amalgamation. An amendment of the Local Autonomy Law in the same year similarly exhorted property wards in general not to injure the unity of the entity to which they belonged.[23]

---

* On property wards see Article 294, paragraph 1, of the Local Autonomy Law. The property ward is managed by an assembly, a general meeting, or a management committee.

The procedure for amalgamation contained a number of interesting features. The governor appointed an Amalgamation Acceleration Committee composed of mayors and assemblymen recommended by their respective prefectural associations, persons recommended by the prefectural boards of education, members of the staff of the prefectural government, and "persons of learning and experience." The Committee studied and discussed the amalgamation plan at the request of the governor and participated in the publicity campaign for it. Towns and villages could jointly establish a council to promote the amalgamation and to draw up an amalgamation plan of their own, provided that they had obtained the opinion of the governor in advance. Similarly, when a plan had been adopted by the villages, it was to be submitted to the governor, who then in turn submitted it together with his opinion to the Prime Minister. The final step was a disposition by the governor based on a resolution of the prefectural assembly, as prescribed by Article 7 of the Local Autonomy Law.

As was noted earlier, in 1952 the governors had been given authority to devise amalgamation plans and to recommend them to the local entities concerned. Before a governor could recommend an amalgamation plan he had to obtain the opinion of the towns and villages concerned, and the governor's request for this opinion had to be made public by the mayor. Then a signature campaign could be started and three-fifths of the voters could present their opinion to the mayor. The mayor had to publicize this opinion and to submit it to the governor within sixty days. It was possible, of course, that this opinion would coincide with the governor's intentions. But if the governor's recommendation did not find acceptance by the local assembly, this fact had to be made public by the mayor. A demand for a referendum could be addressed to the local Election Management Committees, and if in the referendum more than four-fifths of the voters voted in favor of the plan, it was carried out regardless of any assembly resolutions to the contrary. (The amendment of the law in 1954 decreased the required majority to two-thirds.) Thus the resistance of the assembly majority to amalgamation in general, or to amalgamation with the specific entities mentioned in the governor's plan, could be overcome. At the same time a *buraku* that wanted to amalgamate with a neighboring village contrary to the plan could be forced into line by the vote of the other *buraku*, who in the referendum were expected to vote as a block. This procedure was seldom used in practice, because it would have clearly shown the conflicts within the villages, and a demonstration of a lack of harmony is generally avoided by the leaders of rural Japan. Instead, the Autonomy Conflict Mediation Committees were often used to overcome difficulties. But the legal provisions are interesting, because they show the lengths to which the drafters went to close all possible loopholes for obstruction.*

There was also the possibility that the progress of a drive would be impeded by the prefectural assembly, which had to pass a favorable resolution before the governor could put the merger into effect.[24] The interests of individual assembly members were affected because the amalgamations changed the districts from which they were elected. Opposition on the part of the governor or the prefectural assembly could also arise when a locally adopted plan added new areas to a big city which had long been in a conflict with the prefecture. In such cases Article 33 of the Amalgamation Law came into play. If the governor did not act within four months after the application, the city, town, or village concerned could go over his head to the Prime Minister to request an investigation. If the Prime Minister found that the failure of the governor to act violated the national policy of rationalizing the sizes of towns and villages through their amalgamation, he could effect the necessary disposition in lieu of the governor. Here the system of "direct disposition" or "execution by delegation," an important control device of the pre-Occupation era, was brought back to life.

The law set the stage for a great deal of official activity. The amalgamation plans were normally worked out by the Local Affairs Section of the prefectural government together with the Local Affairs Office for each *gun*. The prefectural committees normally went along. To assure acceptance of the plan by the entities concerned, the help of powerful citizens was enlisted and those who aided the drive were awarded letters of thanks by the central or prefectural governments. Sometimes money was spent freely to make a village or *buraku* give up its apathy or resistance. Posters proclaimed the advantages of amalgamation and the dire consequences of failure to cooperate. There were broad intimations that

---

* The same tendency is shown by other provisions of the law. Thus, if a mayor did not fulfill his obligation of notifying the governor of the favorable result of the original signature campaign, the campaign manager could do so directly, and if the assembly did not reject the governor's recommendation but simply pigeonholed it, a referendum could be demanded after four months.

needed financial aid from the national or prefectural governments would not be forthcoming if amalgamation were not approved.[25]

We can now appreciate the outcome of the amalgamation plan. The Autonomy Board had set itself the goal of decreasing the number of towns and villages by two-thirds within the three-year period during which the Amalgamation Law was valid. This meant that 6,281 towns and villages had to be merged with others during this time. On October 1, 1956, the Autonomy Board was able to announce that the drive had been 98 per cent effective and that 6,154 towns and villages had actually merged with other entities.* As a result of the mergers, the number of cities had risen from 285 to 498. The number of towns had decreased slightly, from 1,970 to 1,903, but the number of villages had dropped from more than 7,600 to less than 1,600 and the average population and area of the villages had very nearly tripled. The number of mayors, vice mayors, treasurers, and other local officials had decreased by 18,124 and the number of assemblymen by 90,625.[26] The amalgamations continued under the Law for the Promotion of Construction of New Cities, Towns, and Villages of 1956. Within a year three additional cities had been created and the number of villages had further decreased to 1,365.† The number of local entities of various types changed as follows between the date of the enforcement of the Amalgamation Law and August 1, 1961:

	Cities	Towns	Villages	Total
September 30, 1953	285	1,970	7,640	9,895
August 1, 1961	556	1,938	977	3,471
	+271	−32	−6,663	−6,424

Of course, all this did not happen without arousing controversies. The establishment of Autonomy Conflicts Mediating Committees for solution of disputes among local entities had been provided by the Local Autonomy Law amendment of 1952. The Law for the Promotion of Construction of New Cities, Towns, and Villages made further provision for

---

* An interim report as of April 1, 1955, reveals that some prefectures had exceeded their quota of mergers while others had fallen behind. Kagoshima ranked highest with 135 per cent and Hokkaido lowest with 32 per cent. Nara had reached 34 per cent and Osaka 42 per cent of their quotas. See *Autonomy Yearbook 1955*, p. 18.

† The number of towns showed a slight increase due to the merger of some villages into towns. Tanaka Jiro, Tawara Shizuo, and Ukai Nobushige, *Fuken seido kaikaku hihan* (Tokyo, 1957), p. 9.

the settlement of controversies arising from amalgamations. If other attempts at conciliation—by town and village amalgamation conciliators, appointed by the governor—did not lead to a settlement, the governor was authorized to arbitrate. His arbitral decision obviated the need for any further resolutions of the local entities concerned. In other words, his action was considered as the action of the local entities that normally would have been required—a case of "an execution by delegation," strongly reminiscent of the prewar system. The existence of this sanction was enough. Its actual use by the governor was rarely necessary. The unrest within the affected villages was shown by the number of direct demands connected with the amalgamation issue.[27] Nor did the completion of the merger always lead to the much-vaunted harmony in the new local unit. The tensions engendered flared up in various forms. In some cases the parents of a village, amalgamated into a neighboring town, refused to send their children to the town's junior high school. In a case in Yamanashi Prefecture, in which a local high school was to be closed, the parents not only refused to send their children to the new high school to which they had been assigned, but also went on a tax strike, and the 1,080 voters in the dissatisfied section of the merged unit boycotted the mayoral election in April 1962. In a case in Tochigi Prefecture, more than a hundred disgruntled inhabitants of a merged village became candidates for mayor in an attempt to make a farce of the election and thus to block it.

A bizarre situation arose out of the hotly contested division of a village in Nagano Prefecture between a village in the same prefecture and a city in Gifu Prefecture. When the new administrative units were established in 1958, it became clear that two *buraku* had somehow been overlooked and had not been joined to either unit. The 32 electors were listed on the voting registers of both and thus could vote twice, in two different prefectures. They—and some others in sympathy—refused to pay taxes to either, and by 1962 they had accumulated a tax delinquency of about 4 million yen. There was also the case of the "cold war" between the famous hot-spring resorts of Atami and Yugawara. Both are a few train hours south of Tokyo, but the former is part of Shizuoka Prefecture and the latter is located in Kanagawa Prefecture. The object of the war is a section known as Izumi. In 1955 Izumi residents expressed the desire to be amalgamated into Yugawara, but Shizuoka Prefecture did not want to lose Izumi. According to newspaper reports, it secured loans for certain Izumi hotels that were in financial difficulties and presented gifts of money and livestock to several Izumi families. It tried to persuade the Izumi tangerine growers that their fruit would sell better when labeled "Shizuoka tangerines" rather than "Yugawara or Kanagawa tangerines." The issue was finally taken up by the Autonomy Conflicts Mediating Committee. After a cooling-off period of six years, a decision was handed down: Izumi was to be a part of Atami in Shizuoka Prefecture. Thus offended, the town of Yugawara retaliated: it prohibited the use of its crematory, its parking lots, and the public facilities of its beach areas by Izumi residents; it refused to continue the long-standing arrangement under which Izumi children had attended school in Yugawara in exchange for a yearly payment of 700,000 yen by Atami City; the Yugawara Hotel Owners' Association expelled eighteen hotels in Izumi from membership, doubled the price of hot-spring water for these hotels, and advised its members not to use taxis, masseuses, and geishas from Izumi. It is reported that sixty geishas thereupon left Izumi for Yugawara. The failure of Izumi to achieve amalgamation with Yugawara had dire consequences indeed.[28]

Special Local Public Bodies

The third volume of the Local Autonomy Law is entitled Special Local Public Bodies. When the law was enacted in 1947, this volume consisted of four chapters, dealing respectively with special cities, special wards, associations of local public bodies, and property wards. As was noted earlier, the chapter on special cities was eliminated in the amendment of 1956. In this section we shall deal with the remaining special local public bodies.

Special wards exist only in Tokyo Metropolis. They comprise the area of the former city of Tokyo, which was originally divided into fifteen wards.* By 1932 the number of wards had risen to 35. In 1943 the city of Tokyo was abolished as a unit of local government, but the wards continued their existence as subdivisions of the newly created Tokyo Metropolis, side by side with cities, towns, and villages within the Me-

---

* The fifteen wards were established in the Law for Reorganization of Counties, Wards, Towns, and Villages in 1878. The ward chiefs were then appointed by the central government. The Law Regarding Ward, Town, and Village Assemblies of 1880 provided for elective ward assemblies. After 1889 the regulations for the wards were contained in the city codes.

tropolis. Following the war a rearrangement of the ward area reduced the number of wards to 23. In October 1960 these 23 wards covered 570 of the 2,023 square kilometers of the metropolis. About 86 per cent of the metropolitan population—8,302,565 out of a total of 9,675,601—lived there. The average density of the population in the ward area was 14,578 per square kilometer, as compared with 4,774 for the metropolis as a whole.[29] There are rather distinctive differences between certain groups of wards, notably between those in the Yamate area and those in the Shitamachi area, about which more will be said later. The centrally located Chiyoda and Chuo wards have a daytime population three to four times as large as the number of inhabitants; contrary to the tendency in other wards, the number of inhabitants in these two is actually decreasing. Table 5 shows the area, population density, and population of the various wards as of October 1960 and the increase or decrease in their population between the censuses of 1955 and 1960.

The general rule regarding the status of the special wards is to be found in Article 283 of the Local Autonomy Law: "Except as provided for in Cabinet Orders, the provisions concerning a city in Volume 2 shall be applied to a special ward." But considering the needs of a modern city—in planning, transportation, water supply, sewage, etc.—the division of Tokyo's urban area into 23 separate city-like units was bound to create problems. In the amendment of the Local Autonomy Law of 1952 the original broad grant of functions to the wards was replaced by a list of specific functions, including the establishment and management of certain types of schools, parks, playgrounds, recreational areas, libraries, public halls, and roads. Additional functions may be granted by metropolitan bylaws. Such bylaws may also adjust metropolitan functions and ward functions and assign to the wards the exercise of metropolitan functions. Thus the picture of ward functions and their relation to metropolitan functions is complex. In principle, matters requiring comprehensive planning and coordination, uniformity of execution, or technical expertise are handled by the metropolis. We might add that the tax picture is equally complex. Simply stated, the wards have no truly independent taxing power. They may levy taxes of two kinds: metropolitan taxes, which they are permitted by metropolitan bylaw to impose in lieu of the metropolis (e.g., the prefectural inhabitants' tax may be made a special ward inhabitants' tax and be collected by the wards instead of the metropolis), and taxes created by and for the wards with the con-

TABLE 5

The Wards of Tokyo

Ward	Area	Density of Population Per Sq. Km	Population	Increase or Decrease(*) Since 1955
Chiyoda	11.52	10,162	117,067	*5,678
Chuo	9.65	16,702	161,172	*10,144
Minato	19.01	14,032	266,757	12,165
Shinjuku	18.04	22,938	413,793	65,118
Bunkyo	11.44	22,667	259,311	22,340
Daito	10.00	31,805	318,050	7,992
Sumida	13.90	23,890	332,065	26,475
Koto	25.69	13,640	350,403	72,432
Shinagawa	15.82	27,040	427,780	54,439
Meguro	14.41	20,379	293,660	39,719
Ota	41.70	16,930	705,992	137,494
Setagaya	58.81	11,102	652,883	129,253
Shibuya	15.11	18,640	281,656	32,246
Nakano	15.73	22,307	350,883	61,718
Suginami	33.54	14,501	486,356	80,691
Toshima	13.01	27,826	362,014	61,457
Kita	20.55	20,341	418,000	66,468
Arakawa	10.34	27,608	285,471	32,148
Itabashi	31.90	12,934	412,585	101,360
Nerima	47.01	6,489	305,069	119,255
Adachi	53.25	7,669	408,366	76,185
Katsushika	33.90	11,110	376,637	82,504
Edogawa	45.18	7,007	316,595	61,824
All Wards	569.51	14,578	8,302,565	1,333,461

SOURCE: Tokyo Metropolis, *An Administrative Perspective of Tokyo* (1961), p. 6.

sent of the metropolis.[30] Since the wards differ both in needs and resources, financial adjustments are necessary. These are made by metropolitan bylaws.

The Local Autonomy Law Amendment of 1952 emphasized in general the subordination of the wards to the metropolitan government. The change in ward government which most clearly decreased the independence of the wards and which aroused the greatest controversy concerned the position of the ward chief. Up to this time the ward chief, as well as the members of the ward assembly, had been directly elected. According to Article 281-2, newly established in 1952, the ward chief is now indirectly elected by the ward assembly, subject to the approval of the metropolitan governor.[31] The election of the ward chief by the assembly led sometimes to violence between the conservative and the progressive factions, the latter attempting to prevent the election to which it was opposed in principle. In some cases the police had to be called in and the election was conducted by the conservatives in the absence of the opposition.* A booklet on the Metropolitan Administration in Tokyo, published by the Metropolitan Government for the 1961 EROPA Seminar, summarizes the situation as follows:

All the problems pertaining to special wards lead in the end to the question of the proper relationship between the Metropolitan Government and the wards themselves, or of how to define the character of wards. The solution of these problems may be sought from the standpoint of the history of the wards, social realities, the evils of large-scale municipal administration, and the right balance between democratic decentralization of authority and the efficient centralization of power. If the citizens participate more fully in municipal government through taking more interest in the wards, and if wards are utilized for giving people a civic training, then the democratic value of the special wards will be further increased. From the standpoint of the metropolitan community as a whole, however, the problem of the special wards in Tokyo must be considered in the light of the more efficient and better coordinated administration of the capital city.

Efficient administration requires, as a minimum, both coordination and, in view of the differences between the wards, adjustment among the wards. Only the metropolitan government can carry out this function. On the other hand there is also a political side to the question. Since there is no longer a city of Tokyo, the ward is the only entity of a distinctly urban character to which the inhabitant of the ward area belongs. It is here, in the elections of the ward assembly—and until 1952 in the elections of the ward chief as well—that he finds the type of political outlet elsewhere provided by the city government. The wards differ among themselves sufficiently to make civic participation on the ward level meaningful. Curtailment of the character of the ward as a local entity thus leaves the ward inhabitant at a political disadvantage compared with the inhabitant of cities, towns, or villages.† The solutions proposed

---

* Problems of this type arose in Minato, Shibuya, and Suginami, all wards in the Yamate area.

† A public opinion poll was conducted in 1961 in the ward area on the question: "What method do you think is best for the selection of ward chiefs?" The results were as follows: 47.2 per cent of the respondents favored popular election; 30.1 per cent

emphasize one or the other element in the picture. In 1957 a special committee submitted to the Tokyo Administration System Research Council a plan that would have reduced the status of the wards to that of branches of the metropolitan government, eliminated the taxing powers of the wards, and made the ward chief an appointee of the governor.[32] In 1962 a proposal to put the administration of the capital city under a national ministry would have restored the popular election of the ward chiefs.[33]

We may note parenthetically that the Local Autonomy Law also uses the word "ward" in another meaning. The original version of the law contained provisions for the creation of administrative wards in the special cities (Articles 270 through 277). Together with all other rules regarding special cities, these provisions remained dormant until the amendment of 1956, when they were deleted altogether. But under Article 155 of the Law, certain cities, designated by Cabinet order, had to pass a bylaw dividing their area into wards—in this case without any adjective such as "special" or "administrative"—as jurisdictional areas of the branch offices of the city administration. The five big cities were so designated by Cabinet Order No. 17 of 1947. As of October 1955 Osaka was divided into 22, Kyoto into 9, Nagoya into 12, Yokohama into 10, and Kobe into 8 wards.* These wards are not local entities like the special wards in Tokyo. In addition to being administrative subdivisions of the city, they also serve as election districts and as the jurisdictional areas of Local Election Management Commissions. They differ from the administrative wards envisioned under the abortive special cities system in a significant respect: under that system the ward chief was to be an elected official; under the new dispensation he is appointed from among the city officials, as are all his assistants.

The second type of special local body provided for in Volume 3 of

---

were in favor of the status quo; 2.3 per cent thought appointment by the governor the best method; and 20.4 per cent had no opinion on the question. The ratio of those in favor of popular election was highest among people in the age bracket from 30 to 40 years and among those with more schooling. Party adherence was less a factor than one might anticipate: 47.1 per cent of those who voted for the Liberal Democrats were for popular election. From: Tōsei Chōsakai, *Tokyotōmin no jichi ishiki to tokubetsuku seido ni kansuru yōron chōsa*, p. 36.

* The amendment of 1956 consolidated the various provisions for the division of city areas into wards in the new Article 252-20, according to which the cities designated as "big cities" have to establish wards. This involved no change since those now designated as "big cities" had previously been designated under Article 155, as stated above.

the Local Autonomy Law is the association of local public bodies. These are of three types: partial affairs associations, all-affairs associations, and town and village office affairs associations. All of these are juridical persons, separate from the constituent members. Partial affairs associations may be established by all types of ordinary local public entities, as well as by special wards; the others are limited to towns and villages. In general, their creation is based on an agreement by the constituent members, expressed in articles of association. But partial affairs associations may also be created by the governor, when necessary in the public interest. Otherwise the creation of all types of associations of municipalities requires his permission; associations of prefectures require the permission of the Prime Minister.

A partial affairs association, as the name indicates, is an association for the joint management of a part of the functions of the local entities concerned. These functions may be either proper functions or functions delegated to the local entities or their executive organs, including their administrative commissions. Article 287 provides that the articles of association shall determine the name, constituent members, functions, and location of the office of the association, and, in addition, the organization of its assembly and executive and the manner of election or appointment. Since these associations are not considered local entities in the sense of Article 93 of the Constitution, it is not necessary that their chief executive be elected. The articles must also provide for a manner of defraying the expenses of the association. If the affairs to be managed jointly are identical with those managed by an executive organ of the member entities, that organ shall be abolished. For instance, if village A and village B decide to manage jointly all their educational functions, their respective boards of education will be dissolved. Statistics published in 1952 indicated that at that time partial affairs associations of towns and villages were by far the most common type of association. Prefectures had not formed any associations among themselves, and in only four cases had they joined with municipalities in them.* Cities par-

* Since then the prefectures of Tottori and Shimane have formed a partial affairs association for the development and management of a port. The associations between prefectures and cities all have the same purpose. Examples are the Nagoya Port Management Association between Aichi Prefecture and Nagoya City and the Mōji Port Management Association between Fukuoka Prefecture and Mōji City. Fukuoka Prefecture has also established a Port Affairs Bureau together with Kokura City and another one jointly with Wakamatsu City and Tobata City, based on the Port and Harbor Law. As noted earlier, these cities merged into the new city of Kitakyushu.

ticipated in 14 partial affairs associations among themselves, and in 220 with towns and villages. The bulk, 2,330 in number, had been formed by towns and villages. Joint management of irrigation projects and river improvement was the most frequent object; other purposes were the construction of middle schools and hospitals for infectious diseases, road maintenance, and forest management.[34]

In all-affairs associations, all functions exercised by the member entities are transferred to the association. In this case their individual assemblies and executive organs are abolished. In actuality, this means that the member entities become one ordinary local public entity and that the provisions regarding election of assemblies and chief executives apply to this new unit. Up to October 1, 1952, there were only 21 cases of such voluntary dissolution.

The office affairs associations are actually a type of partial affairs association, restricted to a joint management of the town and village office or part of it. Only 17 associations of this type existed in 1952.

The formation of an association is a rather formalized and cumbersome method of achieving cooperation among local entities. The Kambe Commission felt that simpler ways to promote cooperation should be found and suggested a "formula of joint management without complicated organization."[35] In accordance with this recommendation, the amendment of the Local Autonomy Law in 1952 provided for councils of local public entities, joint establishment of organs, and commissioning of functions.[36] The councils are established by agreement among local public entities and serve purposes of liaison, adjustment, and joint management of functions. They differ from associations in that no new juridical persons come into existence and no new legislative or executive organs are necessary. The councils act only in the name of their members and through them. Councils of this type were established in great numbers after 1953 in order to explore the possibility of amalgamations. The second device, the joint establishment of organs, was meant to be primarily an economy measure. This may be shown by an example. Local entities have to set up inspection commissions in accordance with the Local Autonomy Law and equity commissions in accordance with the Local Public Service Law; the 1952 amendment provides that small entities may establish commissions of this type jointly and thus save expenses. Finally, the commissioning of functions was meant to serve the same purpose: instead of setting up organs of this type, a small town or village was authorized to request a neighboring city that had these organs to carry out their task for them.

The joint schemes provided for in the Local Autonomy Law could have prevented the extinction of local entities by amalgamation, but the legal provisions remained largely unused, for a number of reasons. Cooperation was made difficult by traditional jealousy or animosity between neighboring communities. Some communities feared that cooperation with another entity might be an admission of lack of viability, which would attract the attention of central government and lead to pressure for amalgamation. Finally, Japanese local entities are not accustomed to coping with problems of local government—especially where they concern mainly national functions—on their own initiative. They are used to waiting for "guidance" from above. This guidance, when it was forthcoming, eschewed the slower process of cooperative solutions and championed the more radical measure of rapid amalgamation. It is a significant comment on national-local relations that at this point thousands of towns and villages which would not otherwise have joined with neighbors even in a partial affairs association fell in line with the government's policy and voted themselves out of existence as separate units.

Finally, there is the type of special local public body known as the property ward. This is a part of a city, town, village, or special ward that has its own property or establishment and bears the expenses requisite to it. An assembly or general meeting for the property ward—or, since the amendment of the Local Autonomy Law in 1954, a management committee—may be set up to deal with its affairs. The typical example of a property ward in the past was the *buraku* or *ōaza,* the natural village amalgamated with others during or since the Meiji era. To minimize the resistance to amalgamation at that time, the government allowed the old units to retain their commonly owned forests, meadows, wells, works, net-dyeing vats, fishing racks, shrines, cemetery grounds, and so forth, demanding only that such properties as office buildings, schools, and fire stations be turned over to the new villages. The traditional units thus continued to be given recognition in at least one of their aspects, namely, as an organization for communal ownership and management of property.* Otherwise the *buraku* was not regulated by law.

---

* The original Town and Village Code had regulations for "a part of the town or village which has property or has set up an establishment."

The institution of the property ward was thus for some time the frail bridge that connected the law with the important social units below the town and village level. Around 1910 more than 41,000 of the existing 76,000 *buraku* owned property. The acreage of the *buraku*-owned property was more than three times that of the property owned by towns and villages. The towns and villages derived some revenue from rents and fees for the use of the property they owned. Transfer of the *buraku*-owned property to them would have increased this revenue. Since the national treasury had been depleted by the Sino-Japanese War and the Russo-Japanese War, the national government wanted the towns and villages to execute more national functions and to assume a greater share of the financial burden for them. It was thus interested in increasing local revenue, and a transfer of *buraku*-owned property to the towns and villages seemed to be one way of achieving this end. In addition, the *buraku* were not always prudent in conserving the natural resources they owned. Transferring the forests and grasslands to towns and villages would bring their management under the administrative control exercised over the towns and villages. The government thus had two reasons for the policy for adjustment and unification of *buraku*-owned forests and lands which it instituted in 1910. Some progress was made, not without sacrifice on the part of poor *buraku* inhabitants, whose livelihood had depended on the communal use of the *buraku* property.[37] But many of the *buraku* retained their property and continued their existence as property wards. As we noted, the *buraku* enjoyed a greater degree of governmental and political prominence when the system of neighborhood associations was instituted. After its abolition the Local Autonomy Law continued the former rules regarding property wards in essence.

During the recent mass amalgamations, the history of the Meiji mass amalgamations repeated itself in a sense. Comparatively wealthy villages or *buraku* were certain to resent their amalgamation with substantially poorer ones, which would be "unjustly enriched" by the merger. For this reason the Amalgamation Law provided for the possibility of retention of some property in such cases, again in the form of property wards. We may illustrate the use of this provision by an example: Hinokiyama-mura in Kyoto Prefecture owned a relatively large forest, which it used with some success for the production of mushrooms. When the village was to be amalgamated with three neighboring villages, it balked at the prospect of transferring the forest, which yielded several million yen per year, to the new entity. The governor solved the problem by recommending establishment of property wards in each of the former villages, and the forest thus remained the property of the people of Hinokiyama-mura, although the village itself became part of a new entity, Mizuho-mura. We thus find "old property wards," which were originally the communal property of the traditional units of pre-Meiji days, and "new property wards," which are by-products of the recent merger of the artificial administrative villages that were created in 1889. And, to carry the parallel further, we find the government once again anxious to limit the effect of the concession made in the law. All sorts of pressures are used to achieve a gradual integration of all property within the new towns and villages.

The scanty provisions regarding property wards fail to do justice to the complexity of the actual relations between the *buraku* and the village.* We shall deal with these relations in the next chapter.

Summary

Cities, towns, and villages constitute, in the words of the Local Autonomy Law, the "basic local entities" of Japan. This is meant to describe their legal position, but it also implies that, being closest to the daily lives of the people, they are the center of their strongest identification. It is generally acknowledged that it is this identification that gives meaning to the principle of local autonomy.

Whether the rural village is, indeed, the center of identification for its inhabitants is problematical. Its artificial creation in Meiji times explains the strength of loyalty to sub-units, especially the *buraku,* that remain unrecognized in law. A sense of identification with the legal village could only develop over a period of time. There are some indications that this process had, indeed, started. As more and more institu-

---

* The amendments of the LAL of 1954 and 1956 added to the legal provisions regarding property wards to meet certain problems inherent in the creation of the "new property wards." Of particular interest is Article 296-3, which allows the mayor to delegate certain functions to the management committee of a property ward or its members.

The only Article of the LAL that mentions traditional units by name is Article 260, which states that the creation, abolition, or change of name of an *aza* or *chō* within a city, town, or village shall be effected by the mayor and reported to the governor, who in turn shall give public notice and inform the Prime Minister. But *aza* and *chō* are in this case area designations—used, for instance, as part of the address of an individual—and the article has little legal or social significance.

tions on the village level, such as village schools and village cooperatives, became part of village life and as the functional importance of the
sub-units decreased, the villagers began to think more than before in
terms of the village as a unit. The further development of such thinking
could have been spurred on by giving the villages an appropriate range
of functions, sufficient financial resources, and a significant degree of independence. But, as a minimum, it required for its continuation that
the existing units be left undisturbed for a generation or more, and this
was not to be. The recent mass amalgamations once again established
new units and the population is now to transfer its civic interest to them.
The process of slow growth must start again if the new units are to be
"basic local entities" in more than a legal sense.

The avowed aim of the amalgamations was to create more viable units
and thus to promote local autonomy in the long run.* This meant, un-
avoidably, the extinction of existing units. The problem was to find a
balance between the need for larger units and the need for a basis of
civic spirit on the grass-roots level of government. The government was
not completely oblivious of this problem, as is shown, for instance, by
the requirement in the Amalgamation Law that consideration be given
"to mutual harmony and willing cooperation of the residents." But in
fact, this consideration weighed rather light in the balance. The government could have promoted with greater vigor the formation of associations between villages, at least in villages where the more radical measure of amalgamation ran into resistance. It might have applied its standard of a minimum population of 8,000 inhabitants for the new units in
a less mechanical fashion.† In spite of the injunction in the law, the

---

* Part of this aim was the anticipated saving of local expenses caused by the reduction of the number of officials and assemblymen. There are indications that things
did not always work out that way. Thus an investigation of the expenses for the
offices and assemblies of cities, towns, and villages in Aichi Prefecture showed that
they were actually higher in 1955, after a great number of amalgamations had been
carried out, than in 1953, before the amalgamations. See Hoshino Mitsuo, "Shichōson
gappei no seiji—gyōseijō no mondai," *Toshi mondai*, Vol. 50, No. 3 (March 1959),
pp. 16ff. The report of the Social Science Research Institute of International Christian University, mentioned in note 25 to this chapter, finds a tendency to increase the
number of village officials and to create more specialized sections in the village
offices. It notes improvement in the personnel system and in office procedures.

† Towns and villages that had enough in common to justify amalgamation were
not amalgamated if the new entity would have less than 8,000 inhabitants. On the
other hand, to attain the standard, towns and villages were joined even where social

government did not avoid the disruption of established socio-political affiliations. The continuing difficulties in amalgamated units are proof of this.

Some observers expected that the creation of larger towns and villages would be a step in the transition of Japan's countryside from a communal society to an associative society. (Japanese writers prefer to use Toennies' German terminology, *Gemeinschaft* and *Gesellschaft*.) Narrow local loyalties would be destroyed, the hold of powerful individuals and families over their followers would be broken, social pressures would weaken, and political consciousness would increase. It is not certain that these expectations have been realized, for there is evidence on both sides. In some areas local candidates find that the exercise of traditional controls no longer suffices to assure them election in the new and larger districts that have come into being. They now have to attract votes from outside their old bailiwicks by active campaigns in which they promise to serve the interests of the voters. Elsewhere, however, the increased psychological distance of the village administration seems to have strengthened the ties of the *buraku*.* It may well be too early to reach any conclusions on these long-range effects of the amalgamations.

As stated earlier, the creation of "new cities" raised similar problems. The situation may be somewhat different in regard to the "new industrial cities" that are supposed to arise as a result of the economic development plans discussed in Chapter 8. These are to be units not only in an administrative but also in an economic sense. There are certain similarities between the Law for the Promotion of Construction of New Cities, Towns, and Villages of 1956, on the one hand, and the Law for the Promotion of the Construction of New Industrial Cities of 1962, on

---

basis for the merger was lacking. Where some amalgamations in the area had been accomplished, the remaining entities were then advised to amalgamate with each other. In such cases the invocation of the principle of local autonomy in Article 1 of the Amalgamation Law must have sounded somewhat hollow.

* The report of the Social Science Research Institute of International Christian University states: "The attitude of the village people toward the office has undergone a change, with the result that people in the village feel some psychological distance between them and the village office." The report expresses the opinion that amalgamation may accelerate the collapse of the traditional structure of local government, including the boss system. Hoshino, in the article mentioned above, cites examples for this phenomenon. For a contrary finding in regard to an earlier amalgamation in Toyama Prefecture, see Katagishi Shunji, "Chōson gappei ni okeru 'Mondaimura' no kōsatsu," *Toshi mondai*, Vol. 47, No. 5 (May 1956), pp. 505ff.

the other. But in spite of these similarities the approaches differ. Where structural and administrative considerations provided the impetus in the earlier laws, functional and economic considerations motivate the latter. There is thus an apparent parallel with the changes in the approach to regionalism, which we discussed at the end of Chapter 8.

Political and civic consciousness has long been strongest in the urban centers, as is shown by the history of the Big City Movement. But the special status desired by the big cities was withheld from them while they were still somewhat self-contained units. The revision of the Local Autonomy Law of 1956 brought them a net gain in their corporate autonomy at the very time when the metropolitan explosion had already made their separateness from the surrounding areas of their prefectures somewhat problematical. It is clear now that services have to be planned and provided for in areas that extend far beyond a city's limits. The stimulus can come from above, as it did in the development of the national capital region centering around Tokyo. We noted in the last chapter the beginning of locally initiated plans in the Kansai area. The plans for the Hanshin Regional City, based on the principle of federation, are particularly significant because they were conceived independently from the central government.

The most urbanized part of Japan is to be found in the area of Tokyo's special wards. Here the dilemma between providing for the civic participation of a politically rather sophisticated citizenry and the need for efficient administration of areas necessarily larger than the individual wards—or even their total area—is particularly clear.

Japan shares the problems of metropolitan growth with other highly industrialized countries of the twentieth century. But because in her case the developments of many centuries were telescoped into a few decades, she also faces problems that are all but forgotten elsewhere. On the opposite end of the spectrum from the metropolitan centers, we find rural villages that lag behind in the transition from the values, attitudes, and behavior patterns of an agrarian society to those of a modern, industrial society.

CHAPTER 10

Neighborhood Associations

The Local Autonomy Law does not mention neighborhood associations, and it deals with them only incidentally insofar as it provides for property wards, of which the *buraku* is a frequent example. But one writer has called the *buraku* "the most important unit in the social structure of rural Japan," and another has said that it "plays a more immediate and important role in the daily lives of a larger proportion of the Japanese people than do any of the more formal and better known units of organization."[1] Lack of legal recognition notwithstanding, the *buraku* also plays an important part in village administration and politics. For these reasons, village government in Japan cannot be discussed realistically without reference to the *buraku*.

There are difficulties in describing a unit of this type. The unwary reader may gain the impression that he is being offered a look at "the real Japan" that lies behind the façade of governmental institutions. When he is told that the *buraku* is an indigenous natural group, operating on the basis of traditional mores, he may come to consider it a reflection of the essence of Japanese culture and thus a permanent feature of the Japanese social scene. The Occupation's efforts to change or abolish the *buraku* associations will appear to him a priori culturally inept and thus doomed to failure. When he hears that there are advocates of measures to maintain or reinstitute these units, he will intuitively sympathize with them because he will believe that they are motivated only by a perfectly natural desire to correct a disturbance wrought by alien influence. And yet it seems to me, for reasons stated more generally in Chapter 5, that the indigenous character of the *buraku* and its basis in traditional mores do not justify these conclusions. The view on which they are based neglects the dynamics of the situation. What influence do Japan's industrialization and urbanization have on the traditional basis of the *buraku*? What kind of natural development could be anticipated without governmental interference, either by the Occupation or by conservative Japanese governments? It would seem that the formalization and legalization of the *burakukai* before the war, its "abolition" during the Occupation, and the later proposals for relegalization all have to be viewed in the context of these questions as conscious or unconscious attempts to slow down or speed up the influence of social change.

It has been suggested that the Occupation, instead of legislating against the neighborhood associations, should have made them "a force in democratic education."[2] The adaptation of indigenous institutions to new aims is, in principle, a device of some merit. Democracy and local autonomy depend on civic interest; and the *buraku*—unlike the Japanese village, which is an artificial creation—is close to the daily lives of the villagers. Could it not have been converted into a core of civic interest? Should the Occupation have used the *buraku* rather than the village for this purpose? What are the dynamics of the relationship between *buraku* and village?

The *burakukai* was only one type of the neighborhood associations that were given official recognition in 1940 and prohibited in 1947. The urban counterparts, the *chōnaikai*, followed the same development. In other words, city and country were not differentiated for purposes of dealing with the question of neighborhood associations. But is there in fact enough cultural homogeneity between them to justify this? Is the support they draw from traditional values and behavior patterns equally strong? Are the needs they fill as important in one case as in the other, and if not, does it not follow that rural and urban neighborhood associations have to be treated separately? We shall return to these questions after a brief description of both types of neighborhood associations.

The Traditional Bases of Buraku Life

For purposes of description, we shall select a number of characteristic elements of traditional Japanese society and show how they are reflected in the life of the *buraku*. This involves a good deal of generalization, for the *buraku* is subject to a great number of variations: an agricultural *buraku* may differ from a fishing *buraku* or from a *buraku* of shopkeepers; a lowland *buraku* may differ from an upland or mountain *buraku*; a *buraku* near an urban center may differ from one that is remote from it; and one in the northeast or south of Japan may differ from one in the coastal plains of central Japan. Nevertheless an outline of the traditional bases of *buraku* life will aid us in understanding the *buraku*'s functioning and in appraising its future.

One of the characteristic marks of traditional Japanese society is the emphasis on the importance of the group vis-à-vis the individual. Morality demands that the individual willingly assign a higher priority to the interests of the collectivity than to his own interests. He must not threaten the cohesion of the group by being competitive rather than cooperative, by being self-assertive rather than self-effacing.* Within the group, relations are particularistic, that is, the manner in which one is expected to deal with others depends in each case on the unique position of one actor vis-à-vis the other. This position—his status—is to a large extent ascribed, not achieved. Each person thus has a "proper place," and morality demands that he keep this place. If everyone does this, there will be peace and harmony. Interpersonal relations are of a diffuse nature. Being a tenant, for example, traditionally implied more than just paying rent for the use of the landlord's land, and permitting the use of the land in exchange for the rent payment. Ideally, it involved deference and loyalty on the tenant's part as much as a benevolent paternalism on the landlord's part, not only in matters involving the land, but in general. Thus these relations are given an affective content. Because of the emphasis on affectivity, particularism, and diffuseness, relations are preferred to be personal. Impersonal relations are eschewed. They are "cold" and smack of selfishness on both sides.†

It will be readily apparent that the rules of conduct implicit in this pattern are also those that characterize the traditional Japanese family. To conservatives, this family has long been the proper model for all other Japanese social units; quite aside from other considerations, they

---

*Self-assertion consists, for instance, in taking action independently without reference to the group or in insisting on a course of action because it is "right" in an abstract sense without regard for the consequences for the group.

† This analysis borrows from Professor Talcott Parsons's "pattern-variable scheme," as defined in *The Social System* (Glencoe, 1957) and in Parsons and Shils, *Toward a General Theory of Action* (Cambridge, 1954). See also R. P. Dore, *City Life in Japan* (Berkeley, 1958), p. 440.

would like to keep *buraku* life unchanged because it follows their ideal more closely than do other social systems in present-day Japan. It is significant in this context that however much *buraku* may otherwise differ among themselves, the family is always the prime constituent element. The family in this sense is not the conjugal family of the West. In the northern part of rural Japan and in southern Kyushu a large group consisting of a hierarchy of households linked by kinship or fictive kinship ties is sometimes of importance.[3] Sometimes the "house," a consanguineal group of smaller scale, is the important unit. But the family unit that most frequently forms the basis of *buraku* organization and activity today is the household, a group of relatives usually embracing two or more conjugal families of different generations.* The fact that the family in this sense is the constituent element of the *buraku* becomes apparent in many ways. If one asks for the population figure of a *buraku*, the answer is usually given in terms of the number of families rather than the number of individuals. *Buraku* meetings are attended by one representative for each family, and each family has one vote. The family, not the individual, is the object of most *buraku* decisions, such as those concerning the provision of labor or the making of contributions. Ostracism is applied as a sanction against the family, not the individual. In general, the status of the individual in the community tends to be that of his family.

Tracing these elements of traditional Japanese society to the *buraku*, we find first a strong group cohesiveness. Cooperation in work and in arranging festivals are some aspects of this cohesiveness. Another aspect is indicated by the statement that the *buraku* is "the womb of the election." In effect, the *buraku* resident votes traditionally for a representative of his *buraku* in the village assembly. Voting thus becomes an act of group solidarity, and because this solidarity is prized, the *buraku* prides itself in achieving a nearly complete turnout of voters. A corol-

---

* The fact that today the household is of greater importance than the "house" is itself a sign of the breakdown of traditional units through increased mobility. The old Civil Code still dealt with the "house" as a unit, and subjected all of its members, wherever they lived, to certain controls by the "head of the house." The new Civil Code no longer recognizes the "house." Frequent references in the new Civil Code and in many other laws to "relatives living together" gave, in effect, legal standing to the household. On this subject see Kurt Steiner, "Postwar Changes in the Japanese Civil Code," *Washington Law Review*, XXV (1950), 298.

lary of this system is the absence of active campaigning, which is not only superfluous but also slightly improper in the eyes of tradition-bound villagers.*

Traditional notions of harmony are reflected in the manner in which decisions are made at the *buraku* meetings. In general, voting is avoided. To determine the will of the majority by this method would imply the presence of a minority and thus a split in the solidarity of the group. The technique of recommendation and consensus is a traditional means for achieving the desired appearance of unanimity. After lengthy discussion—in which, in a cautious way, a recommendation may be advanced, modifications suggested, and a compromise reached—the chairman may feel that the time is ripe for an announcement of the consensus of the group; or a member of the group may formulate a recommendation, and then the chairman states that, in the absence of objections, the recommendation is adopted. Since insistence on a solution, proposed by a participant in the discussion, or continuing opposition to it would be considered detrimental to harmony, the pressure in favor of a compromise is strong. When the consensus has finally been announced, objections are hardly ever raised even if some members do, in fact, dissent. To object would show the existence of a rift in the solidarity of the group and would involve the objector in a serious problem of "face" with the individual whose recommendation was challenged. But, as Robert Ward has observed, the absence of objections does not guarantee the loyal support of all participants for the decision taken. "The conflict is often simply removed from the floor of the meeting to less conspicuous areas, where bitter, secret opposition and sabotage are quite possible."[4]

The inhabitants are proud of the harmony of their *buraku*. When they boast of it they often point by way of contrast to some neighboring *buraku* that supposedly exhibits the vice of dissent.† At times harmony

---

* In this chapter we shall only touch upon the role the *buraku* plays in elections. We shall deal with this role in greater detail in Chapter 16.

† This desire for the appearance of harmony also appears on levels above the *buraku*. The writer once asked the mayor of a town well known for the enmity of two contending groups, one headed by the mayor and the other by the chairman of the assembly, whether there were any factions at work there. The answer was an instantaneous "No." The boast of harmony within the unit is often followed by the statement: "This is because our villagers are farmers, who are pure [of heart]."

has to be upheld by social pressure. One of the more formalized sanctions is a type of ostracism most commonly called *mura hachibu*.* This entails the break-off of social intercourse with the ostracized family; the family is omitted when notices of various types are sent around the hamlet; it is excluded from the use of commonly owned farm implements; it receives no cooperation at harvest time; and when fertilizers and seeds were rationed, it did not participate in their distribution. If the *buraku* owns a forest, the ostracized family cannot get firewood from it.

The ostracism is based on a resolution adopted in a special meeting of the *buraku* or some part of it; the meeting is called together by persons of influence after mutual consultation, and the affected family is not represented. The resolution usually refers to the "disturbance brought into the otherwise peaceful *buraku*" as the reason for the sanction. This "disturbance" is occasionally a crime or misdemeanor, but far more frequently it is an act or omission that is quite legal. A few cases may illustrate this point. In 1947 five influential landowners in a rural *buraku* of a city in Kanagawa Prefecture took the lead in ostracizing three farmers for their participation in a prefectural program for the sale of uncultivated land to individuals. In an older case, a family was ostracized because it filed a complaint with the District Procurator against fellow villagers who had used violence in the course of a quarrel regarding the location of a stone fence abutting on the village road.

A case that attracted a good deal of attention to the institution of *mura hachibu* occurred in 1952 in a village in Shizuoka Prefecture. When a by-election for a seat in the House of Councilors happened to conflict with a festival, the heads of the neighborhood associations went from house to house soliciting permission to cast the ballot for those who were too busy to do so themselves and to collect the necessary admission tickets to the polling place. A seventeen-year-old high school girl who took her civics lessons seriously was shocked to note that the visitor to her mother's house had already collected some thirty proxies, and she wrote a letter exposing this illegal election practice. As a result persons of influence in the village came under investigation. The girl's

---

* *Mura* means "village," *hachibu* "eight parts." Some believe that the name indicates an ostracism applied only to 80 per cent of social life, cooperation in case of conflagration and death constituting the other 20 per cent.

family was promptly ostracized because the girl's action had brought dishonor to the village.

Another case occurred in 1957 in a village in Nagano. There a quarrel broke out over the question of whether a clump of trees belonged to the communally owned forest or to an individual family. When the family objected to the cutting down of the trees in order to obtain money for the celebration of a festival, it was ostracized. To have the ostracism lifted, the family had to sign a document waiving all claims and, as a sign of contrition, the members of the family had to go from house to house in the *buraku* bringing presents to each household. Two other families who complained that the penalty was too harsh were in turn threatened with ostracism. When the police arrested the *buraku* leaders on charges of illegal intimidation, the *buraku* showed its solidarity by engaging and paying a lawyer to defend them. In 1958 a woman was elected *buraku* head in a village in Ibaraki Prefecture. Having been absent from the meeting, she denied the validity of the election and refused to serve. She was promptly ostracized as being "too assertive for a woman," by the same people who had elected her earlier despite her sex. In the local elections of 1955, the bosses of a village in Gifu Prefecture had expected that *buraku* solidarity and their control over the various *buraku* would lead to a unanimous vote for their chosen candidate for the position of mayor. To their surprise, he failed to be elected. They then determined among themselves the most likely suspects for the defiance of their authority and obtained their exclusion from *buraku* affairs, which involved, among other things, prohibiting their use of the communally owned grasslands. In the election of 1959 the villagers sought means of reassuring the bosses that they were voting "right," lest they come under suspicion and be ostracized. The matter came to the attention of the authorities when the polls closed in the early afternoon; it was said that all of the eligible votes had been cast, but the Election Management Committee was able to find families who had in fact abstained from voting.[5]

As some of these cases show, the institution is not just an expression of traditional mores. It is also a weapon used by powerful conservative elements to enforce the spirit of conformity that guarantees their continuation in power. The weakening of the consensus about this institution—and of the collectivity orientation on which it is based—is reflected in the increasing number of cases that are being reported to the Civil

Liberties Bureau of the Justice Ministry as infringements of basic rights.*

The other side of group cohesion is group exclusiveness. Outsiders do not "belong." One does not seek contact or cooperation with them, and one does not want them to come into the community.† The boast that one's own *buraku* is harmonious and that others are strife-ridden, and the occasional flare-ups of violence among neighboring *buraku*, are examples of the influence of this sense of exclusiveness. Inhabitants of one *buraku* often feel that they are somehow quite different from those of another *buraku*. Where one of the *buraku* is of more recent origin or of a different social composition, the feeling of exclusiveness reaches particular heights. If the new *buraku* has a higher political conscious-ness, no effort is spared to keep it from gaining stronger representation in the village assembly.‡ It goes without saying that the fragmentation of the village is an obstacle to the emergence of civic spirit, which neces-sarily involves an attachment to units beyond the immediate group.

The importance of concepts of hierarchy differs in various types of villages. Aside from the superiority of the "head houses" in some of them, there is sometimes also a marked difference between the status of the old families in the community and of the newcomers, some of whom may have been in the village for fifty years or more. In some cases the pre-Restoration ranks of warriors and commoners still have a linger-ing influence. Since obligations to those higher in the hierarchy are dif-fuse, and since political relations are not clearly separated from per-sonal and social relations, a family of superior status is in a position to control, by advice and example, entire blocs of votes in local elections.

* The frequency of *mura hachibu* fluctuates in the various prefectures. During 1951 the Civil Liberties Bureau of the Attorney General's Office (now again the Ministry of Justice) and its branches in the Local Legal Affairs Bureaus handled 183 cases of *mura hachibu*. (Based on the monthly report of the Bureau, *Jinken yōgō kyokuhō*, for April 1952, p. 53.)

† Simmons and Wigmore (*Notes on Land Tenure*, p. 83) refer to the practice of villages during the Tokugawa times to pay mortgages of outsiders, lest they become owners of land within the village.

‡ Few tourists who visit the famous Hakone Sightseeing Area and perhaps stay in the highly modern Gora Hotel realize that the settlement of Gora is the object of such a blockade in the village to which it belongs. See *Hakone kankochitai jittai chōsa hōkokusho* (Yokohama, 1953), Vol. V, pp. 27ff. This is a survey of the Hakone Area, sponsored by Kanagawa Prefecture. On the difference of characteristics and atmosphere of neighboring *buraku*, see also Royama Masamichi, *Nōson jichi no hembō*, p. 14.

It is a sign of economic and social change that this position of superiority, traditionally an ascribed one and tied to landholdings of some size, is now sometimes taken over by persons of originally lower standing who achieved wealth and thus gained influence.[6]

Sketchy and generalized though it is, this picture of the manifestations of traditional elements of Japanese society in the life of the *buraku* may have given us some insight into the atmosphere within which the *buraku* and its organs carry out their functions.

Buraku Organization and Functions

Some of the functions of the *buraku* entail no connection with the village office and thus with government, and are rather the spontaneous responses of a close neighborhood group to common problems. Assistance to a member too ill to work or to an aged couple without sons, mutual cooperation in the fields or in house-building, assistance with burials, common planning for festivals (which usually center around the common shrine) or for pilgrimages—all these are functions of this type. They are exercised sometimes by the *buraku* and sometimes by smaller groupings within it. Observers agree that their number and the degree of participation in them are decreasing.[7]

On the other hand, the functions of the *buraku* that we may roughly classify as governmental or administrative have increased. The government first used rural associations (*nōgyōkai*) for the dissemination of new techniques to increase agricultural production. In the agricultural crisis following World War I, it used them for the regulation of supply and for the collective purchase of fertilizer. In the thirties, the informal *buraku* organizations that existed previously became formalized under the prompting of the government, and the *nōka kumiai* (associations of agricultural households) that were established in the *buraku* were given legal status and regulated in the same way as the industrial associations. They carried out their still rather vaguely defined functions under the direction of the town or village *nōgyōkai*. In 1940 they assumed responsibilities in the new national crop requisitioning program under the name of *nōji jikō kumiai* (associations for the furthering of agricultural affairs). Governmental functions and formalization reached their peak with the establishment of the system of neighborhood associations. It will be noted that as a formal adjunct to government the *buraku* is not of great age.[8]

The heads of the *buraku* are almost always selected in the *buraku* meetings, usually by secret ballot. Since the official abolition of the *burakukai* they are usually given such titles as *rinji chōsa in* (special research personnel) or *renraku in* (liaison personnel), but unofficially they are still often referred to by the old title of *buraku chō* (*buraku* headman). The title *renraku in* is quite appropriate since liaison between *buraku* and village office is their most important duty. Often there is a vice headman, a treasurer, a person in charge of road repairs and other public works, a tender of the irrigation system, or such other personnel as appear necessary in the individual *buraku*. The headman and some of the other officials usually receive allowances from village funds. In many cases the headmen assemble in the village office with the mayor about once a month or as occasion demands, get explanations of new regulations and programs, and relay them back to the *buraku*. Often also the headman simply receives notifications from the village office and disseminates the information by means of a circulating bulletin board (*kairanban*).

The headman acts as chairman of the *buraku* meeting and relays its decisions to the village office when some action by that office is required. This is frequently the case. For example, emergency work on roads and ditches damaged by heavy rainfall is usually done by the people of the *buraku* concerned; but larger repairs and building of new drainage facilities and similar public works need funds from the village budget. The *buraku* officials will therefore report to the mayor the need for such works and get the necessary expenses included in the budget. Often this involves a special tax collected from the particular *buraku* or *ōaza* that will benefit from the work.[9] There are other occasions when the interests of the *buraku* have to be advanced in the village office. The *buraku* may want to have a new grammar school established in its vicinity rather than in a *buraku* at some distance; it may want to have the productivity index of the fields within its boundaries reassessed; or it may want to influence the amalgamation plans being drawn up. In all these cases the *buraku* becomes a sort of pressure group, and one based on community solidarity rather than on voluntary association for the pursuit of individual interests.

The *buraku* is also usually the basic unit for the fire brigade. The village may give an allowance for celebrations or the buying of *happi* coats, but it is the *buraku* or *ōaza* that usually buys the fire pump and other equipment. The money comes from semi-voluntary contributions assigned and collected by the *buraku*.*

In addition to being de facto an administrative sub-unit of the village and an area pressure group, the *buraku* serves as an important element in the support system of candidates for elective positions, especially when the candidates are of a conservative persuasion. As noted earlier, in village assembly elections the *buraku* traditionally votes en bloc for a candidate who is to represent it in the assembly. The candidate is determined in advance by the informal leaders of the village. The local "bosses," by using their status or personal relations, are also able to mobilize the *buraku* in favor of candidates in prefectural and even national elections, although their effectiveness diminishes as the distance from the local level increases. We shall discuss this function of the *buraku* more fully in the last chapters of this study.

Urban Neighborhood Associations

So far we have dealt with neighborhood groupings in a rural and primarily agricultural setting. We have shown that these groups in their present formalized appearance did not arise spontaneously, but that there was at least an informal social unit on which the formal organization could be based. Are there any units of this type outside the rural setting? Especially, are there such units in the urban centers of Japan? The size of the "neighborhood" is, of course, an important factor. Cohesion is strongest where the neighborhood is so small that it may be considered a face-to-face group. The larger the city, the less likely is this to be the case.†

Even large Japanese cities are in many respects clusters of historical towns and villages. We find traces of this in the somewhat surprising fact that important thoroughfares in Japanese cities have no names, but

---

* This is only one example of contributions of this sort, which constitute an item of some importance in the village budget.

† Whereas 87.9 per cent of the neighborhood associations in towns and villages consist of fewer than 150 families, this is true of only 26.5 per cent of the neighborhood associations in the six big cities. Among the latter 66.1 per cent consist of more than 200 families, and 27.9 per cent of more than 500 families. The medium- and small-sized cities stand in between these extremes: 66.4 per cent of their neighborhood associations consist of fewer than 150 families, 18.9 per cent of more than 200 families, 3.7 per cent of more than 500 families. Sakuma Tsutomu, "Jumin soshiki no mondai," *Jichi kenkyū,* Vol. 33, No. 7 (July 1957), p. 31.

are cut into segments, each being part of a surrounding area which usually bears the name of a former town or village. Thus the address of a city dweller consists of a house number, the name of a town- or village-like locality, and, possibly, its subdivision.*

While this division of cities into smaller localities is nearly universal, the significance these localities may have in the lives of the inhabitants of different cities, or even of different parts of the same city, varies considerably. Neighborhood groups are normally more important in smaller cities than in larger ones. In the small cities there is comparatively less population mobility and less occupational differentiation; there are few groups to which the inhabitants belong, but these groups have great staying power; the relations between the members tend to involve the whole personality, and cohesion is comparatively strong. The opposite tends to be true of social groups in large cities.[10]

However, within a large city there may be a difference between older and newer parts. In Tokyo, for instance, the eastern part known as *shitamachi* has been fairly well settled for a long time. It was therefore less affected by the influx of new population groups than were other parts of the urban core of the metropolis. Shops, inns, small-scale pro-

---

* There are, of course, some exceptions. When Tokyo's famous shopping street, the Ginza, is mentioned, it is usually the main thoroughfare that is meant. But a typical address still reads about as follows: 4 *banchi* (lot number), 3-*chōme* (subdivision), *Shimouma-chō* (*chō* is another reading for *machi*, meaning town), *Setagaya-ku* (name of ward), Tokyo. The Occupation put up street signs so that its personnel could describe a place as being "at the corner of F Avenue and 30th Street." This remained Greek to the Japanese living or working there. Recently some of the Tokyo wards have launched programs to simplify the address system. These programs involve no deviation from the old concept of giving names to areas rather than to streets; however, the houses are to be numbered consecutively so that, for instance, house number 42 would be between the houses numbered 40 and 44. This is not the case today. It stands to reason that a ward cannot go much farther than this because streets cut across ward boundaries. In Tokyo any more radical reform obviously has to be carried out by the metropolis.

In anticipation of the 1964 Olympic Games, held in Tokyo, names were attached to main thoroughfares. Elsewhere, the municipal level would seem to be the proper level for such reforms. It is symptomatic that the national government is taking a hand in the matter. A bill drafted by the Autonomy Ministry would give municipalities a choice between two formulas: the "gaiku" (block) or the "dōro" (street system). In either case, individual houses—either along a street bearing a name or in a block—are to be numbered consecutively. Municipalities would be obligated to put up signs for block numbers and street names. They would be given a special subsidy to carry the reform into effect. See *Japan Times,* February 12, 1962.

duction plants, and other small independent businesses have often been operated in the same families for generations. Traditional patterns of social life have been changed less than one might expect in areas that are only minutes away from the bustling center of Tokyo. Group cohesiveness and exclusiveness, hierarchical notions, and ties of personal loyalty are still comparatively important for many of the inhabitants. On the other hand, in another part of urban Tokyo known as *yamate* or *yama no te,* rural villages became within a few decades crowded residential areas, dotted with large-scale industrial establishments and lively business districts. Here the expansion in population led to definite changes in the pattern of life. Occupations are diversified. The locality where the individual lives and the one in which he works are often far apart, and the former has become comparatively unimportant to him. The primary group ties—kinship and neighborhood—have become weaker and a new political consciousness, based on diverse interests, has broken through the solidarity of the neighborhood group.

When the establishment of neighborhood associations was made compulsory for the whole country in 1940, few of the urban groups already in existence could look back to a long history. Most of them had come into being either as a response to the mobilization of the population for war or, earlier, in response to the need for neighborly cooperation at the time of a disaster. In Tokyo, the great earthquake of 1923 was particularly important in this regard. Groups of vigilantes (*jikeidan*), organized originally to assist the police in curbing looting and violence in the wake of the disaster, developed later into *chōnaikai.* Of the neighborhood associations existing in 1935, 36 per cent were founded between 1923 and 1927.[11] A Tokyo city bylaw gave them official status in 1938 (although they had been used for administrative purposes unofficially before). From 1940 on, rationing, civil defense, and propaganda provided functions handed down from above. When these came into disuse, new functions had to be sought, even in the old districts, if the associations were to continue. There were no functions that could compare in importance for the inhabitants with the importance of irrigation, public works, or the management of a commonly owned forest for the *buraku* people. Obviously, the sewage system has to be connected with that of the city at large, and the macadamized streets—along which streetcars are running and below which is embedded a maze of gas pipes, water pipes, and cables—cannot be an object of community work.

There do exist some functions of a social character, such as arranging for festivals around the local shrine, but interest in such affairs is unevenly distributed among the hundreds of families in the urban locality. Some people can be counted on to promote them and actively participate in them.[12] But others consider them an anachronism and will not contribute unless some pressure is applied. The same is true for other functions that have been created. Most of these simply require cooperation in affairs that really belong to the city. The city, for example, provides adequate street lighting for the more important streets, but local groups may be formed to erect light poles in quiet side streets, to turn the lights on in the evening and off in the morning, and to exchange the bulbs when necessary.[13] The city police man the police boxes and do some patrolling, but the same local group or another one may also make the rounds at night and protect the shops and houses against burglary or against fire by negligence. Sometimes such a group provides additional facilities for garbage disposal. Often it engages in "civic education," as by distributing leaflets, or it fosters, with the avowed purpose of curbing juvenile delinquency, practice in such traditional sports as *jūdō* or *kendō*.

Since only a small percentage of the inhabitants of the area care to engage in such work, there is a split into participants and mere contributors. In the older parts of the city, the ties between the two may be fairly strong. But in the new parts there is a gulf between them. The creation and execution of these neighborhood functions thus falls to a small group of "powerful men" (*yūryokusha*) or local bosses. To these men, who may start out with a much more limited influence as patrons in a patron-client (*oyabun-kōbun*) relationship, control or sharing control of the neighborhood association means a substantial growth in stature and power. Their control is nearly complete. As R. P. Dore has stated, they are for all practical purposes identical with the association; they effectively make all its important decisions and make their own rules as well.*

---

* Dore, *City Life in Japan*, p. 218. *Oyabun* means part (role or status) of a parent, and *kōbun* means part (role or status) of a child. As its name implies, the system is patterned after the traditional Japanese family. Ideally, the *oyabun* is as benevolent, generous, and protective as a foster parent would be, and the *kōbun* is as loyal and obedient as a foster child. Structural organization within such groups is similar to the Japanese kinship system. Often an *oyabun* has a number of *kōbun* who, in turn, are of "parent-status" to persons below them, and so on, which forms

The names of the urban neighborhood groups vary. When they focus on one function, they are called Crime Prevention Association, Police Assistance Association, or Fire Prevention Cooperative Association. When they combine a number of functions, they may take their name from the locality (*chō*) and add to it the syllable *kai*, meaning association, or they may call themselves *jichikai*, meaning self-government association; sometimes their name will show adherence to traditional notions, as in names such as *kyōwakai*, which means Harmony Association. Organizations with special functions (such as crime prevention) often exist side by side with these more general associations. There is normally a good deal of overlap among their officers, who often are also Welfare Commissioners (*minsei-iin*), PTA officers, youth organization leaders, etc.

Ostensibly these groups are entirely unofficial organizations. In fact, however, they are normally linked with the municipal government in various ways. Crime Prevention Associations, for instance, are connected with the police. A poster of the group is often seen in front of a police box. Often its office is actually located in the police station, although in most cases it is in the home of a leading official. Sometimes the association makes donations to the police, but more frequently it receives a subsidy of doubtful legality from the police budget.*

Neighborhood associations often supplement the services provided by the city, as noted above. Frequently they cooperate with the city government in carrying out certain projects. If, for instance, a drive for

---

a continuous network of relationships. See report by the Ohio State University Research Foundation No. 3 (submitted by Iwao Ishino and John W. Bennet), "The Japanese Labor Boss System" (mimeo., Columbus, 1952), p. 2. The system is ubiquitous in Japanese society.

* These relations lead to laxity in law enforcement, especially when the association is controlled by a strong-arm group. To cite an example: In April 1951, the newspaper *Yomiuri* carried on a campaign for elimination of this evil in the amusement and market section of Shinjuku Ward in Tokyo, charging that the local police station served the interests of the bosses. Dore (*City Life in Japan*, p. 273) mentions in passing that in the neighborhood he describes a manufacturer who by then had completed a prison sentence for wartime peculation was foremost in founding the crime prevention and fire prevention cooperative society. When a new police station is to be established local bosses sometimes ingratiate themselves and establish early and close contact by organizing a Construction Assistance Association for which they collect money in the neighborhood. See the study of Tokyo's Suginami Ward in the special issue of *Tosei*, Vol. 5, No. 10 (October 1960), p. 51.

the extermination of flies and other insects is to be conducted, the city will provide the neighborhood associations with part of the necessary funds out of its budget. The neighborhood associations will collect contributions to add to these funds, purchase the insecticides, and provide the necessary labor. If a road is to be widened in the course of city planning, the leaders of the neighborhood associations facilitate the necessary arrangements with the affected property owners. At times the associations engage in the collection of municipal taxes. For the assistance which they thus render to the city government they frequently receive a subsidy. They then become in fact adjuncts to the local administration.[14]

On the other hand, they also function as local pressure groups vis-à-vis the local administration. For this purpose the neighborhood associations within the city establish a federation. As an example of pressure group activity we may mention the successful drive of the Federation of Neighborhood Associations (*chōkai rengōkai*) of Hachioji City in Tokyo-to to gain exemption of association property from city taxes. Another frequently proclaimed group objective is the legalization of the groups, which is sometimes coupled with a demand for maintenance of their independence.*

The associations normally collect fees from every house in the area. Few families, however opposed to the existence of the associations they may be in private, dare to refuse the small monthly contributions assigned to them, or the special contributions for such purposes as shrine reconstruction, which are solicited in house-to-house visits.† Sometimes

---

* On January 1, 1959, some 3,099 neighborhood associations existed in Tokyo's 23 wards. In about one-half of the wards they had by then established ward-wide federations. In March 1959 about one-half of the neighborhood association chiefs gathered in Hibiya Hall to establish a metropolitan federation. It seemed apparent to many participants that, as a pressure group, they had to orient their activities toward the metropolis rather than toward the wards. If they desired, for instance, to obtain an exemption of their property from local taxation, they would have to address themselves to the metropolitan government which controls the ward taxes. See the special October 1960 issue of *Tosei* and Takagi Shosaku, "Tokyo-to kusei to chōkai rengokai," in *Nippon no atsuryoku dantai,* the 1960 issue of the Annals of the Japanese Political Science Association, pp. 146ff.

† See, for example, Tsuji Kiyoaki, *Nippon kanryosei no kenkyū,* p. 283. According to the Yokohama survey of 1953 (see note 12), the regular monthly contributions were below 60 yen in more than four-fifths of the cases. In only 9 per cent of the cases did they exceed 100 yen. A nationwide survey of the Autonomy Board in 1956 confirms that the fees are small: below 50 yen per month in 35 per cent of the cases, below 100 yen in 55 per cent of the cases, and above 100 yen per month in 10 per cent of the cases. Sakuma Tsutomu, "Jumin soshiki no mondai," pp. 29ff.

unpleasant consequences are threatened if the contributions or additional donations for such purposes as shrine festivals are not given. The less cohesion and uniformity of interests exist in the locality, the more pressure has to be applied.* Like the rural *buraku,* the urban *chōkai* serves as an element in the support system of candidates for elective office. But, as will be shown later, there are differences in the degree to which rural and urban neighborhood associations can be mobilized for this purpose. In this and in other regards, the *buraku* of a completely agricultural village and the various associations in the new parts of the larger cities stand at opposite ends of a vast spectrum.

Summary

We may now return to the questions raised at the beginning of this chapter. It should be apparent that rural and urban neighborhood associations differ in essential respects. The *buraku* looks back to a more or less continuous history, and is to be found even today nearly everywhere in rural Japan. On the other hand, its present formalized appearance and its present governmental functions are of fairly recent origin. Recognition by law and the assignment of governmental functions were part of an effort toward greater mobilization of the population, but they were more than that. The conservative leadership viewed with alarm the erosion of the traditional bases of *buraku* life, which had become apparent even before the war. When the government gave to the neighborhood groups new functions, new status, and increased importance, it attempted to strengthen the values underlying the institution against the tendencies that undermined them.

But utilization by government also contained the seeds of change in the hitherto rather self-sufficient world of the rural hamlet. *Buraku* exclusiveness was counteracted by the need to cooperate in governmental

---

* See, for example, an article in *Tokyo shimbun* on March 25, 1954, which referred to the frequency with which influential members of neighborhood associations visit the houses in the area to obtain contributions toward funds for projects in which they happen to be interested. These bosses, the paper stressed, usually make veiled threats to discriminate against householders who do not comply with their requests. In November 1954 the Justice Ministry responded to mounting complaints against solicitation of funds for construction of shrines and memorials to the war dead by a statement stressing the illegality of the forms of coercion frequently used. The Civil Liberties Bureau reported that complaints regarding forced contributions had jumped from 411 in 1951 to 1,138 in the first 9 months of 1954. See *Nippon Times,* November 16, 1954, p. 3.

efforts from the village to the national level. During the war the new-comers to the *buraku* who fled the bombed-out cities were an additional disruptive element.

All the factors adversely affecting the future of the *buraku* have been magnified in the postwar era. New and improved means of communi-cations and transportation—down to the bicycle—continue to bring the outside world close to the *buraku.* Increasing industrialization means greater mobility for the *buraku* residents. Even those who continue to reside in the *buraku* are less attached to it when they commute to work in a nearby city or town, and when farming becomes only a part-time occupation for them. The increasing mechanization of agriculture makes the farmer less dependent on the cooperation of his neighbors. The com-munal forest, once the main source of fuel, is becoming less important as other fuel becomes available and as electric cooking and heating appliances find their way into farmhouses. Chemical products decrease the importance of the communal grassland as a source of fertilizer. As the thatched roof is replaced by other types of roofing, the need for cooperation of the neighbors in rethatching diminishes. The contractor from the nearest town is also hired more frequently for road repairs that were previously a community effort. Even the rotating bulletin board, the *kairanban,* may fall victim to the loudspeaker of the village inter-communication system.

We have noted that most observers agree that the scope of social *buraku* functions and the degree of participation in them are diminish-ing. Most *buraku* inhabitants admit that there is less cohesion than there used to be, and the older generation frequently complains about the unrest, disobedience, and nonconformist views and practices of the younger people. Clearly the trend of the times is not favorable to the *buraku.*

Government actions affecting the *buraku* have to be viewed against this background. It is true that the Occupation's prohibition of the neighborhood associations had a minimal impact. As noted, the argu-ment was advanced at the time that the *buraku* should have been re-tained—because of its long history and its "consonance with Japanese folkways"—and should have been made to serve democratic ends.[15] Could the *buraku* not have become, in Tocqueville's famous phrase, "the grammar school of liberty"? Tocqueville used this phrase in connection with the town meetings that he observed in New England. There, al-ternative courses of action in comparatively simple local matters were freely articulated, freely discussed, and freely voted on, each individual participant following the dictates of reason in his decision. The attitudes exhibited and fostered there are transferable to the citizens in a functioning democracy—which was, indeed, Tocqueville's point. But the attitudes that the *buraku* serves to foster are not those on which a democratic society can be built; in many respects they are antithetical to democracy—which was precisely why Japanese traditionalists wanted to maintain them. Efforts to retain the institution while changing its character drastically would probably have been as unsuccessful as were the efforts at prohibition.

The argument also has another flaw. While giving great weight to the past, it neglects another time dimension: the future as recognizable in present trends. The Occupation's prohibition of the *burakukai* was clearly not the result of exhaustive sociological studies, but of an exhausted patience with the conservative influence of the institution. But whether this was an element in the Occupation's considerations or not, the Occupation's negative attitude was in consonance with the trends in Japanese society that affect the *buraku* adversely. It may be that as far as the rural neighborhood associations are concerned the Occupation went too far too fast. Obviously it was unable or unwilling to enforce their prohibition thoroughly. Such enforcement would have been difficult because the *buraku* still fulfilled certain functional needs.[16] Perhaps it would have been wisest to be content with the less radical measure: to deprive the *burakukai* of their legal status, their administrative functions, and their governmental support in the hope that a few generations hence they would wither on the vine.*

An element of the problem which is frequently overlooked—although

---

* It would have been necessary in this case to provide an alternative for the services that the *buraku* rendered to the village.

The attempt to abolish neighborhood associations was not the only governmental action affecting them during the Occupation. Considering the importance of the family unit to the *buraku,* the family law reform was bound to have a negative effect on it in the long run. The effect of the land reform is less certain. R. P. Dore (in *Land Reform in Japan,* p. 85) argues that the land reform, which made the inhabitants of the *buraku* more homogeneous, thereby strengthened the traditional solidarity in the *buraku.* It may well be that a continuation of the divisions among the *buraku* people and of the resultant issue between landlords and tenants would have made the institution more brittle and thus have accelerated its demise. By removing the issue, the land reform restored its viability. But considering the strength of all the other factors which erode the *buraku,* it is doubtful whether the land reform provided it with more than a temporary lease on life.

it was quite clear to the creators of the new villages in the Meiji era—is the relationship of the *buraku* and the village. As an artificial and relatively recent creation, and as an agency of government, the village is frequently regarded by the villagers with reserve and apprehension. The *buraku* engages affection to a much higher degree. This attitude stands, of course, in contrast to the new role that village government was to assume under Occupation auspices. Local autonomy on the village level requires that the inhabitants consider the village government as "their government," that they do not shrink back from it but participate in it. The attention of the *buraku* inhabitants had to be turned outside toward the village, not inside toward the *buraku*. Again there is some evidence that such a change is in consonance with existing trends. The village has become more important in the life of the *buraku* people. For example, it is the village that conducts grammar-school education and which, alone or in cooperation with others, builds and supports junior high schools and high schools. There is a P.T.A. (always referred to as such) on the village level and a woman's association that organizes educational and recreational activities. Policy of the youth association is made at the village level. The village farm cooperative provides fertilizer, feed, and tools at discount, is entrusted with savings, and serves as a source of loans. Irrigation is also managed on a village basis or on an inter-village basis, in which case the village represents the interests of its inhabitants. To quote the authors of *Village Japan*:

Mura government (i.e., village government) as the agent of higher professional bureaucracy, has been called on to carry out a growing number of functions having a direct, constant, and highly important bearing on the daily lives and fortunes of its inhabitants. At the same time, the average farmer's legal capacity to participate in and direct the policy and actions of this government has been substantially increased. As a consequence, most persons have a distinctly heightened consciousness of the importance of local government to themselves and their households. They may not yet be strongly resolute in participating meaningfully in the local political process, but they are more interested in this sphere than seems to have been the case before the war. Some of the old mistrust remains, but farmers are no longer so inclined to regard the government of their *mura* as an institution essentially marginal to their wants and welfare.[17]

The effect of the recent mass amalgamations on this change in attitudes has yet to be gauged. As noted in Chapter 9, there are some indications that they increased the psychological distance between the villagers and the new village office and strengthened again the *buraku* ties. In addition, the *buraku* headmen have become more important to the village office. The village covers now a much bigger area. To establish branch offices for various parts of the new village would defeat the purpose of saving local expenses. In this situation the village office uses the *buraku* headmen even more than before as unpaid auxiliary officials. On the other hand, the *buraku* is no longer sufficient as a base for election to the village assembly, and this may have an adverse effect on it as a self-contained unit.

Recent development planning will doubtlessly have a more dramatic impact. The area devoted to agriculture is already shrinking and with it the area of the rural *buraku*. Industrial plants are being established in what was only yesterday a placid countryside. Big apartment complexes (*danchi*) spring up within the confines of existing *buraku*. They are inhabited by thousands of workers and their families, who are typically recruited from outside the area. They establish their own *jichikai*, frequently at first as a pressure group toward their landlord, the Public Housing Corporation. But in due time they find also representation on the local assembly. Their interests and attitudes differentiate them sharply from the old-time villagers. Being in the majority, they are bound to transform the traditional social structures and processes built around the communal core of the *buraku*.[18]

The shrinkage of the area of the rural *buraku* means that the number of people socialized within the world of the *buraku* is diminishing. This will in time have major political consequences. The much-vaunted harmony of the *buraku* militates against the development of political consciousness.* It is still possible to mobilize the *buraku* inhabitants at election time for candidates chosen by the informal leadership. But conservative politicians are beginning to realize that they cannot continue indefinitely to base their future on the lack of political consciousness in the rural areas that once assured them solid and automatic sup-

---

* As long as land reform was an issue, there were differences of interests within the *buraku*. But these were not recognized in the mores of the *buraku*, and the individual was supposed to vote for the *buraku* candidate—usually a landlord—regardless of his interests. Candidates in favor of land reform could not hope to muster sufficient support within a *buraku* and thus had to look for it throughout the village. Those who voted for them thus broke through *buraku* constraints. See Kawanaka Niko, "Chihō jichi ni taisuru fushin no bunseki," *Kōhō kenkyū*, No. 9 (1953), pp. 89ff., especially p. 92; Royama, *Nōson jichi no hembō*, pp. 14ff.

port in election after election. The slack resulting from the weakening of traditional behavior patterns has to be taken up by new types of appeals and by the creation of local party organizations. As the world of the *buraku* shrinks, the possibility of political attitudes increases.

So much for the rural neighborhood associations. Their urban counterparts lack to a great extent such support as the *buraku* has in the customs and the needs—material or otherwise—of its inhabitants. While the *chō* is something more than a mere postal district to the more settled residents, at least in the older areas, it is, as Dore states, "in no full sense of the word a community."[19] When the *chonaikai*, uniformly established throughout Japanese cities in 1940, engaged in rationing goods, digging shelters, fighting fires, or even in propagating patriotism, their activities were accepted and approved of by many as necessary for a nation at war. But many others chafed under the pressures of regimentation and were glad to be rid of them. After the neighborhood associations were prohibited by the Occupation, many viewed with apathy and sometimes with covert hostility the efforts of some of their neighbors to keep them going under some disguise. They paid their contributions but otherwise cooperated as little as possible without creating unpleasantness and incurring the hostility of others. In the neighborhood investigated by Dore "the attitude of the majority was one of negative acceptance."[20] This describes the attitude of an important segment of the inhabitants of other neighborhoods as well. The impetus for the maintenance or renewal of the neighborhood associations came from comparatively small groups.

The ordinance outlawing the neighborhood associations became void on October 24, 1952, when Law No. 18 of April 1952, keeping Occupation ordinances in force for 180 days, expired. There were some reports that the government contemplated a revival of a uniform legalized system of neighborhood associations. But it was clear that important segments of public opinion looked on this prospect with alarm. Thus the *Yomiuri* warned in an editorial on May 7, 1952, that the associations would prove a convenient instrument for enabling local bosses to dominate the community. A *Nippon Times* editorial on May 18, 1952, entitled "Why Revive an Evil?", stated that only local bosses were delighted at the prospect of the revival of the system. It found that the measure would be a tool "to bring back the centralized totalitarianism of the past."

On October 18, 1952, forty women leaders discussed the problem at a meeting sponsored by the Tokyo Metropolitan Board of Education. According to a *Nippon Times* report, one representative favored the formation of community groups "to counteract the postwar tendency towards individualism." The report continues:

She was immediately drowned out by a barrage of protesting voices, pointing out the evils of fire prevention societies, public health associations, and similar groups under multiple titles which have already been in existence for some years in most communities. Such organizations, they declared, are: (1) overrun by men of dubious character; (2) extorting fees and donations under compulsion without clarifying their disbursement; (3) liable to be exploited at election time.[21]

The government has not taken any steps toward the reestablishment of a uniform system of neighborhood associations based on a national law. On September 18, 1952, the chief of the administrative division of the Autonomy Board informed the chiefs of the general affairs bureaus of all prefectures that there was no positive intention at present to reconstruct the neighborhood associations as administrative units, that their revival would be neither encouraged nor forbidden, and that future plans were still under discussion. The report of the Local System Investigation Council recommended against legalization of a uniform system.

The discussion received a new impetus in connection with the recent mass amalgamations. It was argued by some that since the mergers increased the distance between the people and the local administration, neighborhood associations should be officially used to express the desires of the inhabitants vis-à-vis the administration and thus to fill the void. But even among those who favored such a step there was some disagreement as to methods. Individual officials of the Autonomy Board were prone to stress the need for nationwide regulation of neighborhood associations if these were to be legalized in the future. Thus a connection would be established between the top and the bottom of local administration, the neighborhood associations would be clearly juridical persons of a public-law character, and a nationwide regulation of the relations between the officers and members would go far toward preventing the former from becoming bosses. On the other hand, local administrators favored a law that would simply authorize the cities, towns, and villages to establish neighborhood associations by local bylaws. This would allow a locality to rearrange and standardize the areas of neighborhood associations, which presently differ greatly in size and financial capability; it would permit the use of the associations for tax collection purposes; and it would make it legally possible to distribute at election time the tickets for admission to the polling places through the neighborhood associations—a practice which although not unknown is at present strictly illegal, since the associations are not official bodies. *Chōnaikai* officials, although cool toward the idea of a rearrangement of neighborhood associations, liked the idea of official status and the privileges that would go with it (free streetcar and bus tickets and the free use of public establishments are often mentioned) and hoped that greater subsidies from the local administration would be the reward for carrying out tasks delegated by it.[22]

It is not without significance that the *chōnaikai* officials are the group most dedicated to the restoration of neighborhood associations on a formal, legal basis. Unlike the rural *buraku* heads, who perform the chores of their office for a limited period when the lot falls to them in what is a system of limited rotation, the *chōnaikai* officials create and seek their offices; they are likely to keep them for a long time; and while their control over the neighborhood association itself is firm, their control over those living in the neighborhood is not. Clearly, they stand to gain from official recognition. As of this writing, it seems doubtful whether they will achieve it.

CHAPTER 11

The Muddle of Functions

Local units can be said to possess self-government if they are their own masters within a certain area of governmental activity. Within this area they take the initiative, plan, provide the required finances, and execute. Within this area, too, their assemblies and officials are not responsible to the central government, but rather, at least ideally, to the citizens who elected them. Because local issues—such as the sufficiency of police protection or of other local services, the desirability of a certain zoning arrangement, or the need for enlargement of a school—are more easily understood than the complex problems that beset the nation as a whole, it has been argued that the citizen learns on the local level to let reason guide the hand that marks the ballot.* But this presupposes, among other things, that local issues are decided locally.

We often speak of the crisis of local self-government in the twentieth century. The local community cannot cope with many of the economic and social problems of an industrialized society. The scope of governmental activities is increasing everywhere, and national functions expand at the expense of functions that had hitherto been considered as local. While local functions shrink, local government is more and more called upon to cooperate in the execution of national functions. There is a good deal of justification for William Anderson's observation: "What

---

* Similarly, the future national leader may find the local scene a useful training ground. There he takes the first steps in public life and gathers experience as a legislator or administrator. Having made his mark in his own community, he moves on to the next larger political unit until he is ready to appear in the national arena. In both ways the free community is seen as the primary school in which the ways of democracy are learned.

was once local government with the power to make many local decisions, tends to become more local administration of services and rules devised at the center."[1] Yet while this trend is generally recognized, there are few who believe that its inevitable result is complete centralization under which local government becomes nothing more than the local administration of national functions. If there is any merit in the notion of self-government, the problem is to find possible limits to the trend, to create the basis for local-national cooperation where this promises a satisfactory solution, and to redefine the scope of affairs that can still be left to local determination.

For Japan the problem is more complex. It has to be re-examined from two opposing viewpoints. Until a few years ago Japan's political system was thoroughly centralized; now the "principle of local autonomy" has become part of this system. The change requires a curtailment of functions and controls exercised by the national government under the former centralized system; on the other hand, the requirements of modern government set limitations to such a curtailment. The issue really is whether Japan has more centralization than is needed under the circumstances of the twentieth century.[2]

We described the system of functions and controls under the Meiji local government laws in Chapter 3. In Chapter 6 we dealt with the decentralization of police and education and with the failure to implement the recommendations of the Kambe Commission for the reallocation of other functions. In Chapter 7 we referred to the fact that Article 94 of the Constitution has not been used to achieve such a reallocation. It remains to summarize the resulting situation, to illustrate it by specific examples, and to describe recent developments and trends. This we shall attempt to do in the present chapter.

Proper, Assigned, and Administration Functions

The Local Autonomy Law contains a general grant of functions. It follows in this regard its predecessors, the various local government codes of the Meiji era. In its original forms, Article 2 of the law stated that local bodies shall deal with their "public affairs"—their proper functions in the narrow sense of Japanese public law[3]—and with "such affairs belonging to ordinary local public entities with which they were formerly charged by laws and ordinances and with which they will hereafter be charged by laws and government ordinances," i.e., with their assigned functions. The proviso of the former codes that local entities shall deal with these affairs "subject to limitation by laws and ordinances" and "under the supervision of the government" was dropped, as was the recognition of assignment of functions "by custom and practice."

The decentralization of the police created a problem of legislative technique. The functions acquired by the local entities under the new police system were not "proper functions" in the sense in which the term had been used in the past; that is, they were not functions requiring no exercise of governmental authority over the inhabitants. On the other hand, it would have been against the intent of the reform to consider these new functions as a mere assignment by the central government, considering the degree of central control that such an arrangement would have involved. In this dilemma, a third category of functions of uncertain character was added to the two traditional categories. When the Local Autonomy Law was revised in December 1947, Article 2 was amended to include among the affairs that local entities were authorized to deal with, besides "public affairs" and the affairs assigned to them, "other administrative affairs within the areas of the local public entities that do not belong to the national affairs." This category, which came to be known as "administrative affairs," embraced functions that were to be administered locally but which required an exercise of governmental authority. Article 14 of the law was amended at that time to enable local entities to provide sanctions against violations of their bylaws.[4]

In July 1948 a list of affairs with which local entities were empowered to deal "in general" was added in a new paragraph to Article 2.[5] This list, as amended in 1952, includes 22 items, each one comprising a number of functions. A few examples may show the range: maintenance of public order, safety, health, and welfare of the inhabitants and visitors; establishment, management, and regulation of the use of parks, roads, bridges, canals, sewage systems, electric and gas plants, streetcar services, docks, schools, libraries, museums, public halls, hospitals, reformatories, crematories, etc.; prevention of crimes, acts injurious to public morals, disasters, noise, etc.; protection of minors, and of the poor, sick, old, and weak; solution of labor conflicts and advancement of the education of workers; undertaking of profit enterprises deemed necessary for the promotion of public welfare; land development, adjustment, and reclamation; city planning and zoning; improvement of special products; registration and statistics; collection of taxes. The list is impressive.

However, the amendment of 1948 made it clear that the list is by no means an enumeration of functions guaranteed to local entities. There is first the peculiarly vague qualification that they may deal with the affairs on the list "in general"; this is followed by the proviso that they may not deal with these affairs when laws or cabinet orders locate the competence elsewhere. Local entities are, of course, not permitted to deal with national affairs. A list of such national affairs is given, but the law makes it clear that the list is only illustrative. Cities, towns, villages, and special wards must not contravene prefectural by-laws and no local entity may deal with its affairs in a manner contrary to laws or cabinet orders. Any local action violating these prohibitions is declared to be null and void.

The insertion of the list was apparently desired by Occupation officials. But the advantages that local autonomy gained from it were more apparent than real. The list is no more than an illustration of the functions contained in the general grant of the preceding paragraph. It is a jumble of all three categories of functions, including many assigned functions. It contributes little to a clear demarcation of the functions of the various levels of government and, in particular, to the establishment of an area of independent local action. As before the amendment, the existence of such an area depended on the willingness of the central government to refrain from regulating certain functions on the list in the interests of the "principle of local autonomy." Japanese governments, however, have shown little reticence in this regard.*

Until 1956, Article 2 contained no reference to specifically municipal or specifically prefectural functions. This was related to the general no-

---

* Cecil C. Brett in *The Government of Okayama Prefecture: A Case Study of Local Autonomy in Japan* (unpublished dissertation, University of Michigan, 1956), illustrates this point by reference to item 6 of the second paragraph of Article 2 of the LAL, which states that the matters with which an ordinary local public body shall deal include the following: "To establish and manage hospitals, isolation wards, sanitoriums, disinfecting stations, maternity hospitals, residences, hostels, dining halls, baths, public latrines, pawnshops, vocational aid centers, institutions for the aged, relief agencies and other protective institutions, nursery schools, juvenile correction schools, children's welfare establishments, institutions for the physically handicapped, jails, slaughter houses, dust-disposing stations, dirt-disposing stations, crematories, cemeteries, and other establishments relating to health and sanitation and social welfare and to regulate the authority to use them."

Many of these matters are regulated by national laws. Thus hospitals and maternity wards must be managed according to the Medical Services Law of 1948; isolation wards and disinfecting stations are regulated by the Infectious Disease Prevention Law of 1897; baths are regulated by the Public Bath Law of 1948; pawnshops

tion, which was implicit in the law in its original form, that municipalities and prefectures were of equal standing and not two levels in a hierarchy of governments. As noted in Chapter 8, the amendment of the law in 1956 discarded this notion—which had never influenced actual practice—and stressed the existence of two levels of local government. Article 2 was revised in 1956 so that the list of local functions in paragraph 3 is followed by two new paragraphs, one dealing with cities, towns, and villages, and the other with prefectures. Paragraph 4 pays the municipalities the verbal compliment of calling them the "basic local entities," and states that they may deal with the affairs mentioned in the preceding paragraph "in general," except to the extent that these affairs are attributed to the prefectures in paragraph 5. Paragraph 5 refers to the prefectures as "local public entities of large scale, encompassing cities, towns, and villages." They may deal with the affairs mentioned in paragraph 3 when these pertain to large areas or when they have to be executed uniformly; they may also perform functions of liaison and adjustment between cities, towns, and villages and may set standards in matters that are of such a nature that it would have to be considered inappropriate for normal cities, towns, or villages to manage them. This general statement is followed by a list illustrating the various matters with which prefectures shall "principally" deal.* It will be readily apparent that the revision contributes little to a clear demarcation of municipal and prefectural functions.

The crux of the problem of functions lies, however, in the existence of the great number of national laws, which cover the various fields of governmental activity and which are detrimental to local self-govern-

---

are governed by the Public Pawnshop Law of 1927; crematories and cemeteries are subject to the Law Regarding Graveyards and Burials of 1948. As Professor Brett points out, some of the national laws and ordinances contain such detailed provisions that there is little room for local initiative or discretion. For example, the Law Regarding Graveyards and Burials (actually an order of the Dajōkan of 1884, rewritten in the form of a law) lays down conditions for issuance of burial permits of local authorities and provides for ministerial ordinances to determine the circumstances under which the governor may permit the establishment of a graveyard, charnel house, or crematory, to prescribe the manner in which graveyard records are to be kept, and to regulate the use of cremation permits.

* Among the matters on the list are: the planning of the general development of the area and the execution of public works for the development of sources of energy and the conservation of natural resources, including afforestation and flood control; the maintenance of standards in certain matters such as education and public sanitation; the control and management of the police; the regulation of medical affairs;

ment in one or both of two ways: many of them deal with matters that could be left to independent local action; and many also assign to local governments the duty of participating in their execution and of defraying part of the necessary expenses. The origins of this system lie in a time of complete centralization, but the postwar era brought no significant change. In particular, assignments by national laws proliferated in the postwar years as welfare state ideas assumed greater importance and governmental functions increased.[6] To give a detailed picture of the resulting situation would require the discussion of dozens of such laws. This task, which was carried out in the Kambe Report, cannot be attempted within the scope of this introductory study. However, the amendment of the Local Autonomy Law in 1952 facilitated a survey of the situation by appending to the law lists of functions made obligatory on the various types of local entities and their organs by national laws.*

In considering the lists we must recall the two types of assignment known to the Local Autonomy Law as to its predecessors. One is usually called "entity delegation," the other "agency delegation." In the former case, the local entity passes a bylaw implementing the national law on which the assignment is based. In the case of "agency delegation," the national law imposes a function directly on an organ of the local entity —usually its chief executive—which then acts as "national agent."† The

---

labor regulations; licensing and regulation of business enterprises and examinations and licensing in general; inspection of products; liaison between municipalities and the central government; assistance in rationalization of the organization and management of municipalities; adjustment and arbitration among them; and establishment of standards for the execution of municipal functions. To all this is added an enumeration of matters with which the prefectures may deal to the extent to which it is recognized that management by cities, towns, and villages in general is inappropriate, but which the latter may manage nevertheless if they have the requisite size and capacity. These matters pertain, among other things, to high schools and other schools, to libraries, hospitals, transport and other municipal enterprises, and to the promotion of agriculture, forestry, and small- and medium-sized enterprises.

* Subsequent amendments added to the list.

† When Article 2 of the Local Autonomy Law states that an ordinary public body shall deal with affairs with which it was formerly charged by laws or ordinances, and with which it shall hereafter be charged by laws or Cabinet Orders, duly authorized by law, it refers to entity delegation. Article 148, in the chapter on the power of local executive organs, deals with agency delegation. Each delegation, whether of one type or the other, is based on a specific national law. It is well to recall that the Kambe Report recommended that agency delegation should be avoided. The local executive, acting as a national agent, is responsible to the national government, not to the local assembly or electorate. Nevertheless, Article 99 of the LAL provides that the assembly can request explanation and express opinions relating to the assignment.

local organ, acting as "national agent," is subject to national supervision in accordance with Articles 146 and 150 of the Local Autonomy Law. In subsequent chapters we shall deal with this aspect of the matter and also discuss the financial consequences of national assignment. Here we may only note that the national government usually carries only a part of the required finances. All of the delegations are unilateral—that is, the concurrence or agreement of the entity or agency to which a function is assigned is not required. A summary of the lists of laws appended to the Local Autonomy Law as of 1960 is given in Table 6. (For purposes of comparison the number of laws involved according to the original list of 1952 is given in parentheses.)

It will be noted that the prefectures, the prefectural governors, and the prefectural commissions are the object of a particularly great number of assignments. (Each law assigns, of course, not just one but a num-

TABLE 6

*Number of Laws Assigning Functions
to Local Entities or Their Executives*

Appended List No.	Functions Assigned to	Laws Involved	
		1960	*1952*
1	Prefectures	68	(36)
2	Cities	5	(7)
2 (1)	Cities, towns, and villages excluding those assigned under No. 2	49	(32)
3 (1)	Prefectural governors	210	(128)
3 (2)	Boards of education	25	(14)
3 (3)	Prefectural election administration committees	4	(4)
3 (4)	Pref. public safety commissions	5	(7)
3 (5)	Pref. labor commissions	2	(2)
3 (6) (old)	Pref. land commissions	–	(5)
4 (1)	City mayors	29	(21)
4 (2)	City, town, and village mayors excluding those under No. 4 (1)	63	(53)
4 (3)	City, town, and village boards of education	8	(6)
4 (4)	City, town, and village election administration committees	6	(6)
4 (5) (old)	City, town, and village public safety commissions	*	(6)
4 (5) (rev)	Agricultural committees	2	(–)
4 (6) (old)	City, town, and village land committees	–	(4)

* Abolished.

ber of tasks.) This fact explains to a large extent why the difference between the prewar and the postwar prefecture is less striking than one
might have anticipated. In theory, the prefecture changed from a semi-
autonomous body under the executive leadership of a national government official, supervised by the Home Minister, to a fully autonomous
body under the executive leadership of a locally elected and responsible
local official. Because of its dual character the old prefecture was, of
course, heavily engaged in national functions, and carried out limited
self-government functions on the side, as it were. One might have
thought that the change in character would be reflected in a reversal
of the volume of the work devoted to national and prefectural tasks—
that, in other words, the postwar prefecture would be engaged primarily
in independent prefectural functions, carrying out limited national functions on the side. In practice, most of the work of the governor is still
performed by him under the system of "agency delegation," and in regard to this work he is still under national control.

Municipal officials—down to village mayors—also find that most of
their activities are devoted to the execution of national laws, although
they do not find it easy to draw any line at all between assigned and
independent functions. The average citizen, of course, is even less in a
position to do so. The multitude of assignments blurs understanding of
the responsibilities of the various levels of government, and under such
circumstances intelligent civic interest becomes nearly impossible.

The assignment of national functions is not to be condemned in general. It would be uneconomical and otherwise impracticable to have
these functions carried out by an army of national officials blanketing
the country down to the last village, much as this may contribute to a
thorough separation of responsibilities. The idea that local entities and
their officials should cooperate in the administration of such laws as the
Statistics Law, House Registration Law, Passport Law, Alien Control
Order, and Health Insurance Law appears justified. A degree of national control or a nationally established basis for cooperation may well
be necessary for roads, rivers, and canals that extend beyond the boundaries of a single prefecture; and there are other cases in which the considerations requiring some control by a larger unit are not exclusively
geographical.[7]

Nevertheless, it is true that there are many areas of activity that are
occupied by national legislation and centrally controlled through the

assignment system without any clearly apparent need. Such national laws as the Hotel Business Law, Show Enterprise Law, Public Bath Law, Barber and Beautician Law, Cleaning Law, Slaughterhouse Law, and Waterworks Regulations, raise the question whether national regulations of the specific areas of activity and existing national controls are necessary in each case. In the following section, the existing situation is illustrated in regard to certain functions which elsewhere are frequently considered exclusively local in character.

A Few Illustrations

City planning and zoning may in general be considered municipal functions.* The basic law in this field in Japan is the City Planning Law, which dates back to 1919.[8] That law in turn had its antecedents in the Tokyo City Area Renovation Ordinance of 1888, the first Japanese regulation dealing comprehensively with problems of traffic, civil engineering, fire prevention, and urban hygiene. The central government at the time considered it naturally its own task to ensure that Tokyo lived up to its position as the imperial residence, the seat of the government, and the capital of the nation.† Thus a pattern was established: city planning was considered a national affair, to be initiated in areas of national importance and to be directed from above. Local participation consisted

---

* This is not meant to deny that certain circumstances may require the extension of national power into the area of city planning. In Japan, the need for rehabilitation of war-devastated cities led to the Special City Planning Law (Law No. 19 of 1946). This law was absorbed in 1954 by the Land Readjustment Law (Law No. 119). Recent development plans aiming at the dispersion of industry, the prevention of excessive population concentrations, the construction of industrial core cities in certain areas, the restriction of the land devoted to agriculture, and the alleviation of the differences in income levels between more advanced and less advanced areas are bound to affect city planning in some regions of Japan. (For a description of this type of city planning, carried out from a national point of view, see *Municipal Yearbook 1961*, pp. 226ff.) The motives here resemble those of the Town and Country Planning Acts of 1947 and 1954, and, to some extent, those of the Distribution of Industry Act of 1945 in Great Britain. The observations in this section apply only to ordinary city planning.

† One of the characteristics of city planning in Tokyo was from the beginning that certain areas were excluded from consideration. Thus the center of the city is occupied by the Imperial Palace and surrounded by a moat. In spite of the problems which this creates for Tokyo traffic, a change was not discussed until the late 1950's, and then proposals to move the palace to another area were quickly abandoned. In prewar days the military areas (such as the Yoyogi parade grounds) were also excluded from any planning efforts of the civilian authorities.

in the execution of the plan, which was assigned to the mayor as a national agent, and in a sharing of the expenses. During and after World War I industrialization expanded markedly and the population of industrial cities increased greatly. Japanese cities, most of which had developed from old castle towns, were ill-equipped for this influx, and the resulting problem was again considered a national one. The City Planning Law, then enacted and still in force, in its most important aspects thus followed in the footsteps of the 1888 ordinance.[9] It considers city planning a national and not a local function. The competent minister, at present the Minister of Construction, designates the areas in which city planning may be carried out. As of October 1955, all cities, 608 towns and 34 villages were so designated.[10] Designated localities are authorized to draft a city plan. A big city may have a City Planning Committee, usually directly under the mayor, and a staff of city planning experts, often in a separate division or section of the city administration. A smaller entity that lacks these facilities may rely entirely on the City Planning Section of the prefectural government for the drafting of a plan. But even a big city cannot proceed with its plan without the agreement of the governor. The final determination is made by the Minister of Construction, who obtains the advice of the City Planning Commission established in each prefecture as a national agency in accordance with a Cabinet Order. At least formally, the plan has to be approved by the Cabinet.* When the plan is approved, a national subsidy, amounting usually to 50 per cent, is given.[11] The remainder of the cost is to be borne in principle by the local entity concerned. Except in the case of larger cities, the work is usually carried out by the prefecture, which often receives a reimbursement of only half of the necessary expense from the local body which is the object of the plan, so that it actually subsidizes the city planning enterprise.

Many city officials are aware of the subordinate role assigned to them in the entire process. The Kambe Commission recommended that "city planning and city planning works should be municipal affairs to be autonomously decided on and executed by the municipalities." But al-

---

* The City Planning Law is an interesting example of legislative techniques used in prewar Japan. It covers its subject in 27 brief articles. (By comparison, the Land Readjustment Law of 1954 has 148 articles, most of them at least twice as long as the articles of the earlier law.) Details are covered by Cabinet Orders, for which no standards are set. Nor does the law provide any standards for denial or approval of a city plan.

though a basic revision of the City Planning Law has been under discussion for some time, the system established in 1919 is still in force.*

The lack of zoning in Japanese municipalities is rather conspicuous. In the first place, as of 1956 zones were established in only about one-third of the Japanese cities.[12] In the second place, where zones exist, enforcement is rather lax; it is not unusual to find a three-story wooden structure going up in an area where such buildings are specifically prohibited. In the third place, the original regulations prohibiting the establishment of factories in residential areas contained a big loophole: they applied only to work places with more than fifteen employees. However, much of Japanese industry consisted of small establishments—many of them used by large companies that farm work out to them—and these were allowed to mushroom in residential areas without hindrance. Noise, smoke, occasional explosions, and other hazards now plague many neighborhoods, and the degradation of residential environments continues.†

Zoning was put on a new legal basis in 1950 when the Building Standards Law was adopted.[13] According to it, zoning may be effected within city planning districts. The Minister of Construction, acting upon a request by the local entity concerned, may designate residential zones, commercial zones, quasi-industrial zones and industrial zones, as well as so-called special use areas and exclusive use areas within the zones.

---

* Recently the development of certain areas has been entrusted to development corporations established for this purpose with public funds. In Tokyo Metropolis, for example, the Metropolitan Corporation for Town Development is to create three satellite towns. In this case, ninety per cent of the funds came from the metropolitan government and the other ten per cent from the localities concerned. The corporation buys the land, builds roads and houses, and provides for industrial water, sewage, and other services. Another example is the Shinjuku Sub-Center Development Corporation, which is working to change the face of Tokyo's congested Shinjuku district.

† It was described in an editorial in the *Nippon Times* on November 10, 1953, as follows: "Time was when home in Tokyo meant a haven of quiet and a rest for jangled nerves.... Recently, however, an insidious change has been occurring.... A big taxi company, for instance, has moved into the Tameike residential district. ... Taxi drivers move in and out of the garage with a clashing of gears and exuberant blasts of the horn at all hours.... In the Ebisu residential district, a Japanese newsman who built a home three years ago found out the other day that his neighbor had sold the house next door to an industrious businessman whose noisy trade is to break up old cars to make spare parts. In another section it is a sawmill which moved into the midst of a group of peaceloving residents.... The most abhorrent of all the racket comes from the factories and plants which have mushroomed around schools and universities as well as hospitals."

In practice, the zoning plans of smaller cities are usually made upon their request by the prefectural City Planning Section. These plans consist only in a delineation of the various zones; the results of the designation of an area as a zone of one type or the other are fixed by the law, and no leeway is given for local variations.*

Slum clearance is regulated by a law dating back to 1927.[14] According to it, a city desiring slum clearance must apply to the Minister of Construction for designation of the slum clearance district and for approval of the methods to be used in executing the program. When new dwellings have been constructed, the Minister has to approve the "method of their management." In addition, the Minister may designate slum clearance districts on his own initiative; in effect, this amounts to an order to carry out the required improvements.

The centralistic aspects of the Slum Clearance Law may be explained by the time of its origin. But even postwar laws, enacted at a time when local self-government had become basic policy, have perpetuated the centralistic pattern with only minor qualifications. For instance, a Law for Promoting Construction of Fireproof Buildings was enacted in 1952. There is no gainsaying the national importance of the problem in Japan, where traditional building methods involve great hazards of conflagration. At the same time, one would think that matters which vary in each city—such as the location of the fire protection building belt—could be left to local control. But this is not the case. The designation of a fire protection belt is actually made by the Minister of Construction, who makes his decision after consultation not only with the local mayor but also with the prefectural governor and the director of the National Fire Defense Agency.[15]

In 1951 a Publicly Operated Housing Law was passed. Housing construction is to follow plans established every three years. The Minister

---

* The Building Standards Law, as its name indicates, also deals with matters other than zoning. It is interesting to note that governors and mayors are treated as national agents in the supervision of the building officials, whose appointment is obligatory for prefectures and voluntary for cities, towns, and villages. Some of the infringements on local autonomy contained in the original draft were eliminated by objections of the participating staff sections of SCAP, whose interest in self-government had been revived by the visit of the Shoup Mission. The original draft, for instance, allowed the Minister of Construction to designate zones on his own initiative without reference to a request of the local entities concerned.

of Construction sets uniform construction standards for public housing that is to be operated by the local entities; a Cabinet Order fixes the rent to be charged. The income level at which persons are eligible to apply for the lost-cost housing is prescribed by the law and implemented by a Cabinet Order. While the need for national subsidies may justify a degree of national supervision, the fact remains that the law takes most of the program out of the realm of local initiative and determination. The housing problem is an acute one, especially for low-income families, yet for years the national policy benefited primarily middle-class people.[16] By comparison there is the role played by the city in the large-scale public housing program carried out in Vienna after the First World War. There a local tax provided the money, a local agency was in charge of construction, and a local agency controlled renting policies.

With the tremendous increase in the number of cars over the last years, parking became a problem. The need for parking lots became obvious and the parking meter made its appearance. Cities were not allowed to act independently in this matter. A Parking Law, dealing with on-street and off-street parking, was passed by the Diet in 1957. An implementing ordinance of the Construction Ministry states where parking may be prohibited, how much may be charged as a maximum for each ten minutes of parking, the hours in which parking in parking lots may be free, when a building is of such a size that a parking lot has to be provided, how big a private parking lot must be and what equipment (e.g., for lighting) it must have.[17] All this leaves little leeway for the municipal by-law, which is still required to put the measure into effect in the various localities.*

The City Planning Law provides for city parks and greenbelts. In 1956 a City Park Law was passed to set standards for their establishment and management, including the equipment to be provided, the designs of buildings within the parks, and so forth.[18] The law is implemented by

---

* In September 1962 a law went into effect according to which a new car owner must prove that he has a garage or private parking area before he can register his vehicle. The enforcement ordinance specifies that the law shall apply to the 23 Tokyo wards, to Nagoya and Osaka, and to certain parts of Yokohama, Kyoto, and Kobe. The ordinance approved by the Cabinet spells out meticulously the areas of the latter cities which are excepted from its application. It is significant that not even such details are left to the determination of the local governments concerned, which in this case are Japan's largest cities.

an ordinance that spells out the standards in greater detail. Of course, local regulations must be consistent with the law; the passage of such local regulations must be reported to the Minister of Construction, and the same is true for the establishment or abolition of a park or change of the area of a city park. In addition, the Minister of Construction may ask for reports relating to the enforcement of the law, and he as well as the prefectural governor may make recommendations and give technical and administrative advice. The law authorizes the national government to aid financially in the establishment of new parks or the improvement of existing parks by way of a specific subsidy. Aside from the question whether it was necessary or desirable from the standpoint of local autonomy to provide for financial aid in this particular form, it should be noted that the controls are not limited to cases where aid is actually provided.

Enough may have been said to show that the central government still effectively controls many functions that could be considered municipal by any criterion—the degree of national or local interest, the degree of administrative ability required, or the existence of local diversities not offset by an overriding need for standardization.

In the case of functions that are only partly local in nature, the local citizen is even more at a loss to apportion the blame for an unsatisfactory situation. The Road Law, for instance, starts out quite understandably by dividing the roads into Class I National Roads, Class II National Roads, Prefectural Roads, and City, Town, and Village Roads.[19] Unfortunately, no clear-cut pattern of national, prefectural, and local responsibility arises out of this classification. The requirements for permits for construction and repair, the need for subsidies, and the concomitant system of supervision make it difficult to put the responsibility for action in this field on either the prefectural or local level of government. An example may be instructive.

In early 1962 there was much discussion about the need for banning large trucks from the congested Tokyo streets during the daytime hours. The Metropolitan Police Department favored a ban and drafted a policy to be enforced as of April 1962. At first the policy was approved by the Cabinet's ministerial council on traffic affairs. The Transportation Committee of the House of Councilors was then made the sounding board of the trucking companies, which were opposed to the ban. The Transportation Ministry sided with the opponents. The above-mentioned ministerial council thereupon changed its mind and reversed its previous approval of the policy. The National Police Agency and the Transportation Ministry were instructed to discuss ways of relaxing the controls, envisioned in the draft of the Metropolitan Police Department. (At the same meeting in March 1962 the enactment of the law requiring car owners to build garages, to which we referred in the last footnote, was agreed upon.) Needless to say, April came and passed without a solution to the problem. As the *Japan Times* observed in an editorial on March 4, 1962: "There are too many agencies with a finger in the traffic pie." A more intensive study would probably reveal that the degree to which the central government injects itself into the decision-making process in every field frequently hampers the development of bold policies to meet the problems of urbanization.

Local authorities perform most clearly a "proper function" in the sense of Japanese public law when they provide services and utilities to their citizens. The first local public enterprises—transport and gas and electricity supply—were set up in the latter part of the Meiji era. Between the wars local entities began operating housing, public baths, restaurants, markets, slaughterhouses, and other services. These, together with water supply, sewage disposal, hospitals, and sightseeing facilities, constitute the bulk of local public enterprises today. Occasionally local authorities also engage in ice-manufacturing, stone quarrying, and milk production and distribution. Recently the number of local public enterprises has shown a rather spectacular increase. In March 1960 it was 4,007; in March 1961 it had risen to 4,630.

The majority of these enterprises—4,508 out of 4,630—were owned and operated by municipalities, the rest—122 in number—by prefectures. Certain types are normally operated by one or the other level.* Thus,

---

* If the local public enterprise is to be established in an area which is larger than a single municipality, two or more of them may form a partial affairs association. When the area is larger than a prefecture, the problem is sometimes solved by establishing by law a public corporation. Thus the Water Resources Development Corporation was established by Law No. 218 of 1961 to develop the Tone River in the Kanto area and the Yodo River in the Kansai area. The participation of the prefectures concerned in planning the development is fairly restricted. Before the Prime Minister adopts the plan of the Water Resources Development Council, he must hear the opinions of the governors. Nevertheless, the prefectures as well as the affected municipalities have to cooperate in financing and executing the plan. The development is to serve various purposes such as power supply, water supply, and land improvement.

the supply of water for industry is usually a prefectural enterprise, and the supply of drinking water is usually provided by the municipality. But as of 1957 only 44 per cent of Japan's population was served by public water supply enterprises as compared to 95 per cent of the population in England, 90 per cent of the population in Germany, and 80 per cent of the population in the United States.

Sewage disposal services are even more limited in scope. As of 1957 only Tokyo Metropolis, 121 cities, and 17 towns provided such services, and only Tokyo and seven cities had modern disposal facilities. The facilities in Tokyo are far from adequate. Some 68.5 per cent of the inhabitants of the ward area have traditional style toilets. Until about 1949 the disposal of the collected nightsoil was no problem because farmers then used it as fertilizer. But with the recovery of the Japanese fertilizer industry, farmers switched to chemical fertilizers. In addition, the population increase and the improvements in diet doubled the amount of nightsoil to be disposed of between 1949 and 1958, and trebled it by 1961. As a temporary emergency measure, the metropolitan government began dumping excretion into the ocean off Oshima Island, using partly a fleet of wooden tankers, hired from the owners, and partly steel vessels, owned and operated by the metropolitan government. It hopes to abandon this operation in the near future. This requires, on the one hand, an expansion of the existing sewage disposal plants which now dispose of only 37 per cent of the total nightsoil. By 1973 nine such plants are to be completed. On the other hand the plan requires an increase in the number of households with flush toilets and an extension of the required sewage system which at present covers only 21.3 per cent of the ward area. By 1970 this coverage is to be extended to 80 per cent of the area and by 1973 the system is to cover the ward area in its entirety.

A related problem—and one on which Tokyo housewives are likely to be articulate—is that of garbage and trash disposal. The transition from the use of hand-pulled wooden carts to the use of trucks for the collection of garbage was completed only recently. At present about 80 per cent of the garbage is dumped into Tokyo Bay for reclamation purposes. But this operation is approaching the limits of its usefulness. For this reason new incineration plants are urgently needed. It is hoped that by the end of 1970 there will be enough plants of sufficient capacity to burn all the garbage in the ward area.*

* As the *Japan Times* stated in an editorial on February 18, 1962, these problems point up the imbalance between the progress in the standard of living in terms of

In Japan, the distribution of electricity lies in the hands of nine corporations established by law in 1948, each one of them serving a region of the country.* These companies also engage in the generation of electricity, but in this regard they have no monopoly. Local public enterprises may thus generate electricity and sell it to one of the nine corporations. In 1961, some 31 prefectures engaged in this type of local public enterprise; they operated 67 power stations,† and had 27 more under construction. Gas does not rank high as a source of energy in Japan, and the production and supply are largely in private hands; in 1961 only 17 cities owned and operated public gas works.

In the field of transportation, bus lines are the most common object of public enterprise. Fifty-two local entities—all of them on the municipal level except Tokyo Metropolis—operate their own bus lines. Side by side with them are 278 privately operated bus lines and nine operated by the Japan National Railways. Of the sixty tramway systems, those of Tokyo Metropolis and of fourteen cities were operated as local public enterprises; of the 157 local railroads four were operated by cities.

There are 786 local public hospitals, some of them operated by prefectures, others by municipalities; they provide less than a quarter of all hospital beds. Four hundred fifty-three slaughterhouses and 59 markets are local public enterprises. Fifty-five local authorities operate sightseeing facilities of one type or another, including ancient castles opened to the public, lodging houses, and toll roads.

---

individual consumption and in terms of public services. "People are able to buy more for themselves, but they are still lacking the basic services and facilities of a modern community." See also the series of articles by Gyo Hani, entitled "The City in Crisis" in various issues of the same newspaper in March 1962, and Tokyo Metropolitan Government, Bureau of Capital City Development, *City Planning, Tokyo* (1962), pp. 40ff.

* The nine regions are Hokkaido, Tohoku, Kanto, Chubu, Hokuriku, Kansai, Chugoku, Shikoku, and Kyushu. With the exception of the company for the Kanto area—called the Tokyo Electric Power Company—the corporations derive their names from the region which they service. They had their predecessors in nine companies, established in 1941, which absorbed the more than 300 electricity companies existing at the time.

† There are also a number of small private companies, producing electricity and selling it to the nine big electric power companies. In 1953 the Electric Power Development Company was founded, largely with governmental funds, to see to it that the supply of electricity meets the steadily increasing demand for it. By 1958 the capacity of the power stations constructed by this company came close to equaling the capacity of the prefectural power stations. See Karl Hax, *Japan, Wirtschaftsmacht des Fernen Ostens* (Cologne, 1961), p. 177; *Municipal Yearbook 1961*, p. 379.

Another area of public enterprise was opened up to local entities in 1948, when various laws authorized them to operate auto races, motorboat races, horse races, bicycle races, and lotteries. The purpose was not so much to provide for the recreational needs of the local citizens as to improve local finances by collecting entrance fees and betting proceeds. In 1958 there were 229 bicycle race enterprises, 155 horse race enterprises, 66 motorboat enterprises, 8 auto race enterprises, and 52 lotteries managed by local entities (including some managed by associations of local entities).

Until 1952, all local public enterprises were regulated by two different categories of laws. On the one hand, the laws dealing with a specific type of enterprise—for example, the Gas Enterprise Law or the Tramway Law—applied to public as well as to private enterprises. On the other hand, local public enterprises were subject also to the general laws dealing with the administration of local public entities, such as the Local Autonomy Law, the Local Finance Law, and the Local Public Service Law. But the management of public utilities differs from the general administration in various aspects. For example, it requires a different type and degree of expertise; it is supposed to cover its expenses by the income from its own operations, and for this reason different accounting procedures are appropriate; and because its employees are not public servants in the same sense as the officials in the general administration, there are differences in the field of labor relations. These differences were recognized in 1952 when the Local Public Enterprise Law was enacted.[20]

The law deals primarily with the organization and management of public enterprises for the supply of water, gas, and electricity, and for streetcars, local railroads, and other transport services. It applies to these enterprises automatically if they are of a certain size. Thus public water supply works with more than fifty employees, or gas, electricity, and industrial water supply works with more than thirty employees fall under the law. Only the financial provisions of the law apply to public enterprises that have more than twenty employees, but do not reach the size that would make the whole law applicable. Local entities that employ a smaller number of persons in a public enterprise or conduct a type of enterprise not normally encompassed by the law may make the law applicable by a local bylaw, which must be established in accordance with a Cabinet Order. Under the law, the local entity establishes a division in its administrative structure for the management of each public utility.* The day-by-day management is to be entrusted to an administrator who is appointed by the chief executive. The administrator has rather far-reaching powers, including the conclusion of labor contracts and other contracts, the acquisition and disposal of assets, and the levying of fares, fees, and charges. But certain matters, such as the preparation of the annual budget or the submission of pertinent bills to the assembly, are left in the hands of the chief executive, and in regard to others the administrator is subject to the control of the chief executive. Thus the need for efficient professional management is to be satisfied without encroaching on the ultimate responsibility of the chief executive for all aspects of the local administration. However, mayors are often fearful of the independence given to the administrator by the law. For this reason it is not uncommon to find that the mayor himself or the vice mayor heads the division in charge of public enterprises.

The accounts for public enterprises must be kept separate from the general account. The accounting methods also differ. Normally, the enterprises are to operate on a self-paying basis; but in certain instances—as when rehabilitation for disaster damages becomes necessary—funds may be transferred from the general account.

As far as the management of public utilities is concerned, the provisions of the Local Public Enterprise Law supersede the provisions of the more general laws regarding local administration. At the same time local public enterprises continue to be subject to the laws dealing with each type of enterprise. This has certain consequences for the freedom of local action. For example, when a city operates a tramway, it does not freely regulate the fare for passengers, the fee for luggage, the frequency of service, or the speed of the tramway. Because the management of a tramway—whether public or private—is subject to the provisions of the Tramway Law, the administrator in charge has to obtain the permission of the competent minister to regulate these and other matters of this kind.†

* But in practice two or more public utilities are often handled by the same division. Thus Akita City has a Waterworks and Gas Bureau, and, under it, a Gas Section. In Matsue City the Gas Section is a part of the Public Utilities Office.

† It should be noted that the locality also plays only a minor role when a utility is privately managed. The contact of a city with a private streetcar company operating within its boundaries, for instance, consists usually in its permission for the use of city roads, the levying of a fee for such use, and the collection of the fixed property tax. The prefecture has a similar position regarding the use of prefectural roads in the city and the collection of the enterprise tax. The main controls are administered in Tokyo.

A word should be added about the raising of the funds to develop or improve a local public enterprise. The normal method is the issuance of bonds. This requires the permission of the governor (in case of a municipality) or the Autonomy Minister (in case of a prefecture). With few exceptions, local authorities find it difficult to obtain funds from publicly subscribed bonds. These have also the disadvantage of high interest rates. To increase the volume of government funds available to local enterprises at comparatively lower interest rates, the Public Enterprise Financing Corporation was set up in 1957. Its capital consisted wholly of contributions from the government. The corporation issues corporation bonds and thus raises funds for financing its loans to public authorities. Most of the bonds are in the hands of banking institutions.

We may now return to the point that this section seeks to illustrate. National laws cover most areas of local action. As a result, local authorities would have little leeway to do things on their own even if they had sufficient finances. Responsibilities are blurred because in regard to most functions no single level of government is fully in control. It should be noted in closing that local regulations have occasionally developed in areas that are not occupied by national legislation. Thus, prefectural by-laws provide for inspection of prefectural products such as apples (in Aomori and Iwate), mulberries (in Akita, Chiba, Shizuoka, and Tottori), mustard (in Kanagawa), and tangerines (in Oita and Kumamoto); the exportation of fish caught in Lake Biwa is regulated by Shiga Prefecture, and the exportation of beef is regulated by Miyagi Prefecture. To make sure that their action would be *intra vires*, the prefectures in some cases attained an advance opinion from the Attorney General (now again called the Minister of Justice), who at the time could still offer an advisory opinion of the sort obtainable from his counterpart in the United States. He held that when a national regulation has been abolished because it was felt that further control by the state was no longer needed, the area has been vacated by the state and may now be occupied by local legislation. It is significant that in spite of this ruling the Autonomy Board was usually consulted before by-laws even in these areas were enacted.

The Recentralization of Police and Education

In Chapter 6 we noted that the two functions which the Occupation decentralized were those of police and education. Since then some changes in the opposite direction have occurred. If we remember the use made of the police and of the schools by prewar and wartime governments to establish a totalitarian regime, we shall readily understand why these changes were immediately seen as parts of a general "reverse course" and why they created a great deal of political unrest. In the field of education the change was brought about by the Law Concerning the Organization and Management of Local Educational Administration, which replaced the Board of Education Law in 1956.[21] The new law was primarily a step toward the recentralization of education, but it was also a part of the continuing fight of the government against the leftist Japan Teachers' Union (*Nikkyōsō*).* Members of the Union had frequently managed to get themselves elected to prefectural boards of education, and the government wanted to close to the union this avenue of influence over prefectural school administration. The union, on the other hand, had a particular stake in preserving the existing system. This antagonism increased the tensions accompanying the introduction of the bill. However, opposition came not only from that quarter. When the government's intentions of revising the educational system became known, ten of Japan's best-known educators—including the then President Yanaihara and former President Nambara of Tokyo University, President Ohama of Waseda University, President Abe of Gakushuin University, President Royama of Ochanomizu Women's College, and Professor Ouchi of Hosei University—issued a statement criticizing the policy and pointing out the dangers involved.

The bill itself had been foreshadowed by the recommendations of the Ordinance Review Committee and of the Local Systems Investigation Council. It was presented to the Diet by the then Minister of Education, Kiyose Ichiro, who had gained renown before the war as defense counsel for ultra-nationalists and who had defended General Tojo before the International Military Tribunal for the Far East after the war. During the Occupation he had been barred from public office under the purge. As Minister of Education he had publicly questioned the philosophy un-

---

* Earlier, in 1954, the Diet had enacted two laws, proposed by the Yoshida Cabinet, designed to curb the union. The first of these, an amendment to the Special Education Public Service Law, severely restricted the political activities of teachers. The second, the Temporary Law to Insure Observance of Political Neutrality in Compulsory Education Schools, made it punishable to use a teachers' association for the purpose of influencing teachers politically in regard to the instruction of their students. It was directly aimed at the leadership of the Japan Teachers' Union. The laws are No. 156 and 157 of 1954. For details, see Cecil Carter Brett, "Japan's New Education Laws," 23 *Far Eastern Survey* 174 (1954).

derlying the Fundamental Law of Education, pointing out that it neglected national consciousness, and, in particular, that it disregarded such traditional Japanese virtues as filial piety. In explaining the bill, Mr. Kiyose noted, of course, that the board of education system was "adopted somewhat hastily under the Occupation," and stressed that the new system was "more suitable to conditions in Japan today." These were the stock phrases of the "reverse course." As to the issue of centralization he stated: "There is need for an over-all national education setup. . . . The new legislation clarifies the lines of command in the educational structure; it defines anew the powers of the Ministry of Education and of the boards; it brings about some moderate changes that were regarded as necessary since education is an important factor in the future of our country."

The salient points of the law are the following: Members of boards of education are no longer directly elected, but appointed by the governor or mayor with the approval of the local assembly.* The same procedure can be used for dismissal of individual board members. The independence of the boards from the executive is weakened also in other ways. Up to 1956 a board—alone among the administrative commissions created during the Occupation—had the right to draw up a budget of its own, and if this differed from the budget of the chief executive, the board's draft budget had to be presented to the local assembly together with the budget proposal of the chief executive. Now the board's role in budget-making is merely consultative and advising. The superintendents of education are no longer freely appointed by the boards on the various levels. Instead, the appointment of a superintendent at the prefectural level now requires the approval of the Minister of Education, and the appointment of a superintendent on the municipal level requires the approval of the prefectural board.† The municipal boards

---

* Regarding the constitutional question raised by the new law, see Chapter 7, p. 126. The number of the prefectural board members is now five instead of seven. Municipal boards also have five members, but towns and villages may pass a by-law reducing that number to three.

† The superintendent on the municipal level is appointed from among the members of the municipal board. The composition of these boards has some interesting features: in 1960, 71.5 per cent of the total number of board members were over 50 years of age; 32.6 per cent were over 60 years of age. Some 44.6 per cent gave agriculture and fishery as their occupation, but 22 per cent had five years or more of teaching experience. (See Ministry of Education, *Education in Japan, Graphic Presentation,* 1961, p. 39.) In fact, many board members are retired teachers.

no longer have the right to hire and dismiss teachers; instead, this right is now given to the prefectural boards. While supervision of teachers remains a function of the municipal boards, the prefectural boards can give them directions regarding the supervision. Prefectural boards are also authorized in general to give "guidance, advice, and assistance" to the municipal boards. The influence of the Minister of Education is strengthened in a number of ways. We noted that his approval is required for the appointment of a prefectural superintendent of education. In addition, he may give "guidance, advice, and assistance" to both prefectural and municipal boards in a variety of matters including curricula and textbooks.* A companion bill authorized the Minister to request local executives to take necessary measures "if the management of actual administration by the board or superintendent is against the law or not proper for the purpose of education."

One of the aims of the law, as explained by the Minister of Education, Mr. Kiyose, was the establishment of political neutrality in the operation of the boards.[22] Provisions limiting the number of board members who may belong to the same party were retained from the former law. In addition, the law provides that board members may not be officials of any political association and may not be active in any political movement. However, the crux of the matter lies in the change in the system of selection of board members. It may be questioned whether political neutrality is actually ensured by appointment by a chief executive, who at least in the larger entities is connected with a party, and by confirmation by an assembly, which is equally political in composition in this case. But it became clear as soon as the new boards were established that the new system did in fact change their political composition. Since most local chief executives and assembly majorities are conservatives, most board members have conservative leanings and radicals are effectively barred from membership. These conservative boards also tend to be much more pliable to the "guidance, advice, and assistance" of the Ministry of Education.[23]

In the Diet the bill was strenuously opposed by the Socialists, and the

---

* Another bill, the School Textbook Bill, would have put the examination and approval of textbooks under the control of the Minister of Education in consultation with the School Textbooks Examination Council appointed by him. The above-mentioned statement of the ten educators also attacked this bill as an attempt to revive centralized control of education. The School Textbook Bill did not pass.

House of Councilors became the scene of riots which were subdued only after the police had been called in. The bill finally passed on June 30, 1956, and its main parts were enforced as of October 1 of that year.*

Since then the Ministry of Education has played an increasingly active role in the control of education. Thus in 1958 an amendment to the Enforcement Order to the School Education Law introduced a revised uniform curriculum for elementary and lower secondary schools. The Ministry instituted a system of efficiency ratings of teachers and a system of annual achievement tests of the pupils.†

Two further remarks should be made in conclusion. First, the strengthening of central controls over education should not be confused with a concentration or clarification of responsibilities; if anything, these have

---

* It is interesting to note the reaction of the various local government associations to the bill. The National Association of Prefectural Governors and the National Association of Prefectural Assembly Chairmen supported it as reinforcing prefectural control over the municipalities. The National Association of Town and Village Mayors and of Town and Village Assembly Chairmen also favored it, the former undoubtedly because the bill extended their control over the Boards, the latter for reasons that are less clear. The National Association of City Mayors liked the bill for the same reason as the Town and Village Mayors: they had smarted for some time under the "duality" of administration in the field of education and under the independence of the boards. Thus only the National Association of City Assembly Chairmen opposed the bill. See *Kōza chihō jichitai* (Kyoto, 1960), Vol. II, p. 124.

† Every one of these measures encountered violent opposition from the Japan Teachers' Union. A part of the curriculum revision was the reintroduction of moral education courses on a nationwide basis, based on a Ministry of Education Ordinance of September 1959. This was seen as an attempt to return to the traditionalistic indoctrination of the past. Officials of the Ministry who were to explain the new course to the teachers often ran into violence. The system of efficiency ratings by the school principals was seen as an attempt to drive a wedge between principals and teachers and to enlist the former in an effort to weed out teachers who were considered politically undesirable. (In this context the special allowance for principals appeared as a sort of bribe.) Even the achievement tests met with strong opposition when they were first administered in 1961, and as a result more than 1000 teachers were reprimanded, suspended, or discharged. In 1962 the Union instructed its local chapters not to offer further resistance. For details, see Daishiro Hidaka, "The Aftermath of Educational Reform," *Annals of the American Academy of Political and Social Science*, Vol. 308 (November 1956), pp. 140ff; and publications of the Ministry of Education, such as *Education in Japan, a Graphic Presentation* (Tokyo, 1961); *Education in 1960* (Tokyo, 1962); *Revised Curriculum in Japan for Elementary and Lower Secondary Schools* (Tokyo, 1960). An earlier attempt to reintroduce morals courses is described in R. P. Dore, "The Ethics of the New Japan," *Pacific Affairs*, XXV (June 1952), 147.

become more dispersed than they were before. For example, municipal boards establish and maintain public elementary and lower secondary schools, but the teachers of these schools are now appointed and paid by the prefectural boards. (Incidentally, half of the funds from which they are paid are provided by the national government.) The intricate system of supervision, guidance, advice, and assistance—only inadequately reflected in our sketchy outline of the law of 1956 and partly based on other laws, ordinances, or simply practiced without such bases—also diffuses responsibility. In spite of the increase in central control the present system is not monolithic. If seen in perspective, it lies somewhere in between the centralized system of prewar days and the decentralized system instituted by the Occupation.

The police system underwent a similar development. In June 1951 the Police Law was amended to permit towns and villages to abolish their own police and to put their ideas under the jurisdiction of the National Rural Police. Following the procedure of a local plebiscite, as provided in the amendment, all but 139 of the 1,318 towns and villages availed themselves of this means of saving expenses.[24] It will be recalled that Prime Minister Katayama's plan, rejected by SCAP, had limited the autonomous police to localities with more than 50,000 inhabitants. The establishment of an autonomous police in smaller units—down to those with 5,000 inhabitants—may well have been an excess of decentralization. If so, the error appeared to have been substantially rectified by the amendment of 1951.

But even while the amendment was still under discussion, the government revealed plans of considerably greater significance. The campaign of violence in which the Communist Party had increasingly engaged since 1949 was frequently cited in this connection. In April 1951 Prime Minister Yoshida declared that he planned to unify and centralize control over the National Rural Police, the autonomous police, the National Police Reserve, and the Maritime Safety Board. In the same year the Ordinance Review Committee—established after a statement of General Ridgway on May 3, 1951, had given the green light for a reconsideration of Occupation measures—proposed the establishment of a Public Security Ministry.[25] In 1953 the government presented to the Diet a bill aiming at the recentralization of the police. It ran into strong resistance from the opposition parties and the cities, which wanted to retain their police.

The independent press, including its more conservative segments, was antagonistic.* The government's attempt at recentralization proved abortive when the bill failed to pass prior to the dissolution of the Diet.

Undaunted, the government continued its efforts in the following session, backed this time by the recommendations of the Local Systems Investigation Council of October 1953.† On February 15, 1954, it submitted to the Diet a bill which followed these recommendations to some extent—for instance, in abolishing the existing dual system of national and autonomous police—but which had some additional features. Thus, the National Public Safety Commission was to continue, but without its former independence from the Cabinet; its chairman was to be a Cabinet minister. A National Police Agency, replacing the headquarters of the National Rural Police, was to carry out the national police functions of its predecessor and, in addition, was to control the prefectural police, which was to exercise its functions as assigned national functions. The head of the National Police Agency was to be appointed by the Prime Minister after hearing the opinion of the National Public Safety Commission. The Superintendent General of the Metropolitan Police Board of Tokyo, who was to be given a special status as in pre-Occupation Days, was to be appointed in the same manner. The other prefectural police chiefs were to be appointed by the head of the National Police Agency after consultation with the National Public Safety Commission.‡

According to the government, this scheme was intended to abolish the existing dual police system and to establish an "autonomous prefectural police" instead. This explanation, which disregarded, of course, the

---

* Thus the *Nippon Times* declared in an editorial of March 4, 1953, that it was "becoming increasingly clear that an attempt was being made to centralize authority under the pretext of 'correcting' Occupation-inspired measures." It applied to these attempts at "correction" the old Japanese saying about "killing the cow in order to straighten its horns," and, considering the Police Bill in connection with other measures then before the Diet, it warned that "democracy may perish, to be replaced by a highly centralized government which would enable unscrupulous leaders to establish a police state here once again."

† The Council recommended that the dual system of national and autonomous police be abolished and that prefectures and the five big cities be made the units of police administration; that the public safety commissions of these units be maintained, the rest dissolved; and that a central agency be established for purposes of liaison, adjustment of jurisdictions, training, investigations, and maintenance of communications facilities.

‡ It is interesting to note that consultation with the prefectural public safety commission or some other prefectural agency was not required.

strong controls which the central government was to exercise over the prefectural police, failed to allay widespread fears that the bill really aimed at reviving a police state in Japan. The opposition argued that the bill would jeopardize the political neutrality of the police, and, re-calling the frequent instances of police interference in prewar elections, it warned of the dire consequences of such a step. The opposition parties were not alone in appraising the bill in this manner. The conservative newspaper *Sangyo Keizai* stated in an editorial on January 12, 1954, that the government had failed to give sufficient reasons for the proposed re-vision of the police system, and that the real question was whether one wanted to pave the way to a police state or not. On February 17, 1954, the *Yomiuri* pointed out the "formidable evils which will result when the police authority is connected with politics." Prominent legal scholars expressed similar opinions.[26] The building of the National Association of City Mayors displayed streamers proclaiming "Keep the Police in the Hands of the People!" and "Oppose the Revival of the Police State!" Similar streamers spanned the main thoroughfares of the larger cities.

In the House of Representatives the bill was amended in some re-spects by an agreement among the conservative parties. Thus the provi-sion for the appointment of the head of the National Police Agency was changed. Instead of being appointed by the Prime Minister after con-sultation with the National Public Safety Commission, he was now to be appointed by the Commission with the consent of the Prime Min-ister. The power to appoint prefectural police chiefs was transferred from the head of the National Police Agency to the National Public Safety Commission, which had to obtain in each case the consent of the prefectural public safety commission, and, in the case of Tokyo, also the approval of the Prime Minister. Finally, the autonomous police of the five big cities were to be continued for a year. At the end of that year special provisions for the prefectures, in which the five big cities are located, were to come into force. The prefectural public safety commis-sions in these prefectures were to have five members, rather than three as in other prefectures. The additional two members were to be recom-mended by the mayor of the big city within the prefecture with the consent of the city assembly, but they were to be appointed, together with the other members of the commission, by the governor with the consent of the prefectural assembly. The rivalry between the five big cities and their prefectures had clearly led to a compromise.

The bill in this revised form was passed by the House of Representatives on May 15, 1954.* The opposition now aimed at preventing a final vote in the House of Councilors prior to the end of the Diet session. This session had already been extended on May 9, and it was again extended on May 22 and May 31. The government and the Liberal Party were determined to extend the session once more in order to push the bill through the upper house; the opposition was determined to prevent this. Prime Minister Yoshida hurriedly called off his trip to Washington and other Western capitals, which had been scheduled to start on June 4. On June 3, 1954, Socialist Diet members attempted to prevent the speaker from entering the chamber to announce once more an extension of the session. The police were called in, and the Speaker was thus enabled to reach the door of the chamber and to make his announcement with about one minute to spare. The upper house finally passed the bill on June 7, 1954, in the absence of the opposition (including not only the Socialists but also Hatoyama's conservative Democrats), which claimed that the extension of the session was illegal and that the session had actually ended on June 3. There was some discussion about bringing the matter of the constitutionality of the law to the courts, but in the end the issue of restoring the lost dignity of the Diet outweighed all others.† Amidst declarations of repentance from all quarters, the law went into effect. The decentralization of functions thus received its most serious setback

* The new law retains certain features of its predecessors. Thus the country is divided into regions encompassing a number of prefectures for purposes of central police administration. Special provisions apply to Hokkaido, which constitutes a region by itself. Hokkaido is divided into five police areas, each with an area headquarters under a chief who is appointed by the National Public Safety Commission with the consent of the prefectural (Hokkaido) Public Safety Commission. The Tokyo Public Safety Commission has five members. For further details see the official explanation of the new police law published in a special issue of *Toki no hōrei* (No. 139, July 10, 1954) and Tanaka Jiro, *Shinkeisatsu hō oyobi bōei nihō gaisetsu* (Tokyo, 1954). A convenient chart of the police organization is to be found in *Jiji Nenkan*, 1956, p. 203.

† The validity of the new Police Law was subsequently questioned in a suit against the governor of Osaka Prefecture which contested the inclusion of an item for police expenses in the prefectural budget. The plaintiffs argued that the law on which the budget item was based was invalid on two grounds: it was not passed in accordance with regular procedures and it violated the "principle of local autonomy" of the Constitution. The case was finally decided by the Supreme Court in March 1962. As noted in Chapter 7 (the footnote on pp. 121–22), the Supreme Court rejected the plaintiffs' contention.

in a field in which it had its most hopeful beginning and in which the political implications of recentralization were most clearly apparent.*

Summary

This chapter has shown that the allocation of functions to the various levels of government is exceedingly complex. It has done so primarily by reference to laws, however, and we may profitably look at the same problem once more from another angle. Let us assume that an inhabitant of one of Tokyo's wards, plagued by periodic water shortages, wants to find out who is responsible for this situation. Because he knows that there is a Division of Water Supply in the Bureau of Waterworks of the metropolitan administration and because he remembers some discussions on the problem in the Metropolitan Assembly, he is inclined to blame the metropolitan government. But then he comes across an item in his newspaper, such as the following (*Japan Times,* May 10, 1962): "Welfare Minister Hirokichi Nadao said at a cabinet meeting yesterday that if the prevalent dry weather continued the metropolitan water supply would be slashed to only two hours a day. Nadao said he would have to order a switch from the third to the fourth emergency step to lighten the city's water rationing." Is the responsibility then to be put at the doors of the Welfare Ministry? Is the Metropolis not involved? Perhaps, he thinks, the metropolitan administration is still to blame because it failed to enlarge the water reservoirs in order to avoid these recurring "emergencies"; after all, its table of organization shows a Construction Section that is charged with planning, designing, and the technical management of waterworks. But then, the Welfare Minister was also quoted as stating that "the current water reservoir expansion program would be expedited and completed by next March." Is he, and not the governor, responsible for this, too? (If so, our inquisitive citizen may wonder, why should he be concerned about the upcoming gubernatorial election?) Reference to the Local Autonomy Law is not fruitful. Article 2 mentions that it is part of the functions of local authorities "to establish and manage . . . reservoirs . . . and to regulate the rights to use them; to manage water plants and other water supply systems . . . and other services." But,

---

* The scenes of June 1954 were repeated in late 1958 when the Kishi government attempted to revise the Police Duties Law. In the end the government shelved the bill in order to reach an agreement with the opposition regarding the restoration of order in the Diet.

obviously this has to be taken with a grain of salt. So a more thorough study of laws, cabinet orders, and ministerial regulations becomes necessary before our citizen can begin to distribute his blame among central government agencies, the metropolitan administration, and, perhaps, the administration of his ward. (It appears that this ward is always more stringently rationed than others.)

To give another example, an inhabitant of the city of Nara finds that the police force is insufficient to cope with the heavy traffic. Control of the police, he knows, is a prefectural affair. But before he decides whether to criticize the governor or the prefectural Public Safety Commission, he reads (*Japan Times,* March 26, 1962) that Autonomy Minister Yasui Ken delivered a speech in Nara in which he revealed his plan to add 1,000 policemen to the existing force. Obviously, then, the prefecture does not have control over the size of its police forces. Has it no influence at all? These examples could be multiplied at will. Of course, few citizens will make the effort to untangle the jumble of responsibilities. Most find it easier to grumble in general terms about those in power, or to resign themselves to the situation with the comment "*Shikata ga nai*" (It can't be helped). Neither attitude permits the growth of an informed civic spirit.

In the last analysis, there are no clearcut local functions because the central government has, as the saying goes, "a finger in every pie." In the words of the Kambe Report: "In this country it has been considered the almost exclusive business of the State to judge what kind of function is needed and how it should be carried out, and the carrying out of such functions has been made obligatory upon the local public bodies by means of laws and orders and subsidies." Historically this is quite understandable. In an underdeveloped country setting out on a course of modernization—such as Japan in Meiji times—there are at first relatively few people with sufficient knowledge, training, and dedication to advance the new aims. These few work at the national level, and there they normally engage in a variety of tasks.* They determine what needs to be done, and when they assign tasks to others who are as yet less qualified, they naturally lack confidence in them and want to retain control through instructions, permits, inspections, and so forth. The dearth of qualified administrative personnel may thus justify centralization dur-

---

* The case of Yamagata Aritomo, mentioned in Chapter 2, is a good illustration of this point.

ing this initial period. The attitudes thus engendered, however, continue far beyond it.

In Japan these attitudes are reinforced by certain aspects of the traditional value system. The hierarchical notions that are so important in interpersonal relations are transferred to relations between levels of government. It is important to note that hierarchy in this case does not mean that there are levels of authority in regard to specific matters, as in modern organizations. It implies that the relations between higher and lower are not specific, but diffuse, so that those below are expected to defer in general to the wishes of those above, while the latter are expected to reciprocate by being benevolent to the former. A clearcut separation of functions goes against the grain of such a hierarchical relationship. This is especially true of any division of labor between the central government and the local authorities that permits the latter to proceed independently, without any reference to the central government. Centralization, attractive also for other reasons, accommodates these attitudes better than local self-government.

During the Occupation, centralization was to give way to the "principle of local autonomy." But dozens of laws reflecting the attitudes of the past remained on the statute books, and continued to foster these attitudes. A clear separation of functions and the establishment of some area of local independence might have led to a gradual change in them; but the reallocation of functions was not carried out.* Because of this failure even such tendencies toward local self-government as existed were thwarted. Since no scope of independent local activity was ever established, Article 94 of the new Constitution could not function as the guarantor of such a scope. The new dispensation would have required that certain activities be left free of national regulation and supervision. But existing attitudes, especially on the part of the national bureaucracy, militated against such self-restraint.†

---

* At the time of the Occupation not only the government but large segments of Japanese public opinion were somewhat lukewarm toward local self-government. The governments since then have continued in this attitude. However, post-Occupation developments in the fields of police and education indicate that in other circles the appreciation for the potential relevance of local autonomy to the defense against excessive political control from a single power center has considerably increased.

† The contradiction between the policy of local self-government and existing central controls is often explained away by the argument that, even under such a policy, the national government must protect the public welfare of the local inhabitants against the administrative and technical ineptitude, the potential corruptness, and the backwardness of their own local officials.

While a clear division of the activities of the various levels of government along the lines of functions is lacking, another division of work
does exist in actual practice. In many fields the national (and to some
extent the prefectural) government has comparatively little direct contact with the citizens. It controls the activities of the municipal governments, which then act as its line organs. The control is to a large degree
based on law, as we have shown. It is also based on the notion of a
hierarchical order of the various levels of government, which is embedded in administrative tradition. This notion is nurtured by laws that
establish control, and it influences the actual effect of laws that on their
face do not establish controls but only permit "guidance, advice and
assistance."* But not the least important source of national controls is
to be found in the financial dependence of the local entities, with which
we shall deal in the following chapter.

---

* Thus Dore writes: "The Minister of Education's powers to offer 'guidance, advice, and assistance' to local Education Committees (Boards of Education) are exercised in a constant stream of memoranda, outline curricula, and model sets of regulations, and these tend to carry an authority not very different from that of the
directives and regulations of pre-war days." (*Land Reform*, p. 320.)

CHAPTER 12

The Financial Dependence of Local Government

In this chapter we shall deal with questions such as the following: What are the sources of local revenue? How much local revenue is raised locally and how much is received from the central government? How free are the local authorities to find local revenue sources of their own and to determine the rates for taxes or other imposts? Under what conditions and in what form are funds received from the central government granted and apportioned? How much local revenue is expended on local projects and how much on work for the central government? The answers to such questions regarding local revenues and expenditures will throw light on the existing degree of local independence by helping us answer a more general question: How stable is the financial basis of Japanese local government?

The reader will recall that questions of this sort were asked and answered by the Shoup Mission. Finding the situation existing in 1949 and 1950 unsatisfactory, the Mission made detailed recommendations (briefly mentioned in Chapter 6), and so in discussing the present situation we shall show what has become of these recommendations in the intervening years.

We begin with a consideration of the sources of local revenue. Simply stated, these are local taxes; rents, fees and charges; local loans; and subsidies and grants from higher authorities. We shall discuss them in that order.

Local Taxes

Where local autonomy is the aim, local taxes should be the most important source of local revenue. A local entity able to finance its needs through local taxes does not require aid from the central government and thus can be independent from it. Where such independence exists, local citizens can hold their elected officials responsible for the quality of local services. If these services are insufficient in relation to the local tax burden, they can remedy the situation at the next election. If, on the other hand, local taxes are too low to make adequate services possible, the local citizenry will expect its representatives to take the necessary steps to increase the tax revenues and will sanction these steps, painful as this may be at times. But this is feasible only if local authorities are in control of local taxation.

What is the situation in this regard in Japan? How are local taxes determined? Who controls their rates? What portion of the local revenue do they yield? The answers to such questions will emerge from the description of the existing local tax system which follows.

The Local Autonomy Law states in Article 216 the principle that local entities may impose and collect taxes in accordance with the provisions of the law. The law that determines the types and standard rates of local taxes is the Local Tax Law, which, as passed in 1950, incorporated some of the recommendations of the Shoup Mission, including abolition of the last vestiges of the former surtax system (briefly described in Chapter 6).[1]

The local taxes are either prefectural or municipal taxes.* On both levels we have to distinguish between ordinary and special purpose taxes, the latter to be used for specific undertakings and to be levied on persons who stand to benefit from these undertakings. Within the category of ordinary taxes for each level, certain taxes are enumerated in the Local Tax Law. These are called legal ordinary taxes. The others, called extralegal ordinary taxes, are created by the prefecture or municipality with the approval of the national government.

We begin with a consideration of the prefectural taxes. The ordinary prefectural taxes enumerated in the Local Tax Law of 1950 were the newly created Value Added Tax, the Admission Tax, the Amusement, Eating, and Drinking Tax, the Automobile Tax, the Mine Lot Tax, the Fishing Right Tax, and the Hunter Tax. The Fishing Right Tax was abolished in 1952. In 1954 the Value Added Tax was replaced by the Enterprise Tax, and the Prefectural Inhabitants Tax, the Prefectural Tobacco Consumption Tax, and the Real Property Acquisition Tax

---

* Special provisions are made for Tokyo Metropolis, which collects both prefectural and municipal taxes. By bylaw, a part of these taxes may be delegated to the special wards, as noted in Chapter 9.

were instituted; also in that year prefectures were enabled to levy the Fixed Assets Tax—normally a municipal tax—under certain circumstances. The Admission Tax became in the main a so-called "refund tax" collected by the national government. But a part of it, named the Amusement Facilities Use Tax, remained a prefectural tax. The prefectural taxes according to the Local Tax Law in its present form are as follows:

I. Ordinary Taxes
   1. Legal Ordinary Taxes (Enterprise Tax, Prefectural Inhabitants Tax, Real Property Acquisition Tax, Prefectural Tobacco Consumption Tax, Amusement Facilities Use Tax, Eating and Drinking Tax, Automobile Tax, Mining Tax, Hunter Tax)
   2. Extralegal Ordinary Taxes

II. Special Purpose Taxes
   1. Light Oil Delivery Tax
   2. Water and Land Utilization Tax

As noted earlier, the Enterprise Tax is the successor of the Value Added Tax recommended by the Shoup Mission. The Value Added Tax in turn had replaced an earlier Enterprise Tax. However, the Value Added Tax had purposes not shared by either of the Enterprise Taxes. These purposes were connected with the lack of a general sales tax in Japan. A "turnover tax" or "circulation tax," introduced in 1948, proved unpopular. It was also difficult to enforce because enforcement depended upon the cooperation of the thousands of small retailers who conduct a major portion of Japan's domestic trade. For these reasons it was abandoned after a year. Shoup proposed the Value Added Tax as a new technique to avoid the cumulative burden of a sales tax on the various stages between the original sale by a manufacturer and the final sale by a retailer. The proposal aroused a great deal of controversy. Shoup was criticized because the Value Added Tax, designed to fit the specific needs of the Japanese taxation system, was not based on any existing foreign model, and thus had not proven its workability elsewhere—a reasoning that stands in sharp contrast to the attacks on other reforms as foreign importations.[2]

Nevertheless, Shoup's proposal was enacted as part of the Local Tax Law of 1950. The provisions for the Value Added Tax were originally scheduled to become effective for the fiscal year 1951–52. But their enforcement was postponed several times, and in 1954 they were struck from the statute books. Thus the Value Added Tax was stillborn.

The Local Tax Law of 1950 provided for the collection of an Enterprise Tax and a special Net Income Tax as a temporary measure to bridge the gap between the abolition of the Enterprise Tax in its earlier form and the enforcement of the Value Added Tax, planned for the following year. Both of these taxes were based on profit. In the case of the Enterprise Tax, the taxable profit was derived from business; in the case of the Special Net Income Tax it was derived from the profits of professional men such as lawyers, doctors, dentists, and public accountants. The rate of the Enterprise Tax differed for natural and juridical persons (corporations). Businesses and professions were subdivided into certain categories, and the tax rate depended on the category under which an activity fell.

The Enterprise Tax, as instituted in 1954, combined these two taxes and made the temporary arrangement, with certain changes, a permanent one.[3] The present law differentiates three categories of enterprises, and, within each category, enterprises of natural and juridical persons. The third of the categories corresponds largely to enterprises that had previously been the object of the Special Net Income Tax. As for corporations, special provisions apply on the one hand to corporations supplying electricity, gas, or local transport and to life and liability insurance services, and on the other hand to various other corporate enterprises. Certain enterprises—such as the Monopoly Corporation, the National Railways, the Telephone and Telegraph Corporation, as well as agricultural cooperatives and enterprises managed by local entities— are exempted from the tax. While the Enterprise Tax is a prefectural tax, it is levied by the prefectures on the basis of data prepared by the National Tax Offices for purposes of the income and corporation taxes.

The Prefectural Inhabitants Tax is also levied on individuals and corporations. Like the Municipal Inhabitants Tax, it is a hybrid tax, consisting partly of a per capita tax and partly of a percentage of the national Income and Corporation taxes paid in the preceding year. It was established—or rather re-established, as will be shown below in the discussion of the Municipal Inhabitants Tax—in 1954, following a recommendation of the Local System Investigation Council. Its re-establishment was a departure from two important principles of the Shoup Report. The Shoup Mission felt that the municipalities rather than the prefectures needed strengthening if local autonomy was to develop.[4] The Japanese government, on the other hand, was more concerned with strengthening the prefectures, which assumed their new police functions in 1954. It thus reduced the Municipal Inhabitants Tax in order to accommodate the new prefectural tax. The establishment of the Prefectural Inhabitants Tax also violated Shoup's principle of a clear-cut separation of taxes in terms of basis and collection. Now the Prefectural Inhabitants Tax and the Municipal Inhabitants Tax are levied on the same tax base and the municipalities collect not only their own tax but also the prefectural tax.* The cities, which had relied on the Inhabitants Tax for a minimum of certainty and stability, were naturally opposed to the change. The Socialists sided with them in the Diet debates. Defending Shoup's principles, they asserted that the new tax would confuse the tax structure, and contended that a national rather than a municipal tax should be diverted to the prefectures if they needed strengthening. The government, of course, had enough votes to push the bill through.[5]

The Real Property Acquisition Tax is another example of a tax which, having been repealed in consequence of the Shoup Report, was restored in 1954. Its restoration was not based on the recommendations of the Local System Investigation Council, which guided the drafters of the local tax reform of that year in other respects, but on a proposal made by the Autonomy Board. The proposal encountered stiff opposition from the construction industry and the Construction Ministry, which served as a spokesman for the industry's interests within the government. The law, as enacted, shows the marks of this clash: the standard rate, three per cent of the assessed market value of the property, is substantially lower than the rate of the earlier tax of the same name; and the exemptions of 10,000 yen for land, 50,000 yen for old buildings, and 100,000 yen for new buildings are somewhat more generous.

We noted that the Prefectural Inhabitants Tax constituted a departure from Shoup's principle of a clear-cut separation of taxes. In a sense this is true also for the Prefectural Tobacco Consumption Tax, because it, too, has a municipal counterpart. Its establishment in 1954 followed the recommendations of the Local System Investigation Council. Tobacco is a state monopoly in Japan, administered by the Japan Monopoly Corporation, and the profit derived from this monopoly has been an impor-

---

* Following Shoup's principle, Article 21 of the Local Tax Law stated before 1954 that prefectures shall not delegate the collection of their taxes to municipalities. Now an exception is made for the Inhabitants Tax.

tant part of the national revenue since 1898. Since 1954 the local entities—both prefectures and municipalities—levy a tax based on the Monopoly Corporation's tobacco sales to retailers within their areas. The rates, set in 1954, were $\frac{5}{115}$ for the prefectures and $\frac{10}{115}$ for the municipalities.* In 1956 these rates were changed to eight per cent and nine per cent respectively, and in 1958, when the municipalities were to be compensated for the loss of the Bicycle and Cart Taxes, the municipal rate was increased to eleven per cent.

The Amusement Facilities Use Tax is that portion of the Admission Tax that is still levied by the prefectures. The Admission Tax, paid by the visitors of theaters, movie houses, race courses, and similar establishments, became a prefectural tax in 1951 in accordance with one of Shoup's recommendations.† This was the beginning of a protracted controversy. The large cities argued that the tax should not be assigned to the prefectures, which collected it mainly in the cities and then used the receipts mainly for the benefit of the rural areas. The prefectures naturally wanted to keep the tax. In 1954 the national government settled the question by transferring the tax to the National Treasury, which was to distribute nine-tenths of the receipts to the prefectures in proportion to their population.[6] Since 1956 the total receipts from the Admission Tax go to the prefectures. They are allocated in a manner that takes the financial capabilities of the various prefectures into consideration: a certain sum is deducted from the amount for prefectures that show a surplus of revenue over expenditures, and this amount is allocated to less fortunate prefectures.[7] In effect, this puts the urbanized prefectures at a disadvantage. The campaign of the large cities has clearly backfired, for now the tax collected in the cities may be used not only in the rural areas of the same prefecture but also in other prefectures. The Admission Tax thus ceased to be a prefectural tax and became the first example of a so-called "refund tax" in the postwar tax structure—that is, a tax levied by the national government, the receipts

---

* This unlikely rate was the outcome of some pulling and hauling between various ministries. The Local System Investigation Council had envisioned rates of ten per cent and twenty per cent; the first government draft had cut this to five per cent and ten per cent. The Finance Ministry insisted on a further lowering of the rates to $\frac{5}{115}$ and $\frac{10}{115}$.

† Since 1948 it had been distributed by the national government to both levels of local government. One-third of the revenue went to the prefectures, two-thirds to the municipalities.

of which are wholly or in part earmarked as funds from which grants are made to local entities.[8] However, an exception was made for the admission to certain amusement facilities, including cabarets, dance halls, billiard and mah jongg parlors, golf courses, and the ubiquitous *pachinko* (slot machine) halls. The prefectures continue to impose a tax on the users of these facilities. This prefectural tax is the Amusement Facilities Use Tax.

The Eating and Drinking Tax has remained a prefectural tax. It is levied on the guests of bars, restaurants, geisha houses, and hotels, and withheld by the operators of these establishments.[*]

The Automobile Tax is levied on the owners of automobiles, trucks and busses. In 1958, when the municipalities lost the Bicycle and Cart Taxes, they were given the right to levy a tax on light motor vehicles (scooters, motorcycles, and automobiles with less than four wheels), but otherwise the Automobile Tax remained a prefectural tax.[†]

The Mine Lot Tax and the Hunter Tax also still exist as prefectural taxes, although the law in each case has undergone various amendments.

These, then are the legal ordinary prefectural taxes enumerated by the Local Tax Law. In addition, prefectures may also create by by-law so-called extralegal ordinary taxes, which are levied on items not enumerated in the Local Tax Law. Extralegal ordinary taxes were first provided for municipalities in the local tax system established in 1940. Of course, a municipality that wanted to levy a tax of its own devising had to obtain the approval of the central government authorities. In 1946 the authorization for extra-legal ordinary taxes was extended to the

---

[*] As noted in connection with the Admission Tax, it was planned in 1954 to make the Eating and Drinking Tax also a "refund tax." Many officials in the central government still favor this step for purposes of equalization. In 1957 the rates for certain elements of this tax—including the rate on payments to geisha houses—was reduced, apparently on the insistence of the conservative Liberal-Democratic Party. It might be mentioned that geisha houses are traditionally the location for conservative political palavers on all levels.

[†] Originally not only the state and other local public bodies but also the semi-governmental Monopoly Corporation and the National Railways were exempted from it, but in 1952 the latter exemption was dropped, indicating a willingness to restrict the scope of such exemptions. This tendency later found expression in a system of grants to local entities in which property belonging to the national government or to the semi-governmental corporations is located. We shall revert to this point later in this chapter.

prefectures, and in 1948, in the wake of the enactment of the Local Autonomy Law, the requirement of a prior permission was abolished. Instead, the local entities were merely required to report the establishment of new taxes to the Prime Minister, who was authorized to abrogate or alter the local bylaw in question on the basis of an investigation of the Local Finance Committee, then attached to his office. The importance of extralegal ordinary taxes increased in 1950 when, following the recommendations of the Shoup Mission, the number of local taxes actually enumerated in the Local Tax Law was drastically reduced.[*] To prevent excessive taxation of identical tax items by various levels of government, obstruction to the interchange of commodities among the local entities, and violations of the over-all national economic policy, the creation of extralegal ordinary taxes was made dependent on the advance approval of the Local Finance Commission. As was noted in Chapter 6, the Commission had then a certain independence from the central government and exercised a quasi-arbitral function in the settlement of national-prefectural-municipal fiscal relations.[9] But when the Local Autonomy Agency was reorganized in 1952, the authority to give advance permission for extralegal ordinary taxes was vested in the Chief of the Autonomy Board, a Minister of State.[10] The permit system that had existed prior to 1948 was thus essentially restored.[†] The most common objects of prefectural extralegal ordinary taxes are domestic animals, dogs, fruit trees, and gas wells.

Finally, there are the prefectural special purpose taxes. At present there are two: the Water and Land Utilization Tax, and the Light Oil Delivery Tax. The former tax has a counterpart on the municipal level, as noted below. It has the character of an assessment on landowners who benefit from improvements accomplished by public works of the taxing local entity. The special purpose is to pay for these public works. The law contains only an authorization to levy this tax; a bylaw, either prefectural or municipal, must be passed to implement this authorization. Apparently few prefectures are availing themselves of it. The Light

---

[*] In 1948 the Local Tax Law listed 21 legal ordinary taxes on the prefectural level; in 1951 it listed seven.

[†] The reorganization of the Local Autonomy Agency in 1952 will be discussed more fully in the next chapter. As noted there, the Autonomy Board became the Autonomy Ministry in 1960. Today the permission of the Autonomy Minister is required for the establishment of extralegal ordinary taxes.

Oil Delivery Tax was introduced in 1956.[11] Its purpose is to enable the prefectures to pay expenses for road building and repair and to give financial aid to other local entities for their road works. Prefectures in which big cities (as specified in Article 7 of the Road Law) are located must apportion a certain percentage of the tax to these cities. The cities in turn are required to use the apportioned revenue for roads within their area. The percentage is based on the ratio of the area of national and prefectural roads within the city to the area in the prefecture as a whole. The tax is levied on the transfer of specified light oil and of any oil used as automobile fuel (diesel oil), from manufacturers, importers, or their sales agents to retail dealers or consumers. It is levied on the person receiving delivery. The rate, originally 6,000 yen per kilolitre, was raised in 1957 to 9,000 yen, and stands today at 12,500 yen.

We now turn to municipal taxes. The principal legal ordinary taxes of cities, towns, and villages under the original Local Tax Law of 1950 were the Inhabitants Tax and the Fixed Assets (Municipal Property) Tax. Other ordinary legal taxes were levied on bicycles, carts, consumption of electricity and gas, mine products, timber trade, advertising, mineral baths and service girls (defined as geisha, dancers, and other persons similar thereto in their profession). Of these taxes, the Advertising Tax and the Service Girl Tax were abolished as legal ordinary taxes in 1952; and the Bicycle Tax and Cart Tax in 1958. The Mineral Bath Tax was converted into a municipal special purpose tax in 1957. To the remaining ordinary municipal taxes the Municipal Tobacco Consumption Tax, briefly mentioned above in connection with its prefectural counterpart, and the Light Vehicle Tax have to be added. As noted earlier, the latter tax was assigned to the municipalities when the Bicycle and Cart Taxes were abolished in 1958. Previously the tax on motorcycles, scooters, and similar light vehicles had been a part of the prefectural Automobile Tax.

There are also extralegal ordinary taxes and special purpose taxes on the municipal level. Thus the municipal taxes according to the Local Tax Law in its present form are the following:

I. Ordinary Taxes
  1. Legal Ordinary Taxes (Municipal Inhabitants Tax, Fixed Assets Tax, Light Motor Vehicle Tax, Municipal Tobacco Consumption Tax, Electricity and Gas Tax, Mine Product Tax, Timber Trade Tax)
  2. Extralegal Ordinary Taxes

II. Special Purpose Taxes
   1. City Planning Tax
   2. Water and Land Utilization Tax
   3. Common Facilities Tax
   4. National Health Insurance Tax

The Municipal Inhabitants Tax developed historically from a municipal surtax on a prefectural household rate (*kosuwari*). Taxation of the household rather than the individual was related to traditional principles of collective responsibility and to the traditional view of the family as the basic social unit. It was quite appropriate as long as the household, rather than the individual, was the unit of production in a largely agrarian Japan. But as population mobility increased, more and more individuals separated from their families and earned their livelihood independently. The government decided in 1921 to recognize the consequences, at least in the field of taxation, and to extend the tax to such persons. In 1926 the prefectural household rate was abolished in favor of a House Tax, but the municipal tax continued, still levied on the household and on persons who earned their livelihood independently. In the great tax reform of 1940, the tax became known as the Inhabitants Tax and was now levied on absentee landowners and on juridical persons as well. In September 1946 a Prefectural Inhabitants Tax was established. Shoup recommended that the Inhabitants Tax be reserved again to the municipalities, not only because he felt that their finances needed strengthening but also in order to compensate them for the loss of the Admission Tax to the prefectures. Thus the Local Tax Law of 1950 provided for the Inhabitants Tax only as a municipal tax. It was to be one of the main sources of municipal income. For the first time, references to the household were dropped and the tax was imposed on individual persons without any further qualifications. We know already that a Prefectural Inhabitants Tax was re-established in 1954, and that the Municipal Inhabitants Tax was lowered in the process. As noted earlier in connection with its prefectural counterpart, the Municipal Inhabitants Tax is a hybrid tax: it is partly a per capita tax and partly a tax on income. The per capita element of the municipal tax varies for both natural and juridical persons with the size of the municipality. The income element is in fact an addition to the national Income Tax.*

* We may note in passing that the Japan Monopoly Corporation and the Japan National Railways were exempted from this tax. We shall return later to the problem that this constituted.

The Fixed Assets Tax or Municipal Property Tax developed out of a surtax on the national Land Tax. The surtax was granted to the municipalities in the City Code and the Town and Village Code of 1888, and to the prefectures in the Prefectural Code of 1890. The Land Tax itself underwent various changes in 1919, 1926, 1931 and 1940.[12] In 1947 it became formally a prefectural tax (although prefectural tax collectors continued to depend on the assessment made by national tax officials). Municipalities continued to levy a surtax on the prefectural tax. Since land rentals were controlled, the estimated annual prewar rental value remained the base on which the tax was levied. The tax base thus being fixed, the tax rate was increased from time to time in an effort to keep step with the rising inflation. In 1949–50, for instance, the rate of the prefectural tax was 250 per cent, and the municipalities levied a surtax at the same rate. In spite of this, the tax supplied only a negligible amount of revenue.

This was the situation that Shoup encountered. Shoup was in favor of retaining a tax on dwellings—a traditional source of revenue for localities in most countries—and of adding a tax on commercial and industrial business establishments. He recommended that the new tax be based on capital value rather than on annual rental value, and that it be extended to depreciable assets of business enterprises such as machinery, vats, and ovens. Since the tax was to be levied not only on real estate and since, on the other hand, inventories were not to be included in the tax basis, the tax that he proposed was referred to as the "Fixed Assets Tax."* Shoup recommended that this tax should go in its entirety to cities, towns, and villages. One of the reasons for this was his conviction that the development of local autonomy required, above all, a strengthening of municipal finances. But there is a particular advantage in assigning a property tax to the municipal level: the property owners see clearly the connection between their tax payments and the benefits they receive in the form of police and fire protection and similar services. They are thus more likely to exhibit interest in the quality of their municipal government and to participate in municipal affairs than would otherwise be the case. For this reason, the municipalities were to be

---

* Connected with these proposals for widening the scope and changing the base of the tax was the proposal for the abolition of the Real Property Acquisition Tax. As noted earlier, the Real Property Acquisition Tax was reinstated in 1954. At the same time the standard rate for the Fixed Assets Tax, originally fixed at 1.6 per cent, was reduced to 1.5 per cent, and the original maximum rate of 3 per cent to 2.5 per cent. In 1955 the standard rate was further reduced to 1.4 per cent.

more than simply the recipients of the tax; they were to have, in the words of the Shoup Report, "entire responsibility for the tax." In order to assume this responsibility they were to recruit and train real estate assessors and to establish and keep the tax ledgers, showing the valuation put on every parcel of property on the basis of an annual inspection. Shoup believed that even smaller municipalities could do this successfully under certain circumstances. To ensure this, the Local Tax Law, passed subsequent to the Shoup Report, provided that the Local Finance Commission would prescribe the form of the various tax ledgers, maps, and other materials, used in the assessment of property, and would give technical assistance not only in regard to general method and procedure, but also in regard to the appraisal of specific properties. In certain cases, the Commission was authorized to make the appraisal itself. In other cases, in which equity demanded that the tax be distributed among a number of municipalities, it was authorized to make the necessary allocation.* The law also provided that the governor would give guidance and assistance to the municipalities in training the assessors, in using the material or procedures prepared by the Local Finance Commission, and in appraising specific properties in case of special difficulties.† The property ledgers were to be open to public inspection. In each municipality a Property Assessment Review Committee was to be established to decide complaints of taxpayers who found fault with entries in the ledgers. An appeal to the governor and recourse to the courts were made available against its decision. Taxpayers who found that the tax had been imposed on them erroneously or illegally were to be permitted to lodge objections with the mayor, against whose decisions they were to have an appeal to the governor and, ultimately, recourse to the courts.

In spite of all these safeguards, the Japanese government did not share Shoup's belief that even smaller municipalities would be able to administer the tax, especially when it came to large-scale depreciable assets. It was partly for this reason that municipal authority to levy the

---

* For example, when the asset to be taxed, such as rolling stock or electric generation facilities, was operating in more than one community or when the operation of a plant located in one community affected the economy and, especially, the public service expenditures of other communities.

† In keeping with the renewed emphasis on local self-government at the time, Article 402 stated that the authorizations to the Commission or the governor should not be interpreted as giving them the power to direct municipal tax officials.

tax on such assets was limited in 1954, and that the Fixed Asset Tax for assets exceeding a certain amount was transferred to the prefectures.[13] But perhaps a more important reason was the government's desire to strengthen the finance of the prefectures, which took over the police function in the same year. Shoup, who had given first priority to the strengthening of municipal finance, had designed the Fixed Assets Tax, above all others, to guarantee to the municipalities a considerable degree of independence and a comparatively high return. The partial transfer of this tax from the municipalities to the prefectures was a significant reversal of this policy.

We noted previously that the state, local public entities, and certain other juridical persons are exempted from the Municipal Inhabitants Tax. As for the Municipal Property Tax, not only were certain types of properties exempted because of their use—properties in public use by the state or local entities, cemeteries, forest preserves, private schools, etc.—but also all properties belonging to the state, to other local entities, and to the so-called "Three Big Public Corporations" (i.e., the Japan Monopoly Corporation, the Japan National Railways, and the Japan Broadcasting Corporation), regardless of the use to which they were put. The Local Tax Law, as passed in 1950, provided that a tax could be levied on the actual users of the latter properties in certain cases, but these provisions were abolished in 1951.[14] The exemptions, entailing a substantial loss for the municipalities, began to be felt as a problem, and a loosening of the exemption policy was being advocated. One step in this direction was made in 1953, when the scope of the exempted property of the public corporations was defined by Cabinet order. The matter then came under further consideration in 1956, involving this time also the property of the state and of local public entities, such as prefectural property located in a city. It was still considered inappropriate to subject these properties to a local tax, and this for two reasons: for one, it was argued that the local taxing power was granted by the state and thus could not be applied against it or any of its agencies; for another, it was considered inappropriate for the state and local entities at all levels to tax each other because they all shared the purpose of increasing the people's welfare. But it was not considered inappropriate for the state, the prefectures, other local entities, and the public corporations to reimburse the municipalities, on their request for the tax loss that the exemption entailed, in the form of grants. According to laws passed in 1956 and 1957 these grants or contributions—called *nōfukin* in the case of the public corporations and *kōfukin* in the case of the state and other local entities—are equivalent to the property tax.[15]

As mentioned earlier, the other municipal ordinary legal taxes are at present the municipal share of the Tobacco Consumption Tax, the taxes on gas and electricity consumption, on mine products, on the timber trade, and on light motor vehicles. Little need be said about these taxes except that the income derived from them has fluctuated with the changes in the Local Tax Law, which may increase or decrease the rate (as in the case of the Timber Trade Tax) or create new categories of exemptions (as in the case of the Gas and Electricity Consumption Tax).

Municipal extralegal taxes are levied primarily on dogs, on domestic animals in general or on certain types, on orchards, on sewing machines, musical instruments, and safes. Some municipalities tax the use of certain fixed assets (by a person other than the owner who pays the Fixed Asset Tax). Since the Advertising Tax and the Service Girl Tax ceased to be legal ordinary taxes in 1952, some municipalities levy them now as extralegal taxes. In 1955, there were 4,329 cases throughout Japan in which one or the other municipal extralegal tax was levied, but the number of municipalities involved was considerably smaller because some levied more than one extralegal tax. The imposition of these taxes requires a certain degree of local initiative. If we consider the number of municipalities and the variety of extralegal taxes, it becomes clear that only a small percentage of Japan's cities, towns, and villages showed the requisite initiative.*

Finally, municipalities levy special purpose taxes. They, as well as the prefectures, were authorized by the Local Tax Law of 1950 to impose a Water Utility and Land Profit Tax. In addition, municipalities may impose a Common Facilities Tax to meet expenses for common workshops, warehouses, collection depots, and other establishments of a similar nature which are used by only a part of the inhabitants (e.g., by those in one *buraku*). The tax is paid by those who benefit by the facilities in question.

---

* Kyoto City levies a Cultural Sightseeing Establishment Tax of 10 yen on the tourists visiting its castles, shrines, and temples. It uses the proceeds—about 80 million yen annually—partly for the maintenance of existing cultural establishments and partly for the construction of new ones, such as the modern and impressive Kyoto Municipal Assembly Center (Kyoto Kaikan).

In 1951 the National Health Insurance Tax was added to the Municipal Special Purpose Taxes. The National Health Insurance Law at first authorized cities, towns, and villages to join the national health insurance scheme, to administer it locally and, as part of this administration, to collect the premiums. To do so, they had to pass bylaws (which required the approval of the prefectural governor), set up a special account, and report the budget for this account and changes in the original budget to the governor. By 1960, 87 per cent of all municipalities had joined, and as of 1961 the administration of the scheme was made compulsory for all municipalities. In 1951, while participation was still voluntary, an amendment of the Local Tax Law converted the insurance premiums into a special purpose tax levied on the heads of the insured families. This tax continues under the compulsory system. It consists of a flat rate per household, a per capita component (which takes into account the number of persons in the household), an income component, and an asset component. When the revenue fails to meet 50 per cent of the expenditures for medical care benefits in a given year, the municipality may apply through the governor for a national subsidy.[16]

The City Planning Tax was re-established in 1956. It has a history dating back to 1919, the time of the establishment of the City Planning Law. At that time the tax was levied as a prefectural special purpose tax. When the Local Tax Law of 1950 created the Water Utility and Land Profit Tax, it was found that this tax overlapped to some extent with the City Planning Tax since one of its purposes was to pay the expenses for water utility works built in accordance with the City Planning Law. Consequently the City Planning Tax was abolished. But the need for city planning increased as "new cities" were created through mass amalgamations of towns and villages and as the movement into the urban areas continued. The affected cities needed additional tax resources. The argument was advanced that all persons benefiting from city planning—and not only those benefiting from specific water utility works—should be taxed in order to provide the requisite resources. Thus the City Planning Tax, as re-enacted in 1956, is levied on land and houses within city planning areas. The basis for this tax is the value of land or house as used for purposes of the Fixed Assets Tax; the maximum rate is 0.2 per cent. Property on which the Fixed Asset Tax is not levied—such as the property of the state or of other local entities—is also exempted from the City Planning Tax. Lastly, in 1957 the Mineral

Bath Tax was transformed from a legal ordinary tax into a special purpose tax on health and resort facilities.[17]

In the foregoing discussion of prefectural and municipal taxes, we have frequently referred to tax rates prescribed by the Local Tax Law. These rates are standard rates, and were not meant to be compulsory.* On the contrary, the Local Tax Law of 1950 stated specifically that these rates need not be applied, thus implementing the Shoup Mission's principle that local entities should be given power to raise or lower tax rates in response to the needs and desires of local electorates.[18] In spite of these legal provisions the standard rates were considered as virtually compulsory for some years. There were, of course, few entities that could afford a lowering of the rate; but even when such a lowering was feasible, the fear that it would be considered a sign of affluence and would affect national grants and subsidies was sufficient to prevent it. More frequently, the situation would have called for an increase above the standard rate; but such an increase would have had a negligible influence on the total size of the revenue, of which local taxes constituted only a rather minor portion. So, while the financial situation deteriorated, only a few local entities raised their rate above the standard rate. It seemed safer politically—both in relation to the local citizens and in relation to the national government—to levy the standard rate and, for the rest, rely on larger handouts from the national government. It was not until the national government started its plan for local finance reconstruction that the number of local entities charging more than the standard rate began to increase under the "guidance" of the central government.[19]

Other Local Revenue Sources

Little need be said about the other local revenue sources available to local entities according to the Local Autonomy Law. These are rents for the use of their property, fees (such as license fees and examination fees), and allotted charges for establishments benefiting only a part of the locality.† In case of emergency, they may impose statutory labor

---

* They were to be used, for instance, when the basic local revenue was calculated in order to determine the size of the Local Finance Equalization Grant or the Local Finance Distribution Tax to which the locality was entitled. Occasionally, a maximum rate is prescribed in addition to the standard rate.

† A typical example is the charge allotted to a *buraku* or *oaza* in connection with a small irrigation project for its exclusive benefit.

or levies in kind. Matters regarding these revenues must be provided for in local bylaws or regulations.[20]

Although according to the law statutory labor may be imposed only "when it is necessary for the recovery of emergency, disasters, and in other cases of special necessity," contributions by the inhabitants in terms of labor or money are rather common in rural Japan. Thus rural roads or ditches may be repaired by the cooperative labor of the people of a *buraku* or *oaza*, or a contribution in money may be collected for a new school building or for a piece of fire defense equipment. In some cases, the contributions in labor can be considered as a form of mutual aid within a face-to-face group. But the monetary contributions are usually a form of hidden taxation because they are voluntary in name only. The amount is frequently prescribed and collected on the basis of an assessment of the inhabitant's financial capacity, often leaving the contributor in doubt whether the demand is backed by any law or not. While only a small part of the contributions (usually 1 to 2 per cent of the total local revenue) appears in the local budget, the contributions actually constitute a fairly substantial portion of the local revenue. Shoup's estimate was 5 to 10 per cent and it is not likely that this percentage has diminished since then.[21]

Local entities also derive revenue from their public enterprises. Since this revenue goes into a special account and is used to sustain the enterprise from which it is derived, it need not concern us here. The exception is the revenue derived from horse races, bicycle races, automobile races, motorboat races, and lotteries, because these aim at making a profit that will be used for such general purposes of the local entities as the construction of schools or dwellings. As noted earlier, originally only prefectures and disaster-devastated municipalities named by the Local Finance Commission were permitted to hold lotteries. Subsequently, local entities were permitted on application to the Autonomy Board (which took over the functions of the Local Finance Commission) to operate the various types of races mentioned above.[22] This source of revenue has been objected to as immoral, and as leading to "boss rule," "fixing," and other fraudulent practices. Occasional riots have underlined the validity of some of these objections. But the argument carries little weight with the revenue-starved local entities, who are eager to avail themselves of the opportunity of increasing their revenue by entrance fees and betting proceeds. In February 1955 the

Cabinet decided not to approve any new applications, but the fact that this decision had to be reaffirmed in July 1958 attests to the continuing pressure on the part of local entities and perhaps also to a less than perfect implementation of the original Cabinet decision.*

Local Loans

By and large, the purpose of local loans is to allow local entities to undertake large works that they could not finance out of current revenue. These works will benefit future generations, and it is thought proper that those who benefit should contribute to the cost. Loans provide a method to accomplish this. These are the considerations on which the provisions of the Local Finance Law regarding local loans are based.[23] Article 5 of that law, which specifies the purposes for which local loans may be raised, mentions, for example, the establishment of public utility enterprises, disaster, emergency, and rehabilitation enterprises, and the construction of schools, roads, and harbors. A local entity may also raise a loan to enable it to convert an existing loan or to make an investment that will be beneficial in the future. In other words, loans for day-by-day operations are ruled out, as are loans to make up deficits. But as the financial situation of local government deteriorated this principle was frequently circumvented, obviously with the connivance of the central authorities whose permission was necessary. In 1955 the Law to Provide Special Measures to Promote Local Finance Reconstruction created a temporary exception from the principle for local entities with accumulated deficits. These were permitted to float loans for the elimination of the deficits and for the payment of retirement allowances, which were made necessary by the personnel reduction that was an important part of the reconstruction scheme (to be discussed later in this chapter).

Article 226 of the Local Autonomy Law states that "an ordinary local public body shall not require the permission of the competent administrative officer with respect to the raising of local bonds." A proviso, which is added, refers to Article 250, according to which the permission of the Autonomy Minister or the prefectural governor has to be obtained "for the time being" for the raising of loans and for changes in interest rates or modes of repayment unless the loan is a temporary

---

* However, an application of the governor of Tokyo for permission for a sweepstake-type lottery on baseball in order to raise funds for the 1964 Olympic Games was denied.

loan, to be repaid with the revenue of the same fiscal year. In spite of its apparent temporary character this provision in actuality supersedes the general rule of Article 226. Article 250 is implemented by Article 174 of the Cabinet Order concerning the Enforcement of the Local Autonomy Law and by a ministerial ordinance. According to these, prefectures and the five big cities have to obtain a loan permit from the Autonomy Minister, who must consult the Finance Minister in regard to loans exceeding five million yen. Permissions for loans of other local bodies are given by the governor.

Actual practice differs from this legal procedure in typical ways. Municipalities submit their applications to the governor, who consolidates them and sends them to the Autonomy Ministry for informal approval. Similar informal approval is also sought for all prefectural loans. Before giving its approval, the Autonomy Ministry consults the Finance Ministry even if the loan amounts to less than five million yen or if it is a municipal loan. Prior to this consultation, the Finance Ministry also collects applications for local loan permits from both prefectures and municipalities through its branch offices in the prefectures. When agreement between the Autonomy Ministry and the Finance Ministry is reached, the local entities are notified. It is only then that the resolution required by Article 226 of the Local Autonomy Law is adopted by the local assembly, that formal application for the loan is made, and that official permission is granted. Invariably the official permission is received long after the local entities have passed their first budget.[24]

The central government annually sets a limit for the total amount of local loans and issues permissions within that limit.* Applications for loan permits often run to three or four times the fixed total amount, and the competition for permits is therefore keen.

The role that the central government plays in the flotation of local loans is based to a large extent on the fact that it actually supplies most of the funds, either from the Finance Ministry—which largely explains the Ministry's extralegal participation in the permit procedure—or from the deposits of savings and life insurance and annuity premiums of the

---

* Shoup recommended that the limit be set in terms of debt interest rather than in terms of debt principal, so that each locality would be permitted to borrow as long as the annual interest charge did not exceed some stated percentage of its average operating budget. (*Shoup Mission Report*, Vol. I, p. 28). This advice was not followed.

Ministry of Postal Services. Few local entities have the financial capacity to enable them to obtain publicly subscribed funds. In 1960, only the local bonds of Tokyo Metropolis, of Osaka and Hyogo Prefectures, and of the cities of Osaka, Nagoya, Yokohama, Kyoto, and Kobe were issued through underwriting syndicates in the form of securities. Occasionally a prefecture places a loan with a private bank. But in most cases the central government is not only in the position of a supervising authority, but also in that of a creditor.

Proposals for diminishing the role of the central government in providing funds for local loans were advanced by the Kambe Commission and by the Local System Investigation Council. According to the recommendations of the Council, a Central Bank for Local Entities was to be established with capital provided in equal parts by the central government and by local governments. The central government was also to underwrite the loans that the bank would provide. But otherwise the bank was envisioned as a cooperative self-help organization of local entities. A move in this direction was made in 1957 with the passage of the Law to Finance Public Enterprises.[25] The Public Enterprise Finance Corporation, established by this law, serves the purpose of supplying local public enterprises with comparatively low-interest loans guaranteed by the state. But it is, in effect, another central government organ. The capital is furnished wholly by the central government; the Prime Minister and the Finance Minister approve the corporation's planning and, in general, supervise its activities; they also appoint its president and auditor, and their consent is required to the appointment of the members of the governing board. Since the corporation provides loans only to finance public enterprises, the funds of the central government, mentioned above, continue to be the main source of other local loans. Primarily for this reason, approval of such loans is considered a sort of national aid to needy localities. This finds reflection in the policy under which loans are approved. A poor local entity is likely to be given preference, although its capability to repay may be somewhat doubtful and although it may fritter the loan away in small amounts rather than invest it in a way that promises future returns. On the other hand, a comparatively wealthy local entity which needs the loan for some such investment and which is quite capable of repayment may find its request cut.

Along the same lines, it is noteworthy that the local loan level is often raised when partial subsidies for assigned functions are increased. In this case the increased subsidy has to be matched by the local entities, and more local loans are made available to them in order to enable them to do so. Of course, such loans do not give them any additional leeway in supplying locally felt needs.

Subsidies and Grants

There are a number of ways by which disbursements from the national treasury to local entities can be made. Each one differs from the other in the degree of local dependence that results. For example, a subsidy that is earmarked for a specific purpose invites greater dependence than a block grant to the general account of the local entity. A block grant can be used by the local government according to locally felt needs without further central government control; a specific subsidy, on the other hand, requires some supervision, if for no other purpose than to ensure that it is actually used for the function for which it was given. In practice, supervision is not usually kept to this minimum level. Another gauge of local dependence resulting from national subsidies and grants is the extent to which the support is given automatically on the basis of objective criteria. If the criteria are clear-cut and if their fulfillment assures support from the central government at a predetermined level, there is little or no place for behind-the-scenes maneuvering and little opportunity to bring political or personal considerations into play. A block grant, given more or less automatically on the basis of objective criteria, would thus seem to be the system that is most desirable from the standpoint of local independence.

In Japan, the matter of subsidies and grants is complicated by the fact that the functions of the various levels of government are not clearly separated. To compound the confusion, the Local Finance Law—which is the principal guide to national-local financial relations—does not deal with the question of the distribution of the cost of services from the viewpoint of proper, administrative, and assigned functions. Rather, it bases the distribution on the assumption that certain services are in the local or in the national interest, while others are partly in the national and partly in the local interest. The principle is that the level with the predominant interest in the matter has to provide for the necessary expenses in full, while expenses for matters of joint interest are to be borne jointly. Thus, according to Article 10-4, the expenses for affairs mainly related to the interests of the national government are to be borne wholly by the national government, even if these affairs are executed by local governments. Expenses for national elections, for compilation of statistics for the use of the national government, for land adjustment, and a number of other expenses are mentioned as examples. On the other hand, according to Article 9 of the Local Finance Law, expenses for affairs that are mainly in the interest of local entities are to be borne in full by these entities. A number of categories—including expenses for the assembly, personnel, fire defense, promotion of agriculture, industry, and public utilities—are then mentioned as examples. The most complex aspect of the picture is presented by affairs that are supposedly in a joint national-local interest. Expenses for these are to be "shared." Examples include important city planning enterprises and other public works as designated by national laws or Cabinet orders, disaster and epidemic prevention facilities, and facilities for juvenile welfare, health preservation, and certain types of relief. The proportion to which the expenses are to be borne by the national and the local governments is determined by the various laws and Cabinet orders that regulate each of these functions.[26]

Funds from the national treasury thus come to local governments for a number of reasons. They cover varying percentages of the cost. The term for all categories of funds from the national treasury is *kokkō shishutsukin.* Hundred-per-cent subsidies are to take care of expenses for functions that local entities carry out in the national interest. The funds for these expenses are referred to as trust expenses (*itakuhi*). Partial subsidies represent the national government's share in the expenses for functions that are considered to be in the joint national-local interest. The amount paid by the national government is called *futankin,* which is often translated as "national treasury share" or "national allotment."* Finally, there are subsidies given by the national government in support of affairs that are in the local interest. The term for these is *hōjōkin,* but this word is also often used in a non-technical sense for other types of national aid.

* Since prefectures also may delegate functions to cities, towns, and villages, and since some of these affairs are considered in joint prefectural and municipal interest, there are also similar prefectural allotments or shares.

It will be recalled that Shoup recommended that national functions should in most cases be carried out by national officials and that in these cases the hundred-per-cent subsidies should be discontinued. He objected to the theory of joint interest on which the "national treasury shares" are based, and suggested that all functions should be clearly allocated to one level and then carried out and paid for by that level. This suggestion was not put into practice, and the "sharing" of expenses continues with effects which may be illustrated as follows:

A national ministry secures passage of a law that assigns a new function, supposedly of joint national-local interest, to the local entities. The law determines the share of the expenses to be borne by the national government, and the local entities to which the function is assigned have to bear the remainder of the expenses. The Local Autonomy Law and the Local Finance Law provide that whenever the national government delegates its functions to local governments, it must take "necessary measures" to secure to them the required financial resources.* However, according to the prevailing interpretation, this does not mean that it must deliver any funds to them. Rather, the "measure" of the central government may consist in opening up new local tax sources or in increasing existing local tax rates.[27] Ultimately, the financial burden still falls on the local entities.[28] In other words, every law assigning a function to local entities foists on them not only new work—which may require additional personnel—but also an additional financial burden. It obligates them to commit local funds to tasks determined from above, instead of spending them on matters desired by the local authorities and

---

* LAL, Article 229, and Local Finance Law, Article 13. According to the latter provision the government's responsibility to take "necessary measures" may be enforced by dissatisfied local entities. They are permitted to send their opinion through the Cabinet to the Diet, which is then to serve as a sort of arbiter. In practice, such open clashes between the central and local governments do not occur. At least as far as the national government is concerned, another provision of the Local Finance Law is considered to be the solution to the problem. The Ministry that proposes a bill which would burden the local governments financially must consult the Autonomy Ministry in advance of presentation of the bill to the Cabinet. Also, when it presents a budget estimate involving "sharing" of expenses with local government to the Finance Ministry, it must afford the Autonomy Ministry the opportunity of expressing its opinion. Thus, the Autonomy Ministry becomes in theory the guarantor of the rights of local entities. However, this protection by a central government agency is quite different from the self-protection of the local entities against the central government as a whole which is envisioned by Article 13 of the Local Finance Law.

citizenry. One would expect that local officials would oppose this system. However, many of them are so used to carrying out primarily assigned functions with revenues from "above" that they find it difficult to envision a state of affairs in which their main task would be to carry out local projects with locally raised revenues. Their eyes are firmly fixed on obtaining more and greater national shares. The fact that their local entity may sink deeper and deeper into financial difficulties in striving to shoulder the remainder of the cost, and that no money may be left for independent work, is pushed into the background of their thinking.[29] After all, there's always the central government to fall back on for redemption. The effect of this on their sense of local responsibility needs no comment.

As for specific subsidies in the proper and more limited sense, Shoup did not object to the continuation of "promotional subsidies" to encourage local entities to undertake particular functions that they would otherwise not assume or to induce them to improve the quality of local services. But, with this exception, he wanted to replace all specific subsidies by a block grant called the Local Finance Equalization Grant. We mentioned in Chapter 6 that this grant was to replace the former Local Distribution Tax. It was designed not only to assure to local entities their minimum financial requirements year by year and to reduce national controls, but also, as the name indicates, to equalize the financial capabilities of local entities. The basic principles of the Local Finance Equalization Grant were simple. Each local body would submit data to the Local Finance Commission showing its basic financial need and its basic financial revenue. The basic financial need was to be determined by multiplying the units of service in each classification by the cost of each unit required to render local services at an acceptable level under standard conditions. Thus, to cite examples, the unit of service for bridge expenses was the area of bridges; for primary education expenses it was the number of pupils, classes, and primary schools; for labor expenses it was the number of factories and workers; for police expenses it was the number of police personnel, and for fire defense the total floor space of houses. The basic financial revenue was 70 per cent of the standard rates of the ordinary local taxes, as provided by the Local Tax Law. Where the basic revenue was below the basic need, the difference was to be covered by the grant. Ideally, the total of the grants to the individual local bodies was to be included by the government in the national budget.

As noted in Chapter 6, the Local Finance Equalization Grant Law was enacted in 1950.[30] In the fiscal year 1950 the number of subsidies dropped by slightly more than 30 per cent, and in 1951 another 14 per cent of all subsidies were transferred to the Local Finance Equalization Grant. But more than 170 different subsidies continued.[31] Since then new subsidies have been added, and items already covered by the grant have been separated and once again made the object of subsidies.[32] By 1957 the number of all types of treasury payments to local entities was about 600, most of them specific subsidies.*

One of the reasons for Shoup's desire to absorb most subsidies into the equalization grant was that they lend themselves easily to political favoritism. A block grant, computed on the basis of objective legal standards, makes such favoritism more difficult. It is interesting to note that in conferences with SCAP officials at the time of the drafting of the law, the Japanese participants argued with great tenacity for a division of the grant into a general and a special grant. The special grant, amounting

---

* Based on *Jichi ronshū*, Vol. VIII (1957), a special issue devoted to the subsidy system and entitled "Hōjōkin seidoron." As a result of this fragmentation, there were small villages that received as little as 600 yen for one governmental purpose or another. Dore states in *Land Reform in Japan* (p. 222) that "getting money from the government has, in Japanese villages, acquired something of the aspect of a national sport—like 'winning' an extra shirt from the quartermaster in the army—and an ability to channel such grants into his village is the most generally accepted criterion of successful statesmanship in a village mayor." With specific reference to the various subsidies administered by the Ministry of Agriculture and Forestry he observes: "Some of these schemes are the logical outcome of a considered government policy to improve agricultural productivity; some, particularly of the disaster-relief and damage-repair kind which inject hard cash straight into farmers' pockets, have more than one eye cocked to their vote-catching possibilities; some, though certainly justifiable in terms of improving productivity, are less the result of considered policy than of successful piecemeal empire-building on the part of agricultural officials—the spoils of victory in the annual bureaucratic struggle to increase the appropriations of one's own department; about a quarter were wished on the Government in the form of Private Members' Bills (which in Japan may contain financial provisions) by members, mostly of the government party, concerned with the particular interests of their constituents."

He then refers to the "appalling looseness and wastage in administration which prompts a recent report of the Administrative Control Agency to charge that 'an extremely high proportion of these grants in actual operation fall short of their intended effects.' " I do not disagree with his conclusion that in spite of this "these subsidies have undoubtedly done something to encourage agricultural improvements." The question is rather whether these improvements could not have been brought about through more orderly procedures that would be less pernicious to local autonomy.

to ten per cent of the total, was to be less rigidly controlled by legal standards. Finally a compromise was reached and the special grant was recognized in the law "for the fiscal years 1950 to 1952 only." But the special grant was not abolished in 1952; on the contrary, the law was revised so as to make the special grant, reduced to eight per cent of the total, a permanent feature.*

In the past, national grants had fluctuated year by year, depending on the demands of various national policies on the budget. Local entities had no guarantee that their minimum financial requirements would be met. The equalization grant was to change this. At first, Shoup considered making the total grant—that is, the aggregate of the excesses of basic local needs over basic local revenues—a primary charge on the budget. But later he decided not to press this rather drastic idea. Still, Article 3 of the Local Finance Equalization Grant Law in its original form stated unequivocally that "the national government shall each fiscal year . . . measure the financial need and the financial revenue of all local public bodies on the basis of data submitted by each of them, and shall include in the compilation of the national budget as grant the amount necessary and sufficient to cover the excess, if any, of the financial need over the financial revenue." This total excess was to be computed by the Local Finance Commission on the basis of data submitted by the local entities. If the Cabinet intended to appropriate in the national budget a grant of a lesser amount, it had to show how its calculations differed from those of the Commission.[33] The Diet was to serve as arbiter.

These safeguards proved ineffective even during the brief period in which the Commission had a semi-independent status. The grant in the Cabinet's budget draft and in the budget as passed by the Diet always fell short of its recommendation. Later the total grant was fixed in a manner that bore little resemblance to the procedures prescribed in the law. When the Autonomy Board drafted its annual Plan for Local Finance it included an estimate for the grant based on current local budgets, considering price increases and other circumstances. The Finance Ministry invariably cut the proposed national disbursements, in-

---

* Law No. 166 of 1952. In the same year the reorganized Autonomy Board took over the functions regarding computation and allocation of the grant, previously exercised by the semi-independent Local Finance Commission. The Commission became a mere advisory organ. Subsequently the special grant was reduced to six per cent.

cluding those for the grant. The resulting figure was then put into the Cabinet's budget draft and usually approved by the Diet. There was no reference to the total excess of basic local need over basic local revenue, as shown by local data. In May of every year, after the fiscal year had already started, the Autonomy Board issued regulations regarding unit costs (originally the idea was to fix them by law) and made a tentative distribution of a part of the grant. Further calculations, based on the data submitted by the local entities, led to adjustments in the distribution, which in turn required revisions of the various local budgets. Usually the cost for the units of service was calculated below the actual amounts, and the basic financial revenue above them.

The reason for this procedure lay in the priority given to the demands of national functions on the national budget. As before, the problem was "approached from the point of view of the national government in terms of its financial needs, resources, and administrative convenience."[34] Contrary to Shoup's recommendations, the total size of the grant remained dependent on the policies of the national government at a given time.

A device to put the total grant on a more stable basis was recommended by the Local System Investigation Council and adopted in an amendment of the Local Finance Equalization Grant Law in 1954.[35] The amendment changed the name of the law to Local Distribution Tax Law. As the new name indicates, the system instituted by this amendment, which is still in force today, is similar to the distribution tax system that preceded the equalization grant system. The total grant to be distributed now consists of a percentage of certain national taxes, namely, the National Income Tax, the Corporation Tax, and the Sake Tax. The percentage, which is determined by law, was originally 22 per cent; it was increased to 25 per cent in 1956, to 26 per cent in 1957, to 27.5 per cent in 1958, and to 28.5 per cent in 1959. As of this writing it stands at 28.9 per cent.

The switch to the new system was welcomed by the local entities because it put the total size of the grant on a more permanent basis. But this permanence is only relative. The grant fluctuates with the rate and yield of the three national taxes, and the local entities are bound to feel the effects of periods of national slumps or booms; also, there is no guarantee that the percentage of the taxes to be distributed will not be reduced again at some future time when the national government finds itself confronted with other pressing demands.

As far as the method of distribution of the total grant is concerned, the amendment of 1954 did not make any drastic changes. The division between general and special grants has been retained. The general local distribution tax (as the grant is now called) is still allocated basically under the old formula: Basic amount of financial needs less basic amount of financial reserve equals general local distribution tax.

The basic financial need for each item of service is determined by multiplying the units of service by the unit cost. An adjustment coefficient takes into account such factors as a decrease in unit cost in case of a greater number of units, or an increase in unit cost in case of larger areas to be serviced. The basic financial revenue is computed in the case of prefectures as 80 per cent of the local taxes at the standard rates of the Local Tax Law plus certain specified funds from the national government, such as the refunded Admission Tax, the Local Road Tax, and the Light Oil Delivery Tax. In the case of municipalities the computation is similar, but local taxes are included only to 70 per cent of their yield according to standard rates. Thus, the law bases the distribution of the general grant on fairly objective criteria. However, the fact that the total grant is no longer the aggregate of the excess of total needs over total revenues, but is pegged to an extraneous factor—a percentage of national taxes—throws its shadow over actual distribution procedures. These procedures continue along the lines described above. The data submitted by the local entities are often inflated to serve as better starting points for the negotiations with the Autonomy Ministry, which invariably trims the amounts applied for in order to keep the total within the prescribed percentage of the three national taxes. Because of these negotiations, the distribution procedures for the grant tend to resemble those for subsidies.[36]

A word should be added about the handling of the grant for cities, towns, and villages. The original law recognized that the interests of the prefectures and the municipalities were not identical. The cake to be distributed might be too small to satisfy everyone, and the prefectures as well as the municipalities might want to have as large a share as possible. Since the Local Finance Commission could not deal with every individual municipal application without previous screening, it was decided to channel them through the governors, who were permitted to express their opinion when they forwarded the applications to the Commission. In this case the mayor had to be notified and given a chance to defend his application.

Actually the municipalities (with the exception of the five big cities) bring their estimates to the prefectural government for inspection and amendment, or, in the case of towns and villages, for actual preparation of their application. The prefectural governor acts as assistant to the Autonomy Ministry,[37] and supposedly also as the benevolent guardian of the municipalities in his jurisdiction. Thus a measure designed to increase local independence now ties the prefecture more closely to the central government and makes the municipalities more dependent on the prefecture. The local distribution tax still serves purposes of equalization between wealthier and poorer entities.* As noted earlier, some of the "refund taxes" (which are not true local taxes, but national grants) are also used for these purposes.

Shoup's recommendation that the national treasury assume the full burden of disaster rehabilitation was followed only in the fiscal year 1950–51, and discarded thereafter. Since then the national treasury pays the entire cost of rehabilitation only when it amounts to more than twice the estimated ordinary tax revenue for the year. Otherwise it contributes either two-thirds or three-fourths of the cost, depending on the relation between rehabilitation cost and annual tax revenue.[38] Because this contribution does not apply to all rehabilitation expenses, the system prevailing before 1950, under which the national treasury paid two-thirds of the expenses, is being approximated in practice.

Locally Raised Revenue and Revenue from Other Sources

It is extremely difficult to obtain a picture of the degree to which Japan's local entities operate with locally raised revenues and the degree to which they have to rely on revenues received from other levels of government. There are annual fluctuations; prefectures and municipalities differ, and localities within each category differ even more. But to show the general order of magnitude of the two types of revenue sources we may consider the final account for 1959, given in Table 7.

We note that local taxes contributed 36.2 per cent to the total local revenue.† Another 7.4 per cent (income from property, allotted charges,

---

* Thus the prefectures of Osaka, Kyoto, and Kanagawa normally do not receive funds from this source.

† On the prefectural level, the Enterprise Tax is the most important source, followed by the Prefectural Inhabitants Tax; on the municipal level, the Fixed Assets Tax is the most important source, followed by the Municipal Inhabitants Tax.

TABLE 7

Composition of Local Revenue, 1959

Source of Revenue	Prefectures	Municipalities	Over-all
Local Taxes	28.9%	44.1%	36.2%
Refund Taxes	3.0	0.2	1.9
Local Distribution Tax	17.1	11.4	15.3
Other National Treasury Disbursements	31.0	12.5	24.4
Income from Property	1.2	3.6	2.2
Allotted Charges	1.1	0.8	0.6
Fees and Rents	3.5	3.5	3.6
Contributions	0.6	1.8	1.0
Carried Over	1.0	2.2	1.5
Miscellaneous Income	6.0	5.2	5.2
Local Loans	3.5	6.0	4.7
Brought Forward	3.1	3.7	3.4
Total	100.0%	100.0%	100.0%

SOURCE: Based on Autonomy Ministry, *Chihō zaiseijōkyō*, 1959; see also the Autonomy Ministry's pamphlet *The Local Finance System in Japan*, prepared for the 1961 EROPA Seminar.

fees and rents, and contributions) are also of local origin. Of the funds obtained from the national government, the Local Distribution Tax accounted for 15.3 per cent of the total local revenue, and refund taxes and other subsidies for 26.3 per cent. Together these two sources thus provided 41.6 per cent.

A major portion of the revenue with which local entities operate thus comes from "above." The more automatic and objective local distribution tax contributes less to that portion than the other types of national support. The national treasury supports local finance out of funds that come largely from the collection of national taxes. It is thus pertinent to inquire into the distribution of tax resources between the national government and the local governments. The national treasury collects about 70 per cent of the total tax revenue, and the local governments on both levels collect together about 30 per cent. But the national treasury expends ultimately only 34 per cent of that total, while the local entities are the ultimate spenders of 66 per cent. The difference between the local taxes and local expenditures is made up by the various treasury supports. In other words, if the expenditures are considered as given, the need for these supports is largely traceable to the distribution of tax resources.*

Local Expenditures

So far, we have dealt only with the question Where do local revenues come from? The relevance of this question to our purpose of assessing local financial independence is obvious. But it is also pertinent to the same purpose to ask: For what purposes are the revenues expended? Local independence involves a certain leeway for the local entities to determine what tasks they want to undertake and finance. This leeway defines the range of meaningful local policy making and thus the range of self-government. When expenses for assigned tasks preempt the available budget, such a leeway obviously does not exist.

The problem has to be viewed against the larger backdrop of the increasing need for governmental actions that accompanies the transition from an agrarian to an industrial society. Greater governmental integration—the shrinking of the sphere outside governmental consideration, which we described in Chapter 1 as the "vacuum of government"—affects both the national and the local level. As governmental functions expand, governmental expenditures rise. It is noteworthy that in postwar Japan governmental expenditures on the local level have increased more rapidly than those on the national level. The local entities spend slightly more each year out of their general accounts than the national government does out of its general account. Between 1953 and 1959 the ratio between the appropriations on the local level and those on the national level has rather steadily been about 1.1 to 1.[39] But this does not take into consideration that the various disbursements to local governments are included in the appropriation on the national level, while the funds are ultimately expended on the local level. If we adjust for this, we find that out of the total of the national and local general accounts the local entities ultimately spend about twice as much as the national government. Between 1953 and 1959 the ratio of their expenditures to actual national expenditures has fluctuated between a

---

* Direct national government expenditures in Japan are relatively low, in part because defense expenditures are relatively light. The percentages mentioned are taken from *The Local Finance System in Japan*, p. 9. See also Isomura and Hoshino, *Chihō jichi tokuhon*, p. 160.

low of 1.735 in 1953 and a high of 2.018 in 1957. Japan belongs to those countries in which the share of the local entities in the total governmental expenditures is higher than normal.[40]

This indicates that local entities exercise a large number of functions, but it leaves unanswered two questions of crucial significance to local autonomy: To what extent are these functions based on local initiative, and to what extent are the expenditures made from local sources? We know already that in Japan local functions increase largely, if not entirely, by government fiat. The national government, recognizing a need for governmental action, passes a law that requires local aid— including local financial aid—in the execution of the national policy. It assigns a new function and provides for a "sharing of expenses."*

We also know that much of the local revenue from which the expenditures are made does not come from local taxes. Japan, like Denmark, is in a category of countries in which local entities have a higher than normal share in the total governmental expenditure but derive a low percentage of their revenue from local taxes.[41]

Where functions are largely assigned and revenues come largely from above, most of the expenses are likely to be of an obligatory nature. It is not easy to find a distinction between obligatory and non-obligatory expenses in the public accounts.[42] But Local Finance Plans indicate that obligatory expenses account for 69 to 79 per cent of the total.[43] The allocation of local expenditures is shown in Table 8.

Summary

The Shoup Mission Report asked the question: Can Japan afford better local government? It answered the question in the affirmative.[44] But to obtain vigorous local government, the central government would have to take certain steps, including the provision of adequate and independent sources of local revenue "so that substance may be added to the form of local autonomy." The Shoup recommendations described the steps to be taken.

---

* An expansion of local functions based on local initiative is likely to be predicated on financial viability, and thus functions and finances are likely to be in balance. When the initiative comes from the top, this balance is easily upset. Demands may be made which exceed the capabilities of certain local entities. A "sharing of expenses," involving some matching of the national share by a local share, may still saddle these local entities with more expenses than they can sustain.

TABLE 8

Allocation of Local Expenditures, 1959

Expenditures	Prefectures	Municipalities	Over-all
Assembly	0.4%	1.8%	1.0%
Administrative offices	9.0	20.2	14.0
Police	7.0	—	4.3
Firefighting	0.5	3.4	1.7
Construction	18.6	12.2	16.1
Education	32.0	20.0	27.6
Social welfare and labor	8.4	13.8	10.7
Health and sanitation	1.8	3.5	2.4
Industry and commerce	12.5	9.0	10.3
Property	0.7	2.4	1.4
Statistical investigations	0.1	0.1	0.1
Elections	0.3	0.5	0.3
Miscellaneous	2.8	5.6	3.2
Loans	5.8	6.1	6.1
Appropriation preceding year	0.1	1.4	0.7
Total	100.0%	100.0%	100.0%

SOURCE: *Chihō zaisei no jōkyō,* 1959.

When Dr. Shoup submitted the report of his mission, he made it clear that the recommendations would have to be accepted in full if they were to prove workable:

What we are recommending here is a tax system, not a number of isolated measures having no connection with one another. All of the major recommendations, and many of the minor ones, are interconnected. If any of the major recommendations are eliminated, some of the others will thereby become of less value, or even harmful. Consequently, we disclaim responsibility for the results that may follow the adoption of only part of our recommendations.[45]

Upon receipt of the report, Prime Minister Yoshida stated in his letter to General MacArthur of September 15, 1949, that he realized that the recommendations were not to be accepted eclectically, but were to be taken as a whole if they were to serve as the basis for a rational and equitable tax system.

Nevertheless, the recommendations in the field of local finance were emasculated from the beginning. The reallocation of functions was not carried out; disaster relief was not fully absorbed by the national treasury; the borrowing procedures were not changed; and significant parts of the recommendations regarding subsidies and the equalization grant were not followed either in the implementing legislation or in actual practice. The commissions suggested by Shoup were considered a "nuisance" by the Japanese government; the staff assigned to them was numerically inadequate for the performance of their tasks, and their recommendations were consistently disregarded.[46] In time, even those parts of the program that had been adopted were progressively diluted or abandoned.

The fifties were years of crisis for local finance. Throughout this period expenditures increased, especially in the fields of education and social welfare. The number of employees and their salaries rose.* Revenues fell behind and the gap between revenues and expenditures became wider and wider. The term *akaji dantai,* "local entities in the red," came into frequent use in the official vocabulary. In 1951, 15 prefectures showed a deficit in one form or another; by 1952 their number had grown to 35 and in 1955 it was 36. In 1951, 142 cities were "in the red." The following year 205 of them, including four of the five biggest cities, found themselves in this position. And in 1955, four of the five biggest cities and 313 out of the remaining 487 cities showed a deficit. The corresponding figures for towns and villages were 600 in 1951 and 2,389 in 1952. In 1955 the number of "red letter towns and villages" dropped to 1,202, but this decrease was due to a large extent to the decrease in the number of towns and villages following the mass amalgamation wave, rather than to a reversal of the trend toward local deficits.[47] The total deficit actually increased by 6 billion yen during 1955, and this crisis led to adoption of the Law to Provide Special Measures for the Promotion of Local Finance Reconstruction.[48] Its primary aim was elimination of past deficits. For this purpose the flotation of Finance Reconstruction Bonds was authorized and national aid for interest payments was provided. The scheme also aimed at a reduction of expenses by personnel retrenchment. Local entities participating in it could be required to decrease the number of their administrative departments or sections, and prefectural Boards of Education could be required to decrease the number of school personnel in cities, towns,

---

* The increase in the number of employees cannot be accounted for by the growth of the population. The population of Japan rose from 64 million in 1930 to 89 million in 1955; the number of local government employees increased from 140,000 in 1933 to 1,370,000 in 1955.

and villages within their jurisdiction. To provide the funds for the severance payments to discharged employees, special Retirement Allowance Bonds were authorized.* The financial affairs of participating entities came under special controls by the central government, which were both more formal and more stringent than those normal in Japan.† Of course, the development of the Finance Reconstruction Plan for each local entity itself was subject to approval and qualifications by higher authorities.[49]

By May 1956, 596 local entities had applied. These included 18 prefectures, 171 cities, and 407 towns and villages. By April 1960, the number of cities under financial reconstruction had decreased to 152, and that of towns and villages to 328. The number of prefectures still stood at 18. In April 1961 further progress had been made: 16 prefectures, 126 cities, and 293 towns and villages were under "financial reconstruction." In 1962 the scheme applied to 8 prefectures, 104 cities, and 224 towns and villages.[50] The present favorable economic climate of Japan undoubtedly aided the progress of the scheme up to now; if it continues, reconstruction may well be completed according to plan in 1970.

The crisis of the early fifties was only a symptom—exacerbated by natural disasters in 1953, it is true—of a malaise that is inherent in the local finance system. Local finance reconstruction dealt only with the symptoms. The system remained unchanged.

This brings us back to the questions we posed at the beginning of this chapter. We have shown that, with the exception of the rather insignificant extralegal ordinary taxes—which require individual national sanction—all taxes available to local entities are prescribed by national

---

* The law thus provided exceptions to the Local Autonomy Law in regard to the administrative organization of local entities and to the Local Finance Law in regard to the permissible purposes of local loans. The emphasis on personnel retrenchment explains to a large extent the opposition against the law by the Teachers' Union, the local government employees, and the Socialist Party.

† When the Chief of the Autonomy Board found that the financial administration of a local entity was not in accord with the Reconstruction Plan, he could request suspension of excessive expenditures. When he found it necessary to change the original plan, he could request the local entity concerned to do so. But these "requests" had a particular force since he could stop supplying the national assistance for the payment of interest for the reconstruction loans if the requests were not heeded. Periodical reports by the local entities, investigations by the Autonomy Board, and general advice and assistance by the Board were also provided in the law.

laws. These laws also fix the standard rates and the exemptions, and local entities do not feel free to deviate from the legal standard rates. The local tax revenue is thus rather strictly controlled from above. But this control does not ensure fiscal stability: taxes, rates, and exemptions have been changed with bewildering frequency by national legislation. The local tax revenue is at the mercy of the national government from year to year. It is also so low that local entities cannot operate without funds from the national government.

The national government collects about 70 per cent of the total tax revenue. The remaining 30 per cent left to local taxation is clearly not enough to permit local entities to perform their various functions, most of which are affected in some way by a national interest. The situation could be rectified by assigning a greater percentage to local taxation, but the government opposes such financial decentralization. It prefers to keep its tax share and to make up the difference between local revenues and expenditures by shares, grants, and subsidies. These funds from above overshadow in importance the revenue from local taxation. Thus, to sum up, local taxes are not controlled by the local administration, and not being the main source of local revenue, they do not bear a significant relationship to the services which that administration can provide. Under these circumstances one can hardly expect the local citizenry to learn one of the first lessons in the primer of local autonomy, namely, that local officeholders are responsible for the local services that the citizens receive in exchange for their tax payments.

We have also shown that among the funds from the national government, those from specific subsidies outweigh those from the Local Distribution Tax, which is a block grant distributed on the basis of objective criteria. This is significant because the local official applying for a specific subsidy is cast in the role of a poor relation and the national official dispensing the subsidy takes the role of the rich but stingy relative.* The independence of local entities in general is likely to be

---

* The subsidy system has also political ramifications: as long as the national government is in conservative hands, the conservative candidate for local office plays the role of the favored nephew. He can plausibly claim that his relationship with those in power will result in bigger and better national subsidies for the locality, and that it is thus in the interest of the community to elect him rather than his progressive opponent. We shall discuss this influence of subsidies more fully in subsequent chapters.

impaired when they obtain a substantial portion of their revenue from national subsidies. If, in addition, hierarchical attitudes color national-local relations, as they definitely do in Japan, local entities are likely to feel that they are in no position to draw a line at which financial controls from above ought to stop. Central controls therefore tend to encompass all aspects of their financial management. Thus, a local entity that is heavily dependent on national subsidies will be afraid to expend any of its resources for other than obligatory functions without obtaining at least the tacit agreement of national authorities.

A look at local budget-making confirms the financial dependence of local entities. The original budget, computed by March 31, is simply a "skeleton budget," hardly more than an enlightened guess or a "wistful prayer," in the words of the authors of *Village Japan*.[51] The average local entity does not know the size of its operating budget until the various ministries of the central government decide on their subsidies and until the Autonomy Ministry determines its share in the Local Distribution Tax. The original budget—on both the revenue side and the expenditure side—undergoes constant revision in this process, and it is not uncommon for local entities to pass five, six, or even more supplementary budgets in the course of the fiscal year.[52] Since these adjustments are based on negotiations with central government agencies, the fact that the law does not require the formal approval of a national agency before the local budget becomes effective is rather insignificant. In the area of local finance, as in other areas, substance has yet to be added to the forms of local autonomy.

CHAPTER 13

Relations Between the Levels of Government

Local bodies, not being sovereign, are never fully independent from the national government, but the degree and the type of national control may vary. Two common types of control are legal (or judicial) control and administrative control. In the former case, the law specifies the powers of local entities and the powers of the national government to interfere with their actions; the limits thus set to each are enforced by the courts. In the latter case, a general grant of powers to local entities is coupled with a general power of the national executive to supervise the actions of local authorities.

The system of legal control is found in common law countries. Administrative control is relatively new there, and was accepted with hesitation and against much resistance. In these countries there exists a keen awareness that the problem of administrative control is one of limiting its extent and reducing the chances of its arbitrary exercise.[1] The national administrator therefore realizes that an attempt to exercise a greater degree of control than the lawmakers felt desirable will be thwarted by the local entities, who will take recourse to the law. This realization puts a certain constraint on an administrator's impatience with local authories who may not work with the high degree of efficiency that he may feel desirable.

In Japan it is not the system of administrative control but the limitation of that control by law that constitutes a relative innovation. The *daikan* of Tokugawa days worked under orders that gave him almost unlimited authority over his area, and the local officials of the early Meiji era governed under similar broad authorizations. Under the local government codes of the later Meiji era, the local entities had authority to deal with their own affairs, but the control powers of the government over them were still of a very general nature.*

The national bureaucracy thus has always played a role of great importance in Japanese local government. The traditionally low status of the law in Japanese society and the high standing of the persons whose place in society made it natural for them to "govern," the conviction that in the last analysis "governing" and not "public service" is the bureaucrat's business, the long-standing practice of receiving general authorizations and wide discretionary powers, and the absence of a set of values which holds that the less there is of government the better—all these tended to make the bureaucrat impatient of limitations, standards, and procedures that would cramp him in the carrying out of his task. His dedication to this task was not to be questioned. Today, too, the problem is not one of creating an efficient bureaucracy, but one of controlling it.

The bureaucracy held the power in the state virtually alone for some decades after the Restoration. In prewar Japan it was still one of a small number of groups contending for power. As other groups—the political parties, the Zaibatsu, the military—increased in importance early in this century, the story of Japanese politics became one of a succession of struggles and shifting alliances between them. War, defeat, and the Occupation weakened some of the contenders for power. The bureaucracy was hit by the purge and the civil service reforms, but in general its relative importance increased. In part this was natural because the Occupation utilized the bureaucracy for the exercise of its own authority, or, from the Japanese viewpoint, because the bureaucracy, having daily contact with Headquarters, stood between the Occupation and Japan. These circumstances were not auspicious for self-examination and self-denial among bureaucrats.

This does not mean that there are no new trends. In some agencies, experts of one sort or another constitute a new element. With their professional dedication to the programs of their agencies, they may in time become a counterbalance to the "general administrators" who are the core of the old bureaucracy. The relationship between bureaucrats and parliamentarians has improved; bureaucrats no longer contend with the

---

* For example, Article 2 of each of the Meiji local government codes specified that local entities were to perform their duties "under the supervision of the government."

politicians for political power, but try to obtain their policy aims through them.* And while the notion that the bureaucrat is a "public servant" may not have gained full acceptance, the notion of service to the public welfare seems to be replacing the notion of service to the state as personified by the Emperor. Whether these trends will create a climate more hospitable to local self-government is another question.

An eminent Japanese authority states that "the most characteristic feature of the Japanese local government system has been its bureaucratic tendency."[2] Indeed, so close has been the connection that hardly any treatise on the local government system that presents more than merely the legal framework can avoid dealing with the influence of the bureaucracy, and studies of the bureaucracy often deal also with the local government system.[3] This "bureaucratic tendency" may be apparent in the laws drafted and promoted by the bureaucracy—which may, for instance, prescribe a greater degree of administrative control than is required by the necessities of government in the twentieth century. But it may also be reflected in administrative practices that may in effect add to the central controls permitted by the laws.

In this chapter we shall investigate the mutual relations between national and local administrators in law and actuality. We must first trace briefly the development, after the dissolution of the Home Ministry, of the central government agencies primarily concerned with these relations.

Successors to the Home Ministry

The main functions of the Local Affairs Bureau of the defunct Home Ministry were divided into three categories: general local administrations, local finance, and elections. Functions of the first two categories that survived the amendment of the Local Autonomy Law in December 1947 were transferred to the Prime Minister. In the Prime Minister's Office general administration matters were handled by the Local Autonomy Section of the secretariat. A Local Finance Committee, also under the jurisdiction of the Prime Minister, executed some of the powers in the field of fiscal relations which the Local Autonomy Law and other laws vested in the Prime Minister,[4] but its primary purpose was to develop plans for putting local finance on a sound basis. Election manage-

---

* The fact that bureaucrats leave the bureaucracy to become party politicians is another aspect of this changing relationship.

ment, the third category of functions of the Home Ministry's Local Affairs Bureau, was divided. National elections came under the jurisdiction of a newly established National Election Administration Committee.[5] Local elections were administered by local Election Administration Committees in the various prefectures, cities, towns, and villages established in accordance with the Local Autonomy Law.

On June 1, 1949, the functions of the Local Autonomy Section and of the Local Finance Committee were combined, and the Local Autonomy Agency was established as an external organ of the Prime Minister's Office.* It was headed by a Minister of State. According to Article 3 of the Local Autonomy Agency Establishment Law, the agency was to facilitate liaison between the state and local bodies and among the local public bodies themselves, and to support the right of local autonomy "with a view to harmonizing the public interest of the state with the autonomy of the local public bodies." In this way it was to contribute "to the realization of the principle of local autonomy."[6]

If local self-government is seen as the result of a continuing struggle of local entities to achieve and maintain freedom from central control, this statement of the purpose of the agency is inconsistent. On the one hand, the agency was to champion local autonomy, which necessarily implies some independence from the central government. On the other hand, the agency was a part of the central government, and it participated to a significant degree in the exercise of central government control. But the officials of the agency, many of whom had formerly served in the Home Ministry, did not feel that they were laboring under a dilemma. Within a paternalistic framework of thought it appeared natural that a grant of autonomy to weak and backward local entities required a central government agency to guide them in its use, and to protect their interests at the central government level. The idea that they could protect themselves through the courts was not in keeping with traditional views about the status of the law, the courts, and the executive. The preference for administrative protection was the obverse side of the preference for administrative control.

The Shoup Mission recommended abolition of the Local Autonomy

---

* The name of the agency—Chihō Jichi Chō—is sometimes translated as Local Autonomy Board. In this study the title Local Autonomy Agency is used for the agency that existed prior to 1952, and the title Autonomy Board for its successor, the Jichi Chō.

Agency. The Local Finance Commission, which was to take its place, was to be an agency quite different in character. It was to concern itself only with the adjustment of fiscal relations between the various levels of government. To carry out this quasi-arbitral function, it was to have a substantial degree of independence from the Cabinet; and it was to be constituted so as to represent local interests adequately: three of its five members were to be appointed upon recommendation by the six national associations of local chief executives and local assembly chairmen.* The Local Autonomy Agency fought valiantly for its own life. In a memorandum submitted to SCAP's Government Section, it argued that a national organ was needed "to take care of the local public bodies," to protect them from "the arbitrary direction of the various ministries," and in general to represent the needs of local self-government at meetings of the Cabinet and of the Vice Ministers. In the end the Local Autonomy Agency was allowed to continue side by side with the Local Finance Commission, but only after a reorganization that trimmed its functions considerably.

The Local Finance Commission championed the interests of local entities in its recommendations for the Local Finance Equalization Grant and for the total loan limit. Since these recommendations were submitted to the Diet, they were useful to the advocates of local autonomy in that body, although they were sometimes also used by the opposition parties as a new stick with which to beat the government. Yet in the end the Cabinet was always able to avoid following the recommendations, and Shoup's high hopes for the Commission remained unfulfilled.

In May 1951 a statement by General Ridgway, who had succeeded General MacArthur, authorized the Japanese government to review measures introduced by the Occupation. The Ordinance Review Committee established for this purpose recommended that the Local Finance Commission and the National Election Administration Committee be combined with the Local Autonomy Agency. A similar recommendation

---

* The appointment by the Prime Minister required the consent of both houses of the Diet. The six associations are: the National Association of Prefectural Governors, the National Association of Chairmen of Prefectural Assemblies, the National Association of City Mayors, the National Association of Chairmen of City Assemblies, the National Association of Town and Village Mayors, and the National Association of Chairmen of Town and Village Assemblies. Regarding the legislative history of the Local Finance Committee Establishment Law, see Chapter 6, pp. 109ff.

was made in April 1952 by the Administrative Management Agency, a part of the Prime Minister's Office.[7]

These recommendations were put into practice after the Peace Treaty had come into effect. In August 1952, the Local Autonomy Agency was reorganized. It assumed functions regarding certain national elections, and to indicate that its functions were no longer all related to local government, it dropped the adjective "local" in its name. (We shall refer to the reorganized agency as the Autonomy Board.) In connection with the new tasks, an Election Bureau was established within the Autonomy Board and the newly created Central Election Administration Council was attached to it. This Council replaced the National Election Administration Committee, which had been in charge of national elections since the abolition of the Home Ministry. This arrangement continued after the Autonomy Board became the Autonomy Ministry in 1960.[8]

The Autonomy Board also took over the functions of the Local Finance Commission, which, renamed the Local Finance Council, became a mere advisory organ within the Board. In 1953 the Autonomy University, a training institute for local officials, was established as an adjunct to the Board.[9] The chart on page 306 shows graphically the dispersion and reunification of the functions originally exercised by the Local Affairs Bureau of the Home Ministry. It will be noted that the Autonomy Board combines again most of these functions.*

The officials of the Autonomy Board urged for some years that the Board be transformed into a full-fledged ministry, arguing that the enhanced status would enable them to protect local autonomy more effectively. They said, for example, that other ministries, which in their eagerness to implement their programs tended to disregard the adverse effect of added functions and expenses on the already overburdened local entities, would pay more heed to the protests of another ministry than to those of a mere board. In 1953 some newspapers reported that the Local System Investigation Council planned to recommend the reestablishment of the Home Ministry, to be called Naiseishō rather than Naimushō as in prewar days. But the Council's recommendations, submitted later in that year, mentioned only a "unified administrative organ of local administration in the central government, adjusting and absorbing the functions of the Autonomy Board"—an obvious avoidance of the still

* This is not to say, however, that the legal powers it exercises in regard to these functions are equal to those once wielded by the Local Affairs Bureau.

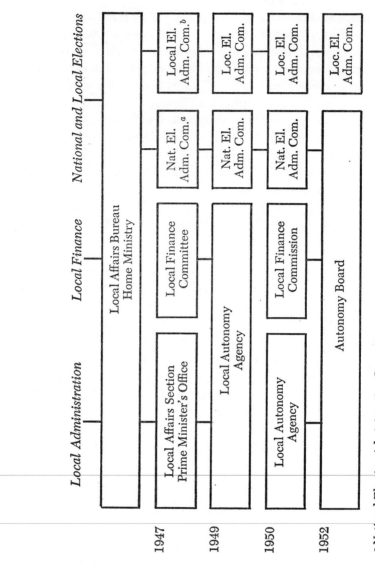

	Local Administration	Local Finance	National and Local Elections
		Local Affairs Bureau Home Ministry	
1947	Local Affairs Section Prime Minister's Office	Local Finance Committee	Nat. El. Adm. Com.[a] Local El. Adm. Com.[b]
1949	Local Autonomy Agency		Nat. El. Adm. Com. Loc. El. Adm. Com.
1950	Local Autonomy Agency	Local Finance Commission	Nat. El. Adm. Com. Loc. El. Adm. Com.
1952	Autonomy Board		Loc. El. Adm. Com.

[a] National Election Administration Committee.
[b] Local Election Administration Committee (on prefectural and municipal levels).

unpopular term "Home Ministry." A proposal for reestablishment of a Home Ministry—by combining the Autonomy Board and the Construction Ministry—was part of a wider plan for administrative reorganization developed by the Hatoyama Cabinet's Administrative Council in February 1956.* A somewhat watered down plan adopted by the Cabinet in March 1956 still envisioned the creation of a Home Ministry. But it was not until March 1960 that a bill transforming the Autonomy Board into a ministry was actually submitted to the Diet by the Kishi Cabinet. At the time, the ratification of the Japan-United States Security Treaty overshadowed all other political issues. When the bill was presented, the Socialists promptly charged that it was another step in recentralization, and, more particularly, that it aimed at preparing the central government for the suppression of opposition to the treaty. The treaty was passed by the House of Representatives on May 19 in the absence of the opposition, which had tried to prevent an extension of the session and had been forcibly ejected by police. From then on the main concern of the government was to keep the Diet in session for an additional thirty days. If it was successful in this, no further action would be required. According to Article 61 of the Constitution, the Treaty would then be considered approved by the Diet on the basis of its approval by the House of Representatives. It was this stormy Diet session, boycotted by the opposition, which in its last days passed a number of laws that otherwise would have aroused great controversy. Among them was the Amendment of the Law for the Establishment of the Autonomy Board.[10] The amendment, which changed the original law's title to "Law for the Establishment of the Autonomy Ministry," became effective July 1, 1960.

Most of the law spells out the various clauses in related laws in which "Autonomy Board" is to be changed to "Autonomy Ministry," and "Chief of the Autonomy Board" to "Autonomy Minister." The Autonomy Board, like its predecessor, the Local Autonomy Agency, was an external organ of the Prime Minister's Office and thus some of the functions of the Prime Minister were, in fact, exercised by the Chief of the Autonomy Board. Now the Autonomy Ministry has become independent of the

---

* On its face, this plan would have combined two of the main fuctions of the former Home Ministry but not the third, its control over the police. However, by this time a certain degree of national control over the police system had already been instituted. The unification of all three main functions of the old Home Ministry could thus be achieved by making the new Home Minister also Chairman of the National Public Safety Commission. The present use of this device will be discussed shortly.

Prime Minister's Office, and the law therefore transfers these functions to the Autonomy Minister.* These changes are of a more or less formal nature; but the law also contains a change of greater substance. It will be recalled that Fire Defense was decentralized under the Occupation. The National Fire Defense Agency, hitherto attached to the National Public Safety Commission and thus somewhat outside the direct command channels of the Cabinet, now became an external organ of the Autonomy Ministry. This approximates the prewar situation more closely than the previous arrangement. The Home Minister's control of the police was approximated, mutatis mutandis, by another method. As noted earlier, the Chairman of the National Public Safety Commission has been a Minister since 1954. It has now become customary to appoint the same person as Autonomy Minister and Chairman of the National Public Safety Commission, and thus to combine the controls over local government and over police by a sort of personal union. Only the Construction Ministry, once carved out of the Home Ministry, remains independent from its successor agency.

Just as its predecessors did, the Autonomy Ministry sees itself as the paternalistic protector of local entities against the attempts of other ministries to extend their control over local activities or to overburden them financially. At times it has actually performed such a buffer function. The motivation in such cases need not necessarily be sought in the Ministry's fervor for local independence; it may be found also in the Ministry's vested interest in remaining the predominant national agency in national-local relations, paralleling the former Home Ministry's interest in being the main channel of national controls. At times, the Ministry actually seems to have pressed for a lesser degree of centralization than that desired by other central agencies.†

The successors to the Home Ministry that we have mentioned have

---

* In the following reference is often made to laws passed before 1960. In these laws certain functions now exercised by the Autonomy Minister or Autonomy Ministry were attributed either to the Prime Minister or the Chief of the Autonomy Board or the Autonomy Board itself. I have retained this nomenclature and have refrained from adding the phrases "now the Autonomy Minister" or "now the Autonomy Ministry" in order to avoid their constant repetition. It is to be understood that in most cases the functions were, nevertheless, transferred as stated above.

† For an example, see the case of the Law for the Promotion of the Establishment of New Industrial Cities, mentioned in Chapter 9, pp. 183–84. A more detailed study of the legislative history of the law may well reveal the existence of a dual motivation for the Autonomy Ministry's position also in this case.

all drafted bills dealing directly with the local government system. Many of these proclaimed in their preambles that they aimed at the realization of the "principle of local autonomy." The true position of the drafters may best be ascertained by the degree to which these bills actually served their avowed aim—that is, by the degree to which they expanded or curtailed local independence. As an example we may consider the amendments of the Local Autonomy Law in 1952 and 1956.

Control and Guidance in Law and in Practice

General rules regarding the relations between the various levels of government are provided in Chapter X of Volume II of the Local Autonomy Law. In Chapter VII there are also special rules for supervision of local executive organs to whom national functions have been assigned.

Before the important revision of the Local Autonomy Law in 1952, Chapter X, consisting of six articles, was entitled "Supervision."* It provided that the Local Finance Commission or the governor may demand financial reports and make inspections and audits; that the Prime Minister (for prefectures) or the governors (for municipalities) may appoint provisional proxies for local chief executives and for local election administration committees after all locally available means of filling these positions had been exhausted; that "for the time being" the permission of the Local Finance Commission or a governor is required for the raising of loans; and that by-laws have to be reported to the Prime Minister or governor. Aside from the fact that the functions of the Local Finance Commission have been taken over by the Autonomy Minister, these provisions are still valid. Prior to 1952 they were, except for a few scattered and relatively unimportant rules for permits and approvals or notifications, the only general rules on the subject of intergovernmental relations. By and large, John Stuart Mill's principle that "power might be localized but knowledge must be centralized" was adhered to.[11]

In 1952 the title of Chapter X was changed to "Relations Between the State and Ordinary Public Bodies and Among Ordinary Local Public Bodies" and the chapter itself was expanded. The articles dealing with relations among local entities contain the provisions for cooperative arrangements among local entities which have been mentioned earlier in this study.[12] The amendment of 1952 also provided for the solution of disputes among local entities or among their organs by Autonomy Con-

---

* A seventh article was deleted by the amendment of December 1947.

flicts Mediating Committees on the national and prefectural levels. These committees are appointed by the Prime Minister or a governor, who may bring the disputes before the committees with or without a request of the parties. The mediation plans worked out by the committees become effective only if accepted by the parties. In 1956 new provisions were added to facilitate the exchange of personnel between levels of government and the dispatch of officials from one local entity to another at the latter's request. These arrangements will be discussed in the next chapter.

Here we are primarily interested in the provisions added in 1952 and 1956 regarding relations between the central government and the local entities. The proponents of these amendments denied any intention to recentralize in violation of the "principle of local autonomy" and claimed that the new provisions simply established a broader legal basis for the type of control which Japanese scholars frequently call "non-power control"; that the range of control remained limited; and that their aim was an efficient system of cooperation and not a system of dominance.* On their face, the provisions established in 1952 seem to substantiate this claim. Thus the Prime Minister and the governors are permitted to give technical assistance and advice to local entities for the rationalization of local organization and activities.[18] When necessary for this purpose, they may demand submission of material. (Similar authorizations are given to the various ministers and to prefectural commissions when they assign matters in their charge to local entities or to municipal commissions.) Technical assistance and advice based on a comprehensive inspection of the local entity in question may be requested by the local executive. These new rules facilitate a greater involvement of authorities on a higher level of government in local affairs, but they do not establish a system of controls.†

---

* "Non-power control" regarding local functions is distinguished from the "power control" that the ministries exercise regarding assigned national functions under Article 15 of the Government Organization Law and Articles 146, 150, and 151 of the LAL. As noted later, in the latter case the control may lead to direct execution of the function by the national government, removal of the local official from office, or suspension of a local action. No such sanctions are provided in Chapter X.

† It should be noted that intergovernmental relations are not exclusively regulated by the LAL. Thus a type of "power control"—a "direct disposition" by the Prime Minister, taking the place of an action by the governor—was provided for in the Law for the Promotion of the Amalgamation of Towns and Villages.

The provisions created in 1956 raise more serious questions. The first of these provisions is Article 246-2. According to it, the Prime Minister may request the local entity or its chief executive to take corrective action when he (the Prime Minister) finds that a local action violates laws or ordinances, or that there is "remarkable deficiency in the proper execution of duties" in regard to certain aspects of financial management or in other regards, or that the action is "clearly detrimental to the public interest." The same applies when he finds that the chief of a local entity clearly neglects the execution of local bylaws, assembly resolutions, or duties based on laws or ordinances. When the local entity involved is a municipality, the Prime Minister may act through the governor. In this case the mayor who objects to the governor's request may bring the matter before the Prime Minister and ask for his opinion.

It will be noted that the authority of the Prime Minister is not unlimited. He can act only in certain situations. However, he is allowed to determine whether such a situation exists and he may base his findings on such unclear criteria as "a clear detriment to the public interest." A violation of national policy may be the cause of his request—for instance, if the cause is a local action that violates laws and ordinances, or a neglect of duties imposed by national law.* But this is not necessarily the case. Article 246-2 is meant to come into play also in regard to purely local matters. Now whenever the issue is local, local autonomy would certainly mean that abuses are to be corrected not by intervention of the national government but by local action, either legal or political. This was the philosophy of the original Local Autonomy Law. The new provisions for national-local relations are clearly not in accord with that philosophy.

It is true that the Prime Minister or a governor can only "request" corrective action, and that the law does not provide a sanction for the failure of the local official to comply with the request. But in the context of actual power relations, this is less important than it may seem. When the relations between the levels of government are, in fact if not in law, those of superiors and subordinates, then the recommendations (provided for in 1952) or requests (provided for in 1956) are not easily disregarded, particularly if such disregard may have financial consequences.

* If the function in question is an assigned national function, the stronger measures of Articles 146 and 150, to be discussed later in this chapter, are at his disposal to assure implementation of national policy.

In other words, the difference between "recommendation," "request," and "instruction," and between "non-power control" and "power control," may be less than the terms suggest. A local executive will think twice before willingly incurring the disfavor of the central authorities by noncompliance, especially since conflict with the central government, even if animated by a desire to safeguard local independence, will not necessarily rally his constituency to him. Under these circumstances it is not enough to study the content of new legal enactments. It is equally important to inquire whether the new laws strengthen or lessen the feelings of subordination that play such an important role. Without any reference to this question the new provisions may sound plausible and innocuous. If they are considered within the context of existing formal and informal intergovernmental relations their centralizing effect becomes quite clear.*

In order to carry out his authority under Article 246-2, the Prime Minister is empowered by Article 246-3 to order the governor to investigate the affairs of a local entity whenever necessary to assure its proper functioning. Other investigations had been authorized prior to 1956. Thus, the affairs of the local entity may also be investigated through the governor at the behest of the Autonomy Minister in connection with his authority under Article 246 to inspect the financial management of local entities. Furthermore, other inspections and audits of local entities are carried out by various ministers or by the governors, either on the basis of laws and ordinances or in connection with subsidies granted to the local entities. Article 246-4—adopted in 1956—now allows a minister or a governor to use the Local Inspection Commissioners for this purpose. "Cooperation" and "efficiency" were given as the reasons for this, but the prize in terms of local autonomy may be a subtle change in the character of these local commissioners. An administrative commission

---

* It appears that the term "request" was chosen in Article 246-2 to denote a stronger duty of obedience than that implied by the term "advise," used for instance in Article 245-3. See Nagano, *Chikujō chihō jichihō* (4th ed., 1959), pp. 802 and 806. We noted that the mayor who has objections to the request of a governor may ask for the Prime Minister's opinion. He must do so within 21 days and the Prime Minister must communicate his opinion to both the governor and the mayor within 90 days. If the Prime Minister's opinion coincides with that of the governor, the mayor must adopt the measures for corrective action that were requested. This appeal procedure also indicates that the possibility of a simple disregard of the request by the objecting mayor was not within the lawmakers' intentions. A quasi-appeal was granted because of the essentially obligatory nature of the "request."

instituted for the purpose of control of the local administration in the interests of the local citizens, and thus given a certain independence from the administration—as shown by the requirement that the local assemblies consent to its appointment—is now assigned a national function and made subject to the control of national officials.*

These, then, are the general rules regarding the relations between the various levels of government set forth in Chapter X of the Local Autonomy Law. It will be noted that the opportunities for central government interference have proliferated since the original law was enacted. While the use of such words as "direction," "instruction," or "order" has been studiously avoided in deference to the "principle of local autonomy," Mill's principle has been progressively abandoned.

When the local entities or their executives carry out assigned national functions they are, naturally, more clearly subordinated to the national government. Special rules govern their relations in this case. Article 15 of the National Government Organization Law provides that "with respect to affairs under his charge each minister may direct and supervise the heads of local public entities in respect to national administrative affairs which they execute, as provided for in Article 150 of the Local Autonomy Law."[14] Article 150 of the Local Autonomy Law states the same thing from the viewpoint of the heads of local public entities. It provides that governors are subject to the direction and supervision of the competent minister, and that mayors are subject to the direction and supervision of the governor and the competent minister in regard to these national affairs. The problem raised by these provisions lies in the dual responsibility of the local chief executive. On the one hand he is a local official and his master is the local electorate. On the other hand, when carrying out assigned functions he acts as agent of the national government and is therefore responsible to it. To solve the conflicts that this situation may create, Article 16 of the National Government Organization Law permits the local chief executive to "make due representation" to the Prime Minister if he deems an order or direction by a minister to be "contrary to the principle of local autonomy." The Prime Minister serves as a sort of arbiter: he may direct the minister to revoke the order or he may let it stand.

Compliance with ministerial directives regarding assigned functions

---

* Significantly, when the inspection is carried out as an assigned function, the results do not have to be made public, as is otherwise the case.

may be enforced by a modified version of an Anglo-Saxon institution, the mandamus procedure. Article 146 of the Local Autonomy Law provides for it as follows: If a governor contravenes laws, ordinances, or dispositions of the minister in charge of the assigned function, or if he neglects the execution of his duties as a national agent, the minister may send him a formal order to perform, with a time limit for compliance. If this proves ineffective, the minister may request the High Court to issue a ruling to the governor.[15] If the High Court recognizes on the basis of a hearing that the request is justified, it issues the ruling, again fixing a time limit. If the governor fails to comply with this ruling and the High Court confirms this fact, the minister, after holding a hearing in the matter, may execute the matter in place of the recalcitrant governor and the Prime Minister may remove the governor from office. Appeals are possible all along the way. A similar procedure is provided for the control of mayors acting as national agents.*

It is obvious that this procedure is rather cumbersome. Yet more than a decade after the original enactment of the law and in spite of dozens of amendments in other regards, the provisions for this procedure remain unchanged. This is all the more remarkable since the protecting hand of the Occupation—whose influence may be seen behind the enactment of these provisions—was withdrawn long ago. It appears that the government does not find it worthwhile to bother to amend the procedure for two reasons: First, the problem at which the procedure aims —non-compliance with orders of the central government on the part of local executives executing assigned national functions—arises very rarely, and when it does arise there are other ways of keeping the recalcitrant official in line, so that up to this writing the mandamus procedures of Article 146 have had to be used only once.[16] Second, post-Occupation Japanese governments have aimed at more far-reaching changes in the relations between the governors and the central government than a mere amendment of Article 146. Thus, if according to some of their proposals

---

* Normally the eight High Courts do not function as courts of first instance. When, pursuant to the creation of the Autonomy Ministry in 1960, certain powers of the Prime Minister were transferred to the Autonomy Minister, the power to remove governors according to Article 146, paragraph 8, was not among them.

Regarding the mandamus procedure against mayors, see LAL, Article 146, paragraph 12. A mayor may be removed by the governor. The court involved in this case is the District Court.

the governors or chief executives of the newly established regions were to be appointed as national officials, they would come under the direct control of the central government and the mandamus procedure would become superfluous.

The paucity of the provisions for supervision in Chapter X of the Local Autonomy Law, as originally enacted, reflected the desire of the drafters to loosen controls where this was possible; Article 146 was to formalize and limit controls where they were essential. It will be noted that even since the expansion of Chapter X by the amendments of 1952 and 1956, the law continues to distinguish between the control of local entities in the case of performance of assigned national functions and their guidance in other cases. This distinction casts the local executive in two different roles in his relations with the national officials or their prefectural agents. But in practice these roles are not differentiated. Rather, the central government exercises very broad powers over the local entities in general, and the prefectural government has a similar position vis-à-vis the municipalities. The revisions of the Local Autonomy Law in 1952 and 1956 simply reinforced this situation.

The control is effected through a number of channels, some formalized, some informal, some official, some semi-official or unofficial. There are, for instance, the various types of notifications (*tsūtatsu*), to governors or division chiefs, issued by the Autonomy Ministry and the various ministries in charge of specific functions. They may be of a general nature, directed to all local entities of a certain type, or they may relate to specific cases and directed to the local entities concerned. A general notification may interpret a law for the local officials and may provide the procedures for carrying the new law into effect. But notifications may also relate to the receipt or use of subsidies by an individual entity or contain an instruction to report or to revise action in consequence of an audit or inspection. Notifications are, furthermore, the main means of exercising ministerial controls under Article 15 of the Government Organization Law and Article 150 of the Local Autonomy Law. In this case they have a clearly authoritative character. On the other hand, notifications that serve only for the guidance of local officials are, at least in theory, not binding; actions in violation are not illegal. The same is true of notifications that lack a legal basis, even if they are on their face authoritative in character. There are some court cases which make this quite clear.[17] But normally such questions of the legal basis or binding quality of a notification are not raised; the notification is obeyed as if it itself had legal force. The issuers of these notifications take full advantage of the situation: notifications supposedly interpreting the law may actually violate the stated intent or spirit of the law; and mere notifications may change established procedures and thereby affect substantive rights granted in the statute itself.* Little wonder that an illuminating article on this subject bears the suggestive title, "Administration by Law and Administration by Notification," and that another article discussing central-prefectural relations finds that there is little actual difference between the notifications a ministry issues to its subordinate local branch offices and those it addresses to prefectural governments.[18]

An informal channel for guidance is provided by the National Association of Governors. Ostensibly, this association of the 46 governors is completely independent from the national government. It functions as a pressure group vis-à-vis the Autonomy Ministry, the other ministries, and the Diet. But it is also used by the Cabinet to ensure the cooperation of the governors in the implementation of national policies. The meetings are ostensibly called by the association itself, but the press reports again and again that the Cabinet has just decided to hold a "gubernatorial conference" at a certain date.[19] In addition, the Autonomy Ministry calls prefectural division chiefs or section chiefs to Tokyo. Thus the meeting of the governors' association in July 1962 was followed within a few days by meetings of all chiefs of prefectural Local Affairs Sections and of all chiefs of prefectural Finance Sections. (Normally these sec-

---

* Under procedures established in April 1946, students could be registered and could vote in the locality in which they lived while attending school. On May 18, 1953, the Election Bureau of the Autonomy Board issued a notification that established new procedures. According to these, the students were to be registered for voting purposes in the locality where they had their permanent home and were to vote there. The political ramifications were obvious: students frequently vote for leftist parties; under the new dispensation many would be unable to vote or would have to vote where leftist votes are of less importance than in Tokyo, Kyoto, and the other urban centers where the universities are located. For these reasons the notification attracted much attention. The question of the legality of the notification was brought to the courts and the case was taken all the way to the Supreme Court. The Supreme Court decision of October 20, 1954, forced the Autonomy Board to reestablish the former procedures. This was done by a new notification dated the following day.

tions are part of the prefectural General Affairs Divisions; frequent ad hoc meetings in Tokyo for prefectural officials keep them in direct and continuous contact with other ministries as well.) Nationwide conferences of prefectural Board of Education members and of prefectural Superintendents of Education provide the Ministry of Education with a downward channel; similar conferences are held in Tokyo for public safety commissioners.

The guidance of municipalities is normally effected indirectly through the prefecture. The primary agency for their guidance is the Local Affairs Section, a part of the General Affairs Section of all prefectural governments. The guidance of towns and villages is effected through the Local Affairs Offices of the prefectures, which are established in the areas of the former *gun,* as noted in Chapter 8. Here again the national associations of local chief executives—which also serve pressure group functions upward—play a role as a downward channel. Thus the National Association of Town and Village Mayors is organized on a prefectural basis and, within the prefectures, on a *gun* basis. The Association of Town and Village Mayors within a *gun* is constituted of all mayors within the jurisdictional area of a prefectural Local Affairs Office. The prefectural association holds a monthly meeting attended by representatives of all *gun* associations at the seat of the prefectural government. Here prefectural policy on a wide range of problems is communicated to the assembled mayors. Somewhat later in the month each *gun* association meets under the chairmanship of the chief of the Local Affairs Office—a prefectural official—to adopt the prefectural policy as its own and to implement it in accord with local circumstances. To quote the authors of *Village Japan:*

In this manner the mayors of all villages in a given *gun,* and to a lesser extent in each prefecture, agree in advance on such matters as the percentage of their villages' revenue that they will allot in their budget to village assembly or personnel expenses, the salaries that they will pay for certain jobs, the rate at which they will set such village imposts as the bicycle and cart taxes, the amount of their contributions to the support of certain prefectural or regional associations, supplementary allowances for teachers, and other similar matters. This procedure obviously circumscribes the village mayors' independent initiative.[20]

In addition, the town or village office is in constant contact with the prefecture in the course of the working day. A number of village mayors who were interviewed by the writer stated that they or members of their staff visited the prefectural Local Affairs Office at least once (and sometimes two or three times) in the course of a day, in addition to making frequent contacts by telephone.

The actual relationship between the central and the local governments is further illustrated by the fact that the Autonomy Ministry distributes to prefectural and municipal executives model by-laws, ready for presentation to the local assemblies with or without adaptation to local conditions. National officials write books and pamphlets, ostensibly of an unofficial nature, but actually designed for the guidance of local officials. Indeed, the forms that guidance and controls take are so many that they cannot be exhaustively enumerated within the framework of a general study such as this. However, two types of institutions, having primary purposes other than the exercise or acceptance of central guidance, should be mentioned here because they either reflect or affect the relations between the central and prefectural governments. These are the Local Branch Offices of the Central Government and the Prefectural Offices in Tokyo.

Local Branch Offices of the Central Government

While various central government ministries maintained branch offices (*desaki kikan*) throughout Japan before and during the war, much of their work was then carried out through the prefectures. Since the governor was a national official, appointed by the central government, there was no problem of control. However, in 1946 it became clear that the status of the governors would soon change, and the ministers became fearful that their grip on the local execution of their programs would thus be weakened. To prepare for this eventuality they hastily established local agencies under their direct control. The number of local branch offices increased rapidly until it exceeded 30,000. The jurisdiction of many of the new offices coincided with the area of a prefecture. This rush in the establishment of new local branch offices was possible because under the Meiji Constitution no legislative action was required. The amendment to the Local Autonomy Law in December 1947, which provided that with specifically enumerated exceptions the establishment of local branch offices henceforth required Diet approval, called a halt to it. There has even been some retrenchment. But according to a survey in

1954, 26,858 branch offices with 618,370 officials still existed at that time. Of these, 309 operated in an area larger than a prefecture.*

The existence of certain national branch offices raises no problems of local autonomy. Examples of this type are post offices, customs offices, immigration and repatriation offices, procurators' offices, and other establishments of the Justice Ministry such as prisons and juvenile detention homes. There is also no objection from this viewpoint to the existence of national tax offices as long as these do not interfere with the administration of the local tax system. This type of national branch office normally antedates the local government reforms. Their functions were never carried out through the prefectural governments. These functions are not only clearly national in scope, but they are also best performed by national officials under direct control of the various ministries. Typically, there is no interaction between these officials and prefectural officials.

It is different with the branch offices established since 1946. Their functions were previously carried out through the governor. Now they are, by and large, assigned to the prefectures. Two consequences are obvious. The first is that there is a great deal of overlapping between the functions of this type of branch office and the functions of the offices of the prefectures. For example, the Statistics Sections and the Agricultural Divisions of the prefectural governments gather statistics relating to agriculture. But there are also 49 Agricultural Statistics Survey Offices of the Ministry of Agriculture and Forestry. The functions of the prefectural Agricultural Divisions also overlap to some extent with those of the 49 Food Affairs Offices of the Ministry of Agriculture and Forestry. The Finance Ministry has 10 Finance Offices on a regional level and below them 42 Branch Finance Offices; the areal jurisdiction of the latter coincides in most cases with a prefecture and their functional jurisdiction regarding the raising of loans by cities, towns, and villages dupli-

---

* The provision of the LAL referred to is Article 156. This amendment was part of a wider program to base the organization of the national government on Diet laws. Article 156 as amended also provided that the national government should pay for the maintenance of its branch offices, thus combating the tendency of these offices to use prefectural facilities without compensation. Article 12 of the Local Finance Law also states that the national government shall not burden the local entities with expenses for the maintenance and work of its branches. The 1954 survey of the number of branch offices is referred to in the above-mentioned article by Kuze.

cates that of the prefectural Local Affairs Section, a part of the Prefectural General Affairs Division.

The second consequence is that the branch offices remove functions supposedly assigned to the prefectures from prefectural control. As a matter of fact, as stated above, the branch offices were established for this very purpose. There is no obvious need for their existence unless one shares the distrust of local autonomy that prompted their establishment. To the extent to which they fulfill their original purpose, they infringe on local autonomy. It is thus not surprising that their abolition has been frequently proposed. In its report of October 1953 the Local System Investigation Council took cognizance of the fact that the 800-odd branch offices exist at three levels: regional, prefectural, and local.[21] In its subsequent report of October 1957 which proposed the establishment of regions, the Council recommended that the functions of the branch offices be transferred, as far as possible, to the new regions, and that the branch offices be then abolished. As we know, this report has not been implemented and the branch offices remain.

The central government is not enthusiastic about the abolition of its branch offices. It fears the political repercussions that are likely to follow the dismissal of the great number of national public servants employed in them. We may assume that another reason is the usefulness of the offices in the supervision of the prefectural administration. The central government finds it convenient to use its officials on the spot to investigate the need for public works for which the prefecture seeks a subsidy, to estimate the proper amount of the subsidy, and to inspect the project in its various stages. But it is not just a matter of convenience. Unlike the inspectors of the various ministries who are sent out from Tokyo, the officials of the branch offices are in constant, informal contact with prefectural officials. Given the financial dependence of the prefectures on the central government, prefectural officials are inclined "to obtain the understanding or advice of" the national officials (whose reports to their ministries may affect the attitude of these ministries to the prefecture) even when the proposed prefectural action lies outside of the functions of the branch office and within the area of prefectural independence. In other words, the existence of national branch offices invites the exercise of a general guidance or control that is, strictly speaking, extralegal.

Two other aspects of national-prefectural relations should be mentioned. In some cases national officials actually work within the prefectural government, staffing, for instance, the prefectural sections dealing with social insurance or land transportation. This is an exception to the principle of separation of the national and local civil service, and we shall revert to it in that context. A recent development adversely affecting prefectural functions is the establishment of public corporations (*kodan*). Examples are the Japan Housing Corporation, the Aichi Water Corporation, the Agriculture Machinery Development Corporation, the Japan Road Corporation, and the Forestry Development Corporation. These corporations execute, partly with funds from the World Bank, enterprises of a magnitude beyond the capacity of the present prefectures. Yet, there is no gainsaying that the functions of the corporations overlap in some cases with those of the prefectures and that the laws establishing the corporations fail to guarantee sufficient consideration of the views of the local population.

Prefectural Offices in Tokyo

In the course of the year a regular stream of officials from every prefecture in Japan pours into Tokyo to conduct negotiations of one type or another with the various ministries.* To house them during their stay, some prefectures established during and immediately after the war lodgings of their own. In the early fifties every prefecture with the exception of neighboring Kanagawa owned such an establishment. Frequently a restaurant attached to it facilitated the entertainment of national government officials. Each prefecture wanted to put its best foot forward when dealing with these officials. Even poorer prefectures thus spent a good deal of money on the maintenance and operation of the Tokyo residence.†

---

* Brett, in his *Government of Okayama Prefecture* (p. 103ff), states that the governor of that prefecture spends about one week in four in Tokyo. Department heads visit Tokyo once every two months on the average for five to seven days. Section heads come up to Tokyo about once in six months for three to four days. The vice-governors of other prefectures often spend nearly as much time in Tokyo as at home. Kyoto's progressive governor, Ninagawa, refused for some years to spend his time on such pilgrimages.

† Entertainment expenses ran sometimes as high as the salaries for the staff. It is said that the relatively poor prefecture of Iwate spent between 20 and 30 million yen on its Tokyo establishment, which is far more modern than the prefectural office building at home. See *Asahi shimbun*, July 30, 1953.

Because of their costliness and their location in the best districts of Tokyo, these establishments were sometimes compared with the mansions that the feudal lords maintained in Edo during Tokugawa times, and humorous observers talked of a "new system of alternate residence" (*sankin kōtai*). The comment was also meant to reflect the feudalistic lord-vassal relationship between the central and prefectural governments, of which the Tokyo residences were considered to be a symptom.

Originally the secretarial staff that provided assistance to the visitors was very small, but it grew steadily until the Tokyo establishments were no longer primarily lodgings but prefectural field agencies. The offices then were often separated from the housing and entertainment facilities. Today all but twelve prefectures have their offices in the splendid modern building of the National Association of Governors, the Todofuken Kaikan.

These offices are normally headed by a prefectural official with the rank of a division chief or section chief. The organization of the office reflects in some cases the structure of the prefectural government; in other cases it is geared to groups of ministries and other central government agencies with which the various sections or officials are to maintain contact.[22] This contact consists at times in actual negotiations. The Tokyo office sometimes opens talks with a ministry which may then be continued and concluded by a visitor from the home office; at other times it works out details after the visitor has completed the preliminary negotiations.

Much of the work of the Tokyo office consists also in the gathering of information regarding actions and plans of the central government agencies, and, especially, regarding changes in policies and changes in ministerial attitudes. This requires daily, direct contact with the ministries. As Brett notes, "visits to ministries often have no other purpose than to cultivate the acquaintance of responsible national officials. Information of value is sometimes picked up from informal gossip."[23] Such information is then transmitted immediately to the home office, usually by teletype, wireless, or through a direct telephone line. On the basis of this intelligence—for instance on the impending allocation of the Local Distribution Tax, of subsidies, and of loan permits—the prefecture may quickly shift its emphasis in the justification of a request or modify its various requests in such a way as to take advantage of its inside knowledge.

When an official from the prefectural government comes to Tokyo, the Tokyo office puts its knowledge of the right people and its store of good will, accumulated by nurturing these contacts, at his disposal. It introduces him in the proper places and arranges for the social niceties which may make his trip more successful.*

As noted earlier, there is a keen competition among prefectures for subsidies and loan permits. Each tries to direct as much central government money into its coffers as possible. In this competition the Tokyo offices play an important part. They are a symptom of the financial dependence of the prefectures.

Large cities, that are unwilling to entrust their cause to the prefecture maintain their own Tokyo offices and participate directly in the contest for national funds. There is also an office for Cooperative Affairs of the Five Big Cities, which has, however, a somewhat different character: it serves as a research and lobbying organization in regard to legislation affecting the big cities. To oppose its efforts in the direction of a transfer of prefectural funtions to these cities, the five prefectures concerned established in 1953 a Five Prefectures Liaison Office as a counter-lobby.

The Effect of Subsidies

In the preceding chapter we showed that financial dependence of local governments is greatest when grants of government funds take the form of specific subsidies. The attitudes displayed in the relations between local and national officials may be illustrated by following the process by which a subsidy is obtained in a hypothetical case.[24] Let us assume that a prefecture wants to undertake a road construction program. After an estimate of the cost is made, an official of the prefectural Public Works Division goes to Tokyo to consult the Ministry of Construction. He appears at the Ministry, accompanied by a staff member of the Tokyo office of the prefecture, and there he delivers first an appropriate gift from the prefecture. Then he presents the purpose of his visit in terms of a petition, couched in carefully chosen and polite words. If the Construction Ministry approves the program submitted

---

* Of course, governors, vice-governors, and division chiefs are often former national officials and find this fact useful in their negotiations. See Brett, *Government of Okayama Prefecture*, p. 106. The good offices of Diet members from the prefecture are also often used.

by the prefecture, the distribution of the necessary expenses is mapped out.* The total appropriation which the Ministry has for subsidies, the importance of the project, and the financial ability of the prefecture serve as rough yardsticks for this plan, but considerations of a political and personal nature, which may even lead to illegal collusion, are not always absent.[25] The result of the negotiations is then reflected in the prefectural budget. If the prefecture has to bear a greater part of the financial burden than anticipated, a supplementary budget is put before the prefectural assembly and passed.

In the course of the negotiations the ministry may attach conditions to the subsidy. This has long been customary practice, but it is now based on a law passed in 1955, which spells out the types of conditions.† Thus the ministry may require that its approval be secured for any change in the plans for the subsidized enterprise, or in the method of defraying the required expenses, or for a temporary or permanent discontinuance of the enterprise; conditions regarding contracts in connection with the enterprise may be added; an arrangement for repayment of the subsidy or a part thereof out of the profits anticipated from the completion of the subsidized work may also be made a condition. But with all this, the ministry's decision regarding the subsidy is not

---

* Normally the negotiations for subsidies involve a number of national agencies. Brett (*Government of Okayama Prefecture*, p. 106) notes that prefectural officials who come to Tokyo for this purpose find it difficult to coordinate the thinking of the various ministries. For example, when the former governor of Okayama sought national aid for the construction of school buildings, he went with his plan first to the Ministry of Education and obtained its approval. He then went to the Autonomy Board which suggested some alteration in the plan. He then tried to work out a revised plan with the Ministry of Education. When the Ministry failed to see eye to eye with the Board, he had to go back and forth between the two until a compromise was arrived at. In negotiating for national aid in the construction of the Asahi River dam, the governor had to contact 37 officials in five ministries before the project could be launched.

† Law Regarding Adjustments of the Execution of Budgets Involving Subsidies (No. 179 of 1955). In addition to legalizing some of the former practices, this law also provides sanctions against local entities that seek to milk the central treasury or to pad their own finances. Such entities may be required to repay funds improperly received or spent, and their officials are made subject to criminal prosecution. Aside from its enforceable provisions, the law is interesting for its exhortations: both central and local officials are reminded that they are dealing with money that comes from the people; national officials are admonished to be impartial when they attach conditions to the grant of a subsidy, and are warned not to interfere excessively nor to make the execution of the enterprises more difficult than necessary.

completely firm. A change in circumstances, as perceived by the ministry, may result in cancellation or reduction of the subsidy or in changes of the ministry's conditions. Not until the enterprise is completed and the final report and the results of the subsequent field investigation of the ministry are in is the local entity informed of the definite amount of the subsidy. Up to this point all budget-making regarding the subsidized enterprise is tentative.

When the road construction is finally under way—performed either by the prefecture or by a contractor who, in accordance with the law, must be selected by competitive bidding[26]—officials of the Construction Ministry come to inspect the work and examine the accounts connected with the program. But this is only one of the audits that follow the receipt of the subsidy. Others are carried out by the Board of Audit, the Finance Ministry, and the Administrative Management Agency. To these inspections must be added the general inspections by the Autonomy Ministry, which are based on Article 246 of the Local Autonomy Law.[27]

When central government officials inspect local activities, the local officials consider it essential to entertain them lavishly to gain or maintain their favor. It has been estimated that some prefectures spend as much as 5 per cent of their total budget on various ways of maintaining the good will of national officials. Sometimes more than half of the subsidy is consumed by expenses for obtaining it.[28] The local officials hope, of course, that these expenses will turn out to be an investment that will yield substantial returns in the future; but at any rate, they see no alternative to bearing them.

When a municipality wants a subsidy the course of action is rather similar, except that its first step must be to convince the prefecture of its need. If, for example, a town wants to obtain a subsidy for a new sewage system, the plan is drawn up by a local official, if the town has a technician for the task, and then inspected and approved by the appropriate prefectural officials. More frequently the plan is drawn up by prefectural officials at the town's request. Then a prefectural official goes to the capital and presents the plan to the Welfare Ministry with the assistance of the Tokyo office of the prefecture. When approval is given, liaison is established with the Construction Ministry and the problem of subsidization is discussed. An arrangement may be arrived at by which the Welfare Ministry subsidizes the approved construction to one-fourth of the total cost, the prefecture adds another one-fourth, four-fifths of the remainder is covered by a loan while the rest comes out of current municipal revenue. The prefectural official negotiates with the Autonomy Ministry for a permit for the loan, and then returns to his prefecture. The arrangements that he has made are accepted by the town for which he has acted almost as a matter of course; after all, the town had no hand in the matter after its initial contact with the prefecture.

The detrimental effects of specific subsidies on the development of local self-government are recognized by most writers and by many local officials. The need for some type of national support of local finance is not questioned, but the form the support takes is widely criticized: there are too many subsidies granted on a piecemeal basis; the method of their allocation is complex, expensive and open to abuse; and the controls that go with the grant of a subsidy are excessive in law and even more so in actual practice.*

Professor Kambe's statement that in Japan "subsidies as a matter of fact deprive local government of its independence" is hardly an exaggeration. The point is not only that subsidies lead to interference of the national government in local affairs. In Japan they reinforce notions of subordination on the part of local officials and prevent the growth on a spirit of responsibility and self-reliance. Professor Kambe points out how essential it is that "petitions for subsidies be considered a disgrace and thus should serve as a warning to the officials of local government."[29] But since subsidies are are so important a source of revenue and since their size can be influenced, the maneuvers to obtain many and generous subsidies rank high in priority in the local official's mind. If, in pursuing the game with great gusto, they get, as a Japanese observer notes, "deeper and deeper ensnarled in their own rope," they seem not to be mindful of it.[30] A spirit of responsibility and self-reliance is indeed an ingredient of a meaningful local autonomy, but under the present system of local finance its growth can hardly be expected.

---

* As mentioned earlier, the present system has also political implications. Conservative candidates for local offices can claim with a certain plausibility that their connections with the national government, which is in conservative hands, will enable them to obtain subsidies for concrete projects in which the voters are interested. They gain thereby an advantage over their progressive opponents. We shall discuss this in connection with gubernatorial elections in Chapter 16.

Summary

In a country in which local self-governing bodies are called upon to assist in the administration of national affairs, their independence is naturally less complete when they act as national agents and more complete when they act on their own initiative and responsibility. Japanese public law reflects this distinction. Central government control over national assignments is provided for in the National Government Organization Law and—with all proper safeguards against controls that may be ultra vires—in Articles 146 and 150 of the Local Autonomy Law. Provisions for supervision of local actions outside the area of assigned functions were rather sketchy in the original version of the Local Autonomy Law. But the sparsity of the legal provisions did not assure a great measure of local independence. In spite of it, it could be said in 1949 that "generally speaking, direct administration as well as supervision and control over the local public bodies by the national government are still so powerful in the present system of administration that a real democratization of local administration and establishment of local autonomy can hardly be expected."[31] What was true in 1949 is even more true today after the expansion of the legal provisions for supervision in 1952 and 1956.

Local entities are not only used to accepting guidance from above, but are afraid of acting without it. Thus if a municipality desires to adopt a by-law on its own initiative, the mayor often shows a draft to the Local Affairs Office of the prefecture before submitting it to his assembly. The same is true for the budget. Governors sometimes seek the advice of the Autonomy Ministry regarding the introduction of bills in the prefectural assemblies. There is a general fear that failure to obtain the understanding of higher authorities in advance may be frowned upon and lead to unpleasant repercussions.

All this is greatly at variance with the letter and spirit of the law. In part the existing situation is a legacy of the centralized government structure of the past. The law was changed but attitudes of long standing did not change with it. Whether they would change in time depended to a large extent on the perception of the existing trends on the part of those who saw themselves in a subordinate role. If, for instance, the central government would have strictly adhered to its differing legal roles in regard to assigned national affairs and to local affairs, the context in which national and local governments met may have subtly changed. The question of intra vires and ultra vires may have been raised—perhaps timidly and only occasionally at first—and reality would have in time corresponded to the law. However, such self-restraint was hardly to be expected. Far from exercising it, the central government bureaucracy not only continued to treat the local entities as subordinate, but also pushed for changes in the law which made it clear that the tendency was not in the direction of loosening but of tightening controls. Their efforts to recreate the status quo ante pay off, even if they fall short of their ultimate aim, as long as they demonstrate that the atmosphere has not changed much after all and thus contribute to the reenforcement of the attitudes of the past. The reestablishment of a ministry in charge of local administration, the Local Autonomy Law amendments of 1952 and 1956, the downgrading of the independence of administrative commissions—all these were only the more conspicuous elements in this process.

The notions of superior and subordinate ranks inherent in a centralized government structure were reinforced in Japan by the value system of a traditionally hierarchical society. In such a society relations between superiors and subordinates are essentially diffuse in nature. The contacts between the great mass of local officeholders and the central government, in which conservatives deal with conservatives, are colored by this diffuseness. In this context, the criteria of intra vires or ultra vires based on specific legal authorization and precisely differentiating the mutual roles in the case of assigned and independent functions, have no place.

But the importance of the traditional value system should not be overrated. Signs of its erosion are plentiful throughout Japanese life. It is important to realize that the subordination of local authorities to the central government is reinforced by factors that would be effective in any cultural milieu. The very practical considerations stemming from the financial dependence of local entities are a case in point. "He who pays the piper calls the tune," in Japan as elsewhere. While conservatives set the mode for intergovernmental relations, the progressive local leader usually feels constrained to comply because he would otherwise invite retaliation. He has not yet learned to entrust his protection in case of deviance to the law and to the courts, which would elsewhere serve as his logical shield.[*]

---

[*] According to Supreme Court statistics, only 4.8 per cent of all administrative cases between May 1947 and December 1957 could be classed as "local government

The traditional value orientation of central government officials may in time come to play a less important role. But it is doubtful whether the administrator whose attitudes toward the local entity are no longer influenced by traditional notions of hierarchy will be more inclined toward the self-limitation of national controls than his predecessor. He reasons may differ, but he, too, is likely to make short shrift of notions of self-government which, from his point of view, stand in the way of maximum efficiency in the implementation of his agency's program.

The attitude of local officials to the present state of intergovernmental relations differs according to the level, size, and economic strength of the authority which they serve.[32] In general, neither the prefectures nor the rural towns and villages are likely to push demands for loosening of central controls. They are not inclined to advocate any changes which, while bringing them greater independence, may also give them even less security than they have now. At times, demands for changes have come from the large cities. Urban administrators may be less influenced by traditional notions; they may be more confident in their own efficiency and ability; they may feel that their own city could be made financially independent. At any rate, their demands have generally taken the form of a call for relief from the tutelage of the prefectures and for a reallocation of functions and financial resources to them.[33]

In the long run these demands may be significant, and may lead to a reconsideration of intergovernmental relations in an atmosphere of greater rationality.* But at present a reduction of the degree of guidance and control that characterizes intergovernmental relations in Japan is not in sight.

---

cases." Close inquiry would probably show that very few of these dealt with intergovernmental issues. Compare with this the body of judicial decisions in Great Britain on the questions whether certain government departments have sufficient statutory powers for specific controls, for withholding a grant, established by Act of Parliament, etc.

* The issue is now seen largely in terms of an ideological antithesis of independence or subordination, and in terms of structures rather than functions. Reconsideration may well start with the question how public goals are best achieved. It may be found that at present certain goals are best achieved at certain levels or in certain places by cooperation. In these cases the groundwork would have to be laid by providing the degree of voluntariness which is implicit in the term "cooperation," and which is denied by the present degree of subordination.

CHAPTER 14

The Organization of Local Entities

According to the Constitution, local entities must have assemblies and chief executive officers, and both must be elected by direct popular vote. Beyond this, their organization is to be regulated by law in accordance with the principle of local autonomy.

These constitutional provisions rule out certain types of organization. Of course, the appointment of chief executives by higher authority is precluded for rather obvious reasons. But granted that the chief executives are to be selected locally, it would have been possible to entrust their selection to the local legislatures and also logically consistent to make them responsible to the legislatures. Both national government and local government would then have been based on the parliamentary system.* As it is, national and local government are organized on differing principles. It is often said that local government follows the lines of the presidential system because the chief executives are directly elected. However, in spite of the method of their selection, local chief executives and assemblies are not independent from each other (as they would be under the presidential system), but interdependent in a manner typical of the parliamentary system.† Under certain circumstances the legislature may achieve the resignation of the chief executive by a vote of no confidence and the chief executive may dissolve the legisla-

* The Prime Minister is designated by the Diet in accordance with Article 67 of the Constitution. In connection with the discussions on constitutional revision, the direct election of the Prime Minister has recently been proposed.

† It will be noted that the constitutional provisions regarding the organization of local entities apply to prefectures as well as municipalities. As for the latter, they make the so-called "strong mayor" system mandatory.

ture and thus take the issue under dispute "to the people." The ultimate responsibility of both branches of government to the electorate is enforced by a system of direct demands, including the possibilities of a recall of the chief executive and a dissolution of the legislature.

The most important law regulating the organization of local government in detail is the Local Autonomy Law. Chapter VI deals with local assemblies and Chapter VII with local executive organs and their relations to the assemblies. Other laws that bear on the subject are those establishing the Boards of Education and the Public Safety Commissions, and the Local Public Service Law.

All of these laws were passed during the Occupation, and each of them was designed to attack the previous system of centralization. Thus, to cite an example, centralization had been achieved in the past to a great extent through controls over the local executive. To facilitate this control from above, the controls of the local assembly over the executive were minimized and local assemblies had to play a role that was distinctly subordinate to that of the executive. In addition, the Home Ministry and the governor had exercised a general disciplinary control over officials. The postwar laws not only abolished the specific control devices we described in Chapter 3; they also redressed the previous imbalance in the relations of the assembly and the chief executive, making the latter more responsive to the former. They limited the importance of the chief executive by creating administrative commissions that took over some of his tasks. They enlarged the functions of the assembly. They separated the local and national public service and put the latter under local control. But as we have shown in preceding chapters, changes in the law are only partly reflected in the actual working of the local government system. In this chapter we shall examine the gap that separates law from reality in the organization of the local entities.

The Organization and Work of the Local Executives

The chief executive of a prefecture is the governor, of a municipality the mayor. Both are now salaried officials elected for terms of four years.[1] Prior to the expiration of their terms they may lose their office by a vote of no confidence in the assembly or by a successful recall, as will be described later.[2]

The local chief executive represents the local entity and coordinates its activities. According to Article 148 of the Local Autonomy Law he administers "the affairs of the local public body concerned" and "such affairs of the national government, other local public bodies, and other public bodies as fall under his powers under laws or ordinances." The former affairs include not only the entity's proper functions, but also functions assigned to it by way of entity delegation; the latter affairs are those assigned to the chief executive by way of agency delegation.[3] As noted earlier, lists of these assignments are attached to the law. In carrying them out, the chief executive acts as an agent of the state, and is subject to national direction. We know already that a great part of the work of the mayor, and especially of the governor, is dedicated to assigned tasks.* In regard to "the affairs of the local public body concerned" also, the chief executive's tasks are first of all administrative. According to Article 149 of the Local Autonomy Law, he is charged, for instance, with the management of property and establishments, with the receipt and payment of funds, with the supervision of the accounts, and with the levying and collection of taxes. He may direct and supervise such public organizations within the local entities as agricultural or fisheries' cooperatives, youth and women's organizations, cultural and welfare organizations (including the Red Cross), for the purpose of adjusting and coordinating their activities. The mayor is also given special powers in case of emergency: he may use private property and may order the inhabitants to participate in preparing defenses against calamity.[4]

In addition to these administrative tasks, the chief executive plays an important role in the local entity's legislative activities. He convokes the assembly, and has the responsibility of presenting to it the annual budget and the prerogative of presenting bills for enactment into bylaws. He promulgates the bylaws after they have been enacted. These bylaws frequently require the issuance of enforcement regulations by

---

* Robert Ward, looking at the functions of the village mayor from the vantage point of the village of Kamo near Okayama, finds that the mayor's most difficult and time-consuming task has long been the local execution of the national crop-requisitioning program; that the mayor's role in the administration of public works is limited by the prefectural and national controls accompanying the financial and technical assistance that is required by all but the smallest projects; and that in the field of relief and public welfare, the mayor's role is largely administrative within the limits prescribed from above. The significance of the mayor's more independent authority as manager of the village property has decreased with the decline in the amount of the property, which is now largely restricted to public buildings. (*Village Japan*, pp. 267f.)

the chief executive. This is, however, only one type of the regulations (*kisoku*) at his disposal. He may issue regulations of a second type when he acts as national agent and is not bound by local legislation. A third type serves him primarily in his capacity as the manager of local property, in which he regulates its use, collects rents, and so forth. Chief executives also issue notifications to the public (*kokuji*) and instructions (*tsūtatsu*) to the local public service personnel.

In the exercise of his tasks the chief executive is assisted by a number of auxiliary organs. Prefectures have a vice-governor and municipalities a vice-mayor, but the Local Autonomy Law permits them to pass bylaws increasing the number of these auxiliary organs or dispensing with them altogether. The accounts, including those concerned with national affairs assigned to the executive, are managed by the chief accountant of the prefecture and the treasurer of the municipality, but in towns and villages the mayor or assistant mayor may perform this duty. These auxiliary organs are appointed by the chief executive, with the consent of the assembly, for terms of four years.[5] All these officials belong to the category of "local public service personnel in the special public service" to which the Local Public Service Law does not apply in principle. Below them are the local officials in the "regular public service," who are divided into secretarial officials and technical officials. Their total number is fixed by bylaw, and they are appointed and removed by the chief executive.

Article 172 thus seems to give to local entities a rather free hand regarding the types and number of officials in the regular public service that they wish to employ. But a number of national laws, each dealing with a specific function, make the appointment of certain officials obligatory. A list of these officials, most of them specialists, was appended to the Local Autonomy Law in 1952.[6] The 57 positions on this list defy easy categorization, but by way of example, we may mention the police and school officials, the various inspectors such as food inspectors, and the various types of welfare workers.* In addition, national laws require the establishment of certain deliberative and advisory councils. An enumeration of these councils may be found in List 7 appended to the Local Autonomy Law. Local entities may also have a part-time expert committee appointed by the chief executive for the purpose of technical investigations.

---

* It should be noted that some of these officials are not supervised by the chief executive but by the Public Safety Commission or the Board of Education.

The organizational structure of the prefectural government is determined to some extent by the Local Autonomy Law.[7] The largest unit within the prefectural administration is called a bureau (*kyoku*) in Tokyo, and a division (*bu*) in the other prefectures. The number of these units differs according to the category into which the prefecture falls. Tokyo Metropolis and Hokkaido each constitutes a special category of its own. The remaining three categories are based on population: one includes all prefectures with a population of more than 2,500,000 inhabitants; another includes all prefectures with a population below that figure but above 1,000,000 inhabitants; the third is constituted by prefectures with a smaller population. According to the Local Autonomy Law, the number of bureaus or divisions ranges from ten in Tokyo to four in the least populated prefectures. Table 9 shows the bureaus or divisions prescribed for prefectures in various categories.

All prefectures have a General Affairs Division, which deals with personnel matters, matters relating to the assembly, and matters "re-

TABLE 9

*Divisions of Prefectural Administration According to the
Local Autonomy Law*

Bureau or Division	Tokyo (Bureaus)	Hokkaido	Prefectures by Population Over 2½ Million	Prefectures by Population 1–2½ Million	Prefectures by Population Under 1 Million
General Affairs	x	x	x	x	x
Finance	x				
Tax	x				
Public Welfare	x	x	x		
Health	x	x	x	x	
Labor	x	x	x		
Economics	x				x
Construction	x				
Public Works		x	x	x	x
Housing	x	x	x		
Harbor	x				
Commerce and Industry		x	x	x	
Agriculture and Forestry		x	x	x	
Development		x			
Public Welfare and Labor				x	
Public Welfare, Health, and Labor					x
Totals	10	9	8	6	4

lating to the general administration of cities, towns, and villages and of other public bodies" within the prefecture. This division also gathers statistics, drafts by-laws, and in general deals with all matters not allocated to other divisions. Tokyo has a Finance Bureau and a Tax Bureau, but in the other prefectures the budget, taxes, and other financial affairs fall within the jurisdiction of the General Affairs Division, which is in many ways the core of the prefectural administration. The larger prefectures have a Division of Public Welfare, a Division of Health, and a Division of Labor; but in prefectures with a population between 1,000,000 and 2,500,000, the Welfare Division also handles labor affairs, and in the smallest prefectures health, welfare, and labor affairs are combined and handled by the same division.

The differences in the economy of the various prefectures is reflected in the legal provisions for the organization of the prefectural administration. In Tokyo a Bureau of Economic Affairs is to handle matters relating to agriculture, industry, forestry and fishing, problems of land adjustment, commodity distribution, and price controls. All prefectures except those with a population of less than 1,000,000 must establish Commerce and Industry Divisions and Agriculture and Forestry Divisions. The smallest prefectures have again an Economics Division combining a number of economic functions.

According to the law, the Tokyo metropolitan government has a Construction Bureau and a Housing Bureau, the former handling city planning, urban reconstruction, roads and rivers, and other public works (except harbors, which fall under the jurisdiction of a special Harbor Bureau). Hokkaido and prefectures with more than 2,500,000 inhabitants have Public Works Divisions (also handling harbor affairs) and Housing Divisions. The smaller prefectures have only Public Works Divisions. In Hokkaido a Development Division is also provided for in the law.* The law permits certain deviations from the pattern it prescribes. A prefecture may establish additional bureaus or divisions if it consults the Autonomy Minister in advance.[8] If a governor wants to decrease the number of bureaus or divisions he may do so, accord-

---

* Prior to the amendment of 1952 there were only two categories: Tokyo and the other prefectures. All prefectures had at least six divisions. Other divisions specified by the Local Autonomy Law could be established by bylaw. The revision of 1952 thus limited the range within which prefectures could determine their organizational structure.

ing to the Local Autonomy Law, on the basis of a bylaw passed by the prefectural assembly; the law enjoins him only not to disturb the balance of the administrative organization of his prefecture with the organization of the national agencies and of other prefectures. In practice, however, he has little leeway. The ministries in Tokyo feel that they have a vested interest in the existence of those divisions in the prefectural administration that carry out their work. The legal nature of the prefecture as an autonomous local entity notwithstanding, they view the divisions of a prefectural government as if they were branches of the ministry. Thus, when a prefecture considers a deviation from existing arrangements, one or another ministry is likely to interfere. The opposition to a change is communicated to the prefecture by letter, telephone, and telegram, often reinforced by the dispatch of an important official to the prefecture. In the past, ministries have sometimes threatened that they would decrease the number of the so-called "subsidized prefectural officials" (part of whose salary is paid by the ministry) or that they would refuse to send a section chief (for a section dealing with a function within the ministry's jurisdiction) if the prefecture persisted in its plan to abolish a division or merge it with another one.[9]

The Local Autonomy Law specifies only the bureaus or divisions to be established by the prefectures. The units below that level are to be established by regulations of the governor. He may "create any necessary section below the bureau or division for the purpose of allotting the affairs which fall within his powers." Here again the Local Autonomy Law seems to give the governor a rather free hand. In reality there are areas in which even the most minute details of the prefectural organization are nationally determined. For example, the establishment and internal organization of social welfare offices, prefectural police headquarters, offices dealing with contagious diseases and with the extermination of rodents and insects are in fact regulated by laws and Cabinet orders.[10] The freedom of the prefectures to organize their own administration is further limited by ministerial ordinances—sometimes lacking a legal basis—and by the interference of the Tokyo ministries, which follows the pattern described above for the bureau or division level. For example, the Local Autonomy Law leaves the establishment of Local Affairs Offices up to prefectural discretion. But when the mass amalgamations of towns and villages into cities would have made it possible for the prefectures to abolish some of their Local Affairs Offices, certain ministers in Tokyo who used these offices as local branches for their work opposed such a move.*

The unit below the division in the prefectural offices is normally the section (*ka*). To cite a rather typical example, the General Affairs Division of the Okayama prefectural government in 1953 was divided into several sections: Personnel Section, Secretariat Section, Documents Section, General Affairs Section, Taxation Section, Local Affairs Section, and Statistics Section. The functions of these sections are in general clear from their names. The Documents Section was, in addition to taking custody of all documents and issuing them, also in charge of drafting prefectural by-laws or else of examining them with an eye to legislative technique and consonance with general legislative policy. The General Affairs Section dealt with the budget, handled liaison with the assembly, managed the Tokyo office of the prefectural government, and took care of a number of miscellaneous tasks. The Local Affairs Section of the General Affairs Division is of particular interest to us. It is the prefecture's agency for relations with the cities, towns, and villages. It deals with the cities directly and with the towns and villages indirectly through the Local Affairs Offices in the various *gun*, to which we have referred earlier. The Local Affairs Offices, which are integral parts of the prefectural administration, are under the jurisdiction of this section.[11]

The official and his staff in charge of a certain part of the section's work (*kakari*) form the lowest unit in the organizational structure. Thus, to cite an example, under the direction of the Chief of the Document Section of the General Affairs Division of the Okayama prefectural government there was in 1953 an official and staff in charge of legislative work (*hōseikakari*) and another official and staff in charge of the other work from which the section took its name (*bunshōkakari*). The section had a total of 24 employees, of whom five were law school graduates.

The Local Antonomy Law does not go into detail regarding the organizational structure of the municipalities. Rather it leaves it up to the

* It may be granted that interference is motivated as much by a zeal for an important and even beneficial national program as by a zeal for centralization as such. The result for local autonomy remains the same—a limitation of the legal scope of the freedom of the local entities to chart their own organization.

mayors to create by bylaw the necessary divisions and sections of the administration. The differences in the complexity of the organization reflect the differences in size, population, economic development, and functions between the urban centers and the remote villages, all of which are encompassed by this rule. In a large city the organizational structure is actually more elaborate than in a small prefecture. In 1961, for instance, the administration of the city of Kyoto was carried on by fifteen bureaus (in addition to the mayor's office, which was in charge of general affairs, including such special projects as the municipal symphony orchestra).[12] A village office, on the other hand, may get along with a simple structure of five or six branches or rather with five or six staff members (*kakari*) each in charge of a part of the work. Thus the village office in Kamo, described by Ward in *Village Japan*, has in addition to the mayor, vice-mayor, and treasurer, individuals in charge of land and requisition matters (*kangyōkakari*); taxation (*zeimukakari*); health insurance (*kenkōkakari*); family records and census (*kosekikakari*); public health (*eiseikakari*); public welfare and statistics (*kōseikakari* and *tōkeikakari*); and agricultural affairs (the clerk of the *nōgyō iinkai*). The *kenkōkakari* has an asistant, and a combined janitor and servant fills out the roster.

Local Administrative Commissions

The organization just described serves, in the words of the Local Autonomy Law, "the purpose of allotting the affairs which fall within the powers of the governor (or mayor)." But not all administrative affairs are executed by the governor or mayor and their staff. Certain affairs are handled by administrative commissions with a degree of independence from the local chief executive. Administrative commissions, which exist both on the national and on the local level, are an innovation introduced during the Occupation. Some of them execute newly created functions, as did the agricultural and land commissions that were instrumental in carrying out the postwar land reform program. Others administer affairs that were formerly under the jurisdiction of the national or local executive in such fields as election administration, public safety, and education. These commissions were established generally in response to certain circumstances encountered by the Occupation.

For one, the very character of the Japanese bureaucracy—exemplified by the often-quoted saying "*kanson mimpi*" (reverence for the officials, disdain for the people)—gave a certain appeal to the notion of "de-bureaucratizing" the administration. The desire to disperse executive functions was also a reaction to the previous concentration of powers in the hands of the executive, which had been intensified by the "leadership principle" of the war period. It was also hoped that the commissions would serve as training grounds for participation in government, which was a new experience, for instance, for the tenant-farmers who became members of the Agricultural Land Commissions. There were also special reasons for the establishment of some of the commissions. For instance, in prewar days elections were managed by local chief executives. The mayors compiled the voter lists, set the date for elections, selected election witnesses, and served as election meeting chairmen. The governors were charged with the general surveillance of the election process. They, in turn, were under the authority of the Home Minister. This system could be justified, at least in theory, as long as those entrusted with the management of elections were not themselves directly elected. The governors in particular were members of the national bureaucracy and thus supposedly neutral in politics.* But after the war, governors and mayors became elected officials and vitally interested in election results. The management of elections could thus no longer be left in their hands. The establishment of Election Administration Committees, endowed with some degree of independency and constituted in a manner to guarantee their political neutrality, seemed to be the answer to the problem.

If a commission is to operate with a degree of independence from the chief executive, its appointment cannot be left in his hands. Therefore none of the commissions described below is the mere creature of the chief executive. But otherwise the way in which the commissions are constituted varies. At one extreme are the commissions that are directly elected either by all the voters or by special constituencies; on the other extreme are those that are appointed by the chief executive with the consent of the assembly. In between stand those indirectly elected by

---

* The theoretical justification had little relation to actual practice. Interference in elections by governors and by the police was rather common. During the twenties elections were often preceded by a strategic shifting of governors. A new cabinet usually replaced incumbent governors with its own henchmen. See Harold S. Quigley and John E. Turner, *The New Japan: Government and Politics* (Minneapolis, 1956), p. 255.

the local assembly and those consisting partly of elected and partly of appointed members. The number of commissioners also varies. The smallest commissions have three members, the largest forty.

The Local Autonomy Law in its original form provided only for the establishment of Election Administration Committees and for inspection commissioners.* In its present form (Article 180-5) the law states that the following commissions have to be established by all ordinary local entities, that is, prefectures and municipalities: Boards of Education, Election Administration Committees, and Personnel Commissions or Equity Commissions. Prefectures must also have Public Safety Commissions, Labor Commissions, Expropriation Commissions, Sea Area Fisheries Adjustment Commissions, Inland Water Fishing Ground Administration Commissions, and inspection commissioners. Cities, towns, and villages have to establish (in addition to Boards of Education, Election Administration Committees, and Personnel or Equity Commissions), Agriculture Commissions and Property Assessment Review Committees. They may also provide by bylaw for inspection commissioners.

The Local Autonomy Law thus provides for the organization of the committees in broad outline. For details (except on inspection commissioners, who are regulated entirely by the LAL) we must turn to various other laws. Thus the Law Concerning the Organization and Management of Local Education Administration of 1956 (the successor to the former Board of Education Law) regulates the Boards of Education. Since we discussed this law in Chapter 11 it is not necessary to go into any details here. We may only note that in 1956 the method of selecting the boards changed from one of the extremes to the other: from direct election to appointment by the chief executive with the approval of the assembly. Simultaneously the powers of the boards in regard to the education budget and in regard to the appointment of the Superintendent of Education were reduced. The law of 1956 also provided for a degree of subordination of the municipal boards to the prefectural boards and of all boards to the Minister of Education, thus legalizing occasional practices that had not been in accord with the original spirit of the law. All in all, the raison d'être of the

---

* The reform of the local government in September 1946 had already paved the way in these regards.

boards is today no longer as clear as it was at the time of their establishment.

Election Administration Committees of prefectures as well as municipalities consist of four members.* They are elected by the assembly of the local entity concerned for three years. To insure political neutrality, the law provides that no two members may belong to the same political party or organization. The committees compile election registers and in general manage local, prefectural, and national elections. Since we shall discuss their work in a subsequent chapter, we may note here only that the relationship between the commissions at the various levels has become complex and somewhat unclear. In principle, prefectural commissions manage prefectural elections, municipal commissions manage municipal elections, and both play a role also in national elections. Thus, the basic election register prepared by the municipal commissions is used in all elections, and the prefectural commissions are in charge of elections of members to the House of Representatives and of those members of the House of Councilors who are elected in prefectural constituencies (rather than by the nation at large). However, according to Article 186 of Local Autonomy Law (as amended) prefectural committees supervise and direct the municipal committees, and according to Article 5 of the Public Offices Election Law (as amended) prefectural committees are subject to the supervision and direction of the Autonomy Minister.† The meaning of the term "supervision and direction" is not defined, and the interpretation is possible that it pertains not only to the purely administrative aspects of the work of the commissions, but also to their decisions in specific cases. At any rate, the establishment of a pyramid of relations between the commissions and their ultimate link with the Autonomy Ministry diluted their original raison d'être.[13]

The Personnel Commissions and the Equity Commissions are based on the Local Public Service Law.[14] Personnel Commissions have to be

---

* Originally the prefectural committees had six members. Later the number of committee members was reduced. Committees for prefectures and for the big cities had four members, those for other municipalities three. Now all committees have the same number of members.

† Except when their work is related to the election of members of the House of Councilors by the nation at large, in which case they are under the Central Election Administration Council, as noted in Chapter 13.

established in prefectures and in the five big cities; they may be established in other cities with a population of more than 150,000 inhabitants. Other local entities must have, either individually or jointly, an Equity Commission. In practice most of the latter commissions are set up on a *gun* basis. The Personnel Commissions recommend measures dealing with personnel administration, or state their opinion on proposed bylaws in this field, develop systems of classification, compensation, and training, and administer any competitive examinations that are held. With the Equity Commissions they hear complaints regarding compensation and working conditions and review in individual cases adverse action taken by the executive against members of the local public service. In other words, the functions of the Personnel Commissions are administrative, quasi-legislative, and quasi-judicial, while those of the Equity Commissions are only quasi-judicial. The commissions, consisting of three members, are appointed by the chief executive with the consent of the local assembly. Political neutrality is assured in the same manner as in the case of the Election Administration Committees.

Since the establishment of the new Police Law in 1954 Public Safety Commissions exist only on the national and prefectural level. We discussed the new arrangement in Chapter 11 and thus need not go into details here. The prefectural commissions manage the prefectural police and carry out such other obligatory duties as are assigned to them by laws and ordinances. A list of these duties is appended to the Local Autonomy Law. (List No. 3.) The commissions consist of five members in Tokyo and in the prefectures in which big cities are located, and of three members elsewhere. They are appointed by the governor with the approval of the assembly. In the prefectures in which the big cities are located—Kanagawa, Aichi, Osaka, Kyoto, and Hyogo—the appointment of two of the five members is based on the nomination by the mayor of the big city in question—Yokohama, Nagoya, Osaka, Kyoto, Kobe—which is submitted with the approval of the city assembly. The term of office of the commissioners is three years. In addition to the usual provisions for insuring political neutrality, the law excludes from service as commissioners all persons who have been police officials or procurators within a period of five years prior to their appointment.

Within the scope of this study it is perhaps not necessary to discuss the more specialized prefectural commissions such as the tripartite local labor commissions, which are based on the Trade Union Law and which deal with mediation or settlement of labor conflicts, or the other commissions based on the Land Appropriation Law and the Fisheries Law. Of the commissions on the municipal level, the Property Assessment Review Committees were mentioned in Chapter 12. The Agriculture Commissions, now engaged in administrative work only on a municipal level, are the successors of the former Land Commissions, whose raison d'être in the administration of the land reform program had disappeared to a large extent when that program was completed. But they took over also the functions of the Crop Adjustment Committees and the Agricultural Improvement Committees. The Agriculture Commissions thus administer the continuing aspect of the land reform program as well as the crop requisition program and the programs for the promotion of agricultural improvements. The method of selection of the committee members proved from the beginning to be a politically delicate matter. The original land commissions which had carried through the land reform had consisted of representatives of tenants, landlords, and owner-farmers in a ratio of 5 to 3 to 2, and the representatives of each group had been elected separately by that group.* The law for the new Agriculture Commissions, passed in 1951 against the opposition of the Socialist Party, abolished this class representation. But the controversy over the composition of the Commissions continued and the law was amended in 1957. The amendment was passed by bipartisan agreement, a rarity in Japan, where sharp opposition between the two major parties is the general pattern of parliamentary politics. The principal of class representation was not reinstituted. Most of the commissioners are elected, but the major is given the power to appoint to the commission one representative each of the agricultural cooperatives and of the agricultural mutual aid societies as well as up to five neutral members recommended by the assembly. The total membership of the commissions varies from 10 to 40.[15]

Inspection commissioners must be appointed in the prefectures. Municipalities may provide for their appointment by bylaw. While the inspection commissioners are grouped together with the other admin-

---

* The original law also provided for the cooption of neutral members, three on the town and village level and five on the prefectural level. See Chapter 6, p. 101.

istrative commissions in the Local Autonomy Law and in most of the commentaries on the commission system, they are nevertheless of a somewhat different character. They do not administer, nor do they have quasi-judicial or quasi-legislative functions. Their task is rather to inspect and to report. In the mind of the creators of the institution, its establishment was a corollary of the new independence of Japanese local government. Prior to the reforms the responsibility for the fair and efficient functioning of local government was supposedly lodged in the national or prefectural agencies which had supervisory powers over the entities on a lower level of the hierarchy: the prefecture insured the satisfactory functioning of the municipalities and the Home Ministry did the same for the prefectures. With the elimination of the concept of tutelage from above, each local entity assumed responsibility for its fair and efficient operation. The inspection commissioners were created to execute this function of self-inspection. Prefectures have four inspection commissioners; municipalities normally have two. However, cities designated by Cabinet order may decide to have four rather than two commissioners. The cities thus designated (Cabinet Order 346 of 1952) are all those with a population of more than 100,000 and any others of smaller population that manage local public enterprises. The inspection commissioners are appointed by the chief executive with the consent of the assembly, one-half of them from among members of the assembly and the other half from among "persons of knowledge and experience." The former members serve during their term as assemblymen, the latter for a period of three years.[16] The management of local enterprises and the financial administration of the local entity are the primary object of inspections. But inspections are not confined to them, and may concern the execution of all functions of the local entity.* The inspection commissioners must conduct a regularly scheduled inspection at least once a year. Special inspections are to be held on demand from the Autonomy Minister, the governor, the local chief executive, or upon direct demand by the local electorate.

* A case brought to the courts in 1954 raised the question whether this includes assembly actions. In that year there was a direct demand from residents of Osaka Prefecture for an inquiry by the inspection commissioners into the propriety of a budget item for the prefectural police in the prefectural budget because—so their argument went—the Police Law of 1954, establishing the prefectural police, was not passed in accordance with the Constitution. (See Chapter 10, p. 213.) The Osaka High Court declared that only actions of the executive could be the object

The governor thus may demand an inspection of the prefectural administration by the prefectural inspection commissioners in his capacity as the prefecture's chief executive as well as an inspection of any municipal administration in the prefecture by the inspection commissioners of that municipality. The prefectural inspection commissioners may also inspect the financial affairs of municipalities receiving aid from the prefecture. Since 1956 ministers and governors may utilize the inspection commissioners on both levels to carry out inspections on their behalf and under their direction. (See Chapter 13, pp. 312f.) These assigned inspections, which are part of the broadened system of controls following the 1956 amendment of the Local Autonomy Law, have little to do with the purposes of self-inspection for which the inspection commissioners system was established. With logical consistency, their results are not made public by the commissioners—as are the results of the other inspections—but only transmitted to the assigning authority.

An appraisal of the record of the administrative commissions must take into account the degree of independence they maintained in their operations. This was, after all, a very significant part of their mission. In this regard is must be noted that the climate in which they operated was not conducive to a bold assertion of the independence with which the law endowed them. From the beginning the Japanese government was hostile to the introduction of the commission system on the national as well as the local level.[17] Local chief executives eyed the system with distrust. They and other critics pointed out that a dispersal of the executive function is likely to decrease over-all efficiency and to lower the sense of responsibility of the executive. Fears of "empire building" by the commissions and of jurisdictional frictions between them and the rest of the executive were also expressed. Some national officials went so far as to blame the financial distress of local governments on the adoption of the commission system at the local level. Various reports

---

of an inspection and that therefore the inspection commissioners could not scrutinize assembly actions, such as the passage of the budget. On March 6, 1962, the Supreme Court decided that assembly resolutions could be the object of an inspection. However, it found that in this case the proposed inspection was designed to scrutinize the passage of a law by the Diet—namely, the Police Law of 1954—and that this was improper because the national government and the local government must remain autonomous within their own spheres of activity.

called for "adjustments in the relationship of the executive organs," or, in other words, for a reduction in the independent status of the commissions.

The first step in this direction was taken in the course of the amendment of the Local Autonomy Law in 1952, when all local executive organs including the commissions were put "under the jurisdiction" (*shokkatsu*) of the chief executive. This is a somewhat vague term, implying a degree of subordination but not the existence of a direct command channel. According to the authoritative commentary of Nagano Shiro (then Chief of the Administration Section of the Autonomy Board), the degree of subordination or independence differs in the case of each type of commission, and must be ascertained by reference to the specific legal provisions governing it. For instance, the new Police Law that put the prefectural Public Safety Commission "under the jurisdiction of the governor" made it clear that this did not vest in the governor the authority to control the operations of the police force, but gave him substantial controls regarding the police budget, the by-laws dealing with the police, and the appointment of the commission itself.[18] The report of the Local System Investigation Council of 1956 called for changes regarding the boards of education and other administrative commissions. These were subsequently enacted, as we have noted.*

Finally, certain general provisions regarding the commissions were inserted in the Local Autonomy Law when it was amended in 1956. Article 180-6 is explicit about the general limits of the independence of the commissions. It spells out certain powers not normally possessed by them, namely the power to draft their own budgets, the power to present draft bills or resolutions to the local assembly, and the power to order receipts and payments. The use of the rather uncommon legislative device of stating the powers *not* possessed by an agency may be explained as a reaction to earlier arrangements that had aimed at guaranteeing the independence of the commissions. Thus the original Board of Education Law granted to the boards of education authority to pre-

---

* Earlier, in 1953, the first report of the Local System Investigation Council had dealt briefly with the commission system. It advocated that all local administrative commissions not based on the requirement of political neutrality or not exercising quasi-legislative or quasi-judicial functions be either abolished or converted into advisory organs.

pare the educational budget, to submit draft measures regarding certain matters (e.g., school bonds or tuition) to the assembly through the chief executive, and to order the chief accountant or treasurer to make payments from the board allotment in the general budget. As mentioned earlier, the boards no longer have these powers nor is there any other administrative commission which has them and which would thus be an example of an exception to the general rule of Article 180-6.

Since 1956 the chief executive may concern himself with the organization of the offices of the commissions and with the size of their staffs. If a commission plans any changes in these respects it must first consult him. He may demand reports from the commissions regarding the management of land, buildings, and other property occupied by them, conduct investigations, and demand changes. Finally, the chief executive can, after consultation with the commissions, delegate some of his functions to them or their staffs. Conversely, the commissions can, after consultation with the chief executive, delegate some of their functions to his auxiliary organs or to the chiefs of branch offices of the local administration. Mr. Nagano states in his commentary that the delegation by the commissions must be "within limits which do not violate the independence of the commissioners and the independence of their functional competence." While this is in accord with the raison d'être of the commissions, it is not made explicit in Article 180-7 of the Local Autonomy Law. If the limits mentioned by Mr. Nagano are not observed, the commissions lose their purpose not by legislative fiat but by a piecemeal abdication.[19]

It is clear that as a result of the amendment of 1956 the line of demarcation between the administrative commissions and the rest of the executive has become less clear-cut. The justification for the change avowedly was the necessity of "guaranteeing the unity of the local entities and the unified exercise of administrative authority." These needs had been considered by the drafters of the earlier laws. The difference lies in the weight assigned to these needs and to the conflicting demands for a degree of independence. The various amendments made rather light of the latter demands.

Certain flaws in the operation of the commissions became apparent soon after their establishment. Because the system was then still a novelty, this had to be expected. Thus the former land commissions tended to leave many of their responsibilities to the clerical staff. The Election

Administration Committees, often heavily staffed with local officials or former local officials, tended to conduct their business in somewhat cursory fashion in infrequent and brief meetings. Instead of using a secretarial staff of their own, prefectural commissions relied sometimes on the official in charge of elections in the Local Administration Section. Municipal committees often consulted their prefectural counterparts before deciding individual cases. Public Safety Commissions often did not control the police officials but were content to play second fiddle to them; in particular, they often entrusted important functions such as the issuance of licenses to the police chief.

Teachers constituted a considerable percentage of the membership of the Boards of Education, an incongruous situation since the teachers were to be supervised in the last analysis by the boards. Prefectural boards exercised influence over the municipal boards, and in some prefectures they even maintained liaison offices for this purpose.[20]

Nevertheless, the commissions could, and in many cases did, contribute to the democratization of the local administration. Their contribution may have grown with increasing experience. But the developments after 1952 sanctioned some of the practices that were inconsistent with the purpose of the commissions and increased the insecurity and timidity on which these practices were based. These developments are seen by many as the symptoms of a return to the unbridled bureaucratic rule of the past. The critics of the government's policy are not blind to the shortcomings of some of the commissions, but they feel that the system should have been given a fair chance to prove itself before being condemned.[21] The future of the commission system in Japan is uncertain, but it is likely that the government will continue to alter the status of individual commissions and thus thwart the purposes of their establishment rather than launch a frontal attack on the system as such.

The Local Public Service

Prior to the Occupation reforms, the prefectures, being semi-autonomous entities under an appointed governor, did not have a public service of their own. Their officials were members of the national public service. Municipal officials were appointed by the mayor, but orders of the Home Minister regulated many aspects of their service and the governor exercised a secondary disciplinary power over them. They were thus indirectly under central government control.

The Occupation reforms aimed at separating the local from the national public service. The Local Public Service Law, enacted in December 1950, divides the local public service into two categories, special and regular public service.* Its provisions apply only to the regular public service. The law lays down the principles for the establishment of the local Personnel Commissions and Equity Commissions, and sets standards for appointments and promotions. Where a Personnel Commission exists, appointments and promotions are normally made from eligibility lists compiled by the Commission on the basis of competitive examinations. (In other localities the administration may use examinations or dispense with them.) But the Personnel Commission may entrust the examinations to national agencies or other local agencies, and it may also put on its own eligibility list persons who had passed the competitive examination for a corresponding position in the national public service. Local entities with Personnel Commissions are required to set up a classification of positions by bylaw, implemented by rules of the Personnel Commissions. Salaries are to be fixed by bylaws, with due consideration of living costs and of the compensation received by national public servants, public servants of other local entities and employees in private enterprise. The law also contains general standards for working hours, working conditions, and for the protection of the welfare of the personnel in case of injury, illness, or retirement. It specifies the causes for disciplinary punishment and the procedure for appeals against adverse action. Politically, most important provisions in the law are those dealing with the restriction of political activities, the prohibition of strikes and other acts of dispute, and the formation of personnel organizations. These provisions parallel to a large extent those of the National Public Service Law. Indeed, the National Public Service Law served as the model for the Local Public Service Law in many respects. But the existence of two separate laws administered by separate agencies symbolized the important new principle of the separation of the local from the national public service.

* Until 1950 prefectural officials continued to be treated under the former regulations. Prior to the enactment of the Local Public Service Law, the Police Law, the Law for Fire Defense Organization, and the special regulations for educational personnel had already established rules for certain local public servants. Also the constitutionally thorny question whether public officials have the right to bargain collectively and to strike had been answered in the negative, at least temporarily, by the amendment of the National Public Service Law of 1948.

There were, however, some exceptions to that principle from the beginning. The supplementary provisions to the Local Autonomy Law stated that prefectural officials engaged in certain functions described by Cabinet order were "deemed to be national government officials for the time being." This system is still in force. At present, personnel engaged in various types of health insurance and pension schemes, in matters concerned with employment security and unemployment insurance, and in matters connected with road transportation have the status of national government officials. These officials are appointed, paid, and—in fact, if not in law—supervised by the central government's ministries of Welfare, Labor, or Transportation.*

In addition there are on both the prefectural and municipal levels so-called "subsidized officials"—that is, local officials who are paid in part by the National Treasury. This arrangement is based on individual laws regulating the functions in which these officials are engaged, such as social welfare, agriculture, and, since 1952, education.

The lines between national and local public service are further blurred by arrangements regarding the recruitment and exchange of personnel, especially for the higher ranks of the prefectural service. We noted that the Local Public Service Law authorized local Personnel Commissions to entrust the conduct of the competitive examinations to the National Personnel Authority or other national agencies, and that it also permitted them to consider a candidate who had passed the national examination as eligible for a local position. Furthermore, the law authorized the Local Autonomy Agency, the predecessor of the present Autonomy Ministry, to cooperate with and give technical advice to local entities regarding their personnel administration. These provisions compromised to some extent the principle of separation of national and local personnel administration. But they must have seemed innocuous enough to pass the scrutiny of the American participants in the drafting of the

---

* According to information supplied by the Autonomy Ministry, the number of officials of these ministries working in prefectural offices on April 1, 1962, was as follows: Ministry of Welfare, 13,209; Ministry of Labor, 2,251; Ministry of Transportation, 1,568; total, 17,028. For the legal provisions, see LAL, Supplementary Provisions, Articles 5 and 8, and Cabinet Order No. 19 of 1947; also Nagano, *Chikujō chihō jichihō*, p. 1089. In theory, the governor supervises the chief of the section in which these officials are working (e.g., the Unemployment Insurance Section). In fact, governors have little control. The real control channel leads over the appropriate local branch office of the ministry concerned to the ministry in Tokyo.

law.[22] Yet these provisions were soon used rather widely for arrangements that were contrary to the basic purposes of the law. Recruitment into the prefectural service took place either formally through the prefectural Personnel Commissions, or informally through the central government. In practice the lower positions were staffed through the formal channel, the higher positions through the informal channel. These arrangements were welcomed by many prefectural administrators who had from the beginning viewed the separation of the national and the local public service with some apprehension. They feared that the prefectural public service would not attract personnel of sufficiently high caliber. More specifically, they were concerned whether the graduates of the Law Faculty of Tokyo University, which traditionally was the main pool for the replenishment of the national bureaucracy, would be willing to enter prefectural service. No such problem had existed under the old system, since the Home Minister had simply assigned to the prefectures a number of graduates who had entered the Ministry. But now, it was said, the best graduates would apply for service in the national government, which carries greater prestige, and the prefectures would have to content themselves with second-rate men. The informal staffing arrangements served, in their minds, to overcome this problem.[23] Another practice that soon became common was the exchange of personnel between the national and prefectural governments. The prefecture would draw up a list of officials desiring to enter (or reenter) national service and send it to the Autonomy Board. The Board would take some of the officials and place the rest in one of the Tokyo ministries. Officials from Tokyo would replace them in the prefectural administration.[24]

This arrangement was not only against the spirit of the establishment of the Local Public Service Law; for some years it also lacked a legal basis. But later the Local System Investigation Council recommended that the exchange of personnel between the state and the local public entities and among the local public entities themselves be promoted, and the amendment of the Local Antonomy Law in 1956 sanctioned and regularized the practice. Detailed provisions now regulate the dispatch of officials from one local entity to another, including the dispatch of prefectural officials to municipalities, in such respects as the status of the dispatched officials, salary, allowances and travel expenses to be paid to them by the receiving entity or by the dispatching entity, and so forth. There are also provisions dealing with similar questions regard-

ing the rights of officials who at one time were national officials and subsequently became prefectural officials or vice versa.[25]

The existing system enables the prefectures to obtain the services of
persons who would otherwise not be available to them. But it also has
certain disadvantages. The separation of the prefectural service from
the national service is today more a myth than a reality. The young official recruited in Tokyo identifies with the prefecture in which he serves
only to a limited extent. His real ties are with the central government.
He stays in the prefecture only until he has risen to a position that makes
it possible for him to return to Tokyo, which is what he has hoped for
all along. The return of such officials drains experienced personnel from
the prefecture. Implicit in the system is an admission on the part of the
prefectures that their service is inferior to the national service.

If the local public service was to be independent, it had to be sufficiently able to perform its tasks. Measures for the training of local officials were thus called for. Some prefectures and municipalities saw this
need and established training institutes and other means for in-service
training. But the improvement of the quality of the local personnel was
not left in their hands for long. In 1953 the Autonomy University was
established in Tokyo under the auspices of the Autonomy Board (now
the Autonomy Ministry). It offers courses of varying length to selected
officials of prefectures and municipalities. Much of the instructional
staff is drawn from experts on local government in various universities.
There is little criticism of this institution, which undoubtedly serves a
useful purpose and apparently serves it well. The point is rather that
the problem of improving the quality of the local public service, which
should have been the concern of local governments, was taken over
and solved by the central government in a manner that is bound to
create new links between it and local officials throughout Japan.

We may illustrate the actual limits of local—or at least prefectural—
independence in the field of personnel administration by a case that
occurred in Chiba Prefecture early in 1963. As noted earlier, the Local
Public Service Law sets certain basic standards for working hours and
other working conditions but otherwise leaves their determination up
to the local entities. Article 24 only enjoins them "in fixing working hours
... to give adequate consideration to the avoidance of imbalances between their personnel and the personnel of the national government and
of other local entities." Chiba's new governor, noting that many of his

employees spent as many hours on the train as they did in the office on Saturdays, instituted a system under which half of them had a free Saturday every other week. This meant cutting the work week from 44 to 42 hours. The Autonomy Ministry, fearing that the case might establish a precedent, declared its opposition to the scheme; so did Prime Minister Ikeda at a Cabinet meeting at which it was decided that the Minister of Postal Services, whose home was in Chiba, should intercede with the governor. The Autonomy Minister and the Chief Cabinet Secretary issued a statement calling for a suspension of the system, and by the end of the week the governor gave in, explaining that he did so under orders from the government, although he was still convinced of the merits of his plan. The plan had been in effect for two Saturdays.*

Local Assemblies and Their Work

The Local Autonomy Law contains provisions regarding the organization, powers, and procedures of local assemblies. According to these, the size of an assembly depends on the size of the population. Prefectural assemblies have a minimum of 40 and a maximum of 120 members. The lower limit applies to prefectures with a population of 700,000 inhabitants or less. If the population exceeds 700,000 but falls short of one million, one assembly member is added for each 50,000 inhabitants. If the population exceeds one million, one assembly member is added for each additional 70,000 inhabitants. The size of the assembly provided in the law is open to change in one direction: since 1952 prefectural by-laws may determine that the number of assembly members in the prefecture shall be smaller than that stated in the Local Autonomy Law. As of July 1, 1961, only one prefecture, Tottori, had the minimum number of assembly members prescribed by the Local Antonomy Law; Tokyo Metropolis alone had the prescribed maximum number.

Municipal assemblies have a minimum of 12 and a maximum of 100 members. According to the law, membership of the assemblies of towns and villages ranges from 12 to 30, and that of city assemblies from 30 to 100. Cities with a population of 300,000 have 48 assembly members.

---

* See, for example, *Asahi Evening News*, January 11, 12, 15, and 19, 1963. There were some questions regarding the internal procedures by which the new work schedule had been instituted. But it appears that the Autonomy Ministry was most concerned about the substance of the scheme and about the independent attitude shown by the governor.

Cities in which the population exceeds that number but falls short of 500,000 add four assembly members for each additional 100,000 inhabitants. Cities with a population of more than 500,000 add four assembly members for each additional 200,000 inhabitants. Municipal bylaws may reduce the number of assembly members below the number provided in the law. In January 1961, 122 cities had passed such bylaws. The Osaka City assembly had 78 members instead of the legally permissible number of 96; and 59 cities had assemblies of less than 30 members, the minimum number according to the Local Autonomy Law.*

The Local Autonomy Law permits towns and villages to provide by bylaw for a general meeting of all voters instead of an assembly, but the only village which at one time used this form of direct democracy has since been merged with a neighboring town, so that there is at present no example of a general meeting in Japan. In general, Japanese local assemblies, while large by the standards of local councils in the United States, do not differ greatly in size from equivalent assemblies in France. This is not surprising. The provisions of the Local Autonomy Law are based on those of the Meiji codes which, in turn, followed in this regard their French counterparts.[26]

We shall deal with the election of assembly members in a later chapter. We may note here only that their normal term of office is four years, and that they receive a remuneration, but not normally a salary sufficient for their maintenance.†

It is difficult to draw any sort of profile for local assemblies as such.

---

* Based on a survey of the National Association of City Assembly Chairmen in January 1961 (*"Shi gikai no soshiki ni kansuru chōsa"*). Of the then existing 555 cities, 526 (94.8 per cent) had replied to the questionnaire. The survey showed that 34 per cent of the cities that reduced the number of their assemblymen were under Local Finance Reconstruction. Since Autonomy Ministry officials had frequently stressed the advisability of decreasing local expenses by reducing the number of assemblymen—although assembly expenses, in fact, constitute a minimal percentage of the total—this seems to indicate that many cities which took this step did so under some prodding from above.

† However, the remuneration of the chairmen of the assemblies of the larger prefectures is higher than the salary of the lowest paid governors. In January 1962, eleven prefectural assembly chairmen received monthly salaries exceeding 100,000 yen. The remuneration of assembly members exceeded that amount in four prefectures. The minimum salary for prefectural assembly members was 50,000 yen (six prefectures). Based on statistics of the office of the National Association of Prefectural Assembly Chairmen (*Shiryō*, No. 76).

After all, that term applies to the assembly of a rural village on the one hand and to that of an urban prefecture such as Tokyo Metropolis on the other. While the Local Antonomy Law deals with all local assemblies without differentiation in one and the same chapter, a great deal of actual diversity among the assemblies is to be expected. Farming is of course the prevailing occupation of the assemblymen in the villages. But even in towns with a fairly substantial number of families of merchants and employed persons, farmers often hold a greater number of seats than their proportion to the population would justify. In the cities, assemblymen engaged in tertiary industries form the largest occupation block, followed by assemblymen engaged in primary industries. In the smaller cities this order is reversed. In prefectural assemblies, assemblymen engaged in primary industries also constitute a substantial percentage of the total number.[27]

Even in the assemblies of cities and prefectures the number of lawyers is low. This fact is noteworthy in view of the great importance of lawyers in politics in the United States and in other Western countries. The explanation lies not only in the small number of lawyers in the country, but also in the relatively low status of the lawyer in the community. In return, the low percentage of lawyers in the assemblies has certain consequences. For example, it affects the style of assembly operations. Assemblymen who are not lawyers often feel that they are really amateurs in the business of legislation, and this feeling colors their attitude toward the executive.[28]

Although the overwhelming majority of the members of all types of assemblies are men, there are differences in the closeness with which this male predominance reaches one hundred per cent. A survey of city assemblies in 1954 showed that in the smaller cities (those with a population of less than 50,000), women then had 1 per cent of the seats, while in the Big Cities they held 3 per cent of the seats. In the 1959 local elections, women won 5.5 per cent of the seats in the assemblies of the Tokyo special wards, 3.7 per cent of the seats in the assemblies of the Big Cities, 1.4 per cent of the seats in the assemblies of other cities and in prefectural assemblies, and 0.6 per cent of the seats in town and village assemblies. All the chief executives elected were men.[29]

The composition of the various types of assemblies in terms of the party affiliation or independence of their members as of April 1, 1960, is shown in Table 10 on page 356.

TABLE 10

Party Affiliation in Local Assemblies, 1960

	Prefectures		Cities		Towns and Villages	
	No.	Per Cent	No.	Per Cent	No.	Per Cent
Liberal Democrats ..	1,768	66.89	2,650	14.79	2,204	3.45
Socialists	444	16.82	1,329	7.42	901	1.41
Democratic Socialists.	146	5.52	259	1.45	89	0.13
Communists	11	0.41	274	1.53	351	0.55
Smaller groups	82	3.10	180	1.00	48	0.08
Independents	192	7.26	13,222	73.81	60,381	94.38
Total	2,643	100.00	17,914	100.00	63,974	100.00

SOURCE: Wada Hideo, *Kempō no gendaiteki dammen* (Tokyo, 1961), pp. 417–18.

It will be noted that most town and village assemblymen are independents. In cities the ratio of independents differs with the size. The larger the city, the more likely the connection of a substantial part of the assembly members with a political party. In the 1954 survey it was found that in the smaller cities 76.45 per cent of the assembly members were independents. In the next larger cities the percentage was 67.06 per cent, in the third group 66.7 per cent, and in the fourth group (cities with a population of over 150,000) 45.8 per cent. In the big cities it was only 11.1 per cent. In prefectural assemblies most members are affiliated with a party. We shall discuss this matter in greater detail in the following chapters, but a few comments may be appropriate in the present context. Most independents are of conservative persuasion, so that it is no exaggeration to state that local assemblies quite generally have a conservative majority. This is significant in a number of ways. Traditional notions of harmony, held by conservatives, affect the operations of the local assemblies and their relations to the chief executive, especially if he, too, is a conservative. As far as local autonomy is concerned, conservatives are more likely to subscribe to hierarchical notions regarding relations to the central government; and so long as the central government is also in conservative hands, the political tensions that might otherwise foster tendencies toward independence are absent.

On the prefectural level, assemblymen may form organizations (often called "clubs") with names that do not correspond to any party label.

Thus in the Kyoto prefectural assembly there is not only a Liberal Democratic Club but also a New Liberal Democratic Club and a Liberal Comrades Association in addition to the organizations of Socialist, Democratic-Socialist, Communist, and Independent assembly members. In Hyogo, the organization of the Liberal-Democratic assembly members is called Kōsei-Kai ("Fairness Association," a title chosen also by similar organizations in three other prefectures). Despite their names, these organizations often constitute the active part of the party on the prefectural level, and their meeting rooms in the prefectural assembly buildings often serve simultaneously as the prefectural party headquarters.

The assemblies of prefectures and big cities are normally divided along party lines or, at least, along the lines of a general "conservative" or "progressive" persuasion. This type of division is sometimes to be found also in other cities, but more frequently their assemblies are divided along the lines of factions, usually based on personal relations.* There may be a pro-mayor and an anti-mayor faction, the latter often headed by the chairman of the city assembly; or there may be factions of old-timers and newcomers. Factions may also consist of the representatives from the older parts of the city and of the representatives from newly added areas. Factions based on area interests or loyalties are most frequent in town and village assemblies; in fact, at this level the assembly members are usually considered to be delegates for a small community, such as the *buraku*.

The meetings of the assembly are convened by the chief executive. Before the amendment of the Local Autonomy Law in 1952 six regular meetings a year were required; since then the law states that regular sessions should be called not more than four times a year. In addition there may be extraordinary sessions. One-fourth of the assembly may demand the convocation of a session.

In 1961 all prefectural assemblies held four regular sessions, each lasting an average of fifteen days. Twenty-nine assemblies held extraor-

---

* The two types of divisions are not mutually exclusive. For example, Liberal Democratic assemblymen are frequently divided along the lines of personal factions. Most frequently these factions are adherents of one or the other Diet member from the prefecture. See Ward, *Village Japan*, pp. 424ff; Brett, *The Government of Okayama Prefecture*, pp. 112ff.

dinary sessions, some as many as three or four; the average length of
these was three days. Thirty-two prefectures held their regular sessions
in February, June, September, and December; five held their first session of the year in March, but otherwise adhered to the norm; four deviated from it in other ways; and five held to no regular schedule.[30]

Before the enactment of the Local Autonomy Law the chief executive
—the governor or mayor—presided over the meetings of the assembly.
Since then each assembly elects from its own membership a chairman
and a vice-chairman. According to the law, they hold office during their
entire four-year terms as assemblymen. In actuality the chairmanship
usually rotates among the more powerful assembly members. A gentle-
man's agreement is reached before the election under which the elected
chairman abdicates his post after a year or two in favor of another assemblyman with substantial backing. It is possible to hand the prestige-
giving position of chairman around in this fashion because it can be
expected that the agreements among the conservative leadership group
will be compiled with by the conservative assembly majority. There is
little danger that a member of the progressive camp could be victorious
in the selection of a successor to the retiring incumbent.*

According to a 1959 survey taken by the Autonomy Ministry, 31 (or
67 per cent) of the 46 prefectures, 60 per cent of the cities, and 32 per
cent of the towns and villages had, in fact, assembly chairmen for one
or two years.[31] The chairman is assisted by the executive office, which
prefectural assemblies must and city assemblies may establish. This
innovation, and the separation of the task of the assembly chairman
from that of the chief executive, are in line with the policy of the postwar reforms intended to increase the relative importance of the assembly.

As another step in the same direction, the Local Autonomy Law provides for the establishment of standing and special committees by local
by-laws. Based on this provision, all prefectures and most cities—537
out of 540 in 1960—have established standing committees. The special
committees deal with matters especially referred to them by the assembly and are created for this purpose on an ad hoc basis. The standing
committees are authorized to consider and to report on bills and on the

* In 1961 none of the chairmanships in prefectural assemblies was held by a Socialist; only two prefectural assemblies (Kyoto and Osaka) had Socialist vice-
chairmen.

budget and to carry out investigations of such matters as fall within their scope of jurisdiction. On important matters they may hold public hearings.

Originally the number of standing committees was unrestricted. Prefectural assemblies usually had committees corresponding to the divisions of the executive office and, in addition, a steering committee, a rules and discipline committee, and others. Tokyo Metropolis also had committees to report on the affairs of each of the special wards. In the cities the number of standing committees varied, of course, according to their size. But in most cases it was seven or eight, except in the big cities, which had from nine to sixteen. It is typical of the general tendency of the Local Autonomy Law amendment of 1956 that it limited the permissible number of standing committees. Now Tokyo may have a maximum of twelve; Hokkaido, prefectures with a population of 2,-500,000 or more, and the large cities with more than 1,000,000 inhabitants may have a maximum of eight; prefectures with a population above 1,000,000 inhabitants and cities with more than 300,000 inhabitants a maximum of six; and smaller prefectures, cities, and towns and villages a maximum of four. In actuality, the number of standing committees sometimes falls below the legally permissible maximum. The Tokyo Metropolitan Assembly has eight standing committees roughly corresponding to the bureaus of the metopolitan administration.* Six other prefectural assemblies also have eight standing committees; twenty-five have six, two have five, eleven have four, and one (Niigata) has three.

The operation of the standing committees varies greatly. In the big cities and in some prefectures they may use their investigative powers on their own initiative with an eye to clarifying what legislative action in a given field is required. In some cases their public hearings attract a good deal of public attention. The interests of various groups are then represented before the committees and opposing views are aired. The committee members develop a degree of technical specialization that they bring to bear on the discussion of bills referred to the committee by the plenum. They thus in fact perform the functions envisioned by

---

* They are the committees for general affairs and capital city development; for finance and taxation; for welfare and education; for health, economy, and public sanitation; for construction and labor; for housing and ports; for transportation and waterworks; and for police and fire protection.

the creators of the institution. Often, however, the standing committees serve primarily as communication channels between the local executive and the local legislature. According to the Local Autonomy Law they are to discuss only matters specifically referred to them by the whole assembly when they meet while the assembly is not in session. In actuality, standing committees—especially in smaller municipalities— usually meet prior to the assembly sessions to hear explanations of draft bills that the executive plans to put before the assembly, to listen to statements by the officials in charge regarding the reasons for the introduction of the bills, and to exchange questions and answers. Thus the executive learns in advance of the assembly meeting whether its proposal will be acceptable; the assembly members enjoy the prestige of being informed about the executive's intentions; and sometimes the bills are amended at this stage. The committees thus serve to foster harmony between the two branches of the local government and to prevent the loss of face that defeat of a measure in the full assembly would entail. Committee meetings are then really pre-assembly conferences between officials and assembly members rather than second stage in the local legislative process.

On the municipal level the regular committees are often replaced by a Committee of the Whole (Zenin Kyogikai). (In this case the real standing committees go into action only in rare cases when a highly technical matter is up for consideration.) This Committee of the Whole may also discuss draft bills before they are put before the formal assembly session. Amendments may be agreed on at this stage rather than in a formal meeting either of the assembly or of a committee. When all problems are threshed out in these informal sessions the bill is submitted to the formal assembly session. Of course, it passes the assembly smoothly, normally without any further question. The assembly session becomes a formality, devoid of importance or interest to the citizen. The provision that assembly sessions must be public is in these cases without much meaning or purpose.*

In some of the small cities or towns the standing committees may

---

* Sessions of the Committee of the Whole are normally not open to the public. Only eleven cities adopted bylaws throwing committee sessions open to the public. On the other hand, Yokohama and four other cities passed bylaws specifically excluding the public from sessions of the Committee of the Whole. See *Chihō jichi shiryō*, No. 223 (July 1, 1960), p. 8.

have altogether only a formal existence, based on the rather vague notion that this contributes to a smooth operation of the legislative process. Sometimes bills are immediately put before the plenum of the assembly and all deliberations—including exchanges of questions and answers—take place there. After the bill has been approved, it is referred, as a mere matter of form, to the standing committee.[32]

On the other hand, some prefectural assemblies use, in addition to the formal committee system, parliamentary techniques that take into account the existence of parties. A bill may be discussed in a meeting of representatives of the parties before it goes to the appropriate committee and a compromise may be worked out there, rather than in the committee. In big cities, there may be a similar arrangement in the form of a "compromise group," in which representatives of the parties—or, in case of the conservatives, of various factions within the party—participate.

So much for the organization of the assemblies. In regard to their powers, the Local Autonomy Law states that they enact bylaws, determine the budget, approve the final account, decide on the creation, management, and disposal of the permanent property, enter into certain contracts and perform a number of other functions, such as the election of the Election Administration Committee and the approval of certain appointments by the chief executive. They have a broad investigative authority supported by the power of subpoena. They may examine the management of the affairs of the local entity and demand reports. They may summon the chief executive and the administrative commissions for examinations not only regarding the administration of the proper affairs of the entity but also regarding national affairs assigned to the executive branch.

The provisions of the law regarding assembly proceedings are somewhat sketchy. Members are given the right to present bills on any matter except the budget, which must be presented by the executive. A majority of the full membership of the assembly constitutes a quorum. In certain cases a session may be held even in the absence of that quorum; this may be done, for example, if a session has been called twice in regard to the same matter, but less than half of the membership have responded. As noted previously, assembly sessions are normally to be open to the public. For most decisions a simple majority of those present suffices. Tie votes are broken by the chairman. Minutes are to be kept and to be forwarded to the chief executive. Municipal assemblies must forward reports of their session to the governor, prefectural assemblies to the Autonomy Minister. Beyond these general rules, each assembly is free to adopt its own rules of procedure.[33]

Of course, actual procedures differ for the various types of assemblies. Obviously they are more complex in case of the assemblies of prefectures or big cities than in case of small villages. But certain statements are valid in general. Thus almost all bills at all levels are presented by the chief executive, the legal provisions for member bills notwithstanding.[34] Also, the executive participates in legislative proceedings to a degree that is not apparent from the legal provisions. According to the law, the chief executive may present explanations regarding the budget and other matters to the assembly. Otherwise, he and other members of the executive are to appear before the assembly when summoned by the chairman. In actual practice, the chief executive is present at every session, occupying usually a permanent desk facing the assembly. His subordinate officials also occupy permanent desks, as do representatives of the administrative commissions along with their officials, such as the superintendent of education.* Finally, in all assemblies deliberations of the budget, including the number of supplementary budgets passed each year, consume most of the time.

Beyond this, generalizations regarding the work of the assemblies become more difficult. The number of bylaws differs with the type and size of the locality. It depends also on the number of national laws in any given year that require local legislative action. In a prefecture, thirty or more bylaws (including amendments to existing bylaws) may be passed in a session; in a village, the number may be below ten for a year. Often the bylaws amount to little more than authorizations to the chief executive providing only the most general standards for his discretion.[35] In a prefecture or large city the bills have been prepared by the division in charge, and have often been passed by a legislative council and approved and submitted to the assembly by the chief executive,

---

* Speaking of the Okayama Prefectural Assembly, Brett notes that it is not unusual for the officials of the executive branch to outnumber the assembly members (*The Government of Okayama Prefecture*, p. 92). The practice of executive attendance is a legacy of prewar days. As Brett states, "in view of the deference which has traditionally been accorded to officials in Japan, one cannot but suppose that the representatives are inhibited to some extent at least in carrying on their deliberations in the presence of such an imposing body of officials." Executive attendance is also common in meetings of the standing committees, as noted earlier.

who normally explains his legislative program in the first meeting of the session. The titles of the various bills are read, the members are referred to the printed material distributed to them for study, and the meeting is adjourned. When the session reconvenes, interpellations to the executive are in order. In large assemblies the time available for questions may be allotted to the various parties or groups within the assembly in accordance with their strength. As Brett states, the interpellation period is practically the only opportunity for assembly members to state their views on the floor, and they are likely to make the most of it. The questions are answered by the chief executive or one or more of his officials; the answers may show some adroitness, or they may be patently noncommittal or excessively brief. Nevertheless, this is likely to be the liveliest part of the session. Then bills are formally assigned to standing committees and the plenum is adjourned for a few days. In the standing committees some bills evoke no comment at all, others prompt some inquiries from the officials present at the committee meeting, or even some debate. But all bills normally pass without resort to a formal voting procedure. When they are reported out to the plenum (occasionally with a comment by the committee chairman that the committee's unanimous approval of the bill does not imply the absence of all criticism), further debate in the assembly is the exception rather than the rule. The chairman of the assembly asks whether there are any objections to the recommendations of the committees. The assembly replies, "No objection," and the bills are adopted.[36]

The procedures are simpler in smaller localities. But, and this is one further generalization that seems permissible in all assemblies, the bills introduced by the executive are almost certain of passage. The same is true for the budget, although, as stated earlier, a great deal of time may be consumed by item-by-item explanations by the executive and by questions from the floor.

One of the explanations for this fact is to be found in the informal contacts between the executive and the legislature prior to the assembly sessions. We referred to this point briefly in discussing the use of the standing committees as communications channels. As Brett demonstrates in a chapter of his study aptly entitled "Legislation by Negotiation," the assembly actually enters the lawmaking process at a time when the bills are still in the drafting stage. By the time they are put before the assembly, the amending has already been done and passage is assured.

The sessions of the assembly thus naturally proceed with great "smoothness." This smoothness is considered highly desirable by most executives and assembly members. In smaller units it is often proudly claimed that proceedings are smooth because of the harmony existing in the community, and the unusual cases where an objection was raised and actual voting was necessary are considered a blotch on the record of the local entity. The importance attributed to harmony reflects the conservative attitudes of the local assemblies and of most chief executives.

However, while the conservative emphasis on harmony and ideological homogeneity of the two branches of local government is important, perhaps the most important reason for the smoothness of the legislative procedure lies in the character of the bills to be passed by the assemblies. The fact that almost all by-laws are proposed by the executive and that they are usually adopted without change may make the assembly appear to be a rubber stamp of the executive. Actually, the reason for the compliance of the assembly lies less in the overpowering strength of the executive than in the fact that the passage of the bylaws is in reality a routine matter, for most of them are required by national law.[37] In this case the question whether the bill is desirable or not is beyond any argument.

There remains the matter of details and form. But this matter, too, is largely removed from debate because the bill has been handed down from the central government or the prefecture in the form of a model bylaw. Governors and other prefectural officials have received orientation or guidance at their meetings with national officials in Tokyo. The model bylaw may also have been discussed at a meeting of the National Association of Prefectural Assembly Chairmen. Where a municipal bylaw is required, the mayors received their guidance from the Local Affairs Section of the prefectural government or from the chief of the prefectural Local Affairs Office in their *gun*. Thus even details and form are largely predetermined. At most, the mayor may make minor changes in the model bylaw to adapt it to local circumstances. But by and large, he is likely to feel that legal technicalities are better left to the experts who drafted the model bylaw, and the assembly is likely to share this feeling.[38] In its legislative activities the entire local apparatus, not only the assembly, serves to a large extent as a rubber stamp of the central government.

There are of course exceptions to this rule. When the issue to be resolved by the local assembly is purely local, the normal passive solidarity of the assembly may well break down. This is morely likely to happen in connection with the budget than in connection with the adoption of bylaws. Thus on the village level the question where a new school building or a new meeting and recreation hall is to be located, or which road repair is to be given priority, may lead to a clash between the representatives from the various *buraku* whose interests are affected and, occasionally, to a clash between the mayor and a group of assembly members.

There is one further activity of the assembly which deserves mention. Under Article 124 of the Local Autonomy Law an individual citizen or a group of citizens may present a written petition to the assembly through an assemblyman. On the prefectural level, where such petitions are quite frequent, many originate from towns and villages. They call to the notice of the prefectural authorities some undesirable condition—such as the deplorable state of a road or a bridge in the village—and request amelioration. The assembly—or, more frequently, one of its committees—discusses the petition and, if it concurs, passes it on to the appropriate executive official and requests a report on his disposal.*

The Relationship Between the Executive and the Assembly

As noted earlier, the local chief executive is chosen by direct popular election. In this regard he is independent of the local legislature and his position resembles that of an executive under the presidential system

* Brett (*The Government of Okayama Prefecture*, p. 122) finds that this more traditional device performs the functions envisaged for direct demands for assembly action. Among the petitions that he mentions in his study are the following: objections of a village to the reactivation of a former Japanese Army proving ground for use by U.S. forces; a request from the prefectural P.T.A. for an increase in the prefectural assistance for private schools; a request from a village for a prefectural subsidy to enable it to buy two mechanically operated water pumps; a request from a group of railway workers for reduction of their property tax. Some petitions were forwarded to the national government, such as a petition for the establishment of a new railway station, a petition against the establishment of a powder magazine by the National Defense Agency, and various petitions for subsidies.

In 1961, prefectural assemblies handled a total of 12,864 petitions under Article 124 of the LAL (*seigan*). They also dealt with 8,890 petitions that were informally presented without fulfilling the requirements of Article 124 (*chinjō*). Petitions dealing with public works ranked high in number in many prefectures. (Based on statistics of the office of the National Association of Prefectural Assembly Chairmen, *Shiryō*, Nos. 91 and 92.)

of democratic government. His responsibility to the electorate—rather than to the assembly—is enforced also by the provisions for the recall of the executive. On the other hand, the parliamentary system is emulated in the provision that the assembly can force him out of office by a vote of no confidence unless he decides to dissolve the assembly and to take the disagreement "to the people" by way of a new election.

This blending of systems reflects the pragmatic approach of the Occupation officials who played a role in the drafting of the law. They saw various needs—the need for increasing political consciousness on the local level and the need for diminishing executive control over the assemblies, for instance—and attempted to respond to each of them. In view of the highly centralized character of the former system, they also felt it necessary to insure that the executive on the higher level—the prefectural governor in the case of municipalities, the Prime Minister in the case of prefectures—had no power to interfere in local executive-legislative relations on a lower level. The law, as originally enacted, made it quite clear that the local decision-making process was to be autonomous in this sense. However, the amendments of 1952 and 1956 deviated to some extent from this principle. The existing provisions regarding the relations of the chief executive with the assembly are, therefore, complex. They may be summarized as follows.

The chief executive has, first of all, a general if limited veto power. He may return an assembly's resolutions concerning a by-law or the budget for reconsideration within ten days, specifying the reasons for his objection; if the assembly passes its original resolution again by a two-thirds majority, the veto is overruled. The exercise of this general veto power is in the discretion of the chief executive. Chief executives find it rarely necessary to use this power. This is not surprising in view of the general picture we have just given of the informal relations between the two branches. At the same time the cases in which this general veto power was exercised serve as a reminder that deviations from this general pattern do exist. Between January 1, 1955, and June 30, 1960, the cases numbered 9 on the prefectural level and 67 on the municipal level.*

In addition to this general discretionary veto power, the chief execu-

* On the prefectural level three cases occurred in Fukuoka Prefecture, which experienced much executive-legislative friction during this period. The other six cases occurred in Nagano and Hiroshima (two each), in Okayama, and in Nagasaki. In

tive has a mandatory veto power: he is obliged to ask for reconsideration of an assembly action in four situations. The first of these is of special interest because the governing provisions of the original Local Autonomy Law were amended in a significant way in 1956. If the chief executive considers an act of the assembly—a resolution or an election—to be ultra vires or illegal, he must cause the assembly to reconsider it. Originally the law provided that he may file a lawsuit against the assembly if it failed on reconsideration to amend its action. The courts, and not some higher authority in a hierarchy of governments, were to be the guardians of legality.[39] In the last analysis, they still are, because the possibility of bringing the issue before the courts was not abolished in 1956. However, the local chief executive must now request first an investigation by higher authority, i.e., by the governor or the Autonomy Minister. Such a request must be made within 21 days. Acting as arbiter, the higher authority may hand down a decision within 90 days. If it finds the chief executive's objection justified, it rescinds the assembly's action. Only after this type of recourse has been used can the party that is dissatisfied with the arbitral decision bring an action in the courts.

There is also another way of resolving the conflict without going to the courts. We mentioned in Chapter 13 the Autonomy Conflict Mediating Committees, which since 1952 may be established to settle disputes not only between local entities but also between organs of the same entity. Having received a request for investigation, the governor or Autonomy Minister may appoint such a committee and submit the conflict to it for mediation. The amendments of the law thus have gone to con-

---

one case the veto was overridden by the assembly; in two cases the assembly on reconsideration followed the governor's proposal; and in six cases it passed a compromise measure. The cases on the municipal level were distributed over 22 prefectures and 49 municipalities, 13 of them cities. The veto was overridden in 15 cases, a modified bill was passed in 4 cases, and the mayor had his way in 32. (In 16 cases the assembly had not, or had not yet, acted on the request for reconsideration.) The statistics are based on the Autonomy Ministry's *Chihō jichi geppō*, No. 30-31 (March 1961).

The exercise of the veto often indicates not just a policy disagreement but real animosity between the chief executive and the assembly majority. This may be illustrated by a case in Hokkaido in which the assembly decreased the mayor's salary very drastically, stating that he lacked the proper qualifications and that his private life was not in accord with the dignity of his office. The mayor asked for reconsideration, but the assembly passed the measure again with the required two-thirds majority.

siderable length to diminish the likelihood of court actions. One may well sympathize, in general, with the desire to avoid them. The point which needs to be stressed in this case is that the alternatives infringe on the principle of the separateness of the local decision-making process and confirm notions of subordination of one level of government to the next higher one in a hierarchical structure.[40] Since cases of this type are exceedingly rare on the municipal level and virtually nonexistent on the prefectural level, the confirmation of such notions is perhaps the most important result of the change in the law.*

The second situation in which the chief executive is obliged to cause the assembly to reconsider its action occurs when he finds that a resolution "cannot be executed in respect to revenues and expenditures." The resolution need not deal directly with the budget, with taxes or other financial matters. It is sufficient that the chief executive believes that the measure involves expenditures which the local entity cannot afford. When his effort of changing the assembly's mind fails, he has no further legal recourse. No special majority is needed to overrule him.[41]

The third case of a mandatory request for reconsideration has to do with the "obligatory" expenses of the local entity—that is, expenses which it has to defray on the basis of laws or ordinances, or on the basis of orders of a competent ministry. Examples are expenses constituting the prefecture's share in the maintenance of national roads, or expenses that are necessary for the performance of obligatory local functions. If the assembly strikes out or reduces such expenses in spite of the demand for reconsideration, the chief executive may appropriate and disburse the required amount without further reference to the assembly. This device is a modified version of the "execution of the original draft" (*genan shikkō*) of the former local government codes. But it is applicable only within a much more narrow scope and does not involve a direction from a "supervising authority."[42]

---

* There was no case on the prefectural level between January 1, 1955, and June 30, 1960. Two examples on the municipal level may illustrate the type of conflicts that fall into this category. In a municipality in Chiba the assembly passed a resolution to annul its election of the local Election Administration Committee and to hold another election. The mayor asked for reconsideration, stating that a resolution to annul a legally held election is illegal. The assembly stuck to its resolution, whereupon the mayor asked for investigation by the governor. The governor sided with the mayor's view and rescinded the assembly resolution. In a municipality in Hiroshima the assembly elected a new chairman although the incumbent had not yet resigned. The election was canceled by the governor upon the mayor's request for investigation.

Finally, the chief executive must request reconsideration of an assembly resolution that strikes out or reduces emergency expenses necessary to meet a disaster or to provide for its recovery, or expenses for the prevention of epidemics. If the assembly insists on its action, the chief executive has a choice: he may accept his defeat (in which case the reconsidered assembly resolution remains in effect, even if passed by a simple majority), or he may consider the assembly action as a resolution of no confidence and dissolve the assembly within ten days or resign.[43] In practice the last three situations rarely arise. No case was reported on the prefectural level between January 1955 and the end of June 1960.[44]

Normally the resolution of no confidence is of course the assembly's ultimate weapon to resolve its conflicts with the executive. A quorum of two-thirds is required, and three-fourths of the assembly members present have to vote for the resolution to obtain its passage. The chief executive may within ten days dissolve the assembly and take the issue "to the people" by way of a new assembly election. If he fails to do so he loses his office. He also loses his office if after dissolution of the assembly that passed the no confidence resolution, the new assembly again passes a vote of no confidence. For the second vote of no confidence a two-thirds quorum is also required, but a simple majority of those present suffices for its passage. It may be noted that the power of dissolution is narrowly circumscribed. In this regard the present system differs conspicuously from the prewar system, under which a broad dissolution power was in the hands of the Home Minister. A prewar governor or mayor who requested the dissolution of his assembly did not endanger his own position. Their postwar successors, however, take a risk. For, if the electorate sides with the assembly—that is, if the election results in an assembly with a majority that is again opposed to the chief executive—the defeat of the executive is final. At least in law, the former predominance of the chief executive has been abolished and a balance between his position and that of the assembly has been established.

The legal provisions for no confidence votes and dissolutions are used rather sparingly. On the prefectural level, only four cases are on record between January 1, 1955, and June 30, 1960. Three motions for a vote of no confidence against the Socialist Governor of Hokkaido—in November 1955, October 1957, and April 1958—failed to pass. So did a motion in the prefectural assembly of Gumma in March 1956. On the municipal level, motions for vote of no confidence do sometimes pass, leading occasionally to the resignation of the mayor, but more frequently to a dissolution of the assembly. In the period mentioned above, 19 such motions were made in 17 cities; of these 8 passed and 11 failed. In 6 of the 8 cases in which the motion succeeded, the mayor reacted by dissolving the city assembly; in the other 2 cases he resigned.* There were also 63 no confidence motions in 60 towns and villages; 30 failed and 33 passed. Those that passed led to the resignation of the mayor in 2 cases, to a dissolution of the assembly in 27 cases, and in the remaining 2 cases to the assembly's reconsideration of the no confidence vote after passage.

Another aspect of executive-legislative relations is the scope of the actions that the executive can take without prior reference to the assembly or—in the terms of Japanese public law—the scope of his "discretionary dispositions." The intention of the drafters of the Local Autonomy Law to abolish the former predominant position of the executive is also apparent in the provisions regarding this scope. There are two types of such "discretionary dispositions." One type is based on a resolution of the assembly that delegates to the chief executive the authority to dispose of a specified "matter of a minor nature" that would normally fall within its jurisdiction. The chief executive must report his disposition to the assembly. Aside from such delegations by the assembly, the chief executive may act at his own discretion in four situations. They are: (1) If the assembly has not been established (for example, because the former assembly was dissolved or resigned *en bloc* and the new assembly has not yet been constituted). (2) If no meeting of the assembly can be held even under the exceptional circumstances in which sessions are permissible in the absence of a quorum (for example, because even at the third call only one assemblyman appears). (3) If the chief executive determines that action has to be taken before the assembly can be convoked. (4) If the assembly "fails to pass a resolution on any such matter as shall be resolved therein."[45]

In these cases the chief executive must also report his disposition to the next meeting of the assembly and ask for its approval. According to the interpretation of the Autonomy Ministry, failure to obtain such approval does not affect the legal validity of the disposition. The political effect, of course, is another matter.[46] It will be noted that the four cases of non-delegated discretionary dispositions have one thing in common:

---

* It appears that no confidence resolutions usually occur in smaller cities, indicating that they are used more to resolve factional conflicts than party conflicts. See *Chihō gikai no jittai chōsa*, 1954, p. 58.

the chief executive can make a disposition only if the assembly has not acted. He cannot replace an assembly action by a disposition of his own because he feels that an assembly measure is "injurious to the public interest," as was the case under the Meiji system.*

Summary

The present chapter indicated, to begin with, the extent to which local entities have control over their own organizational structures. On the prefectural level this control is limited by laws, by Cabinet orders, and by ministerial ordinances. Above all these looms the influence of national ministries that feel free to interfere in the prefectural organization because the prefectures, in spite of their character as "fully autonomous local entities," serve primarily national ends. Municipalities have slightly more freedom, although the general atmosphere of local government (including the inadequacy of most municipal finances, the financial dependence on higher levels of government, and the general notion of subordination to control by higher authority) do not favor innovation and experimentation.

The Occupation's attempt to debureaucratize local administration by creating semi-independent commission outside of the regular executive has largely been undone. On the one hand, the independence of these commissions from the chief executive has been reduced; on the other hand, the connections of some of these commissions to their counterparts on a higher level (or to a national ministry) have been strengthened. Practices that were at variance with the purposes of the establishment of the system have been ratified and reinforced by subsequent legislation.

The Occupation also attempted to establish an independent local public service. This purpose was achieved only partially, especially on the prefectural level, where it was most important. The top-to-bottom coordination of the past has been somewhat reduced, but large groups

---

* The most conspicuous case of the use of these legal provisions occurred in Fukuoka Prefecture in 1956. At the time, the governor used discretionary dispositions to put into effect 88 measures. The assembly, deeply embroiled in a conflict between the governor and the Board of Education regarding an increase in the number of teachers in elementary schools and high schools, had failed to pass these measures prior to the closing of its session of March 1956. Regarding the recall movement against the governor, see Chapter 16.

of important prefectural officials are still linked in a number of ways to the central government bureaucracy.* Here, as elsewhere, the amendment of the Local Autonomy Law in 1956 tended to sanction prior extra-legal arrangements that were not in agreement with the spirit of the postwar reforms, and thus to lessen the effectiveness of these reforms.

As for local executive-legislative relations, the postwar reformers aimed at strengthening the assembly's position vis-à-vis the chief executive. They introduced a number of legal devices to achieve this aim. Yet, the legislative record of most assemblies seems to indicate that the chief executive is still in a predominant position. His bylaws and his budget are normally passed without change. If we ask what the assembly does in its sessions, we may well answer in Robert Ward's concise phrase: "It discusses and it approves."[47] This is not to say that it is without influence on local decision making. Its influence may be exercised through informal contacts with the executive that lead to "legislation by negotiation." It may express itself, at least on the prefectural level, through criticism of the executive in formal question periods. Yet, the assembly does not normally exhibit the degree of independence that it was expected to have under the reformed system. A combination of factors—aside from those leading to executive predominance over legislative bodies elsewhere—accounts for this. On the prefectural level, the legacy of bureaucratic dominance over the people and their representatives, reflected by the prominent attendance of officials at assembly and committee metings, is one of these factors. Another factor is the dominant conservatism of local politics. Traditional notions of harmony, shared by executives and legislatures, put a taboo on the actual use of the legal devices by which an assembly could assert its position. But perhaps the most important factor is the narrowness of corporate autonomy—the limited scope of independent local legislative activity. Most of the local

---

* As usual, SCAP statements tended to equate the adoption of a legal reform with its successful implementation. In a lecture prepared by the Local Government Division of SCAP's Government Section in 1947 or 1948 there occurred the following statement: "Before the enactment of the Local Autonomy Law the Department [that is, the *bu*, or division of the prefecture] was an integral division of the old government system; it was a part of the bureaucratic ladder of organization. The official as *buchō* [division chief] looked with longing eyes toward Tokyo for recognition and promotion. Today that system does not exist." (SCAP, Government Section, Local Government Division, Paper No. 4, "Administrative Functions and Responsibilities," mimeo., p. 3.)

legislative activity exhausts itself in the adoption of measures handed down from above. The executive who proposes these measures in the local assembly, and the assembly that discusses and adopts them, do not act in a context of independence in which the detailed legal provisions regarding their relationship could become meaningful.*

This situation is not likely to change unless local independent functions and local finances increase and thus provide room for greater local initiative which for the time being seems very improbable.

---

* Lectures prepared by the Local Government Division of SCAP's Government Section proclaimed optimistically that henceforth local legislative bodies in Japan would rank in power with their counterparts in England, the United States, and other Western democracies. "Under the old regime," so the lecture continued, "the assembly was a hollow representation of a democratic legislative body. It was too often the rubber stamp of a distant central government. . . . Today the assembly is a legislature of real power and responsibility. It is a free organ or agent of government." (SCAP, Government Section, Local Government Division, Paper No. 3, "Powers and Responsibilities of the Legislative Body," mimeo., n.d., p. 1.) The degree to which the local legislature is still "the rubber stamp of a distant central government" is the measure of the failure of the reforms in this area.

Robert Ward points out that the assembly which enacts a required bylaw placates the offices of the prefecture or of the national government that originated it and saves "face" for the mayor, who must work and get along with these extra-village authorities. On the other hand, the mayor will be guided in the execution of the bylaw by the discussions in the assembly. "The assembly indirectly but effectively demarcates the areas in which it desires or will tolerate effective administration of the letter of the law vis-à-vis those where it would prefer partial or merely ritualistic enforcement." (*Village Japan*, p. 364.)

It should be noted that in purely local matters clashes of interests—involving sometimes the executive in its relations to groups in the assembly—do occur, traditional notions of harmony notwithstanding.

CHAPTER 15

Citizen Participation in Local Government, I

When the Occupation set out to foster local autonomy, it aimed at establishing grass-roots democracy. This concept is based on certain assumptions about political leadership, which may be stated briefly as follows: Political power on the local as well as the national level flows upward from the people to the leadership. Leadership is not an a priori status but is based on support by the people. Government exists to serve the interests of the people, and the people determine what best serves their interests.* They make their will known in elections. The candidates for public office present alternatives for civic and political action in their campaigns; the people, by expressing their support for the alternative that seems best calculated to serve their welfare, make the final decision. A candidate is thus chosen primarily for his views on civic matters.

The people are not, of course, all of one mind in regard to what is the best choice, but the candidate and viewpoint that finds support from a majority or plurality is considered "the people's choice." This is significant for the rotation of offices: if in the next election there is a shift of public opinion so that the majority supports a new contender for office, the leadership changes. The fact that there are different viewpoints among the electorate and that each election thus results in the victory of a majority and in the defeat of a minority is fully accepted as natural. It is not viewed with alarm as a breakdown of the unity and harmony of the people. It suffices if the people are unified in their support for the rules of the game.

---

* All of this is no more than a paraphrase of Lincoln's definition of democracy as "government of the people, by the people, and for the people."

While the voter is supposed to be mindful of the interests of the community as a whole when he casts his ballot, he is not expected to leave his own interests out of consideration. A degree of self-orientation is accepted.* It is quite normal for a candidate to appeal to special interests and thus win the support of individuals and of groups formed to pursue a shared interest. Still, voting remains in the end a matter for the individual, who supposedly casts his ballot on the basis of a rational choice. Attempts to influence the individual's vote by means other than an appeal to his reason are frowned upon.

Reality differs from this ideal picture to some degree in all countries and at all stages of political development. We may assume that the character and strength of the traditional value system at a given time is one of the factors that account for these deviations. In Japan the traditional value system includes a number of notions that conflict with the notions underlying the ideal image of the electoral process.

We noted earlier that Japanese tradition assigned to the people a passive role. Government was not theirs; there were those who governed and those who were being governed. The former were superior in status, and demanded and commanded; the latter were inferior, and complied and obeyed. Political leaders thus were not made by the people. Political leadership was rather a natural result of the status—primarily based on ascription—that certain persons held in society. The attitudes engendered by such a system may be expected to persist even after the introduction of elections. To vote may become simply another duty imposed by those who govern, an expression of support for those already in a

---

* The theoretical dilemma of a possible clash of the interests of a group with the interests of the community as a whole is solved in various ways. One way is to consider the political system simply as a mechanism for the reconciliation of pluralistic interests. This view denies the existence of any interest of the community that transcends the interests of various groups, aside from its interest in achieving their reconciliation. Self-orientation is then not only permissible; it becomes the grist for the mills of the polity. The Burkean postulate that the elected candidate ought not to represent the interests of his electorate but ought to be a free agent, guided only by his convictions regarding the general good, is actually another way of solving the dilemma. In practice the dilemma is often solved by a denial of the clash between the interests of the community and the interests of a given group. The group convinces itself and attempts to convince the electorate that its interests are identical with those of the community.

In this and in the following chapter the pattern-variable scheme of Professor Talcott Parsons is frequently referred to for purposes of analysis. (See also Chapter 10.)

position of power. The question of whom to vote for resolves itself without too much difficulty in a society in which everyone supposedly owes loyalty and obedience to someone above him. One votes for one's superior or for the candidate he sponsors.

It follows that in elections of this type the views of the candidates on political and civic issues and their relationship to the views and interests of the voters are not really important. Far from dictating the direction of future policies, these elections leave the determination of policy up to those whose right to govern is merely ratified by the vote. It follows further that campaigns which appeal to views and interests are not only superfluous; they are also inconsistent with basic assumptions about the proper relations between persons of superior and inferior status. These and other human relations are seen as particularistic. As far as elections are concerned, this means that the vote is generally not given to a candidate because he has certain universalistic qualifications—not, for example, because he is "a good man" in terms of his civic views or in terms of his ability, but because he has a certain personal relationship to the voter. This relationship is diffuse, not specific. It is not limited to any clearly demarcated sphere, such as the political, but extends to all spheres of social life. In other words, it is a relationship between person and person, not one between a candidate and a voter in an election.

Superior and inferior statuses are, of course, less clear when achievement orientation replaces ascription and when social mobility increases. But within limits, diffuse interpersonal relations can also be created in this situation and can be used to mobilize election support. This may be done by exhibiting a continuing sympathetic interest in the voter's personal affairs, by advising him in crisis situations, by granting favors to him and his family, and in many other ways. The diffuse obligation—the *on* in Japanese terminology—that the candidate puts on the voter assures his vote more or less automatically and continuously. In this case, too, the appeal is not directed to the specifically political interests of the voter; it aims at more than the voter's vote in the forthcoming election. We may expect that where traditional values have carried over into a situation with comparatively fluid status relationships, the appeal to the person as a whole will be a favorite political technique.

The traditional preference for diffuse rather than specific interpersonal relationships is not the only element in Japanese tradition that militates against rational appeals to individual interests to obtain votes.

The pursuit of individual interests itself is frowned upon because in Japanese tradition the emphasis lies on the interests of the collectivity. It follows that an appeal to the voter as a member of a collectivity is in line with traditional mores, while an appeal to his interests as an individual runs counter to them. The collectivity in question, of course, is the community to which the individual belongs, not an association which he joined to pursue his individual interests. The *buraku* was, and to some extent still is, such a community. Because the individual is expected to assign the highest priority to the collective interest, he is expected to vote for the candidate who supposedly represents the collectivity interests, even if his individual interests would incline him to vote for some other candidate. Abstention from voting amounts to shirking a duty to the collectivity. In other words, we may expect a high degree of social pressure to vote, and, more particularly, to vote in conformity with all the others who belong to the collectivity. Such voting gives the impression of unity within the group. We mentioned earlier the quest for harmony—or at least for its outward appearances—that is stressed in Japanese tradition. An open clash of interests is to be avoided, and so the best elections are those that are uncontested. Campaigns that articulate clashes of interests are undesirable in themselves, and equally undesirable because of their result: an obvious division of the electorate and of the representatives into a majority and a minority standing in opposition to each other. It should be clear that these notions stand in contrast to the notions underlying the ideal type of democratic elections.

Of course, the hold of traditional notions on the voters differs in various areas of Japan. It is stronger in rural areas than in urban areas, and affects certain elections more than others. Prefectural elections may differ from village elections, assembly elections from mayoral or gubernatorial elections. We shall call the type of election behavior that is most completely in accord with traditional values the "conservative" pattern, and the type of election behavior that is most completely in accord with the Western ideal of elections the "progressive" pattern. If we think of these patterns as end points on a continuum, we may expect actual election behavior in various types of elections to be located at different points on it.

In this chapter we shall explore three elements in the patterns of election behavior—the voting rate, the rate of competition among candidates for a given position, and the degree of party affiliation or independence—

on the basis of election statistics. In the next chapter we shall examine the six types of local elections in some detail, and in the process relate our findings in this chapter to those observations.* But first we shall discuss briefly the legal framework for local elections.

Legal Provisions

Universal male suffrage was instituted in Japan in 1925. After the war women were given the right to vote. The Constitution of 1947 states in Article 15:

> The people have the inalienable right to choose public officials and to dismiss them.
> All public officials are servants of the whole community and not of any group thereof.
> Universal adult suffrage is guaranteed with regard to the election of public officials.
> In all elections, secrecy of the ballot shall not be violated. The voter shall not be answerable, publicly or privately, for the choice he has made.

As mentioned earlier, Article 93 of the Constitution provides that the chief executives of all local public entities, the members of their assemblies, and other local officials, as determined by law, shall be elected by direct popular vote within the several communities.

These basic rules are implemented by the Public Offices Election Law, which deals with both national and local elections.[1] Voters in local elections must be 20 years of age and must have resided within the local entity for three months. To be eligible as a member of a city, town, or village assembly, or of a prefectural assembly, one must be over 25 years of age and have the voting right in the locality. The same age requirement applies to mayors, but governors must be 30 years of age. In neither case does the law require residence. This is significant, particularly in the case of gubernatorial elections, because it makes it possible to "import" a candidate from the outside.

As a rule, the election district for municipal assembly elections is the city, town, or village in its entirety. But in cities designated in accordance with Article 155, paragraph 2—that is, in effect, the five big cities—the administrative wards serve as election districts. Other cities may establish election districts by bylaw, fixing the number of assemblymen

---

* In the next chapter we shall also deal with the other method of citizen participation in local government, the method of engaging in direct demands.

to be elected in each district in proportion to its population. Fifty-three additional cities have done this.* The election districts for prefectural assembly elections are the cities and the counties (*gun*).† In the elections of mayors and governors the local entity as a whole—city, town, village, or prefecture—serves as the election district.

The voter does not need to register for elections; he is registered automatically by the local Election Administration Committee. The basic voter list includes all persons who are over the age of twenty years and who have resided in the locality for at least three months prior to September 15 of a given year. It is drawn up yearly on the basis of various official records. After completion, it is opened for public inspection. Persons who feel aggrieved by the omission of their names may first raise an objection to the committee, and, as a last resort, may bring a suit against the chairman of the committee if the objection does not lead to the desired result. Just before each election a supplementary list is compiled. It contains the names of persons who were not included in the basic list but who have since completed the requirement of three months residence in the locality. These lists are valid for all elections, national as well as local.

Certain persons are excluded from becoming assembly members or chief executives. Thus the Local Autonomy Law states that no one is to be concurrently a member of a local assembly and a member of the Diet or another local assembly. It also bars paid officials of a local entity from membership in its assembly. Other laws provide the basis for exclusion of judges, members of boards of education, and other administrative commissions, and certain officials of the national railroads and of the monopoly corporations. Until 1956 persons who entered into contract work with a local entity were not disqualified from becoming assembly

---

* See the survey regarding the organization of city assemblies conducted by the National Association of City Assembly Chairmen in January 1961. The survey shows that 37 of the 53 cities were so-called "new cities," created by amalgamations. These were all cities with a population below 100,000. The division of the small cities into election districts reflects the desire for separate areal representation of their component units. Thus we find that Kyoto City (population 1,284,746 on October 1, 1960) has 9 election districts, while the "new city" of Kohama in Fukui Prefecture (population 36,236) has 10.

† The recent amalgamations, expanding the city areas at the expense of the *gun* areas, have led to significant changes in the districts for this type of elections. As a result, many prefectural assemblymen are now elected in single-member districts. See Chapter 16, p. 436.

members, although they could not become chief executives. By making use of the *oyabun-kobun* system (a fictive kinship relation) which is particularly strong in the construction trades, such contractors sometimes became important forces in the assembly and thus had a chance to influence its decisions in ways designed as much to serve their personal interests as those of the community at large. In the major revision of the Local Autonomy Law in 1956 this loophole was plugged, not only in regard to assembly positions but also in regard to those of vice-governor, certain top auxiliary organs of the chief executive, and inspection commissioners.[2]

For each election, the local Election Administration Committee selects an Election Meeting Chairman. One of his tasks is to receive the written notification of candidacy for each candidate. This notification may be submitted by the candidate himself or by one or more registered voters who recommend a candidate with the latter's consent.* A deposit is required for candidates in all elections except those on the town and village level.

Election campaigns are severely limited by the law in terms of time, expense, and permissible practices. No electioneering is permitted before the notification of candidacy has been filed, which can be done only after the election date has been announced. It is generally recognized that the shortness of election campaigns favors the incumbents, since the line between servicing the needs of constituents and actual voter solicitation is difficult to draw. Premature campaigning on the part of a new candidate is more easily recognized. Certain campaign activities are financed by public funds. Thus in some elections so-called competitive speech meetings are held, at which all candidates appear and make their views known to the public.† These meetings are arranged by the local Election Administration Committee and the costs are borne by the national treasury. The candidates also receive free a specified number of postcards, posters, and transportation tickets. The law strictly regulates the number of newspaper advertisements, posters, and election cards, the number of speeches on radio and television, the number of trucks or other vehicles that may be employed, and many other matters.

---

* As we shall note later, the practice in this regard differs significantly in various types of elections.

† Since 1952 candidates may send a representative if they are unable to attend the competitive speech meeting (Public Offices Election Law, Article 154 as amended.)

It also sets a limit to the amount of money that may be spent by candidates and their supporters, but the permitted maximum for campaign expenses is usually exceeded.* Certain practices are forbidden. These include not only the buying of votes, but also house-to-house visits by candidates or canvassers and the serving of food or drink—except tea— for campaign purposes. The problems of enforcing these restrictions are many and vexing. After every election there are thousands of arrests and prosecutions. Still, many of these restrictions are more often than not ignored.

The municipal Election Administration Committees appoint a voting overseer for each polling place, as well as three to five voting witnesses to assist him. When the voter arrives at the polling place he shows his polling booth entry card, which is checked against the voting list. The voter then receives a ballot, enters the booth, and writes the name of his favorite candidate on the ballot. He then puts the ballot in the ballot box. Secrecy of the ballot thus seems to be assured.† The ballots are taken to a "ballot-counting place" and are there counted in the presence of ballot-counting oversers and ballot-counting witnesses. All these are appointed by the Election Administration Committee. The above-mentioned Election Meeting Chairman collates the returns from the various voting districts and reports the result of the election to the Election Administration Committee. The Committee then announces the final returns.

Local elections are held every four years. Under the existing system of "unified local elections" all entities of a certain type hold their elections on the same day. The elections for prefectural offices and the elections in the five big cities are normally held first. A week later elections are held for the positions of mayors and assemblymen in the other cities and in the towns and villages. But in certain localities elections occur in between the dates for these unified local elections. The reason may be the resignation, death, or recall of a mayor or governor, the recall of an

---

* Professional politicians frequently complain that elections are getting more and more expensive. The free campaign aids received by the candidates are only of limited help. They can be used for general appeals to the electorate, but much campaigning consists in less overt and less general appeals, which are equally costly.

† However, as will be shown later, in small localities there is less secrecy than meets the eye, and the voting witnesses, whose ostensible purpose it is to ensure fairness, often exert conscious or unconscious pressure on the voters to vote in conformity with direction of locally powerful individuals.

entire assembly, or the termination of the term of office of officials elected in such by-elections.*

Degree of Participation in Local Elections

Japanese local elections are generally characterized by high voting rates. A high turnout of voters is considered to be very desirable. The semi-official Fair Election Movement (Kōmei Senkyo Undō) urges the voters to cast their ballots; newspaper editorials do the same and if the turnout is high they congratulate the voters and the country.[3]

But voting rates give us only the number of votes cast.[4] At best, they give us only certain clues as to what the vote means in terms of political consciousness or civic interest. We shall look for these clues by comparing the rates in various types of elections in urban and rural areas.

We start with an investigation of voting rates in the elections of town and village assemblies. The statistics for the first postwar local election in 1947 do not differentiate between various types of municipal assemblies, so that a figure for town and village assembly elections alone is not available.[5] The nationwide voting rate in elections was 95.92 per cent in 1951, 92.33 per cent in 1955, 92.50 per cent in 1959, and 91.97 per cent in 1963.† These town and village assembly election rates are, of course, spectacularly high; if we compare them with the rates in other types of local elections in Japan, we find that they top all others. There are some differences between the rates in various prefectures. Data for 1955 and 1959, for instance, show that towns and villages in predominantly rural prefectures had the highest rates.[6] On the other end of the scale were the towns and villages in Tokyo Metropolis. Some urbanized prefectures stood slightly above the national average in both elections, while some comparatively rural prefectures showed low voting rates. Thus, the voting rate in town and village assembly elections does not seem to be simply a function of the urbanization or rurality of the prefecture; but it can still be stated that towns and villages in rural prefectures tend to show higher rates than those in urbanized prefectures.[7]

In the elections of town and village mayors the voting rate is lower than in the elections of assemblymen. The national average in 1951 was

---

* At present only about 20 of the 46 governors are normally elected at the time of the unified elections.

† Figures for the 1963 elections are given where they were available at the time of this writing.

95.84 per cent, in 1955 it was 92.04 per cent, in 1959 it was 91.12 per cent, and in 1963 it was 90.25 per cent.[8] All prefectures that ranked in first to fifth place in either 1955 or 1959 were rural in character.[9] The lowest voting rates occurred in Kanagawa in 1955 (85.35 per cent) and in Osaka in 1959 (83.46 per cent), and the second lowest rate in Tokyo in both years (86.27 and 83.69 per cent).[10] Thus, the pattern is rather similar to that of the town and village assembly elections. The voting rates tended to be higher in rural prefectures than in urban prefectures.

When we turn to elections in the cities, it is well to remember that the term "cities" encompasses units that are quite different from one another. Cities range from small, recently amalgamated semi-rural "new cities" to the highly urban five big cities. In addition, Tokyo's special wards are classified as cities. If we separate various types of cities and compare the voting rates for their assemblies with the voting rates for town and village assemblies, we obtain the following picture (Table 11).

We note that the voting rate in city assembly elections is lower than that in town and village assembly elections. Among the cities, the voting rate in the most urbanized units—the Tokyo wards and the five big cities—is conspicuously lower than in the rest of the cities. The general tendency of an inverse ratio between urbanization and voting rate is quite clear. This tendency is apparent also when we look at the voting rates for city assemblies in the various prefectures. The highest voting rates appeared in the cities of rural prefectures that also ranked high in the two types of elections discussed previously, namely, Fukushima, Yamanashi, Yamagata, Toyama, Shimane, and Gumma. To these must be added Tochigi and Nagano, both relatively rural in character. Cities in urbanized prefectures tended to show lower voting rates.[11]

TABLE 11

Voting Rates in City Assembly Elections

Election Year	Tokyo Ward Assembly Elections	Assembly Elections in Five Big Cities	City Assembly Elections		Town and Village Assemblies
			Incl. Tokyo Wards, Five Big Cities	Excl. Tokyo Wards, Five Big Cities	
1951	75.30%	72.92%	84.31%[a]	90.56%	(95.92%)
1955	61.51	62.26	76.80	85.00	(92.33)
1959	65.40	65.09	78.96	85.81	(92.50)

[a] This figure is based on Autonomy Board, Election Bureau, *Senkyo nenkan* (January 1953), p. 129.

TABLE 12

Voting Rates in City Mayor Elections

| Election Year | Tokyo Ward Chief Elections | Mayor Elections in Five Big Cities | City Mayor Elections | | Town and Village Mayor Elections |
			Incl. Five Big Cities	Excl. Five Big Cities	
1951	75.46%[a]	74.18%	84.10%[a]	90.01%[a]	(95.84%)
1955	–	61.76	79.57	83.73	(92.04)
1959	–	67.17	81.93	85.76	(91.12)

[a] The 1951 election was the last direct election for Tokyo ward chiefs. The figures in the third and fourth columns for that year include or exclude the Tokyo wards in addition to the Five Big Cities. The figure in the third column is based on the Autonomy Board's *Senkyo nenkan* (January 1953), p. 129.

The voting rates for city mayor elections, and how they compare with voting rates for town and village mayor elections, are given in Table 12. Again, cities have lower voting rates than towns and villages, and the rates drop as the urban character of the units becomes more marked. Investigation of the voting rates in the various prefectures shows that the tendency toward high voting rates in rural prefectures exists also in this type of election, although the prefectures with high voting rates are not completely identical with those ranking high in other elections. The prefectures in the urbanized Kanto and Kansai districts—especially Tokyo, Kanagawa, and Kyoto—showed low voting rates, as did Hokkaido.[12]

We noted earlier that in towns and villages more voters vote for assembly candidates than for mayoral candidates. It is interesting also to compare the two voting rates on the city level. If we exclude the most urbanized units, we find that voters in the remaining cities behave in this regard in much the same way as voters in towns and villages. The record in the five big cities shows certain fluctuations (which in itself is not without significance). But in two out of the three elections, in 1951 and 1959, the voting rates for mayoral candidates were higher than those for assembly candidates. The same was true for the ward chief elections in Tokyo in 1951, the only election in which the comparison could be made.

Let us now consider voting rates on the prefectural level. Since cities (*shi*) and counties (*gun*) serve as election districts for assembly elections, and since the statistics distinguish between these areas also in gubernatorial elections, we are able to compare voting rates in the urban parts (*shibu*) and the rural parts (*gumbu*) of the prefectures as well as voting rates in various prefectures. We focus first on prefectural assem-

TABLE 13

Voting Rates in Prefectural and Municipal Assembly Elections

			City Assembly Elections	
Election Year	Prefectural Assembly Elections	Town and Village Assembly Elections	Excl. Tokyo Wards, Five Big Cities	Incl. Tokyo Wards, Five Big Cities
1951	82.99%	95.92%	90.56%	84.31%
1955	77.24	92.33	85.00	76.80
1959	79.48	92.50	85.81	78.96

bly elections. Table 13 compares the nationwide voting rates in these elections with the voting rates in various municipal elections.

We note that prefectural assembly elections attract fewer voters than town and village assembly elections and city assembly elections, at least if we exclude the Tokyo wards and the five big cities from consideration. In the most urbanized units—and only in those—prefectural assembly elections sometimes have a greater appeal than elections for the city or ward assembly.* This is a significant fact. It indicates that the pressures that elsewhere lead to the high voting rates in local assembly elections are relatively weak in these units while political consciousness and, therefore, interest in prefectural (rather than municipal) elections is relatively high. But political interest is no match for the pressures that drive rural voting rates up. Even in prefectural assembly elections the voting rates are higher in rural than in urban prefectures. In the last two elections the prefectures with the highest voting rates were all rural, those with the lowest voting rates all urban.[13]

Within the prefectures, the county areas (gumbu) tend to show higher voting rates than the city areas (shibu). On a nationwide basis the voting rates for gumbu were 83.26 per cent in 1955 and 84.74 per cent in 1959; for shibu they were 72.19 per cent in 1955 and 76.41 per cent in 1959. Even in prefectural assembly elections—where the more pronounced political coloring could lead us to expect that the politically

---

* In the Tokyo wards the voting rate for the prefectural assembly election was higher than that for the ward assembly election in 1959 (68.9 per cent as against 65.4 per cent), but lower in 1955 (57.6 per cent as against 61.5 per cent). See the Report of the Tokyo Metropolitan Election Administration Committee on the 1959 elections, Shōwa 34 nen 4 gatsu chihō senkyo no kiroku, pp. 92 and 162. In 1963 the prefectural assembly elections had a nationwide voting rate of 76.85 per cent.

TABLE 14

Voting Rates in Gubernatorial Elections and Prefectural
Assembly Elections

Election Year	Gubernatorial Elections	Prefectural Assembly Elections
1951	82.58%	82.99%
1955	74.85	77.24
1959	78.25	79.48

less conscious rural areas show a lower voting rate than the politically more conscious urban areas—the inverse relationship between urbanization and voting rate holds true.[14]

In gubernatorial elections the nationwide voting rates were 82.58 per cent in 1951, 74.85 per cent in 1955, 78.25 per cent in 1959, and 74.62 per cent in 1963. Reference to Table 12 shows that those rates are lower than those for either town or village mayor elections or city mayor elections. They are also somewhat lower than those in prefectural assembly elections, as shown in Table 14. A comparison of the voting rates of individual prefectures is more difficult because, for the reasons mentioned earlier, not all prefectures elect their governors at the time of the unified local elections. Thus there were only 19 gubernatorial contests in the unified elections of 1955 and 1959. However, the voting rates in these contests confirm the general tendency toward high voting rates in rural prefectures and low voting rates in urban prefectures noted in other types of elections.[15] This is all the more remarkable because the contests in Tokyo and Osaka in particular were important tests of strength between the "conservative" and the "progressive" camps. As in prefectural assembly elections, political interest cannot push the voting rates in urban prefectures up to the level sustained by other forces in rural prefectures.

In gubernatorial as in prefectural assembly elections, the nationwide *gumbu* voting rate is higher than the nationwide *shibu* voting rate. In 1955 and 1959 the *gumbu* rates were 82.57 and 83.71 per cent; in the same years, the *shibu* rates were 70.02 and 75.53 per cent.

It is significant that the *gumbu* voting rate exceeds the *shibu* voting rate considerably in highly urban prefectures. Thus in 1955 Tokyo's *gumbu* voting rate was nearly 17 per cent above its *shibu* voting rate.[16]

If we consider the conservative strength in rural areas, this fact explains to a large extent the conservative victories in those prefectures.

Our investigation of voting rates has shown three general tendencies: elections in small units draw heavier votes than those in larger units; elections in rural areas draw heavier votes than those in urban areas; and elections for assemblies draw heavier votes than those for chief executives. Parenthetically, the first two tendencies hold true even if we extend the scope of our investigation to national elections. (The third tendency, of course, is not applicable on the national level.) National elections tend to show a lower voting rate than local elections, including prefectural elections; the highest voting rates occur in rural prefectures, the lowest in urban prefectures; and within most prefectures the *shibu* voting rate is lower than the *gumbu* voting rate.[17]

Many Western observers may well be surprised by these tendencies in Japanese elections, because they are the very opposite of the tendencies with which they are familiar at home. For example, in England and the United States, in national elections a voting rate above 60 per cent is common, while in local elections voting rates above 50 per cent are rather rare. Quite aside from this, the above-mentioned tendencies are difficult to explain so long as we start with the assumption that the vote is an expression of political or civic interest. Is such interest in Japan especially high? Is it highest in regard to the affairs of towns and villages? Is it most prevalent in rural areas? It may be well to consider some opinion polls regarding popular attitudes toward local affairs. How much do Japanese voters, who cast their ballots in such great numbers in local elections, know about these affairs, and how much do they care about them? There are many polls, both nationwide and local, that deal with these questions. A few examples may suggest the answers.

A survey conducted in 1949 by the Public Opinion Research Branch of the Civil Affairs Section of the Occupation's I Corps, which covered six prefectures in western Japan, showed that knowledge about local officeholders was relatively slight. Among the respondents, 74 per cent knew the name of the mayor of their locality, but only 65 per cent remembered how he had been selected; 67 per cent knew how assemblymen were selected, but 54 per cent did not know the terms of office of either the mayor or the assembly.

In a nationwide poll conducted by the National Public Opinion Research Institute in March 1951, 40 per cent of the respondents stated that they were too busy with the affairs of their daily lives to have time for local affairs.* In addition, 53 per cent said they knew nothing about the financial affairs of their local entity.

In another nationwide poll conducted by the Jiji Press in January 1956, under a plan worked out by the Autonomy Board, the question was asked: "Do you believe that the people in your city (town, or village) pay attention to the activities of the government of the city (town, or village)?"[18] Of the respondents, 16.6 per cent felt that their fellow citizens "pay a good deal of attention," 46.2 per cent felt that they "do not pay much attention," and 37.2 per cent did not know how to answer the question. As for their own interest in prefectural affairs in particular, the answers of those interviewed were as follows: 4.4 per cent stated that they were very much interested, 19.8 per cent claimed some interest, 33.4 per cent professed not to have much interest, and 42.4 per cent stated that they had absolutely no interest. Thus if we group the last two answers together we find that 75.8 per cent stated that they had little or no interest in prefectural affairs. However, there was a significant difference in the responses to these two questions in urban and in rural areas. Interest in municipal affairs was higher in the rural areas than in the city areas (where only 9 per cent stated that their fellow citizens paid a good deal of attention). But interest in prefectural affairs was higher in the cities. Of the interviewees living in villages, 51.6 per cent had absolutely no interest in prefectural affairs while only 31.8 per cent of those in the big cities and 33 per cent of those in other cities claimed to have no interest. Yet, as we have seen, in prefectural elections the rural voting rates are higher than the urban voting rates, and the voting rates in prefectural elections in general are surprisingly high when we consider the high percentage of those who profess little or no interest in prefectural affairs.

In the same poll, the respondents were also asked whether the activities of mayors and assemblymen sufficiently reflected the desires and opinions of the inhabitants. To this question 53.2 per cent answered, "I

---

* Both surveys inquired also into the respondents' familiarity with the term "local autonomy." In the first survey, 50 per cent confessed unfamiliarity with the term, and of those who knew the term 22 per cent had only a vague idea of the meaning. In the second survey, 46 per cent did not know the meaning of "local autonomy." The data of the first survey are taken from a mimeographed report of Headquarters, I Corps, to GHQ, dated September 15, 1949. The second survey was reported by *Kyōdō News* on June 5, 1957.

don't know," 15.8 per cent "yes," 19.6 per cent "to some extent," and 11.4 per cent answered "no." The reason most frequently given for a negative answer was that the officeholders lacked zeal (22.6 per cent); the failure of the citizens to communicate their opinion ranked next (12.1 per cent), followed by the assertion that those in power were managed by bosses (10.5 per cent). Insufficiency of the budget was mentioned by 5.9 per cent of the total. But significantly enough, the respondents in the big cities (12.5 per cent) and in other cities (8.0 per cent) cited this reason more frequently than those in towns (1.8 per cent) or villages (3.9 per cent). Finally, 36.4 per cent were unable to give a reason for their negative reply. Of those who felt that their mayors and assemblymen were somewhat responsive to the citizenry, 57.2 per cent failed to give a reason for their qualified answer. Those who stated a reason referred to a lack of zeal on the part of officeholders (13.0 per cent). Insufficiency of the budget was mentioned by 8.8 per cent (14.0 per cent in the big cities), bossism by 5.4 per cent. (Bossism was given as a reason by 7.7 per cent of the village inhabitants and by 6.2 per cent of the town inhabitants, but only by 2.0 per cent of those living in big cities and by 3.3 per cent of other city inhabitants.)

A poll dealing with the interest in national and local elections was conducted in February 1956 by the newspaper *Yomiuri* on the basis of a national stratified random sampling.[19] To the question "Which elections are you more concerned with, general or local?" 46 per cent stated that they were more concerned with national elections, 20 per cent expressed more concern with local elections, 19 per cent declared themselves equally concerned with both, while 5 per cent stated they were not interested in either. Ten per cent answered "I don't know."*

On the basis of these polls we can hardly assume that the voting rates

---

* The composition of those expressing concern for national or local elections differed markedly in terms of occupation, schooling and age. Among professional and salaried people interest in national elections was highest (67 per cent and 56 per cent). Among agriculturalists and fishermen it was lowest (18 per cent). The reverse was true regarding the interest in local elections (12 per cent and 17 per cent for the first named groups, 49 per cent for agriculturalists and fishermen.) Interest in national elections increased with higher schooling and was more prevalent among the younger age groups. Older people and those with less education also answered more frequently "I don't know." It should be noted that in spite of the low interest in national elections among those in rural occupations, the voting rate in these elections is highest in rural areas.

in various Japanese elections accurately reflect the real degree of political or civic interest among the voters. Many voters obviously cast their ballots for other reasons.

Ratio of Candidates to Positions

According to the ideal picture sketched at the beginning of this chapter, elections are contests between candidates who compete for office on the basis of their views on public policy. A candidate convinces a sufficient number of the electors that his views are better than those of his opponents or that their interests would be served best by putting him into office; they vote for him and he wins the vacant position. On the other hand, the traditional value system militates against such contests, because they smack of disharmony and self-interest. The degree of competition is thus an important factor in any determination of the extent to which various local elections in Japan reflect traditional notions.

We should mention at the outset that it is possible to avoid contests altogether by ensuring, in the language of Article 100 of the Public Offices Election Law, that in assembly elections "the number of candidates according to the ... notifications of candidacy by candidates for public office ... does not exceed ... the fixed number of members to be elected," or that in the election of a chief executive "the number of candidates according to the notifications of candidacy is ... only one." In these cases no balloting is held. The Election Meeting Chairman declares in the election meeting that the candidates are the persons elected for the position in question.

We start with an investigation of the ratio of candidates to positions in the elections of town and village assemblies. The ratio was 1.3 candidates per seat in the local elections of 1947, 1951, 1955, and 1959; in 1963 the ratio dropped to 1.2. This is, of course, a conspicuously low ratio. It is equally remarkable that it remained the same throughout all postwar elections, although the number of assembly seats changed drastically during this period as a result of amalgamations.[20] Urbanized prefectures do not differ from rural prefectures in this respect. There seems to be a tendency for certain regions—Kyushu and Tohoku, in particular—to show a ratio slightly above the average. But the ratio is fairly steady throughout the country.[21] The low ratio indicates, of course, the occurrence of uncontested elections. In 1955, 12 per cent of the assemblymen were elected without contest; in 1959 the figure was 7.2 per cent, and in 1963 it was 4.6 per cent. The overwhelming majority of assemblymen who were elected without contest were independents.[22]

In the elections of town and village mayors the ratio of candidates to positions is also low, although it is somewhat higher than in town and village assembly elections. The ratio of candidates to positions was 2.0 in 1947, 1.9 in 1951, 1.8 in 1955, and 1.9 in 1959.[23] Here also urban and rural prefectures show no marked differences.*

Selection without contest is particularly frequent in mayoral elections in towns and villages. In 1955, 37.2 per cent of the towns and villages selected their mayors without balloting; in 1959 the proportion was 34.2 per cent. When we consider that in more than one-third of the cases there was only one candidate for the position of mayor and that yet there were nearly two candidates for each position on a nationwide basis, it becomes clear that in some contests more than two candidates vied for the single position at stake. Mayors who won their positions without contest were almost invariably independents.[24]

In the cities the picture is somewhat different. Elections for city assemblies are more competitive than elections for town and village assemblies. If at first we omit from consideration the five big cities and the Tokyo wards, we find that in the remainder of the units classified as cities, the ratio of candidates to assembly seats was 2.5 in 1947, 2.2 in 1951, 1.9 in 1955, and 1.6 in 1959.[25]

These ratios are, of course, not high; but they are higher than the ratios in town and village assembly elections. It will be noted that the ratio is decreasing. This downward trend may be partly due to the creation of "new cities" of semi-rural character. We may assume that the factors that accounted for the low ratio in the towns and villages before amalgamation continue their effect when these units are amalgamated, and that they depress the overall ratio for cities. The decreasing ratio may reflect also the consolidation of the power of local politicians who created in the years since 1947 more or less unassailable bailiwicks, thereby discouraging competition. (In this sense, the ratio in the first postwar election that followed the purge and the land reform may be

---

* Tokyo had a ratio slightly above the average in 1955 (2.00) and the highest ratio in the nation in 1959 (3.47). But other urban prefectures did not significantly differ from rural prefectures.

considered atypically high.) As for the larger cities within the group, the decrease in the ratio may reflect the increasing influence of national politics. Japan had for all practical purposes a two-party system from 1955 to 1960. Candidates from smaller groups and independent candidates may have been squeezed out during this period by candidates of the two big parties. In this context the drop in the competition rate in the big cities and in the Tokyo wards, noted below, is significant. (A similar trend is noted below for prefectural assembly elections.)

Few city assemblymen obtain their seats without contest. Their number was 37 in 1955 and 44 in 1959, 0.4 and 0.2 per cent of the total respectively. This ratio is, of course, much lower than that in case of town and village assembly elections. In both types of assembly elections almost all who win their seats in this manner are independents. But there is a subtle difference: while the majority of uncontested winners of town and village assembly seats are "pure independents"—i.e., independents without any political leanings and regular party support—most uncontested winners of city assembly seats are classified as "conservative independents."[26]

In the elections of assemblymen in the five big cities, the ratio of candidates to seats was 3.3 in 1951, 2.7 in 1955, and 2.0 in 1959.* In the big cities the competition ratio is thus always higher than in the rest of the cities. The tendency of the ratio to decrease is even clearer in their case, probably because they are affected by all the factors mentioned above. They absorbed semi-rural communities and local politicians entrenched themselves in them. Being more highly politicized, the big cities also felt the impact of the emerging two-party system more than the smaller units. Neither in 1955 nor in 1959 did an assemblyman win his seat without contest. In Tokyo's special wards the ratio of candidates to seats was 2.4 in 1947, 3.1 in 1951, 2.4 again in 1955, and 2.0 in 1959. There were no uncontested winners.[27] The downward trend between 1951 and 1959 is noticeable also in this case.

We turn next to the elections of city mayors. In cities other than the five big cities the ratio of candidates to posts was 3.0 in 1947, 2.2 in 1951, 2.3 in 1955, and 2.2 in 1959. We note that city mayor elections are more

---

* The statistics for 1947 do not separate the five big cities from the other cities. In 1963, the ratio was 1.8. In that year two assemblymen (0.5 per cent) won without contest.

competitive than town and village mayor elections or city assembly elections.[28]

Selection without contest in city mayor elections is more frequent than in city assembly elections, but less frequent than in town and village mayor elections. The percentage of city mayors so selected was 11 per cent in 1955 and 17.7 per cent in 1959. Where a contest is held, it is sometimes a three-cornered contest. Most city mayors who win their positions without contest are independents.[29]

The mayors of the five big cities are always elected by actual balloting. In 1947, when all five mayoral positions were to be filled, there were 17 candidates, a ratio of 3.4 candidates per position. In the unified elections of 1951, three positions were at stake and two candidates competed for each of them. In the unified election of 1955, seven candidates competed for the two vacancies (a ratio of 3.5), and in 1959 six candidates competed for the same two vacancies (a ratio of 3.0). The ratio in the big cities was thus always higher than that in the rest of the cities. Finally, if we look at the two instances in which the chiefs of the Tokyo wards were directly elected, we find a ratio of 3.1 candidates per post (69 candidates for 22 posts) in 1947 and a ratio of 2.5 candidates per post (45 candidates for 18 posts) in 1951. There were no uncontested elections.

Let us now consider elections on the prefectural level. In the 1947 prefectural assembly elections, 7,115 candidates competed for 2,490 seats. This is a ratio of 2.9 candidates per seat. In 1951, 1955, 1959, and 1963, the ratios were 2.3, 2.1, 1.8, and 1.7 respectively.[30] These ratios are higher than those in town and village assembly elections and slightly higher than those in city assembly elections, except for the assembly elections in the big cities.

We note that the ratio decreased also on this level. On the other hand, the percentage of uncontested elections increased between 1955 and 1959. In 1955, 74 candidates became prefectural assemblymen without contest. They filled 2.8 per cent of the seats at stake. They came from 54 districts in which no balloting was necessary because the number of candidates equalled the number of assemblymen to be elected. Actual balloting took place in 972 other districts. In 1959, 251 candidates coming from 115 districts won without competition and filled 9.5 per cent of the vacant assembly seats. Balloting took place in 1,015 other districts. It appears from this that the uncontested elections occurred generally in districts which on the average sent fewer members to the assembly than the rest of the districts.* We shall discuss these phenomena in greater detail in the next chapter. It may suffice here to point out that the decrease in the competition ratio in prefectural assembly elections is related to an increase in uncontested elections, which in turn is related to the creation of smaller districts. The changes in the size of the districts were the results of the mass amalgamations, which thus affected the competition ratio also on this level, although somewhat more indirectly than on the municipal level. The other factors—the consolidation of influence in the hands of a smaller number of politicians and the emergence of the two-party system—also probably played a role.

On the prefectural level the uncontested elections went mainly to candidates affiliated with a conservative party. Relatively few seats were won without contest by independents, and the number of pure independents who won their seats in this manner was very small.†

In the gubernatorial races the competition was keenest in 1947, when 207 candidates vied for the 46 posts. This was a ratio of 4.5 candidates per post. In the unified elections of 1951, with 34 governorships up for election and 94 candidates, the ratio was 2.8 candidates per seat. In 1955, 21 governorships were contested by 48 candidates, and the competition ratio dropped to 2.3. In 1959, 20 contests attracted 53 candidates, so that the competition ratio increased to 2.7. As in the case of city elections— and differing from town and village elections—the ratio on the prefectural level is higher for the post of chief executive than for the post of assemblyman. In general, the competition for gubernatorial positions is higher than that for mayoral positions in towns and villages and in cities, except in the five big cities.

* The average district sent 2.55 members to the assembly in 1955 and 2.35 in 1959. The districts in which no balloting was necessary sent an average of 1.37 members to the assembly in 1955 and an average of 2.18 in 1959.

† In 1955 there were still two great conservative parties, the Liberal Party and the Democratic Party. Candidates of these two parties won 41 of the 74 uncontested seats (23 and 18 respectively). Of the remaining 33 seats, 22 were won by independents, 7 were won by candidates of the Right Wing Socialists and Left Wing Socialists, the two Socialist parties existing at the time; the remaining 4 seats went to candidates of smaller groups. Of the independents, 15 were conservative independents, one a progressive independent, and 6 pure independents. In 1959, the lion's share of uncontested seats—180 out of 251—went to Liberal Democrats; 34 went to Socialists. Candidates affiliated with the two big parties thus won 214 of the 251 uncontested seats. Candidates of smaller groups won seven of them. Thirty of these seats went to independents. Twenty of these independents were conservative independents, seven were progressive independents, and only three—half of the number of 1955—were pure independents.

Uncontested elections occur even at this level. In 1955, two pure independents became governors without contest, and in 1959 a conservative independent won without contest.* There is no correlation between the competition ratio and the degree of urbanization of the prefecture, but the contest in Tokyo is always keenest. In 1955 six candidates aspired to the position of governor, in 1959 nine.

If we correlate voting rates and competition ratios in various types of elections we find that the least competitive elections show the highest voting rates and the most competitive elections show the lowest voting rates. Thus, by far the lowest ratio of candidates to seats occurs in town and village assembly elections, which have the highest voting rates. In the cities, where the competition ratio is higher, the voting rate is lower. The elections to the position of chief executive are normally more competitive than those to the assemblies, but their voting rates are lower. In general, there is an inverse relationship between the competitiveness of the type of election and the turnout of voters.

Party Affiliation and Independence

On the national level, policy alternatives are articulated by the political parties, and the candidates' views are normally those of the party to which they belong. A vote for a party-affiliated candidate that expresses support for one or the other policy alternative is in accord with our ideal picture of elections. On the other hand, the articulation of policy alternatives to gain votes and the use of the vote to ensure realization of one or the other alternative is not in keeping with certain elements in the traditional Japanese value system. It may thus be assumed that candidates are less likely to be party-affiliated where the hold of tradition is strong. In this sense the degree of party affiliation or lack of party affiliation of the victorious candidates may provide some clues for the existence of the conservative or progressive patterns of election behavior.

This is the basis of our interest in the degree of party affiliation; however, a few caveats are in order. We are dealing here with local, not national, elections. The policy issues on this level may not be those with

* It appears that a candidate who hopes to win in this manner must declare himself to be an independent. A victorious pure independent in this case is likely to be not a candidate without party support, but rather a candidate backed by both big parties. The governorships filled without contest were those in Shimane and Okayama in 1955 and in Tokushima in 1959. In 1963, the competition ratio increased to 2.9, but there were four candidates who had no competition.

which national parties concern themselves. For this reason a candidate may articulate his views on local public issues and thus win support without party affiliation. In other words, a vote for an independent candidate may be a reflection of the progressive pattern, rather than of the conservative pattern. The opposite is equally true: a voter may cast his ballot for a party-affiliated candidate, regardless of that affiliation and regardless of the candidate's policy views, because of a personal relationship that he has with him either directly or through intermediaries. In this case the vote reflects the conservative, not the progressive, pattern. Furthermore, the voter may cast his ballot for an independent candidate because he considers his qualifications superior to those of his competitors, whatever their respective policy views. In this case the voter's considerations are rational because they relate to the overt purpose of the act of voting. Because the criteria he employs—qualification for office—are universalistic in character, his vote for an independent candidate is then not based on the evaluations that are typical for the conservative pattern. Finally, we may consider the case in which the vote is cast for a certain candidate because of his relationship to the voter, but in which this relationship is not diffuse but specific. Examples of such a particularistic and specific relationship occur when the vote is bought by a bribe or by a promise to obtain for the voter a specific advantage. In this case—which resembles a contract—the relationship is limited in two ways: in time, because it is concluded once the candidate has fulfilled his promise; and in scope, because it is focused narrowly on only one segment of the social life of the interacting persons. In this regard the vote, even if cast for an independent candidate, does not reflect the conservative pattern, under which the relationship between candidate and voter is not only particularistic but also diffuse.*

Nevertheless, the categories of party affiliation may be useful, especially in the case of Japan. While it is true that an independent candidate may articulate policy views on local civic issues and may get elected because these views appeal to the voters, in Japan this is rarely the case. One of the reasons for this is the narrowness of corporate autonomy. Wherever issues play a role at all, political considerations of national scope have a tendency to overshadow local civic considerations.† Can-

---

* Within the scope of this survey it is not intended to create a complete model of citizen participation in local elections. The remarks above are meant to be suggestive.

† It should be noted that Japanese parties normally proclaim their stand on various issues at the time of local election campaigns.

didates whose appeal is not based entirely on the conservative pattern are also likely to be party-affiliated for other reasons. Because local entities depend on national subsidies, conservative candidates of this type are likely to stress their relationship to persons in positions of power on the national level, persons who are also conservatives. Progressive candidates are, in general, more likely to base their appeal on the progressive pattern and to be party-affiliated.[31]

We noted that party-affiliated candidates may obtain votes because of their personal relationship with individual voters. Indeed, candidates can and do appeal to the voters on both traditional and untraditional grounds. Even if we realize that only a part of their support is gained by such untraditional appeals as their affiliation with a party, the extent to which they find it useful to use that appeal may yet serve as a rough indicator of the presence of elements of the progressive pattern. The untraditional appeal based on the candidate's qualifications may well be used by independent candidates, as noted above. But because of the limited emphasis on local civic issues there is reason to assume that in Japan this appeal is used just as frequently by party-affiliated candidates. (Its use is more prevalent in elections of chief executives than in those of assemblymen, as noted in the next chapter.) Appeals to particularistic, specific relationships between candidate and voter may also be used by party-affiliated and independent candidates. But the existence of these cases is, in fact, not very significant. The "deal" is not usually made between the candidate and the voter, but between the candidate and an election broker or "floating boss" who, in turn, controls votes on traditional grounds. Thus, where the vote for an independent candidate is based on untraditional profit considerations on the level of the intermediary, it is still likely to be a vote according to the traditional pattern in the last analysis.*

---

* One final comment: we are dealing here with the appeals of the candidates and the motives of the voters. Voting statistics show only whether the candidates were affiliated with a party, and how many voters voted for party-affiliated candidates; they fail to show whether the affiliation motivated them to do so. It would have been tempting to use public opinion polls instead, and there is no dearth of polls asking voters whether they prefer to "vote for a party" or to "vote for the person of the candidate." The difficulty lies in the fact that these polls do not differentiate among the various reasons for the latter preference. A "vote for the person of the candidate" is a vote according to the progressive pattern, when the criterion was universalistic, such as the qualifications or experience of the candidate; but it is based on the conservative pattern when the criterion was particularistic and diffuse, as in the case of existing obligations of loyalty.

We start our investigation again with the assembly elections on the municipal level. In 1947, 90.5 per cent of all the assembly seats in Japan's cities, towns, and villages were filled by independent candidates; 2.9 per cent of the seats went to candidates of the Democratic Party, 2.5 per cent to candidates of the Liberal Party, 2.9 per cent to Socialists, 0.2 per cent to Communists, and 1 per cent to candidates affiliated with various small parties.[32]

The percentage of independents was even higher in 1951, when they occupied 94.3 per cent of the vacant seats. In 1955 it was 94.4 per cent, in 1959 88.9 per cent.[33]

The percentage of independents is higher in towns and villages than in cities. Thus in 1955, 98.2 per cent of the elected town and village assemblymen were independents. If we omit the five big cities and the Tokyo wards from consideration, the percentage of victorious independent candidates for city assembly seats was 84.9 per cent. In the Tokyo wards the percentage was 30.2 per cent, and in the five big cities it was a mere 17 per cent. In 1959, 96.4 per cent of the elected town and village assemblymen, but only 75.3 per cent of the elected city assemblymen, were independents. In the Tokyo wards the percentage of independents was 20.9 per cent, in the five big cities 13.4 per cent. However, no clear dichotomy emerges between urban and rural prefectures. Osaka and Fukuoka ranked—with Tokyo—below the national average, but Kanagawa, Kyoto, Aichi, and Hyogo ranked above it. The situation in 1959 was similar. In both elections the percentage of independent assemblymen in Hokkaido was comparatively low (96.1 per cent and 93.2 per cent respectively).

Although the percentage of independent town and village assemblymen is high in all prefectures, it is higher in some prefectures than in others. In 1955 all town and village assembly seats in Fukui and all but one of the seats in Yamagata, Ibaraki, Shimane, and Oita went to independents. In Tokyo, on the other hand, only 91.4 per cent of the victorious town and village assemblymen were independents. In 1959 the nationwide ratio of independent town and village assemblymen dropped from 98.2 per cent to 96.4 per cent, as noted above. There was no prefecture in which all seats were captured by independents. In Akita and Ibaraki all but two of the seats went to them. In Tokyo only 85.7 per cent of the elected town and village assemblymen were independents. In 1963 the percentage of independent town and village assemblymen dropped to 95.0 per cent, that of independent assemblymen in the five big cities to 10.3 per cent. In the remainder of the cities and the Tokyo wards together the percentage was 62.6 per cent, which was 8.1 per cent lower than in 1959.

If we separate the victorious independent assemblymen into the three categories of "pure," "conservative," and "progressive," we note that on the town and village level the percentage of those who are classified as pure independents is high. In 1955, 58.3 per cent of the total number of successful independents were so classified. In 1959 the percentage was 53.7 per cent.[34] In the cities—other than the five big cities and the Tokyo wards—the percentage of victorious pure independents is lower. The percentage was 38.5 per cent in 1955 and 31.9 per cent in 1959.[35] In the five big cities, 54 independents were elected in 1955. Of these 9 (16.6 per cent) were pure, 37 were conservative, and 8 progressive. In 1959, 16 (34 per cent) of the 47 victorious independents were pure, 26 were conservative, and 5 progressive. In the Tokyo wards, 88 of the 283 independents successful in 1955 were pure (31.1 per cent), 164 were conservative and 31 progressive. In 1959, 202 ward assembly seats went to independents. Of these 46 (22.7 per cent) were pure, 146 conservative, and 10 progressive. Thus the majority of independents in towns and villages are pure while the majority in cities are conservative.

We turn now to the elections of municipal chief executives. Table 15 shows the results of the elections for municipal chief executives between 1947 and 1959 in terms of party affiliation or independence: in

TABLE 15

*Party Affiliation or Independence of
Municipal Chief Executives*

Year	Demo-crats	Liberals	Socialists	Commu-nists	Small Groups	Inde-pendent	Total
1947	405	383	264	11	105	9273	10441
	(3.9%)	(3.7%)	(2.5%)	(0.1%)	(1.0%)	(88.8%)	
1951	56	245	55		19	6351	6726
	(0.8%)	(3.6%)	(0.8%)		(0.3%)	(94.5%)	
1955	9	11	10	1		1806	1837
	(0.5%)	(0.6%)	(0.5%)ᵇ	(0.05%)		(98.3%)	
1959ª	41		20	1	1	1341	1404
	(2.9%)		(1.4%)	(0.1%)	(0.1%)	(95.5%)	

ª By 1959 Democrats and Liberals had merged to form the Liberal Democratic Party, and the Socialist Party was reunified.
ᵇ Total polled by the Left Wing Socialists and the Right Wing Socialists. The breakdown was 3(0.15 per cent) for the Left Wing and 7(0.35 per cent) for the Right Wing.

general, the ratio of independents is somewhat higher among successful mayoral candidates than among successful assembly candidates.*

Again, the ratio of independents is higher in towns and villages than in the cities. In the cities—excluding the five big cities—independents captured 93.6 per cent of the mayoral positions in 1955 and 78.9 per cent in 1959. In 1955 the two conservative parties won 4.7 per cent of the posts; in 1959 this percentage had risen to 12 per cent. The Socialists fared even better. In 1955 the Right Wing Socialists and the Left Wing Socialists together captured only 1.7 per cent of the city mayor positions, but in 1959 the reunified Socialist Party won 9.1 per cent of the positions.[36] The same phenomenon can be noted in city assembly elections. In 1963, independents became mayors in 77.4 per cent of the cities, other than the five big cities. This was a decrease of 1.5 per cent from 1959.

In the big cities only two mayoral contests took place in 1955 and in 1959. In 1955 both positions went to conservative independents; in 1959 one was won by a conservative independent and the other by a Liberal Democrat.†

The independent town and village mayors are more likely to be "pure independents" than the independent city mayors. This is shown by Table 16.

It will be noted that in the towns and villages the percentage of pure independents dropped in 1959, while that of conservative independents rose. Still, the percentage of pure independent town and village mayors was higher than that of pure independent city mayors. The percentage of pure independents dropped in 1959 also in the cities while that of conservative independents rose. It appears that more and more inde-

---

* In this, as in many other regards, the election of 1947 was an exception. It appears that mayoral elections are affected to some extent by the developments of national politics. The fall of the Socialists from the crest of 1947 to the depths of 1951; the strengthened grip of the Liberals on the government after the elections of 1949; the confusion in the conservative and in the progressive camp prior to the mergers of late 1955 and the consolidation of the political scene after these mergers all seem to be reflected in fluctuations in party affiliation and independence. The comparison of the ratio of independents in 1955 and 1959 may suggest that mayoral candidates are more willing to accept a party label when the party system is stabilized.

† The mayors of the big cities are normally independents, but "independence" in their case has the same connotations as in the case of governors, which are noted below. After the elections of 1963, Yokohama had a Socialist mayor (replacing a Liberal Democrat), Osaka a progressive independent mayor, Nagoya a conservative independent mayor, and Kyoto and Kobe pure independent mayors.

TABLE 16

*Independent Town and Village Mayors and City Mayors
by Types, 1955 and 1959*

Type of Independent	1955		1959	
	Town and Village Mayors	City Mayors	Town and Village Mayors	City Mayors
Pure	914 (55.7%)	50 (31.1%)	540 (44.9%)	35 (25.2%)
Conservative	650 (39.6)	93 (57.8)	619 (51.5)	87 (62.6)
Progressive	79 (4.7)	18 (11.1)	43 (3.6)	17 (12.2)
Total	1643 (100%)	161 (100%)	1202 (100%)	139 (100%)

pendents, both in cities and in towns and villages, are obtaining conservative endorsement. This suggests that pure independents lean to conservatism.*

In the elections of prefectural assemblies the majority of the winners are party-affiliated. In 1947, when 2,490 seats were to be distributed, 803 (32.2 per cent) went to independents, the rest to party men. The Democratic Party captured 604 seats (24.3 per cent), the Liberal Party 491 seats (19.7 per cent); the Socialists followed with 411 seats (16.5 per cent). Four seats went to Communists (0.2 per cent) and 177 (7.1 per cent) to smaller parties and groups. In 1951, 782 (29.8 per cent) of the 2,616 seats at stake went to independents. As in the other local elections of 1951, the Liberals forged ahead of the Democrats, winning 1,074 seats (41.1 per cent), while the Democrats occupied only 284 prefectural assembly seats (10.9 per cent). It will be noted that the Liberals also outnumbered the independents. The Socialists won 334 (12.8 per cent) of the seats, the Communists 6 (0.2 per cent). The representation of smaller parties in prefectural assemblies decreased to 136 seats (5.2 per cent).

In 1955 the percentage of successful independents rose to 857 (32.8 percent). This increase was accompanied by a sharp drop in the representation of the Liberal Party: only 606 (23.2 per cent) of the 2,613 seats at stake went to them. The Democrats obtained 594 seats (22.7 per

---

* This would not be true only for Japan. Thus R. M. Jackson notes in *The Machinery of Local Government* (London, 1958), p. 55: "An Independent is often a party man. It is noticeable that this happens more frequently on the Right than on the Left. A Socialist is normally concerned to make it quite clear that he is one. . . ."

TABLE 17

Independent and Party-Affiliated Municipal and Prefectural Assemblymen

Election Year	Municipal Assemblymen				Prefectural Assemblymen			
	Indep.	Cons. Parties	Prog. Parties	Small Parties	Indep.	Cons. Parties	Prog. Parties	Small Parties
1947	90.5%	5.4%	3.1%	1.0%	32.2%	44.0%	16.7%	7.1%
1951	94.3	3.6	1.6	0.5	29.8	52.0	13.0	5.2
1955	94.4	2.7	2.6	0.2	32.8	45.9	16.7	4.6
1959	88.9	5.8	5.1	0.2	15.7	59.9	21.7	2.7

NOTE: Municipal Assemblymen are those of all cities, towns, and villages. The electorate is thus roughly identical with that of the prefectural assemblymen. The column "Conservative Parties" shows the total of the Liberal and Democratic representation in 1947, 1951, and 1955. Similarly, the column "Progressive Parties" includes the representation of Socialist parties, the Labor-Farmer Party (in 1955), and the Communist Party.

cent), a substantial increase over 1951. The Socialists, split into two parties, won a total of 420 seats (16.1 per cent).* The Labor-Farmer Party, which later in the year joined the reunited Socialists, won 6 seats (0.2 per cent) and the Communists increased their representation to 10 seats (0.4 per cent). The number of winners affiliated with smaller parties dropped further to 120 (4.6 per cent).

The elections of 1959 saw the principal conservative parties united in the Liberal-Democratic Party and the two socialist parties reunited. The Liberal Democrats won 1,592 of the 2,656 assembly seats (59.9 per cent), adding substantially to the number of seats held by the two conservative parties in the previous elections. The Socialists also increased their representation; they gained 562 seats (21.2 per cent). On the other hand, the number of successful independents dropped sharply to 419 (15.7 per cent), and the representation of smaller parties decreased to 71 seats (2.7 per cent). The Communists occupied 12 seats (0.5 per cent).†

Table 17 permits us to compare the percentages of independent and party-affiliated assemblymen on the municipal and the prefectural level.

* In the prefectural assembly elections and in the municipal assembly elections the Left Wing Socialists were slightly more successful than the Right Wing Socialists. In the gubernatorial elections and in the elections of mayors the Right Wing Socialists were more successful.

† As in the case of mayoral elections, the fluctuations in party affiliation and independence of successful candidates for prefectural assembly seats seem to reflect developments in national politics.

It is immediately apparent that the percentage of independents on the two levels is quite different. It is considerably lower on the prefectural level. It also fluctuates more on that level.*

The representation of progressive parties increased on both levels between 1951 and 1959. Small party representation decreased steadily. The fluctuations thus occur primarily in conservative party representation. Decreases in that representation coincide with increases in the percentage of independents and vice versa. This is particularly clear on the prefectural level. It appears that the quality of "independence" on the two levels is somewhat different and that independent prefectural assemblymen are on the whole more politically oriented than independent municipal assemblymen. More intensive investigation would probably show that some candidates for prefectural assembly seats ran in some elections as independents and acquired a conservative party label in others. This is the more likely since most of the successful independents are conservative independents. In 1955, 63.2 per cent of the victorious independents were so classified, while 16.6 per cent were classified as progressive and 20.2 per cent as pure. In 1959, 63.7 per cent were conservative independents, 19.1 per cent were progressive independents, and 17.2 per cent were pure independents.[37]

The percentage of independent assemblymen varies among the prefectures. In general, urban prefectures show a smaller percentage than rural prefectures.[38] There are also variations among the prefectures in regard to the "purity" of the successful independent candidates. In some prefectures—including the urban prefectures of Kanagawa, Osaka, and Hyogo in 1955 and Tokyo and Hyogo in 1959—all independents were either conservative or progressive. In others—mainly rural, but including the urban prefecture of Aichi in both elections—all independents were pure.

Considering the comparatively high degree of politization of the prefectural assemblies, indicated by the prevalence of party-affiliated mem-

---

* The elections of 1947 held at the time of the purge and the land reform showed an abnormally high degree of politization. The percentage of independents on the municipal level may be considered abnormally low. For the same reasons the representation of the progressive parties was abnormally high. The percentage of independent prefectural assemblymen dropped further to 12.7 per cent in 1963. In that election the political arm of the Sōka Gakkai, the Kōsei Remmei, captured 56 (2.1 per cent) of the assembly seats.

bers, we may expect to find most of the governorships also in the hands
of party men. However, in the past governors tended to be independents
and even today the percentage of independent governors is higher than
that of prefectural assemblymen. In 1947, when all 46 governors were
to be elected, 31 (67.4 per cent) of the winning candidates were independents. The Democrats, the Liberals, and the Socialists each managed
to elect four governors, while the remaining three posts were captured
by smaller parties. In 1951, 31 posts were contested. This time 24 governorships (77.4 per cent) went to independents, four to Liberals, and
three to Socialists; the Democrats and the small parties were unsuccessful in their bids. In 1955, with 21 posts at stake, independents won 18
(85.6 per cent), the Democratic Party, the Liberal Party, and the Socialist Party each won one governorship. Finally, in 1959 there were 20
gubernatorial contests; fourteen of these (70 per cent) were won by
independents, four by Liberal Democrats, one by the Socialists, and
one by a representative of a smaller group. It will be noted that the percentage of victorious independents in 1959 was lower than in 1955. Some
of the independents subsequently affiliated with the Liberal Democrats,
so that on the eve of the 1963 elections 23 of the governors were Liberal
Democrats, 21 were independents, and one was a Socialist.* The percentage of independent governors seems to be declining. Furthermore,
most of the victorious independents gained their position with the support of a political party. Thus of the 18 independents who gained or regained office in the unified election of 1955, 11 were conservative, two
were progressive, and only five were pure independents. Of the 14 independents elected or reelected in 1959, 9 were conservative, 2 were progressive, and 3 were pure independents. The support given to an independent gubernatorial candidate by a party must not be thought of as
more half-hearted than the support given to a party candidate. When a
conservative independent fights a Socialist candidate or when a progressive independent fights a Liberal Democratic candidate, all the re-

---

* In 1959 the governor of Ibaraki represented a prefectural group. In 1963 one
governorship was vacant. In the 1963 election 12 (60 per cent) of the 20 governorships went to independents, a further drop from the percentage of 1959 (70 per
cent). As a result of that election, 24 governorships were held by Liberal Democrats,
21 by independents, and 1 by a Socialist. Of the independents, 12 were conservative,
4 progressive, and 5 pure.

sources of the principal parties are employed for the independent as well as for the opposing party candidate.* Occasionally a contest in which two independent candidates oppose each other is in reality also a confrontation between the two big parties.†

In either case the denomination of one or both of the candidates as "independent" is a formality dictated by considerations of prefectural or national politics but frequently forgotten in the heat of the battle by candidates and voters.‡ Furthermore, not even classification as pure independent necessarily means that the gubernatorial candidate received no party support. In most cases it indicates rather that the candidate received the support of both major parties. His opponent is then normally a candidate of the Communist Party. Thus, the relatively high percentage of independent governors is not an indication that party politics are less important in gubernatorial elections than in prefectural assembly elections.

Because the election appeal of progressive candidates is likely to be a political appeal, progressive strength in the various types of elections is of interest to us. Table 18 shows this progressive strength in the elections of 1955 and 1959. The table shows that progressive chances are better in cities than in towns and villages and better on the prefectural level than on the municipal level. The first point hardly needs further comment. But we may note that the fact that progressive chances increase with the urbanization of the unit in which the election takes place is confirmed by a comparison of progressive strength in the assemblies of the big cities and in the assemblies of other cities. In the big cities, progressives occupied 32.7 per cent of the seats in 1955 and 38 per cent of the seats in 1959—substantially more than in the remainder of the cities.

---

* In 1959 the contest in Tokyo was an example of the first case, that in Osaka an example of the second case.

† A good example is the gubernatorial contest in Tokyo in 1963. The governor of Hyogo, Mr. Sakamoto, who had been backed by the Socialists in 1954 and 1959, resigned in 1963 to enter the Tokyo race. He had again the full support of the Socialists. He was opposed and defeated by the incumbent, Dr. Azuma, who had the full support of the Liberal Democrats in this bitterly fought contest. Yet, neither candidate carried a party label. Dr. Azuma ran as a conservative independent, Mr. Sakamoto as a progressive independent.

‡ A similar pattern can be observed in some contests for the position of mayor of one of the big cities.

TABLE 18

Progressive Strength in Various Types of Elections

Type of Election	1955	1959
Town and Village Assemblies........................	8.7%	8.6%
City Assemblies (except Big Cities and Tokyo Wards).....	16.4	19.4
Prefectural Assemblies	22.1	24.6
Town and Village Mayors...........................	5.2	3.9
City Mayors	11.6	18.6
Governors	14.3	15.0

NOTE: All successful candidates who belonged to the Socialist Party (or to the two Socialist parties in 1955), to the Labor-Farmer Party, and to the Communist Party, or who were classified as progressive independents, are here considered "progressive."

As for the second point, it may be well to carry the comparison beyond the municipal and prefectural level to the national level. In the elections to the two Houses of the Diet, progressives occupy about one-third of the seats. Thus progressive representation is greatest on the national level, decreases on the prefectural level, and is smallest on the municipal level.* Table 18 also shows that progressives occupy a greater percentage of assembly seats than of the chief executive positions. However, if we consider that it takes a greater percentage of the electorate to put a mayor or governor into office than to elect a minor segment of the assembly, we realize that actually progressives do better in elections of chief executives than in assembly elections.†

* Commentators often write about the "inverted pyramid of progressive strength." Progressive chances appear to be in an inverse relation to the size of the electoral unit. However, size is hardly the determining factor in this case. We are probably closer to the truth if we consider size only as an indicator for the degree of politization and state that progressive chances appear to be in a direct relation to the degree of politization of the various types of elections.

† There are no prefectures with progressive majorities, but there are always some prefectures with progressive governors. Similarly, there are hardly any city assemblies with progressive majorities; yet, in the unified elections of 1959 more than 30 of the 175 mayors elected were progressives. In Fukuoka, where a Socialist governor was elected in 1959, the winning candidate obtained 958,131 out of 1,700,160 votes in his contest with a conservative independent. But in the assembly elections the combined progressive vote was only 730,758 out of 1,699,793 votes. The Socialist governor faces an assembly in which 33 Socialists and four progressive independents are outnumbered by 31 Liberal Democrats and 10 conservative independents, with 4 representatives of minor groups and 4 pure independents holding the balance.

Summary

If we arrange our main findings regarding voting rates, competition rates, and party affiliation in accordance with the various types of elections, we may summarize them as follows:

Town and village elections are characterized by extremely high voting rates. The rate for assembly elections is even higher than that for mayor elections. In both types of elections on this level the highest voting rates occur in rural prefectures. Urban prefectures tend to show a comparatively lower rate, the nadir being reached in the towns and villages of Tokyo Metropolis. In the town and village assembly elections, the number of candidates is not much larger than the number of available seats. The ratio held steady in all postwar elections at 1.3 candidates per seat, regardless of the changes in the number of seats. Many assemblymen are, in fact, elected without contest because the number of candidates in the town or village is identical with the number of seats in its assembly. The assemblymen who win their seats in this manner are almost always independents, as, indeed, the overwhelming majority of all town and village assemblymen are independents. The majority of these independents are pure independents. In the elections of mayors more than one-third of the towns and villages have only one candidate who thus obtains his post without balloting. On the other hand, the ratio of candidates to positions is somewhat higher than in the case of assembly elections, so that where balloting becomes necessary, more than two candidates may vie for the post. The percentage of independent town and village mayors is higher than that of independent assemblymen. But the percentage of pure independents is slightly lower.* Finally we noted that the chances for progressive candidates are very slim on this level.

Elections in cities differ from elections in towns and villages in several respects. For one, the voting rates in assembly elections and in mayor elections are lower. If we exclude the most urbanized units, the elections of the mayors produce a lower turnout than the assembly elections, but the difference is less marked than in towns and villages. In the most urbanized units the tendency is in the opposite direction: mayoral contests tend to attract a higher percentage of the voters. City elections

---

* In 1955, 58.3 per cent of the independent town and village assemblymen, but only 55.7 per cent of the independent town and village mayors, were pure. In 1959 the percentages were 53.7 per cent and 44.9 per cent. See p. 400 and Table 16.

both for mayor and assemblymen are more competitive than the corresponding town and village elections. Only relatively few city assemblymen are chosen without contest. The percentage of independent city assemblymen is lower than the percentage of independent town and village assemblymen, although it is still quite high. Independent city assemblymen are less likely to be "pure" than their counterparts in towns and villages. The ratio of independent city mayors is also lower than the ratio of independent town and village mayors, and independent city mayors are less likely to be "pure." While the great majority of city mayors is conservative, the percentage of progressive city mayors is not as negligible as that of progressive town and village mayors.

The difference in the character of the units bearing the denomination "city"—ranging from agglomerations of recently amalgamated towns and villages to highly industrialized urban centers—is reflected in various ways: in the truly urban centers the voting rate is lower, the competition rate is higher, and there are fewer independents and relatively more progressives in their assemblies.

Prefectural elections are characterized by a voting rate that must be considered low if compared with municipal elections. The voting rate is highest in predominantly rural prefectures, lowest in predominantly urban prefectures. Within the prefectures, rural districts produce a higher voting rate than urban districts. This is true for prefectural assembly elections as well as for gubernatorial elections. The voting rate is slightly lower in the latter elections than in the former. Nevertheless, prefectural elections are more competitive than municipal elections, and gubernatorial elections more competitive than prefectural assembly elections. The candidates for the prefectural assemblies are predominantly party-affiliated, and even independent candidates are often supported by a party. Governors are frequently independents, but that term is not to be taken at face value, for there are few governors who did not receive party support at the time of their election. Progressives are more successful on the prefectural than on the municipal level, but less successful than on the national level.

In the next chapter we shall describe the process that leads to these phenomena and, in doing so, relate them to the conservative and progressive patterns of election behavior.

CHAPTER 16

Citizen Participation in Local Government, II

Assuming that the hold of tradition is stronger in rural than in urban areas and stronger in smaller units than in larger ones, we may expect the conservative pattern of election behavior to emerge most clearly in town and village elections. The high voting rate, low competition rate, and the high percentage of independent candidates may then be considered as symptoms of the conservative pattern. It remains to demonstrate that these symptoms are indeed related to elements of the traditional value system, and to describe in some detail the mechanisms of this relationship. Having thus established one end point of the continuum, we shall then investigate the degree of remoteness of other elections in terms of the strength or weakness of the symptoms and in terms of the strength or weakness of the related elements of the traditional value system.

Town and Village Assembly Elections

We noted earlier that Japanese tradition places a heavy emphasis on collectivity orientation.[1] The individual actor—in his role as voter, as in other roles—is to be guided not by his interests, but by the interests of the collectivity to which he belongs. The collectivities that are traditionally most important in rural Japan are the family and the cooperative living group, the buraku.*

---

* The voter is involved in a number of collectivities in a broad sense. These include the political units in which the elections take place, namely, the village, town, or city, the prefecture, and ultimately the state. According to our ideal picture of elections, the vote is expected to be collectivity oriented, at least to some extent, in regard to these units. But this presupposes a separation of the political role from other roles. Otherwise, collectivity orientation will tend to be strong in small, relatively undiffer-

Loyalty to the family, of course, may conflict with loyalty to the *buraku*—for example, if a member of the family living in another *buraku* is a candidate. In these cases, family loyalty is likely to win out. In such a clash between the demands of two diffuse relationships, the actor is typically permitted to fulfill the demands of the diffuse relationship of the higher order. No stigma is attached to this, as would be the case if a younger son of the family would vote for a candidate in another *buraku* because of individual personal interests or political convictions. The likelihood of conflicts between family loyalty and *buraku* loyalty is somewhat diminished by the fact that families are usually settled in the same *buraku*.

In general, however, the families in the *buraku* are expected to vote for a candidate from the *buraku* who will represent the interests of the *buraku* in the assembly of the town or village. In other words, assembly elections are, in effect, elections of delegates to the assembly in which the various *buraku* are expected to vote as units. Since the entire town or village normally constitutes the election district, two requirements have to be met to ensure that the *buraku* obtains maximum representation in the assembly. First, *buraku* residents who have the right to vote must actually exercise it. Voting thus becomes a duty to the collectivity, not a matter of individual interest or discretion. A turnout of nearly one hundred per cent becomes a matter of pride, because group solidarity is highly valued. The village leadership is of course in accord with those sentiments; some villages provide a bonus for *buraku* in which every voter casts his ballot, and abstention from voting comes under social opprobrium.[2] Collectivity orientation thus supports the extremely high voting rates in town and village assembly elections. Second, all *buraku* residents must vote for the same candidates. Each *buraku* desires to obtain as many seats on the assembly as is possible, considering the number of its votes. The chances for this are best if the number of candidates from the *buraku* equals the number of seats it can obtain and if all voters vote for these candidates. If the number of candidates is larger,

---

entiated units (or social systems) and weak in the larger political units. This is, in fact, still largely the case in Japan. The resultant "fragmented" character of Japanese society has often been noted. An act in accordance with the interests of a sub-collectivity, such as the *buraku*, may yet be self-oriented in terms of the surrounding larger unit, such as the village. When we speak of collectivity orientation, we mean this type of orientation.

the *buraku* vote will be split and the chances for maximum representation will be diminished. Thus the *buraku* leadership usually determines the number of candidates that the *buraku* can elect, and selects the candidates, often in a *buraku* meeting, by the device of "recommendation and consensus." The *buraku* then votes en bloc for these candidates, who are of course sure of election if all voters behave as expected. If a *buraku* is so small that it would fail to elect an assembly member by itself, it is likely to work out an informal cooperative arrangement with other *buraku* to assure representation of its interests in the assembly.[3] In its purest form this system makes the actual casting of ballots superfluous. If the informal leadership group in the village agrees on the number of assembly seats to which each *buraku* or group of *buraku* is entitled, and if, honoring this informal agreement, the *buraku* present only the corresponding number of candidates, the total number of candidates will equal the number of assembly seats and no balloting need be held. We noted that 12 per cent of all town and village assemblymen in 1955 and 7.2 per cent in 1959 were selected in this manner. Thus the system does not work to such perfection in the majority of towns and villages. But it works well enough to keep the competition ratio extremely low. Even in the cases where actual balloting takes place, it is often a mere formality because the outcome of the election can be predicted accurately in advance. *Buraku* solidarity, and family and other ties primarily of a personal nature,* determine the voter's ballot in nearly every case in a manner known to the informal leadership.[4]

The fact that the vote in the traditional pattern is essentially a "fixed vote," determined by geographical and other loyalties, should be kept in mind because it is important also in other settings. We may note that in town and village assembly elections the overwhelming prevalence of the "fixed vote"—in other words, the almost complete absence of a "floating vote"—makes campaigns unnecessary. For the candidate representing a *buraku*, the fixed vote suffices.

Only a candidate who does not represent a geographical community but the interests of one or the other group of voters, such as landlords,

---

* Thus, a voter may feel obliged to vote for a candidate from another *buraku* because he has customarily served as go-between in the marriages of family members or has been instrumental in settling a dispute in which the family was involved, or is the son of the former landlord of a tenant farmer who has now become a farmer-owner, or stands otherwise in an important diffuse relationship to the voter.

tenants, non-farmers, or Socialists, needs to campaign actively because he has to obtain support of the members of that group throughout the village. The occasional participation of such candidates in the election is regretted by tradition-bound village leaders for a number of reasons. The candidate deviates from the valued principle of group solidarity; he stresses issues that divide the group; and a vote along the lines of interests and issues inevitably creates a majority and a minority, thus revealing a breakdown of unity and harmony. (Another reason, less frequently mentioned, is the fact that deviant candidates defy the informal leadership and undermine the existing leadership structure.) Finally, vigorous campaigning is not the proper "political style" in the traditionalistic Japanese countryside. The self-assertion that such campaigning requires is embarrassing and even offensive to people who consider self-effacement a virtue because the group and not the individual is important. Ward relates the more typical case of a candidate for the assembly of the village of Kamo whose entire campaign within his *buraku* "consisted of an appearance at the *buraku* assembly where, at the headman's urging, he delivered himself of the following resounding statement: '*Kondo tatte imasu kara, dōka yoroshiku onegai shimasu*' ('Since I am standing for election this time, please, do what you can')."[5] Indeed, why should he have given a longer oration? Before he announced his candidacy he had held conversations with leading residents of the two *buraku* that he was to represent; the notification of his candidacy had been submitted to the Election Meeting Chairman with the signatures of the headmen of these *buraku*; the headmen had informed their people of the candidacy, and the candidate himself had informed his relatives in other *buraku*. Calculations showed that these votes would ensure the candidate's election. No more was necessary.

The fact that the notification of candidacy had not been submitted by the candidate himself but by the two *buraku* headmen deserves some comment. Such recommendations (*suisen dotoke*) are connected with the political style of self-effacement. They occur frequently in town and village assembly elections, less frequently in city assembly elections, and very rarely in the elections of assemblymen of the big cities and of the Tokyo wards.[6] Together with the absence of overt campaigning, the notification of candidacy by persons of status may thus constitute an additional indication of the prevalence of the conservative pattern of elections.

Since most candidates do not appeal to any particular interest that transcends *buraku* lines, it is only natural that most of them are pure independents. At the same time, candidacy within this traditional framework is itself an indication of a conservative orientation. In other words, the prevalence of independents in the assemblies of Japanese towns and villages has connotations that are absent in other cultural milieus in which the assemblymen of small local units are also normally without party affiliation.

We mentioned the informal political leadership group and its influence on assembly elections. Since in Japanese villages status and influence are general and not differentiated, the political leadership group is normally identical with those who have prominent economic and social status.[7] Thus the members of the group typically come from old and well-established families* of better than average lineage or ancestry (for example, families of former samurai or of former village headmen), are middle-aged or elderly, and have some leisure to nurture their leadership status because they have freed themselves from the obligations of full-time farming. This list of characteristics indicates the importance of ascriptive status. The informal leadership often overlaps, of course, with those who hold formal office; members of certain families are rather regularly nominated and elected to the town or village assembly.[8]

The picture we have sketched here explains the high voting rates, the low competition ratio, and the high percentage of independents in village assembly elections. But it still remains an abstraction, to which reality conforms only in degrees. Deviations from it which are indicative of the influence of various social changes take many forms. Thus collectivity orientation is not always the only explanation for the high turnout of the voters and for the voting of each *buraku* as a block. Some villagers may well cast their vote willingly for a delegate from their *buraku* not only to express group solidarity but also because they find that their primary and most immediate interests really do coincide more with those of their *buraku* neighbors than with those of any group outside. By voting for a *buraku* delegate they want to assure, for example, that the irrigation system and the roads that they use will be adequately

---

* Ward postulates the rule "The more local, the better," and notes that one is still a relative newcomer if his family has lived in the community only for a generation or two.

maintained through appropriations out of the village budget, and that their crop delivery quota will be kept in line with their ability to deliver at a given time.*

Nor is the *buraku*-oriented vote always as spontaneous as we have suggested. Social pressure is frequently applied and the threat of sanctions for deviance is often made articulate. Non-voting is easily noticeable in rural villages. Local bosses sometimes let it be known before the election that they "can tell whether a voter voted right by looking at his face" or that they "have a friend among the voting overseers, so that they will know whether a voter voted right."[9] To be able to prove that they voted "right," voters sometimes slip a piece of cardboard under the ballot and press down hard when writing in the candidates' names, so that they can show the imprint in case they are suspected of having broken rank; sometimes they simply hand the completed ballot open to a voting overseer instead of dropping it in the ballot box.[10] Sometimes a local boss collects the polling place admission tickets from voters so that he can cast the vote for them. The families requested to surrender their tickets find it as difficult to deny the request as the voting overseers find it difficult to prevent such illegal proxy votes. The threat of sanctions—especially of ostracism (*mura hachibu*)—is sometimes employed to keep politically conscious persons from disturbing the "harmony of the *buraku*" by nominating themselves as candidates. Finally, ascription is not always the basis of membership in the informal leadership group. Even where a person of ascriptive status is accorded leadership position, performance considerations may not be absent. Thus a descendent of a former samurai family or of a family of local functionaries of Tokugawa or Meiji times may be a member of the leadership group not only because of the villagers' regard for this superior as-

---

* The land reform eliminated the biggest challenge to this pattern of voting; without it, the immediate interests of tenant farmers would have oriented them more and more to vote with others who favored such a reform, regardless of *buraku* boundaries. The difference between the *buraku*-oriented vote, based on traditional considerations, and the same type of vote based on the above-mentioned view of the *buraku* as a geographical pressure group may be subtle. There is, nevertheless, a real distinction in the motivation. Yet the two cases have much in common. For example, in both cases the expectations of the voter are very modest. He does not aim at any improvement in local administration; his horizon does not encompass the village, except as its administration relates to the *buraku*; he does not attempt to control those in authority, but only hopes that the efforts of the *buraku* delegate will induce them to give a little more to the *buraku* and to demand a little less from it.

criptive status, but also—and perhaps more importantly—because the villagers consider his political connections in neighboring villages and at higher political levels and his political knowledge and experience as practical assets.[11] Furthermore, the boss without inherited prominence who has achieved wealth and used it to extend his influence over others is no rarity. An "influential person" of this type is likely to make up by a certain aggressiveness for the spontaneous deference that is withheld from him by the villagers.

Buraku differ in these and other regards from one another.[12] But by and large the *buraku* is the "womb of the election," above all (although not exclusively) in the elections of town and village assemblymen. These elections show the conservative pattern most clearly because *buraku* life tends to preserve the pertinent aspects of the traditional value system.

Town and Village Mayor Elections

Town and village assemblymen are perceived primarily as *buraku* delegates. The mayor, on the other hand, is clearly an officer of the local entitity as a whole. Since the *buraku* and not the town or village is the focus of the inhabitants' collectivity orientation, the election of a mayor engages their natural solidarity to a lesser degree. Thus the voting rate in these elections tends to be lower. This may seem somewhat paradoxical because the mayor holds without doubt the most important office in the village.

The *buraku* nevertheless plays an important role also in mayoral elections. Frequently these elections are seen as contests between the more populous *buraku*. The vote of a single *buraku*, however, is insufficient to elect a mayor. Arrangements with the leaders of neighboring *buraku* may add to this vote, in which case the candidate becomes, in effect, the candidate of one section of the village encompassing a number of *buraku*, in a contest with another section of the village. Of course, members of the candidate's family and others who stand in some particularistic and diffuse relationship to him are expected to vote for him. His supporters also make use of their ties with persons living outside their *buraku*. The need for more votes than the *buraku* can provide thus leads to a greater likelihood of campaigns. Much of this campaigning is discreet and covert. But overt campaigns are much more frequent than in town and village assembly elections. Overt campaigning, however, need not—and usually does not—consist in the enunciation of policies that the candidate promises to pursue in office.

Self-effacement is proper also for mayoral candidates, but it comes less naturally in their case.* The fact is that the position of mayor requires a certain ability, knowledge, and experience. As Ward states in *Village Japan,* the mayor should have a thorough practical knowledge of the problems of farming and irrigation, a fair amount of training and ability in the field of local finance, and a certain familiarity with public administration at the local level, since he has to deal with the experts on these matters in the prefectural government.[13] However, while these considerations may influence the selection of candidates, they are normally not stressed in the campaign by the candidates, who, rather than offend sensibilities by self-assertion, prefer to rely on the fact that their qualifications are already known to the voters.

Of course, the spectacle of candidates competing openly for the same position is not welcome in conservative communities. Attempts to avoid such competition by pre-election agreements among the informal leaders of the village (or rather, of the various *buraku* in the village) are frequent. They are often successful: as we noted in the preceding chapter, there is usually no balloting in more than one-third of Japan's towns and villages because only one candidate for the post of mayor is nominated. Connected with the role that the informal leadership plays as well as with the candidates' posture of self-effacement is the manner in which the notification of candidacy is submitted. In 1955, 1,581 candidates submitted their own notifications, while 1,767 others permitted themselves to be "drafted" by way of a *suisen dotoke*; in 1959 the corresponding figures were 1,326 and 1,162.†

---

* Not a few candidates win by some appeal to human sympathy. A good example is the case of the candidate in Atsumimachi in Aichi Prefecture who pleaded, "I have been a candidate three times and failed three times. Please elect me mayor, if only for three days." This plea also stressed the traditional virtue of sincerity (*makoto*). See Sugiura Mimpei in *Chūō Kōron,* Vol. 47, No. 6 (June 1959), p. 240.

† The story of the uncontested mayor election in Kamo Village in 1947 is related in some detail in *Village Japan* (p. 414). The former mayor had been purged and had to be replaced. The vice-mayor, who had been in the village office since 1936, had his "campaign" organized by two former headmen of his *buraku*. This discreet campaign was highly successful. The candidate was nominated by the headmen of all the village's *buraku*, ten of the twelve village assemblymen, and an assortment of other local notables. Understandably, no one cared to challenge the choice of such an assemblage and no balloting was necessary. This is perhaps the more noteworthy because the

When a pre-election agreement on a single candidate fails, a contest becomes unavoidable. This may be a contest among the larger *buraku* or sections of the town or village clustering around them, as noted earlier. But occasionally there are personal factions among the informal leaders who compete with each other. The geographical base of influence of the members of each faction is important in this case, too, but at least some covert "politicking" is necessary to attract additional votes. Finally, there is also the possibility that notions of at least a semi-political nature enter into the contest, that "those who are worldly and educated and those of little outside experience and little sympathy with changes in the social system" oppose each other as progressives and conservatives.[14] Compared with assembly elections, the contest in the larger arena of the village tends to be somewhat more open.* There is enough competition in the two-thirds of the villages where actual balloting is held to bring about an over-all ratio of candidates to positions that is higher than the ratio in case of assembly elections.

Where a candidate competes as a "progressive"—often in defiance of pre-election arrangements by the local leadership—his campaign is of necessity somewhat more vigorous. He may not be able to count on all the votes even from his own *buraku;* nor can he hope to swing other *buraku* to his side. What he lacks in a geographical base and in the "fixed vote" based on personal relationships must be made up by the votes of the villagers who agree with him. The latter possibility exists to some extent because *buraku* cohesion is less strong in mayoral elections than in assembly elections. Progressive chances for capturing the mayoral position are thus somewhat better than the chances for capturing a

---

candidate appears to have been handicapped in two ways: he was not a native of the village, and he had been adopted into his wife's family to provide it with a male heir. On such adopted husbands (*mukoyōshī*), see, e.g., *Village Japan*, p. 238.

* When the mayor of Kamo, elected without contest in 1947, tried for a second term in 1951 he was opposed by two candidates. His opponents were a well-known political figure, who like the incumbent lived on the west side of the village, and a teacher in the local primary school with some political experience, who came from the more populous east side. The schoolteacher won the contest. The reasons given by the villagers are interesting indications of the considerations that determine votes in such contests. The fact that two candidates came from the west side split the western vote and thus operated in the winner's favor. His position as teacher (*sensei*) gave him status, and, according to some, enlisted the P.T.A. in his behalf. Last but not least, both his opponents were regarded as participants in past failures and scandals, while the winner was a "new face" (*Village Japan*, p. 415).

majority in the village assembly.* Still, the overwhelming majority of mayors are independents who are either conservative or pure.

Ascribed status is still important in rural Japan but the candidates for the position of mayor are not always members of outstanding local families, as was the case before. During the period of land reform it seemed best to bypass persons of superior ascriptive status who were landlords, and to nominate someone who could claim neutrality in regard to this divisive issue. Thus non-farmers—schoolteachers, priests, vice-mayors, officials of agricultural associations or of private companies—often became the first directly elected and salaried mayors in Japanese towns and villages.[15] After the land reform ceased to be an issue, the professional requirements of the office prevented a return to the selection of mayors on the basis of ascriptive criteria. Achievement or performance criteria such as education and experience will probably continue to influence the nomination and election of candidates for the chief executive position.

Elections to City Assemblies

In the introduction to Chapter 15 we stated that we expect the influence of the traditional value system, and hence the conservative pattern of election, to be more prevalent in rural areas than in urban areas. The data presented in that chapter confirmed this expectation if high voting rates, a high percentage of uncontested elections, a low competition ratio, a high percentage of independent candidates, and a low degree of issue orientation or politization can be taken as symptoms of the conservative pattern. In general, all these symptoms are more clearly apparent in town and village elections than in city elections. Earlier in the present chapter we pointed out that traditional values not only discourage campaigns but also dictate a certain style for candidates. They must be self-effacing, not self-assertive. We found an indication of this in the high percentage of candidates in towns and villages who do not submit the notification of candidacy themselves, but prefer the so-called *suisen dotoke*, the notification of their candidacy by local notables. In city assembly elections, on the other hand, most candidates submit their own nominations.[16] In this regard also, city elections seem to be less traditional than town and village elections.

---

* There were 7 Socialist, 1 Communist, and 79 progressive independent town and village mayors after the election of 1955, and 5 Socialist and 43 progressive independent town and village mayors after the election of 1959.

But cities differ greatly among themselves. Some of them are more urban than others, whatever criteria we apply for the use of this term. There are big cities and small cities, older cities and recently amalgamated new cities, cities with higher and lower percentages of inhabitants in primary industries, cities in remote rural prefectures, and cities that are really parts of large metropolitan regions.

Our data in Chapter 15 suggested that the strength or weakness of the traditional or progressive pattern differs with the urban character of the cities. The election behavior in some cities is rather close to that in towns and villages. In other cities elements of the progressive pattern which have little importance in rural Japan are conspicuous. In other words, the various types of cities constitute a continuum in themselves. The most urbanized units—the big cities and the special wards of Tokyo —are the end point of this continuum on the progressive or untraditional side.* The new cities created by amalgamation are the end point on the conservative side.

The description of town and village elections shows that under the conservative pattern the vote of the individual is largely determined by his belonging to a geographical community, the *buraku*. To be successful, a candidate must, above all, be supported by this community. This support is the core of the "fixed vote" that is given to him more or less automatically. Since the fixed vote is based on considerations that are closely related to elements in the traditional value system, we can state that the greater the relative importance of the fixed vote, the clearer the conservative pattern of the election. We noted in Chapter 10 that geographical communities of sorts exist also in cities, and it is pertinent to our inquiry to investigate their role in providing the fixed votes of candidates in elections.†

In cities that have recently been created out of towns and villages, the *buraku* continues to exist. We could expect politics to go on as before were it not for the changes in the institutional setting that go along with the status of a city. The most important of these changes is the

---

*Closer inspection shows that even these units differ significantly among one another in their degree of progressiveness. We shall show later some of the differences among the election patterns in the Tokyo wards.

† Family relations are, of course, another component of the fixed vote in cities as well as in towns and villages. I was told that a former assembly chairman of the city of Tsuchiura apparently relied heavily on the vote of the 80 "houses" in the city that were related to him, and on the status that the family connections bestowed upon him.

reduction in the number of assemblymen. For example, six villages of 2,000 inhabitants each, five villages of 5,000 inhabitants each, and a town of 18,000 inhabitants had together a total of 178 town or village assemblymen. When these twelve units are amalgamated into a city of 55,000 inhabitants, they elect together only 36 city assemblymen. Before amalgamation, representation of each of the larger *buraku* and of groupings of smaller *buraku* was feasible on each of the twelve assemblies. If the new city as a whole constitutes an election district—as is the norm according to the law—the support of even the largest *buraku* is not likely to suffice to put an assemblyman into office. Agreements for support of a common representative of a number of *buraku* are necessary in every case. The area encompassed by the agreement must be much larger than before. Since a greater number of *buraku* is involved and since it is likely that a number of them would like to furnish the common representative, agreements become more difficult. The neat arrangements under which there are no supernumerary candidates become nearly impossible. If an agreement among the leaders of the various *buraku* can be reached, the vote for the recommended candidate becomes less automatic. After all, that candidate may no longer be a man from the same *buraku* or even from a neighboring *buraku* with which friendly relationships have been maintained over the years; he may be an outsider from another section of the village that has long been the object of parochial antagonism. The sentiments that sustain the fixed geographical vote are thus weaker in certain parts of the candidate's constituency, and the slack has to be taken up by overt or covert campaigning. The candidate may "nurture" his constituency by establishing more and more diffuse relationships with the families of voters which will pay off at election time. By bestowing favors of various sorts—not excluding gifts of money—he may put a general obligation on the recipients, who would feel ashamed if they would not vote for their benefactor at the next election. But the candidate may also appeal to his constituency by making explicit what was implied in the case of the pure *buraku* delegate: he may declare his understanding of the concrete needs of the *buraku* and promise to work for their fulfillment. The *buraku* inhabitant will thus be told that a vote for a certain candidate is in the interest of the *buraku* because that candidate will see to it that the road to outlying fields or to the main irrigation ditch is repaired with city funds, or that a new school is constructed close by, or that building a meeting hall for the young men is given higher priority. But this is a game that can be played by more than one candidate if the *buraku* is uncommitted. If no agreement has been reached among the leadership or if the leadership is not in firm control, the *buraku* may be raided by outsiders. Deprived of the usual guidelines, voters may then even stay away from the polls.

These results, highly undesirable from a traditional viewpoint, may be partly averted if the election district for the assembly seats is narrowed, so that towns or villages which were separate before the amalgamations remain separate election districts, each sending a specified number of members to the assembly. It is significant that a number of cities, most of them small and new, have passed by-laws establishing such election districts, and that the number of election districts in them is relatively large.[17] Whether this will suffice to sustain the conservative election pattern in these units in the long run remains to be seen.

In the larger cities, solidarity within neighborhood areas is weaker to start with. The arguments in favor of geographical representation on the city or ward assembly carry less weight, and the control of the informal leadership over the neighborhood association and the control of the association over the vote of the residents is less sure. Nevertheless, neighborhood associations of various descriptions play a significant role in city elections. The degree of their cohesion and thus their usefulness for political purpose differs in various cities and often in various parts of the same city. In Kyoto, for instance, the administrative wards are the election districts for city assemblymen. But the districts for the elementary schools—the *gakku*—are the center of a certain community sentiment. Organized as federations of several *chōnaikai*, they serve as contact points between the city administration and the *chōnaikai* and often also as balloting districts.* The people within the school district take a lively interest in "their" school and find it important to send a representative of the district to the city assembly. Thus the candidates for city assembly seats who control a school district stand a better chance of success than those who have no such geographical base to build on. In other words, the school districts are easily converted into bailiwicks (*jiban*) for city politicians. The conversion of districts, originally serving

---

* An indication of the official recognition of the *gakku* is the fact that the tax receipts show not only the administrative ward and the *chō* as part of the address, but also the *gakku*. There are 163 *gakku* but 228 balloting districts. The larger *gakku* are divided into two or more balloting districts.

a different function, into bailiwicks occurs also elsewhere. In Osaka the network of neighborhood associations was resurrected after SCAP's attempts at interdiction under the auspices of the Red Cross. The Red Cross system of district and block organizations now provides one of the most important elements in the support system of conservative candidates in that city.[18]

As for geographical organizations in the special wards of Tokyo, we mentioned in Chapter 10 the differences between the Shitamachi area and the Yamate area, and noted that the latter bears the brunt of the social increase in the population of Tokyo. There is also a good deal of mobility within the area of the 23 *ku,* which makes the population of the *ku* in the Yamate area in particular less stable.[19] In addition, most men spend their working day outside the ward in which they reside. The neighborhood thus plays a relatively minor role in their lives. While many of them are members of a *chōnaikai,* of a *tonarigumi,* or of the P.T.A., the degree of their participation is slight, particularly if compared with their participation in organizations with a non-geographical focus.[20] We observed in the case of town and village assembly elections that *buraku* solidarity is reflected in high voting rates. It is thus noteworthy that in the elections to the ward assemblies the western Yamate wards have voting rates below the average, while the more stable—and con-servative—wards in the center and northeast of the ward area have voting rates above the average.[21] The role that neighborhood associations in Tokyo play in ward assembly elections is shown by the example of Shitayama-chō—a neighborhood that "could hardly be called Yamate, but which is not quite Shitamachi"—related in Ronald Dore's excellent book *City Life in Japan.*[22] The chief of the neighborhood association, a Mr. Sakura, had ambitions in 1951 for using his position to become a candidate for a seat on the ward assembly. He called a meeting of neigh-borhood leaders at his house to discuss policy regarding the forthcoming elections. He started out by stating that it would be a good thing if someone from the neighborhood would be elected, because the only way anything could be done in the ward was by pressure exerted by a ward assemblyman. Unless someone with an interest in the neighborhood was elected, the roads in it would never be improved and the school would never get its wing repaired. The candidate should be a "man of charac-ter," not someone who was interested in the salary which nowadays, under the deplorable new system, was paid to ward assemblymen. The listeners agreed with this emphasis on the interests of the geographical collectivity and the quality of the candidate, but when the vice-chief of the neighborhood association proposed that Mr. Sakura himself should be the candidate, there was little enthusiasm. Another member of the inner group, whose name was mentioned, denied any ambition for the office. In the end it was proposed to put the weight of the neighborhood association behind a candidate from an adjoining neighborhood, who was equally concerned with the local primary school, where he had been P.T.A. president before Sakura (a tacit acknowledgment that actual interests extended beyond neighborhood boundaries); he would be grateful for the extra votes, it was said, so that he could be relied upon to get the main road through Shitayama-chō improved as a quid pro quo. This proposal was adopted. The names of the Shitayama-chō leaders appeared on the posters of the candidate as "supporters" and the word was passed around that the interests of Shitayama-chō demanded his support. By and large he got the support; the number of his votes showed that many must have come from Shitayama-chō. Eighteen months after his election the main road was improved.

In this case the candidate received a welcome addition to his own fixed vote—a sizable portion, though no longer all, of the vote of his own neighborhood—by the action of an adjoining neighborhood. Such additions are often necessary because the support of a single urban neighborhood does not always suffice for winning a seat on the city or ward assembly. To strengthen their control over their own neighborhood and to win votes in other parts of the election district, candidates often create "supporters' associations" (*kōenkai*). These are not political clubs —if politics is thought of as being related to policy—but loose associations of followers, who are linked to the candidate by personal bonds. The candidate sometimes invites the members to expense-paid visits to a hot spring; he sends gifts, congratulations, or condolences at appropriate occasions; he listens sympathetically to their individual and collective needs, promising to work toward their fulfillment when this is feasible through action of the city or ward; and he assists them in their contacts with govermental agencies.* The personal relations thus established pay

---

* Such associations are also formed, even by party-affiliated candidates, in other local elections (as noted later), and in national elections. It is reported that they are

off in electoral support by the families, friends, and neighbors of the members. The relations resemble patron-client relations because of their particularistic and diffuse character; but the important point is that they arise not spontaneously because of some ascribed status of the patron, but are created and nurtured by him for a clearly conceived purpose.

Already existing organizations may be utilized for the same purpose of gaining additional votes. In a Japanese city one encounters a variety of systematically organized interest groups. Some of these are bound to an area. For example, each of the great shopping streets or areas of Osaka's Minami-ku has one or more street organizations representing the combined interests of all the shops and businesses of its particular locality.[23] Organizations of this type can also be found in other parts of Osaka and in other cities. In addition, there are interest groups without a geographical focus. The various trade associations, professional associations, and agricultural associations, the employers' associations, the League of Medium and Small Industries, and the labor unions—so important in left-wing politics—are prime examples. There are also women's organizations, widows' organizations, old people's clubs, and many others.* Candidaes for the city or ward assembly are usually active in many of those organizations. And, in addition, they usually hold a variety of official or semi-official positions. Thus Ward describes the calling card of a prominent local political figure in Osaka's Minami-ku as follows:

On its face its owner describes himself as a member of the city's Election Administration Commission, chairman of a major branch of the city's Red Cross organization, and director of the association of subway shopping areas. On the back he lists his chairmanships and directorships in twelve other organizations ranging from the Association of Natives of Mie Prefecture Resident in Osaka to the Minami-Ku Cooperative Society for Fire Prevention and Public Security.[24]

A study of Tokyo's Suginami Ward reveals the positions of various types held by 28 important members of the ward assembly. Seven of

---

used to pass out money and goods and to make up for door-to-door campaigning, prohibited by the Election Law to prevent such bribery. See, e.g., Sakuji Horikoshi, "Reform of Japan's Election Law," *Asahi Evening News*, March 8, 1962.

*Ward found that the 1955 edition of the Minami-ku directory has 70 printed pages listing the names and top officers of such groups and their local branches.

them—including the chairman of the assembly—were chiefs of neighborhood associations (*chōkai*). Six of them had positions in a crime prevention association, four had positions in a fire defense organization, and one, who held positions in both, was also a member of the Agriculture Commission and a Social Welfare Commissioner. Another was also chairman of the Local Shrine (*ujiko*) Worshippers' Association. The chairman of the ward assembly occupied—in addition to the position as chief of a *chōkai*—the chairmanship of the Agriculture Commission and of the Association for Problems of Juveniles in the ward. He also was a member of the National Health Insurance Administration Council. Of the seven neighborhood association chiefs four were elected on the Liberal Democratic ticket, the others being independents. The chairman of the ward assembly was also the managing director of the local branch of the Liberal Democratic Party. Of the other 21 members of the assembly whose connections are given, 16 were officers of crime and fire prevention associations or organizations for young people. Four were chairmen of associations of merchants on various thoroughfares or in various areas. There was a sprinkling of positions in agricultural cooperatives, the P.T.A., the alumni association of a local secondary school, the Association for Families Bereaved by the War, and in other organizations. Altogether, 86 affiliations or positions are mentioned for the 28 persons on the list. Of these twenty-eight 16 were Liberal Democrats, although only 3 held significant positions in the local party branch. The remaining 12 were independents.[25]

As is clear from this, party affiliation also plays a role on this level. Branches of the major parties exist in all larger cities. With the exception of the Communist party branches, which are beehives of constant activity, these branches are usually more or less dormant except at election time. Still there are differences in the degree to which they are important to the party-affiliated candidate. A Communist candidate may rely on them nearly exclusively to guide his campaign. A Socialist candidate may get his main support from the trade-union organizations in the area, particularly if he is a trade-union official. Otherwise he expects to get assistance from the party branch and to attract progressive votes by emphasis on the party platform and on party slogans. But often he also uses other appeals. He may be a joiner of certain organizations not classified as conservative, and may even create his own supporters' association. To the Liberal Democratic candidate, the party branch may be less important. His main reliance may rest on the votes in his neighborhood, the votes based on personal relations—including those coming from his supporters' association—and the votes based on his many and varied connections in the area.

The tenuous character of party affiliation and the latent conflict between the role of the conservative local politician as a party man and as a representative of purely local interests is illustrated by two occurrences in Aomori and Mie prefectures. The government's desire to give added emphasis to technical education led to the decision to establish 12 higher technical schools (on the pattern of the prewar *semmon kōtō gakko*) throughout Japan. There was first some competition among the various prefectures to get one of the schools located within their areas. Both Aomori and Mie were successful. Then there ensued a competition between two cities in each prefecture—Aomori and Hachinohe in one case, Yokkaichi and Suzuka in the other—to be chosen as the site of the new school. The decision was in effect up to the prefectural assemblies, both controlled by the Liberal Democratic Party. In both cases the Liberal Democratic assemblymen of the city that lost out left their party in a huff.*

To the conservative candidate, then, the affiliation with the local party branch at election time may then be no more than another connection with persons whose political influence can get him votes and a temporary expedient to facilitate his campaign. But in a big city, party affiliation often looms large in the consciousness even of conservative candidates.† In any case, the candidate for the assembly of a city differs from his counterpart in towns and villages. Urban political leadership is not of the same generalized and undifferentiated nature as rural political leadership. It is apt to be a full-time specialized activity.‡ All local politicians —the terminology begins to fit on this level, whereas one should hesitate

* See *Chihōjichi shiryō*, No. 259, 260 (January 15, 1962), p. 26.

† In big cities the district for city assembly elections is identical with that for prefectural assembly elections, although the number of seats to be filled from the district differs. Candidates for prefectural assembly seats, most of them party-affiliated, thus enter into mutually useful cooperative relations with two or three candidates for city assembly seats, who then normally assume the same party label. See p. 439 below.

‡ This is possible because the activities of the city politician are accompanied by financial compensations of various types which make up for the neglect that his business or profession may suffer. See Ward, *Urban-Rural Differences*, p. 144 and *passim* (cited in note 11 to this chapter).

to use it on the town and village assembly level—draw their political support from a combination of sources. Collectivity orientation in an urban neighborhood is a far cry from that in a rural *buraku*. Nor are the neighborhood leaders the accepted and deferred-to persons of recognized superior status that the "influential persons" of many villages are even today.[26] A variety of techniques must thus be used to amass the necessary number of votes. These techniques include the creation of a generalized personal bond, the appeal to specific local community interests, the appeal to the interests of an organized interest group, and the appeal to the voter's political convictions. Campaign styles vary accordingly among candidates in small cities and big cities and among conservative and progressive candidates. The emphasis put on the various elements of the support system and on the various techniques appropriate in each case, are reflections of the conservative and progressive patterns. For instance, in a city like Osaka, which stands at one extreme of the above-mentioned continuum, political support systems are, as Ward states, not qualitatively different from those in many Western metropolises.[27]

City Mayor Elections

The general milieu of city mayor elections is, of course, the same as that for city assembly elections. Because of the broad scope of the term "city," marked differences in the election patterns of units bearing that designation exist in both types of election. But just as town and village mayor elections differ in some aspects from town and village assembly elections in spite of the identity of their milieu, so city mayor elections differ from city assembly elections. In both cases the differences stem from three interrelated facts: only one position is to be filled; the position is an executive position; and the election district is the local entity as a whole. While the representation of geographical communities is often a consideration in voting for assemblymen, this is less likely to be the case in the mayoral elections. Since the solidarity of geographical communities, which accounts largely for the high voting rates in assembly elections, is not involved, the voting rates in mayoral elections are lower. This is, in fact, the case in cities in which geographical communities still have great significance—that is, in the smaller, less urbanized cities. In the larger cities, however, the voting rate in mayoral elections tends to be higher than that in assembly elections, as noted in Chapter 15.

The reason is probably twofold. Because the solidarity of geographical communities is less strong than in small cities, the voting rates in assembly elections are relatively low; and because political sophistication is stronger, the interest in the contest for the most important position, that of the chief executive, is relatively high.*

This leads us to a general observation of some importance. Traditional attitudes influence the election pattern in cities side by side with untraditional attitudes that are absent in a rural setting. Because traditional attitudes are less strong in cities, the symptoms of the conservative pattern are, in general, less pronounced. But the presence of untraditional attitudes, such as political interest, must also be taken into account. The relatively high voting rates in city mayor elections, which we have just noted, are an example of the fact that the election pattern in cities is the result of an interaction of these factors.

The complicated interplay between traditional and progressive elements in the election patterns of cities makes it difficult also to give a single explanation for the comparatively high percentage of uncontested city mayor elections, and for the apparent increase in that percentage.[28] On the town and village level, uncontested elections are the sign of an emphasis on harmony and solidarity and of a firm control of the political process by conservative, informal leadership. In cities, too, the cause for the lack of a contest may be as traditional as an informal arrangement between local bosses, which no one cares to challenge by an independent candidacy. Such arrangements are more likely to be made in small cities. The creation of the new cities thus increased the likelihood of uncontested elections.† But the lack of contest may also reflect the consolidation of the power of the incumbent mayor, who may have been able to build up a political machine so powerful that it discourages other contenders. As this happens in more localities, the percentage of un-

---

* Aside from the big cities, the phenomenon of higher voting rates in mayoral elections appears also in other cities in urbanized prefectures. Thus in Hyogo Prefecture the rates were as follows for 1955 and 1959: city mayor elections, 80.81 and 82.77 per cent; city assembly elections, 78.67 and 79.53 per cent. In 1963 the big cities showed voting rates of 67.55 per cent in the mayoral elections and a voting rate of 65.60 per cent in the assembly elections.

† For example, when two towns and a number of villages are amalgamated into a new city, the mayor is expected to come from one of the two towns. The informal leaders of the towns may decide among themselves which town should furnish the candidate for mayor. The other town is then usually given the post of vice-mayor as a consolation prize. In the absence of self-styled candidates, there will then be only one candidate for the post, and no balloting is necessary.

contested elections rises.[29] The reason for the lack of competition may also tie in with the increasing politization of city mayor elections. Like an independent candidate for the governorship, an independent candidate for the position of mayor in a larger city may be one who is endorsed by both major parties. In this case also his position remains unassailable as long as he enjoys this dual endorsement, and his reelection is likely to be uncontested. *

Similar considerations may explain the apparent decrease in the overall competition ratio in city mayor elections.† This phenomenon is, of course, connected with the increase in the percentage of uncontested elections. In addition, the consolidation of the party system after the 1955 elections may have discouraged candidates from smaller parties in the more politically oriented cities. Although the low competition ratio in rural Japan ties in with notions of harmony, it would be hasty to assume that the trend toward lower competition rates in the cities indicates a return to tradition.

We noted that the percentage of independent city mayors is lower than that of independent town and village mayors and that independent city mayors are less likely to be "pure."‡ This indicates a greater degree of politization in the cities, but it does not quite reveal its true extent. The independence of a candidate for town and village mayor may be the natural outcome of the environment of the election. If he is sure to win on the basis of the votes of the farmers without regard to the few non-farmers—merchants, workers, and "salarymen"—who live in the village, he is likely to be an independent, because he shares with his electors an aversion to political cleavages. In the city the diversity of occupational and social backgrounds is likely to be much greater. Even a newly amalgamated city may have more than just a negligible percentage of voters who are non-farmers, especially if in the process of amalgamation it came to include a post office, a railroad station, a factory or two, and

---

* Mayors who started as progressive independents with Socialist support sometimes make peace with the Liberal Democrats during their tenure of office, obtain their support, and are then reelected as pure independents, often without opposition.

† This trend becomes clearer if we include the 1963 elections. As noted in Chapter 15, the competition ratio was 3.0 in 1947, 2.2 in 1951, 2.3 in 1955, and 2.2 in 1959. In 1963 it was 2.0.

‡ The percentage of independent mayors is declining. This becomes clearer if we add the results of the 1963 elections to our considerations. In 1963 the percentage of independent town and village mayors dropped 1.2 per cent to 96.8. In the case of city mayors the percentages were 93.6 in 1955, 78.9 in 1959, and 77.4 in 1963.

perhaps an electricity substation. If the candidate for mayor would affiliate with a party, some of the votes of one or the other group would elude him. But he can gain votes from all segments by projecting the image of an able, politically independent administrator. This stance, based on careful political assessments rather than on adherence to the traditional value system, is, in fact, often taken by candidates in small and medium-sized cities. As the number of voters of progressive inclination increases with increased urbanization, one of the candidates may see sufficient chances for victory in making a special appeal to them and may then style himself a progressive, although the ideological difference between him and his opponent—who is likely to be the incumbent—may be rather slight. Sometimes this pays off, but when it does the progressive mayor usually has to face a conservative assembly majority.*

All this indicates that campaigns in city mayor elections are more overt than those in town and village mayor elections. Most candidates register their candidacy themselves. Only 98 out of 409 candidates in 1955 and 73 out of 395 candidates in 1959 had the notification of their candidacy submitted by other local notables. In neither year was there a case of such a *suisen dotoke* in any of the big cities.

Ascriptive status does not play a significant role. Candidates feel that they have to convince the voters that their ability, educational background, and administrative or political experience make them desirable chief executives. Of course, other appeals are also used. The range of techniques is similar to that employed in city assembly elections. But, since the arena of the contest is the entire city, the fixed vote based on geographical community and family connections does not have the relative importance in the support system of mayoral candidates that it has in the support system of assembly candidates. The support system of mayoral candidates is thus likely to be more complex. To nurture the floating vote, supporters' associations, taking their name from the candidate, are often established well in advance of the elections. The candidate also woos young men's organizations and women's groups. He joins and is active in professional, social, and cultural groups of a wide range. These may include, in addition to the groups already mentioned, groups that take a stand on specific issues, such as trade with China or the

* As industries are dispersed into more and more of the smaller cities, and as apartments (*danchi*) for their employees and for commuters to nearby large industrial centers spring up in the hitherto rural parts of smaller cities, this tendency is likely to increase.

banning of nuclear weapons tests. Interest groups and parties play a relatively large role in the support system and contribute a significant percentage of the campaign funds and of the votes. As a matter of fact, when we speak of the fixed vote in mayoral elections in larger cities, we think as much or more of the predictable vote of policy-oriented groups— the trade unions being the core of the fixed votes of the progressive candidates—than of the predictable vote of groups without such an orientation.

This is particularly true in the so-called "big cities." Mayoral elections there are considered to be of national significance. The party-affiliated candidate has the approval and active support of the Diet members and prefectural assembly members elected by his party in the district. But even candidates who formally run as independents may in fact have been selected by the leadership of one of the parties. The campaign manager is often a person of some prominence in the national party headquarters. The campaign organization of the mayoral candidate may parallel that of the gubernatorial candidate, and there may be informal or even formal connections between the two, aiming at a division of labor in the campaign within the city area.[30] In the case of Liberal Democratic candidates or even in case of conservative independent candidates it is not uncommon for the Prime Minister and members of the Cabinet to participate in the mayoral campaign. The mass media are employed to carry the candidate's appeal to the masses of the voters throughout the city. Posters with the candidate's name in large letters, his picture, his party affiliation (if any), and the names of prominent supporters are displayed in all parts of the city. Altogether, a conscious effort is made to impress the candidate's name on those who are likely to vote for the name they know. Loudspeakers repeat again and again that name and a request for the listener's vote. All this is not very different from the mayoral elections in many a Western metropolis—or, in the Japanese context, from prefectural or national elections.

Prefectural Assembly Elections

The districts for the election of prefectural assemblymen are the cities and counties (*gun*) in the prefecture. The elections thus take place in the general setting of city elections and in the general setting of town and village elections. But, in contrast to the elections in these settings, their purpose is to staff the assembly of a political unit of a large scale. One consequence of this difference is that the separate interests and loyalties of sub-units of towns and villages and of cities that affect municipal elections are not directly involved. Inasmuch as the solidarity of these sub-units accounts to a large extent for the conspicuously high turnout of voters in municipal elections—and especially in town and village assembly elections—we could easily assume that prefectural assembly elections would show a low voting rate. However, as was shown in Chapter 15, this is not the case. To be sure, prefectural assembly elections attract a lower percentage of the electorate than town and village assembly elections. But in rural prefectures the voting rate still approaches sometimes 90 per cent, and even in urban prefectures the *gumbu* voting rate usually exceeds 80 per cent.

We know that the reason for these high voting rates cannot be found in a great concern for prefectural affairs. The *Jiji Press* poll of January 1956, to which we referred in Chapter 15, showed that three-fourths of the respondents had little or no interest in these affairs and that this lack of interest was especially pronounced in rural areas.[31] Yet, the voting rates for prefectural assemblies are higher in rural prefectures than in urban prefectures and higher in the rural parts of the various prefectures than in the urban parts. In the absence of a direct engagement of community solidarity, what accounts for these high voting rates?

To explain this phenomenon, a word needs to be said about the relations of prefectural politicians to their constituencies, especially if these constituencies are rural in character. In discussing town and village elections, we mentioned the informal leadership group which determines the number of assembly seats for each *buraku*, assures that the *buraku* vote as units for certain candidates, and attempts to achieve agreement among the various *buraku* on a single mayoral candidate. This group is made up of "influential persons" (*yūryokusha*).* The influence of each member of the group extends over a clearly defined area within which collective action is common. The relations of the *yūryokusha* to the members of the collectivity are diffuse, not specifically limited to any aspect of life, such as politics. These "influential persons" on the *buraku* level form the smallest mesh in a network that stretches upward to the prefectural politician from a rural constituency. Operating within the apolitical atmosphere of the traditional *buraku*, they are able to deliver en bloc the votes of those who are subject to their influence.

---

* We noted that the influence may be based on ascribed or achieved status, the latter case having recently become more prevalent than before.

When a prefectural assembly election approaches, the voters ask them for advice on how to vote, or they are told how to vote and obey.

Above those influential on the *buraku* level we are likely to find bigger "bosses"—often referred to as *chihō no seijika* ("local politicians") or *chihō no yūryokusha* ("locally influential persons")—who control a number of towns and villages within the *gun*. Their influence also extends over a clearly defined area, sometimes known as *nawabari* ("roped-off place" or "domain").[32] This influence is exercised indirectly on the lowest level through the *yūryokusha*, to whom the bigger bosses are normally linked by personal relations of a diffuse character. In turn, these intermediary bosses with their local connections are the constituent elements of the *jiban* or bailiwick of the prefectural politician.[33] They serve as his eyes and ears in the constituency and "nurse" it for him in his absence. When a son is born to a family of some standing, the local politician presents it with a *tai* (a sea bream) as a token of congratulations and good wishes. When a notable in one of the villages dies, he sends a wreath and advises the prefectural politician on the appropriate size of the monetary gift to be given to the widow. When a local businessman opens a new store, he sends a wreath of flowers, which is then prominently displayed in front of the store. He bolsters in all these ways at one and the same time both his own influence and that of the prefectural politician.

The links upward are subtly different from each other. The *buraku* inhabitants may defer more or less spontaneously to the advice of the *yūryokusha* in the *buraku* in the case of town and village assembly elections, especially if the *yūryokusha* are persons of ascribed status. But to mobilize the same vote at the bidding of a local politician for a prefectural candidate—neither one of them a member of the community—requires additional incentives, at least in the form of entertainment. The expenses for these incentives are paid by the local politician. When he makes his rounds among the *buraku* bosses in order to instruct them which candidate is to receive their support, he leaves with them a sum of money, euphemistically called *meishigawari* ("in lieu of a calling card").* The ability to provide entertainment for the villagers adds, of course, to the "face" and position of the *buraku yūryokusha*. The link

---

* Although house-to-house visits for campaign purposes are forbidden by the election law, they are nevertheless very common. In Okayama, where the *buraku* bosses are known as *kui* or *kue* ("stakes"), this procedure is known as *kuiuchi* ("the driving of stakes"). See *Village Japan*, p. 430.

between him and the local politician may be essentially of a diffuse, personal nature; however, it is strengthened by a mutuality of interests that has a specifically political coloring. The link between the local politician and the prefectural politician may be of the same mixed nature. But sometimes the only nexus is that of mutuality of interests, or even simply a cash nexus. This is the case if the local politician has no constant allegiance at all, but sells the vote that he controls to the highest bidder. The existence of such "floating bosses" is often decried and their use is actually a distortion of the traditional value system. They are, nevertheless, used by prefectural politicians to overcome deficiencies in the strength of their *jiban*.*

A prefectural assembly candidate in a rural area thus accumulates blocks of votes from areas that are controlled by his lieutenants or by bought "floating bosses." Almost the entire vote comes from this *jiban*; the "floating vote," which would have to be secured by overt campaigning, is negligible. Within the *jiban* he achieves a high concentration of favorable votes, amounting to between 70 and 90 per cent of the total. Beyond the boundaries of the *jiban* his vote falls off rapidly. In other words, the candidate does not attract votes throughout the election district—the *gun*—but is essentially elected by an area that is only part of it. If this area—his *jiban*—is large enough and the concentration of votes in it is high enough, he is successful.[34]

There exists thus a peculiar parallelism between town and village assembly elections and prefectural assembly elections in a rural setting. The *jiban* corresponds in a sense to the *buraku*. Of course, there is an important difference. The traditional *buraku* is a closely knit community and the successful candidate is its delegate to the village assembly, where his main duty is to see that the *buraku's* interests are represented. The *buraku* inhabitants vote for him primarily out of a sense of duty to the collectivity and do so rather spontaneously. The *jiban* of the prefectural politician, on the other hand, has no *a priori* existence. It consists of a number of towns and villages that do not form a unit in the consciousness of the inhabitants and that may, indeed, have conflicting interests and other causes for antagonism. What makes these towns and villages a unit at election time is merely the fact that they are—to use a metaphor common among Japanese politicians—"in the net" of the same

---

* At the prefectural level, the selling and buying of votes constitutes one of the most frequent violations of the election law.

candidate. Still, the parallelism between town and village assembly elections and prefectural assembly elections explains to a large extent the high voting rates in prefectural assembly elections in rural prefectures, and in the rural parts of all prefectures, in spite of an avowed lack of interest in prefectural affairs. In these elections, too, the vote is cast primarily out of a sense of obligation. The obligation is to a person to whom the voter stands in a direct and diffuse face-to-face relationship, even if he has no such relationship to the candidate himself. Collectivity orientation plays a lesser role, but is nevertheless important. Candidates often reinforce their *jiban* by promises to work for the allocation of prefectural funds to locally desired public works. In addition, constant admonitions from governmental and semi-governmental agencies make a high voting rate a source of pride for the village. Social pressure is applied to achieve a high rate and the individual often casts his ballot in response to it.*

The adaptation of the conservative pattern to prefectural assembly elections is easier in some prefectures than in others. We noted in Chapter 15 that the lowest voting rates in these elections occur in prefectures with important urban centers. In such prefectures, the difference of the voting rates in town and village assembly elections and in prefectural assembly elections is likely to be marked. In Tokyo Metropolis, for example, the town and village assembly elections drew 83.85 per cent of the voters to the polls in 1955 and 82.61 per cent in 1959; the metropolitan assembly elections had voting rates of 59.63 per cent and 70.13 per cent respectively. If we analyze the voting rate in the metropolitan assembly elections of 1955 according to the various area components of the metropolis, we find that the rate in the outlying islands was highest (82.1 per cent), followed by the rate in the *gumbu* (73.3). As for the *shibu,* the rate in the various cities in the metropolitan area was 72.1 per cent and the rate in the most urbanized part, the area of the 23 wards, was 57.6 per cent. Within the *gumbu* the voting rates regularly show differences depending on the rurality of the various *gun* and their distance from the urban core of the metropolis. Nishitamagun and Minamitamagun show a higher voting rate than Kitatamagun, which is adjacent to the ward area.†

---

* The village with the highest voting rate often receives a prize from the prefectural government.

† Similarly, Musashino City on the western outskirts of the ward area shows a low voting rate compared with Ome City, which is smaller and adjacent to the more rural

We turn to a brief consideration of the competition ratios in prefectural assembly elections. If the multi-member election districts for prefectural assembly elections are each neatly divided into the number of *jiban* that corresponds to the number of seats from the district, and if the number of candidates thus equals the number of assembly seats to be filled, no balloting is necessary in the district. We noted in Chapter 15 that in 1955 no balloting was necessary in 54 districts, and that 2.8 per cent of the successful candidates won without competition.* In the 1959 elections, the number of districts in which no balloting was necessary rose from 54 to 115 and the percentage of candidates who won their seats without competition from 2.8 to 9.5 per cent.† The competition rate dropped from 2.3 in 1951 to 2.1 in 1955 to 1.8 in 1959. At first glance, this might seem to reflect a strengthening of the conservative election pattern. However, the explanations that we advanced for similar changes in the competition ratio on the city level—such as consolidation of the party systems and of the power of officeholders—may well apply here also. In addition, the decrease in the competition rate in prefectural assembly elections is connected with the mass amalgamations after 1953. The changes in city and *gun* boundaries amounted to a redrawing of the districts for these elections.[35] There were in 1959 relatively more single-member districts than before and relatively fewer districts, sending

---

Saitama Prefecture. Within the ward area the differences between Yamate and Shita-machi, noted in connection with ward assembly elections, exist also in prefectural assembly elections. The more traditional Shitamachi area tends to show higher voting rates than the Yamate area, which is largely inhabited by white-collar workers and members of the intelligentsia, whose political interest runs relatively high.

* Not all of the districts were multi-member districts. If we omit from our consideration those prefectures in which all districts without balloting were single-member districts, we find that a perfect division of multi-member districts among the candidates occurred in more than 10 per cent of the districts of the following prefectures: Niigata, Toyama, Ishikawa, Fukui, Shimane, Hiroshima, Yamaguchi, and Saga. These are all rural prefectures. In the most urbanized of these prefectures, Hiroshima, three single-member districts and one two-member district were involved. In Ishikawa, on the other hand, the system worked in a four-member district and in a two-member district. See *Chihō senkyo kekka shirabe* 1955, pp. 78f.

† Unfortunately, the Autonomy Board's report on the 1959 elections does not show how many of the districts were single- or multi-member districts. We can therefore not demonstrate, as we did for the 1955 elections, that the *jiban* system avoids competition most effectively in rural prefectures. No elections were necessary in more than 10 per cent of the districts of 18 prefectures. All but two of the prefectures mentioned in the preceding footnote were among them.

more than two members to the prefectural assemblies. This is shown in Table 19.

It will be noted that the number of single-member districts rose between 1951 and 1959 from 182 to 424. Now in a four-member district there may easily be more than four persons who believe that they have a chance to be elected. There may be five politicians with a local *jiban* of sorts or four politicians with a *jiban* as well as a progressive candidate hopeful of accumulating sufficent votes in the district on the basis of a political platform to beat the candidate with the weakest *jiban*. As soon as there are more than four candidates for either reason, balloting becomes necessary. But where a single-member district coincides with the *jiban* of a prefectural politician, the possibility of successful competition is slim and the election is likely to remain uncontested. This relationship between the type of district and the likelihood of an uncontested election is shown in Table 20. This table makes it clear that the increase in the number of incontested elections is related to the increase in the number of single-member districts.*

We noted that the links between the participants in the process that assures the prefectural assembly candidate the votes of his *jiban* are primarily apolitical, and could thus be used by both conservative and progressive politicians. But on the lowest level the process rests on traditional attitudes of the villagers. For this reason, the process is most frequently the stock-in-trade of conservative politicians. Occasionally the process is used to good advantage by right-wing Socialists, especially by those who were connected with the prewar peasant movement; but in their case, the area *jiban* competes in importance with other elements of the support system, such as the organized trade-union vote.

We have shown that the conservative pattern of elections, modified to some degree because of the greater distance between the voter and the candidate, puts its stamp on prefectural assembly elections in rural areas. But as stated at the outset, these elections also take place in the cities. Normally, each city constitutes an election district (except for the five big cities, which are divided into a number of districts). The elections in

---

* The proliferation of single-member districts has political consequences. Socialists and Communists do poorly in them. Only 12.5 per cent of the prefectural assemblymen elected in such districts in 1959 were Socialists, while in districts sending four members to the Assembly, 22.5 per cent of the successful candidates were Socialists and in still larger districts the percentage was 28.8. (Based on Kawaguchi, "Chōson gappei to senkyo jiban," p. 251.)

TABLE 19

Number and Percentage of Various Types of Districts for Prefectural
Assembly Elections in 1951, 1955, and 1959

Type of District	Election Districts						Seats					
	1951	Per Cent	1955	Per Cent	1959	Per Cent	1951	Per Cent	1955	Per Cent	1959	Per Cent
Single-member	182	20.5	335	32.6	424	37.5	182	7.0	335	12.8	424	16.0
Two-member	260	29.6	302	29.4	346	30.6	520	19.8	604	23.0	692	26.0
Three-member	153	17.4	156	15.2	151	13.4	459	17.6	468	17.9	453	17.1
Four-member	135	15.3	105	10.2	110	9.7	540	20.7	420	16.1	440	16.6
Five-member	78	8.9	59	5.8	41	3.6	390	14.9	295	11.3	205	7.7
Six-member and over	73	8.3	69	6.7	58	5.1	525	20.1	492	18.8	443	16.7
Total	881	100.0	1,026	100.0	1,130	100.0	2,616	100.0	2,614	100.0	2,657	100.0

SOURCE: Kawaguchi Tei, "Chōson gappei to senkyo jiban," in Nōson sōgō kenkyū, Vol. 14, No. 2 (April 1960), p. 249.

TABLE 20

Number and Types of Districts with Uncontested Elections

Year	Total	1-Member	2-Member	3-Member	4-Member
1951	22	18	3	1	—
1955	54	38	13	2	1
1959	115	77	33	4	1

SOURCE: Kawaguchi, "Chōson gappei to senkyo jiban," p. 250.

the cities—the *shibu* of the prefecture—run the gamut from a close re-semblance to the rural pattern to a close resemblance to the pattern of comparable elections in the West. The remarks at the beginning of the section on city assembly elections regarding the wide variety of "cities" are applicable here. Where the progressive pattern prevails, the tra-ditional support system on the basis of an area *jiban* is relatively less important. Candidates organize their own supporters' associations. Occu-pational organizations, from trade unions to bathhouse-owner associa-tions, are joined and courted for the votes they may bring. Politically organized support plays a significant role. Campaigns are more overt. In short, the prefectural politician running in a city district uses the same type of support system as the city politician. As a matter of fact, city assemblymen often serve as links between the voters and the pre-fectural assembly candidate, just as the informal leaders known as "local politicians" do in the countryside. The mutual advantages in this case are even clearer, since all participants are officeholders.* The district for city assemblymen and prefectural assemblymen is normally the same—although it fills a greater number of seats in the city assembly than in the prefectural assembly. Thus a prefectural assembly candidate often cooperates with two or three city assemblymen, supporting them in their campaigns as they support him in his.

We noted in Chapter 15 the relatively high politicization of prefec-tural assembly elections. This is not a surprising phenomenon in elec-tions of large scale. Among other things, it ties in with the mixture of support systems that prefectural politicians must employ.† In this con-text it is important to realize that the prefectural assemblyman is not the end point of the network we described. That network normally stretches upward to a Diet member from the same district, who is, of course, affiliated with a party. If the Diet member is a Liberal Democrat, the connection usually extends only to him personally and not to the faction to which he belongs. In other words, prefectural assemblymen who have connections with Diet members from the same faction do not form a faction in the prefectural assemblies. The factionalism of the

* This is not to say that the "local politicians" in the countryside have no official leadership positions. Often they are village mayors, assembly chairmen, or important assembly members.

† It is likely that even prefectural politicians from rural areas will be pushed toward the employment of other means in addition to their interpersonal relations with in-formal leaders. The inroads of the well-organized politico-religious Sōka Gakkai in the election of 1963 may be a foreboding of the need for additional appeals.

Liberal Democratic Party is not reflected in these assemblies. The case of the Socialists is somewhat different. Connections with Diet members exist in this case, also; but because right-wingers and left-wingers draw electoral support from different unions, these ideological factions are likely to be reflected on the prefectural assembly level. The relations between the prefectural and the national politician are often based on loyalty. Not infrequently the prefectural politician is the *deshi* (disciple) or *kobun* of the national politician and received his *jiban* from him. But in every case the relationship is mutually useful. The prefectural assembly candidate, running in a relatively large district, needs campaign funds and welcomes the halo and the "political mileage" with which endorsement by a national figure provides him. In turn, the prefectural politician is useful to the Diet member much in the same way in which the local politician is useful to the prefectural politician. He helps the Diet member to nurse his constituency; he contributes the votes of his own *jiban* to those of the larger *jiban* of the national politician and, on a more formal level, he serves as the latter's local campaign manager. This aspect is illustrated by Isomura and Hoshino when they state: "It is said that the success or defeat of a Diet member depends on his control of prefectural assemblymen in his district, and the success or defeat of the latter depends on his control over the mayor and assemblymen of cities, towns, and villages in his district."*

Gubernatorial Elections

In the elections for the governorships of the forty-six prefectures of Japan, the prefectures as a whole serve as election districts. But the elections attract attention far beyond the prefectural boundaries; they are, in fact, of national interest. The governorship is a conspicuous and in many ways a pivotal position, and persons of national stature, such as politicians and bureaucrats, enter the contests.† Campaigns frequently deal with issues of national and international scope, and the top leaders of the parties stump in support of candidates.

---

* *Chihōjichi tokuhon*, p. 200. The connection between Diet members and prefectural assemblymen is of great significance to the composition of the Liberal Democratic Party. It facilitates recruitment into that segment of the party that consists of "pure politicians" in distinction to the segment consisting of ex-bureaucrats. On this point see Robert A. Scalapino and Junnosuke Masumi, *Parties and Politics in Contemporary Japan* (Berkeley, 1962), p. 56.

† This is possible because of the lack of a residence requirement for candidates.

One would expect elections of such political importance to engage the participation of a relatively high percentage of the politically sophisticated urban voters. But are there any indications to that effect? We know already that of all types of local elections, gubernatorial elections have the lowest voting rate, that the urban prefectures show the lowest voting rate in the country, and that within these prefectures, the *shibu* rate is lower than the *gumbu* rate. This may be somewhat surprising, but it does not prove that political interest is not a factor in determining the voting rates in the urban areas. It simply demonstrates again that the political interest in the urban areas is no match for the various social pressures that produce the extremely high voting rate in rural areas. Since these social pressures are relatively weaker in an urban setting, and since political interest cannot take up the slack, urban voting rates are lower than rural voting rates even in gubernatorial elections.

To find an answer to our question, we must compare the voting rates in gubernatorial elections with those in other elections within the urban areas. Let us look at the voting rates in the most urbanized area, Tokyo Metropolis. We noted that in Japan the elections for the chief executive typically draw a lower voting rate than those for the assembly. But in Tokyo this is not necessarily the case. In 1955 the voting rate in the metropolitan assembly elections was 59.63 per cent, while that in the gubernatorial elections was 68.32 per cent. In 1959 the two rates were nearly equal, 70.13 and 70.12 per cent. The gubernatorial contests between Yasui and Arita in 1955 and between Azuma and Arita in 1959 were pitched political battles between the conservative and progressive camps. It is likely, therefore, that the higher voting rate in the gubernatorial contests was based on the interest that these contests evoked among the politically sophisticated voters of the metropolis. When we focus our attention on the voting rate in gubernatorial elections in the ward area of Tokyo, we note a marked fluctuation between the elections. In 1955 the rate in the total ward area was 57.6 per cent, but in 1959 it was 68.9 per cent. As indicated previously, the social pressures typical of the conservative pattern lead to consistently high voting rates; political interest, on the other hand, is likely to differ in various elections. For this reason a marked fluctuation in voting rates, as shown in Tokyo, is itself an indication of an influence of political interest on the voting rate.

Another indication can be found by a comparison of the voting rate in the gubernatorial elections with those in ward assembly elections. In the ward elections the social pressures of the conservative pattern are exerted on the inhabitants to a much higher degree than in the gubernatorial elections. In 1955 the over-all voting rate in ward assembly elections was 61.5 per cent, nearly 4 per cent higher than in the gubernatorial elections of that year. But in 1959 the picture was reversed: the ward assembly election showed a voting rate of 65.4 per cent, which was 3.5 per cent lower than the voting rate in the gubernatorial election of the same year (68.9 per cent).* In addition, the differences among the various wards are noteworthy. A comparison between the rates in the more tradition-minded wards of the Shitamachi area and the less tradition-minded wards in the Yamate area shows the following picture: In 1955, the Shitamachi wards had a ward assembly voting rate that was considerably higher than the gubernatorial voting rate. On the other hand, in some of the less conservative wards the difference between the two voting rates was slight, and in one of them, Setagaya ward, a slightly higher percentage of voters (51.4 per cent) voted in the gubernatorial race than in the ward assembly election (51.0 per cent).[36] It would appear from this that in the conservative wards the voting rates dropped sharply when social pressure lessened—as is the case in the gubernatorial elections as compared with ward elections—while in the less conservative wards political interest in the gubernatorial contest takes up the slack to a large extent. In 1959 the same phenomenon appeared in a different form. As noted, in that year the over-all voting rate in the gubernatorial contest was higher than the voting rate in the ward assembly elections. This in itself is highly significant as a sign of existing political interest. But again there was a difference between the Shitamachi wards and the Yamate wards. In two of the Shitamachi wards, Edogawa and Adachi, the pattern of a higher ward assembly voting rate persisted (the difference being 1.2 per cent and 0.4 per cent respectively), and in other wards of the Shitamachi area the gubernatorial voting rate was not very much higher than the ward assembly voting rate. In the more progressive wards, on the other hand, a much higher percentage of voters cast their ballots in the gubernatorial contest than in the ward assembly contest.[37] The pattern was thus similar to that of 1955; again there was evidence that the heightened interest in

* It will be noted that the ward assembly election rates held more constant than the gubernatorial election rates. In the former case the increase over 1955 was 3.9 per cent, and in the latter case it was 11.3 per cent.

the politically more important contest was reflected in the voting rates of Tokyo's more progressive wards.*

As far as the ratio of candidates to positions is concerned we may assume at the outset that in gubernatorial races notions of harmony and the propriety of the avoidance of competition play no role. The number of candidates depends rather on calculations regarding chances for success, on the availability of the necessary campaign funds, on considerations of personal or party prestige, and on similar considerations that would come into play in any other cultural setting.

Most gubernatorial contests are between two candidates.[38] A ratio of roughly 2 to 1 leads easily to the assumption that the contest is normally between candidates representing two principal parties. But this assumption would neglect the existence of a third category of candidates, the independents. As a matter of fact, the ratio of independent candidates for gubernatorial positions is still quite high. However, as noted in Chapter 15, "independence" is not to be taken at face value. A contest involving one or even two independent candidates may nevertheless be a confrontation between two political camps. The contests in 1959 in Tokyo and Osaka may serve as examples. In Tokyo the conservative

* Further indications along these lines are provided if we widen our focus to include national elections. We noted in Chapter 15 that in Japan, contrary to Western experience, voting rates in local elections tend to be higher than those in national elections. In Tokyo this is not always the case. Tokyo's voting rate in the House of Representatives election of April 1953 (61.89 per cent) and of February 1955 (66.35 per cent) was higher than that in the Metropolitan Assembly election of 1955 (59.63 per cent). On the other hand, the Metropolitan Assembly election of 1959 showed a higher voting rate (70.13 per cent) than the House of Representatives election of November 1960 (63.42 per cent). Again it will be noted that in contrast to the constancy in voting rates where the conservative pattern is strong, the voting rates on both levels showed fluctuations. We may assume that where the conservative pattern is weak, there are voters who go to the polls in certain elections because their political interest is aroused but who stay away from other elections in which this is not the case. In the House of Councilors election, in which the smallest district is the prefecture—150 councilors are elected from prefectural constituencies, 100 from the nation at large—the conservative type of social pressure is at a minimum and the voting rate throughout the country is notoriously low. In Tokyo we find that the difference between the voting rates in the various wards in the House of Councilors elections is not nearly as great as the difference in voting rates in ward elections. In the absence of great pressure, the conservative wards do not produce their usual high voting rates. In progressive wards the pressure is even less strong, but because of higher political interest progressive wards match the voting rates of the conservative wards in this type of elections. A comparison of city mayor and city assembly elections earlier in this chapter also indicates a higher degree of political awareness in urban areas.

candidate, Dr. Azuma, ran as an independent against the Socialist candidate, Arita; in Osaka the progressive candidate, Obata, ran as an independent against the Liberal Democrat, Sato. In these cases the "independence" was purely formal. The support by the two main parties in terms of campaign organization and finances was as complete as if the candidates had run under the party's designation. But not all two-sided contests involving independents follow this pattern. Occasionally the contest is between a candidate supported by both main parties—who then runs as an independent and is sure of election—and a Communist candidate.* Occasionally also, two conservative candidates may compete against each other and in this case they run normally as conservative independents. It would thus be too simple to view each two-sided gubernatorial contest as a reflection of the bipolar character of Japanese politics.[39]

We noted that uncontested elections occur occasionally. At this level an uncontested election is a sign of the towering strength of one candidate and of the hopelessness of competition. Typically the governor thus elected is the incumbent seeking re-election as an independent. Altogether the chances for incumbents to be re-elected are very good. In 1959 ten of the 13 incumbents who ran emerged victorious; in 1955 eleven of the 16 incumbents who ran were re-elected, and in 1951 twenty-two of the 31 contests were won by incumbents. In the 1963 election, 18 out of 20 candidates for governorships were incumbents, and all of them were successful. As a result, there were two governors who had been elected four times, six governors who had been elected three times, and 21 governors who had been elected twice; only nine governors served their first term. There is now some agitation for a limitation on the number of terms governors may serve.[40] A number of reasons may account for this remarkable staying power of Japanese governors. The incumbent is able to grease his own machine by patronage; he is less handicapped in his campaigning by election law restrictions; and tradition-minded voters are reluctant to vote against a person occupying a high position.

We noted that a high percentage of the governors are independents. Historically, one of the reasons was the prevalence of ex-bureaucrats

---

* In 1959 there were seven Communist candidates, none of them successful. All of them ran against independents, and in six cases out of the seven there was only one independent opponent. In the seventh case, the Communist candidate was opposed by three conservative independents.

among gubernatorial candidates. In 1947, when all 46 positions had to be staffed by the elections, 31 were captured by independents. In 24 cases the incumbent governor—who had originally been appointed under the old system by the central government—was returned to his post in his new character as "the people's choice." Two other candidates who were successful had been appointed governors in other prefectures. In addition, two successful candidates who did not hold gubernatorial positions in 1947 had been governors before. Altogether 32 former governors competed. Of the six who were defeated, two were defeated by other former governors.[41] Four additional gubernatorial contests were won by candidates who formerly held high positions in the central government.* The prevalence of ex-bureaucrats among governors continued after the 1951 election. In a number of contests the vice-governor advanced to the post of governor, and many of the vice-governors were also ex-bureaucrats. Of the 48 persons who had become vice-governors between 1947 and 1950, 24 were former Home Ministry Officials, 4 were former officials of Japan's colonial administration or of the defunct Superintendencies-General, and a majority of the remainder were former officials of various ministries. Only 10 were former municipal officials or had no background in public administration.

The number of independent governors who are ex-bureaucrats is augmented by candidates who avoid a party label for various reasons. There is the governor originally elected with the support of a party who has been able during his tenure of office to attract support also from prefectural politicians of the other party and who then gets himself easily re-elected as an independent;† there is also the gubernatorial candidate who runs against a Communist opponent with support from

---

* The election of ex-bureaucrats to gubernatorial positions is particularly interesting in view of a public opinion poll conducted on August 31, 1946, about seven months prior to the election, by the newspaper *Mainichi*. In this poll only 11 per cent of the respondents, asked to characterize the type of people who should be elected as governors, stated a preference for bureaucrats, while 14 per cent preferred party politicians and 75 per cent preferred "civilians," i.e., people from various walks of life specifically excluding the bureaucracy and the party hierarchy. See Oka Yoshisato and Tsuji Kiyoaki, "Sengo taisei no seisaku to kikō," in the 1953 *Annals of the Japanese Political Science Association*, p. 47. The subsequent statement in the text regarding vice-governors who became governors is based on the same article, p. 44.

† This occasionally includes a Socialist governor who has made his peace with factions of the conservative parties in the assembly.

both major parties and consequently does not accept either party label; and there is the candidate who feels that his chances would be diminished by a Socialist label and who succeeds in getting himself elected as a progressive independent. All these pressures against overt party affiliation explain why the percentage of independent governors is still relatively high. But pressures in the opposite direction do exist. We noted a drop in the percentage of independent candidates between 1955 and 1959. The number of party-affiliated governors has been increasing and this tendency is likely to continue.

Gubernatorial candidates, of course, also use the various types of support systems available to Japanese politicians. But the emphasis on one or the other type differs from case to case. In rural prefectures and in the rural parts of urban prefectures the essentially apolitical links of direct or indirect personal and social relations are of great importance. Candidates use these links also in urban areas. But in urban areas where they are likely to yield a smaller percentage of the "fixed vote," political appeal plays a more important role. The overt part of the campaign is then very conspicuous. In addition, conservative and progressive candidates may differ in the emphasis they place on one or the other type of support system and their "fixed vote" may differ in nature, that of the progressive candidate being more associational in character. Occasionally the progressive candidate in a highly urbanized prefecture may wage an almost entirely unconventional campaign and emerge victorious. The campaign management is often in the hands of a senior prefectural politician who also serves as campaign manager for the Diet member from his area at times of general elections. But when the spotlight of national interest is focused on the contest, the national party leadership may assume a very important role in the management of the gubernatorial campaign. No efforts are spared, for instance, by the Liberal Democrats when a Socialist governor—such as Governor Tanaka of Hokkaido who held office from 1947 to 1959—is to be pushed out of office or when an urban prefecture, such as Aichi, is to be prevented from falling into progressive hands. Campaigns in urban prefectures where the Socialists feel that they have a chance to win the governorship also engage the efforts of the national leadership of that party. In some of these cases the vote is rather close. The gubernatorial contest in Osaka Prefecture in 1959 was won by the Liberal Democratic candidate Sato by a mere 15,374 votes out of a total vote of nearly two million.

One particular argument used by conservative candidates in their fight against progressive opponents—whether either of the candidates is party-affiliated or not—deserves special mention. If the governor has a "direct connection"—the term always used is *chokketsu*—to the central government, so the argument runs, subsidies will flow more freely and more generously into the prefecture. The validity of this argument is often confirmed during the campaign by members of the Cabinet and other leaders of the ruling party. Thus the influential Liberal Democratic leader Kawashima Shojiro wrote in *Shukan Asahi* on March 1, 1959, about a month before the elections of that year:

> It profits [the prefecture] if the governor belongs to the government party. If I may speak out of my experience as chief of the Autonomy Board, we did not look much after the needs of places with Socialist governors. At present the work of the prefecture is largely work on behalf of the state. Financially, too, the prefecture depends on the state. If there were no state subsidies the prefecture could actually not carry out its work. That is to say, under a governor who does not have a direct connection with the government, the work cannot be carried out.

Prime Minister Kishi also stressed the importance of a prefectural government "having direct connections with the center" in campaigning for conservative governors in that year.[42] It is something of a question whether political favoritism in the distribution of subsidies is actually as far-reaching in its consequences for the prefecture as these rather blatant campaign statements make it appear.* But it is quite likely that voters are swayed by the argument, which ties in with various old sayings counseling non-opposition to those in authority, such as "nagai

---

* One progressive governor whom I interviewed denied this. He pointed out that the loopholes in the Local Distribution Tax Law which give discretion to the central government—the provisions for the so-called "Special Distribution Tax"—are, after all, rather limited. He did not deny that the discretion may be used for purposes of political favoritism, nor that Diet members of the government party actually lobby for the exercise of such favoritism in national ministries that dispense subsidies, especially the Autonomy Ministry. But he felt that such lobbying was in fact less successful than the *chokketsu* argument would assume, because the administrators in the ministries are more inclined to think in terms of needed projects than in party political terms. The plausibility of this statement is enhanced by the fact that many contacts with the central government are carried out by the higher ranking officials of the prefectural bureaucracies, who, even in a prefecture with a progressive governor, are likely to be former central government officials and thus to have their own connections with the central government bureaucracy. On the other hand, it is well to recognize that progressive governors and gubernatorial candidates have an interest in denying the validity of the *chokketsu* argument. All things being equal and funds being limited, conservative governors are probably given a certain preference.

mono ni makarero" (roughly, "kings have long arms"). The fact that some progressive gubernatorial candidates prefer to run as independents, that some independents become Liberal Democrats, and that some Socialist governors shed their party label when they stand for reelection may well be in part a tacit acknowledgment of the effectiveness of the argument.

Gubernatorial elections in urbanized prefectures show a greater admixture of elements of the progressive pattern than any other local election. It may thus be worthwhile to conclude by describing the abovementioned contest in Osaka Prefecture in 1959 in greater detail. The contest was widely heralded as one of the first important confrontations between the unified conservative and the unified progressive camp.* We mentioned earlier that the Liberal Democratic candidate was opposed by a progressive candidate who ran as an independent. The progressive candidate, Mr. Obata, was endorsed by the Socialist Party, the Communist Party, the major labor unions, and by various politically oriented associations in which he had been active, such as the Kansai branch of the Committee for Reestablishment of Diplomatic Relations with the Soviet Union and China and various peace groups. In the calculations of the campaign managers, these organizations constituted the bulk of the "fixed vote." Labor was estimated to supply most of it, and the campaign organization of the progressive candidate for mayor of Osaka City also was to contribute to it. To obtain votes from small and medium businessmen, the progressive candidate stressed the benefits that Sino-Japanese trade would bring them. But much of his overt campaign addressed itself to national and international issues, above all to the issues of averting a return to totalitarianism and of maintaining peace. Referring to the fact that his opponent, Mr. Sato, had last held the position of chief of the Self-Defense Agency, he would ask: "Whom do you prefer as governor, the War Movement's Sato or the Peace Movement's Obata?," adding that giving governmental power to a war-loving man could only result in high-handed authoritarian government.

Obata himself, like his opponent a graduate of Tokyo University, had

---

* The reunification of the Right Wing Socialists and the Left Wing Socialists on the one hand and the merger of the Liberals and the Democrats into the Liberal Democratic Party on the other hand occurred after the unified local election in 1955. The split-off of the Democratic Socialists from the Socialist Party had not yet occurred in 1959. The following description is based mainly on Nishikawa Seiji, "Osaka fu chiji, shi chō senkyo no jittai," in *Toshi mondai*, Vol. 50, No. 8 (August 1959), pp. 22ff.

once been governor of Aichi Prefecture. Addressing himself to his opponent's argument of the usefulness of having "direct connections with the center," he called for an end to the evil practices that prevented voters from electing the man of their choice, if indeed such practices existed; and at the same time he attempted to show the fallacy of the argument by pointing out that Yamaguchi, the home prefecture of both Prime Minister Kishi and Finance Minister Sato, was not doing well by any means, its most direct connections with the central government notwithstanding.

Mr. Sato was an example of a prominent national politician chosen by the Liberal Democrats to ward off the danger of a Socialist victory in an important urban prefecture. He had previously been elected to the House of Representatives, had been elected three times to the House of Councilors, had been parliamentary vice-minister of Education and, as mentioned above, the minister in charge of the Self-Defense Agency. He had resigned this last position to become a candidate for governor of Osaka Prefecture. At one time he had been chairman of the board of Otani Gakuen, a Buddhist school. Alumni of that institution were instrumental in establishing his supporters' association, the *Satokai,* and in obtaining the support of other Buddhist groups. The votes thus assured—the *Satokai* alone was estimated to account for 100,000 votes—were an important part of Mr. Sato's "fixed vote." To this were added votes assured by the support of the incumbent governor of Osaka Prefecture and the mayor of Osaka City, who was running for a third term; votes from the overlapping *jiban* of Liberal Democratic Diet members and of conservative prefectural and city assemblymen, including the votes brought in by the network of neighborhood associations and Red Cross organizations. But in order to add to this "fixed vote" enough of the "floating vote" to gain victory, Mr. Sato also had to engage in large-scale political campaigning. He promised "prosperity for Osaka on the basis of free enterprise," "development of industry and promotion of trade," sometimes indicating that he felt that what was good for Osaka's heavy industry was good for Osaka. Other slogans used in his campaign were "Hope to youth and peace to women," and "a bright prefectural government through love and understanding."* In his speeches Mr. Sato

* The emotions evoked by the use of the word *akarui*—often used for political appeals—are difficult to define and are only imperfectly reflected by the usual translation "bright." Decency, orderliness, and harmony are all implied. Posters showing open-faced, clean-cut young men and women walking together into a sunny future aim at a similar emotional reaction.

broadly hinted that his opponent was a Communist, calling on his audi-
ence to "save the native soil from the grasp of the Reds." The use of the
argument for assuring a direct connection with the central government
by electing a Liberal Democrat has already been noted.

Both campaign organizations were headed by national figures. In
Mr. Sato's case the vice-president of the Liberal Democratic Party, Mr.
Ono, was its chief. In Mr. Obata's case, the Socialist Party delegated
Mr. Matsubara for the same task, but he had to abandon it in mid-
campaign for a House of Councilors by-election. The campaign organization reflected in each case the heterogeneous components of the candidates' support system and was thus quite complex. Mr. Obata's over-
all campaign policy was decided by a conference of representatives of
the Socialist party, the Communist party, the trade unions, and of various
organizations such as youth groups and peace groups. In order to unify
the campaign work for the progressive gubernatorial candidate and the
progressive mayoral candidate within Osaka City, it was decided that
in Osaka City the organization for the mayoral candidate, Mr. Nakaba—
a former vice-mayor of Osaka City—would also conduct the gubernatorial campaign. Mr. Nakaba had established his supporters' association,
the *Nakabakai*, some eight months prior to the campaign. This arrangement introduced an essentially conservative element, local bosses tied
together by personal relations, into Mr. Obata's over-all support system.
On the other hand, it appears that the labor vote was somewhat neglected within Osaka City and that the trade unions did not go all out
in support of Mr. Nakaba because he avoided a clear-cut progressive
stand in his pronouncements. Outside Osaka City, where the campaign
was not tied to Mr. Nakaba's mayoral campaign, it proved more effective. Mr. Obata won 50.1 per cent of the *gumbu* vote, but only 49.4 per
cent of the *shibu* vote. The over-all vote was close, Mr. Sato winning
50.5 per cent of the total and Mr. Obata trailing with 49.5 per cent.*

We have now discussed the six main types of local elections to posi-

---

* The mayoral contest in Osaka City was won handily by the conservative candidate, Mr. Nakai, who garnered 62.4 per cent of the vote as against Mr. Nakaba's 36.2
per cent. A third candidate won the remaining 1.4 per cent. However, Mr. Nakaba
was successful in the mayoral election of 1963, while Mr. Obata was again defeated
by Mr. Sato, this time by a margin of 243,000 votes.

In the prefectural assembly election of 1959, the vote was also close. After the

tions in local government in Japan.* But there is one other way by which the Japanese electorate can make its participation in local government felt. This is the method known as direct demand, and we turn to it now.

Direct Demands

The system of direct demands apparently owes its existence to a proposal of the Local Government Division of SCAP's Government Section. It recommended itself as a means of civic and political education.† The existence of similar institutions in American local government undoubtedly also played a role. Officials of the Home Ministry opposed the introduction of direct demand, fearing that the institution would be abused or used too frequently, thus depriving the electoral process of much of its meaning. These fears proved to be unfounded. In general, the institution has served its purposes reasonably well, although it is sometimes used in ways that were probably not anticipated by its proponents.

There are four types of results that may be obtained by direct demand. As will be noted, in all cases the initial step is to persuade a certain percentage of voters to write their names in a signature book. Various provisions of the law are designed to ensure the absence of deception,

---

election the prefectural assembly consisted of 39 Liberal Democrats, 30 Socialists, 2 Communists, 3 progressive independents, 3 conservative independents, 2 pure independents, and 7 representatives of smaller groups. An indication of the increasing politicization of the prefectural assembly was the drop in successful independents. Before the election there were 12 progressive and 5 conservative independents in the Osaka Prefectural Assembly. After the election independents occupied a total of 8 seats, as noted; the number of progressive independents had dropped from 12 to 3. On the other hand, the number of Socialist assemblymen had risen from 17 to 30.

* There are also other elections, such as those to the Agriculture Commissions, but we have omitted the election to bodies with specialized functions from the scope of our investigations.

† It is interesting to note that Sun Yat-sen introduced the referendum, the initiative, and the recall into China as principles of democracy. To serve the purpose of political education, direct demand must lead to a speedy resolution of the issue. It is essential that the period between the collection of signatures and the result of the movement—for instance, the retirement of the mayor—be as short as possible. However, the safeguards against abuse inserted in the Local Autonomy Law in 1950 prolonged this period. The result is sometimes that the mayor who is to be recalled or the assembly which is to be dissolved serve out their time in office while the proceedings are still pending.

coercion, and other interferences with the free expression of the right of direct demand.

The first type of direct demand aims at the enactment, amendment, or abolition of a bylaw. One-fiftieth of the voters may address such a demand to the local chief executive. The signature books are first presented to the municipal Election Administration Committee for certification that those who signed are persons whose names appear on the election lists. Provision is made for public inspection of the signature books after the certification has been given. If there are objections, the municipal Election Administration Committee determines their validity and rules accordingly. The appeals against such a ruling go to the prefectural Election Administration Committee if the direct demand concerns a prefectural bylaw. The ultimate recourse is a suit filed with the High Court, which has jurisdiction over the area.* If the direct demand concerns a municipal bylaw, the complaint against the ruling of the municipal Election Administration Committee takes the form of a suit filed with the local District Court. There is no regular appeal against the decision of that court, but it is possible to bring an action in the Supreme Court, whose decision is final. When the chief executive receives a direct demand regarding a bylaw, he calls the assembly and presents the demand, together with his own opinion of it, for the assembly's consideration. The assembly is of course free to accept or reject the demand—that is, to enact or not to enact the desired bylaw or amendment or to abolish or not to abolish the bylaw against which the demand was directed.† In the beginning, direct demands of this type sometimes aimed at the reduction of local taxes, which seemed to confirm the apprehensions of the opponents of the direct demand system.‡ In order to protect the hard-pressed local entities against the po-

---

* This is one of the exceptions to the general rule that High Courts function as courts of appeal against decisions of District Courts.

† As will be noted, Japanese voters do not have the right of popular initiative under which the electorate could adopt a measure directly.

‡ It should be noted, however, that only one direct demand of this type on the municipal level led to the actual adoption of the desired bylaw, and even in this case the assembly made certain amendments. Of the 20 cases of such direct demand on record, 12 occurred on the prefectural level and 8 on the municipal level. All direct demands on the prefectural level ended in failure—in five cases because the required number of signatures was not obtained, and in seven cases because the direct demand was rejected by the assembly. Seven of the cases on the municipal level also

tential loss of revenue, and in order to restore the budgetary prerogatives of the chief executive, the Local Autonomy Law was amended in
1948 to exclude bylaws relating to the levying and collection of taxes
and other imposts from the scope of direct demands of this type.

The second type of direct demand calls on the inspection commissioners to inspect the management of an enterprise carried on by the
locality, the volume of local revenues and expenditures, and the administration of local affairs in general. The affairs that may be inspected
on direct demand include not only those under the jurisdiction of the
chief executive but also those handled by the various administrative
commissions. Again, the signatures of 2 per cent of the local electorate
are required. The result of the inspection is to be reported to the assembly, to the chief executive, and to the administrative commission
concerned. The representatives of those who made the demand also
have to be notified and public notice has to be given.

The third type of direct demand aims at the dissolution of the assembly. In this case the signatures of one-third of the voters are required.
The demand is addressed to the Election Administration Committee,
which submits the issue to the vote of the electorate. The assembly is
dissolved if a simple majority of the voters express themselves in favor
of dissolution. However, such a direct demand is possible only after a
year has passed since the election of the assembly or since the last vote
on a direct demand for dissolution.

The fourth type of direct demand is known in Japan by the English
name "recall." It comprises three cases.* The aim may be the dismissal
of an assemblyman, the dismissal of the chief executive, or the dismissal
of some other official, such as the vice-governor, the vice-mayor, the
chief accountant, the treasurer, or a member of one of the administrative commissions. All three cases require the signatures of one-third of
the voters. A difference exists between the first two cases and the third
one. The persons against whom the recall is directed in the first two
cases—assemblymen or chief executives—hold elective positions. The
recall is therefore effected by a popular vote, which is called by the

---

ended in failure—one because the number of signatures was insufficient, and six because of rejection by the assembly.

* This presentation follows the arrangement in the Local Autonomy Law. If we
speak in the following of the six types of direct demand, we shall mean the first-
mentioned three types and the three cases of recall.

Election Administration Committee when it is satisfied that those who present the demand have met the required conditions. When a simple majority of the voters expresses itself in favor of the demand, the persons against whom the recall is directed must vacate their positions. As in the case of direct demand for assembly dissolution, the voters cannot oust a chief executive or assemblyman whom they have elected less than a year before. In the third case, the demand is directed against officials who are appointed by the chief executive with the consent of the assembly or are elected by the assembly. It is therefore not passed on by the electorate but is addressed to the chief executive, who must submit it to the assembly. The official concerned loses his office if three-fourths of the assembly members present consent to the demand. A quorum of two-thirds is required. The time limit in this case is one year for assistant governors and other auxiliary organs of the executive, and six months for members of the various commissions.

These, in brief, are the rules for direct demands in the Local Autonomy Law.[43]

Table 21 shows the number of direct demands of all six types during the period from the enforcement of the Local Autonomy Law in 1947 to the end of May 1960. It will be noted that the frequency of direct demands fluctuated over the years. The number was high in 1948 and particularly in 1949, when it reached its highest point with 245 direct demands on record. The following three years showed a decrease in numbers to a low of 68 in 1952. But then the number rose again, and, with the exception of 1957, every succeeding year showed a somewhat higher number than 1952. This increase reflects the tensions introduced by the mass amalgamation drive of 1953–57 and by the promotion of the establishment of new cities, towns, and villages that followed it.

Table 21 also shows that most direct demands occur on the municipal level. Closer investigation reveals that on that level the overwhelming number of direct demands occur in towns and villages rather than in cities.[44] We note that on the municipal level direct demands aim most frequently at the dismissal of the chief executive or the dissolution of the assembly. If we add to these the demands for dismissal of assemblymen, we account for 851 of the 1,191 cases on that level. Further investigation reveals, however, a significant difference between the aims of direct demands in cities and in towns and villages. While the great majority of the demands occur in towns and villages, direct demands for the enactment or abolition of bylaws and for inspections are rela-

TABLE 21

Number and Type of Direct Demands, May 3, 1947, to May 31, 1960

Year	Demands Regarding Bylaws			Demands for Inspection			Demands for Dissolution of Assemblies			Demands for Dismissal of Assembly Members			Demands for Dismissal of Chief Executives			Demands for Dismissal of Auxiliary Personnel			Total		
	P[a]	M[b]	Total	P	M	Total	P	M	Total	P	M	Total	P	M	Total	P	M	Total	P	M	Total
1947	–	1	1	1	–	1	–	–	–	–	–	–	–	–	–	–	–	–	1	1	2
1948	12	10	22	–	12	12	–	67	67	–	19	19	–	74	74	–	1	1	12	183	195
1949	3	17	20	1	25	26	–	89	89	–	16	16	–	91	91	–	3	3	4	241	245
1950	–	4	4	–	12	12	–	35	35	–	6	6	–	39	39	–	–	–	–	96	96
1951	3	3	6	1	20	21	–	13	13	–	5	5	–	25	25	–	–	–	4	66	70
1952	–	5	5	–	13	13	–	14	14	–	6	6	–	29	29	–	1	1	–	68	68
1953	–	3	3	–	20	20	–	14	14	–	10	10	–	27	27	–	–	–	–	74	74
1954	1	4	5	–	14	14	–	25	25	–	12	12	–	31	31	–	2	2	1	88	89
1955	–	10	10	–	30	30	–	16	16	1	2	3	–	24	24	–	–	–	1	82	83
1956	–	7	7	–	15	15	–	10	10	–	11	11	–	24	24	–	2	2	–	69	69
1957	–	10	10	–	12	12	–	7	7	–	24	24	1	12	13	–	–	–	1	65	66
1958	–	10	10	–	17	17	–	13	13	–	15	15	1	14	15	–	–	–	1	69	70
1959	–	24	24	1	19	20	–	5	5	–	10	10	–	8	8	2	–	2	3	66	69
1960	1	11	12	–	3	3	–	3	3	–	–	–	–	6	6	–	–	–	1	23	24
	20	119	139	4	212	216	–	311	311	1	136	137	2	404	406	2	9	11	29	1,191	1,220

[a] Prefectures.   [b] Municipalities.

SOURCE: Autonomy Ministry, *Chihō jichi geppō*, No. 29 (December 1960), pp. 10 and 11.

tively more frequent in cities than in towns and villages.* On the prefectural level, direct demands regarding bylaws are more frequent than
all others, as can be seen in Table 21. In other words, in the cities and
on the prefectural level, the focus of the direct demand is more likely
to be on a specific issue of local politics, and the solution sought is an
equally specific one. The focus of direct demands in towns and villages
is in many cases quite diffuse—as the examples below will show—and
the solution goes to the official status of the opposition as a whole, not
to its defeat on a specific issue. Many of the cases reflect tensions between the chief executive and the assembly, or, to put it differently,
tensions between factions dominated by the chief executive and factions
hostile to him. It appears that demands for dismissal of the chief executive in particular are often used when attempts at obtaining a vote of
no confidence have failed or do not appear promising.[45]

As for the results of the direct demands, the official statistics give us
only an approximate picture. The cases in which the number of those
entering their names in the signature books falls short of the legally required percentage of the voters are lumped together with the cases in
which the direct demand was not pressed beyond the presentation of
the signature books and with the cases in which the signatures were
collected but the books not presented. In these cases the demands may
or may not have been ineffective. For example, the chief executive on
his own may have submitted to the assembly a bill of the demanded
content before the signature books were presented, in which case the
demand really achieved its end. On the other hand, the signature books
may not have been presented because the campaign was given up as
hopeless. In the statistics, all of these cases appear together under the
category of "other cases." With this in mind, we may now consider the
following record of the results of the direct demands of each type.

I. Demands for adoption or abolition of a bylaw, 139 cases
   A. Prefectural level, 20 cases
      1. Submitted to the assembly, 13
         (a) Rejected, 12
         (b) Adopted with amendments, 1
      2. Other cases, 7

---

* For instance, 47 of the 119 demands regarding bylaws and 55 of the 212 demands for inspection occurred in cities. On the other hand, if we consider together
the demands for the dissolution of the assemblies and for recall of assemblymen or
chief executives, only 53 out of 851 cases occurred in cities.

B. Municipal level, 119 cases (47 in cities, 4 in special wards)
    1. Submitted to the assembly, 82
        (a) Rejected by the assembly, 69
        (b) Adopted with amendments, 7
        (c) Adopted, 6
    2. Rejection of the direct demand, 8
    3. Other cases, 29

We note that on both levels the majority of the demands was rejected by the assembly. Only one prefectural bylaw and 13 municipal bylaws were clearly traceable to direct demands in the 13 years covered by the statistics.

By comparison, the level of effectiveness in direct demands for inspection is high, as shown by the following:

II. Demands for inspection, 216 cases
    A. Prefectural level, 4 cases*
    B. Municipal level, 212 cases (55 in cities, 2 in special wards)
        1. Accepted, 159
        2. Rejected, 16
        3. Other cases, 37

In the case of demands for dissolution of the assembly and demands for dismissal of individual assemblymen or of the chief executive, the electorate votes on direct demands that fulfill the legal requirements regarding the number of signatures. The cases are thus first divided into those in which balloting was actually held and those in which no balloting was held. Where balloting was held, the majority may vote either for or against the dissolution or dismissal. This is reflected below as "passed" or "not passed." Where no balloting was held, this may have been for a number of reasons. If the demand was one for the dissolution of the assembly, no balloting may have been necessary because the assembly resigned en bloc, thus preventing a ballot. This then would achieve the aim of the direct demand. On the other hand, the direct demand may have been rejected by the Election Administration Committee or withdrawn by those who submitted it. Such a case would fall

---

* All four cases fell into the category of "other cases" described above. For instance, a direct demand in Wakayama for inspection of the financial management of the building of a prefecturally owned deep-sea fishing vessel led to a request for the same inspection by the assembly, and the aim of the direct demand was thus achieved before the signature collection was even completed.

into the ubiquitous category of "other cases," mentioned above. The breakdown is as follows:

III. Demands for dissolution of the assembly, 311 cases
    A. Prefectural level, no cases
    B. Municipal level, 311 cases
       1. Balloting held, 114
          (a) Passed, 74
          (b) Not passed, 40
       2. No balloting held, 197 (19 in cities)
          (a) Assembly resignation en bloc, 51
          (b) Direct demand rejected, 34
          (c) Direct demand withdrawn, 23
          (d) Other cases, 89

Leaving aside the category of "other cases," we note that 125 out of 311 cases led to the desired aim, the premature end of the tenure of the assembly, either by dissolution or by en bloc resignation.

Demands for recall of assemblymen may be directed against one or more assemblymen. As a matter of fact, they are more frequently directed against a group of assemblymen than against a single individual. The number of assemblymen involved is thus considerably higher than the number of cases. For instance, the 37 cases on the municipal level between May 1947 and May 1950 involved 150 assemblymen. Direct demands of this type are often used in the struggle of factions within the assembly, the tie between the members of the faction under attack being more often personal or regional (all of the members coming from the same *buraku,* for instance) than political. Here, too, the balloting was in some cases forestalled by resignation, and this is reflected in the statistics.

IV. Demands for recall of assemblymen, 136 cases
    A. Prefectural level, 1 case*
    B. Municipal level, 136 cases (6 in cities)
       1. Balloting held, 42
          (a) Passed, 33
          (b) Not passed, 9
       2. No balloting held, 94
          (a) Resignation of assemblymen, 28
          (b) Direct demand rejected, 11
          (c) Direct demand withdrawn, 16
          (d) Other cases, 39

* The only case on record, which involved seven assemblymen, occurred in Ishikawa Prefecture in 1955; in this case the signature books were not presented within the legally prescribed period.

Thus 61 out of 136 direct demands were at least partially successful, either because of the outcome of the ballot or because of the resignations of at least some of the assemblymen concerned.

In the case of demands for recall of chief executives, the categories are the same as in the preceding two types of demands. The results were as follows:

V. Direct demands for recall of chief executives, 406 cases
   A. Prefectural level, 2 cases*
   B. Municipal level, 404 cases (24 in cities)
      1. Balloting held, 127
         (a) Passed, 70
         (b) Not passed, 57
      2. No balloting held, 277
         (a) Resignation of mayor, 82
         (b) Direct demand rejected, 40
         (c) Direct demand withdrawn, 36
         (d) Other cases, 119

There were thus 406 cases, of which 152 (all on the municipal level) led to the recall or resignation of the chief executive. Resignations without balloting were actually slightly more numerous than completed recalls. This phenomenon is probably connected with the general importance of resignation as an aspect of the Japanese political style. The politician who goes down to defeat fighting wins little sympathy, but there is some virtue in "accepting one's responsibility" and in sacrificing oneself for the harmony of the collectivity by resigning, even if the self-sacrifice is somewhat less than spontaneous.

In the case of demands for dismissal of auxiliary personnel, an affirmative vote in the assembly rather than an affirmative vote of the electorate is required. The categories are thus similar to those in the case of demands regarding by-laws, except that in the present case there is the possibility that the demand may achieve its purpose without a vote of the assembly because the official concerned resigns from his post.

---

* In December 1958 a demand for the resignation of the governor of Tokyo Metropolis was initiated in connection with the question of expanding U.S. air bases in the area; the movement never reached the signature-presentation stage and was abandoned in January 1959. The other case, directed against the governor of Fukuoka Prefecture, started in November 1957. The demand did not immediately achieve its aim because the Election Administration Committee found that the number of valid signatures fell short of the number required under the law; the case is nevertheless important because Fukuoka was the only prefecture in which a Socialist governor replaced a conservative in the subsequent local elections of 1959.

VI. Demands for dismissal of auxiliary personnel, 11 cases
   A. Prefectural level, 2 cases*
   B. Municipal level, 9 cases (1 in a city)
      1. Submitted to the assembly, 4
         (a) Rejected by the assembly, 3
         (b) Consented to by the assembly, 1
      2. Not submitted to the assembly, 5
         (a) Resignation of official concerned, 1
         (b) Rejection of direct demand, 1
         (c) Other cases, 3

This is by far the least frequent type of direct demand. On the municipal level there has been no case since 1956.

Some examples may illustrate the purposes for which the various types of demands are used. In the foregoing it has been suggested that the institution is utilized sometimes as a weapon of one personal faction against another personal faction. In these cases both factions are likely to be conservative and their views on specific issues play no role in the conflict. But there are also cases in which direct demands are the weapon of the progressive minority against the conservative leadership and then the political flavoring is, of course, strong. Perhaps the most famous examples of direct demands are those aiming at the abolition of bylaws regarding mass meetings, demonstrations, and parades, frequently referred to as Public Peace Ordinances (*kōan jōrei*). As noted in Chapter 7, these ordinances were adopted in various cities and prefectures during the Occupation, beginning with the Public Peace Ordinance of Fukui City of July 7, 1948. In many cases the adoption of the ordinance was accompanied by disorders in the assembly halls and by riots and violence outside. The question of constitutionality was not decided by the Supreme Court until 1960. During this period, there were also some attempts to abolish the ordinances by way of direct demand, notably in Tokyo Metropolis, and in the cities of Kyoto, Kawasaki, and Niigata. None of them achieved success.

In Tokyo 91,134 ballot signatures were collected in September 1951.

---

* Both occurred in Tokyo in 1959, and both were directed against the Metropolitan Election Administration Committee. The first of these attacked the committee as a whole, claiming that it was unduly influenced by the governor, so that proper administration of elections was made impossible; the demand was abandoned within a month. But two months later a second demand was initiated, accusing one of the committee members of improper interference with a public notice of the election; this demand never reached the stage of presentation of signature books and was therefore also abortive.

This was well above the legally required number of 78,487 and the demand thus had to be submitted to the Metropolitan Assembly. The assembly rejected it on February 7, 1952. In the meantime, the signature collection campaign in the city of Kyoto had also been successful. The legally required number of signatures was 13,120, but 62,868 persons signed the signature books. The ultimate fate of the movement in Kyoto, however, was the same as in Tokyo: on March 30, 1952, the demand was rejected by the city assembly. As these examples show, this type of direct demand lacks effectiveness as a tool for the progressive minority because most local assemblies, having a conservative majority, refuse to adopt the desired measure.

Other frequent objects of direct demands are bylaws regarding the establishment of election districts, the fixed number of assemblymen or local officials, the salaries of officials in the "special local public service," and the location of the office of the city, town, or village.*

Direct demands for inspections arise from a variety of reasons, some form of graft being a frequent cause. When the mayor of the city of Sendai attended the Pan-Pacific Mayors' Conference in Seattle and spent 1,970,000 yen on the trip, an investigation was instituted on the basis of a direct demand. The result was a finding by the inspection commissioners that the bylaw covering the subject of official travel was so loose that the actions of the mayor were covered by its scope and thus not illegal; the inspection commissioners suggested the enactment of a more rigid regulation. The construction of schools often gives rise to direct demands of this type. The inspection may concern, for instance, the cost or quality of construction or the amount of incidental social expenses. Sometimes the direct demand aims at an investigation of the methods used and the funds spent to induce industrial companies to locate a plant in a city. Some cases are connected with the amalgamation movement, the administration being accused of unjustified expenditures or of making dispositions that are ultra vires.

Sometimes the manner in which the officials in question, most fre-

---

* It is interesting to note that the last-mentioned case nearly always occurs in towns and villages. Of the seven cases of this type recorded between June 1, 1956, and May 31, 1960, only one occurred in a city. This ratio differs significantly from the over-all ratio between direct demands regarding bylaws in cities on the one hand and in towns and villages on the other, which was 26 to 59 for the same period. The reason is probably to be sought in the desire of the various *buraku* within a town or village to see the office located in their own proximity rather than at the location decided on by the town or village assembly.

quently the mayor and his staff, carry out their duties in general comes under investigation. An interesting case of this sort occurred in 1953 in the village of Niijimamoto in Tokyo Metropolis. As frequently happens, a number of investigations were demanded together. One of the investigations concerned the collection and distribution of goods for victims of the disastrous typhoon "Ione." In the same demand the question was raised why a part of a subsidy for the destruction of pine bark beetles was given to certain shrines in the area, and whether such a use of public funds was not contrary to the constitution.* The inspection commissioners found that no improper or unconstitutional use of public funds was involved because the shrines received the funds for the purposes for which the pine beetle subsidy was intended. In this and in most other cases, the inspection commissioners exculpated the officials against whom the demand was directed. Sometimes the result was only a slap on the wrist, in the form of a report to the effect that the official acts complained of, while not illegal, were to be regretted and should be avoided in the future. In only a few cases did the inspection commissioners roundly condemn the acts of the executives. Still, if the purpose of this type of direct demand is to assist the citizens in keeping the officials "on their toes," it may be said that it is not completely ineffective.

When we turn to direct demands for dissolution of local assemblies, we approach the area in which the institution is frequently used in a traditional context. This is apparent not only in the overwhelming prevalence of cases in towns and villages and in the paucity of cases in cities; it is also clear from the reasons given for the demands. Accusations abound that an assembly has "isolated itself from the people," that its "policy runs counter to the people's will," that it practices "deception and tyranny." And of course there is the standard complaint of lack of harmony in the form of an accusation that the assembly's "bickering is throwing the administration into confusion" or that its members are "lacking in political morality." In one case, in the village of Nishiwaki

* The reference was to Article 20 of the Constitution, which states that "No religious organization shall receive any privileges from the State . . ." and especially to Article 89, which states that "No public money or other properties shall be expended or appropriated for the use, benefit, or maintenance of any religious institution or association or for any charitable, educational, or benevolent enterprise not under control of public authority." This provision is echoed in the Local Autonomy Law, Articles 212 and 230.

in Wakayama Prefecture, the peculiar accusation was made that the assembly members created a disturbing agitation by supporting an opposition candidate for the position of mayor (i.e., that they failed to support the one candidate selected by the informal leadership of the various *buraku*, and thus made it necessary to conduct actual balloting). Also indicative of the traditional atmosphere in which this new legal institution is often used is the fact, noted above, that in many cases balloting is forestalled by the resignation of the entire assembly. It is in this category, furthermore, that the tensions of the mass amalgamation movement became most apparent. Between January 1, 1952, and the end of May 1956 there were 72 direct demands of this type on the municipal level. In 33 cases the reason for the demand referred specifically to problems arising out of the amalgamations. Frequently the reason stated was simply "opposition to the merger," agreed upon by the assembly.

Direct demands for the recall of one or more individual assemblymen also typically occur in a rural setting. The reason is sometimes an accusation of neglect of duty, abuse of authority, or graft (for instance in connection with a school construction or other construction). In some cases the assemblymen concerned were considered a disruptive element because they "opposed the mayor and by word and deed earned the distrust of the villagers," or because "disagreeing with the way of thinking of the townspeople, they did not respect the people's will in the assembly, were irresponsible in their arguments, lacked the proper qualities of assemblymen, and turned a deaf ear to all councils of self-reflection." On the other hand, an abortive direct demand in a city of Aomori Prefecture was directed against two assemblymen who were "not suited for their posts because they were bosses." In 6 of the 30 cases (involving 98 assemblymen) that occurred between January 1, 1952, and May 31, 1956, problems connected with amalgamations were cited as the reason for the recall movement. In about 20 per cent of the cases, the assemblymen resign before the actual balloting on the recall.

Accusations of the type mentioned in connection with the recall of individual assemblymen are also frequently the basis for demands for the recall of chief executives. The chief executive is sometimes accused of having "forced through an unwanted amalgamation." A case that occurred in a town of Aomori Prefecture in December 1951 is exceptional and interesting because nearly the entire range of appeal provisions came into play. The mayor was accused of ulterior motives in his nominations of members of the various administrative committees and in his decisions regarding road repairs; of improper conversations regarding the planned expansion of the primary school building with a bidder for the construction; of discriminatory treatment of office staff members and of extravagance in spending funds for entertainment. The Town Election Administration Committee rejected the demand without even inspecting the signature books. This rather unusual action was justified as follows: "The reasons for the direct demand are absolutely trumped up; the demand is used as a political tool; the demand is damaging to the independence of local government and, because it throws the town government into confusion, it is injurious to the public welfare." The representatives of those who signed the recall then resubmitted the signature books, stating that their rejection was illegal. But the committee was adamant and rejected the books again. In October 1952 the representatives brought a lawsuit against the committee to the District Court, which decided in their favor. Against this decision the committee appealed to the High Court, but that court upheld the decision. Undaunted, the committee appealed to the Supreme Court. The Supreme Court rejected their appeal in December 1953, and the committee thus had to inspect the signature books. Upon scrutiny it found that 8 of the 11 leaders of the recall movement were disqualified because they were local officials, and so finally, in February 1954, it rejected the demand for this reason.

One of the most famous cases of a recall of a chief executive occurred in October 1952 in Shibuya Ward in the Yamate area of Tokyo. It was started by a civic group, the Shibuya Shinwa Kai (Shibuya Friendship Association), which was founded after the ward assembly had shown itself unwilling to pass a resolution of no confidence against the ward chief lest it be dissolved by him. The group was headed by the former president of Aoyama Gakuin College, Abe Yoshimune. The ward chief, one Sato Kenzo, was involved in a scandal in which he, six officials of the ward office, and six executives of various companies, including the president of a large construction company, were arrested. Sato himself was accused, among other things, of having accepted a bribe to award the construction company the contract for the construction of a metropolitan model school and of having embezzled public funds in the amount of many millions of yen. The direct demand accused Sato also of dishonorable conduct in connection with the clearance and rebuilding of the notoriously congested area in front of Shibuya Station. Some 49,516 valid signatures were collected, about 1,300 more than the legally required number. Balloting was held in April 1953. The affirmative vote (22,787) outnumbered by far the negative vote (4,421). Mr. Sato fought the movement with two lawsuits, one directed against the validity of the signatures and one against the validity of the balloting. Both were pending for years. The first of these cases in which the Shibuya Ward Election Administration Committee figured as defendant was decided in the last instance by the Supreme Court on July 18, 1961. Mr. Sato lost his appeal. He then withdrew the other suit directed against Tokyo Metropolitan Election Administration Committee on August 21, 1961.[46] Belatedly, the efforts of the Shibuya Shinwa Kai were vindicated.

The only case of a recall movement against a governor occurred in Fukuoka Prefecture. It was initiated by an ad hoc civic group called the "Council for Political Development," which stated that it was neither progressive nor conservative but above partisanship and interested only in justice and fairness in the prefectural administration. The case was often referred to as the "case of the fraudulent appropriation of 100 million yen," because that sum had been lent, out of the prefectural tax fund, to a Tokyo bank facing bankruptcy. When the scandal broke in March 1957, the persons primarily implicated were the vice-governor and the treasurer, who were soon indicted for bribery and the misuse of public funds. But the Council for Political Development felt that the governor, Mr. Tsuchiya, whose seal had been used in the transaction, should assume responsibility, especially since the "appreciation money" or kickback of 10 million yen, paid by the bank, was used for political purposes benefiting the governor. Mr. Tsuchiya, however, blamed the whole affair on the two main culprits. He felt that because the money was restored to the prefectural fund no harm was done to the people of the prefecture; therefore he had no cause for resignation. The collection of signature books began November 1957 and by the following January 879,786 signatures had been collected. But as a result of the investigations of various municipal Election Administration Committees, which ruled on objections regarding the validity of some of the signatures in the period between January and April 1958, the total number of valid signatures throughout the prefecture was declared to be 648,647. This number was below the legally required number of 722,105, and the

recall movement failed. However, later developments showed that it
was by no means without effect. In 1959 the incumbent governor, Mr.
Tsuchiya, was defeated by his Socialist opponent, Mr. Uzaki.*

These two cases of the recall of a chief executive are interesting for
a number of reasons. For one, they show that the phenomenon of civic
reform organizations is not unknown in Japan, at least on the prefectural
level or in an urban setting.† For another, they show that direct demands
can serve, in addition to their overt purposes, the purpose of dramatizing
grievances and arousing civic interest. Finally, if we compare these two
cases with some of the cases in a rural setting mentioned earlier, they
show us that direct demands, like elections, reflect the broad spectrum
of political behavior patterns in Japan and the varying influences of
tradition and change on these patterns.

Summary

The last two chapters have shown that the behavior of Japanese voters
differs in various local and institutional settings. Town and village assembly elections in rural prefectures are closest to what we called the
"traditional pattern"; among local elections, gubernatorial elections in
urban centers are closest to the "progressive pattern." But elements of
both patterns are always present, and the difference lies in the composition of the mixture in every case. This is not surprising. There are many
threads leading back and forth between rural and urban Japan. A great
percentage of the population of the cities was born and brought up in
the villages; on the other hand, industrialization and the expansion of
the means of transportation and communications have made continuous
inroads into rural life.

---

* The governorship of Fukuoka Prefecture has been in Socialist hands since then
because Mr. Uzaki was re-elected in 1963. In the same election the newly created industrial city of Kitakyushu in Fukuoka Prefecture also elected, as its first mayor, a
Socialist.

† The initiation of such a movement in a rural setting is often discouraged by various means, including violence. For example, when a recall movement against a village assembly in Ibaraki Prefecture was initiated by the local Young Men's Association, members of a terrorist organization locked the leaders of the movement into a
room in the village office, forced them by threats to suspend the signature collection
campaign, and burned the signature books that had already been signed by more
than the legally required number of voters. See *Mainichi shimbun*, February 15,
1950, and Report of the Civil Liberties Bureau of the Attorney General's Office on
this case, which is in my possession.

However, the transformation of traditional values and behavior patterns has been much more rapid in the large industrial cities than in the countryside. The existence of continuities should not blind us to the great gap that separates the end points of our continuum.*

This gap has important consequences for the body politic as a whole. The tradition-oriented electoral behavior on the local level in rural areas, based on the power structure of towns and villages, is utilized by national politicians through prefectural politicians and local bosses, who act as intermediaries. It benefits the conservatives more than the progressives, and so the conservatives are always certain of a majority in the Diet. Japan, it has been said, has not a two-party system in which the major parties alternate in the control of the government, but a one-and-a-half-party system: a party that is always in power and a perennial minority party.

Political groups which are unable to influence national policy, which have been excluded from positions of power for long periods of time, and which see no hope of gaining power in the near future, generally tend to frustration. But in Japan this frustration is aggravated because the opposition feels that it represents the politically conscious and articulate segment of the population, and that the "public opinion" it represents is constantly disregarded by the ruling party, which controls the masses of politically unsophisticated rural voters and is able to exercise its power without regard for the correctness or incorrectness of its policies. The opposition claims that this is "tyranny of the majority," and a perversion of true parliamentary democracy.† The conservatives, on the other hand, have more than a practical stake in the continuation of the traditional pattern of political behavior. Many of them also have a deep ideological commitment to the value system on which this behavior is based. There are some conservatives who view the erosion of traditional values with great alarm; they consider it the result of alien

* The existence of this gap explains the fascination that backward areas hold for Japanese social scientists. Edward Norbeck wrote in his *Takashima, A Japanese Fishing Community* (Salt Lake City, 1954): "To many Japanese urbanites the customs described in these pages are to a good measure strange and unknown, because they disappeared from urban areas many years ago" (p. 185).

† Regarding the concepts of the "one-and-a-half-party system" and of the "tyranny of the majority," see Scalapino and Masumi, *Parties and Politics*, pp. 53, 147. The latter concept was much discussed by Japanese intellectuals at the time of the crisis regarding the Japanese–U.S. Security Treaty in May and June 1960.

influences; they see any deviation from the traditional social and political behavior pattern as a sign of radicalism and lack of patriotism, and hope to stem the tide by governmental action. They are in the forefront of what for some years has been called the "reverse course." There is thus no full consensus in Japan about what the political process ought to be, although most participants now pay lip service to parliamentary democracy. This lack of consensus is the root cause of a deep-seated malaise that profoundly affects the operation of the political institutions of the nation. The incidents of political violence in post-Occupation Japan are symptoms of it.

On the other hand, encouraging signs are not lacking. Recent events have shown to some conservative politicians that they cannot hope to base their future indefinitely on the lack of political consciousness in the rural areas, which hitherto assured them of solid support in election after election. They see the solution to their emerging problem in building up local party organizations to fill the vacuum created by the weakening of the traditional behavior pattern, and in stressing policies with wide popular appeal to various population groups.* With the progress of these efforts, the importance of issues will increase and the politically stultifying impact of traditional ideas will in time diminish.† The expression of differing views will be accepted as a matter of fact, rather than being viewed as an intolerable disruption of the moral order. A new consensus regarding the political process will make it possible to apply new techniques for the adjustment of conflicting interests. Until then the political socialization provided by local government will continue to retard the establishment of a new consensus as well as the develop-

---

* On the Liberal Democratic efforts in this direction, see Scalapino and Masumi, *Parties and Politics*, pp. 82ff. It is likely that the successes of the Sōka Gakkai in the House of Councilors elections of 1962 and in the local elections of 1963 will give further impetus to these efforts. In 1963 the Kōsei Remmei, the political arm of the Sōka Gakkai, won 56 prefectural assembly seats, 38 seats in the assemblies of the big cities, and 721 seats in assemblies of other cities and of the Tokyo wards. Although not all the voters for the Kōsei Remmei came from the conservative camp, it is apparent that many voters faced with the dilemma of voting for candidates recommended by this proselytizing, politico-religious organization or for candidates to whom their votes went in the past on the basis of personal relations were choosing the former alternative.

† The villagers may well continue to vote for conservative candidates, but the basis on which they cast their ballots will have changed. Their vote will denote a political preference based on a scrutiny of the appeals of competing candidates and groups.

ment of democratic attitudes. Only when the local political process itself has become democratic will local government become the training ground for democracy envisioned by de Tocqueville, John Stuart Mill, and Lord Bryce. The democratization of local politics is an important challenge confronting present-day Japan.

Under present circumstances it must be expected that such a change in the local political process will lead to a greater influence of party politics on it. In fact, this tendency is already apparent.* This is a development that Yamagata dreaded from the beginning because he wanted to keep local government the preserve of the bureaucracy, which was then an independent participant in the political arena. Today, many decry the inroads of party politics into local government because they feel that parties inject a divisive influence into local government. In this form the argument may be applied also to groupings in local assemblies that advocate differing local policies. Yet local groups of this type—"Rathausparteien" in the German terminology—would be very much in line with the spirit of local autonomy. The argument thus tends to support not only the existing low political consciousness, but also the existing low civic consciousness.

Others, in Japan and elsewhere, find only that the affairs of a local entity should not or cannot be decided on the basis of the principles or interests of national parties because there is no Republican or Democratic, no Conservative or Progressive way of providing the services that are the concern of local governments. Local assemblies, they say, should not consist of party politicians, but of civic-minded inhabitants who employ their qualifications, including their detailed knowledge of local conditions, to arrive at policies that are beneficial to the community. In other words, local policies should be determined only by local considerations. Yet in present-day Japan the flimsiness of corporate autonomy—the absence of clear independent functions and the lack of independent financial resources—leaves little room for significant local policy making. The main effort of local governments is directed toward

---

* It is most noticeable on the prefectural and city levels, but it is not confined to them. A comparison of the 1963 election with the 1959 election shows a decrease of 10 per cent in the number of independent governors, of 3 per cent in independent prefectural assembly members, of 3.1 per cent in assembly members of big cities, of 8.1 per cent in assembly members of other cities and of wards, and of 1.5 per cent in city mayors. The number of independent town and village mayors decreased by 1.2 per cent, that of independent town and village assemblymen by 1.4 per cent.

the next higher level and, in the final analysis, toward the national level; the main problem is how to obtain grants and subsidies from them. The conservative campaign argument for a "direct connection with the center," which promises rewards for those entities that align themselves politically with the party in power, is symptomatic. It strengthens the orientation toward national politics, although conservatives often voice their disapproval of this orientation. Socialists also find that they are hamstrung in all their endeavors unless they obtain control of the central government. Thus, once the local voter ceases to vote in accordance with traditional political behavior patterns, he is likely to vote for or against the party in power at the national level. To reverse this trend it would be necessary to make the local political process more autonomous by giving a greater latitude to independent local decision-making. Civic autonomy presupposes a greater degree of corporate autonomy than that granted to local entities in Japan today.

We may now return to some of the larger questions raised in the Introduction. Throughout this study we have noted that reality falls short of the constitutional ideal of local autonomy for two interrelated reasons. On the one hand, the institutional reforms of the Occupation remained a halfway house, especially in the area of functions and finances; on the other hand, attitudes inherited from the past—such as the persistence of hierarchical notions in the minds of national bureaucrats and local officeholders and the slight regard for the legal process as a means of solving problems of intergovernmental relations—prevented the local entities from assuming the role that the reforms supposedly assigned to them. Local autonomy did not fail in Japan; it was never fully established. To have made it a reality at least three things were required: first, a completion of its institutional framework; second, sufficient time for the new system to take firm roots in the consciousness of local citizens and officeholders; and last but not least, enough self-restraint in the use of tutelary powers by the national bureaucracy to indicate that a change in local attitudes was possible and, indeed, desired under the new dispensation. In 1952, as the Occupation drew to its close, a group of leading Japanese jurists, re-examining the laws of the Occupation period, took note of certain faults in the operation of local governments and of the then incipient tendency of revisionism. They stated:

Attempts at the revival of a centralized administration are no more justifiable than the accusation against the inefficiency of local administration. The local autonomy provided for in the Constitution and outlined in the Shoup recommendations deserves to be given a better chance for development. . . . It is imperative to prepare and improve the foundation before condemning the legislation for its alleged inapplicability.[47]

The conservatives in power and the national bureaucracy showed no inclination to heed this counsel. They had exhibited a negative attitude toward the reforms from the beginning.* With the end of the Occupation it became clear that the local government reforms were to be among the first objects of the conservative revisionism that was later dubbed the "reverse course."[48] The unfinished institutional structure left by the Occupation was defended by the Socialists—who by then had acquired the reputation of being "anti-American"—although often without success. Secure in their majority in the Diet, conservative governments revised the Local Autonomy Law, the Local Tax Law, the Local Finance Equalization Grant Law, and many other laws affecting local government. In some cases these revisions aroused apprehensions about the future direction of the national society. The recentralization of the police and of education demonstrated to many who had been somewhat lukewarm to local autonomy in the beginning that decentralization could play a role in preventing a recurrence of the experiences of Japan's totalitarian past. The opposition to these measures thus was not confined to the Left. In spite of this opposition, and in spite of incidents of violence of the type mentioned earlier, the bills were passed by the permanent majority in the Diet. In other cases, the government refrained from putting certain measures before the Diet because it realized, from the public debate that the announcement of its plans engendered, that pushing them through would have repercussions that it preferred to avoid. The plans to return to a system of nationally appointed governors or to substitute centrally controlled regions for the present prefectures belong to this category. Thus limits were set to the reverse course, and the local government system was not completely recentralized. But neither can today's system be characterized as a system of local autonomy.

---

* See the references to their "last-ditch stands" in regard to some of these reforms in Chapters 5 and 6. At that time, the Socialists, although generally in favor of the Occupation reforms, apparently did not assign a high priority in the over-all scheme to the decentralization of local government.

At the time of the establishment of the Meiji local government system, Japan was, in the terms of present-day social science, a "developing country." It was not unnatural that the new national leadership, faced with the task of rapid modernization, was disinclined to grant a substantial measure of corporate and civic autonomy to local units. The limited personnel of sufficient ability and knowledge to assist in the advancement of the new national goals was employed at the national level. Deprived of such talent, the local units could not be relied upon to maintain the proper standards of administrative efficiency. Thus only limited functions could be entrusted to them. At the same time governmental integration proceeded apace and it became necessary to enlist the cooperation of the people at large. This cooperation could be secured by fostering their political consciousness or by mobilizing existing habits of obedience to authority for the achievement of national goals. Recognizing these habits as a valuable asset, and unencumbered by any commitment to democracy, the national leadership preferred the second alternative. To stem the development of political consciousness it used dynastic and nationalistic appeals, stressed traditional values, suppressed deviation and, after some experimentation, confirmed the leadership of the traditional local elite. When the creation of elected local assemblies became necessary, the national leaders feared that these assemblies would become politicized and would retard the local implementation of national policy. They met this danger by limiting the decision-making scope of the assemblies, by isolating the local executives from the assemblies and from the electorate, and by subjecting the executives—and local decision-making in general—to central controls. The prefecture, with its appointed governor, served as the pivot of centralization.[49]

This system was maintained despite the momentous economic and social developments of the succeeding decades. The conservative estimate of the capabilities of local units was not revised in spite of the growth of urban centers. In the period following the First World War, certain tensions became apparent. Demands for an increase in local autonomy were voiced and minor adjustments in the local government system were made. But in spite of the extension of universal suffrage to local elections and in spite of signs of a rising political consciousness, conservative politicians continued to favor traditional patterns of political behavior, which assured them of easy election victories but obstructed the development of civic consciousness as much as the development of political consciousness. Later, militarism, national mobilization, and war interrupted all tendencies toward corporate or civic autonomy.

The Occupation picked up the interrupted trend. The results of its efforts on the institutional level have been mentioned previously. On the political level, the local purge and the land reform opened access to local leadership to new groups. The purge was, of course, a temporary phenomenon. But the land reform had lasting results. It removed the one political issue—the issue of landlord-tenant relations—which in the past had disrupted the solidarity of the *buraku*.[50] Faced by the dilemma of voting for the designated representative of his *buraku* or for a Socialist who represented his interest as a tenant farmer, the tenant was sometimes tempted to take the latter choice. The land reform removed the dilemma. In this sense, the solidarity of the *buraku*—which had weathered the interdiction of the Occupation—was restored and with it the traditional pattern of local citizen participation in the villages was strengthened. Yet, in other respects social change has been weakening the *buraku* for decades. The recent emphasis on the industrial development of backward areas, and the growing mechanization and the shift to capital-intensive production in agriculture is likely to accelerate this trend. The question should be whether to try to speed up the period of transition or to retard it. Short-range political considerations may becloud this issue for conservatives.* But if our diagnosis of the malaise

---

* Socialists have at times indicated an awareness of it, but have given a relatively low priority to it because of their preoccupation with national politics. The 1954 platform of the Right Wing Socialist Party contained the sentence "the democratization of local government is a sine qua non for the realization of a peaceful revolution." The platform of the Left Wing Socialist Party linked the expansion of freedom and democracy to the maintenance of the system of public elections of local chief executives—then endangered by conservative plans to return to a system of appointive governors—and to thorough democratization of the administrative organization of local public bodies. Later the unified Socialist Party also had a platform plank calling for the thorough democratization of local administration and the protection of local autonomy and finance. See *Comparative Platforms of Japan's Major Parties*, translated and arranged by Cecil H. Uyehara, Michio and Shimako Royama, and Shijuro Ogata (Fletcher School of Law and Diplomacy, 1955, mimeographed), pp. 36ff. In 1958 the Sōhyō campaign policy suggested the establishment of resident organizations in cities, towns, villages, and *buraku* with the purpose of establishing contact with farmers, fishermen, and small businessmen to discuss freely measures of fighting local bosses, bringing democracy to local areas, and assuring the free selection of candidates. This trend achieved a new impetus after the 1960

in the Japanese body politic is correct, it is vital to Japan's political health that the politically backward part of the nation join in the political modernization, and that a new basic political consensus be established.

The erosion of the solidarity of traditional communities, such as the *buraku,* raises the even more fundamental question of what is to replace it. If this question receives no answer, Japan is likely to turn into a completely atomized mass society, and history has shown that such a society is a more fertile ground for totalitarianism than for democracy. One possible answer lies in the development of a variety of voluntary organizations to meet the various needs of the individual, including his need to relate to others in a context proximate to his other needs. The local entity could be the locus of many of these organizations, none of which would encompass all phases of the life of the members, as traditional groups did, but each of which would fill some of their needs and, for this reason, would engage their voluntary participation. Since some of the needs must be filled by governmental action, local government could play a similar role. However, to play this role—to engage the interest, identification, and voluntary participation of the citizens—local government needs a certain freedom to promote civic activities that will satisfy the desires of its citizens. In other words, local entities must not be simply agencies of the state, but must stand between the individual and the state.* And so we return to the problem of corporate autonomy. Can Japan today grant greater corporate autonomy, at least to some local units, without retarding needed economic development?

As we have said, the restricted scope of corporate autonomy in Japan is traceable to the requirements of rapid modernization in Meiji times. At that time the grant of a scope of autonomy beyond the capabilities of the existing local units may have retarded the process. In order to advance it, local units were subordinated to central controls. But just as too much autonomy granted too soon may retard development, so too

incidents. In January 1961 the Socialist organ, *Gekkan shakaitō* (No. 43, January 1961, p. 42), contained an article by the chief of the agricultural section of the party which advocated organizing party workers in local entities and *buraku,* and building up a system that would start with the *buraku* and extend all the way up to the nation. The purpose was to increase the political consciousness of the local population.

* It is in this context that the argument against the intrusion of national parties into local government has perhaps the greatest cogency. This intrusion prevents local government from playing the role envisioned above.

little autonomy granted too late may do the same, because the national leadership fails to make use of an existing local potential. There may well be a time when it becomes of advantage to replace local subordination with local cooperation. The questions to be asked are whether the existing central controls are justified in regard to all, some, or none of the local units, or whether their continuation has become dysfunctional even to the goals of further development. These questions need to be asked again and again, for yesterday's answers need not be correct today and are likely to be wrong tomorrow.

Notes

Notes

1. Oda Yorodzu, *Principes de Droit Administratif du Japon* (Paris, 1928), p. 187.

2. Walter Wallace McLaren, *A Political History of Japan during the Meiji Era, 1867–1913* (New York, 1916), p. 58. Similarly, Etsujiro Uyehara wrote in *The Political Development of Japan, 1867–1909* (London, 1910), p. 29: "Under the feudal regime local autonomy existed to a considerable extent, so that the Shogun's government, paradoxical as it may seem, was de facto decentralized rather than centralized." Sir George Sansom in his *Japan, A Short Cultural History* (London, 1946), p. 460, concurs: "Within their own fiefs the barons enjoyed a very full measure of autonomy." See also Norman Jacobs, *The Origin of Modern Capitalism and Eastern Asia* (Hong Kong, 1958), p. 87, for the statement that in Japan local responsibility and autonomy were guiding assumptions from the earliest days of feudalism and that under the Tokugawa there was a constant localization of political authority.

3. The quotations are, in order, from K. Asakawa, "Some Aspects of Japanese Feudal Institutions," *Transactions of the Asiatic Society of Japan* (hereafter cited as *TASJ*), XLVI (1918), 101; Frank Brinkley, *A History of the Japanese People from the Earliest Times to the End of the Meiji Era* (New York, 1914), p. 637; D. B. Simmons and John H. Wigmore, "Notes on Land Tenure and Local Institutions in Old Japan," *TASJ*, XIX (1891), 49. More recently, Thomas C. Smith, in *The Agrarian Origins of Modern Japan* (Stanford, 1959), p. 203, has stated that the Tokugawa gave the villages "an extraordinary degree of autonomy" after removing the warriors from them, but that the self-sufficiency of the villagers had roots that stretched far back into the past.

4. Lafcadio Hearn, *Japan, An Attempt at Interpretation* (New York, 1905), p. 278.

5. Brinkley, *A History of the Japanese People*, p. 576; J. C. Hall, "Japanese Feudal Laws," *TASJ*, XXXVIII, Part IV (1911), p. 292. (Hall's work appeared in various issues of the *Transactions*. Unless specifically indicated, all references here are to the portion in volume XXXVIII.)

6. James Murdoch, *A History of Japan* (London, 1926), Vol. III, p. 19.

7. See, e.g., Sansom, *A Short Cultural History*, p. 449.

8. It is of course true that the *tozama* were considered by the Tokugawa as vanquished foes or as neutrals of somewhat suspect loyalty. But even their relationship to the Tokugawa was considered that of vassals to their lord. On the distinction between early and later European feudalism see, e.g., Joseph R. Strayer, "Feudalism in Western Europe," in Rushton Coulborn, ed., *Feudalism in History* (Princeton, 1956), pp. 18ff.

9. John H. Wigmore, "Materials for the Study of Private Law in Old Japan," *TASJ*, XX suppl. (1892), pp. 84ff.

10. In this chapter Tokugawa domains and other fiefs are not differentiated. For a more detailed description of local administration in both shogunal domains and other fiefs, see K. Asakawa, "Notes on the Village Government in Japan after 1600," Part II, *Journal of the American Oriental Society*, XXXI (1901), pp. 155ff and especially p. 160.

11. *Ibid.*, p. 155.

12. See, e.g., Simmons and Wigmore, "Notes on Land Tenure," p. 55, and Asakawa, "Notes on Village Government," Part II, p. 157.

13. Regarding the position of the *goshi*, who ranked above the ordinary peasants and who in certain areas constituted the village aristocracy and held the village offices, see E. Herbert Norman, *Soldier and Peasant in Japan: The Origins of Conscription* (New York, 1943), pp. 58ff. But see also Thomas C. Smith, "The Village in the 17th Century," *Journal of Economic History*, XII (1952), 1, for the fact that there was a village "aristocracy" of peasant rank, which was distinguished by large landholdings, a degree of social exclusiveness, and a monopoly of local administrative and political power. The distinction between the *goshi* and this group was that the former, according to Smith, retained warrior rank, although they remained on the land, while the latter were former warriors who were incorporated into the peasant class.

14. Smith, *Agrarian Origins*, p. 59; Andō Shōeki, an eighteenth century critic of feudalism, complained about the latter attitude: "Today these headmen, provided as they are with rice and money by their fellow villagers and others in the vicinity, lord it over them like officials or elders, lecture them and rebuke them with abusive language and punish the guilty if any such should be found." E. Herbert Norman, *Andō Shōeki and the Anatomy of Japanese Feudalism*, *TASJ*, 3rd ser., II (1950), 105.

15. See, e.g., Murdoch, *A History of Japan*, Vol. III, pp. 44 and 802; Simmons and Wigmore, "Notes on Land Tenure," pp. 141ff; Brinkley, *A History of the Japanese People*, p. 642.

16. The terms "diffuseness" and "specificity" are used here in the sense of Talcott Parsons' pattern variable scheme, as developed in *The Social System* (Glencoe, Ill., 1951), pp. 46ff.

17. In coining this word, Tsuda combined the Chinese characters for power or authority (*ken*) and reason (*ri*). Later the character for *ri* was replaced by one signifying "interest," and it is this combination of characters

that is used today. On this topic, see Nobushige Hozumi, *Lectures on the New Japanese Civil Code as Material for the Study of Comparative Jurisprudence* (Tokyo, 1912), Chapter IX, "The Introduction of the Notion of Right."

18. Regarding the relative importance of towns in the social development of East and West in general, see Maurice Zinkin, *Asia and the West* (London, 1951), pp. 9ff; also G. B. Sansom, *The Western World and Japan* (New York, 1950), p. 7; and for a comparison between the more self-assured *chōnin* culture of the pre-Tokugawa era with its more docile counterpart in the *genroku* period, see Norman, *Andō Shōeki*, pp. 82ff.

19. See Norman, *Andō Shōeki*, p. 4; Sansom, *A Short Cultural History*, pp. 359ff; Ishikawa Yeiyo, "Cities in Japan," *Contemporary Japan*, XVII, Nos. 1–3 (1948), 22; Yosaburo Takekoshi, *The Economic Aspects of the History of the Civilization of Japan* (New Haven, 1930), Vol. I, p. 362.

20. Norman, *Andō Shōeki*, pp. 3, 423 and the same author, *Soldier and Peasant in Japan*, pp. 6f; also Takekoshi, *Economic Aspects*, Vol. I, pp. 275ff.

CHAPTER 2

1. Etsujiro Uyehara, *The Political Development of Japan, 1867–1909* (London, 1910), p. 41.

2. Itani Zenichi, "The Economic Causes of the Meiji Restoration," *TASJ*, 2nd ser., XVII (1938), 204.

3. Hearn, *Japan*, p. 327.

4. The story of these forerunners of the Meiji Restoration is skillfully told by G. B. Sansom in *The Western World and Japan*, especially pp. 258, 261, 267, and 271.

5. Walter W. McLaren (ed.), "Japanese Government Documents," *TASJ*, XLII (1914), 1 (hereafter cited as McLaren, *JGD*).

6. Nobutaka Ike, *The Beginnings of Political Democracy in Japan* (Baltimore, 1950), p. 33.

7. The description of the events leading up to the abolition of the fiefs is based mainly on McLaren, *JGD*, pp. 7–33; George M. Beckman, *The Making of the Meiji Constitution* (Lawrence, Kansas, 1957), pp. 8–17; and on the excellent study *Jichi gojūnenshi* (Fifty Years of Self-government), published by the Tokyo Shisei Chōsakai (Tokyo Institute of Municipal Research) in 1941, pp. 16ff (hereafter cited as TIMR, *Fifty Years*).

8. This is shown, for instance, in the defense of the Conscription Act of 1872 by Tani Tateaki. See Norman, *Soldier and Peasant*, p. 42.

9. The number of *fu* had been decreased from nine to three in August 1869. McLaren, *JGD*, p. 28.

10. TIMR, *Fifty Years*, p. 21; McLaren, *JGD*, LXXXVII; Ukai *et al.*, *Nihon kindaihō hattatsushi* (Tokyo, 1958), Vol. V, pp. 26ff.

11. Cf. Kikegawa Hiroshi, "Meiji chihō seido seiritsu katei," *Toshi mondai*, XLIV, No. 8 (August 1953), p. 101. Mr. Kikegawa, formerly a research associate of the Tokyo Institute of Municipal Research, is also the author of

Fifty Years. The above-mentioned series of articles which appeared in *Toshi mondai* between August 1953 and February 1955 was published in book form in 1955 under the title *Meiji chihō jichiseido no seiritsu katei.*

12. This is a somewhat oversimplified description of the district arrangement, for actually there were some differences in the various *ken.* Some *ken* established a system of large districts (*daiku*) and small districts (*shoku*). In 1872 this system was officially adopted by a decree of the Finance Ministry. Large *ku* were placed under a *kuchō*, small ones under a *kochō.* See Kikegawa, "Meiji chihō seido," pp. 17ff. Between 1872 and 1879 separate school districts (*gakku*) existed for purposes of educational administration. On these and their relation to the local government districts as well as to the traditional village communities, see Chiba Masaji, *Gakku seido no kenkyū-Kokka kenryoku to sonryoku kyōdōtai* (Tokyo, 1962).

13. The basic decrees of the Council of State were *Fukoku* 170 of 1871 and *Fukoku* 117 of 1872. For an analysis of the entire development, see TIMR, *Fifty Years,* pp. 2, 30, 31, 33; Kikegawa, "Meiji chihō seido," pp. 15–22; Kaino Michitaka, *Iriai no kenkyū* (2nd ed., Tokyo, 1949), pp. 306ff. The large and small districts had no names, but were simply numbered. See Ukai *et al., Nihon Kindaihō,* p. 27.

14. Royama Masamichi, *Nōson jichi no hembō* (Tokyo, 1948), p. 1.

15. Beckman, *The Making of the Meiji Constitution,* pp. 33f and Appendix II (Okubo's opinion on constitutional government, 1873).

16. See, e.g., McLaren, *Political History,* pp. 117, 126, 128, and 132; for the early organization of the Home Ministry, see McLaren, *JGD,* pp. 36–41.

17. McLaren, *JGD,* pp. 426–32.

18. TIMR, *Fifty Years,* p. 39.

19. McLaren, *Political History,* p. 112.

20. Beckman, *The Making of the Meiji Constitution,* pp. 35–38; McLaren, *JGD,* pp. lxxvi to lxxx, 505–29; Kikegawa, "Meiji chihō seido," pp. 35f.

21. In 1881, Okuma provoked a government crisis by his advocacy of the immediate convocation of a national assembly.

22. Beckman, *The Making of the Meiji Constitution,* pp. 28–33 and Appendix I.

23. McLaren, *Political History,* p. 132. The analysis of the reasons for the grant of local assemblies is based, in addition to McLaren's work, on TIMR, *Fifty Years,* pp. 6ff, and on Nagahama Masatoshi, *Chihō jichi* (Tokyo, 1952), p. 22. The entry in Kido's diary is quoted in *Fifty Years,* p. 18.

24. The terms "law," "rules," and later "system," were used interchangeably. There was no difference either in genesis or in effect.

25. See his report to the President of the Council of State, Sanjo Sanetomi, quoted in TIMR, *Fifty Years,* p. 45. It should be noted that in spite of Okubo's realization the practice of appointing one *kochō* for a number of villages was renewed in 1884, and that compulsory amalgamations of villages occurred throughout the period of the Three New Laws.

26. A convenient outline of the laws comprising this system may be found

in TIMR, *Fifty Years*, pp. 52ff; a summary in English may be found in Taka-hashi Teizo, "The Local Government System of Japan," *Doshisha Law Review* (International edition), No. 2, 1957, pp. 3–7.

27. The Fukushima incident is described in some detail in Chitoshi Yanaga, *Japan Since Perry* (New York, 1949), p. 157. Mishima's zeal against the political parties was rewarded in 1885, when Yamagata was Home Minister, by his appointment as superintendent-general of the Tokyo Metropolitan Police Board.

28. TIMR, *Fifty Years*, p. 384.

29. See, e.g., Yamagata Aritomo, *Chōheiseido oyobi jichiseido kakuritsu no enkaku*, in Kokka Gakkai, *Meiji kensei keizaishiron* (Tokyo, 1919), p. 401. This discourse by Yamagata (hereafter cited as Yamagata, *Conscription and Self-Government*) forms the basis of many observations in this section.

30. For material on this subject, see Ito Hirobumi, *Kempō shiryo* (Tokyo, 1935), especially Vols. 2 and 3; Suzuki Yasuzo, *Nihon kempōshi gaisetsu* (Tokyo, 1941) and *Jiyū Minken Undō* (Tokyo, 1948); and, in English, Uyehara, *Political Development*, and McLaren, *JGD*.

31. Yanaga, *Japan Since Perry*, p. 118.

32. Yamagata, *Conscription and Self-Government*, p. 401.

33. Quoted in Suzuki Yasuzo, *Nihon kempōshi gaisetsu*, p. 341.

34. See the explanation, attached to the City, Town, and Village Code, reprinted in TIMR, *Fifty Years*, pp. 252ff at p. 257.

35. Yamagata was thus following the lines of thought of Aoki and Kido to which we referred earlier. Aoki, who had been a student in Prussia, advocated to Kido the establishment of a well-organized local administration before the promulgation of a constitution. During Ito's sojourn in Germany, Aoki was minister to that country and acted as interpreter for Ito when the latter attended Gneist's lectures. See Beckman, *The Making of the Meiji Constitution*, pp. 32, 71, and 72. It appears that Ito originally had shared Aoki's ideas.

36. These reasons are perhaps most clearly indicated in Yamagata, *Conscription and Self-Government*. They can also be inferred from his instructions to local government officials (see, e.g., McLaren, *JGD*, p. 419) and from his speeches before the Assembly of Local Governors (see, e.g., Wm. Theodore de Bary, ed., *Sources of the Japanese Tradition* [New York, 1958], p. 708).

37. Yamagata, *Conscription and Self-Government*, p. 397.

38. Quoted in Wm. Theodore de Bary, *Sources of the Japanese Tradition*, p. 708, from Tokutomi Ichiro, *Koshaku Yamagata Aritomo den*, II, 1097–1103.

39. See Ito's opinion on the establishment of local government in *Hisho ruisan: Hōsei kankei shiryo* (Tokyo, 1934), Vol. II, pp. 375ff.

40. Herman Roesler, Ito's adviser on the Constitution, as well as Albert Mosse, presented opinions on this draft.

41. The chronological account of these developments is based mainly on Yamagata, *Conscription and Self-Government*, pp. 397ff, and TIMR, *Fifty Years*, pp. 76ff. The development of the Prefectural and County Codes is de-

scribed on pp. 295ff. See also Kikegawa, "Meiji chihō seido," pp. 133ff, and George O. Totten, *Japanese Municipal Government under Meiji and Taisho, 1868–1925* (unpublished Master's thesis, Columbia University, 1949). The term "Sei," used only in the titles of these laws, means literally "system" or "order." It is here translated as "Code" meaning an act of the legislature that covers a broad area but that does not have a higher standing than any more specific legislation.

CHAPTER 3

1. In 1919 Dr. S. H. Wainwright could still write of "Japan's Transition from the Rule of Persons to the Rule of Law," *TASJ*, Vol. XLVII (1919), pp. 155ff. The transition, which is an aspect of a change of emphasis in interpersonal relations from particularism to universalism and from diffuseness to specificity, is still not completed.

2. For a discussion of these types of control, see Chapter 13.

3. TIMR, *Fifty Years*, p. 559. This work deals with the various amendments in substantial detail on pp. 399ff, 454ff, 516ff, and 559ff. A perceptive analysis is to be found in Nagahama, *Chihō jichi*, p. 18ff; and there is a brief synopsis in English in Sato Tatsuo, "Development of Local Self-Government in Japan," in *Waseda Journal of Political Science and Economics*, No. 116 (1952), pp. 14ff.

4. On the role of the prefecture, see Chapter 8 and Takagi Shosaku's comment on my paper: "The Japanese Prefecture: a Pivot of Centralization," presented to the annual meeting of the American Political Science Association in September 1956, in *Toshi mondai*, Vol. XLVIII, No. 4 (April 1957), pp. 107–17.

5. Harold S. Quigley, *Japanese Government and Politics, An Introductory Survey* (New York, 1932), p. 296.

6. See the Law Concerning Government Organization and the Regulations Concerning the Authority of Local Government Officials (*Chihōkan kansei*).

7. A brief résumé of this "Big City Movement" will be given in Chapter 9. See also Quigley, *Japanese Government and Politics*, p. 305; Goto Ichiro, "The Problem of 'Special Cities' in Japan," *Waseda Journal of Political Science and Economics*, No. 116 (Tokyo, 1952), pp. 28ff.

8. The number is arrived at from the tables in Tokyo Shisei Chōsa Kai, *Nippon Toshi Nenkan*, Vol. 16 (1952), Statistical Part, pp. 6ff. (This reference work will hereafter be cited as *Municipal Yearbook*.)

9. TIMR, *Fifty Years*, pp. 265ff. For an analysis of the effects of these measures, see Kaino, *Iriai*, pp. 308ff.

10. Regarding these developments, see TIMR, *Fifty Years*, pp. 431ff and 500ff. The abolition of the *gun* was effected by Law No. 63 of 1921 and by Imperial Ordinance No. 147 of 1926. On the local affairs offices of the prefectures, see Chapter 13.

11. Article 2 of each of the Codes. The numbering of the articles has not changed substantially since the revision of the Prefectural Code in 1899 and of the City Code and Town and Village Code in 1911. In the following footnotes the reference to articles is based on the Codes as revised.

12. Charles A. Beard, *The Administration and Politics of Tokyo* (New York, 1923), p. 45.

13. A classic work on the question of "proper and assigned functions" is Miyazawa Toshiyoshi, *Koyūjimu to ininjimu no ron* (Tokyo, 1943). A good discussion of the problem may be found in Hara Ryonosuke, "Chihō kōkyō dantai no jimu no han-i ni tsuite," *Toshi mondai kenkyū*, No. 2 (May 1949), p. 3.

14. See Watanabe Sotaro, *Jichi seidoron* (Tokyo, 1931), pp. 359ff.

15. Prefectural Code, Article 127; City Code, Article 157; Town and Village Code, Article 146. (In the following, the references to articles in the various Codes are given in the same order unless noted differently.) An exception to the general rule, stated above, existed for the raising of local loans, including the determination and alteration of the method of raising them, the rate of interest, and the method of repayment. In this case the authorization of both the Home and Finance Ministers was necessary. See Articles 134, 166, and 146, respectively.

16. See, e.g., Watanabe, *Jichi seidoron*, pp. 406ff; Oda Yorodzu, *Principes de Droit Administratif*, pp. 210ff.

17. Articles 129, 161, and 141, respectively.

18. Article 173 of the City Code. As noted earlier, the appointment was formally made by the emperor.

19. Articles 135 to 136, 167 to 169, and 147 to 149, respectively.

20. See Quigley, *Japanese Government and Politics*, p. 302. Quigley's observation in 1932 was limited to city government, but it held true for all types of local governments.

21. In the beginning, many towns and villages sent their budgets to the higher authorities for approval, although there was no legal provision for it. See Fujita Takeo, *Nihon chihō zaisei seido no seiritsu* (Tokyo, 1941), p. 186.

22. Prefectural Code, Articles 82, 88, 129; City Code, Article 161; Town and Village Code, Article 74.

23. Quigley, *Japanese Government and Politics*, p. 296. The pertinent provisions are Prefectural Code, Articles 83 and 85; City Code, Articles 90 and 91; Town and Village Code, Articles 74 and 75. This particular device dates back to the era of the Three New Laws. See McLaren, *JGD*, p. 310.

24. City Code, Articles 163 and 164; Town and Village Code, Articles 143 and 144. See also Article 80 of the Prefectural Code.

25. Articles 131, 162, and 142, respectively.

26. City Code, Article 170; Town and Village Code, Article 150.

27. Prefectural Code, Articles 41, 78; 82 to 86; City Code, Articles 87, 90 to 92; Town and Village Code, Articles 72, 74 to 76.

28. Fujita, *Nihon chihō zaisei seido*, pp. 179ff; see also, by the same author,

"Nihon chihō zaisei no tokushitsu to kadai," in *Shisei,* Vol. 3, No. 1 (January 1954), p. 12.

29. Chapter 5 of the Prefectural and Town and Village Codes and Chapter 6 of the City Code. The Local Tax Law was Law No. 24 of 1926. Some of the developments in the field of local finance and taxation are mentioned in Chapter 12. An important change was the establishment of a new local tax system in 1940, which provided for the first time for independent taxes in addition to surtaxes.

CHAPTER 4

1. For a description of this development, see Charles B. Fahs, *Government in Japan: Recent Trends in Its Scope and Operation* (New York, 1940), especially pp. 27ff.

2. City Code, Articles 88 and 94, and Town and Village Code, Articles 72 and 78, as amended in 1943.

3. Nagahama Masatoshi, *Chiji kōsen no shomondai* (Tokyo, 1946), pp. 40ff; Tsukui Tatsuo, "Tonarigumi seido" in *Nippon hyōron,* November 1943.

4. Home Ministry Ordinance No. 17 of September 11, 1940, for the Guidance in Establishing *Buraku-kai,* etc., and Home Ministry Instruction to all Governors No. 91 of the same day. The text of these documents and a commentary on them may be found in Harima Shigeo, *Buraku-kai, chōnai-kai nado no soshiki to sono unei* (Tokyo, 1940). This booklet gives a good insight into the spirit of the establishment of these organizations.

5. For a list of such organizations and the laws and ordinances covering them, see Harima, *Buraku-kai, chōnai-kai,* pp. 12ff.

6. Hozumi Shigeto, "The *Tonarigumi* of Japan," *Contemporary Japan,* Vol. XII, No. 8 (August 1943), p. 983.

7. Harima, *Buraku-kai, chōnai-kai,* pp. 17 and 60; Tamura Hiroshi, *Goningumi seido no jissho-teki kenkyū* (Tokyo, 1936), pp. 86ff.

8. Home Ministry, *Survey of Chōnai-kai in the Six Big Cities,* April 1941.

9. Sato Kennosuke, "How the *Tonarigumi* Operates," in *Contemporary Japan,* Vol. XIII, No. 7–9 (July–September 1944), pp. 782–85.

10. Home Ministry Administrative Memorandum No. 430, November 1941.

11. The amendment of the City Code was Law No. 80 and that of the Town and Village Code was Law No. 81, both of March 1943. At the same time the Prefectural Code was amended by Law No. 79 and the Hokkaido Assembly Law was amended by Law No. 82. An analysis of these revisions is given in Nagahama, *Chiji kōsen,* pp. 54ff, and in Fujita Takeo, "Chihō seido no kakkiteki kaikaku," in *Toshi mondai kenkyū,* No. 39 (1944), p. 158.

12. Law No. 89 of 1943 (*Tokyo-tōsei*).

13. Home Ministry Instruction No. 31, June 1, 1943.

14. Quoted in Nagahama, *Chiji kōsen,* p. 51.

15. Maruyama Mikiji, "New Regional Administrative Councils," in *Contemporary Japan*, Vol. XII, No. 8 (August 1943), p. 978. Interestingly enough, the writer protests on the next page that the appointments of the presidents of the regional councils by the Prime Minister did "not encroach upon the sphere of provincial autonomy."

16. The basic ordinance establishing the Regional Administrative Councils was Imperial Ordinance No. 548 of June 30, 1943. For the place of the establishment of the councils in the program of production control, see T. A. Bisson, *Japan's War Economy* (New York, 1945), pp. 109ff.

17. Imperial Ordinance No. 350 of June 10, 1945. Tōkai and Hokuriku were combined into one region and the prefectures comprising the various regions were rearranged.

18. Statement of the Japanese government, submitted to SCAP in October 1945, mentioned in Government Section, SCAP, *The Political Reorientation of Japan* (Washington, D.C.), Vol. I, p. 132.

19. Tsuji Kiyoaki, *Nihon kanryosei no kenkyū* (Tokyo, 1953), p. 154.

CHAPTER 5

1. Edwin O. Reischauer, *The United States and Japan* (rev. ed., Cambridge, 1957), p. 229.

2. See, e.g., George A. Warp, "In Our Image and Likeness," *National Municipal Review*, XLII (1953), 175.

3. A SCAP report described the dominant faction in the Liberal Party, centering around Prime Minister Yoshida, as one that "preferred to return to former methods of Japanese administration." Home Minister Uyehara, appointed in January 1947, also belonged to this group. SCAP, *Summation of Non-Military Activities*, No. 16 (January 1947), p. 29.

4. The Policy Statement was amended and approved as the "Basic Post-Surrender Policy for Japan" by the Far Eastern Commission in June 1947. The Far Eastern Commission was established as a policy-making and reviewing authority for the Occupation by the Moscow Agreement of the Foreign Ministers on December 27, 1945. The texts of the Potsdam Declaration, the Moscow Agreement, and the Basic Post-Surrender Policy can be found in Japanese Foreign Ministry, *Documents Concerning the Allied Occupation and Control of Japan* (Tokyo, 1949), Vol. I, pp. 7, 171, 179. (This compilation will hereafter be cited as Japanese Foreign Ministry, *Documents*.) See also Edwin M. Martin, *The Allied Occupation of Japan* (New York, 1948), Appendixes A and B.

5. SCAP, General Order No. 8. The text of this order will be found in the report of Government Section, SCAP, *Political Reorientation of Japan* (Washington, n.d.), Vol. II, p. 796. This work consists of two volumes, the first describing the progress of the Occupation reforms in the political field from 1945 to 1948, the second containing a collection of pertinent documents. It will

hereafter be cited as *Government Section Report*. A sequence was planned, but never completed, or at least never published. In reading the first volume, it is well to bear in mind its origin.

6. Japanese Foreign Ministry, *Documents*, Vol. I, p. 111.

7. *Government Section Report*, Vol. II, p. 785.

8. *Ibid.*, Vol. I, pp. 117, 260f.

9. This contributed later to the failure of the efforts to reallocate functions among the various levels of government. An allusion to the problem is made in *Government Section Report*, Vol. I, p. 270.

10. SCAPIN No. 222, November 1, 1945. A SCAPIN was a memorandum from SCAP to the Japanese Government, issued under the authority vested in it by the terms of surrender. A collection of the more important SCAPINs may be found in Japanese Foreign Ministry, *Documents*. Regarding the creation and abolition of the Regional Administrative Affairs Bureaus, see also *Government Section Report*, Vol. I, p. 133.

11. City Code, Article 88, 88-2; Town and Village Code, Articles 72-3, 72-4, and 78, as amended in 1946. (Notations of the form 88-2 refer to new Articles added to the original numbered sequence. See note 13 to Chapter 9.)

12. See Takagi Shosaku, "Chōnaikai no hōseika wo meguru mondai," *Toshi mondai kenkyū*, Vol. 10, No. 6 (1959), p. 34.

13. Home Ministry Instruction of December 22, 1945, relating to the reformation and guidance of *burakukai* and *chōnaikai*.

14. This summary of events is primarily based on *Government Section Report*, Vol. I, pp. 29ff and 286ff, Vol. II, pp. 496–98; see also Takagi, "Chōnaikai no hōseika," p. 34.

15. Cited by Takagi, "Chōnaikai no hōseika," p. 35, from a report in *Asahi* of January 24, 1947.

16. Home Minister Omura's statement of January 29, 1947, may be found in *Government Section Report*, Vol. I, p. 287.

17. Cabinet Order No. 15, May 3, 1947; for the English text, see *Government Section Report*, Vol. II, pp. 701ff. The Local Autonomy Law, which went into effect on the same day, prohibits the delegation of the administrative and financial affairs of government to private and semi-governmental bodies.

18. For an exposition of different views on the matter, see Ralph D. Braibanti, "Neighborhood Associations in Japan and Their Democratic Potentialities," *Far Eastern Quarterly*, VII (1948), 139, and John Masland, "Neighborhood Associations in Japan," *Far Eastern Survey*, XV (1946), 355.

19. SCAPIN No. 93 is reprinted in *Government Section Report*, Vol. II, pp. 436ff. As a result of this directive the incumbent Home Minister was removed and the Cabinet of Prince Higashikuni resigned. SCAP, *Summation of Non-Military Activities*, No. 1, September–October 1945, p. 3.

20. *Government Section Report*, Vol. I, pp. 135f.

21. *Ibid.*, Vol. II, p. 708.

22. *Ibid.*, Vol. I, p. 136.

23. *Official Gazette Extra*, No. 68, First Session of the National Diet, House of Representatives, November 29, 1947, p. 2.

24. Laws No. 238 and 239 of 1947.

25. *Government Section Report*, Vol. I, p. 138. Of 48 persons who held the position of vice-governor between 1947 and 1950, 25 had a "pure" Home Ministry background. See Oka Yoshisato and Tsuji Kiyoaki, "Sengo taisei no seisaku to kikō," in *Sengo Nippon no seiji katei* (Tokyo, 1953), p. 44. This interesting volume constitutes the 1953 Annals of the Japan Political Science Association. It will hereafter be referred to as JPSA, *Annals 1953*.

26. *Official Gazette Extra*, No. 12, 90th Session of the Imperial Diet, House of Representatives, July 5, 1946, pp. 11, 13, 15.

27. Nagahama, *Chiji kōsen*, p. 1.

28. Explanation of Home Minister Omura, *Official Gazette Extra*, No. 12, 90th Session of the Imperial Diet, House of Representatives, July 6, 1946, p. 3.

29. See interpellations by Iwamoto Nobuyuki, Matsunaga Bukkotsu, Nakamura Kiochi, Ohara Hiroo, and Isoda Masanori in *Official Gazette Extra*, No. 12–14. Mr. Yao's interpellation is in No. 13, p. 12.

30. See, e.g., *ibid.*, No. 12, pp. 1ff; No. 13, pp. 4, 12.

31. *Ibid.*, No. 14, pp. 16f.

32. Laws No. 26 to 29 of that date.

33. *Government Section Report*, Vol. II, p. 758.

34. For the Occupation's version, see *Government Section Report*, Vol. I, pp. 88–112. After the end of the Occupation, a number of articles on the subject appeared in Japanese periodicals. Reference to a number of these "now-it-can-be-told stories" is made in *Nippon Times*, May 16, 1953, p. 4. Sato Tatsuo, former Chief of the Cabinet Legislation Bureau, who was engaged in drafting of the constitution on the Japanese side, wrote a series of articles entitled, "Nihonkoku kempō seiritsushi," in the magazine *Jurist* beginning in May 1955 (No. 81). These articles were later published in revised form as a book under the same title. Volume I of this authoritative work appeared in November 1962. Robert E. Ward discussed the "Origins of the Present Japanese Constitution" in *American Political Science Review*, L (December 1956), p. 980. The genesis of the constitution was studied extensively by the Japanese government's Constitution Research Committee, which submitted its report on this phase of its work in the spring of 1961. The various drafts of the constitution are contained in *Government Section Report*, Vol. II, pp. 605ff. A notable omission is the original Government Section draft. This draft may be found in Sato Tatsuo, "The Origin and Development of the Draft Constitution of Japan," *Contemporary Japan*, Vol. XXIV, Nos. 4–9 (1957), and in *Kokka gakkai zasshi*, Vol. 68, Nos. 1 and 2 (September 1954), pp. 1–37.

35. *Government Section Report*, Vol. I, p. 105.

36. "Kempō dai hassho kakusho" in a collection, published by the Autonomy Board, entitled *Chiho jichi rombunshū* (Tokyo, 1955), p. 40.

37. *Ibid.*, p. 53. Mr. Sato adds that he does not know whether SCAP had actually come around to the Japanese point of view on charters.

38. SCAP, *Summation,* No. 17 (February 1947), p. 24.

39. Sato, *Kempō dai hassho,* pp. 44, 53.

40. *Government Section Report,* Vol. II, p. 661; also Martin, *The Allied Occupation of Japan,* p. 64. The Far Eastern Commission statement regarding requirements of the new constitution was issued at a time when the constitution bill was already before the Diet. Apparently it was based on an earlier directive by the State-War-Navy Coordinating Committee in Washington. Colonel Kades of Government Section referred to the importance attached by the Far Eastern Commission to the popular election of local government executives in a conference with Japanese government officials in early March 1946. Sato, *Kempō dai hassho,* p. 44.

41. *Official Gazette Extra,* No. 5, 90th Session of the Imperial Diet, House of Representatives, June 26, 1946, p. 3.

42. For the resolution of the House of Representatives, the constitution of the Council, its terms of reference, the record of its meetings and its report, see *Kaisei chihō seido shiryō,* a continuing collection of material relating to the local government reform published for the use of government agencies by the Domestic Affairs Office and its successor agencies. The material mentioned is contained in Volume III (March 1948). The *Government Section Report* which discusses the work preparatory to the drafting of the Local Autonomy Law in Vol. I, pp. 270ff, does not mention the Council.

43. *Government Section Report,* Vol. I, p. 261.

CHAPTER 6

1. SCAP *Summation,* No. 17 (February 1947), p. 24.

2. SCAPIN, No. 93, October 4, 1945.

3. SCAP *Summation,* No. 2 (November 1945), p. 36; *ibid.,* No. 4 (January 1946), p. 36.

4. The reorganization of the Japanese police is described in *Government Section Report,* Vol. I, pp. 291–304. The Government Section memorandum is on pp. 293–96. The Japanese plan is to be found in *Government Section Report,* Vol. II, pp. 699f.

5. The correspondence between Prime Minister Katayama and General MacArthur is in *Government Section Report,* Vol. II, pp. 703–6. The Police Law (No. 196 of 1947) can be found on pp. 106ff.

6. Police Law, Articles 4, 27, and 40.

7. Police Law, Articles 2, 31, 41, 43, and 54.

8. Police Law, Articles 4, 5, 8, 10, 20, 21, 24, 26, 43, and 44.

9. Constitution of Japan, Article 9.

10. Police Law, Articles 4 and 63–65.

11. The principal SCAP directives in this regard were dated October 22 and December 31, 1945. See Foreign Ministry, *Documents,* Vol. II, pp. 205 and 219.

12. For these developments, see SCAP, Civil Information and Education Section, *Education in the New Japan* (Tokyo, 1948) (hereafter cited as CIE *Report*), especially Vol. I, pp. 141ff, and Vol. II, p. 89, and the Educational Reform Council's report, *Educational Reform in Japan* (Tokyo, 1950). See also Daishiro Hidaka, "The Aftermath of Educational Reform," *Annals of the American Academy of Political and Social Science* (hereafter cited as *Annals*), Vol. 308 (November 1956), pp. 140ff.

13. For the development of the FEC directive, see CIE *Report*, Vol. I, p. 150; for its text, *ibid.*, Vol. II, pp. 11ff.

14. Fundamental Law of Education (Law No. 25 of 1947); reprinted in *Government Section Report*, Vol. II, p. 865. In June 1948, the Diet by resolution declared the Imperial Rescript on Education to be invalid and inconsistent with the new Constitution.

15. Law No. 27 of 1947. The law was revised in 1949 to provide for the establishment of junior colleges.

16. Law No. 170 of 1948. The Occupation aimed also at the transfer of universities, with some exceptions, to the local boards. But the Educational Reform Council opposed this idea successfully and the recommendations of the United States Education Mission were modified. See *Educational Reform in Japan*, pp. 32ff. The Board of Education Law is reprinted in *Government Section Report*, Vol. II, pp. 1207ff.

17. See Board of Education Law, especially Articles 3, 4, 9, 29, 48, 49, 56, and 63; Local Autonomy Law, Articles 112 and 149; see also the Opinion of the Attorney General, No. 33, of June 25, 1949.

18. Regarding the government's division on the question of postponement, see Asahi Shimbunsha, *Asahi nenkan*, 1953, pp. 273f; Hidaka, "The Aftermath of Educational Reform," p. 153; also, *Nippon Times*, August 29 and September 4, 1952.

19. Law of Fire Defense Organization (Law No. 226 of 1947).

20. Osaka Municipal Office, *Report on the Survey of the Administration of the City of Osaka* (Osaka, 1950), p. 1.

21. The Occupation's story of the purge is told in *Government Section Report*, Vol. I, pp. 8ff. See especially pp. 29ff for the extension in 1947. SCAPIN 550 may be found in *ibid.*, Vol. II, p. 482; the implementing ordinances and purge statistics in Vol. II, pp. 496–564.

22. SCAP, Natural Resources Section, Report No. 136, *The Japanese Village in Transition* (Tokyo, 1950), p. 201. This report will hereafter be cited as NRS, *Japanese Village*.

23. On this subject, see R. P. Dore, *Land Reform in Japan* (London, 1959); Andrew J. Grad, *Land and Peasant in Japan* (New York, 1952); Laurence I. Hewes, *Japan—Land and Men* (Ames, Iowa, 1955); John E. Eyre, "Post Occupation Conditions in Rural Japan," *Annals*, Vol. 308 November 1956), pp. 113ff; SCAP, National Resources Section, Report No. 127, *Japanese Land Reform Program*, and the above-mentioned NRS, *Japanese Village*.

24. Dore, *Land Reform*, p. 133, states that the original draft of the Minis-

try of Agriculture had permitted a maximum holding of tenanted land of three *chō*. By raising the limit to five *chō*, the Cabinet reduced the estimated amount of land to be transferred from 1,300,000 *chō* to 900,000 *chō*, and the number of landlords affected from 1,000,000 to 100,000. For other accounts, see Ministry of Agriculture and Forestry, Agricultural Land Bureau, *Agricultural Land Reform Legislation* (Tokyo, 1949), pp. 3ff; Grad, *Land and Peasant*, pp. 46ff; Hewes, *Japan—Land and Men*, pp. 53ff.

25. SCAPIN 411 is reprinted in NRS, *Japanese Village*, p. 258.

26. Laws Nos. 43 and 42, respectively.

27. The former landlords thus received less than they could have received on a free market, had such a market been permitted to exist. A lawsuit instituted on the basis that their property was taken without the "just compensation" provided by Article 29 of the Constitution was rejected by the Supreme Court in December 1953 (*Supreme Court Reports, Civil Affairs*, Vol. VII, No. 12, p. 1523). See also Dore, *Land Reform*, pp. 432ff.

28. Eyre, "Post-Occupation Conditions in Rural Japan," p. 114.

29. Thus the local elections of 1947 showed a remarkable decrease in the number of landlords elected to village assemblies and an increase in the number of owner-operators, tenant farmers, and non-farmers elected. Mayors were less frequently landlords and more often non-farmers of some status who stood on the sidelines of the landlord-tenant conflict. See NRS, *Japanese Village*, p. 193; Dore, *Land Reform*, p. 326.

30. However, traces of the former position of the landlords remained even within the land reform program. Although only three out of ten members of the Land Commissions were landlords, landlords held more chairmanships than either owner-cultivators or tenants. Grad, *Land and Peasant*, pp. 50 and 52.

31. Dore, *Land Reform*, p. 421. Dore's book is a mine of information for students of the land reform in all its ramifications.

32. For this development in general, see Robert A. Fearey, *The Occupation of Japan, Second Phase: 1948–50* (New York, 1950).

33. SCAP, *Report on Japanese Taxation by the Shoup Mission* (Tokyo, 1949). The report consists of four volumes. The following discussion is based mainly on Vol. I, pp. 8–11 and 21–31, and on Vol. III, pp. A1 through A31.

34. *Shoup Mission Report*, Vol. III, p. A1.

35. *Ibid.*, p. A18.

36. Law No. 111 of 1948; regarding the earlier system, see Shiomi Saburo, *Japanese Finance and Taxation, 1940–1956* (translated by Shotaro Hasegawa) (New York, 1957), pp. 47f.

37. Law No. 415 of 1949.

38. The Local Finance Equalization Grant Law was Law No. 211 of 1950. For the pertinent findings and recommendations of the Shoup Mission, see *Shoup Mission Report*, pp. A21ff. For details regarding the implementation of Shoup's recommendations, see Chapter 12.

39. These laws were, respectively, Law No. 226, Law No. 211, and Law No. 210, of 1950.

40. Based on a press statement of the Shoup Mission on September 21, 1950.

41. *Shoup Mission Report,* Vol. I, p. 29; upon the establishment of the Local Finance Commission the Local Autonomy Agency in the Prime Minister's Office was to lose some of its functions.

42. Local Administration Investigation Committee Establishment Law No. 181 of 1949.

43. Local Administration Investigation Committee, *Recommendations Concerning Redistribution of Administrative Affairs* (Tokyo, 1950) (hereafter referred to as *Kambe Report*), p. 5; *Shoup Mission Report,* Vol. III, p. A6.

44. *Kambe Report,* pp. 13f.

45. *Ibid.,* pp. 15–17.

CHAPTER 7

1. See, e.g., Tanaka Jiro, *Shinkempō to chihōjichi* (Tokyo, 1948), pp. 104ff. (This treatise, together with one by Kiyomiya Shiro, appeared as Volume 11 of *Shinkempō taikei,* a series of booklets outlining and explaining the new Constitution); Juridical Society, *Commentary,* pp. 1355ff; Watanabe Sōtaro, "Chihōjichi gainen no sai kōsatsu," *Toshi mondai kenkyū,* No. 1 (February 1949), p. 1. The discussions on this problem are frequently based on the theories of German legal philosophers such as Gierke and Jellinek.

2. Juridical Society, *Commentary,* p. 1372.

3. *Ibid.,* p. 1380.

4. Sugimura Shosaburo, "Kōwago ni okeru chihōjichi," *Kokka gakkai zasshi,* Vol. 65, No. 4 (1950), p. 4.

5. See, e.g., Yanase Ryokan, "Kempō dai hachishō ni tsuite," *Jichi kenkyū,* Vol. 28, No. 6 (June 1952), p. 3; "Kempō to chihōjichi," *ibid.,* Vol. 29, No. 11 (November 1953), p. 3; "Chihōjichi no honshitsu," *Kōhō kenkyū,* No. 9 (October 1953), p. 76. For opposing views see, e.g., a series of articles in the February 1953 issue of *Jurist;* Kaino Michitaka, "Chihōjichi no honshitsu ni tsuite," *Kōhō kenkyū,* No. 9, p. 84; Ukai Nobushige, "Kempō ni okeru chihōjichi no honshi," *Toshi mondai,* Vol. 44, No. 2 and No. 4 (February and April 1953).

6. Juridical Society, *Commentary,* pp. 1374ff.

7. Tsunehisa Mimachi vs. Setagaya Ward Assembly, Chief of Setagaya Ward, Governor of Tokyo and the State, *10 Supreme Court Reports (Civil Cases),* 86 (1956). The Supreme Court had taken the same basic position previously in other cases. The Setagaya case is briefly reviewed in Nathaniel L. Nathanson, "Constitutional Adjudication in Japan," 7 *American Journal of Comparative Law* 198 (1958).

8. The amendment of the Local Autonomy Law in 1952 is described in

Chihōjichi Kenkyū Kai, *Chihōjichi nenkan* 1954 (Tokyo, 1953), p. 21. (This yearbook, published under the auspices of the Autonomy Board, is a valuable source of factual information and statistics. It will hereafter be referred to as *Local Autonomy Yearbook 1954.*) A record of public hearings on the amendment may be found in *Kaisei chihō seido shiryō,* Vol. 8 (Tokyo, 1953), p. 278ff. Opposing views regarding its constitutionality are expressed, e.g., in Sugimura Shosaburo, "Fu-Ken no kempōjō no chi-i ni tsuite," *Toshi mondai kenkyū,* Vol. 5, No. 5 (May 1953), pp. 5ff; and in Juridical Society, *Commentary,* pp. 1382, 1393.

9. For a résumé of various arguments, see the special issue of *Hōritsu jihō,* Vol. 34, No. 5 (May 1952), especially the article by Arikura Ryokichi, "Tokubetsu kuchō sennin iken hanketsu ni tsuite." In the case before the Tokyo District Court, sociological considerations were also advanced. The prosecution, upholding the constitutionality of the present system of ward chief selection, argued that the wards were different from the basic local public entities because they were not the locus of a community spirit. The lower court did not agree, but the Supreme Court advanced similar considerations in its decision, as noted above.

10. An indication of the government's position is given in Juridical Society, *Commentary,* pp. 1375 and 1381 (fn. 2); the above brief outline of the government's position, which omits some of the finer points, is partly based on personal discussions with Japanese government officials concerned with the matter.

11. *Dō* is from Hokkaido, which would form one of the regions; *shū* means "province" or "state," in the sense of the various states of the United States. The Dō-Shū system is discussed more fully in Chapter 8.

12. Sugimura, "Fu-Ken no kempōjō no chi-i ni tsuite," pp. 5ff., and "Kempō no chihōjichi jōshō ni okeru mondaiten," *Kōhō kenkyū,* No. 9 (October 1953), pp. 95ff. Professor Sugimura holds in particular that there need not be a "double structure" of local entities, i.e., a prefectural and a municipal level.

13. See, e.g., Article 127 of the German Weimar Constitution and Article 117 of the Italian Constitution of 1947.

14. See Kempō Chōsakai Jimukyoku, *Teikoku kempō kaisei shingiroku,* Tokyo, n.d., Vol. XII; Juridical Society, *Commentary,* p. 1401. This explanation was not clear, as was pointed out by one of the questioners, Mr. Sawada, since delegated affairs also involve coercive power, which according to Mr. Omura were to be included under the term "management of affairs." The lack of clarity carries over into Article 2 of the Local Autonomy Law, as amended by Law No. 169 of 1947, which divides the functions of local entities into public affairs, assigned affairs, and administrative affairs. The exact nature of the last category—i.e., whether they are local affairs or national affairs entrusted by a general delegation—is not clear. See Tanaka Jiro, *Gyōseihō kōgian* (Tokyo, 1950), Vol. II, p. 90.

15. See, e.g., Kanamori Tokujiro, *Kempō yuigon* (Tokyo, 1959), p. 205ff.

16. Regarding the "Laws for Temporary Adjustment," see Alfred C. Oppler, "The Reform of Japan's Legal and Judicial System under Allied Occupation," *Washington Law Review* XXIV (1949), 290.

17. Juridical Society, *Commentary*, p. 1400.

18. Justice Holmes in Noble State Bank v. Haskell, 219 U.S. 104 (1911).

19. On the provenience of Article 95 see Juridical Society, *Commentary*, pp. 1409ff; also Ukai Nobushige, "Chihōjichi ni okeru tokubetsuhō no mondai," *Jichi kenkyū*, Vol. 27, No. 10 (October 1951), pp. 3ff.

20. Law No. 220 of 1950. On the problem raised by this law and on other questions involving Article 95 of the Constitution, see Sato Tatsuo, "Chihō tokubetsuhō no mondai" in his collection of essays, *Senryoku sono ta* (Tokyo, 1953), pp. 110ff. The procedure to be followed in case of special laws is provided for in the Diet Law, Article 67; in the Local Autonomy Law, Articles 261 and 262; and in the Enforcement Order to the Local Autonomy Law, Articles 180 to 183.

21. The first special laws were the Hiroshima Peace Commemoration City Establishment Law and the Nagasaki International Cultural City Establishment Law (Laws No. 219 and 220 of 1949). A number of laws of the same type were enacted in 1950. By 1951 there were fifteen of them.

22. Law No. 126 of 1950.

23. For a contrary view, see, e.g., Ukai Nobushige, *Kempō* (Tokyo, 1956), p. 261.

24. *Japan News*, June 11, 1951, p. 5.

25. Law No. 234 of 1951.

26. The Capital Construction Law is Law No. 219 of 1950, and the Capital Region Development Law is Law No. 83 of 1956. The government's position regarding the latter law was authoritatively established by the Chief of the Cabinet Legislation Bureau in Hayashi Shuzo, "Dai 24 kokkai de seiritsu shita shutokenseibihō to kempō dai 95 jō ni tsuite," *Jichi kenkyū*, Vol. 32, No. 5, pp. 3ff. The Law Restricting Industrial and Educational Establishments in the Built-Up Area within the Capital Region, passed in 1959, was also not considered a special law.

27. See Article 265, par. 7 of the Local Autonomy Law.

28. See, e.g., Ukai Nobushige, "Constitutional Trends and Developments," *Annals of the American Academy of Political and Social Science*, Vol. 308, (Nov. 1956), pp. 1ff.

29. The drafts can be found in the special issue of *Hōritsu jihō* of June 1956, entitled "Kempō kaisei."

30. *The Sample Survey on Social Stratification and Mobility in the Six Largest Cities of Japan*, published by the Japan Sociological Society in December 1952, shows (pp. 44 and 46) that in rating various occupations the prefectural governor was everywhere given the highest rank. Judges came out in second or third place. In the rural community, investigated for purposes of comparison, the judges ranked below the officials of large companies. The survey was published in English in mimeographed form.

CHAPTER 8

1. See, e.g., LAL, Articles 2, 7, 8, 14, 151, and 153.
2. See, e.g., *Japan Times*, August 12, 1957, p. 8.
3. *Nippon Times*, January 18, 1954, p. 4. It will be recalled that at the time Hokkaido had a Socialist governor.
4. In this public opinion poll, conducted in Tokyo Metropolis by Yoron Kagaku Kyokai on October 28, 1954, the following question was asked: "The Constitution provides that the governor of a prefecture shall be elected by direct election. Some people would prefer the governor to be appointed by the national government. What do you think about that?" The returns were:

I	In favor of direct elections	76.7%
II	In favor of appointment	9.7
III	Don't know	12.7
IV	Other answers	0.5
V	No response	0.4
		100.0

The following tabulation shows the percentage breakdown by occupation, age, and sex:

	I	II	III	IV	V
By occupation					
Salaried people	87.6	7.6	4.8	—	—
Merchants and industrialists	84.0	7.7	7.1	0.6	0.6
Laborers	74.2	14.0	10.7	1.1	—
Housewives	76.7	8.1	14.8	0.4	—
Students	86.1	2.3	11.6	—	—
Professionals	77.0	19.2	3.8	—	—
Agriculturalists	25.0	12.5	56.2	—	6.3
Not employed	58.0	17.1	22.7	1.1	1.1
By age					
20–29	83.3	5.6	10.3	0.4	0.4
30–39	82.9	7.5	9.6	—	—
40–49	79.7	7.5	11.8	0.5	0.5
50 and over	59.8	19.3	19.3	1.1	0.5
By sex					
Men	81.7	10.0	7.5	0.8	—
Women	71.6	9.5	17.8	0.3	0.8

From Allan B. Cole, *Japanese Opinion Polls of Sociopolitical Significance, 1947–57* (Fletcher School of Law and Diplomacy, 1960), p. 459.

5. *Asahi Evening News*, February 13, 1954, p. 1.
6. For the prewar situation, see Charles A. Beard, *The Administration and Politics of Tokyo* (New York, 1923), especially Chapters 2 and 3.

7. Public Offices Election Law (Law No. 100 of 1950), Article 15.

8. The discussion occurred at the Third General Meeting of the Fourth Local System Investigation Council, January 29, 1957. On the problem see Kikegawa Hiroshi, "Saikin no gunno meguru shomondai," in *Toshi mondai,* Vol. 48, No. 4 (April 1957), pp. 426ff.

9. See, e.g., the somewhat whimsical article by Oya Sōichi, "Nippon renyōka no kōzō," in *Chūō kōron,* August 1962, p. 43.

10. Stenographic Record, Imperial Constitution Amendment Draft Committee (*Teikoku kempō kaiseian iinkai giroku*), pp. 380–83; *Official Gazette Extra,* No. 23, 92d Session of the Imperial Diet, House of Representatives, March 23, 1947, p. 10.

11. Second report of the Local Administration Investigation Committee, September 22, 1951; see the above-mentioned issue of *Jichi ronshū* (November 1954), p. 159.

12. *Mainichi* (Osaka, English edition), April 24, 1952, p. 1.

13. Quoted in *Jichi ronshū* (November 1954), p. 173.

14. The reports of 1953 and 1957 are both entitled *Chihō seido no kaikaku ni kansuru tōshin.* The 1957 report is appended to Tanaka Jiro, Tawara Shizuo, and Ukai Nobushige, *Fuken seido kaikaku hihan* (Tokyo, 1957).

15. For details see, e.g., Tokyo Metropolitan Government, Capital Construction Division, *Problems of an Excessively Grown City, and the Development of Capital Region* (1957) and *City Planning, Tokyo* (1962); Royama Masamichi, "Tokyo and Osaka," in W. A. Robson, *Great Cities of the World* (2d edition, 1957), pp. 741ff; the pamphlet *Planning for Redevelopment of the National Capital Region,* prepared by the Autonomy Ministry for the EROPA Seminar of 1961; and the various reports of the National Capital Region Development Commission.

16. See the pamphlet *Outline of Regional Development Programs in Japan,* published by the Autonomy Ministry for the 1961 EROPA Seminar.

CHAPTER 9

1. See the quotation from Royama Masamichi in Chapter 2, p. 25.

2. Japan Sociological Society, *Sample Survey of Social Stratification and Mobility in the Six Large Cities of Japan* (Tokyo, 1952), p. 27.

3. Consulate General of Japan, San Francisco, *Japan Report,* Vol. 1, No. 10 (December 27, 1955), p. 6; Vol. 4, No. 6 (March 25, 1958), p. 9. Regarding the creation of an additional city with more than one million inhabitants, Kitakyushu, see below, p. 184.

4. *Municipal Yearbook 1956,* p. 34.

5. *Ibid.,* p. 1; see also 1952 edition, p. 19; 1958 edition, p. 64; 1961 edition, p. 1.

6. *Ibid.,* pp. 32–34.

7. *Ibid.,* pp. 6ff.

8. *Local Autonomy Yearbook 1954,* Table 5; *Shisei,* Vol. 3, No. 5 (May 1954), p. 2.

9. See the Statement of Opinion appended to Hara Ryonosuke *et al., Chihō seido kaikaku no mondaiten* (Tokyo 1953), p. 172.

10. The figures are based on *Municipal Yearbook, 1961,* pp. 6ff. A comparison with the population figures as of 1953 and 1955 shows the rapid growth of these urban centers:

	1953	1955
Osaka	1,956,176	2,547,316
Nagoya	1,030,635	1,336,780
Yokohama	951,189	1,143,687
Kyoto	1,105,734	1,204,084
Kobe	813,642	979,305

11. Law No. 1 of 1922.

12. Goto Ichiro, "The Problem of Special Cities in Japan," *Waseda Journal of Political Science and Economics* No. 116 (October 1952), pp. 28–40; and Osaka City, Department of General Administration, *A Memorandum on Special Municipality* (Osaka, 1947), pp. 6–9.

13. See, e.g., Osaka Municipal Office, *Special Municipality Series* (1947) and *Report on the Survey of the Administration of Osaka* (1950); also *Five Major Cities' Views on Reallocation of Functions* (August 1950), *Tokubetsu shisei riyūshō* (1951) and *Tokubetsu shisei hantai riyūshō ni tsuite* (1952). The three last-mentioned pamphlets were published by the Office for Cooperative Affairs of the Five Big Cities in Tokyo.

14. Law No. 147 of 1956. (As noted earlier, when new articles are inserted in a Japanese law it is customary not to revise the numbering of the articles, but to add a second number to that of the preceding article. Thus Article 252-2 does not mean the second paragraph of Article 252, but a new article inserted after Article 252.) Articles 252-2 to 252-16 were inserted by the amendment of 1952, and Articles 252-17 to 252-20 by the amendment of 1956.

15. From the Autonomy Ministry's pamphlet, *Local Government in Japan* (Tokyo, 1961), p. 5.

16. Law No. 117 of 1962.

17. Law Regarding Special Regulations for the Amalgamation of Cities (No. 118 of 1962). The previous amalgamations affected towns and villages that were merged with each other or with adjoining cities.

18. These figures are based on *Local Autonomy Yearbook 1954,* Statistical Part, Table 6, pp. 14–15, and on *Local Autonomy Yearbook 1955,* p. 18. Regarding the amalgamations of 1940–41, see Saitamaken, Chihōka, *Saitamaken shichōson gappeishi* (Urawa, 1960), Vol. I, p. 348.

19. *Shoup Report,* Vol. III, p. A-8; *Kambe Report,* Chapter III, Section II, pp. 24ff.

20. LAL, Article 2, paragraph 10, and Article 8-2.

21. The Law for the Promotion of the Amalgamation of Towns and Villages is Law No. 258 of 1953. It was amended by Laws No. 79 and 226 of 1954 and expired in September 1956. The law was formally introduced as a member bill, but it actually carried out the policy of the national government. See Nagahama Masatoshi, "Shinshi ni kansuru hitotsu no mondaiten," *Toshi mondai,* Vol. 47, No. 5 (May 1956), pp. 425ff; also Kato Kazuaki, "Chōson gappei to chōson zaisei," *Toshi mondai kenkyū,* Vol. 7, No. 11 (November 1955), pp. 155ff.

22. Law No. 164 of 1956.

23. Amendment of the Local Autonomy Law by Law No. 193 of 1954, Articles 296-2 to 296-6. The use of paternalistic exhortations without sanctions is obnoxious to many progressive legal scholars, who believe that the failure to make a clear distinction between law and morality is a sign of the feudalistic frame of mind of conservative lawmakers.

24. LAL, Article 7.

25. See, e.g., Hoshino Mitsuo, "Seijiteki kanten yori mita shinshi no kihonmondai," *Toshi mondai,* Vol. 47, No. 5 (May 1956), pp. 432ff and, by the same author, *Nihon no chihō seiji* (Tokyo, 1958), p. 196. For a case study of an amalgamation, in English, see Social Science Research Institute, International Christian University, *The Power Structure in a Rural Community— the Case of Mutsuzawa Mura* (Tokyo, 1960), pp. 32ff. This study is based on the longer Japanese report of the same Institute, *Nōson no kenryoku kōzo.* See also Richard K. Beardsley, John W. Hall, and Robert E. Ward, *Village Japan* (Chicago, 1959), pp. 395f. For an official report on five amalgamations in five different prefectures demonstrating the benefits of amalgamations, see Autonomy Board, Administration Division, *Gappei chōson no keiei to sonkensetsu no jittai* (Tokyo, 1955).

26. From *Ashai Nenkan 1957,* p. 301; for a discussion of the change in the scale of cities, towns, and villages, see Takagi Shosaku, "Shichōson kibo no hensen," in *Kōsei no shiryō,* November 1961.

27. See Chapter 16.

28. Reports of troubles connected with mergers are frequent in the Japanese press and periodicals. The examples cited are based mainly on *Mainichi* (English edition), April 9, 1955 and September 18, 1961; *Asahi shimbun,* April 14 and May 13, 1962.

29. Based on Tokyo Metropolitan Government, *An Administrative Perspective of Tokyo* (1961), p. 6.

30. LAL, Article 282; Local Tax Law, Article 736. It should be noted that Article 40 of the Police Law of 1947 created one Public Safety Commission for all 23 wards together.

31. On the question of the constitutionality of the amendment, see Chapter 7, pp. 123ff.

32. *Japan Times,* December 15, 1957, p. 8. Charles Beard made a similar

suggestion in 1923 in *The Administration and Politics of Tokyo* (New York, 1923), p. 42. Of course, at that time there still existed a city of Tokyo.

33. See Chapter 8, footnote on p. 158.

34. *Local Autonomy Yearbook 1954*, Statistical Part, Table 4, p. 7. For a description of a partial affairs association regarding irrigation, see Beardsley, Ward, Hall, *Village Japan*, p. 135.

35. *Kambe Report*, Chapter III, Section III, pp. 27f. The LAL (Articles 210 and 211) contained provisions for the possibility of joint use of establishments, but these, too, were rarely used.

36. LAL, as amended by Law No. 617 of 1952, Articles 252–2 to 252–16. The LAL, as enacted in 1947, had a special chapter dealing with similar councils. This chapter was deleted in December 1947.

37. Fujita Takeo, *Nihon chihō zaisei hattenshi* (Tokyo, 1949), pp. 157–67.

CHAPTER 10

1. The first quotation is from A. R. Radcliff-Brown's introduction to John F. Embree, *Suye Mura, A Japanese Village* (Chicago, 1939), p. xii. This work by the late Dr. Embree is the forerunner of the numerous village studies undertaken in more recent years, and it is something of a classic in the field. The second quotation is from Robert E. Ward, "The Socio-political Role of the Buraku (Hamlet) in Japan," *American Political Science Review*, XLV (1951), 1025. (Hereafter cited as Ward, *Buraku*.) Much of the following discussion is based on this excellent, concise presentation of the subject matter. Richard K. Beardsley, John W. Hall, and Robert E. Ward collaborated on the monumental work on *Village Japan* (Chicago, 1959), referred to earlier. This is a detailed, intensive study of a *buraku* in Okayama Prefecture. Chap. XII, "The Community and Local Government," and Chap. XIII, "The Community and the Political Process," are of special importance to students of local government.

2. Ralph J. E. Braibanti, "Neighborhood Associations in Japan and Their Democratic Potentialities," *Far Eastern Quarterly*, VII (1948), 139ff. George A. Warp, "In Our Image and Likeness," *National Municipal Review*, XLII (1953), 176, goes a step farther and states: "we abolished the essentially democratic neighborhood associations because they had been misused during the war."

3. Regarding this group, often referred to as *dōzoku*, see, e.g., *Village Japan*, p. 269; Richard K. Beardsley, "The Household in the Status System of Japanese Villages," *Occasional Papers of the Center for Japanese Studies*, No. 1 (1951), 62. The importance of the *dōzoku* is greatest where there is the least population mobility. In remote fishing villages, the *dōzoku* forms a group for small-scale fishery. See SCAP, Civil Information and Education

Section, *Some Aspects of the Fishery Right System in Selected Japanese Fishing Communities* (Tokyo, 1948), p. 2.

4. Ward, *Buraku*, p. 1031; *Village Japan*, pp. 354f; see also Fred N. Kerlinger, "Decisionmaking in Japan," *Social Forces*, XXX (1951), 36.

5. These examples are based on reports of the Civil Liberties Bureau to the writer in his capacity as Chief, Civil Affairs and Civil Liberties Branch, Legislation and Justice Division, Legal Section, SCAP, on articles in the *Nippon Times* (e.g., July 1, 1952), later called the *Japan Times* (e.g., Dec. 18, 1958); on articles in *Shūkan asahi* (e.g., June 7, 1959); and in other periodicals. The case of the Shizuoka schoolgirl was enough of a cause célèbre to be recalled in newspaper articles ten years later. See, e.g., *Mainichi shimbun*, June 7, 1962, for an interview with the victim turned heroine, under the title "This One Vote . . . I Was Right!"

6. See Nobutaka Ike, *Japanese Politics, An Introductory Survey* (New York, 1957), pp. 75ff.

7. See, e.g., Embree, *Suye Mura*, Chaps. IV and VIII; Edward Norbeck, *Takashima, A Japanese Fishing Community* (Salt Lake City, 1954), p. 102; SCAP, Natural Resources Section, *The Japanese Village in Transition* (Tokyo, 1950), p. 198; and *Village Japan*, pp. 474ff.

8. On this subject see also Robert E. Ward, "Patterns of Stability and Change in Rural Japanese Politics," *Occasional Papers of the Center for Japanese Studies*, No. 1 (1951), 2; *Village Japan*, pp. 351ff. In an earlier chapter we referred to the fact that villages are often subdivided into *ōaza*—usually the old Tokugawa village—and these again into *buraku*. Where this pattern exists, some of the functions that we shall ascribe to the *buraku* are carried out by the *ōaza*. However, even in this case the *buraku* usually participates in them in the form of a sub-unit of the *ōaza*. The *ōaza* sometimes has a limited number of officials—such as a person in charge of public works—but no organization that is as formal as that of the *buraku*.

9. Local Tax Law, Articles 702 to 733. Regarding the connection between the village and the *buraku*, see Paul S. Dull, "The Political Structure of a Japanese Village," *Far Eastern Quarterly*, XIII (1954), 175; *Village Japan*, pp. 349ff.

10. See Isomura Eiichi, "Toshi no shakai shūdan," *Toshi mondai*, Vol. 44, No. 10 (October 1953), pp. 1369–84.

11. R. P. Dore, *City Life in Japan*, p. 454 (n. 233), quoting Isomura Eiichi, *Ku no kenkyū* (1936), p. 242. Dore's book is a masterful detailed description of a postwar Tokyo neighborhood lying between Shitamachi and Yamate, both geographically and in character. See also the table of statistics regarding Tokyo neighborhood associations, reprinted from a 1943 survey, in Ukai Nobushige *et al.*, *Nihon kindaihō hattatsushi*, Vol. 6 (Tokyo, 1959), p. 167.

12. Older and less educated people and small businessmen are the groups most favorably inclined to the existence of urban associations. Isomura Eiichi, *Toshi shakaigaku* (Tokyo, 1953), p. 233. See also the report on a public

opinion poll conducted by the Tokyo Metropolitan Government entitled *Tokyo tosei ni tsuite* (Tokyo, 1954), p. 9. According to a later survey taken in March 1956, the membership—characteristically counted in terms of households—was highest in the central area of Tokyo and east of the Sumidagawa River, and lowest in the *yamate* district. When the Occupation decreed the abolition of the neighborhood associations, their offices had been turned over to the wards, to young men's associations, to the Red Cross, to crime or fire prevention societies, or to the leaders of the neighborhood associations as individuals. After 1952 some of these offices were returned to the reconstituted neighborhood associations, but in 1955 the homes of leading officials still served as offices in nearly three-fourths of the cases. Some 97 per cent of the chiefs of the associations were over forty years of age, and more than half of them were over fifty years of age. The officials were directly elected by the membership in only nine per cent of the cases. In 45.1 per cent, the chiefs were selected in the general meeting (*sōkai*), frequently without any balloting, the general meeting expressing only approval of those selected previously by the officers. In 24.3 per cent, the chief was selected by the officers without reference to others. There was usually no quorum requirement for the general meeting, which normally convened only about once a year. Sometimes its functions—including the approval of the budget and the selection of officers—were taken over by a meeting of the officers to which others of unspecified nature could be invited. Some 83 per cent of the associations were subdivided into 20 to 50 units of 10 to 20 households each, clearly the successors of the wartime *tonarigumi*.

See Tōkyō-to, Sōmukyoku, Gyōseika, *Chōkai, jichikai nō jittai chōsa hōkokusho* (March 1956). The method used—visits by Metropolitan officials to ward offices and ward branch offices and to officers of neighborhood groups to which questionnaires were submitted—may have resulted in some bias. A similar survey was conducted in Yokohama in 1953. Its report, entitled *Chiiki jichi dantai jittai chōsa hōkokusho*, is extensively quoted in Hoshino Mitsuo, *Nihon no chihō seiji* (Tokyo, 1959), p. 68. According to it, 67 per cent of all households in Yokohama belong to some area organization.

13. For a detailed description and analysis of this aspect, see Takagi Shosaku, "Chihō jichitai to gairo shōmei," in *Toshi mondai*, Vol. 53, Nos. 2–4 (February to April 1962).

14. The survey of the Tokyo Metropolitan Government (mentioned in note 12 above) shows that at the time some 80 per cent of the existing associations had the name *chōkai* (63 per cent) or *jichikai* (17.2 per cent). Other names were Harmony Association, Cooperative Association, or Friendship Association. In some cases groups reconstituted as neighborhood associations retained their former names as fire or crime prevention societies, etc. The motive for establishing the association was expressed in 48.7 per cent of the cases in terms of "promoting solidarity," "mutual help," and "friendship," and in only 22.5 per cent in terms of functions such as sanitation or safety. In 4.5 per cent "liaison with officials" was given as the motive. More than 90 per cent

of the associations performed such functions as collective expression of congratulation or condolence, the prevention of crimes, the distribution of insecticide, and the carrying out of tasks delegated by ward officials. Cooperation in the big spring housecleaning campaign, in road and ditch cleaning, in fire protection, and in night-watch service were frequent functions. At least half of the associations organized shrine festivals, parties to pay respect to old people, or other recreational affairs.

15. Braibanti, "Neighborhood Associations," p. 141.

16. According to a survey by the Autonomy Board in 1956, organizations similar to the outlawed neighborhood associations in area and functions were established within three months of the abolition in 94 per cent of the rural areas and in 77.9 per cent of the country as a whole. Sakuma Tsutomu, "Jumin soshiki no mondai," *Jichi kenkyū*, Vol. 33, No. 7 (July 1957), p. 29.

17. *Village Japan*, p. 279.

18. For a detailed investigation of the effects of urbanization on the town of Hino in Chiba Prefecture, see International Christian University Publication II-A, *Chiiki shakai to toshika* (Tokyo, 1962).

19. Dore, *City Life*, p. 269.

20. *Ibid.*, p. 278.

21. *Nippon Times*, October 19, 1952, p. 3; see also the negative comments in *Asahi*, October 6 and 24, 1952. Nevertheless, the ward assembly of Chiyoda ward in Tokyo passed "standards for the organization and management of *Chōkai* in Chiyoda ward," in August 1953. This was the first Tokyo ward to take such action. See Chiyoda Kuyakusho, *Chiyodaku shi* (Tokyo, 1960), Vol. III, pp. 950–54.

22. See, e.g., Takagi Shosaku, "Chōnaikai no hōseika o meguru mondai," *Toshi mondai kenkyū*, Vol. 10, No. 6. (June 1959), pp. 31ff; and the round-table discussion, "Burakukai, chōnaikai," in *Jichi kenkyū*, Vol. 36, Nos. 1 and 2 (January and February 1960).

CHAPTER 11

1. William Anderson, ed., *Local Government in Europe* (New York, 1939), p. xvii.

2. For a discussion of this problem, see Nagahama Masatoshi, "Chihō jichi to chihō bunken," *Kōhō kenkyū*, No. 9 (October 1953), p. 99.

3. See Chapter 3, p. 49.

4. LAL, Articles 2 and 14, as amended by Law No. 169 of 1947. Art. 14 also authorizes the prefectures to enact by-laws relating to the administrative affairs of the municipalities that take precedence over municipal by-laws.

5. LAL, Article 2, as amended by Law No. 179 of 1948.

6. For a comparison of national functions assigned to the prefectures in 1937 and 1953, see the excellent series of articles by Kuze Kimitaka, "Fuken

ni okeru chihō jichi no jittai," in *Jichi kenkyū,* Vol. 33, Nos. 2, 3, 4, and 6 (February through June 1957). The above-mentioned comparison is shown in Table 1 of the first article.

7. *Kambe Report,* Chapter II, Part II, p. 16.

8. Law No. 36 of 1919.

9. Takagi Shosaku, "Toshi keikakuhō," in Ukai Nobushige *et al., Nippon kindaihō hattatsushi,* Vol. 9 (1960), pp. 129ff.

10. *Municipal Yearbook 1956,* p. 151.

11. City Planning Law, Articles 6–2, as amended by Law No. 168 of 1949.

12. *Municipal Yearbook 1956,* p. 151. Zoning was first introduced by the City Area Building Law, established in the same year as the City Planning Law.

13. Law No. 201 of 1950.

14. Law No. 14 of 1927.

15. Law No. 160 of 1952. The distribution of financial responsibility in the law is quite complex. The state may grant a subsidy for that part of fireproof buildings within the belt which is between the fourth floor above ground and the first floor below ground.

16. See, e.g., the editorial in *Japan Times,* April 19, 1959.

17. The Parking Law is Law No. 106 of 1957. The ordinance was dated December 13, 1957.

18. Law No. 79 of 1956.

19. Law No. 180 of 1952.

20. Law No. 292 of 1952. The following discussion is based mainly on Takagi Shosaku, "Shiei jigyo no kikō to unei," in *Toshi mondai,* Vol. 42, No. 2 (February 1958), on the *Municipal Yearbooks* for 1956 (pp. 311ff), and 1961 (pp. 370ff), and on the pamphlet on "Local Public Enterprises in Japan," prepared by the Autonomy Ministry for the 1961 EROPA seminar in Tokyo.

21. Law No. 162 of 1956. A companion bill, the Law for the Adjustment of Related Laws Accompanying the Enforcement of Law No. 162, became Law No. 163.

22. See *Japan Report,* Vol. II, No. 13, July 15, 1956.

23. See the appraisal of the activities of the new boards one year after the coming into force of the law in *Asahi shimbun,* Oct. 2, 1957.

24. Law No. 233 of 1951. Another aim of the law was to increase cooperation between the National Rural Police and the autonomous police. The above figures are from *Local Antonomy Yearbook 1954,* p. 152.

25. *Kyōdō News,* April 25; *Nippon Times,* April 27, 1951; *Nippon Times,* July 27, 1951.

26. For a survey of such opinions, see *Toshi mondai,* Vol. 45, No. 7 (July 1954), p. 161. Fears of a return to the past were not alleviated by subsequent staffing policies of the government. In early 1958, for instance, the government decided to name Yasui Eiji, Home Minister and Welfare Minister in the second Konoe Cabinet (1940), to the National Public Safety Commission. *Japan Times,* January 22, 1958.

CHAPTER 12

1. For a comparison of the local tax system before and after Shoup, see Saburo Shiomi, *Japanese Finance and Taxation, 1940–1956* (New York, 1957), pp. 90–91. For a description of the circumstances under which the Local Tax Law was passed in 1950, see Chapter 6, p. 108. Since then the law has been amended a number of times each year. Much of the sub-chapter on local taxes is based on the Autonomy Board's *Chiho zaisei no genjō bunseki*, May 1955; on Ministry of Finance, Taxation Bureau, *Outline of National Tax in Japan, 1956*; and on a pamphlet prepared by the Autonomy Ministry for the 1961 EROPA Seminar entitled *The Local Tax System in Japan*.

2. *Shoup Mission Report*, Vol. II, pp. 200ff. For a detailed discussion see Ito Hanya, "The Value-Added Tax in Japan," *Annals of the Hitotsubashi Academy* (October, 1950), pp. 43–59. Bronfenbrenner and Kogiku note in their article on "The Aftermath of the Shoup Tax Reform," 10 *National Tax Journal* 240 (1957) that this type of tax became familiar after experiences in France and in the state of Michigan.

3. The temporary provisions for the Enterprise and Special Net Income Taxes may be found in Article 740 of the Local Tax Law in its original form. They were later revised by Law No. 226 of 1950. In 1954, the Local Tax Law was substantially amended by Law No. 95. At that time the standard tax rate for the Enterprise Tax was lowered and the deductions for individuals were raised.

4. *Shoup Mission Report*, Vol. I, p. 23.

5. The Prefectural Inhabitants Tax was established by the amendment of the Local Tax Law by Law No. 95 of 1954. For a sketch of the legislative history of that important amendment, see *Toshi mondai*, Vol. 45, No. 5 (May 1954), pp. 190ff.

6. This solution of the dispute between cities and prefectures was proposed by the Local System Investigation Council. The laws in question are the Admission Tax Law (No. 96 of 1954) and the Admission Distribution Tax Law (No. 102 of 1954). The transfer was effected against fairly strong opposition, especially since the original plan also called for a transfer of the Amusement, Eating, and Drinking Tax. A sketch of these developments is given in *Toshi mondai*, Vol. 45, No. 5 (May 1954), p. 190.

7. Law No. 20 of 1956.

8. The question whether "refund taxes" or "locally remitted taxes" are to be considered as local taxes or as national grants was answered by the compilers of the volume on *Local Government Finance and Its Importance for Local Autonomy* (published in 1955 at The Hague by the International Union of Local Authorities on the basis of reports prepared for the Rome Congress, 1955) as follows: "We drew the dividing line between local taxes and national grants at taxes which, though levied and administered entirely by the central government authorities, accrued to the benefit, either wholly or in part, of the local areas in which they were collected. From the point of view of grants,

the borderline case is the grant made from taxation specially levied for the purpose and dependent, as regards amount, on the *national*, not the *local*, yield" (p. 24). By these criteria the Admission Tax is no longer a local tax.

Another "tax" of the same type is the Local Road Tax. This is a percentage of the national Gasoline Tax, which is granted to the prefectures and to the five big cities for the purpose of road construction and repairs. In 1954 the Gasoline Distribution Tax Law (Law No. 190) provided that one-third of the receipts would be distributed among the prefectures and the five big cities. Since 1955 the Local Road Tax Law (Law No. 105) and the Local Road Allocation Tax Law (Law No. 113) provide for this distribution on a somewhat changed basis. At the time, a tax of 13,000 yen was levied on each kilolitre of gasoline; two-thirteenths of this amount—that is, 2,000 yen—was designated as the Local Road Tax, to be distributed to the prefectures and the cities specified in Article 7 of the Road Law. In 1957, when the rate of the Gasoline Tax was raised from 13,000 yen to 18,300 yen per kilolitre, the Local Road Tax was raised to 3,500 yen. The method of distribution is similar to that for the Light Oil Delivery Tax, a prefectural special purpose tax described in this chapter.

It should be noted that the pre-Occupation "refund taxes" had previously been abolished in 1948. From the viewpoint of local self-government a disadvantage of "refund taxes" is that they decrease the sense of responsibility of local officials. They flow in from the outside and are more freely expended than taxes which have to be collected from the local population by those who spend the money. Central government officials, on the other hand, see in "refund taxes" a means of equalizing the resources of wealthier and poorer entities.

9. See Chapter 6, p. 110.

10. Local Tax Law, Articles 260 and 669; Law Regarding the Adjustment of Related Laws pursuant to the Enforcement of the Autonomy Board Establishment Law (No. 262 of 1952), Article 14.

11. Amendment of the Local Tax Law (Law No. 81 of 1956).

12. Thus the rental value of the land became the tax basis in 1931. From 1940 on the Land Tax, while still collected nationally, was refunded to the prefecture in which it had been collected. It thus became a borderline case between national and prefectural taxes. The surtaxes levied by prefectures and municipalities continued.

13. Law No. 95 of 1954. The amount depends on the population of the municipality: the greater the population, the higher the maximum value of the assets that the municipality may tax.

14. For the exemptions in the Local Tax Law, see Articles 296 and 348; for the tax on users, Articles 344 to 347.

15. The laws relating to these grants are Law No. 82 of 1956 and Law No. 104 of 1957. Some assets, such as property used by the Imperial Family, official residences, and welfare institutions remain fully exempted.

16. The National Health Insurance Law dates back to 1922. It was sub-

stantially amended by Law No. 60 of 1948, Law No. 47 of 1950 and Law No. 90 of 1951. To meet the expenditures for the guidance and supervision of municipalities within their areas, the prefectures are also granted a national subsidy. The amendment to the Local Tax Law that converted the insurance premiums into a special purpose tax was Law No. 95 of 1951. Neighborhood associations are often used to collect this tax, although the legality of this procedure is open to question. (See LAL, Article 243.)

17. Law No. 60 of 1957.

18. Local Tax Law, Article 1, par. 1, item (5); *Shoup Mission Report*, Vol. III, p. A9.

19. Horike Yoshiro, "Chihō zaisei seido kaikaku no shomondai," *Toshi mondai kenkyū*, Vol. 5, Nos. 8 and 9 (October and November 1954), especially No. 8 at p. 97; and Soyama Hiroshi, "Shōwa 31 nendo chihō kōkyō dantai no kessan no gaikyo to mondaiten," *Jichi kenkyū*, Vol. 34, No. 3 (March 1958), pp. 13–24.

20. LAL, Articles 217 to 225, especially 218.

21. *Shoup Mission Report*, Vol. III, p. 413.

22. Lottery Law (No. 144 of 1948); Horse Race Law (No. 158 of 1948); Bicycle Race Law (No. 209 of 1948); Small Car Race Law (No. 208 of 1950); Motorboat Race Law (No. 242 of 1951).

23. The Local Finance Law is Law No. 190 of 1948.

24. Based in part on a mimeographed report of the Local Finance Commission, entitled *Japan's Local Finance: How Shoup Recommendations Are Being Implemented*, submitted to SCAP in August 1950. There is no reason to believe that procedures changed after the Autonomy Board became a Ministry.

25. Law No. 83 of 1957.

26. To correct revenue differentials between more and less advanced areas and to promote a more balanced economic development of the country, the Law for Exceptions to the Rate of National Shares Concerning Public Works for the Development of Less Advanced Areas was enacted in 1961. It increases the national treasury share for designated large-scale works, designed to build up a new industrial foundation in case of areas which fall below a clearly defined "financial index." The increased rate is objectively computed on the basis of a formula given in the law. For a summary of the law in English, see the pamphlet *Outline of Regional Development Programs in Japan*, prepared by the Autonomy Ministry for the 1961 EROPA Seminar, pp. 17ff.

27. Nagano Shiro, *Chikujō chihō jichihō* (Tokyo, 1953), p. 652. This work is an authoritative commentary on the LAL by the then Chief of the Administrative Section of the Autonomy Board.

28. Fujita Takeo, in *Nihon no chihō zaisei* (Tokyo, 1959) points out that Japanese governments have long been accustomed to assigning national functions to local governments without granting them adequate financial resources, especially at times when the national treasury is hard pressed by new demands.

29. As will be noted later, local expenditures have increased rather spectacularly over the last years. This increase was accompanied by an increase in subsidies. But the true significance of this phenomenon becomes clear only when we compare the expenses for subsidized works as part of local expenditures, as shown in the following tabulation (which uses a unit of 1,000,000 yen):

Year	A Local Expenses	B Subsidies	B/A	C Local Share	C/A	B + C = D Tot. Spent for Subs. Works	D/A
1950	5,023	1,055	21.0%	493	9.8%	1,548	30.8%
1951	6,328	1,182	18.7	744	11.7	1,926	30.4
1952	8,002	1,572	19.7	947	11.8	2,517	31.5
1953	9,149	2,714	29.3	1,804	19.6	4,518	48.9
1954	9,804	2,722	27.8	1,838	18.7	4,560	46.5
1955	9,829	2,757	28.0	1,867	19.0	4,624	47.0

Based on Finance Ministry, Secretariat, Investigation Section, *Nihon no zaisei* (Tokyo, 1955), p. 264.

The last column (D/A) shows that subsidized programs consume an increasing portion of the total local expenditure: from 30.8 per cent in 1950 to 47.0 per cent in 1955. The total amount expended on these programs (D) increased by 199 per cent in the six years under consideration, and subsidies (B) increased by 162 per cent. But the local share of expenses for subsidized programs (C) increased by 279 per cent. In spite of the increase in subsidies, local entities bore a heavier financial burden in 1955 than in 1950.

30. Law No. 211 of 1950. See Chapter 6, p. 109.

31. Horike, *"Chihō zaisei,"* No. 9, p. 80.

32. A noteworthy early example was the revival of the separate subsidy for compulsory education. An attempt in this direction had been made by the government with the support of the Civil Information and Education Section of SCAP immediately after passage of the Local Finance Equalization Grant Law, but had been quashed by Government Section, then the guardian of local autonomy. After the end of the Occupation a Law for Charging Expenses for Compulsory Education to the National Treasury (Law No. 303 of 1952) was passed, according to which the national government defrays one-half of the salaries for teachers in compulsory education—a prefectural responsibility—by means of a specific subsidy. Press and public opinion in general considered this law as an aspect of the recentralization of education. the Ministry of Education, on the other hand, pointed out that as long as the Local Finance Equalization Grant did not meet all local needs, local entities might not spend their scarce resources on education unless this was assured by a specific subsidy for the purpose. A subsequent effort of the central government to transfer the payment of teachers' salaries completely to the national treasury was condemned by most of the press, including the influential *Mainichi* and *Sangyo keizai* (see their editorials on January 24, 1953) and by the often conciliatory *Nippon Times,* which characterized it

in an editorial on January 26, 1953, as "bonehead action." The bill did not pass. The Local System Investigation Council, in its report of October 1953, specifically advised against the system proposed in the unsuccessful bill.

33. Article 6 of the Local Finance Equalization Grant Law.

34. *Shoup Mission Report,* Vol. III, p. A23.

35. Law No. 101 of 1954.

36. See Masao Kambe, "Independence of Local Finance," *Kyoto University Economic Review,* Vol. XXIV, No. 1 (April 1954), p. 11.

37. The Ministry's Ordinance 359 of 1952 defines the duties of governors in regard to the calculation of the grant and its distribution to cities, towns, and villages.

38. Law for Special Regulations Regarding the Charge of Disaster Rehabilitation Expenses to the National Treasury (No. 189 of 1950) and Law Regarding the Charge of Public Works Disaster Rehabilitation Expenses to the National Treasury (No. 97 of 1951), amended by Law No. 209 of 1952.

39. The ratio was lowest in 1953 with 1.019, and highest in 1957 with 1.130. Most of the data in this subsection are based on the pamphlet *The Local Finance System in Japan,* and on the Autonomy Ministry's Annual Reports on the State of Local Finance, *Chihō zaisei no jōkyō hōkoku.*

40. The International Union of Local Authorities in its report, *Local Government Finance and Its Importance for Local Autonomy* (The Hague, 1955), contains a classification of 24 countries along these lines on p. 18.

41. *Ibid.,* p. 19.

42. Budgets classify the expenses normally according to broad categories which do not reflect this distinction. See, e.g., the budget of Okayama Prefecture, outlined in Ardath W. Burks, *The Government of Japan* (New York, 1961), p. 214.

43. The percentage is higher in the case of prefectures, lower in the case of cities. Subsidies go primarily to work of an obligatory nature. The following summary, taken from Ogita Tamotsu, *Chihō zaisei kōwa* (Tokyo, 1959), p. 65, is based on the 1955 Local Finance Plan:

	With Subsidy	*Without Subsidy*	*Total*
Obligatory expenses	45%	34%	79%
Non-obligatory expenses	2	19	21
Total	47%	53%	100%

44. *Shoup Mission Report,* Vol. III, p. A3.

45. *Ibid.,* Vol. I, p. ii.

46. Regarding the government's attitude toward these commissions, see *Asahi shimbun,* April 17, 1951, editorial.

47. See *Local Finance Report,* especially for 1956 and 1957. It is true that the total amount of deficits in 1955 (64,200 million yen) was 700 million yen less than in 1954. But this decrease was somewhat illusory. In 1955 the floating of so-called Local Finance Reconstruction Loans was authorized un-

der the reconstruction scheme described below. In the table from which the
above figures were compiled these loans show up as revenue. If we deduct
them and take into consideration the failure of local entities to pay their share
for national enterprises, we find that the total deficit increased by 6 billion
yen during 1955. The real extent of the crisis was obscured for a while by
the Korean war boom, which had a favorable effect on local tax revenues
(especially the revenue from the Enterprise and Corporate Inhabitants taxes).

48. Law No. 195 of 1955.

49. All local entities with a deficit in 1954 were made eligible for participation in the scheme. They applied to the Chief of the Autonomy Board,
theoretically after the governor or mayor had received his assembly's consent
to the Local Finance Reconstruction Plan which he had prepared. This plan
then had to be approved by the Chief of the Autonomy Board who could
attach conditions to his approval. In actuality the usual informal consulta-
tions between the governor or mayor and the Autonomy Board preceded the
making up of the plan and the assembly's action.

If a plan worked out by the chief executive in agreement with the Autonomy Board did not find the consent of the assembly, or if the assembly
modified the plan in a manner unacceptable to the Autonomy Board, the
chief executive could ask for a reconsideration by the assembly, and if the
assembly did not come forth with a resolution in thirty days or before its
session ended, he could submit the plan without affirmative assembly resolution. The situation in these cases was strongly reminiscent of the pre-war
system: the chief executive, put into the position of serving two masters, was
extricated from it by loosening the assembly's control over his action.

50. Based on Autonomy Ministry Secretariat, *Jichi benran, 1962.* (Tokyo,
1962) p. 86.

51. Hall and Ward, *Village Japan*, p. 385.

52. For a discussion of local budget making, see, for example, *Jichi ronshū*,
Vols. XIV and XV (September 1961), two special issues entitled "*Chihō zaimu
kaikei seidoron*," especially Vol. XIV, pp. 100ff.

CHAPTER 13

1. Regarding the development of administrative control in England, see E.
L. Hasluck, *Local Government in England* (Cambridge, 1948), pp. 16, 96ff;
and R. M. Jackson, *The Machinery of Local Government* (London, 1958),
pp. 213ff. D. N. Chester, *Central and Local Government: Financial and Administrative Relations* (London, 1951), pp. 5ff and 323ff, makes some interesting criticisms and proposals on the subject.

2. Tanaka Jiro, *Shinkempō to chihōjichi*, p. 122.

3. See, for example, Tsuji Kiyoaki, *Nippon kanryō sei no kenkyū* (Tokyo,
1953). On the subject of the Japanese bureaucracy, see also Hugh McDonald
and Milton J. Esman, "The Japanese Civil Service," *Public Personnel Re-*

view, VII (1946), p. 213; Milton J. Esman, "Japanese Administration," *Public Administration Review*, VII (1947), p. 100; John Maki, "The Role of Bureaucracy in Japan," *Pacific Affairs*, XX (1947), p. 391; Tsuji Kiyoaki, "The Cabinet, Administrative Organization, and the Bureaucracy," *The Annals of the American Academy of Political and Social Science*, Vol. 308 (November 1956), p. 10; and Nobutaka Ike, *Japanese Politics, An Introductory Survey* (New York, 1957), Chapter 8, "The Bureaucracy."

4. Local Finance Committee Law, No. 155 of 1947.

5. National Election Administration Committee Law, No. 154 of 1947.

6. Local Autonomy Agency Establishment Law, No. 131 of 1949.

7. Regarding these recommendations, see Ardath W. Burks, "A Note on the Emerging Administrative Structure of the Post-Treaty Japanese National Government," *Occasional Papers of the Center of Japanese Studies*, No. 3 (1952), p. 47.

8. The main function of the Council is to manage the election of the 100 members of the House of Councilors who are elected by the nation at large. Other national elections—including the elections of the other 150 members of the House of Councilors, who are elected by prefectural constituencies—are managed through the prefectural Election Administration Committees. These are directed and supervised in this aspect of their work by the Autonomy Minister. This link with a Ministry, avoided under the preceding arrangement, was not the only change in election management introduced in 1952. Without going into the details of a matter that is outside the scope of this study, we may note that the Council does not have the quasi-legislative authority of its predecessor. It does not issue ordinances, but only proposes their issuance to the Ministry. It does not have an independent secretariat, but uses the Election Bureau of the Ministry instead. See Chihō Jichi Kenkyū Kai, *Jichi ronshū*, Vol. V, "Chihō gyōsei iinkai seidoron" (Osaka, 1965), pp. 173ff.

9. Autonomy Board Establishment Law, No. 261 of 1952; Autonomy University Establishment Law, No. 99 of 1953.

10. Law No. 113 of 1960.

11. John Stuart Mill, *Representative Government* (New York, 1875), p. 304.

12. See Chapter 9, pp. 200–201. The arrangements are the establishment of councils of local entities, the joint establishment of certain organs, and the commissioning of functions.

13. LAL, Article 245-3.

14. Law No. 120 of 1948.

15. The original government draft of the LAL provided simply that the governor or mayor may be dismissed by the Home Minister. This was revised by the House of Representatives to necessitate a legal action by the government, aimed at dismissal, before an Impeachment Court, which was to be created. See *Official Gazette Extra* No. 23, 92d Session of the Imperial Diet,

House of Representatives, March 23, 1947, p. 9. The present version stems from the amendment of the LAL in December 1947.

16. This use of Article 146 concerned an order of the Governor of Tokyo to the mayor of the town of Sunakawa, where an American air base is located. The planned expropriation of surrounding land in order to enlarge the base led to a heated political controversy. Although the mayor as national agent was required by the Land Expropriation Law and by the Law for Special Measures Resulting from the US-Japan Administrative Agreement to issue a public notice (which then enabled surveyors to enter the land to be expropriated), he refused to do so, contending that the governor's order was illegal because the maintenance of American bases violated Article 9 of the Constitution. His refusal created a situation in which the conditions for the mandamus procedure under Article 146 were present, and the governor instituted appropriate action. He won the case in the first instance. The District Court did not entertain the question of constitutionality. It found that within the sphere in which he acts as a "national agent" the mayor has to obey the orders of the governor, so long as they are legal in a formal sense and not impossible to execute, regardless of his opinion of their constitutionality. Neither Article 99 of the Constitution, which obliges all public officials to "respect and uphold the Constitution," nor Article 138-2 of the LAL, which enjoins local chief executives to carry out their duties based on their own judgment and responsibility, give the mayor the right to refuse orders in regard to matters that are under national control. (Decision of Tokyo District Court of July 31, 1958, *Gyōsei jiken zaibanreishū*, Vol. 9, No. 7, p. 1515.)

The mayor appealed to the Supreme Court. The case then became enmeshed in several other cases concerning the expansion of the base, including the famous Sunakawa Case, which brought the question of the constitutionality of maintaining U.S. air bases in Japan into sharper focus. (See Alfred C. Oppler, "The Sunakawa Case: Its Legal and Political Implications," 76 *Political Science Quarterly* 241.) The Supreme Court rendered its decision on July 17, 1960. It found that the mayor, who is elected by the local constituency, is not in a relation of direct subordination to the governor. The national government is given certain powers of control within the area of assigned functions, but its orders must not conflict with the "principle of local autonomy." In accordance with the rule of law, conflicts between a governor and a mayor in cases of Article 146 of the LAL have to be decided by the courts. The courts have to rule on the merits of the contentions of the parties. The District Court failed to do this. Therefore, the Supreme Court quashed the original verdict and sent the case back to the District Court. (Supreme Court, *Minji hanreishū*, Vol. 14, No. 8, p. 1420.) The District Court, in its decision of March 28, 1963, found on retrial that the governor's order was valid, and the order was subsequently carried out. (The mayor who was the defendant in the case had passed away by then.)

17. Decision of Supreme Court of October 27, 1952, *Minji hanreishū,*

Vol. 7, No. 10, p. 1141; Decision of Nagoya District Court, *Gyōsei jiken zaibanreishū*, Vol. 5, No. 4, p. 838.

18. Tanaka Jiro, "Horitsu ni yoru gyōsei to tsūtatsu ni yori gyōsei," *Jichi kenkyū*, Vol. 32, No. 7 (July 1956), p. 3ff; Kuze Kimitaka, "Fuken ni okeru chihō jichi no jittai," *Jichi kenkyū*, Vol. 33, No. 2 (February 1957), pp. 79ff and p. 92.

19. Gubernatorial conferences were held regularly by the Home Ministry in prewar days. On this function of the National Association of Governors, see Cecil C. Brett, *The Government of Okayama Prefecture* (unpublished doctoral dissertation, University of Michigan, 1956), p. 107.

20. *Village Japan*, p. 370. On the associations of town and village mayors, see also Robert E. Ward, "Some Observations of Local Autonomy at the Village Level in Present-Day Japan," *Far Eastern Quarterly*, XII (1953), 196; and Paul S. Dull, "The Political Structure of a Japanese Village," *Far Eastern Quarterly*, XIII (1954), 180. For an analysis of the pressure group aspects of the six national local government associations, see Ari Bunseki, "Chihō roku dantai," in *Nippon no atsuryoku dantai*, the 1960 issue of the Annals of the Japanese Political Science Association, pp. 49ff.

21. The National Association of Governors favored the abolition of branch offices. See National Association of Governors, *Opinions Regarding the Reform of the Local System, Part I*. Examples usually mentioned in this context are the Labor Ministry's 46 Labor Standards Offices, its 46 Women's and Minors' Offices, its 337 Labor Standards Inspection Offices and its 421 Public Employment Stabilization Offices; the 8 Branch Offices of the Ministry for Commerce and Industry; the Transportation Ministry's 10 Sea Transport and 9 Land Transport Offices with their branches; and the Construction Ministry's 6 Local Construction Offices.

22. According to Kuze, whose article on the actuality of local autonomy in the prefectures furnished much of the material for this part of the study, the number of staff members in the Tokyo offices in 1957 ranged from 79 in the case of Hokkaido to 4 in the case of nearby Gumma. Kuze, "Fuken ni okeru chihō jichi," cited in note 18 above.

23. Brett, *Government of Okayama Prefecture*, p. 104.

24. The following description is largely based on interviews with prefectural and municipal officials.

25. Professor Kambe Masao in his article on "Independence of Local Finance," *Kyoto University Economic Review*, Vol. XXIV, No. 1 (April 1964), pp. 1ff, referring to the Annual Report of the Board of Audit for 1954, states that "bribes are advanced to members of the Diet as well as to government officials." The Takushima scandal of 1956, concerning an official of the Ministry of Agriculture and Forestry of comparatively low rank, involved the spending of 100 million yen; the collusion in this case took the form of a kickback of funds to the official who had obtained the exorbitant subsidy.

26. LAL, Article 243.

27. A study based on twelve prefectures showed the following picture regarding the average number of inspections in each of them in the course of 1953:

Agency	Inspections	Days	Officials
Board of Audit	13	59	49
Ministry of Finance	19	51	52
Ministry of Agriculture and Forestry	11	28	23
Ministry of Welfare	5	18	11
Ministry of Education	2	5	5
Ministry of Construction	8	38	22
Prime Minister's Office*	14	46	37
Ministry of Transportation	2	9	6

* At the time both the Autonomy Board and the Administrative Management Agency were external organs of the Prime Minister's Office.

Source: Kuze, "Fuken ni okeru chihō jichi," pp. 20ff. Kuze notes that it is likely that these figures, based on information from the General Affairs Divisions, are likely to fall short of the actual total of inspections in regard to subsidized works carried out by the various divisions of the prefectural governments. In addition to these formal inspections, the branch offices of the various ministries often check on the prefectures by telephone or correspondence in connection with their normal liaison with the prefectural offices. A case study of a subsidy from the Ministry of Agriculture and Forestry may be found in Brett, *Government of Okayama Prefecture*, pp. 172ff.

28. Kuze, "Fuken ni okeru chihō jichi," p. 82; *Asahi shimbun*, April 17, 1951, editorial.

29. Both quotations are from Masao Kambe, "Independence of Local Finance," *Kyoto University Economic Review*, Vol. XXIV, No. 1 (April 1954), p. 15.

30. Kuze, "Fuken ni okeru chihō jichi," p. 28.

31. From a memorandum entitled "Opinion Concerning the Allotment of Public Affairs between the State and the Local Public Bodies," submitted by the Local Autonomy Section of the Prime Minister's Office to SCAP's Government Section on May 12, 1949.

32. Brett, *Government of Okayama Prefecture*, p. 102, notes that age also plays a role. Older officials in the prefectural government of Okayama exhibited at best a passive acceptance of the present system; at times they expressed nostalgia for the "good old days."

33. Sometimes they have advocated the abolition of the prefectures. See National Association of City Mayors (Zenkoku Shichō Kai), *Warera wa jichi wa kō shūchō suru* (Tokyo, 1953), pp. 2f.

CHAPTER 14

1. As of January 1, 1962, the monthly salaries of governors ranged from 230,000 yen for the governor of Tokyo to 85,000 yen for the governor of Tottori. The average was 127,886 yen. The salary of the governor of Tokyo is higher than that of a Cabinet Minister (185,000 yen). Based on statistics of

the office of the National Association of Prefectural Assembly Chairmen (*Shiryō*, No. 76, published February 6, 1962). See also *Japan Times*, February 12, 1962.

2. Public Offices Election Law, Article 10; LAL, Articles 19, 140, and 204.

3. Nagano, *Chikujō chihō jichihō*, pp. 425ff.

4. LAL, Articles 159 and 160. The supervision over public organizations is a remnant of the wartime trend toward integration, noted in Chapter 4.

5. The positions of assistant accountants and assistant treasurers may be created by bylaw. In the original version of the Local Autonomy Law their appointment also required the consent of the assembly, but this requirement has since been dropped. A local entity may also have accountants appointed by the chief executive from among the local secretarial officials. Prior to the amendment of 1952 the appointment of a vice-governor was mandatory (LAL, Articles 161-71).

6. LAL, Appended List 6.

7. LAL, Article 158.

8. An example is the actual organization of the Tokyo Metropolitan Government. Under the governor three vice-governors are in charge of various aspects of the metropolitan administration. In 1961 the first vice-governor was in charge of the Bureaus of General Affairs, Finance, and Taxation (established in accordance with the Local Autonomy Law, as noted above) and of the Bureaus of Capital City Development and of Olympics Preparation. The latter bureaus are additions to the pattern prescribed by the law. (The Bureau of Olympics Preparation was established in anticipation of the 1964 Olympic Games, in Tokyo.) The first vice-governor also supervised the Office of General Planning, the Office of the Chief Accountant and the Office of Public Relations; he coordinated the relations of the Board of Education, of the Public Safety Commission, and of other administration commissions with the rest of the metropolitan administration, and he was concerned with the affairs of the Tokyo Metropolitan University and of the four junior colleges managed by the metropolitan administration. The second vice-governor was in charge of the Bureaus of Public Welfare, Public Health, Labor, Economic Affairs, and Housing as well as of the Metropolitan Welfare Home and the Central Wholesale Market. The third vice-governor supervised the Bureau of Construction, the Harbor Bureau, the Bureau of Public Sanitation, the Bureau of Transportation, and the Bureau of Waterworks and Sewerage. The last three bureaus are not required by law. There were thus 15 subdivisions of the metropolitan government that had the status of bureaus. In 1961–62 there were 155,106 persons on the payroll of Tokyo Metropolis (of these, 51,467 were connected with the Office of Education, 30,167 with the Metropolitan Police Department, and 16,021 with the Bureau of Transportation). For details, see Tokyo Metropolitan Government, *An Administration Perspective of Tokyo*, 1961, pp. 15ff.

9. Regarding the extralegal limitations imposed by the ministries and examples of actual cases, see the article series by Kuze (*Jichi kenkyū*, Vol. 33,

No. 4, p. 93). "Subsidized officials" and sections staffed by national officials will be discussed later in this chapter.

10. Lists 5, 6, and 7 appended to the Local Autonomy Law specify certain administrative agencies or deliberative councils that must be established, and certain types of officials that must be appointed. These lists give a good survey of the limitations of the above-quoted general rule of Article 158 of the LAL.

11. For a brief discussion of the Okayama prefectural administration in 1961, see Ardath W. Burks, *The Government of Japan* (New York, 1961), p. 206. See also Cecil C. Brett, *The Government of Okayama Prefecture* (unpublished dissertation, University of Michigan, 1956), pp. 56ff.

12. On the administrative organization of the city of Osaka, see W. A. Robson (ed.), *Great Cities of the World* (London, 1954), p. 728; for the administrative organization of Okayama City, see Burks, *The Government of Japan*, p. 212. The administrative organization of Osaka Prefecture and of Osaka City are compared in Osaka Municipal Office, *Report on the Survey of the Administration of the City of Osaka* (Osaka, 1950), p. 30. The description of the office of the village of Kamo may be found in *Village Japan*, p. 366.

13. For a discussion of this question, see *Jichi ronshū*, Vol. V, "Chihō gyōsei iinkai seidoron" (Osaka, 1956), pp. 175ff.

14. Law No. 261 of 1950. See also LAL, Article 202-2.

15. On the legislative history of the laws of 1951 and 1957, see Dore, *Land Reform in Japan*, pp. 425–31; the Agricultural Commission of the village of Kamo is described in Ward, *Village Japan*, p. 373.

16. LAL, Articles 195 to 202; see also Article 75 and Articles 246-2 to 246-4, newly established in 1956. The institution has been compared to the Chinese censorate. See Ralph J. E. Braibanti, "Executive Power in the Japanese Prefectural Government," *Far Eastern Quarterly*, IX (1950), 241.

17. On the national level the constitutionality of administrative commissions was questioned on the basis that according to Article 65 the "executive power shall be vested in the Cabinet," and that the Cabinet can only be made responsible to the Diet if it has the executive power, but not if it is deprived of part of it by independent commissions. It is significant that during the Occupation not less than three of General MacArthur's infrequent letters to the Prime Minister dealt with the subject of the semi-independence of the various commissions. After the Occupation ended, a number of the commissions on the national level—such as the Local Finance Commission, the National Election Administration Committee, and the Radio Regulatory Commission—were integrated into the regular departments of government.

18. LAL, Article 138-3; Nagano, *Chikujō chihō jichihō*, p. 399.

19. See LAL, Articles 180 to 180-7, 213-2, 239-3, and 239-4, and Nagano's commentary to these articles.

20. A thorough study of the actual working of some commissions was published by the Institute of Social Science of Tokyo University under the title *Gyōsei iinkai: riron, rekishi, jittai* (Tokyo, 1951).

For an excellent description of the operation of the Public Safety Commission of Okayama Prefecture, see Brett, *The Government of Okayama Prefec-*

ture, pp. 214, 222–37. Some of Brett's findings may be summarized as follows: the Public Safety Commission had come under the influence of police headquarters ("the dog was being wagged by the tail—not gently but vigorously"); its conferences were held at headquarters, the Chief Superintendent of Police served as its "official" secretary, and the commission's executive secretary was relegated to routine matters; the commission adopted rules that made it impossible to make decisions or take actions independently of police headquarters; the attitude of the Chief Superintendent to the commission was one of tolerance or condescension, for the true line of authority did not run from police headquarters to the Public Safety Commission but to the Police Agency in Tokyo.

21. See, for example, Ukai Nobushige, "Chihō jichi to gyōsei iinkai seido," in the collection of essays *Chihō jichi rombunshū* (Tokyo, 1954), p. 277; Royama Masamichi, "Nippon-kanryo no kuni," *Kaizo* (September 1952), pp. 72ff.; *Jichi rombun,* Vol. 5, "Chihō gyōsei iinkai seidoron," pp. 11ff.

22. See Local Public Service Law, Articles 17, 18, and 59. In the discussion of the bill in the Local Administration Committee of the House of Representatives, the representatives of the People's Democratic Party moved an amendment to eliminate the possibility of a delegation of power by local Personnel Commissions to other agencies, but the motion was defeated. (Report of the Local Administration Committee of December 5, 1950, in *Official Gazette Extra,* December 10, 1950, p. 98.)

23. By the first decade of the twentieth century all important offices in prefectural governments were held by Tokyo University graduates. See Robert A. Scalapino and Junnosuke Masumi, *Parties and Politics in Contemporary Japan* (Berkeley, 1962), p. 9, citing Kurihara Teiichi, *Chihō kankai no hensen* (Tokyo, 1930), and Tanaka Sōgōrō, *Nihon kanryo seijishi* (Tokyo, 1954). The Occupation tried to increase the relative importance of other universities, but failed. The graduates of Tokyo University are still recognized as a sort of elite. It is not uncommon for candidates who failed in the national examination to take the prefectural examination later.

24. Brett, *The Government of Okayama Prefecture,* p. 98, states that a local official going to Tokyo loses ranks while a national official who comes to the prefecture usually goes up a step. On the interchange of national and local officials, see also Matsumura Kiyoyuki, "Chihō kōmuin no jinji kōryu," in *Chihō jichi rombunshū* (Tokyo, 1954), p. 311.

25. LAL, Articles 252-17 and 252-18, and Supplementary Provisions, Article 8.

26. LAL, Articles 91 and 95. For the earlier provisions, see Prefectural Code, Article 5; City Code, Article 13; and Town and Village Code, Article 11 (all in the version prior to their replacement by the LAL). Regarding the size of French assemblies, see, for example, Brian Chapman, *Introduction to French Local Government* (London, 1953), p. 35. William A. Anderson, *Local Government in Europe* (New York, 1939), p. 202, contains a translation of the corresponding provisions of the French Municipal Code of 1937.

27. According to the above-mentioned survey of city assemblies of January

1961, 32.3 per cent of the assemblymen were engaged in agriculture and forestry and 1.9 per cent in fishery; 14.5 per cent were businessmen, 20.5 per cent employees of companies, and 7.9 per cent officials of organizations. The rest were engaged in various secondary and tertiary industries, with the exception of 4.2 per cent who had no occupation and 5.1 per cent nondescript "others."

An earlier survey of 15 cities published jointly by the National Association of City Assembly Chairmen and the Osaka Municipal Government Research Institute in 1954 (*Chihō gikai no jittai chōsa*) showed that men engaged in agriculture and forestry formed the largest occupational segment of the assemblies in cities with a population of less than 50,000 (30.89 per cent) and in cities with a population of 50,000 to 100,000 (24.56 per cent). On the other extreme stood the big cities, in which this group occupied only 4.4 per cent of the seats. Among the winners of the prefectural assembly elections of 1959, company employees formed the largest group (31.6 per cent), followed by those engaged in agriculture and forestry (26.7 per cent). See Autonomy Board, Election Bureau, 1959 *Chihō senkyo kekka shirabe*, p. 25.

28. In 1959, lawyers constituted 1.2 per cent of the victorious candidates in the prefectural assembly elections. According to the 1954 survey of city assemblies, all the professions together constituted 15.9 per cent of the assemblies of the big cities, and 4.4 per cent to 5.8 per cent of the assemblies of other cities. Yasumasa Kuroda, in *Political Socialization: Personal Political Orientation of Law Students in Japan* (unpublished Ph.D. thesis, University of Oregon, 1962), indicates that the legally trained bureaucrat in Japan plays a role functionally equivalent to that of the lawyer in the United States, and discusses some of the consequences.

29. 1959 *Chihō senkyo kekka shirabe*, p. 21. The 1954 survey is the above-mentioned *Chihō gikai no jittai chōsa*.

30. For the legal provisions, see LAL, Articles 101 and 102. The statements regarding sessions of prefectural assemblies are based on statistics of the office of the National Association of Prefectural Assembly Chairmen (*Shiryō*, No. 91, and *Zenkoku todofuken gikai benran*, July 1, 1961).

31. This survey is mentioned in Wada Hideo, *Kempō no gendaiteki dammen* (Tokyo, 1961), p. 397. The survey of the National Association of City Assembly Chairmen in 1961 indicates that the percentage in the case of cities may actually be higher. According to it, city assembly chairmen rotated in 73.5 per cent of the cities that responded (93 per cent of all cities); in 61.8 per cent of these cases rotation was annual. The successor to the chairman, who resigned according to agreement, was selected either by election in the assembly or by a method known as *shimei suisen* (nomination and recommendation), which presupposes that no assemblyman demands an election by vote and all assemblymen consent to the selection of the one candidate who has been nominated. The legal basis for this procedure is LAL, Article 118, paragraphs 2 and 3. It is also used in other elections conducted by the assembly. For a case in which the incumbent prefectural assembly chairman reneged on

his promise to resign after two years, and in which a no confidence resolution was passed against him as a consequence, see Brett, *The Government of Okayama Prefecture*, pp. 113ff. On the rotation of assembly chairmen, see also Kudan Juro, "Chihō gikai no unei wo miru," *Shisei*, Vol. 2, No. 10 (October 1953), p. 42.

32. On the operation of standing committees in the municipalities, see the joint publication of the National Association of City Assembly Chairmen and the Osaka City Government Research Office, *Chihō gikai no jittai chōsa*, p. 109ff.

33. LAL, Articles 112 to 123.

34. In 1957, 19 of the 46 prefectural assemblies were not presented with any member bills at all. The other 27 prefectural assemblies dealt with a total of 51 member bills. Forty of these dealt with matters concerning the assembly itself, such as its internal organization or precedure or the compensation of its members. Of the eleven remaining bills, which were of a more general nature, seven were defeated. From Tomohisa Shigekazu, "Chihō gikai ni okeru giin rippō no genjō to mondaiten," *Toshi mondai*, Vol. 50. No. 1 (January 1959), pp. 42–44. Statistics of the Office of the National Association of Prefectural Assembly Chairman (*Shiryō* No. 90) show that in 1961, 19 prefectural assemblies dealt with 24 member bills, most of them concerning assembly matters. Member bills on the municipal level are equally rare.

35. In 1962, 185 by-laws were in force in Hyogo Prefecture. Of these 42 affected the local inhabitants, i.e., they constituted an exercise of the local "police power." (Examples are the regulations regarding the possession of dogs, and other regulations requiring licenses.) The remainder dealt with the organization of the prefectural government, the local personnel, the management and use of prefectural buildings, parks, hospitals, etc., and with accounting procedures. The Administration Section of the Autonomy Ministry issues a collection of local bylaws, *Chihō jichi jōreishū*, mainly for the use of officials. This collection permits an analysis of local legislation activity.

36. This description is largely based on Brett's *The Government of Okayama Prefecture*, which contains a number of interesting details. It is typical of procedures at this level. At the same time it goes without saying that not all sessions of all prefectural assemblies—or even all sessions of any one of them—follow the pattern exactly. For example, actual voting does occur occasionally.

37. See the great number of bylaws which begin with a reference to a national law in the above-mentioned collection, *Chihō jichi jōreishū*; also Fujii Sadao, "Hitsujōteki jōrei kitei jikō zenzō no keikō to sono igi," *Jichi kenkyū*, Vol. 25, No. 6 (June 1949), p. 17. The system used by these national laws is that of "entity delegation." Laws using the system of "agency delegation" are implemented locally by regulations, as stated earlier.

38. For a perceptive discussion of the legislative activities of the village assembly of Kamo in Okayama prefecture, see Ward, *Village Japan*, p. 362ff.

In that village, all bylaws had their origin in model bylaws handed down from above, and all were adopted without change by the assembly.

39. LAL, Article 176, paragraphs 4 and 5, in their original form.

40. This infringement is most apparent when the higher authority rescinds an assembly action on a subordinate level. But the higher authority cannot at the same time substitute a disposition of its own, as it could under the former codes. The amendment of Article 176 should be considered in connection with the changes in Chapter 10 of the LAL, which were mentioned in the preceding chapter.

41. This interpretation is based on Nagano, *Chikujō chihō jichihō,* pp. 526ff.

42. The chief executive may appropriate and disburse the amount that he originally proposed in full or in part. This case is an exception to the general rule of Article 96, LAL, that the annual expenditures are to be determined by assembly resolution. The pertinent provision is LAL, Article 177, paragraph 2, item 1. For a commentary, see Nagano, *Chikujō chihō jichihō,* pp. 528f.; regarding the "execution of the original draft," see Chapter 3, pp. 75f.

43. In this case—involving the application of LAL, Article 177, paragraph 2, item 2 and paragraph 4—the normal conditions for a vote of no confidence, a quorum of two-thirds and a majority of three-fourths, need not be present.

44. A somewhat confused case involving Article 177 arose in the town of Komae in Tokyo Metropolis. The question whether the town should amalgamate with Setagaya Ward or with the city of Chōfu split the assembly into two factions. Each faction started a direct demand for the recall of the other faction. There was also a movement for the recall of the mayor. When the budget for 1958 came up for discussion, no decision had been reached on these demands. The assembly reduced the mayor's budget by 5 million yen, slicing 1 million off his budget for health expenditures. The mayor considered the reduced budget a measure that "cannot be executed in respect to revenues and expenditures," and requested reconsideration under Article 177, paragraph 1. But when the assembly remained recalcitrant, he changed his approach. He dissolved the assembly, declaring that he considered the reduction of the health expenditures a vote of no confidence under Article 177, paragraph 4. The Governor of Tokyo, noting that the dissolution was based on neither an explicit vote of no confidence (Art. 178) nor an implied vote of no confidence (Article 177, paragraph 2, item 2 and paragraph 4), requested an explanation from the mayor. When no explanation was forthcoming he used the authority bestowed upon him by the LAL amendment of 1956. Finding that the mayor's action was illegal he requested that it be remedied (Article 246-2). The mayor in turn ordered the treasurer to expend the funds for the health budget that had been cut by the assembly. When the treasurer refused, the mayor fired him without consultation with the assembly by way of a "discretionary disposition" (Article 179).

45. The meaning of the phrase "any such matter as shall be resolved therein" (in the assembly) is open to controversy. According to Nagano, it

encompasses not only resolutions required by law, but also those required by actual circumstances. See LAL, Article 179. Discretionary dispositions by delegation are dealt with in Article 180.

46. Autonomy Board, *Gyōsei jitsurei*, August 15, 1951.

47. Ward, *Village Japan*, p. 363.

CHAPTER 15

1. Law No. 100 of 1950; see also LAL, Articles 17 to 21.

2. LAL, Articles 92-2, 166, 168, 180-5.

3. Thus, on April 26, 1951, the *Nippon Times* wrote that the local elections just held "marked a new high in democratic Japan," that "a great deal of the credit must go to the interest of the people in the process of local government," and that "it is a matter of congratulation that the people have responded so unanimously to their duty as democratic citizens." The editorial concluded: "Here is proof that the democratic principles which were introduced less than six years ago as an integral part of national existence are a living and growing force."

4. This section is based almost entirely on statistics published by the Election Bureau of the Autonomy Board after each round of unified local elections, under the title *Chihō senkyō kekka shirabe*, especially the volumes on the 1955 and 1959 elections.

5. The voting rate for all types of municipal assemblies (including city and ward assemblies) was 81.17 per cent.

6. Yamanashi Prefecture was leading in both years with a rate of 95.94 per cent and 95.45 per cent respectively. Tottori placed second in 1955 with 95.81 per cent and third in 1959 with 95.15 per cent. Toyama had the fourth highest voting rate in both 1955 and 1959 (95.54 per cent and 94.85 per cent respectively). Fukushima was eighth in 1955 (94.98 per cent) and second in 1959 (95.32 per cent). Gumma was sixth in 1955 (95.46 per cent) and seventh in 1959 (94.49 per cent). In all these prefectures except Toyama more than 50 per cent of the population is engaged in primary industries. In Toyama 46.1 per cent of the population is so engaged.

7. The voting rates in Tokyo were 83.85 per cent in 1955 and 82.61 per cent in 1959. Osaka had the second lowest voting rate in 1959 (87.05 per cent) and ranked well toward the bottom of the list in 1955 (90.98 per cent). Kanagawa had the fifth lowest rate in 1955 (89.68 per cent) and was below the national average also in 1959 (91.58 per cent). These are the prefectures with the highest percentage of inhabitants in secondary and tertiary industries. If we consider other prefectures of comparatively urban character, we find that Kyoto stood above the national average in 1955 (93.04 per cent) but slightly below that average in 1959 (92.40 per cent). Similarly, Fukuoka stood below the national average in 1955 (92 per cent), but above that average in 1959 (93.64 per cent). Aichi showed a voting rate slightly above the national average in both elections (92.78 per cent and 92.74 per cent respectively).

Hyogo also topped the national average (93.48 per cent and 94.56 per cent respectively). Rural prefectures with low voting rates were Aomori (90.74 per cent and 90.35 per cent), Chiba (88.99 per cent and 90.73 per cent), and Kochi (88.46 per cent and 90.30 per cent).

The influence of the proximity of a highly urbanized area may be seen in the voting rates in towns and villages in various parts of Tokyo Metropolis. Those in Kitatamagun, which adjoins the ward areas, tend to have a lower voting rate than those in the more remote Nishitamagun. In 1959 their respective voting rates were 79.45 per cent and 92.48 per cent. (In town and village mayor elections they were 82.37 per cent and 87.02 per cent.) See Tokyo Metropolitan Election Administration Committee, *Shōwa 34nen shigatsu jikkō chihō senkyō no kiroku* (Tokyo, 1959), pp. 228, 252.

8. As in the case of assembly elections, the statistics for 1947 do not differentiate between the elections for the various municipal chief executives, that is, mayors of cities, special wards, towns, and villages.

9. High voting rates in 1955 and in 1959 occurred in Toyama (96.01 per cent and 94.05 per cent respectively), Tottori (95.39 per cent and 95.32 respectively), and Yamagata (95.56 per cent and 94.38 per cent respectively). Gumma, with the second highest voting rate in 1955 (95.66 per cent), ranked much lower in 1959 with 93.52 per cent, but was still considerably above the national average. The same was true of Fukushima, which ranked fourth in 1955 (95.31 per cent). Its 1959 voting rate was 93.49 per cent. Shimane, which had the highest rate in 1959 (95.40 per cent), had a less conspicuously high rate in 1955 (94.31 per cent). But this rate was nevertheless well above the national average. Similarly, Kumamoto, ranking third in 1959 (94.71 per cent), also had a voting rate which was higher than the national average in 1955 (94.21 per cent).

10. Of the most urbanized prefectures, Tokyo, Osaka, Kyoto, and Fukuoka had voting rates below the national average in both elections. Kanagawa, which had the lowest rate in 1955, rose above the national average in 1959 with a voting rate of 93.03 per cent. Aichi and Hyogo had voting rates above the average in both elections (Aichi, 92.63 per cent and 92.93 per cent; Hyogo, 94.80 per cent and 92.99 per cent), but neither of them ranked anywhere near the top. The rural prefectures of Aomori, Chiba, and Kochi, which had low rates in town and village assembly elections, tended to show low rates also in the town and village mayor elections of 1955 and 1959. Only Aomori's rate in 1959 (92.15 per cent) was above the national average. Even then it ranked only 22d among the 46 prefectures.

11. The lowest rates in 1955 occurred in Hokkaido (78.17 per cent), Hyogo (78.67 per cent), Kanagawa (79.28 per cent), Miyagi (79.41 per cent), and Tokyo (79.59 per cent); the lowest rates in 1959 in Miyagi (76.24 per cent), Tokyo (78.74 per cent), Osaka (79.24 per cent), Hyogo (79.53 per cent), and Chiba (80.78 per cent). Osaka, Hyogo, Tokyo, and Kanagawa are, of course, highly urbanized. Chiba adjoins Tokyo. Miyagi has a high percentage of inhabitants in primary industry but contains the important city of Sendai. It will be noted that some of these prefectures belonged to this category

only in one of the two elections. However, these prefectures (i.e., Hokkaido and Kanagawa in 1959 and Osaka and Chiba in 1955) had a voting rate well below the national average also in the other election. Nevertheless, it appears that the degree of urbanization is not the only factor influencing the voting rate in individual prefectures.

12. In addition to such prefectures as Yamagata, Fukushima, Yamanashi, and Gumma, high voting rates occurred in Gifu and Akita in 1955 and in Fukui and Kumamoto in 1959. These are all rural prefectures. But in 1955 Kagoshima, a predominantly rural prefecture, showed a conspicuously low voting rate of 75.56 per cent, thus emphasizing the existence of factors aside from the rural-urban dichotomy that may influence voting rates in certain prefectures or in certain elections. (In 1959 Kagoshima's rate in city mayor elections was 83.54 per cent.) In 1963 the voting rate in the 5 big cities was 67.55 per cent, in the remainder of the cities 81.78 per cent.

13. The prefectures with the highest voting rates in prefectural assembly elections were:

1955		1959	
Yamanashi	89.44%	Shimane	89.93%
Gumma	88.63	Yamanashi	89.97
Shimane	87.71	Gumma	87.44
Tittori	87.70	Fukui	87.41
Oita	87.29	Tottori	86.62

The prefectures with the lowest voting rates in prefectural assembly elections were:

1955		1959	
Tokyo	59.63%	Kyoto	67.22%
Kyoto	67.22	Tokyo	70.13
Osaka	68.28	Osaka	71.07
Kanagawa	68.66	Hyogo	71.26
Hyogo	70.61	Kanagawa	72.58

14. It happens occasionally that in prefectures without important urban centers (e.g., Niigata, Tokushima, and Oita in 1955, and Iwate, Niigata, and Oita in 1959) the *shibu* voting rate is slightly higher than the *gumbu* voting rate. But in prefectures with important urban centers, the difference between *shibu* and *gumbu* voting rates is often quite marked, as the following table shows:

	1955		1959	
	Shibu	*Gumbu*	*Shibu*	*Gumbu*
Tokyo	58.64%	75.39%	69.61%	79.41%
Osaka	65.59	86.54	70.31	83.76
Kanagawa	66.49	82.60	71.52	82.88
Aichi	72.12	83.13	72.89	82.94
Kyoto	63.65	82.84	64.58	83.31
Hyogo	64.56	84.88	67.51	84.78
Fukuoka	71.81	78.28	78.43	84.53

15. The highest voting rates occurred in the following rural prefectures:

	1955		1959
Oita	87.30%	Shimane	89.56%
Nagano	85.81	Fukui	86.51
Miyazaki	84.89	Wakayama	85.98
Mie	84.79	Saga	85.21
Akita	84.62	Miyazaki	85.18

The lowest voting rates occurred in the following prefectures:

	1955		1959
Tokyo	59.62%	Tokyo	70.12%
Osaka	68.28	Osaka	70.76
Kanagawa	68.32	Kanagawa	72.58
Fukuoka	74.17	Iwate	77.15
Hokkaido	77.86	Oita	79.60

There were no contests at the time of the unified local elections in these years in the urbanized prefectures of Aichi, Kyoto, and Hyogo. The gubernatorial elections in those prefectures showed the following rates:

Aichi	1/30/55: 75.34%	Kyoto 4/16/54: 61.17%	Hyogo 12/12/54: 61.30%
	1/2/59: 75.72%	3/17/58: 42.29%	11/12/58: 42.99%

(Based on Autonomy Ministry, Election Bureau, *Senkyo nenkan*, March 1960, p. 318, and December 1960, pp. 222ff.) If we take these elections into consideration, we find that the prefectures with the lowest voting rates were all urban prefectures.

16. For Tokyo, Kanagawa, and Osaka the voting rates were as follows:

	1955		1959	
	Gumbu	*Shibu*	*Gumbu*	*Shibu*
Tokyo	75.38%	58.59%	79.39%	69.61%
Kanagawa	83.52	66.27	82.88	72.52
Osaka	86.53	60.66	80.98	70.00

It is noteworthy that the politically important election of 1959 produced a relatively high *shibu* rate, thus reducing the usual gap.

17. The first statement is true for elections to the House of Representatives and to the House of Councilors. Only the House of Representatives elections of 1955 drew a slightly higher voting rate (75.84 per cent) than the gubernatorial election of the same year (74.85 per cent). But this rate was still lower than that in other local elections in 1955, including the prefectural assembly elections. The voting rate in elections to the House of Representatives fluctuated between 74 per cent and 77 per cent between 1951 and 1959.

As for the second statement, the highest voting rates in the House of Representatives elections of 1953 were to be found in Yamagata, Gumma, Shimane,

Nagano, Saga, Tottori, Fukushima, and Fukui. These prefectures—all rural in character—had a voting rate above 83 per cent, while the national average was 74.22 per cent. On the other hand, the lowest turnout occurred in Osaka, Kyoto, and Tokyo, followed by Kanagawa, Tokushima (the only rural prefecture in the group), and Hyogo. Aichi also ranked below the average. The situation was similar in 1955. The national average voting rate was 75.84 per cent. The 17 prefectures with a voting rate above 80 per cent were all rural prefectures, while Tokyo, Kyoto, Osaka, and Kanagawa had voting rates below 70 per cent. Hyogo (70.66 per cent) and Aichi (75.11 per cent) also were below the average. In the House of Representatives election of 1958, the picture remained relatively unchanged, although the national average voting rate increased to 76.99 per cent and Aichi had a voting rate above that average.

A comparison of *gumbu* and *shibu* voting rates in the House of Representatives elections of 1953, 1955, and 1958 shows the following picture:

	Gumbu	*Shibu*
1953	80.28%	66.06%
1955	80.60	71.90
1958	81.18	74.19

(Based on the Autonomy Ministry's *Senkyo nenkan,* March 1960, pp. 235 and 245; December 1960, p. 128.) See also Jun'ichi Kyogoku and Nobutaka Ike, *Urban-Rural Differences in Voting Behavior in Postwar Japan,* Stanford University Political Science Series No. 66 (1960), and Robert E. Ward, "Urban-Rural Differences and the Process of Political Modernization in Japan: A Case Study," in 9 *Economic Development and Cultural Change* (No. 1, Part II, October 1960), pp. 135ff.

18. The results of this poll can be found in *Toshi mondai,* Vol. 47, No. 3 (March 1956), pp. 106–7. This entire number is devoted to the study of the relations between citizens and city government.

19. See Allan B. Cole (editor and compiler), *Japanese Opinion Polls with Socio-Political Significance, 1947–1957* (Boston, 1960), p. 415. This volume contains also a number of other polls of interest for students of local politics.

20. In 1947, 231,121 candidates competed for 183,224 seats; in 1955—after the start of the mass amalgamation movement—55,152 candidates competed for 43,948 seats; in 1959, 39,085 candidates competed for 31,238 seats.

21. For example, in 1955 and 1959 no prefecture reached a ratio of 2:1. In both years Kagoshima Prefecture had the highest ratio (1.77 and 1.65 respectively), followed by Miyazaki Prefecture (1.70 and 1.61). Both prefectures are in Kyushu. In 1955 Fukui had the lowest ratio of candidates per seat (1.06); Shizuoka had the lowest ratio (1.10) in 1959. Tokyo had a ratio above the average in both elections (1.43 and 1.31), but the other urban prefectures showed ratios slightly below the average.

22. In 1955, 5,235 of the 5,283 town and village assemblymen who gained their seats in this manner were independents; in 1959, 2,238 assemblymen were elected without contest, 2,184 of them independents. Independents pre-

dominate in town and village assemblies in general, as shown on p. 398. But the proportion of independents is even higher for those elected without contest.

23. Here, too, the numbers of positions and candidates show the influence of the mass amalgamations. They were as follows:

	1947	1951	1955	1959
Positions	10,210	6,807	1,675	1,227
Candidates	19,957	12,846	3,092	2,333

24. All but seven of the mayors so chosen—612 out of 619 in 1955, 413 out of 420 in 1959—were independents. In 1963, 41 per cent of the town and village mayors were elected without contest.

25. The mass amalgamations resulted in an increase in the number of cities and city assembly seats. In 1951, 16,992 candidates competed for 7,626 seats; in 1955, 16,261 candidates competed for 8,716 seats; and in 1959, 15,281 candidates competed for 9,537 seats. The equivalent competition ratio in 1963 was not available at the time of this writing.

26. For example, in 1955 there were 5,235 uncontested winners of town and village assembly seats who were independents. Of these, 3,101 (59.5 per cent) were classified as pure independents, 1,839 as conservative independents, and 295 as progressive independents. In 1959, 1,211 (55.4 per cent) of the 2,184 independents, victorious without contest, were pure independents. On the city level in 1955, 35 out of 37 city assemblymen selected without contest were independents. Of these 35, 23 were classified as conservative independents, 1 was classified as a progressive independent, and 11 (31.4 per cent) were pure independents. In 1959 the contrast was even clearer. Of 44 uncontested winners 41 were independents. Thirty-three of these were conservative independents, 2 were progressive independents, and 6 (14.6 per cent) were pure independents. It will be noted that the percentage of pure independents seems to decrease. In 1963, 34 city assemblymen (0.27 per cent) won without contest.

27. The actual numbers were as follows:

	1947	1951	1955	1959
Positions	895	941	938	970
Candidates	2,182	2,932	2,289	1,914

Because the Tokyo wards are multi-member districts it is not necessary that the number of candidates is twice that of the number of seats to prevent uncontested elections. For example, if in a ward 60 candidates are nominated for the available 40 seats, an election has to be held although the ratio is only 1.5. In 1959 the actual overall ratio was 1.97.

28. The actual numbers were:

	1947	1951	1955	1959
Positions	204	182	172	175
Candidates	620	399	394	381

29. In 1955, 21 mayoral candidates were victorious without contest; 2 of them were Liberal Democrats, the remaining 19 were independents. Of these 19, 10 (52.6 per cent) were pure independents and 9 were conservative independents. In 1959, 27 of the 31 city mayors, selected without contest, were independents. (Two were Liberal Democrats and 2 Socialists.) Of the 27 independents, 10 (37 per cent) were pure independents, 15 were conservative independents, and 2 were progressive independents. The percentage of pure independents decreased in this case also. In 1963, 21 per cent of the city mayors were selected without contest.

30. The actual figures were:

	1947	1951	1955	1959
Positions	2,490	2,617	2,613	2,656
Candidates	7,115	6,010	5,536	4,860

31. On this point see Robert A. Scalapino and Junnosuke Masumi, *Parties and Politics in Contemporary Japan* (Berkeley, 1962), p. 121.

32. Based on statistics compiled by SCAP, Government Section, and published in mimeographed form ("The Elections of April 1947," p. 72), Independents won 173,196 of the 191,391 seats to be filled. Of the 183,224 assembly seats in towns and villages, 167,924, or 91.6 per cent, were taken by independents. The report indicates (p. 59) that 75 per cent of the independents were, in fact, supported by conservative parties.

33. In 1951, 170,279 seats were at stake. In 1955 the number of seats to be distributed was only 53,911, because the mass amalgations had reduced the number of villages and also because in many villages assemblymen were permitted by the Amalgamation Promotion Law to continue in office for an additional year.

34. The actual figures were:

	1955	1959
Pure independents	25,176	16,174
Conservative independents	14,715	11,920
Progressive independents	3,277	2,025
Total	43,168	30,119

35. The actual figures were:

	1955	1959
Pure independents	2,853	2,526
Conservative independents	3,729	4,557
Progressive independents	821	830
Total	7,403	7,913

36. While the two conservative parties together won 7.1 per cent of the seats in 1955, their successor, the Liberal Democratic Party, won 12.6 per cent of the seats in 1959. The Socialists, who had won 5.9 per cent of the seats in

1955, when they were still divided, captured 9.9 per cent of the seats in 1959, when they were reunited.

37. The actual figures were:

	1955	1959
Pure independents	173	72
Conservative independents	542	267
Progressive independents	142	80
Total	857	419

38. Both in 1955 and 1959 the five most urbanized prefectures fell below the national average. In 1955, independents occupied more than 50 per cent of the assembly seats in seven prefectures, all rural in character. In 1959, when the national average was 15.7 per cent, more than 25 per cent of the assembly members were independents in twelve rural prefectures. In Kagoshima, independents held 90 per cent of the seats in 1955, 33 per cent in 1959.

CHAPTER 16

1. See, for example, Chapter 10, pp. 209–15; Chapter 15, p. 377.

2. Villages also compete with one another in group solidarity. To heighten the appearance of solidarity, a village in Saitama Prefecture dropped aged and illiterate voters from the election register and thus achieved a turnout of 99.1 per cent in the elections of 1951. See *Nippon Times*, April 29, 1951.

3. Niike *buraku*, the object of the study on *Village Japan* by Beardsley, Hall, and Ward, competed with 29 other *buraku* for the 16 seats on the assembly of the village of Kamo. It had about 70 votes, but about 100 votes were necessary to elect an assemblyman. Cooperative arrangements were worked out with four other *buraku* in the same *oaza*. The five *buraku* together elected three candidates, furnished by the largest *buraku* and "dutifully supported by the voters of the other *buraku*" (p. 410).

4. See, for example, Kanagawa Prefecture, *Hakone kanko chitai jittai chōsa hōkokusho* (Yokohama, 1953), Vol. I, p. 16. (This interesting survey was prepared by a team under the direction of Prof. Tanaka Jiro of Tokyo University.) Also *Village Japan*, pp. 412f.

5. *Village Japan*, p. 413.

6. In 1955 there were 27,815 candidates for town and village assemblies, nominated by *suisen dotoke*, while 29,259 others submitted their own notification of candidacy. In 1959 the corresponding figures were 19,258 and 20,590. (Unless another source is stated, statistical data in this chapter are from Autonomy Board, Election Bureau, *Chihō senkyo kekka shirabe, 1955 and 1959.*) The figures for city assembly elections are given later in this chapter.

7. *Village Japan*, p. 405.

8. To cite a perhaps extreme example, in 1953 it was found that three-fourths of the assembly members of the village of Sengoku near Hakone—well known to foreign tourists for its splendid golf courses—had the same family

name. (See the survey of the Hakone Region cited in note 4 above, especially Vol. I, p. 16, and Vol. V, p. 26.)

9. From a survey carried out under the direction of Professors Yamaoka and Yamada of Shimane University and published in 1960 by the Election Administration Committee and Fair Election Promotion Movement of Shimane Prefecture under the title *Shimane ken ni okeru seiji ishiki to tohyō kōdō*. A follow-up was published under the same title in 1961.

According to the same survey, only 13.9 per cent of the respondents throughout the prefecture replied in the negative to the question whether they had received requests to vote in a certain way in elections. (The survey was not limited to any specific type of election.) In addition to the cases in which a *buraku* meeting had decided on the candidate for whom to vote, requests came from "influential persons" (*yūryokusha*); from relatives, school friends, and other friends; from candidates or their campaigners; from local youths' or women's organizations; and from such occupational groups as agricultural cooperatives, fishing cooperatives, and labor unions. When asked with reference to village elections whether they believed that recommendation by the *buraku* was a good thing, 37.6 per cent answered affirmatively and 43 per cent negatively; 16 per cent felt that both *buraku*-recommended candidates and "independent" candidates were all right, and 3.4 per cent did not know how to reply.

See also Kyogoku Jun'ichi and Masumi Junnosuke, "*Seiji ishiki ni okeru zenshin to teitai*," in the 1953 Annual of the Japan Political Science Association, p. 128; Sugiura Mimpei, "*Waga machiwa senkyo no hanazakari*," in *Chūō Kōron*, Vol. 47, No. 6 (June 1959), p. 240.

10. All voting is done by writing in names. When this was still done by Japanese brush, the voter would press the palm of his hand on the wet writing to secure proof of correct voting. The same or similar tactics are applied in national elections. In connection with the general elections of 1958 a voting overseer related that at the polling place to which he was assigned, 15 voters asked others to write for them, and 7 of these "announced aloud the names of their candidates for all to hear. They did so with the obvious intention of letting others know for whom they were voting, although it was quite evident that they could write if they wanted to." Quoted from *Mainichi*, May 5, 1958, in Kenzo Yoshimura, "Personal Connections as an Important Factor in the Determination of Voting Behavior in Japan," *Waseda Political Studies*, No. III (1960), p. 47.

11. Robert E. Ward, "Urban-Rural Differences in the Process of Political Modernization in Japan: A Case Study," 9 *Economic Development and Cultural Change* (No. 1, Part II, October 1960), p. 145 (hereafter cited as Ward, *Urban-Rural Differences*). The interested reader will find this case study valuable in adding details—and at times qualifications—to the generalizations offered in this chapter.

12. Even *buraku* within the same village may differ in their "conservatism," and this may be reflected in their voting rates. See, e.g., International Chris-

tian University, Social Science Research Institute, *Nōson no kenryoku kōzō* (Tokyo, 1959), p. 403. In the survey in Shimane Prefecture, mentioned earlier, only 8 per cent of the respondents in Matsue City and 18.4 per cent in the fishing village of Gozu stated that they had been requested by "influential persons" to cast their vote in a certain way; in fishing, mountain, and more remote farming villages up to 56.5 per cent of the respondents considered *buraku* recommendation of candidates a good thing.

13. *Village Japan*, p. 365.

14. The quote is from John B. Cornell, "Matsunagi, The Life and Social Organization of a Japanese Mountain Community," in *Two Japanese Villages*, University of Michigan Center for Japanese Studies (Occasional Papers No. 5), p. 210.

15. Regarding the influence of the land reform, see Royama Masamichi, *Nōson jichi no hembō* (Tokyo, 1948), p. 397. For a discussion of the differences between the honorary, non-professional "elder" type of pre-reform village mayor and his salaried, civil servant type post-reform counterpart, see *Village Japan*, p. 365.

16. In 1955 this was done by 12,716 out of 16,374 candidates, in 1959 by 12,627 out of 15,334 candidates.

These figures do not include candidacies in Tokyo wards and in the five big cities. In these units the percentage of *suisen dotoke* dwindles into insignificance. In the big cities only 24 out of 857 candidates in 1955 and 12 out of 718 candidates in 1959 did not submit their own notification. In the Tokyo wards the corresponding figures were 54 out of 2,302 in 1955 and 43 out of 1,922 in 1959.

17. See Chapter 15, p. 536.

18. Ward, *Urban-Rural Differences*, p. 152.

19. A study of the voters of Meguro-ku in the Yamate area showed that 97.3 per cent of them had moved into the *ku* since 1925, more than half of them in the decade between 1942 and 1952. Many of the newcomers had previously lived in other Tokyo wards. Twenty per cent of them had come to Meguro from outside Tokyo. See Isomura Eiichi, "Daitoshi ni okeru shimin to senkyo: Tokyo-to no baai," *Toshi mondai*, Vol. 46, No. 3 (March, 1955), p. 15.

20. A study of Nerima-ku, cited in the above-mentioned article by Professor Isomura, shows the following picture in this regard:

Organization	Frequency of Membership	Degree of Participation
Chōnaikai	21.8%	37.6
Tonarigumi	11.8	30.6
P.T.A.	45.0	39.3
Occupational organizations	13.1	68.9
Agricultural organizations	7.2	62.5
Religious organizations	15.4	64.7
Hobby clubs	12.7	78.5
Women's organizations	12.2	58.8
Others	6.8	86.8

21. In 1951, for example, the average voting rate for the 23 wards was 75.3 per cent. The highest voting rates occurred in Arakawa ward (83.6 per cent), Daito and Sumida wards (83.2 per cent), and Edogawa ward (82.6 per cent). At the other end of the scale were such wards as Setagaya (66.3 per cent), Nakano (68.4 per cent), Meguro (68.6 per cent), Shinjuku and Minato (each 69 per cent), and Suginami (69.2 per cent). As Professor Isomura points out, in wards of the latter type—the habitat of white-collar workers and of the intelligentsia—the influence of the neighborhood is stronger on women, whose life is more likely confined to it, than on men. This is reflected in the uncommon fact that in these wards the female voting rate in ward assembly elections is higher than the male voting rate.

The data are taken from the article by Isomura cited in note 19 above. See also Tokyo Metropolis, Election Administration Committee, *Chihō senkyo no kiroku* (Tokyo, 1951); *Municipal Yearbook 1952*, p. 59. For a characterization of Daito ward, see Royama Masamichi, *Seiji ishiki no kaibō* (Tokyo, 1949), pp. 24ff.

22. (Berkeley, 1958.) The description of the neighborhood is on p. 14; the narration of the events in 1951 is a paraphrase of footnote 240, on p. 454. The nomenclature has been changed to make it consistent with that employed in the present study. Thus a "borough" in Dore's terminology is here called a "ward," and a "ward" is called a "neighborhood." The name Shitayama-chō is not the real name of the neighborhood but a composite to indicate that its characteristics put it betwixt and between Shitamachi and Yamate.

23. Ward, *Urban-Rural Differences*, p. 151.

24. *Ibid.*

25. Tōsei Chōsakai, *Dai toshi ni okeru chiiki seiji no kōzō—Suginamiku ni okeru seiji, gyosei, shimin* (Tokyo, 1960), p. 84.

26. Dore, *City Life in Japan*, p. 282.

27. *Urban-Rural Differences*, p. 159. This may serve as a reminder that elements of the conservative pattern are also present, often in a somewhat changed form, in the West. A new element, not accounted for in the foregoing, is the recent emergence of a militant politico-religious organization, the Sōka Gakkai, which puts forward its own candidates in local and national elections. In 1963 the Kōsei Remmei, the political arm of the Sōka Gakkai, captured 10.3 per cent of the assembly seats in the big cities and 5.7 per cent of the assembly seats in other cities and in the Tokyo wards.

28. As noted in Chapter 15, this was 11 per cent in 1955 and 17.7 per cent in 1959. In 1963 it was 21 per cent. As before, there was a contest for the mayoral position in the two big cities that elected their mayors in 1963.

29. It should be recalled that city mayors were directly elected for the first time in 1947. Where the incumbent was a candidate he won in 61.2 per cent of the cases in 1955 and in 70.3 per cent of the cases in 1959.

30. For a description of the gubernatorial election in Osaka prefecture and the mayoral election in Osaka City in 1959, see Nishigawa Seiji, "Osaka-fu chiji, shichō senkyo no jittai," *Toshi mondai*, Vol. 50, No. 8 (August 1959), pp. 22ff.

31. John B. Cornell observes in his study of the mountain village of Matsunagi that "very few persons are interested enough in politics outside the *mura* to attend the electioneering meetings held at the school during a prefectural campaign." (This study is cited in note 14 above; the quote is from p. 210.) For the *Jiji Press* poll, see Chapter 15, p. 388.

32. *Village Japan*, p. 427.

33. *Ibid.*, p. 432. Ward's description of the *jiban* of prewar national politicians is in general applicable to the *jiban* of present prefectural politicians. For a lucid explanation of *jiban*, see also Nobutaka Ike, *Japanese Politics: An Introductory Study* (New York, 1957), p. 197.

34. For graphs showing the electoral support of successful candidates, see Kawaguchi Tei, "Chōson gappei to senkyo jiban," in *Nōgyō sōgō kenkyū*, Vol. 14, No. 2 (April 1960), p. 239. (*Nōgyō sōgō kenkyū* is published by a research agency of the Ministry of Agriculture and Forestry.)

35. It will be recalled that in this movement towns and villages were merged with adjacent cities or combined to form new cities. When this happened to all towns and villages within a *gun*, the *gun* disappeared altogether. When only some towns and villages within a *gun* became part of a city—whether an already existing city or a "new city," created by amalgamation —the *gun* shrank in area and population, and the number of assemblymen it elected to the prefectural assembly decreased. A particular problem arose in this case when the *gun* had shrunk to such an extent that it had become too small to serve as election district altogether. The Public Offices Election Law in its original version authorized the prefectures to combine several small election districts by bylaw. In 1958 the law was amended to make such combinations mandatory when the population of an election district had become less than one-half of the quotient arrived at by dividing the total population of the prefecture by the total number of prefectural assembly seats. When the population of the election district was higher than one-half of the quotient but lower than the full quotient, the prefectures were authorized but not obligated to combine the district with another district. At the time of the 1959 elections many remnants had not yet been combined with other districts.

36. For example, the difference between the two voting rates was 5.5 per cent in Adachi ward, 5.7 per cent in Daito ward, 6.8 per cent in Katsushika ward, 6.9 per cent in Edogawa ward, 7.1 per cent in Sumida ward, and 7.6 per cent in Koto ward. All these wards are in Shitamachi. In the Yamate wards of Minato, Shinjuku, Shinagawa, and Ohta the difference was less than 1 per cent.

37. For example, the difference was 2.9 per cent in Daito ward, 0.4 per cent in Katsushika ward, 1.1 per cent in Sumida ward, and 2.4 per cent in Koto ward. On the other hand, in Minato ward the difference was 6.3 per cent, in Shinagawa ward 6.7 per cent, in Ohta ward 7.2 per cent, and in Setagaya ward 10.3 per cent. The exception in the Yamate area occurred in Shinjuku ward, where the ward assembly elections surprisingly attracted a slightly higher percentage (0.8) than the gubernatorial elections. The reasons for this

deviation, which may have resulted from local factors, need further investigation. The above figures are based on Tokyo Metropolitan Election Administration Committee, *Report on the Local Elections of April 1959 and the House of Councilors Elections of June 1959*, especially pp. 92, 162, 251.

38. The first elections of governors in 1947 and the Tokyo elections more generally show a higher ratio. In 1955 four contests were between three candidates, Tokyo had six candidates, and two elections were uncontested. The remaining 14 contests were between two candidates. In 1959 five contests were between three candidates; in one case there were four candidates; Tokyo had nine; and one election was uncontested. Twelve contests were between two candidates.

39. Isomura and Hoshino, *Chihōjichi tokuhon* (Tokyo, 1961), p. 203.

40. By contrast, only 10 of the 40 new contenders in 1959 and 10 out of the 31 new contenders in 1955 were successful. If we look at gubernatorial elections which were held in between the unified local elections, a similar picture emerges. Between January 1, 1953, and December 31, 1957, 29 such elections took place: in 10 cases because the governor's tenure of office expired (the governor not having been elected at the time of a unified election) and in 19 cases because of resignations. In the first-mentioned 10 cases, 7 of the incumbents ran again, 6 being reelected. In the other 19 cases, 14 of the governors who had resigned ran again and 9 were reelected. Autonomy Board Election Bureau, *Senkyo nenkan 1953–1957* (March 1960), p. 317.

41. See SCAP, Government Section, *Political Reorientation of Japan*, Vol. 1, p. 331.

42. Kawaguchi, "Chōson gappei to senkyo jiban," p. 238. See also *Asahi shimbun*, April 20, 1959.

43. Articles 74 to 88. It should be noted that the laws that provided the basis for the mass amalgamation drive also temporarily created new types of direct demands, including a type of referendum that can supersede assembly resolutions. In this regard, see Chapter 9.

44. For example, there were 221 direct demands for dissolution of assemblies or for dismissal of chief executives or assemblymen between January 1, 1952, and May 31, 1956; only one—the demand for dismissal of the ward chief of Shibuya ward in Tokyo—occurred in a local entity classified as "city." With the creation of new cities, the number of direct demands in cities increased somewhat. Of the 155 direct demands of the same type which occurred between June 1, 1956, and May 31, 1960, four occurred in cities. See Autonomy Ministry, Election Bureau, *Senkyo nenkan 1958–1959* (Tokyo, December 1960), p. 233.

45. Isomura and Hoshino, *Chihōjichi tokuhon*, p. 99. The statistics in this section are based mainly on publications of the Autonomy Ministry, namely, *Senkyo nenkan 1953–1957* (March 1960), *Senkyo nenkan 1958–1959* (December 1960), and *Chihō jichi geppō*, No. 23 (November 1956) and No. 29 (December 1960). Some of the data regarding the individual cases are from *Chihō jichi shiryō*, No. 146 (April 1957), pp. 6ff. The *Chihō jichi shiryō* is

published monthly by a private research organization in Tokyo called the Chihō Jichi Kenkyushō.

46. The Supreme Court decision is to be found in *Supreme Court Reports, Civil Cases,* Vol. 15, No. 7, p. 832; the second case was pending at the Tokyo High Court as Case No. 1 of 1954 when it was withdrawn.

47. From a round-table discussion of leading jurists, translated from the February 1952 issue of the legal periodical *Jurist,* in *Contemporary Japan,* Vol. XXI, Nos. 10–12 (1953), pp. 361f.

48. On this point, see my article "Local Government in Japan: Reform and Reaction," *Far Eastern Survey,* XXIII (1954), pp. 97ff.

49. This function of the prefecture is discussed in my paper "The Japanese Prefecture: A Pivot of Centralization," mimeographed (presented at the meeting of the American Political Science Association in 1956). This paper is discussed by Takagi Shosaku in *Toshi mondai,* Vol. 48, No. 4 (April 1957), pp. 107ff.

50. See George O. Totten, "Labor and Agrarian Disputes in Japan Following World War I," in 9 *Economic Development and Cultural Change* (No. 1, Part II, October 1960), p. 187.

Bibliographical Note

The treatment of Japanese local government in Western languages has hitherto been confined to articles in periodicals and to sections of books covering wider topics. On the other hand, the Japanese literature on the subject is enormous. There are numerous treatises on local government as such and quite a few monographs on specific aspects of local government. The periodical literature on the subject is staggering in its quantity and variety. In order to make this bibliographical note useful not only to specialists on Japan who can read Japanese but also to those interested in comparative local government, a double standard has been applied: articles and pertinent sections of books written in English have been included, while similar material in Japanese has been excluded.

Bibliographies

Material in Western languages is listed in Borton, Eliséeff, Lockwood, and Pelzel, *A Selected List of Books and Articles on Japan* (Cambridge, 1954), which also cites the standard bibliographies in English, French, and German. *The Far Eastern Bibliography,* published until 1954 in each August issue of the *Far Eastern Quarterly* and later as a separate September issue of the *Quarterly* and its successor, the *Journal of Asian Studies,* contains a section on Japan. Fred W. Riggs, "Notes on Literature Available for the Study of Comparative Public Administration," *American Political Science Review,* XLVIII (1954), 515–37, has some entries on Japan. I published a bibliography on "Japanese Local Government" in the same *Review* (L, 1956, pp. 1126–33) as part of an article by Harold Zink entitled "Selected Materials for a Comparative Study of Local Government." The present bibliographical note is a greatly extended and revised version of that article.*

Those who can read Japanese will find the Bibliographical Series of the

---

*I express my thanks to the American Political Science Association for its permission to use the earlier bibliography as the basis for the present note.

University of Michigan Center for Japanese Studies of great value. John W. Hall, *Japanese History: A Guide to Japanese Reference and Research Materials* (Ann Arbor, 1954) emphasizes the period before the Meiji Restoration. Robert E. Ward, *A Guide to Japanese Reference and Research Materials in the Field of Political Science* (Ann Arbor, 1950) has appeared in a revised edition, co-authored by Robert E. Ward and Hajime Watanabe, which has the title *Japanese Political Science: A Guide to Japanese Reference and Research Materials* (Ann Arbor, 1961). The focus of the earlier edition was on the period prior to the Occupation, while the revised edition stresses the results of Japanese scholarship since 1945.* Sixty-six per cent of the entries in the revised edition are new and did not appear in the first edition. The revised edition contains a list of bibliographies on local government and administration (p. 22) and deals in Chapter XXIV with local government and politics on eleven pages that contain more than 100 entries. Other chapters, especially those on constitutional law, administrative law, and public administration also have entries of interest to students of local government. The present bibliographical note overlaps, of course, to some extent the pertinent parts of *Japanese Political Science*. I shall be glad if it can be considered, aside from the coverage of English material, as a useful supplement to that admirable work.

The Union of Japanese Societies of Law and Politics has published annually since 1950 in English the *Japanese Science Review: Law and Politics*, which in some years takes the form of an annotated bibliography; local government is treated primarily under administrative law, but the entries are broader than this heading indicates. In Japanese, bibliographies of current publications appear, without annotation, as appendixes to various periodicals which are listed below. In 1952, when the occupation reforms were first subjected to intensive reconsideration, the National Association of City Mayors published *Chihō seido kaikaku ni kansuru ikenshū* (A Collection of Opinions on the Reform of the Local Government System), which contains synopses of articles that appeared in 1951 and 1952. While not limited to local government, *Sengo hōgaku bunken sō mokuroku* (Bibliography of Postwar Legal Literature), published since 1954 by the editors of the law journal *Horitsu jihō* (Law Times) should be mentioned. It lists monographs as well as articles primarily in the field of law, but includes important works in the fields of politics, economics, and sociology. A mimeographed bibliography of local government, *Chihō jichi bunken mokuroku*, based on the library holdings of the Tokyo Institute for Municipal Research (Tokyo Shisei Chōsakai), acquired between 1945 and March 1955, was published in that year by the Social Science Research Institute of Tokyo University (Tokyo Daigaku Shakai Kagaku Kenkyū-sho). The Tokyo Institute for Municipal Research publishes from time to

---

*Wartime and postwar research is also emphasized in Professor Ward's "Survey of Political Science Literature on Japan," *American Political Science Review,* XLVI (1952), 201–13.

time bibliographies on specific subjects such as town and village amalgamation (1956), urban sociology (1959), and neighborhood associations (1960). Articles on local government in major Tokyo newspapers, such as *Asahi, Mainichi, Yomiuri, Nihon keizai,* and *Tokyo Times,* are indexed in *Chihō jichi kankei shimbun kiji sakuin,* edited by the library of the Tokyo Metropolitan Assembly. A steady flow of official and semi-official publications is produced by various governmental agencies on the national and local level. Much of this material is very useful, but it has always been difficult to keep track of it. Ward and Watanabe deal with "Guides to Official Publications" on pp. 13–15 and with "Official Publications of Local Governments" on pp. 188–91.* On the national level the National Diet Library's *Kanchō kankōbutsu sōgō mokuroku* (General Catalog of Government Publications), published annually since 1952, is most useful, although coverage lags two years behind the date of publication. As for local publications, I would echo some statements by Ward and Watanabe, namely that there are records on practically everything, that the best sources of information are the working libraries of prefectural and major municipal governments and that local authorities are most helpful in facilitating the work of the serious researcher, especially if he has an introduction from some other authority. Ward and Watanabe give a suggestive list for several major jurisdictions (Tokyo Metropolis, Kyoto Prefecture, and Kyoto City), and other examples are given later in the present Note.

Periodicals

One of the oldest and best of the Japanese periodicals dealing specifically with local government is *Toshi mondai* (Municipal Problems), now in its 54th volume. It is published monthly by the Tokyo Institute of Municipal Research. It contains articles of high quality that deal primarily with problems of public administration. During recent years articles on local politics in the broadest sense have appeared in it with increasing frequency. Some issues deal with a single topic, e.g., problems of civic organizations (October 1953), city planning (February 1954), housing (March 1954), citizens and local elections (March 1955), the relationship between city administration and citizens (March 1956), problems of newly established cities (May 1956), the local elections of 1959 (August 1959) or the use of leisure time (February 1960). Each number contains a valuable section on current affairs and a topically arranged list of articles in Japanese and Western periodicals. Similar in many ways is *Toshi mondai kenkyū* (Journal of Municipal Problems), published since 1949 by the Toshi Mondai Kenkyūkai (Association on Municipal Problems), an organization sponsored by the Osaka Municipal Government.† Here

---

*The International House of Japan Library News also deals in its issue of October 1963 (No. 21) with Government Publications.

†Where a publication shows both a Japanese and an English title—as in the case with the *Journal*—the English title is used in this bibliography, whether it is an exact translation of the Japanese title or not.

the emphasis on practical administrative problems is somewhat heavier and the focus is often on problems in the Osaka area.

The legal and administrative aspects of local government are almost exclusively the subject of *Jichi kenkyū* (Studies of Self-government), which has been published monthly since 1925 by the Ryōsho Fukyūkai (Association for the Distribution of Good Books). It regularly contains articles by central government officials—in addition to contributions by noted academic authorities—and an appendix summarizing new laws, ordinances, regulations, and notifications from central governmental agencies, especially the Autonomy Ministry and its predecessors, to the prefectural governments. The semi-official national associations of local governments publish monthly a number of periodicals. Thus the National Association of Governors publishes *Todofuken tenbō* (Prefectural Prospects); the National Association of City Mayors publishes *Shisei* (City Government); and the National Association of Town and Village Mayors publishes *Jichi kōron* (Self-government Forum). The last-named association also publishes the *Chōson shūhō* (Town and Village Weekly). *Tōsei* (Metropolitan Government), published monthly since 1955 by the Tōsei Chōsakai (Metropolitan Government Research Association), deals with problems of Tokyo Metropolis.* Monthly publications under the auspices of the Autonomy Ministry—formerly the Local Autonomy Agency and the Autonomy Board— are *Chihō jichi* (Local Self-government), edited by the Chihō Jichi Seido Kenkyūkai (Association for the Study of the Local Self-government System), and *Jichi jihō* (Local Self-government Review), edited by the Chihō Zaimu Kyōkai (Local Finance Association). Both appear monthly (since 1948) and both contain specialized articles on current issues of local administration and finance, designed primarily for the information of local government officials. *Jichi ronshū* (Collection of Essays on Self-government) appears at irregular intervals, normally two to four per year. It is published by the Jichi Kenkyūkai, a research association sponsored by the Osaka Prefectural Government. Each issue is devoted to a timely topic such as regionalism (October 1954 and February 1959), local administrative commissions (March 1956), the local finance system (September 1956), the prefectural system (June 1957), direct demands (April 1959), the local public service (December 1959), or local finance accounting (two issues in September 1961). Each subject is introduced by one or two articles, followed by a report of a round-table discussion of experts and by a collection of pertinent material, including at times, in addition to official documents, excerpts from the literature or from newspaper reports on the subject in question.

An independent periodical, published two or three times a month by a private organization, the Chihō Jichi Kenkyūjo (Local Self-government Research Institute), in *Chihō jichi shiryō* (Materials on Local Self-government). Its 16 pages frequently contain reports on actual occurrences in the admin-

---

*Regarding some of the research reports published by the same association, see 46–51. See also the earlier edition of this guide, pp. 20, 43ff; Hall, *Japanese History*,

istration and politics of various local entities and thus supply a welcome counterbalance to the often overly legal, theoretical, or abstract treatment of other periodicals. The Japan Socialist Party issues *Chihō seiji* (Local Politics) and the Japan Communist Party *Gikai to jichitai* (Assemblies and Local Entities), both appearing monthly. The National Federation of City and Ward Election Administration Committees has published bimonthly since 1952 *Senkyo jihō* (Election Review). It carries research reports, judicial decisions, and other materials in the field of local elections.

Of course, articles on local government are often found also in periodicals of wider scope. The legal aspects are considered in the various law reviews, sometimes in special issues devoted to a topic of local government.* Thus *Kōhō kenkyū* (Public Law Review), the semi-annual organ of the Japanese Association of Public Law, devoted its issue of October 1953 (No. 9) to a symposium on local government; *Jurist* dealt in its issue of August 15, 1960 (No. 208) with the court decisions regarding local public peace ordinances; and *Hōritsu jiho* (Law Times) considered the problem of the election or appointment of the chiefs of the Tokyo wards in its issue of May 1962 (No. 390). The *Dōshisha hōgaku* (Dōshisha Law Review) and other law reviews also frequently contain articles of interest to the political scientist. Among the journals in the fields of political science, economics, and sociology, the venerable *Kokka gakkai zasshi* (Journal of the Political Science Association), published monthly since 1887 at Tokyo University and now serving as the official organ of the Japanese Political Science Association, is of particular importance. The *Seiji gakkai nempō* (Annuals of the Japanese Political Science Association) devotes each yearly issue to a specific subject (for example, "Japanese Politics under the Occupation," or "Pressure Groups in Japan") and often reflects recent trends in political science research in Japan. The quarterly organ of the Japanese Sociological Society, *Shakaigaku hyōron* (Sociological Review), and the bimonthly publication of the Institute of Social Science of Tokyo University, *Shakai kagaku kenkyū* (Journal of Social Science), frequently contain articles of political interest. So does *Waseda seiji keizaigaku zasshi* (Waseda Journal of Political Science and Economics). The Graduate Division of Political Science of Waseda University also publishes, in English, *Waseda Political Studies*.† Similar publications in English with occasional articles of interest to the student of local government in general or local finance in particular are the *Kyoto University Economic Review*

* A list of law reviews is in Ward and Watanabe, *Japanese Political Science*, pp. 46–51. See also the earlier edition of this guide, pp. 20, 43ff; Hall, *Japanese History*, p. 71f; *Japanese Science Review*, No. 3 (1952), pp. vii–ix. Japanese guides to periodical literature, including legal periodicals, are listed in Ward and Watanabe, *Japanese Political Science*, pp. 15–20.

†The issue of October 1952 contained articles entitled "Development of Local Self-government in Japan" by Sato Tatsuo, and "The Problem of Special Cities in Japan" by Goto Ichiro. The issue in 1960 (no month indicated) contained an election survey in an urban and a rural area.

and the *Osaka Economic Papers,* published by the Economics Department
of Kyoto and Osaka Universities.*

Yearbooks and Statistical Literature

   A basic source for statistics on a broad number of subjects is the official
Nihon tōkei nenkan (Statistical Yearbook of Japan), issued by the Bureau of
Statistics in the Prime Minister's Office. The postwar series, beginning in
1949, identifies the data in Japanese and English. The results of the quinquen-
nial censuses are published by the same bureau as *Kokusei chōsa hōkoku*
(Report on the Nation Census), preceded by an indication of the census
year (e.g., 1950 or 1955). From 1948 until 1954, the Chihō Jichi Kenkyūkai
(Local Self-government Research Association), an organization consisting
primarily of officials of the Autonomy Board, edited the *Chihō jichi nenkan*
(Local Autonomy Yearbook). It contained an account of developments during the preceding year in the fields of administration, finance, personnel, and
elections, the gist of new laws and directives to local officials, a detailed
chronology, and pertinent statistical data. *Nihon toshi nenkan* (Municipal
Yearbook of Japan), published originally by the Tokyo Institute of Municipal
Research and since 1955 (Vol. 17) by the National Association of City Mayors,
is a treasure-house of information and statistics regarding city government
and its functions and finances. *Senkyo nenkan* (Election Yearbook), published
by the Election Bureau of the Autonomy Ministry, contains detailed data
on national and local elections (including those based on direct demands),
held during the period covered by each issue, as well as a résumé of changes
in election laws and of proposals for electoral reform. This yearbook has appeared since 1950 at irregular intervals. In 1960, two issues were published;
the March issue covered the period between 1953 and 1957, the December
issue the period 1958–59. The same bureau also publishes a detailed report
following each unified local election—that is, at four-year intervals—under
the title *Chihō senkyo kekka shirabe* (Survey of the Results of Local Elections).

   As indicated earlier, there are many other reports of an official or semi-
official nature published by governmental agencies at the various levels. Only
a few can be mentioned here. Of fundamental importance to the field of local
finance is the Autonomy Ministry's *Chihō zaisei no jōkyō hōkoku* (Report on
the State of Local Finance). The same agency's *Chihōzei no genjō bunseki,*
published irregularly, is, as the title indicates, an analysis of the actual situation of local taxation. The ministry also publishes *Jichi geppō* (Monthly Report
on Self-government), containing regulations and statistics on specific topics.
A small handbook presenting statistical data of a general nature is the min-

   * On local finance, see, for example, Kambe Masao, "Independence of Local Fi-
nance," *Kyoto University Economic Review,* XXIV (1954), 1–15, and Kinoshita
Kazuo, "Current Problems of Local Finance in Japan," *Osaka Economic Papers,*
II (1954), 41–52.

istry's *Jichi benran* (Self-government Handbook). The Economic Planning Board publishes in English monthly reports as well as the yearly *Economic Survey of Japan,* which contains sections dealing with public (including local) finance. The annual report of the Ministry of Education, *Education in Japan,* also appears in an English edition. (There is also a yearly graphic presentation of the report under the same title.) The Supreme Court publishes the *Gyōsei jiken soshō nenkan* (Yearbook of Administrative Law Cases).

On the prefectural level, there are first the annual statistical reports, usually issued as *X ken tōkeisho,* with "X" as the name of the prefecture (Statistical Yearbook of X Prefecture), and their summary versions, entitled variously *X ken tōkei tekiyō* (Statistical Abstract of X Prefecture) or *X ken sei ichiran* (A Glance at the Government of X Prefecture), or *X ken sei yōran* (Handbook of the Government of X Prefecture), or *X ken gaiyō* (Outline of X Prefecture). There are also more specific reports on the administrative organization, the budget, and a variety of functions. The big cities and many other cities, and even some towns and villages, publish similar reports. The Election Administration Committees of prefectures and large cities often publish detailed statistical reports on specific elections. Examples are Tokyo Metropolitan Election Administration Committee, *Chihō senkyo no kiroku* (Record of Local Elections) and Kyoto City Election Administration Committee, *Kyoto shichō senkyo kekka shirabe* (Survey of the Results of the Election of the Mayor of Kyoto City).

Historical Material

Within the scope of this note it is not possible to do justice to the richness of the material on the history of local government or on the history of individual units that is available in Japanese. The reader is referred to John W. Hall's *Japanese History,* mentioned above, and to his "Materials for the Study of Local History in Japan: Pre-Meiji Records," *Occasional Papers of the University of Michigan Center for Japanese Studies,* No. 3 (Ann Arbor, 1952). The original version of Robert Ward's bibliography and, to a lesser degree, the revised version also contain references to material for the post-Meiji period. (In the revised version, see especially pp. 182–84.) Yamagata Aritomo, often considered the founder of the Meiji local government system, gave his account of its establishment in *Chōhei seido oyobi jichi seido kakuritsu no enkaku* (History of the Establishment of the Conscription and Self-government Systems), which is part of *Meiji kensei keizai shiron* (Historical essays on Meiji constitutional government and economy), published by the Kokka Gakkai in 1919. A more detailed account of the establishment and development of the Meiji system can be found in *Jichi gojūnenshi* (History of Fifty Years of Self-government), published in 1941 by the Tokyo Institute of Municipal Research. The compiler of this work, Kikegawa Hiroshi, published his subsequent research on the subject in 1955 under the title *Meiji chihō jichi seido no seiritsu katei* (The Establishment of the Meiji System of Local Government).

A unique collection of materials regarding the prefectures of the early Meiji era has recently become available on microfilm. This is the *Fuken shiryō* (Materials on Prefectures), collected by the various prefectural governments under directions of the cabinet from 1874 on. The materials consist of 2,166 volumes, each containing about 300 handwritten pages (378 reels on microfilm). Arranged by prefectures, they cover such categories as history, geography, demography, folk customs, government and politics, law, tax systems, budgets, military services, police and security, education, agriculture, and industry. Also included is a political history of the Meiji era.

Documents pertaining to the establishment and development of the prefectural system were published in 1941 by the Jichi Shinkō Chūōkai (Central Association for the Promotion of Self-government) under the auspices of the Home Ministry, in a massive volume entitled *Fukenseido shiryō* (Materials on the Prefectural System). Older works on the development of the Meiji system are Miyatake Gaiketsu, *Fuhanken seishi* (History of the System of Urban Prefectures, Fiefs, and Rural Prefectures), published in 1884, and Omori Shoichi and Ichiki Kitukuro, *Shichōson seishikō* (A Volume on the History of the City, Town, and Village system), published in 1916.

The effect of the establishment of the town and village system on the traditional village communities has engaged the interests of a number of scholars. Kaino Michitaka, *Iriai no kenkyū* (A Study of Village Commons, 2d ed., 1949) is something of a classic in the field. Recently, Chiba Masaji probed the development of their relationship in *Gakku no kenkyū: Kokka kenryoku to sonraku kyōdōtai* (A Study of School Districts: National Power and Village Community, 1962). Fujita Takeo's *Nihon chihō zaisei hattatsushi* (History of the Development of Japanese Local Finance, 2d ed. 1951) is a standard work on its subject.

In English, an unpublished M.A. thesis by George O. Totten, III, deals with *Japanese Municipal Government under Meiji and Taisho, 1868–1925* (Columbia University, 1949). Okuma Shigenobu, *Fifty Years of New Japan* (New York, 1909) includes an essay on local government by S. Shimizu. Pertinent material may also be found in Walter W. McLaren, "Japanese Government Documents," *Transactions of the Asiatic Society of Japan*, Vol. 42 (1914). Of course, most books on recent Japanese history refer to the establishment of the Meiji local government system. W. W. McLaren's *Political History of Japan during the Meiji Era: 1867–1913* (New York, 1913); Chitoshi Yanaga, *Japan Since Perry* (New York, 1949); and George M. Beckmann, *The Making of the Meiji Constitution: The Oligarchy and the Constitutional Development of Japan, 1886–1891* (Lawrence, Kan., 1957) are useful examples. There is a chapter on local administration in Harold S. Quigley, *Japanese Government and Politics* (New York, 1932); Hugh Borton, *The Administration and Structure of the Japanese Government* (Department of State Publication 2244, Far Eastern Series 8, 1945) shows the development from 1937 to 1945. Oda Yorodzu, *Principes de droit administratif du Japon* (Paris, 1928) also deals with local administration (pp. 176–223 and *passim*). A case study, now of historical interest, is Charles A. Beard, *The Administration and Politics of Tokyo: A Survey and Opinion* (New York, 1923).

Legal Material

The text of laws, ordinances, and regulations is promulgated in the *Kampō* (Official Gazette), published by the Finance Ministry's Printing Office since 1883. A supplement under the title *Kampō gōgai* contains the records of the proceedings of both Houses of the Diet. For the convenience of Occupation officials, the *Kampō* and *Kampō gōgai* for the period from April 1946 to April 1952 appeared also in an English version (*Official Gazette*, English Edition). From September 1953 to February 1954 a private company, the International Public News Agency in Tokyo, published excerpts from the *Kampō* in English under the title *Japan's Official Gazette*. While the *Kampō* appears nearly daily during Diet sessions, the *Hōrei zensho* (Compendium of Laws and Ordinances) is issued monthly and divided into sections—such as "laws," "government ordinances," "ministerial ordinances"—within which the materials are arranged by their serial numbers. This is also an official publication published by the Finance Ministry's Printing Office.

Private collections of laws are issued annually by major publishers under the title *Roppō zensho* (Compendium of the Six Codes). These handy volumes, printed on thin paper, are the vade mecum of every legal scholar, practitioner, and student in Japan. They contain, in addition to the six basic codes which constitute their core, the up-to-date texts of several hundred laws, including the more important laws in the field of local government. There is also a compendium of local government laws, *Chihō jichi roppō*, published irregularly by Gakuyōshobō.

The Autonomy Ministry compiles the *Chihō jichi kankei hōreishū* (Collection of Laws and Ordinances Regarding Local Self-government). It also publishes *Chihō gyōzaisei jitsurei* (Concrete Cases Regarding Local Administration and Finance), which presents the official interpretation of laws and illustrates their application to actual cases. Its *Chihō gyōsei hōki* (Laws and Regulations on Local Administration), published in seven volumes in 1958, covers the major laws and regulations and their numerous amendments since the enactment of the Local Autonomy Law in 1947. The Local Autonomy Section of the Secretariat of the Prime Minister's Office issued in 1948 a looseleaf booklet in English entitled *Laws Concerning Local Autonomy*. It contains the text of the Local Autonomy Law and supplementary enforcement orders and was kept up to date by insertion sheets until 1951. The Local Autonomy Agency and the Local Finance Commission published an English translation of the Local Tax Law and some related laws in 1950.

For a study of the legislative history of important measures in the field of local government the records of the Local Administration Committees of both Houses of the Diet (*Chihō gyōsei iin kaigiroku*) are important. They are published by the House in question. The forerunners of the present Autonomy Ministry—the Local Autonomy Agency and the Autonomy Board—

published collections of recommendations, drafts, official statements, committee debates and Diet debates under the title *Kaisei chihō seido shiryō*. There are two editions. The earlier one in eight volumes covers the period from 1947 to 1951; the later one in four volumes covers the period to 1955.

Important legal reforms are sometimes based on proposals of special commissions. The *Report on Japanese Taxation by the Shoup Mission* deals with the tax system in general, but contains also important recommendations regarding local functions and finances. It was published by SCAP in 1949. A supplementary *Second Report on Japanese Taxation* is available in an edition published by the Japan Tax Association in 1951. Both are in English and Japanese. On the basis of the Shoup Mission's recommendations, the Chihō gyōsei chōsa iinkai (Local Administration Investigation Committee), under the chairmanship of Professor Kambe Masao, was created in 1949. It submitted its report, *Gyōsei jimu saihaibun ni kansuru kankoku* (Recommendations Concerning Redistribution of Administrative Functions) in 1950. Although the recommendations were shelved, the report is useful because it sheds light on a problem of continuing importance. After the Occupation, the Japanese government began to revise the Occupation-sponsored reforms and created for this purpose the Chihō Seido Chōsakai (Local System Investigation Council). The Council published its first report, *Chihō seido no kaikaku ni kansuru tōshin* (Report Concerning the Reform of the Local Government System) in 1953. Major parts of this report and of some, although not all, of its successors have been implemented by subsequent legislation.*

Pertinent court decisions may be found in the Supreme Court Reports, *Saikō saibansho hanreishū* (Compilation of Supreme Court Decisions) and *Gyōsei jiken saiban reishū* (Compilation of Decisions in Administrative Cases), both of which appear monthly. The above-mentioned *Gyōsei jiken soshō nenkan* (Yearbook of Administrative Law Cases) is useful because it contains charts and tables.

Prefectures and larger cities publish their by-laws in printed form and the proceedings of their assemblies in printed or mimeographed form (*X ken gikai* or *X shikai kaigiroku*). A classified loose-leaf compilation of prefectural by-laws, edited by the Autonomy Ministry or its predecessors, is *Chihō jichi jōreishū* (Collection of Local Government Bylaws). Some prefectures also publish topical compilations of their by-laws and insert sheets at various intervals.

Secondary Material on the Postwar System

(1) Material in English. The Occupation gave an official account of its

---

*An exception is, for example, the Council's report on the reform of the prefectural system, published in 1957. The reports always arouse a great deal of comment and criticism. For a critical analysis of the report of 1953, see *Toshi mondai*, Vol. 44, No. 11 (November 1953). A monograph by Tanaka Jiro, Tawara Shizuo, and Ukai Nobushige, *Fuken seido kaikaku hihan* (A Critique of the Reform of the Prefectural System, Tokyo, 1957) deals with the report of 1957, which may be found there as an appendix.

endeavors from 1945 to 1948 in the report of SCAP's Government Section, *Political Reorientation of Japan: September 1945 to September 1948* (Washington, Government Printing Office, 1949). The first, a narrative volume, contains a section on local government (pp. 260–89). The second, a collection of documents, includes translations of the various constitution drafts—omitting significantly the original Government Section draft—and of some of the basic laws, such as the Local Autonomy Law, the Police Law, the Board of Education Law, and the Law Abolishing the Home Ministry. It also contains important SCAPINs, memoranda exchanged between the Occupation and Japanese government agencies and statements by General MacArthur.

The Autonomy Ministry published a series of pamphlets for the benefit of the participants in the seminar of the Eastern Regional Organization for Public Administration (usually referred to as the EROPA Seminar), held in 1961 in Tokyo. The first of these pamphlets gives an overview of local government in Japan.* Others deal with the local finance system and the local tax system, with local public enterprises, and with various regional development plans. Some prefectural and municipal governments published additional pamphlets on development plans in their areas (for example, Chiba Prefecture's *Keiyo Industrial Area* and Nagoya City's *City Planning for the City of Nagoya*). Altogether the output of material in English, especially in the field of development planning, has increased noticeably of late. There are, in addition to the reports of teams of experts, such as the Joint Japan–United Nations Team on the Hanshin Metropolitan Region, English-language pamphlets on planning by the Tokyo Metropolitan Government and by other local governments which, despite their frequently apparent public relations purpose, contain a wealth of useful data.

Good introductions to Japanese local government are to be found in chapters on that subject in textbooks on Japanese government published in the United States. Among these are Harold S. Quigley and John E. Turner, *The New Japan* (Minneapolis, 1956); Ardath W. Burks, *The Government of Japan* (New York, 2d ed., 1964); and Theodore McNally, *Contemporary Government of Japan* (Boston, 1963). The Occupation reforms and their aftermath are perceptively discussed in Kazuo Kawai, *Japan's American Interlude* (Chicago, 1960), pp. 103–10. The development of the present local tax system is shown in Saburo Shiomi, *Japanese Finance and Taxation: 1940–1956* (translated by Shotaro Hasegawa, New York, 1957). R. P. Dore, *Land Reform in Japan* (London, 1959), provides interesting insights into local politics.

A number of articles on various aspects of Japanese local government have appeared in American journals. Ralph J. Braibanti dealt with "Executive Power in the Japanese Prefectural Government" in *Far Eastern Quarterly*, IX (1950), 231–44. Contrary views on the neighborhood associations were

---

*It is similar to the survey reports submitted periodically by the Tokyo Metropolitan Government to the International Union of Local Authorities. One of these reports is reprinted in the Union's volume on *Local Government Finance and Its Importance for Local Autonomy* (The Hague, 1955), pp. 224–41.

given in Braibanti's "Neighborhood Associations in Japan and Their Demo-
cratic Potentialities" in *Far Eastern Quarterly*, VII (1948), 136–64, and by
John Masland, "Neighborhood Associations in Japan" in *Far Eastern Survey*,
XV (1946), 355–58. Robert E. Ward called our attention to "The Socio-
Political Role of the Buraku (Hamlet) in Japan" in an article in the *American
Political Science Review*, XLV (1951), 1025–40. He contributed further to
our understanding of rural political behavior in "Patterns of Stability and
Change in Rural Japanese Politics," *Occasional Papers*, No. 1 (1951), pp.
1–6. He described village government in "Some Observations of Local Auton-
omy at the Village Level in Present-Day Japan," *Far Eastern Quarterly*, XII
(1953), 183–202. George A. Warp published two critical articles in the
National Municipal Review, vols. XLI and XLII: "Americanization in Japan"
(October 1952) and "In Our Image and Likeness" (April 1953). I discussed
"The Japanese Village and Its Government" in *Far Eastern Quarterly*, XV
(1956), 185–99, and outlined Occupation and post-Occupation developments
in "Local Government in Japan: Reform and Reaction," *Far Eastern Survey*,
XIII (1954), 97–102.

(2) *Material in Japanese*. The volume of Japanese literature on the postwar system of local government confronts the bibliographer with an embar-
rassment of riches. As in other countries, professors at leading Japanese universities often write textbooks on the subjects they are teaching, and there
are literally dozens of texts dealing with local government. (In addition, texts
on administrative or constitutional laws deal broadly with the subject.) As
productive scholars, Japanese academicians also explore specific aspects of
the subject in monographs. Scholars frequently serve on governmental commissions, and this involvement in current developments often results in additions to the monographic literature. Public officials also often write books in
the area of their expertise; thus officials of the Autonomy Ministry, of the
Finance Ministry, and of other agencies on the national or prefectural level
contribute to the literature on local government law, administration, finance,
etc. It is impossible to list even a representative fraction of these works in a
short bibliographical note, and it must suffice to call the attention of the student of local government to the work of such scholars as Hara Ryonosuke,
Nagahama Masatoshi, Royama Masamichi, Sato Isao, Sato Tatsuo, Sugimura
Shozaburo, Tagami Joji, Tawara Shizuo, Yanase Ryokan, and Yoshitomi Shigeo, as well as to the work of such public officials as Hayashi Keizo, Nagano
Shiro, and Suzuki Shunichi.*

Much of the literature emphasizes law and theory, but in some more recent
books the emphasis is on administrative practice or the approach is political
or sociological. If I list in the following the titles of a few books, it is because
their authors have not been previously mentioned, or because I found them

---

* Some works by these authors are mentioned in Ward and Watanabe, *Japanese
Political Science*, in Ward's earlier *Guide*, and in various issues of the *Japan Science
Review*. The notes to the present study cite specific works of most of these authors.

helpful even though they are not among the standard works in the field, or because I believe that they can serve as a valuable introduction to the subject. In the last-named category, Isomura Eiichi and Hoshino Mitsuo, *Chihō jichi tokuhon* (A Reader in Local Self-government, Tokyo, 1961) is particularly useful; it is very readable and much more sophisticated in its approach than the title promises. Wada Hideo, *Chihō jichi no riron to dōtai* (Theory and Dynamics of Local Self-government, Tokyo, 1960) is a collection of essays, some of them dealing with basic problems of local administration in a general way and others presenting case studies of such problems as the relationship of party ideology to localism. A chronology of significant postwar developments is appended. A number of books deal with actual or proposed revisions of the postwar system. Hara Ryonosuke, *Chihō seido kaikaku no mondaiten* (Problematical Issues of the Reform of the Local Government System, Tokyo, 1953), and the same author's *Chihō seido kaikaku no kihon mondai* (Basic problems of the Reform of the Local Government System, Tokyo, 1957) belong to this category. The latter work is a collection of essays. Similar to it in nature is Tanaka Jiro, *Chihō seido kaikaku no shomondai* (Various Issues of the Reform of the Local Government System, Tokyo, 1955). Royama Masamichi, *Chihō seido no kaikaku* (The Reform of the Local Government System, Tokyo, 1953) also discusses various problems and proposals for their solution. The problems discussed are, of course, those of particular concern at the time of publication; but the importance of these books is by no means ephemeral, partly because the shifts in concern are significant and partly because many of the problems are still current.

An advisory group of the Zen Nihon Jichi Dantai Rōdō Kumiai (Japan Union of Local Government Workers) edited *Kōza chihō jichi dantai* (Lectures on Local Entities), a collection of five volumes by various authors, dealing with the history and theory of local autonomy, local functions, the local public service, and the relations of local inhabitants to their government. Some fifty prominent scholars and officials contributed to *Chihō jichi rombunshū* (Collection of essays on Local Autonomy), published under the auspices of the Autonomy Board by the Chihō Zaimu Kyōkai (Local Finance Association) in 1954. The occasion for this publication was the first anniversary of the passage of the Law for the Promotion of Amalgamation of Towns and Villages, but the essays cover a wide range of topics.

A comprehensive and authoritative commentary on the Local Autonomy Law is Nagano Shiro, *Chikujō chihō jichihō: Kaishaku to sono unyō* (The Local Autonomy Law, Article by Article: Interpretation and Application). It was first published in 1953 and a completely revised version appeared in 1959. A useful text on the Local Autonomy Law is Sugimura Shozaburo, *Chihō jichihō* (The Local Autonomy Law), published in 1956. Takahashi Teizō, *Chihō jichihōron* (On the Local Autonomy Law, 3d ed., Tokyo, 1962) adds to the commentary references to judicial decisions and an index of cases cited. It contains an introduction dealing with the development of the local government system and a selective bibliography on prewar and postwar writings.

In the field of local finance Professor Fujita Takeo is probably the foremost academic authority. His works on the postwar system include *Gendai chihō zaisei no riron* (Theory of Present Local Finance, 1951), *Nihon chihō zaisei-ron* (On Japan's Local Finance, 1955, rev. ed. 1959), and *Nihon no chihō zaisei* (Japan's Local Finance, 1959). Among the writings of officials in the same field, those of Ogita Tamotsu include *Chihō zaisei seido* (The Local Finance System, 1951), and *Chihō zaisei kōgi* (Lectures on Local Finance, 1959). Shibata Mamoru and others published in 1954 *Chihō kōfuzeihō kaisetsu* (Commentary on the Local Distribution Tax Law). Commentaries and treatises on other laws in the field of local government include Suzuki Shunichi, *Chihō kōmuinhō no kaisetsu* (Commentary on the Local Public Service Law, Tokyo, 1950), and Tanaka Jiro, *Shinkeisatsuhō oyobi bōei nihō gaisetsu* (Outline of the new Police Law and of the Defense Law, Tokyo, 1954). The Chihō Jichi Seido Kenkyūkai (Association for the Study of the Local Self-government System) published in 1951 a series of twelve booklets by central government officials on various subjects (such as the Local Autonomy Law, the Local Public Service Law, local government revenues and expenditures, and local budget-making) under the general title *Jihō jichi sōsho* (Local Self-Government Series).

Monographs that analyze the actual functioning of specific institutions are published less frequently than straight legal commentaries. The Shakai Kagaku Kenkyūjo (Institute of Social Sciences) of Tokyo University published in 1951 a volume on the actual operation of administrative commissions, including those on the local level, under the title *Gyōsei iinkai: riron rekishi, jittai* (Administrative Commissions: Theory, History, and Actuality). Local commissions in particular are treated by Hara Ryonosuke and other scholars from the Kansai area in a volume entitled *Chihō gyōsei iinkai seido no jittai bunseki to hihan* (Analysis and Critique of the Actuality of the Local Administration Commission System, Osaka, 1952). Local assemblies were analyzed in 1952 in Tanaka Hitsuichi *Chihō gikai uneiron: sono riron to jissai* (On the Activities of Local Assemblies: Their Theory and Practice) and in 1954 in a joint publication of the National Association of Chairmen of City Assemblies and the Osaka Governmental Research Institute, entitled *Chihō gikai no jittai chōsa* (Investigation of the Actual Conditions of Local Assemblies). Kanamaru Saburo and Wakabayashi Senji deal with local legislation in *Jōrei to kisoku* (Bylaws and Rules, Tokyo, 1949).

The mass amalgamation drive of 1953–57 directed the attention of many scholars to the political and sociological aspects of local government. An example of the resulting literature is Shima Yasuhiko (ed.), *Chōson gappei to nōson no hembo* (Town and Village Amalgamations and the Transformation of Agricultural Villages), published in 1958. The problems and effects of the mass amalgamation were frequently discussed in case studies. Some of these are mentioned in the next section. Local politics, rather than the institutions of local government, are emphasized in Hoshino Mitsuo, *Nihon no chihō seiji* (Japanese Local Politics), published in 1958.

Case Studies and Public Opinion Surveys

In English, there is first of all the monumental study of the *buraku* of Niike in Okayama Prefecture by Richard K. Beardsley, John W. Hall, and Robert E. Ward, entitled *Village Japan* (Chicago, 1959). The chapters by Robert Ward entitled "The Community and Local Government" and "The Community and the Political Process" are important contributions to an understanding of these subjects. Two doctoral dissertations done at the University of Michigan deal with government and politics in Okayama, where the University's Center for Japanese Studies was located for some years. In 1956 Cecil C. Brett wrote *The Government of Okayama Prefecture: A Case Study of Local Autonomy in Japan,* and in 1962 Alfred B. Clubock wrote *Electoral Politics in Rural Japan: A Case Study of Okayama Prefecture.* Differing in scope, approach, and method, each of the two dissertations is useful in its own way. Paul S. Dull, "The Political Structure of a Japanese Village," *Far Eastern Quarterly,* XV (1956), 185–99, deals with a village in the same prefecture. There are a number of rural community studies of at least tangential interest written by anthropologists, beginning with John Embree's study, *Suye Mura: A Japanese Village* (Chicago, 1939). A thoughtful article by Richard K. Beardsley entitled "Community Studies in Japan," *Far Eastern Quarterly,* XIV (1954), 37–55, deals with the work of Japanese and American scholars. The subsequent work of John B. Cornell, Edward Norbeck, and Robert J. Smith must also be mentioned. The report of SCAP's National Resources Section, *The Japanese Village in Transition* (Tokyo, 1950), focuses on the effects of the land reform, including its political effects, in thirteen villages.

English-language studies of urban communities that deal with the institutions of local government or the local political process are fairly rare. Masamichi Royama describes the administration of Tokyo and Osaka in his contribution to William A. Robson, *Great Cities of the World: Their Government, Politics, and Planning* (2d ed., London, 1957, pp. 719–55). R. P. Dore, *City Life in Japan: A Study of a Tokyo Ward* (Berkeley, 1958) investigates the life of the inhabitants of a Tokyo neighborhood, including their political attitudes and behavior. Its treatment of the local neighborhood association is outstanding for its clarity, empathy, and urbanity. Robert E. Ward, "Urban-Rural Differences and the Process of Modernization in Japan," *Economic Development and Cultural Change,* Vol. IX, No. 1, Part II (October 1960), pp. 135–65, compares the political process in rural Okayama and urban Osaka. A special issue of *Waseda Political Studies* (Vol. III, 1960) deals with voting behavior in a smaller city and a farming community in a national election, but is nevertheless useful to students of local politics.* So is the article by Jun'ichi Kyogoku and Nobutaka Ike on "Urban-rural Differences in Voting Behavior in Postwar Japan," which appeared in the above-mentioned issue of *Economic Development and Cultural Change,* pp. 167–85. Allan B. Cole,

---

*This is an abbreviated English version of Yoshimura Tadashi and others, *Tōhyō kōdō no kenkyū* (A Study of Voting Behavior), published in 1959.

Japanese Opinion Polls of Socio-political Significance, 1947–57 (Cambridge, 1960) contains the results of some polls on attitudes toward local government.

Japanese scholars have become increasingly interested in gauging political consciousness, especially of the rural population. Among the first important studies of this problem is Royama Masamichi, *Nōson jichi no hembō* (The Transformation of Self-government in Agricultural Villages), published in 1948. In the following year Professor Royama edited *Seiji ishiki no kaibō* (An Analysis of Political Consciousness), based on surveys in an urban and a rural election district in Tokyo. The same group of scholars (Royama Masamichi, Ukai Nobushige, Tsuji Kiyoaki, Kawahara Jikichiro, and Nakamura Kikuo) collaborated and published in 1955 a case study of the general election of October 1952 and, in a supplement, of the general election of April 1953, under the title *Sōsenkyo no jittai* (The Actual Conditions of General Elections).

The Autonomy Board publishes at times (as in December 1958 and March 1961) the results of public opinion surveys in connection with general elections, usually under the title *Sōsenkyo no jittai: yoron chōsa kekka no gaiyō* (The Actual Conditions of General Elections: Summary of the Results of Public Opinion Polls). The polls in this case are conducted by the Central Public Opinion Survey Institute. Prefectural and municipal election administration committees also conduct surveys of this type. Thus, the Kyoto City Election Administration Committee published in 1962 the results of a survey on the general election of 1960 under the title *Kyotoshi ni okeru senkyo ni kansuru yoron chōsa no gaiyō* (Summary of a Public Opinion Poll Regarding the Elections in Kyoto City). A similar report was published by the Election Research Association of the University of Nagoya's Law Department together with the Nagoya City Election Administration Committee under the title *Daitoshi ni okeru senkyo to shimin no seiji ishiki* (Elections and Political Consciousness of Citizens in a Big City). Two slim volumes, published in 1960 and 1961 by the Shimane Prefectural Election Administration Committee, report the surveys of Professors Yamaoka and Yamada of Shimane University. They bear the title *Shimaneken ni okeru seiji ishiki to tōhyō kōdō* (Political Consciousness and Electoral Behavior in Shimane Prefecture). While the focus is in some cases on general rather than on local elections, the general problem of the degree of political consciousness is basic also to the study of local politics. As the present study shows, on the grass roots level local and national politics are intricately intertwined.

Investigations of the socio-economic bases of local politics received a new impetus with the mass amalgamations of 1953–57. Fukutake Tadashi edited in 1958 *Gappei chōson no jittai* (The Facts About Amalgamated Towns and Villages), a case study of an amalgamation in Shizuoka Prefecture. A brief but illuminating discussion of the effects of the amalgamations on the *jiban* (bailiwicks) of prefectural politicians is Kawaguchi Tei, *Chōson gappei to senkyo jiban* (Town and Village Amalgamations and Election Constituencies), which appeared in April 1960 in the series *Nōgyō sōgō kenkyū* (Coordinated Agricultural Studies), published under the auspices of the Ministry of Agriculture and Forestry. The Social Science Research Institute (Shakai Kagaku Kenkyūsho) of the International Christian University publishes a series of interdisciplinary studies, in Japanese, English, or in both languages. One of these, *Nōson no kenryoku kōzō* (The Power Structure in a Rural Community), published in November 1959, deals with a village in Chiba which was in the throes of amalgamation proceedings at the time of the investigation.*

Another one of these studies focuses on a somewhat related problem, the effect of planned industrial development and the concomitant urbanization on hitherto rural areas. *Chiiki shakai to toshika* (Local Community and Urbanization), published in 1962, shows the effect in the case of a village in Chiba Prefecture. An earlier study by Fujisawa Hiromitsu, *Chihō shōtoshi no seitai* (The Ecology of Small Regional Cities) contains a sociological analysis of the problem in general and a case study based on a city in Yamanashi Prefecture. It was published in 1958 by Nōgyō Sōgō Kenkyūjo (Institute for Coordinated Agricultural Studies) of the Ministry of Agriculture and Forestry. Ide Yoshinori, who collaborated in the two above-mentioned studies of the Social Science Research Institute of the International Christian University, published in 1963 together with Ishida Yū the results of their investigations of agricultural villages in Kagoshima Prefecture under the title *Chiiki shakai ni okeru seiji to gyōsei* (Politics and Administration in a Local Community). Economic and socio-political surveys are sometimes sponsored and published by prefectural governments. An example is the five slim volumes published by Kanagawa Prefecture in 1953 under the title *Hakone kanko chitai jittai chōsa hōkoku shō* (Report on a Survey of Actual Conditions in the Hakone Sightseeing Area). The survey was conducted under the direction of Professor Tanaka Jiro of Tokyo University. Interesting insights into village politics can be gained from case studies in a popular vein, such as Namie Ken, *Mura no seiji* (Village Politics), published in 1953, and Sugiura Mimpei, *Chōkai giin ichinensei* (A Freshman in the Town Assembly), published in 1957. Both were written by assemblymen, the latter book by a Communist member of the assembly of a town in Aichi Prefecture who was serving his first term.

While the political behavior of the rural population holds a particular fascination for Japanese social scientists, there have also been some studies of urban areas. Examples of polls conducted in such areas, aside from the above-mentioned election studies, are *Tokyo tōsei ni tsuite* (On Tokyo Metropolitan Government), published by the General Affairs Office of Tokyo Metropolis in 1954; *Dai toshi ni okeru chiiki seiji no kōzō: Suginamiku ni okeru*

---

* An abridged English version was published in the same year. There are, of course, many works on Japan's rural society, including some case studies of the political power structure. Examples are listed in Ward and Watanabe, *Japanese Political Science*, pp. 153ff.

seiji, gyōsei, shimin (The Structure of Local Politics in a Big City: Politics, Administration and Inhabitants in Suginami Ward), published by the Tōsei Chōsakai (Metropolitan Government Research Association) in 1960; another publication of the same association in 1961, *Tokyo tōmin no jichi ichiki to tokubetsuku seido ni kansuru yoron chōsa* (Public Opinion Survey on the Local Consciousness of Inhabitants of Tokyo Metropolis and the System of Special Wards); and *Osaka shi ni okeru toshi gyōsei ni kansuru yoron chōsa* (Public Opinion Survey on the Administration of Osaka City), which appeared as a special issue of *Toshi mondai kenkyū* in March 1954. General surveys of attitudes toward local self-government have been published by the National Public Opinion Institute attached to the Prime Minister's Office, usually under the title *Chihō jichi ni kansuru yoron chōsa* (as in 1951) or *Chihō jichi ni tsuite no yoron chōsa* (as in 1952). (Either title may be translated as Public Opinion Survey on Local Self-government.)

Thus, while the traditional legal-institutional, administrative or historical orientation is still prevalent in much of the Japanese literature on local government, there is an increasing accumulation of data for studies of political attitudes and processes. Monographs of larger scale that utilize such data within a clearly stated conceptual framework are as yet relatively few in number. But an increasing portion of the periodical literature departs from the traditional approach, and, all in all, the work done over the last years along these lines promises to add new dimensions to our knowledge and understanding of Japanese government and politics on the local level.

Index

Du